Handbook of Moral and Charact
Second Edition

M000205281

There is widespread agreement that schools should contribute to the moral development and character formation of their students. In fact, 80% of US states currently have mandates regarding character education. However, the pervasiveness of the support for moral and character education masks a high degree of controversy surrounding its meaning and methods. The purpose of this handbook is to supplant the prevalent ideological rhetoric of the field with a comprehensive, research-oriented volume that both describes the extensive changes that have occurred over the last 15 years and points forward to the future. Now in its second edition, this book includes the latest applications of developmental and cognitive psychology to moral and character education from preschool to college settings, and much more.

Larry Nucci is Adjunct Professor in the Graduate School of Education at the University of California, Berkeley and Editor-in-Chief of the journal *Human Development*.

Darcia Narvaez is Professor in the Department of Psychology at the University of Notre Dame and Executive Editor of the *Journal of Moral Education*.

Tobias Krettenauer is Professor in the Department of Psychology at Wilfrid Laurier University, Associate Editor of the *Journal of Moral Education* and Consulting Editor for *Child Development*.

Educational Psychology Handbook Series
Series Editor: Patricia A. Alexander

Handbook of Moral and Character Education

Second Edition

Edited by Larry Nucci, Darcia Narvaez,
and Tobias Krettenauer

Routledge
Taylor & Francis Group

NEW YORK AND LONDON

Second edition published 2014
by Routledge
711 Third Avenue, New York, NY 10017

and by Routledge
2 Park Square, Milton Park, Abingdon, Oxon OX14 4RN

First edition published by Routledge 2008

Routledge is an imprint of the Taylor & Francis Group, an informa business

© 2014 Taylor & Francis

Library of Congress Cataloging in Publication Data
Handbook of moral and character education / edited by Larry Nucci, Tobias Krettenauer, Darcia Narvaez – Second edition.
   pages cm. – (Educational psychology handbook)
   Includes bibliographical references and index.
   1. Moral education–Handbooks, manuals, etc. 2. Personality development–Handbooks, manuals, etc. I. Nucci, Larry P. II. Krettenauer, Tobias. III. Narvaez, Darcia.
   LC268.H264 2014
   370.11'4–dc23   2013034759

ISBN: 978-0-415-53233-4 (hbk)
ISBN: 978-0-415-53238-9 (pbk)
ISBN: 978-0-203-11489-6 (ebk)

Typeset in Minion
by Wearset Ltd, Boldon, Tyne and Wear

CONTENTS

FIGURES

TABLES

EDITORS

Larry Nucci is Adjunct Professor of Human Development in the Graduate School of Education at the University of California, Berkeley and Professor Emeritus of Educational Psychology at the University of Illinois at Chicago. He has published extensively in the areas of social and moral development and directs the Domain Based Moral Education (DBME) lab at UC Berkeley. He is Editor-in-Chief of the journal *Human Development*, the author of *Education in the Moral Domain* (Cambridge University Press, 2001) and *Nice is Not Enough: Facilitating Moral Development* (Pearson, 2009) and editor of four other volumes including *Moral Development and Character Education: A Dialogue* (McCutchan, 1989) and *Conflict, Contradiction and Contrarian Elements in Moral Development and Education* (Erlbaum, 2005).

Darcia Narvaez is Professor of Psychology at the University of Notre Dame. After college, she was a church musician, K-12 music teacher, middle school Spanish teacher and owned her own business. She also earned a Masters of Divinity. She earned her Ph.D. in Educational Psychology from the University of Minnesota, where she became a tenured faculty member and was the executive director of the Center for the Study of Ethical Development. She publishes extensively on moral development and education. Her books include *Moral Development in the Professions* (with Rest; Erlbaum, 1994); *Postconventional Moral Thinking* (with Rest, Bebeau, & Thoma; Erlbaum, 1999); *Moral Development, Self and Identity* (with Lapsley; Erlbaum, 2004); *Personality, Identity and Character* (with Lapsley; Cambridge University Press, 2009); *Evolution, Early Experience and Human Development* (with Panksepp, Schore, & Gleason; Oxford University Press, 2013); *Ancestral Landscapes in Human Evolution: Culture, Childrearing and Social Wellbeing* (with Valentino, Fuentes, McKenna, & Gray; Oxford University Press, 2014); and *Neurobiology and the Development of Human Morality: Evolution, Culture and Wisdom* (Norton, 2014). She is Executive Editor of the *Journal of Moral Education*.

Tobias Krettenauer is Professor in the Department of Psychology at Wilfrid Laurier University, Canada. He received his Ph.D. in Developmental Psychology from the

Max Planck Institute for Human Development in Berlin, Germany, and earned his Habilitation degree at Humboldt University Berlin. His research on morality, self, and emotions has been funded by several grants from the German Research Foundation and the Social Sciences and Humanities Research Council Canada and has been published in internationally renowned journals. Currently, he is Associate Editor of the *Journal of Moral Education* and Consulting Editor for the journal *Child Development*.

CONTRIBUTORS

Noriyuki Araki is Professor of Education at Fukuyama University, Hiroshima, Japan.

James Arthur is Professor and Head of the School of Education and Director of the Jubilee Centre for Character and Values in the University of Birmingham, United Kingdom.

Robert Atkins is Professor of Childhood Studies and Nursing at Rutgers University, Camden, NJ, and Director of the Robert Wood Johnson's Foundation New Jersey Health Initiatives program.

Muriel J. Bebeau is Professor of Primary Dental Care–Health Ecology and Director of the Center for Ethical Development at the University of Minnesota.

Marvin W. Berkowitz is Sanford N. McDonnell Professor of Character Education and co-Director of the Center for Character and Citizenship at the College of Education, University of Missouri—St. Louis.

Melinda C. Bier is Associate Director of the Center for Character and Citizenship, College of Education, University of Missouri—St. Louis.

Tonia Bock is Associate Professor of Psychology at the University of St. Thomas, Saint Paul, Minnesota.

Peter Brunn is Director of Strategic Partnerships of the Developmental Studies Center, Oakland, CA.

Elizabeth Campbell is Professor of Education at the Ontario Institute for Studies in Education, University of Toronto, Canada.

Richard F. Catalano is Dobb Professor for the Study and Prevention of Violence and the Director of the Social Development Research Group in the School of Social Work at the University of Washington, Seattle.

Guozhen Cen is Professor of Education at the Shanghai Teachers University, Shanghai, China.

Anne Colby is Consulting Professor at the Stanford Center on Adolescence, Stanford University, Stanford, CA.

Matthew Davidson is Vice President and Director of Education at the Institute for Excellence in Ethics, Manlius, NY.

Wolfgang Edelstein is Director Emeritus of the Max Planck Institute for Human Development, Berlin, Germany.

Maurice J. Elias is Professor of Psychology at Rutgers University, New Brunswick, NJ.

Constance Flanagan is Professor in the School of Human Ecology at the University of Wisconsin—Madison.

Erin Gallay is a graduate student in the Social Foundations of Education at Eastern Michigan University, Ypsilanti, MI.

Jessica Harrison is a doctoral student in Psychology at Portland State University, OR.

Daniel Hart is Distinguished Professor of Childhood Studies and Psychology, and Director of the Institute for Effective Education at Rutgers University, Camden, NJ.

J. David Hawkins is Endowed Professor of Prevention in the School of Social Work at the University of Washington, Seattle.

Charles C. Helwig is Professor of Psychology at the University of Toronto, Canada.

Carolyn Hildebrandt is Professor of Psychology at the University of Northern Iowa.

Elisabeth Kals is Professor of Social and Organizational Psychology at the Katholische Universität Eichstätt Ingolstadt, Eichstätt, Germany.

Amy Kranzler is a doctoral student in Psychology at Rutgers University, New Brunswick, NJ.

V. Megan Kash is a doctoral student in the Institute of Child Health, University College London.

Vladimir Khmelkov is Vice President at the Institute for Excellence & Ethics, Manlius, NY.

Tobias Krettenauer is Professor of Psychology at Wilfrid Laurier University, Waterloo, Canada.

Daniel Lapsley is Professor and Chair of the Department of Psychology, University of Notre Dame, IN.

In Jae Lee is Professor of Education, Seoul National University of Education, Seoul, Korea.

Thomas Lickona is Professor and Director of the Center for the 4th and 5th Rs at the State University of New York, Cortland.

M. Kyle Matsuba is Professor of Psychology at Kwantlen University, British Columbia, Canada.

Verna E. Monson is a research fellow at the Holloran Center for Ethical Leadership in the Professions at the University of St. Thomas School of Law.

Laurel S. Morris is a doctoral student in Psychology at the Behavioral and Clinical Neuroscience Institute of the University of Cambridge, UK.

Markus Müller is Professor of Social and Organizational Psychology at the University of Siegen, Germany.

Darcia Narvaez is Professor of Psychology at the University of Notre Dame, IN.

Larry Nucci is an Adjunct Professor in the Graduate School of Education, University of California, Berkeley and Professor Emeritus of Educational Psychology at the University of Illinois at Chicago.

Fritz K. Oser is Professor of Education at the University of Freiburg, Switzerland.

Sarah J. Parker is Director of the Reeds Center, New York.

Walter C. Parker is Professor and Chair of Social Studies Education at the University of Washington, Seattle.

Cristi Pinela is a doctoral student in Psychology at Portland State University, OR.

F. Clark Power is Professor of Liberal Studies at the University of Notre Dame, IN.

Deborah W. Powers is a doctoral student in Human Development at the Graduate School of Education, University of California, Berkeley.

Alisa Pykett is a doctoral student in the School of Human Ecology, University of Wisconsin.

Robert W. Roeser is Professor of Psychology at Portland State University, OR.

Peter L. Samuelson is a faculty member of the Fuller Graduate School of Psychology, Pasadena, CA.

Kristin K. Sheehan is Program Director of Play Like a Champion, University of Notre Dame, IN.

John Snarey is the Franklin N. Parker Professor of Human Development and Ethics, Emory University, Atlanta, GA.

Paul C. Stey is a doctoral student in the Department of Psychology, University of Notre Dame, IN.

Cynthia Taylor is a doctoral student in Psychology at Portland State University, OR.

Sharon To is a doctoral candidate in the Department of Applied Psychology and Human Development, OISE, University of Toronto, Canada.

John W. Toumbourou is Professor and Chair of Health Psychology, Deakin University and is an Honorary Associate at the Centre for Adolescent Health (Murdoch Children's Research Institute), Australia.

David R. Vago is an associate psychologist in the Department of Psychiatry at Brigham & Women's Hospital and is also an instructor at the Harvard Medical School, Cambridge, MA.

Marilyn Watson was Director of Programs at the Developmental Studies Center and Program Director of the Child Development Project and currently is an independent author and scholar, Vacaville, CA.

Roger P. Weissberg is Professor of Psychology and CEO of the Collaborative for Academic, Social, and Emotional Learning (CASEL), University of Illinois at Chicago.

Thomas Wren is Professor of Philosophy at Loyola University of Chicago, Evanston, IL.

Shaogang Yang is Professor of Psychology at Guangdong University of Foreign Studies, Guangzhou City, China.

Jun Yu is a doctoral candidate in the Department of Psychology, Idaho State University.

Betty Zan is Associate Professor of Education and Director of the Regents Center for Early Developmental Education, University of Northern Iowa.

1

INTRODUCTION AND OVERVIEW

Larry Nucci, Darcia Narvaez, and Tobias Krettenauer

The first edition of the *Handbook of Moral and Character Education* published in 2008 responded to a need for a single volume resource that would present the work of leading researchers and scholars in the growing field of moral and character education. The interest in moral education has not subsided since publication of the handbook. There remains widespread agreement that schools should contribute to students' moral development and character formation. As was the case in 2008, 80% of states have mandates regarding character education. Internationally, many nations such as Canada, Korea, Japan, and China mandate moral/character education as part of their national curriculum. Within Europe the interest in moral education is often subsumed under the broader topic of citizenship education where basic concerns for developing compassionate and morally engaged children and youth are at the heart of these efforts. The broad international scope of interest in moral and character education is evidenced by the fact that the Association of Moral Education, which held its 2011 meeting in China, includes members from more than 35 countries around the globe.

With publication of the first edition, we began the process of moving beyond the controversies and debates that have plagued moral and character education by bringing together a collection of chapters by the top researchers and scholars that reflect the state of the art in the field. Since the publication of the first edition, new work has opened up additional approaches to moral education, and has expanded the connections to related areas such as citizenship education. This second edition includes updates of the foundational chapters from the first volume along with new chapters that address emerging work in areas of social and emotional development, applications of mindfulness to moral education, sport as a context for moral growth, moral development and ecology education, and a new section on citizenship education. In addition, the new edition responds to the growing international scope of moral and character education by including authors from Europe and Asia who are addressing issues of moral philosophy, moral development, character, and citizenship within democratic societies. More than half of the chapters in the second edition are covering topics or include authors not within the first edition of the handbook. All of the chapters that appeared in the first volume have been edited and updated. In many cases these changes have been substantial.

PART I: DEFINING THE FIELD: HISTORICAL, PHILOSOPHICAL, AND THEORETICAL FOUNDATIONS

In broad terms the debates over moral and character education divide along three dimensions. One broad distinction is between those who view character formation and morality as centered on the cultivation of virtues and those who argue that morality is ultimately a function of judgments made in context. The former, who often trace their ideas within Western culture back to Aristotle, emphasize the importance of early dispositional formation and the influence of the social group. Often these virtue-based approaches to character education incorporate an emphasis on the attachment to groups and the role of society in forming the young as described by Emile Durkheim (1925/1961). Traditional character educators generally fall within this perspective. On the other hand, those who emphasize the role of reason and judgment draw their philosophical arguments from rationalist ethics with its emphasis on autonomous justification for moral actions based on principles of justice or fairness (Rawls, 2001). The focus is upon the development of moral reasoning drawing from the seminal work of Piaget (1932), and the Socratic approach to education. A third broad dimension is the degree to which educators place an emphasis upon the role of emotion. Traditional and developmental approaches address in different ways the role of emotion in moral and character development. However, the foregrounding of emotion is best seen in approaches that fall within the category of attachment theory, social emotional learning and mindfulness education. These latter approaches are discussed in detail in chapters in Parts II and III of the book.

In Part I authors address the basic philosophical, historical and theoretical issues undergirding contemporary moral and character education. The first chapter of this section (Chapter 2) by Thomas Wren "Philosophical Moorings" takes us through the Western philosophical schools of thought that buttress traditionalist and developmental approaches to moral education. His is not a "cliff notes" reading of these philosophical positions, but rather a critical analysis of their relative adequacy as bases for moral education. In Chapter 3, Gouzhen Cen and Jun Yu expand the attention to philosophical underpinnings by providing an overview of traditional Eastern philosophical traditions of Confucianism, Daoism, and Buddhism that have informed moral and character education in Asian societies as well as current applications of contemplative practices through mindfulness education in the West.

James Arthur picks up the thread in the discussion of philosophical positions that stress the promotion of virtue through his vigorous defense in Chapter 4 of traditional approaches to character education. His chapter provides a contemporary rebuttal to Kohlberg's analysis of the limits of virtue-based moral theories, and attempts to recover the role of traditional educational practices that have had a long history in the Anglo-Saxon approach to character education.

In Chapter 5 "Lawrence Kohlberg's Revolutionary Ideas: Moral Education in the Cognitive-Developmental Tradition," John Snarey and Peter Samuelson provide an historical overview of the work of Lawrence Kohlberg that spawned the re-awakening of interest in moral education in the 1970s and formed the starting point for all subsequent developmentally-based approaches to moral education. They offer insights into the history and personal motivations for Kohlberg's efforts and his later struggle to reconcile the fundamental insights from his own work with Durkheim's sociological perspective on moral education.

Daniel Lapsley and Paul Stey extend the discourse on virtue and reason opened by Wren in Chapter 2 by extending it to contemporary philosophical and psychological considerations of the connections between morality and the self. In Chapter 6 "Moral Self-Identity as the Aim of Education," these authors explore whether the developmentalist emphasis on reason can suffice as a basis for moral education in the absence of an effort to also impact the development of the "self." They review some of the struggles associated with Kohlberg's initial approach to moral education with its absence of a connection to the student as a moral person (issues that Snarey and Samuelson touch on in Chapter 5). However, Lapsley and Stey do not dwell on that historical debate, but endeavor to place the issue squarely within the philosophical and theoretical nexus that is at the heart of the dialogue represented in the handbook.

Part I concludes with Elizabeth Campbell's thoughtful analysis in Chapter 7 of the ethical dimensions of teaching, and the ethical dimensions of what it is to be a teacher. Her plea for moral autonomy and responsibility within the teaching profession is one that must be heeded if any of the ideas presented in this handbook are to reach fruition.

PART II: THEORY-BASED APPROACHES TO MORAL AND CHARACTER EDUCATION

Much of the forward looking work in moral and character education is taking place at the level of theory development and theory testing. These efforts employ advances in developmental and cognitive psychology in a reciprocal process to inform research and theory for teacher preparation and classroom practices in the area of moral education. Larry Nucci and Deborah Powers lead off this section with Chapter 8, "Social Cognitive Domain Theory and Moral Education." This updated chapter outlines the basic premises of social cognitive domain theory and reviews research that has demonstrated that concepts of morality (fairness, human welfare) are universal and form a conceptual system distinct from convention, religious prescription, and personal issues. The chapter presents recent work on developmental patterns within domains, and presents research on the applications of domain theory to classroom practices. The revised chapter provides a table with examples matching up development within each domain with illustrative connections to the regular academic curriculum. The chapter concludes with recent work at two universities employing social cognitive domain theory in the preparation of pre-service teachers to engage in moral education.

In Chapter 9 "Developing Ethical Expertise and Moral Personalities" Darcia Narvaez and Tonia Bock bring together several cognitive and neurobiological lines of research to make recommendations for moral character development. They suggest that the traditionalist and cognitive developmental approaches to moral character development can be unified in instruction for moral expertise development. The Integrative Ethical Education model spells out a five-step, empirically-derived approach for intentional character education that moves from caring relationships to self-authorship. Attention to the neurobiology of moral development occurs when classroom practices foster engagement and communal imagination over self-protective concerns.

Marilyn Watson (Chapter 10) focuses the lens of moral education on the role that classroom structure and affective relationships have for meeting the developmental needs of elementary school children. Watson employs attachment theory and self-determination theory (SDT) to generate an approach to classroom structure and behavioral management called "Developmental Discipline" that engages the child's intrinsic motivations for autonomy, belongingness, and competence. Developmental discipline comprised a central element in the approach to moral and character education formulated by the Developmental Studies Center. The revised chapter includes a discussion of Watson's ongoing work to infuse developmental discipline within teacher education.

Whereas considerable attention has been given to moral and character education at the elementary school level, far less attention has been paid to other age groups. Chapter 11 by Carolyn Hildebrandt and Betty Zan, "Constructivist Approaches to Moral Education in Early Childhood," presents the theoretical assumptions and research on classroom practices of a developmentally-based approach to moral development in early childhood settings. Their work builds from extensive research and experience in the application of Piagetian theory to classrooms in collaboration with their late colleague Rheta DeVries.

The most radical theory driven effort at transforming school culture to promote moral development has been the "Just Community Schools" initiated by Lawrence Kohlberg and his colleagues. Chapter 12 by Fritz Oser, "Toward a Theory of the Just Community Approach: Effects of Collective Moral, Civic, and Social Education," updates the chapter on the just community from the first edition by Clark Power and Ann Higgins D'Alessandro. Oser's chapter reviews the history of the development of the just community approach, and captures the European experience with this form of moral education. He provides an additional theoretical perspective that extends Kohlberg's assumptions and develops the notion that a key element in moral development and the educational success of the just community is the confrontation of young people's experiences with moral misconduct.

A new direction for moral education is the integration of contemplative educational practices through what is termed "mindfulness." In Chapter 13, "Contemplative Education: Cultivating Positive Mental Skills and Social-Emotional Dispositions through Mindfulness Training," Robert Roeser and his colleagues describe the underlying Buddhist assumptions behind mindfulness, and the current educational theory and research that supports the movement toward integrating the use of meditative mindfulness techniques to heightening students' emotional sensibilities and awareness of their own motivations and desires, and to strive toward a more compassionate approach to social interaction. Roeser and colleagues' chapter spells out the directions for future research in this emerging field.

This section of the handbook ends with Chapter 14, "Research-Based Fundamentals of the Effective Promotion of Character Development in Schools," by Marvin Berkowitz and Melinda Bier in which they present a narrative summary of what has been learned regarding effective educational practices from the decades of research on character education.

PART III: SCHOOLS-BASED BEST PRACTICES

In Part III the emphasis shifts from current theory-based work on moral and character education to a focus on approaches that are grounded in school-based practices.

This is not to say that these school-based approaches are not also connected to theory and research. The section starts off with Chapter 15 by Peter Brunn, "Pedagogy for the Whole Child: Developmental Studies Center's Approach to Academic, Moral and Character Education," that presents the current work of the Developmental Studies Center that began as a theory driven and heavily researched program. This chapter presents arguably the most successful effort to date to apply what has been learned from developmental psychology to the classroom. The thrust of Brunn's chapter, however, is on how its approach has evolved over time to accommodate to the realities of classrooms and schools as it functions to address both the academic as well as social and emotional needs of children.

Brunn's discussion of the schools-based work of the Developmental Studies Center is followed in Chapter 16 by a review of the current status of schools-based efforts to address students' social and emotional learning (SEL), and how attending to SEL can complement efforts to address moral education and character formation. Maurice Elias and his colleagues, Sarah Parker, Megan Cash, and Roger Weissberg are among the leaders of the movement that led the Obama administration to place an emphasis upon issues of students' emotional safety and social emotional learning as core educational goals for American schools.

In Chapter 17, Matthew Davidson and Thomas Lickona, "Smart & Good Schools: A New Paradigm for High School Character Education," address factors that they argue serve to integrate the combined goals of high schools to produce students who attain high academic success while also fostering moral character. In this revised chapter they make the case that moral virtues such as honesty and fairness must be supported by performance virtues such as perseverance and hard work if moral values are to be enacted within a person's actions.

The final two chapters in this section present approaches to moral and character education in the Asian countries of Japan and Korea. In Chapter 18, "An Application of Kohlberg's Theory of Moral Dilemma Discussion to the Japanese Classroom and its Effect on Moral Development of Japanese Students," Noriyuki Araki reviews the research examining the effectiveness of applying moral dilemma discussions in Japanese classrooms. His chapter also addresses the limitations that Japanese schools encountered with their efforts to enact traditional forms of character education. In Chapter 19, "Moral and Character Education in Korea," In Jae Lee provides a comprehensive overview of how the Korean educational system works to integrate elements from both character and moral education orientations in order to make the best fit between traditional Korean cultural traditions and contemporary educational research.

PART IV: MORAL EDUCATION IN RELATION TO CIVIC ENGAGEMENT AND CITIZENSHIP AND DEMOCRACY EDUCATION

This section is new to the second edition of the handbook and provides chapters that link moral development with programs that foster civic engagement, citizenship, and democracy education. This section begins with Chapter 20 by Walter C. Parker, "Citizenship Education in the United States: Regime Type, Foundational Questions, and Classroom Practice," that reviews the history of citizenship education in the United States. As Parker outlines, this has been a topic that has generated controversies about both the goals and teaching methods to be employed. This is followed by Anne Colby's updated

Chapter 21 on fostering civic engagement among students in colleges and universities. Her chapter reviews the research examining the impact of college experience on the moral development and civic engagement of young adults. As this chapter makes clear, the process of moral development does not end in adolescence, and the college years afford an important context for the furtherance of moral growth. Chapter 22 by Wolfgang Edelstein and Tobias Krettenauer shifts the focus from North America to Europe and describes current efforts to integrate citizenship and democracy education across a very diverse range of cultures with divergent governmental histories. Their chapter reviews the range of approaches being attempted to engage in democratic education throughout Europe, and the challenges posed by the oftentimes non-democratic history of various countries and cultures within Europe. The section ends with the most recent and perhaps most ambitious effort at democratic education taking place in China. Sharon To, Shaongang Yang, and Charles C. Helwig present an eye-opening set of studies in Chapter 23, "Democratic Moral Education in China," indicating that democracy and moral education are gaining ground among Chinese educators and the new generation of students.

PART V: MORAL AND CHARACTER EDUCATION BEYOND THE CLASSROOM

Education is often defined in terms of practices that schools and teachers use to influence student learning and development. Children's and adolescents' moral development and character formation, however, are not simply the result of schooling. The chapters in Part V address how formal programs for community service, informal learning experiences through the media, and other modes of learning beyond the classroom can influence moral and character development. Richard Catalano, John Toumbourou, and David Hawkins lead off this section in Chapter 24, "Positive Youth Development in the United States: History, Efficacy and Links to Moral and Character Education," with their revised chapter examining what has become known as "positive youth development." This approach inverts the usual attention to youth disorders by focusing upon areas of youth competence or strength with the goal of anticipating problems before they emerge. In Chapter 25, "Community Contribution to Moral and Character Development," Constance Flanagan, Alisa Pykett, and Erin Gallay enlarge the discussion by discussing the ways in which communities contribute to the moral development and character formation of children and youth through community involvement and institutions designed to work with children beyond the school context. Flanagan et al. underscore the importance of membership and developmental experience in community-based organizations. They discuss the processes of moral development, how a moral self develops through membership and identification with a community where one has mutual obligations. Community environmental action projects profit from the empathy and interdependence individuals have developed together and help young people enlarge their concerns as they develop skills for citizenship. Their chapter is followed in Chapter 26 by an updated comprehensive examination of the impact of efforts to engage youth through service learning. Daniel Hart, Kyle Matsuba, and Robert Atkins in "The Moral and Civic Effects of Learning to Serve" define what is meant by service learning and civic engagement, describe the elements of effective programs, and offer powerful evidence that such beyond-the-classroom experiences shape the moral development and character formation of young people, including urban youth who face daily challenges of gang involvement, drug use, and street violence.

Chapter 27 by Elisabeth Kals and Markus Müller, "Education for Sustainability: Moral Issues in Ecology Education," addresses an emerging concern in this age of climate change and global development, namely how to educate young people to acknowledge their moral and ethical responsibilities toward the environment. This chapter is new to the second edition.

It is often said that sports build character. That cliché is critically examined by F. Clark Power and Kristin Sheehan in Chapter 28, "Moral and Character Education Through Sports." They take us beyond the bromides to look at the psychology of morality within the context of sports, and to explore the kinds of sports experiences that genuinely tap into and build students' moral character. Engagement in sports and sports teams is a form of involvement in community.

Finally, Muriel Bebeau and Verna Monson in Chapter 29, "A Theoretical and Evidenced-Based Approach for Designing Professional Ethics Education," review decades of research on the impact of professional education on the moral development of health professionals. On the basis of this research they offer a grounded theory for the integration of moral education within professional preparation generally and across disciplines. This chapter closes the circle with the discussion of the ethical dimensions of teaching introduced by Elizabeth Campbell in Part I of the book.

This second edition of the *Handbook of Moral Development and Character Education* reflects the state of the art and science of the field. This is an area of research and practice that has grown over the past five decades as the general public and political leaders have come to realize like leaders in centuries past that education is about more than academic learning. As Theodore Roosevelt once said, "To educate a man in mind and not in morals is to educate a menace to society." Still, perspectives vary in how best to go about the process of education for moral development, and whether the emphasis should be placed on the cultivation of virtue, or the development of moral judgment. Moreover, there are concerns about the premature application of developmental research to school practices (Nucci & Turiel, 2009). Nevertheless, there is a convergence of opinion around the need to continue research and inquiry in this area, and to encourage schools and teachers to include attention to moral development in their educational practices. It is our belief that this second edition will serve as a valuable resource for efforts to engage in both research and practice in the area of moral development and character education.

REFERENCES

Durkheim, E. (1925/1961). *Moral education.* Glencoe, IL: The Free Press.

Nucci, L., & Narvaez, D. (2008). *Handbook of moral and character education.* New York: Routledge.

Nucci, L., & Turiel, E. (2009). Capturing the complexity of moral development and education. *Mind, Brain, and Education, 3,* 151–159.

Piaget, J. (1932). *The moral judgment of the child.* New York: Free Press.

Rawls, J. (2001). *Justice as fairness: A restatement.* Cambridge, MA: Harvard University Press.

Part I

Defining the Field

Historical, Philosophical, and Theoretical Foundations

2

PHILOSOPHICAL MOORINGS

Thomas Wren

As with the rest of human life, morality and moral education have an outside and an inside. Seen from the outside, morality provides a way of getting along with others, and from the inside it is a way of getting along with oneself. In other words, moral education is at once a necessary condition for social control and an indispensable means of self-realization. Most of us, including philosophers and psychologists as well as parents and educators, assume that these two functions of morality sustain each other: what is good for society is good for our kids, and vice versa. Although Nietzsche and a few other so-called rugged individualists have rejected this assumption I will not spend time defending it in this chapter. Instead I will focus on the second of these two perspectives, the "inside view."[1] My motives for doing this are twofold. First of all, I want to unpack the general understanding, shared by contemporary educators of all persuasions, that morality is a form of self-realization. Also, I want to situate this understanding within the philosophical tradition of what, using the term in its broadest possible sense, I will simply call "human development."

Specialists in the fields of education and psychology may object that not all conceptions of moral education are developmental, and that is certainly true if we understand development in the biological sense of an organic unfolding of innate powers, taking place within a reasonably stable environment that sustains but does not itself shape the developmental process. It is also true if we understand development in a nonbiological but equally narrow sense as an ordered progress through cognitive stages, each of which has its own logical structure.[2] But our everyday concept of human development is not so narrow: there what is distinctive is not its inevitability or logical structure, but its normativity. Plainly put, most of us think of development as a movement from a less desirable state to a better one, even though in the case of human development the "betterness" at issue—namely, human flourishing—is subject to philosophical debate.

In what follows I will trace the way philosophers have formulated the fundamental developmental idea of human flourishing, since I believe that the history of their struggles to understand what it means to be human have shaped the ways in which contemporary moral educators understand their own enterprise. I am tempted to say that here as elsewhere in the history of ideas, ontogeny recapitulates phylogeny. However, to say this would oversimplify the way theories emerge within an intellectual tradition. It would be more realistic, I believe, to think of traditions, including our philosophical tradition, as providing necessary albeit usually unnoticed moorings for a specific theory or practice such as character education or moral judgment development. Thanks to these moorings a theory or practice is secured, stabilized, and thereby rendered intellectually plausible and practically useful. This point applies across the board, but as we will see in the following pages it is especially true for the theory, research, and practice of moral and character education.

When I spoke just now of "our philosophical tradition" I had in mind the usual pantheon of Western philosophers, beginning of course with the Greeks. One could begin even further back, since ancient non-Western thought is rich with insights into the moral dimension of selfhood—or better, the liberation from the demands of the self. However, the non-Western part of our story is well covered in the next chapter, so let's begin with what might be called the early Greek cognitive-developmental conception of human development.

SOCRATES AND PLATO

For Socrates (469–399 BCE) and Plato (428–347 BCE),[3] human development consisted in increasingly adequate knowledge of the ideal forms and, at the highest level, knowledge of the form of the Good. This form or idea (the usual two translations of the Greek *eidos*) is supremely intelligible, and other forms "participate" in its goodness because they too are thoroughly intelligible albeit more limited in their referential range. Since even sensible things and images participate in the intelligibility of their respective forms (the tire on my car can be understood as representing, imperfectly, the idea of a perfect circle), they too have a derivative sort of goodness. Furthermore, something of the same sort also holds for the cognitions directed toward these forms and things: perceptual knowledge is good but intellectual knowledge is better. The movement from less to more adequate modes of thinking is represented in Plato's famous Allegory of the Cave (more on this in a moment).

Although the Good was the highest in a hierarchy of ideal forms, it could be known indirectly in the course of knowing lower forms that reflect its goodness—indeed, one can get a glimmer of the highest form from the most banal perceptual experience. This idea is not as arcane or counterintuitive as it might first seem. We use lofty ceremonial language to commend saints and heroes for their goodness, but we also smack our lips after eating a hot dog and say, quite unceremoniously, "Mmm, that was good!" Banalities such as the hot dog commendation have been the subject of language-analytic theorizing by metaethical philosophers since G. E. Moore, but they also illustrate something very important in Plato's theory of the forms. In our lived experience the theoretical distinction between knowing and willing disappears. In ordinary, nonproblematic circumstances—say on a perfect day at the stadium when the home team is winning and lunch was a very long time ago—to see or smell a hot dog cooking on the grill is by that very fact to want it. In other words, the hot dog is *perceived as desirable* or, as Plato would say, it is apprehended "under the form of the Good."

This account also applies to more lofty forms of cognition. Christian philosophers and theologians influenced by Plato have hypothesized that the beatific vision enjoyed by the saints in heaven is at once a face-to-face knowledge of God and a perfect loving union with him. And theorists of human development have said the same thing about knowledge of the Good qua *moral*, namely that it is the ideal form of Justice: to know it is to choose it. Jean Piaget and Lawrence Kohlberg are examples of this sort of moral cognitivism.[4] The philosopher William Frankena is another. In his classical article on metaethical internalism, he argued that the very locution "X is the good [or right] thing to do" entails a motivational claim on the part of the speaker that he or she is at least somewhat inclined to do X" (Frankena, 1958; see also Wren, 1991).

But neither contemporary cognitivists nor ancient Platonists ever thought that it is easy to attain a direct, internally motivating vision of the Good itself. Piaget and Kohlberg postulated a series of logically structured stages through which one must pass on the way to the complete fusion of moral knowledge and moral virtue. Plato, on the other hand, simply told a story, his famous Allegory of the Cave. In it he describes a group of prisoners who have been chained together since birth and can only see shadows on the wall in front of them, cast by a fire behind them against crude two-dimensional replicas of things in the outside world, which of course the prisoners have never seen nor even imagined to exist. One of the prisoners is dragged outside the cave where, after becoming accustomed to the bright light of the real world, he attains true knowledge or what we might call the higher stages of Platonic cognitive development. He sees for the first time and with increasing acuity the really real things (here read: eternal truths and values) that were so poorly imaged in the cave. Eventually he also sees the Sun itself, which like the Good, is the source of all things. The story does not have a happy ending, though. He later returns to the cave, where he is reviled by the prisoners for his inability to predict the goings and comings of the shadows on the wall. As often happens with those who try to enlighten others, he is eventually killed.

The beauty of virtue. Plato's most famous account of virtue is his discussion of justice in the *Republic*, where he compares the tripartite structure of the soul (mind, spirit, and appetite) to the three classes of an ideal society (rulers, guardians, and workers). Each of these three classes has a distinctive function—ruling, protecting, and producing or consuming goods—which when done well exhibits the virtues of wisdom, courage, and temperance respectively. A just society is one in which all three classes work well and harmoniously together. Similarly, an individual who is wise, courageous, and temperate is said to be just in a global sense that corresponds to what we mean today by calling someone a very righteous or moral person.

So far so good. But here as in Plato's other dialogical writings, it is important to recognize what precipitated his famous parallel of personal and societal justice. Much earlier in the dialogue Socrates had been shocked by the cynical claim, represented by the sophist Thrasymachus, that justice is nothing more than an instrument of self-interest. In opposition, Socrates argued that justice (and by extension, virtue in general) is not a means but rather a good in itself, a "thing of beauty" (*to kalon*). But what does this mean? Is Plato grounding his moral theory in purely aesthetic value? Not at all.

Although he expounded his comparison of a just person and a just society without going into detail about any of the constitutive virtues, it is clear from this and other parts of the *Republic* that he believed each virtue has its own status as an ideal Form or eternal truth, and hence can be known directly in roughly the same way as are the other Forms or eternal truths, such as the one embodied in the tire of my car. In the latter case the eternal truth is the mathematical formula for a circle ($c=\pi d$); in the former (the moral judgment) it is a moral principle. Supposedly those who are truly wise understand the hurly burly of daily life in these terms, which in the moral context means that our judgments about what to do are based "on principle" in a double sense: the principle provides a motivational component as described above and also a justificatory rationale. Understood in this way, Plato's teaching on the virtues fits with the rule-oriented moral theory of Immanuel Kant and his contemporary heirs—who include not only philosophers like John Rawls but also cognitive developments such as Piaget and Kohlberg—as well as with the disposition-oriented theory of Aristotle and his heirs—who include not only philosophers like Alasdair MacIntyre but also most of the character educationists featured elsewhere in this volume.

ARISTOTLE

After Socrates' death in 399 BCE, Plato taught in the academy until he died, during which time Aristotle (384–322 BCE) was a student and then, after Plato's death, the founder of a rival school, the Lyceum. The institutional rivalry between these two schools is of little historical interest, but the intellectual rivalry between Aristotle and those of Plato's disciples who remained true to their teacher's intellectual idealism is important. The contrast is supposedly illustrated in Raphael's famous painting *The School of Athens*, in which Plato and Aristotle are pictured together, the one pointing heavenward toward the realm of the ideal Forms and the other gesturing downward to the earth which, for Aristotelians, was the truly real world.

Plato's notion of human development was fundamentally backward-looking—the prisoner in the cave was really trying to go back to a pristine state that he had lost, but for Aristotle human development was as forward-looking as any other sort of organic development. It was a goal-seeking sort of process, not a form-recalling one. It was, in a word, teleological. Just as the internal dynamism or *telos* of an acorn is to grow into an oak tree, so the *telos* of human beings is to develop into fully functioning, happy, flourishing rational animals. And that is what organisms do when nothing goes wrong. Of course things can go wrong and often do, for people as well as acorns. Even so, the acorns have an easier time of it, since they cannot err. Unless certain external conditions are absent (the acorn falls onto a sidewalk rather than fertile soil) growth is guaranteed, for the simple reason that acorns are not conscious of the end-state they are moving toward.

With this we come to what may be the two most important yet least understood parts of Aristotle's theory of human development and, accordingly, his conception of character and character education. The first part is his conception of the human *telos* as living in conformity with reason. Such a life may appear from the outside to be hopelessly conventional, but if the "reason" to which a person conforms is his or her *own* reason and not just an external social norm then it is clearly wrong to equate good character with mindless conformity. Even so, Aristotle is often read in the latter way, owing to the second part of his theory of human development, namely his account of character acquisition as "habituation." These two themes, "conformity with reason" and "habituation," need to be disentangled if we are to understand the relation between classical Aristotelian virtue theory and contemporary theories of moral education.

There is an important ambiguity in Aristotle's use of the term "reason" in the context of moral character and virtue. Sometimes he seems to mean the individual's own historically situated cognitive faculty and at other times he echoes Plato's notion of Reason as a transcendent reality that by its very nature always seizes upon the truth. The latter impression is strengthened by W. D. Ross's famous translation of the *Nicomachean Ethics* (1984), where the original Greek *orthos logos* is rendered as "right rule" (1138b25).[5] However, more recent scholarship regards this choice as far too Kantian, so that now the preferred translations are "right reason" and "practical wisdom." Indeed, the more colloquial (and more literal) phrase "straight thinking" may be even closer to what Aristotle has in mind, but this is not the place to quibble over terminology. What is important is that for Aristotle moral reasoning was an interpretation of here-and-now situations, not the imposition of antecedently known eternal principles onto the empirical phenomena of the present moment.

Over the last 20 or 30 years this point has been made repeatedly by Aristotle scholars, but it is only slowly percolating into the respective literatures of moral development and character education. In his early work Kohlberg (1970) dismissed virtue theory as an essentially noncognitive bundle of habits that were not only conceptually and psychologically disconnected from each other (character being considered as "a bag of virtues") but also too situation-specific to be the subject of any realistic education program. He eventually qualified this view (see Power, Higgins, & Kohlberg, 1989) but the line had been drawn, and character educationists such as W. Bennett (1991) who resisted the Kohlbergian characterization of virtue as knowledge of the good also implicitly resisted the idea at the heart of Aristotle's own view, namely that virtue is cognitive through and through. It is, as he put it in the *Ethics*, "a character state concerned with choice, lying in the mean relative to us, being determined by reason and the way the person of practical wisdom would determine it" (1107a1).

This idea of practical wisdom or *phronesis*—sometimes rather misleadingly translated as "prudence"—is the core of what we might call Aristotle's interactive model of cognitive developmental and social learning moral psychology. Moral goodness and wisdom are necessary conditions for each other, in that a person cannot be fully good without practical wisdom nor practically wise without also being virtuous. So put—and this was the way Aristotle himself put it (1144b31–2)—this famous dictum may sound like a chicken-and-egg sort of circular argument. But if we temporarily suspend the chronological question of which precedes which, and instead analyze separately what Nancy Sherman (1989) has called the four areas of practical wisdom, we can see what Aristotle had in mind. We can also see the general outlines of what he would have said about the current disconnection between the cognitive developmental and character formation models of moral education.

The four areas of practical wisdom that Sherman identifies (while adding that there may be more) are perception, deliberation (choice-making), collaborative thinking, and habituation. Each of these areas has its own logical geography and developmental course, and of course all four overlap in important ways. Each has been the subject of arcane debates among philosophers, classicists, and philologists, but their basic features are reassuringly familiar to anyone who has raised children or engaged in any sort of moral education. The first area, perception, is essentially interpretative, since it is the ability to pick out the salient features of a situation. The person with good moral perception can "read the scene" in much the same way as a person with good social skills knows what to say at a funeral, an art critic sees when things come together in a painting or concert, a military commander realizes when the battle is turning, or a coach quickly sizes up the other team's strengths and weaknesses.

This description of perception begins with the concrete situation and is therefore quite different from the top-down account of moral reasoning that is also identified with Aristotle, namely the practical syllogism. In the latter account moral cognition is modeled on deductive inference, where a major and minor premise logically entail a conclusion. Analogously, the so-called practical syllogism (Aristotle himself never used this term) combines a general value statement such as "My goal is X" with a factual statement about the here-and-now situation such as "Doing Y on this occasion will lead to X," from which the conclusion follows, "Therefore I should do Y."[6] True, the practical syllogism model incorporates perception—after all, the situation-specific minor premise would be impossible without it—but only as an accessory to the transsituational and personally neutral value or moral principle that constitutes the major premise. For this reason it would be a mistake to reduce Aristotle's notion of perception to the task of applying abstract principles to specific situations. Moral cognition and its developmental story run in the opposite direction: our general knowledge of what counts as courageous, just, etc. is the resultant of many specific interpretations of real world situations. Perception is part of the moral response, not its prelude. As Sherman aptly puts it, "Pursuing the ends of virtue does not begin with making choices, but with recognizing the circumstances relevant to specific ends" (p. 4).

One might object that some people are just born with greater social sensitivity than others, and that it would be unfair to regard them as more moral than someone who, perhaps because of a harsh upbringing or a cognitive processing deficit, often fails to pick up important social cues. However, Aristotle sees the distribution of moral sensibility as an educational problem, not a fairness issue. He would applaud the "sensitivity training" that is now part of our corporate culture as well of the school and the family. He would, I think, see such efforts as constituting an essential component of moral education.

But of course seeing and doing are not identical. They are different moments of virtuous action, and this difference takes us to Aristotle's second area of practical wisdom, which is the deliberation that precedes choice-making. Like sensitivity, deliberative thinking is a skill that can be learned, in moral as well as nonmoral contexts. Here again we can think of the corporate sector, where management trainees are expected to participate in workshops and other sorts of programs in which they learn how to improve their ability to determine which actions are most appropriate means toward selected ends. This ability includes such subskills as being able to prioritize multiple goals and to integrate them in ways that minimizes conflict. The analogy with moral deliberation should be obvious, regardless of whether training in this area is done formally or informally. Instruction, modeling, trial and error, vicarious experience through historical or literary narratives, debates about hypothetical cases—moral educators have used such practices for centuries.

Aristotle's third area of practical wisdom is collaborative thinking, which is both the source and the fruit of hands-on collaboration. Collaboration can be on any scale and at any level of sophistication: within the family, among friends, civic activity, and even across national boundaries. In every case the cognitive requirement is the ability to take the perspective of another, and the affective requirement is the tendency to care about whatever is revealed when one takes such a perspective. Its most primitive version is collaboration for mutual benefit, but Aristotle believed that it is in our nature as "polit-ical animals"—*zoon politikon*—to care about common goods such as the quality of our family life itself, the preservation of our friendships, the prestige of our city, and so on. This expansion of our horizons includes an increased sensitivity to social complexity: children develop better understandings of why their parents worry about the things they do, lovers learn new things about their own motivations, citizens discover in public debate issues they never dreamed of, and so on. Social bonds are not blind attachments but rather richly cognitive relationships, shaped not only by day-to-day interactions with family members, friends, and associates but also by what is now called civic education. The pedagogies for civic education are controversial—what is the correct ratio of discip-line to creativity, how to combine respect for authority with critical thinking, etc.—but there is little doubt that Aristotle thought collaborative thinking, like perception and deliberation, is something that can be learned, and that this learning process was an integral component of moral education.

As we turn to the fourth area of practical wisdom, habituation, it might seem that here Aristotle's emphasis will be on noncognitive processes. Many commentators as well as moral educators who invoke Aristotle have interpreted him in that way, but within the scholarly community the tide shifted a few decades ago (see Burnyeat, 1980; Rorty, 1980; Nussbaum, 1986; Sherman, 1989; Sorabji, 1973–1974). Those who continue to favor the noncognitive interpretation take quite literally Aristotle's distinction between the intellectual and moral virtues, according to which the latter consist in habits that regulate the "irrational" parts of the soul—i.e., the passions. These habits, Aristotle tells us, are acquired in childhood by means of external shaping factors such as discipline, good example, and above all by the repetition of good acts. In this way, we are told, the child develops moral virtue as a "second nature," a phrase that character education theo-rists sometimes confuse with simple conformity.

The problem with that interpretation of Aristotle is that, as Sherman explains, "it leaves unexplained how the child with merely 'habituated' virtue can ever develop the capacities requisite for practical reason and inseparable for full virtue" (p. 158). As we have seen, Aristotle insisted that full virtue is possible only with practical wisdom (1144b30–33), which includes the heavily cognitive areas or dimensions of perception of salience, choice-making abilities, and collaborative thinking. It is far more plausible, as an interpretation of Aristotle but also as a description of our own children's early devel-opment, to suppose that habituation includes not only rewards and punishments but also reasoned explanations as to why certain actions are rewarded or punished, certain persons are held up as models, and so on. For a child to lack adult-level practical wisdom does not imply that he or she has no cognitive capacities for reading situations, making choices, or taking the perspective of others. Furthermore, a closer look at what Aristotle said about the so-called nonrational parts of the soul—i.e., the passions or emotions—shows that even the crudest responses of fear or anger or desire have cognitive dimensions and hence can be directed by one's own intelligence as well as by external pressures.

To sum up so far, it seems that each of Aristotle's first three areas of practical wisdom has its own educational agenda or pedagogy. Perception is developed through sensitivity training, which includes teaching children how to pick out the morally salient features of a situation. Deliberative thinking is developed through what might be called managerial pedagogy, which shapes the ability to set goals and figure out how to meet them. And collaborative thinking is developed through perspective-taking training and, on a larger scale, civic education. But what about his fourth area, habituation? Does it have its own pedagogy too?

Yes and no. Aristotle went to great length to explain how moral teachers—typically parents—should use discipline, modeling, and consistent repetition to enable the learner to acquire the right habits. This is the pedagogy of habit formation, but it should not be understood as radically distinct from the other three areas of practical wisdom. Virtue is itself a habit and so are all its component skills. For instance, children develop the habit of reading common household social situations (perception) by observing their mother's sensitive response to a sibling's unspoken needs, they develop an established habit of carefully weighing the pros and cons of any course of action (deliberation) by doing so on repeated occasions, and they expand their interpersonal horizons to civic readiness (collaborative thinking) by emulating leaders whom they see praised and honored for their service to the community. For Aristotle moral education was organic, not modular: each component pedagogy made its own contribution to the goal of living a life in conformity to reason, but as it did so it provided the necessary conditions and platforms for the other pedagogies. This integration of functions was only to be expected in a fundamentally teleological philosophical system such as Aristotle's.

Aristotelian teleology has as its contemporary counterpart recent psychological and educational theories in which reality, especially moral reality, is understood in developmental terms. It should therefore come as no surprise to learn that cognitive developmentalists such as Piaget and Kohlberg sometimes compare Aristotle's account of habituation to their own accounts of the early stages of moral competence (see Power et al., 1989, p. 134). Such comparisons are plausible, but we should not identify Aristotle too closely with any contemporary psychological theory. His recognition of the importance of external pressures such as discipline, good example, trial and error, and above all the repetition of good acts is also compatible with the more cognitive approaches of social learning theory, such as Martin Hoffman's (2000) "induction,"[7] which emphasizes the role of reason-giving in parent–child relationships, or Walter Mischel's (1968, p. 150) "observational learning," which is mediated by perceptual–cognitive processes. It is safest to say that Aristotle's theory of habituation and, for that reason plus others, his entire ethical theory is underdetermined as far as contemporary moral psychology is concerned. Even though much of what he says in the *Nicomachean Ethics* and elsewhere is clearly incompatible with hard-core behaviorist or associationist approaches to moral socialization, and even though his account of moral education has important developmental features, it leaves open important questions such as whether the acquisition of moral habits is best understood in stage-structural terms, according to which the cognitive capabilities discussed above (perception, etc.) either advance in tandem or are clustered in distinct and increasingly complex ways during the child's developmental career. Perhaps the best way to characterize Aristotle's thought in this important area is to say that it seems to be more a refinement of common sense than deep psychological theory. That moral virtue is indeed part of the human *telos* is old news.

BRITISH EMPIRICISM

We now skip over the transformations of Aristotelian teleology wrought by the Roman Stoics who turned philosophy into a "therapy of desire" (Nussbaum, 1994) and later by the medieval scholastics who baptized the very idea of goal-seeking and treated it as part of the larger story of divine providence and salvation history. We even rush past the opening century of modernity, when in the 1630s René Descartes rejected the teleological model itself, dismissing it as the keystone of the existing ramshackle edifice of unwarranted assumptions, beliefs, superstitions, and appeals to tradition. These were all important phases in the history of philosophy and the formation of our contemporary views of human nature, but they are not of special relevance to contemporary theories and practices of moral education or character formation. However, the so-called "empiricist" phase that came next was not only relevant but amounted to a radical break with what was then the established view of human development.

John Locke. And so we come to rest in the following century, and take up the so-called Father of British Empiricism, John Locke (1632–1704). Uninspired by the worn-out scholasticism current when he was a student at Oxford, Locke cheerfully embraced Descartes' repudiation of tradition as the font of wisdom. However, he rejected its accompanying theory of innate ideas and other cognitive structures. In this respect Locke and the empiricists who followed him had the same ambivalence toward Descartes that Aristotle had toward Plato's notion of self-standing ideal forms.

What psychologists now call human development was a relatively unanalyzed notion in British empiricism. Locke never directly challenged the general Aristotelian model of human flourishing, which he inherited from scholastic philosophy and the conventional Christianity of the sixteenth and seventeenth centuries. Here as elsewhere, he took a common sense approach to human nature, as did the philosophers who followed him. However, he replaced Aristotle's dynamic notion of human development as the unfolding of an inner teleology with his own relatively static notion of experience as receptivity to external perceptions or "inputs." For instance, Locke believed our moral understanding is shaped by a combination of natural prosocial "sentiments" and experiences (observations) of prosocial behavior in others.

Locke's famous image of the mind was a "blank slate" (*tabula rasa*). It lies at the heart of the conception that he and other empiricists such as David Hume and Adam Smith had regarding what counted for them as human development. The blank slate metaphor has two parts: (1) there are no innate ideas (certain ideas such as the moral principle of the Golden rule and principles of identity and contradiction are self-evident, but that does not make them innate), and (2) experience is the only stylus that can write on the slate. There were, said Locke, two sources of experience: *sensation* (which was the primary source, derived from sensible objects external to the mind), and *reflection* (the secondary source, entirely internal to the mind). Among the latter are moral ideas, but Locke left it to his successors to spell out exactly how these ideas emerge.

David Hume. The most important of these successors, especially in matters of moral psychology, is undoubtedly David Hume (1711–1776). Like Locke he located moral ideas and their corresponding passions under the category of "ideas of reflection" since they were not immediate perceptions of an external reality. He shared Locke's belief that their mutual predecessor Thomas Hobbes had gone too far in his account of psychological egoism, according to which all action, even moral action, is motivated solely by self-interest. Their more moderate position was that motives of benevolence as well as self-interest are operative in human affairs. However, in his *Enquiry concerning the Principles of Morals* (1751) Hume went on to argue that the way we actually make moral judgments is to approve or disapprove certain actions rather than to describe any unique moral quality they might have. Since as far as he could tell most of the actions we approve of happen to increase public utility, he concluded that we have a natural tendency (motivation) to consider and promote the well-being of others. The "calm passion" of benevolence combines with "pleasurable impressions" such as knowing one is esteemed by others, and thereby creates what learning theorists would later call schedules of internal reinforcement.

In sum, Hume believed that morality is based on affectivity, not rationality, that our nature includes not only the power to reason but also two types of passion, namely self-regarding and other-regarding sentiments, and that successful social systems cultivate both sorts of affectivity. Moral development consists in the cultivation and balance of the sentiments, but he did not think there is any special cognitive framework within which this development must take place.

There are several reasons for this absence, but the main one is Hume's associationist theory of knowledge in general. Wielding Ockham's razor, he did away with the assumption that ideas necessarily have a one-for-one correspondence to the components of external reality. Whatever coherence the world (or the self) seems to have is, he claimed, a matter of the simple application to our mental life of three natural laws of association, namely the laws of resemblance, contiguity, and causality (which is basically contiguity in time rather than space). Note that what is associated in these laws are not things or events in the world but introspectible entities, namely ideas, taken in the broad sense as including the internal contents of all experience.

The educational implications of this skeptical disconnect between the way our ideas are configured and the way the external world is configured are profound, and they are especially profound in the case of moral education. What is learned are regular relations between certain kinds of experiences and certain kinds of perception, typically the sentiment-laden perception that one is the object of other persons' approval or the experience of benevolent feelings. How these relationships are learned varies. Sometime the learning in question is the simple repetition of a pair of ideas or mental events such as the smell of cigarette smoke and the pain of a sublethal electric shock, and sometimes it is a very complicated set of resemblances and correlations such as what the social learning theorist Albert Bandura has called "observational learning," which is to say watching human models. As he explains,

> By observing others, one forms rules of behavior, and on future occasions this coded information serves as a guide for action…. Throughout the years, modeling has always been acknowledged to be one of the most powerful means of transmitting values, attitudes, and patterns of thought and behavior.
>
> (1986, p. 47)

Absent from this quotation is any hint of *why* or *how* the simple experience or set of experiences of seeing a model perform a certain action leads one to form a rule for that action. Like Hume, Bandura applied Ockham's razor to lop off any epistemological account of the correlation between observation and rule-formation. Although he prefers to be called a "social cognitive theorist" Bandura's approach to observational learning is at bottom as epistemologically barren as Pavlov's classical conditioning paradigm or B. F. Skinner's radical behaviorism (see Wren, 1991, ch. 3). The same could be said of any program of moral education that was governed by Hume's three laws of association as closely as Bandura was in the passage just quoted.

KANT

It was perhaps inevitable that Hume's skepticism about our moral and scientific knowledge of the external world would generate a counter-skepticism about the validity of the entire empiricist program. However, when the reaction came it was not a return to the straightforward realism of classical philosophy but rather an entirely new conception of philosophical inquiry, known from its very beginnings as "transcendental critique." Its founder was Immanuel Kant (1724–1804), who began his philosophical career in much the same way that Locke did a century earlier, working within the scholastic dogmatism that had somehow lingered on during the modern era. This came to an end for Kant when, in what must have been the philosophical equivalent of a midlife crisis, he read Hume's work and, as he later put it, awoke from his dogmatic slumbers.

The rationalists inspired by Descartes and the empiricists inspired by Locke shared the same goal of explaining how our concepts can match the nature of objects, but Kant changed the program. Taking what is now called a constructionist approach, he argued that philosophers must show how the structure of our concepts shapes our experience of the world. He broke this huge task into two parts. The first was to establish the conditions under which (Newtonian) scientific knowledge—and by extension any experience whatsoever—is possible, which he did in the *Critique of Pure Reason* (1781/1998). Then, using similar categories and methods of argument, he went on to establish the conditions of the possibility of any *moral* experience, first in his famous *Foundations for the Metaphysics of Morals* (1785/1959) and then in the more formidable *Critique of Practical Reason* (1788/1956).

Unlike the empiricists, Kant had a clear and radically new conception of human development: personal autonomy. Paradoxically, the way one becomes autonomous is by obeying the law, especially the moral law. But one must obey the law for the right reasons, which is to say from motives of duty rather than the "inclinations" of self-interest. (Note that Kant saw nothing intrinsically wrong with acting from inclination, as long as one does not do so *instead of* acting from duty. He was, in fact, something of a bon vivant according to many reports.) Kant unfolded his idea of moral autonomy as follows. Since a truly good person is one who has internalized and follows the moral law, the core conception of moral agency is not the teleological notion of human flourishing or virtue but rather the *deontological* notion (from the Greek word for duty, *deon*) of following a self-imposed rule. Simply put, when I act from inclinations—which range from crude sensual desire to the composite desire for happiness—I am letting my actions be ruled by something other than my own will. I am properly described as acting under the rule of something "other," which Kant called heteronomy of the will. But when I act in accord with a law that I generate and impose on myself as a rational member of the human community, I am self-ruled, which is of course the literal meaning of the word autonomy. Like all legislation, the moral law is formulated as a set of prescriptions, commands, or *imperatives*, which Kant divides into sorts: hypothetical and categorical.

"*Hypothetical*": As the term suggests, hypothetical imperatives, like hypothetical statements, have an "if-then" structure, linking an antecedent condition and a consequent action or action-mandate. The action that is the object of the command is considered good simply because it is a means to achieve an ulterior end or proposition (the antecedent): "If you want *y*, do *x*," or negatively, "Avoid *x* if you want *y*." Seemingly moral injunctions such as "Keep your promises if you want people to trust you," and "Don't steal if you want to avoid problems with the police," are hypothetical in form and for that reason not really part of the moral law.

"Categorical": In contrast, a truly moral action has neither antecedent nor consequent components. Its rightness is simply unconditioned, that is, independent of considerations of external goals or circumstance. There are no "ifs, ands, or buts": the action is commanded simply because it is considered to be of value in itself. Thus the general form of a moral imperative is "Do *x*" or "Don't do *y*"—as in "Keep your promises" and "Don't steal."

Of course it is possible to issue obviously nonmoral commands that are categorical in the trivial sense that no antecedent is uttered, as when a parent says, "Wash your hands before coming to the table." What makes a truly moral imperative different from "Keep your promises" is, then, something over and above the simple absence of an antecedent term. This "special something" is, Kant believed, a formal quality of the *maxim* underlying the action in question, a point that Kohlberg (1981, p. 135 *et passim*) later seized upon in order to differentiate his judgment-oriented approach from the content-oriented approach typical of character education.

To examine this quality we first need to understand Kant's notion of a maxim or, to use a phrase common in contemporary analytic philosophy, the relevant act-description. Kant's own example is a person who normally tells the truth but is prepared to lie if doing so is to his or her advantage. Such a person has adopted the maxim "I will lie whenever doing so is to my advantage," and is acting on that maxim whenever he or she engages in lying behavior. Of course many maxims have nothing to do with morality, since they are purely pragmatic policies such as straightening one's desk at the end of each workday or not picking up hitchhikers.

Now we can identify the "special something" that makes a maxim a moral maxim. For Kant it was the maxim's *universalizability*. (Note that *universalizability* is a fundamentally different concept than *universality*, which refers to the fact that some thing or concept not only should be found everywhere but actually is. However, the two concepts sometimes flow into each other: human rights are said to be universal not in the sense that they are actually conceptualized and respected in all cultures but rather in the sense that reason requires that they *should* be. And this is a moral "should.") However, in the course of developing this idea, Kant produced several formulations of the Categorical Imperative, all of which turn on the idea of universalizability. Commentators usually distinguish the following five versions:

1. *"Act only according to a maximum that at the same time you could will that it should become a universal law."* In other words, a moral maxim is one that any rationally consistent human being would want to adopt and see others adopt. The above-mentioned maxim of lying when doing so is to one's advantage fails this test, since if there were a rule that everyone could or even should lie under such circumstances no one would believe anyone—which of course is utterly incoherent. Making such a maximum standard practice would destroy the very point of lying.

2. *"Act as if the maxim directing your action should be converted, by your will, into a universal law of nature."* The first version showed that immoral maxims are *logically* incoherent. The phrase "as if" in this second formulation shows that they are also untenable on *empirical* grounds. Quite simply, no one would ever want to live in a world that was by its very nature populated only by people living according to immoral maxims.

3. *"Act in a way that treats all humanity, yourself and all others, always as an end, and never simply as a means."* The point here is that to be moral a maxim must be oriented toward the preservation, protection, and safeguarding of all human beings, simply because they are beings which are intrinsically valuable, that is to say ends in themselves. Of course much cooperative activity involves "using" others in the weak sense of getting help from them, but moral cooperation always includes the recognition that those who help us are also persons like ourselves and not mere tools to be used to further our own ends.

4. *"Act in a way that your will can regard itself at the same time as making universal law through its maxim."* This version is much like the first one, but it adds the important link between morality and personal autonomy: when we act morally we are actually making the moral law that we follow.

5. *"Act as if by means of your maxims, you were always acting as a universal legislator, in a possible kingdom of ends."* Finally, the maxim must be acceptable as a norm or law in a possible kingdom of ends. This formulation brings together the ideas of legislative rationality, universalizability, and autonomy. What Kant had in mind can be illustrated by imagining an ideal parliament of partisan but nonetheless civil senators or deputies who have, over and above their personal feelings, deep-seated respect for each other *as legislators*, typically accompanied by courtly rhetoric such as "I would respectfully remind my esteemed colleague from the great state of ___ that…"

Like most philosophers who discuss the way we think about moral issues, Kant took as his normal case a fully functional adult living in a basically decent environment. But cognitive developmental psychologists who focus on children's moral reasoning processes have also worked in the long shadow of Kant ever since Jean Piaget wrote his *Moral Judgment of the Child* (1932/1965). This work is now a classic scholarly resource for moral educational theory. The same can be said of much of the work by Lawrence Kohlberg, whose first publication in 1958 was a doctoral study based on Piaget and whose last publications appeared posthumously as late as 1990 (Kohlberg, Boyd, & Levine, 1990). In both cases they charted the development of the child's ability to make moral judgments about the rightness or wrongness of specific (though hypothetical) actions, and in both cases claimed to discover an ordered set of stages that began with what Kant called heteronomous principles of action and ended with autonomous principles.

The logical structures of Piaget's and Kohlberg's stages are, of course, well known, but what is not always clear is the dynamic by which the child moves through the sequence. Here we find no help from Kant, who apparently assumed that a clear-thinking person of any age would have an intrinsic motivation to think and act autonomously, even though moral struggle always remained a logical as well as empirical possibility. Surprisingly, one of the best accounts of our tendency to reason autonomously can be found in Aristotle's treatment of collaborative thinking. As we saw above, he posited an innate prosociality (the human person as *zoon politkon*) that was realized in the quest for shared goods at various levels of inclusiveness. Aristotle's conceptions of human flourishing and moral standards were typically ethnocentric, but there does seem to be an important affinity between his idea that people are political animals and Kant's idea of moral agents as "universal legislators in a possible kingdom of ends." If so, then the developmental dynamic in question may be connected in important ways with the Kantian constructionist epistemology that

Piaget and Kohlberg deployed. As they explain in various contexts, children (and adults, at least in Kohlberg's scheme) move from one stage to the next because of interactions that take place between them and other persons: conflicting social demands, questions proposed by others who think differently, responsibilities for distributing resources, and so on. Toward the end of his career Kohlberg decided that classroom discussions of moral dilemmas were far less effective as occasions of moral growth than were real-life experiences of decision-making. With this realization came the "just community" approach to moral education, which in spite of its Kantian conception of moral reasoning seems to incorporate much of Aristotle's own understanding of practical wisdom.

However, the deep gap between Aristotle and Kant remains. As we saw above, Aristotle believed that practical wisdom, which for him was the supreme moral virtue, is something quite different from principled reasoning. Whereas Kant thought that we first formulate and adjudicate moral maxims and then apply them to concrete situations, Aristotle thought that we first pick out the goods that are at stake in a given situation, then work out the best way to balance these goods in a coherent and publicly responsible way, and then—but only if one is inclined to be a moral philosopher as well as a moral agent—distill all these considerations into a set of moral principles such as those found in his discussion of distributive justice in Chapter 3 of the *Nicomachean Ethics*.

THE AFTERMATH

The history of moral philosophy did not end with Kant, but the parts that have most influenced moral educators did, with of course a few exceptions. One of the most important exceptions is Arthur Schopenhauer (1788–1860), whose conception of the world, including the human world, as the representation of a cosmic force or "Will" influenced Freud and those educators who understand morality primarily in Freudian categories. However, Freud himself insisted that Schopenhauer's influence was incidental to his own discovery of the unconscious and related primary processes, and it seems safe to say that whatever Schopenhauer's influence on Freud really was, it has had no direct impact on moral educators in the English-speaking world. Something of the same sort holds for the moral theories of G. W. F. Hegel (1770–1831) and Nietzsche (1840–1900), whose influence on nineteenth and twentieth century ethical philosophy is not matched by any direct impact their works had on moral education.

Another important exception is John Dewey, who anticipated the cognitive developmental view that human beings advance in their understandings of moral issues in a progressive way. His application of this general psychological principle to the classroom— the controversial "progressive education" pedagogy—foreshadowed the just community approach mentioned a few lines earlier. As Power et al. (1989) once explained, "our basic expectation, derived from the theories of Dewey and Piaget, was that participation in the governance of a small school community would stimulate growth of moral reasoning more than would participation in the more traditionally governed high schools" (p. 266).

Philosophers continue to add their voices to the dialogue of moral and character education, but for the most part they do so by retrieving—or better, refurbishing— the parts of the philosophical tradition that we have surveyed in this chapter. Among more recent moral philosophers the figure of the late John Rawls (1921–2002) towers over all, but without denying his importance it is clear that much of the power of his social contract theory of justice and its consequent importance for moral educators is an extension of the Kantian approach, as he himself readily acknowledged. Similar retrievals have been made by virtue theorists such as Alasdair MacIntyre (1929–) who advocate a return to the teleological conception of character found in Aristotle, and utilitarian philosophers such as Richard Brandt (1910–1997), whose contributions to the moral education debate were drawn from the deep well of Humean empiricism.

The Global Order. As the twentieth century drew to a close, the difference between virtue-based and principle-based accounts of morality became a philosophical theme in its own right, articulated in what is often identified as the liberal-communitarian debate. Virtue-based accounts portrayed moral agents as motivated by commitments and loyalty to those with whom they share traditions, nationalities, and other sorts of communal bonds. Here the historical roots are in Aristotle's notion of virtue, especially as it operates in friendship relationships. In contrast, principle-based accounts saw moral agents as motivated not by communal ties (except incidentally) but rather by a sense of duty that is grounded in universal and impartial principles of justice prefigured by Kant's Categorical Imperative. Over the last few decades the debate between virtue-oriented and duty-oriented moral philosophers has focused on a variety of issues that have their own educational implications (Wren, 2005). However, since the beginning of the present millennium many of the virtue vs. duty issues have been absorbed into still more complex discussions of *globalization* and its moral implications. In what follows I will quickly frame those discussions and then indicate their relevance to moral education.

It is sometimes remarked that today's moral and political discussions of globalization recapitulate the opposition between cosmopolitanism and nationalism that has been with us since the days of Hellenistic and Roman Stoics. As an abstract generalization in the history of ideas this claim is true enough, but it fails to take seriously the fact that questions about our responsibilities to distant others have a new urgency, thanks largely to technologies and international structures that have emerged in the wake of colonialism and the cold war. Our general obligation to those in far-off lands is no longer a second-tier responsibility, to be addressed only after our more important local obligations have been sorted out and fulfilled.

The complex philosophical structure of our moral responsibility to distant others is part of a still larger evaluative question that already lies at the center of civic education and is beginning to show up in the theory and practice of many moral educators: *What are the normative implications of the increasingly powerful forces of globalization?* Any serious answer to that question must recognize that moral educators and philosophers (as well as public policy specialists and hands-on decision-makers who deal with ethically complex issues of international relations) need a distinctive "ethics in a world of strangers" (Appiah, 2006). And any answer to that question will also have to go beyond the now-familiar philosophical distinction between communitarian and liberal ethical theories. Whatever use that distinction might still have in philosophical accounts of personal decision-making, it seems to be of little help in designing and morally assessing collective strategies and policies concerning large-scale transnational issues such as forced industrial development, governmental corruption, or conflicts between tribal practices and democratic institutions.

In short, we need to develop new philosophical and educational approaches that deal with justice and other moral issues on a global scale. The standard communitarian approach presupposes existing ties to friends, relatives, and fellow nationals. For that reason it would be illogical to expect it to provide an ethic for a world of strangers, even when the concept of community is expanded to include the regional loyalties of, say, citizens in Latin America or the European Union. Admittedly, not everyone would agree with this assessment. (The pioneer of globalization studies, Roland Robertson [1938–], would certainly disagree.) However, the tendency toward boundary maintenance is now a well-documented characteristic of ethnic and cultural groups (see Barth, 1969), and so it seems empirically as well as logically wrong to view communitarianism as a self-standing globalization ethic.

A somewhat different lack of logic undermines the liberal understanding of global ethics. Philosophers who take that approach to moral questions (e.g., Kant, Mill, Rawls) tend to treat our relation to distant others as a motivationally barren, purely logical connection. For instance the only connection that Kant's Categorical Imperative or the Golden Rule formally acknowledges between "others" and oneself is a common rationality and vulnerability to fear, pain, and death. Whatever validity or motivating force this quintessentially liberal notion might have in personal or small group relationships, it seems clear that in today's globalized world the relationships and corresponding moral obligations we have regarding distant others are much more complex, and that this complexity should be recognized by moral educators. For instance, it is plausible that in the course of our everyday use of the natural resources which multinational corporations have exploited from developing nations through dishonest "rent transfers" (typically a euphemism for certain bribes at the highest levels of government) we become accomplices to the crimes committed by corrupt governments against their own people. Under this interpretation (elaborated by Thomas Pogge, 2002), we have a moral obligation to make restitution, directly or indirectly, to the citizens of that country for the stolen goods we have purchased from its leaders or corporate accomplices, just as we would have an obligation to restore a stolen car to its rightful owner even though we had purchased it unwittingly.

There are many other moral issues generated by globalization that moral educators could and should address. One of the most frequently discussed of those issues is the distribution of resources from wealthy to poor nations. Another is the seemingly paternalistic export of participatory democracy and human rights mandates to non-Western peoples who have other political traditions. National sovereignty is challenged by morally charged efforts to control emissions on a global scale, and policies regarding immigration, free speech, and access to education are now seen as human rights issues. Social, political, and economic problems that used to be local or national issues are now subject to international assessment, as are their remedies and, by implication, the ethical standards for those remedies, especially standards couched in the language of human rights. In a word, civic virtue has taken on a whole new meaning, one that calls for new approaches to the civic dimension of moral education.

More specifically, over the last decade or two it has become increasingly clear that civic virtue should be understood and taught as a special case of moral virtue (see McLaughlin, 1992, and my expansion of his ideas in Wren, 2013). With this new understanding has come a new emphasis on collective action, since there is little that a single individual can do to address justice or benevolence issues in far-off lands, in international contexts, or on any sort of large scale. For this and other reasons *voluntary collective action* now seems to be an important aspect of moral education in global contexts. That the global not-for-profit sector is one of the most effective and accessible fields for such action is shown by the remarkable increase in the number of international NGOs since 1990 as well as by the explosion of literature devoted to this new version of what the medieval philosopher Thomas Aquinas (1225–1274) called "commutative justice," namely the responses that individuals and groups should make to the legitimate claims which other individuals and groups—no matter how distant—have on them (*Summa Theologica* [1265–1273/1945], II, II Q61a1; see also Edwards and Gaventa, 2001).

CONCLUSION

So where does this leave us? Good answers to that question are to be found throughout this book. To return to the "mooring" metaphor that introduced the present chapter, we should keep in mind that the various assertions, denials, interpretations, and methodologies offered throughout this volume are not free-floating intellectual constructions but rather are moored to long-standing but still-evolving philosophical traditions. However, they are moored in different ways and tied to different mooring posts, by which I mean that their underlying assumptions are drawn from significantly different philosophical conceptions of what it means to be—and to develop into—a fully human person. Understanding how their respective philosophical infrastructures differ will not resolve the complex theoretical and practical differences among moral educators, but it will enable them to take each other's perspective more thoroughly and, let us hope for the sake of our children and ourselves, more productively.

NOTES

1. For an example of the "outside view," consider Robert Dreeben's (1968) structural functionalist conception of the school as

   an agency of socialization whose task is to effect psychological changes that enable persons to make transitions among other institutions; that is, to develop capacities necessary for appropriate conduct in social settings that make different kinds of demands on [students] and pose different kinds of opportunities. (p. 3)

2. This point has been discussed at length by Ger Snik and other contributors to a volume entitled *Philosophy of Development: Reconstructing the Foundations of Human Development and Education* (van Haaften, Korthals, & Wren, 1997). As Snik explains, "The question is not whether we should use the notion of development but only what specific conception of development is most appropriate in educational contexts" (Snik, 1997, p. 202).

3. Here as elsewhere it is hard to separate their respective views of the Forms since most of what we know of Socrates comes from his role in Plato's dialogues, especially the *Phaedo* and the *Republic*. Following the usual practice in Plato scholarship, I have used the Stephanus method of pagination when referring to specific passages in Plato's works (see Plato, 1997).

4. In the introduction to the first volume of his collected writings Kohlberg (1981, p. xxix) presents an eight-point summary of the elements of Plato's conception of justice that he incorporated in his own work. His third point is especially relevant here: "Virtue is knowledge of the good. He who knows the good chooses the good."

5. Ross's translation of the *Nicomachean Ethics* is contained in Aristotle, 1984. A much better overall translation of the *Nicomachean Ethics* is the one by C. Rowe, contained in Aristotle, 2002. Note, by the way, that in my discussion of Aristotle I have followed the usual practice of using line numbers (the Bekker numbers) rather than page numbers since there are so many different translations of Aristotle's work.

6. Some philosophers prefer to say the conclusion is not "I should" or any other sort of statement but rather the decision itself to do Y—or even the act of doing Y.

7. Hoffman defines this oddly named parenting technique as "the type of discipline … in which parents highlight the other's perspective, point up the other's distress, and make it clear that the child's action caused it" (2000, p. 143).

REFERENCES

Appiah, K. (2006). *Cosmopolitanism: Ethics in a world of strangers.* New York: W.W. Norton.

Aquinas, T. (1265–1273). *Summa theologica,* trans. by the English Dominican Fathers. In A. C. Pegis (Ed.), *The basic writings of St. Thomas Aquinas.* New York: Random House, 1945.

Aristotle. (1984). *Nicomachean ethics,* ed. W. D. Ross, revised by J. O. Urmson, trans. In Jonathan Barnes (Ed.), *The complete works of Aristotle: The revised Oxford translation* (Vol. 2). Princeton, NJ: Princeton University Press.

Aristotle. (2002). *Nicomachean ethics* (C. Rowe, trans.). Oxford: Oxford University Press.

Bandura, A. (1986). *Social foundations of thought and action.* Englewood Cliffs, NJ: Prentice-Hall.

Barth, F. (1969). *Ethnic groups and boundaries. The social organization of culture difference.* Oslo: Universitetsforlaget.

Bennett, W. J. (1991). Moral literacy and the formation of character. In J. Benninga (Ed.), *Moral character and civic education in the elementary school* (pp. 128–137). New York: Teachers College Press.

Burnyeat, M. (1980). Aristotle on learning to be good. In A. O. Rorty (Ed.), *Essays on Aristotle's Ethics* (pp. 259–281). Berkeley: University of California Press.

Dreeben, R. (1968). *What is learned at school.* Reading, MA: Addison-Wesley Publishing Company.

Edwards, M., & Gaventa, J. (Eds.) (2001). *Global citizen action.* Abingdon, UK: Earthscan.

Frankena, W. (1958). Obligation and motivation in recent moral philosophy. In A. I. Melden (Ed.), *Essays in moral philosophy* (pp. 40–81). Seattle: University of Washington Press.

Hoffman, M. L. (2000). *Empathy and moral development: Implications for caring and justice.* New York: Cambridge University Press.

Kant, I. (1956). *Critique of practical reason* (L. W. Beck, trans.). Indianapolis and New York: Liberal Arts Press. (Original publication 1788).

Kant, I. (1959). *Foundations of the metaphysics of morals* (L. W. Beck, trans.). Indianapolis: Bobbs-Merrill. (Original publication 1785).

Kant, I. (1998). *Critique of pure reason* (P. Gruyer & A. W. Wood, Eds. and trans.). Cambridge: Cambridge University Press. (Original publication 1781).

Kohlberg, L. (1958). *The development of modes of thinking and choices in years 10 to 16.* Ph.D. dissertation, University of Chicago.

Kohlberg, L. (1970). Education for justice: A modern statement of the Platonic view. In T. Sizer (Ed.), *Moral education: Five lectures* (pp. 57–83). Cambridge: Harvard University Press.

Kohlberg, L. (1981). From *Is* to *Ought*: How to commit the naturalistic fallacy and get away with it. In L. Kohlberg, *Essays on moral development. Vol. I: The philosophy of moral development.* New York: Harper & Row.

Kohlberg, L., Boyd, D., & Levine, C. (1990). The return of stage 6: Its principle and moral point of view. In T. Wren (Ed.), *The moral domain: Essays in the ongoing discussion between philosophy and the social sciences* (pp. 151–181). Cambridge: MIT Press.

McLaughlin, T. H. (1992). Citizenship, diversity and education: A philosophical perspective. *Journal of Moral Education, 21* (3), 235–250.

Mischel, W. (1968). *Personality and assessment.* New York: Wiley.

Nussbaum, M. (1986). *The fragility of goodness: Luck and ethics in Greek tragedy and philosophy.* Cambridge: Cambridge University Press.

Nussbaum, M. (1994). *Therapy of desire: Theory and practice in Hellenistic ethics.* Princeton, NJ: Princeton University Press.

Piaget, J. (1932/1965). *The moral judgment of the child* (M. Gabain, trans.). NY: The Free Press.

Plato. (1997). *Plato: Complete works.* (J. M. Cooper & D. S. Hutchinson, Eds.). Indianapolis: Hackett Publishing Company.

Pogge, Thomas. (2002). *World poverty and human rights: Cosmopolitan responsibilities and reforms.* Cambridge, UK: Polity Press.

Power, F. C., Higgins A., & Kohlberg, L. (1989). *Lawrence Kohlberg's approach to moral education.* New York: Columbia University Press.

Rorty, A. O. (1980). The place of contemplation in Aristotle's *Nicomachean Ethics.* In A. O. Rorty (Ed.), *Essays on Aristotle's Ethics* (pp. 377–394). Berkeley and Los Angeles: University of California Press.

Sherman, N. (1989). *The fabric of character: Aristotle's theory of virtue.* Oxford: Oxford University Press.

Snik, G. (1997). Conceptual development and education. In A. W. van Haaften, M. Korthals, & T. Wren (Eds.), *Philosophy of development: Reconstructing the foundations of human development and education* (pp. 199–210). Dordrecht: Kluwer Academic Publishing.

Sorabji, R. (1973–1974). On the role of intellect in virtue. *Proceedings of the Aristotelian Society, 74,* 107–129.

van Haaften, A. W., Korthals, M., & Wren, T. (Eds.). (1997). *Philosophy of development: Reconstructing the foundations of human development and education.* Dordrecht: Kluwer Academic Publishing.

Wren, T. (1991). *Caring about morality: Philosophical perspectives in moral psychology.* Cambridge: MIT Press.

Wren, T. (2005). The liberal-communitarian debate. In R. E. Freeman & P. Werhane (Eds.), *The Blackwell encyclopedia of management: Business ethics,* rev. edition (pp. 311–315). Oxford: Blackwell Publishing.

Wren, T. (2013). Civic virtue is not enough. In D. Schrader & E. Nowak (Eds.), *Educating democratic competencies* (pp. 325–342). Frankfurt am Main: Peter Lang Dialogos Series.

3

TRADITIONAL CHINESE PHILOSOPHIES AND THEIR PERSPECTIVES ON MORAL EDUCATION

Guozhen Cen and Jun Yu

There's a saying in China: "The three teachings of Confucianism, Daoism, and Buddhism are like the legs of a tripod; you cannot lack even one." Though this was first spoken more than 1,000 years ago, it underscores the importance of these three traditional philosophies in Chinese culture, even today. *Xiao* or filial piety, is one of the most important Confucian values, and has been used to teach children in East Asia how to respect and care for their parents and ancestors for thousands of years. The Daoist idea of "letting things take their own natural course" is still a very popular belief in China. Meanwhile, the Chinese language itself has more than 500 idioms that reflect Buddhist teachings and principles, such as, "Good deeds create good karma, and bad deeds create bad karma" (Zhu, 2006).

These three traditional philosophies served as the primary sources for guidance in China's moral education until the mid-nineteenth century. Today, the official basis for moral education in China comes from Communist ideology, though it is clear from the examples above that Confucianism, Daoism, and Buddhism still remain influential to a certain extent in Chinese society. In this chapter we will introduce these philosophies and then explore their perspectives on moral education. More specifically, we will introduce each major philosophy, the moral values it promotes, the goals of moral cultivation it sets, and the pathways through which one can reach these goals, as well as major implications for moral education.

CONFUCIANISM

Brief Introduction to Confucianism

Confucius (551 BC–479 BC) is the founder and the most prominent representative of Confucianism, and his thoughts encompassed morality, education, and politics during the end of the Spring and Autumn Period (770 BC–476 BC; Cihai Bianji Weiyuanhui, 1990). This period was a tumultuous time in Chinese history where there were multiple states constantly at war with each other in a struggle to gain power over an area that is part of today's modern China. This milieu led to a troubling collapse in etiquette and good manners in society. In an attempt to offer a solution to this crisis in manners, Confucius developed the philosophy which we today refer to as Confucianism. Confucius' ideas are mainly recorded in the *Analects*. There were eight schools of Confucianism during the Warring States Period (475 BC–221 BC), with the schools of Mencius and Xunzi as the most important ones.

Confucianism is a system of thought that is centered around Confucius' theory of *ren* (Tang & Zhang, 1999). For Confucius, the basic meaning of *ren* is to love people ("Analects," n.d.). This encompasses feelings—such as love and empathy—and behavior, and is primarily focused on interpersonal relationships. In other words, *ren* is about how to treat others and how to behave yourself. This idea of loving others inherent in *ren* is reflected in two different sayings in Confucianism. First, "do not do to others that which you yourself would not want to be done to you." Second, "if you want to become successful yourself, you must first help others become successful; and if you want to be understood by others, you must first understand them." These highlight the selflessness, compassion, and acceptance of others that are at the heart of *ren*. Confucius proposed *ren* as the highest moral ideal and principle for an individual and a society. He advocated that individuals should aspire to become a person who is *ren*, while society itself—including its rulers—should operate in a way that is consistent with the principle of *ren*. Through learning and self-cultivation, people can better manage the family, make the country orderly, and bring peace to the world.

What characteristics does a *ren* person have? From Confucius' perspective, such individuals exercise self-restraint and are courteous. They are humble, benevolent, loyal, and generous toward others, and hardworking and frugal in their lives. They also live courageously and are persistent in pursuing their moral ideals. Confucius said that a truly *ren* person would be willing to die rather than compromise their ideals and live in a way that would be inconsistent with being *ren*. Overall, a *ren* person could be understood as possessing perfect goodness and operating in the highest spiritual level in which the will of the heavens and humanity are united (Feng, 1989).

Confucius' Perspectives on Moral Education

According to Confucius, everyone is born the same—it is education and self-cultivation that makes a difference in an individual's moral character. Confucius believed that education should be available to everyone regardless of status which is consistent with his idea of *ren*—to love everyone. So he started private education that was open to everyone, which was revolutionary for his time, when only nobles had access to education. He maintained that the goal of education—along with self-cultivation—is to help individuals become *ren*.

To become *ren*, one must possess those qualities valued and promoted in Confucianism. The most important of these qualities are *li* or propriety, *xiao* or filial piety, *ti* or brotherly love, *zhong* or loyalty, *shu* or tolerance, *yi* or righteousness, *zhi* or wisdom, and *xin* or integrity.

Li or propriety originally referred to ceremonial procedures in life, such as weddings and funerals. But it also was about the proper etiquette for living, and showing respect for gods and ancestors. Additionally, *li* reflected the inherent hierarchical structure in society—where, for example, certain ceremonies were once only reserved for nobles.

In *li*, people should behave according to the specific etiquette or procedures in certain situations and according to their status. For example, you should use the appropriate title when addressing an individual; when you meet a respected individual, an elder or a teacher, you should show respect by kneeling or bowing before them; and when you sit around the table, you should choose your seat according to your status as compared to your dining companions. In promoting *li*, Confucius underlined that there were differences among individuals in terms of a person's status or age. He considered it important that people behave in a way that fits their status or age, as this can ultimately promote harmony within society. When society is harmonious and orderly, it is consistent with the ideal of *ren*.

Xiao or filial piety and *ti*—love and respect among siblings—can be thought of as the idea of *ren* as it applies to families, helping to maintain order and harmony among family members. *Xiao* is where an individual shows respect to their family's elders and ancestors. Some examples of how one might demonstrate *xiao* in their family include taking care of one's parents in their old age, marrying and having children to carry on the family lineage, and visiting and worshipping the graves of ancestors on a regular basis. Similar to *li*, Confucius also recognized that there are differences among family members, and these differences are the basis for how children should treat their parents, grandparents, and ancestors. *Ti* originally referred to love and respect for one's elder brothers, but could be broadly seen as being applicable to relationships between all siblings. Confucius considered *xiao* and *ti* the foundation for *ren* because he believed that moral behavior started in the family. If people could behave appropriately in their families, then they could expand that moral behavior to society as well.

Zhong refers to loyalty in interpersonal relationships, as well as the idea of fulfilling your duties or responsibilities to your country, work, family, and friends. What behaviors are consistent with *zhong*? For example, if someone assigns you a task, you should try your best to work hard and complete the task. Parents should fulfill their responsibility to properly rear their children, just as teachers should fulfill their responsibility to properly teach students; in both cases, parents and teachers should act as models. Also, students should study hard, finish their homework, and learn what is required of them by their teachers and schools. *Zhong* is important because, in order to achieve the kind of order and harmony of a society that embodies *ren*, you need to be able to trust in others—that they will do what they are expected to do.

Shu, or tolerance, means to put oneself in another's place and be able to forgive others. This idea is embodied in the Confucian saying, "do not do to others that which you yourself would not want to be done to you." In other words, you should take others' perspectives and empathize with them before doing something that might affect them. According to Confucianism, this kind of tolerance reflects the idea of loving others, which is at the heart of *ren*. In urging people to think first about how their actions could impact others—including harm to others—*shu* can help reduce and resolve interpersonal conflict, helping to create a more harmonious interpersonal environment.

Yi or righteousness broadly refers to morality and justice, but in a more narrow sense refers to a standard by which one judges what is right and wrong, good and bad. Confucius advocated righteousness for the public and society instead of for individuals. In other words, he believed that when one is facing a situation where personal interest is at stake, one should first consider its benefit to the greater good. In the end, if the greater good is more important than personal interest, then one should make the choice for the greater good, even if it is harmful to you at an individual level. There is a selflessness in the principle of *yi* which is consistent with the idea of loving others in *ren*—in this case, to the point where others and society matter more than your own interest.

Zhi or wisdom refers to both knowledge and wisdom. Confucius valued education. In promoting the value of *zhi*, he wanted people to learn how to differentiate between right and wrong—and also use this understanding to guide themselves towards proper moral behavior, instead of merely being controlled by one's own impulses or desires. In order to reach this level of understanding, Confucius recommended that people study *li* or propriety, know people through what they say, know the limits of one's knowledge, listen and read more, and find and follow the good in the world. Only through the acquisition of knowledge and wisdom can one have a proper understanding of Confucian values and aspire to become someone who is *ren*.

Xin or integrity refers to honesty and consistency between deeds and words, and primarily is shown through one's behavior. In other words, you should be sincere to yourself and towards others; people should be able to trust in your words—that you will do what you say you're going to do. If what you do and say is consistent, then others can trust in you. Likewise, if you can trust in others, this will enhance your relationships. Otherwise, without trust, people will cheat each other or be suspicious of one another, which leads to a society that is not prosperous—the opposite of a harmonious and orderly *ren* society. Therefore, *xin* is the foundation for all interpersonal relationships and can help one become successful.

While all of these values form the basis for becoming an individual who is *ren*, how can one achieve this? According to Confucius, first you should aspire to become *ren*. Confucius considered this goal-setting as a primary task in moral education. Once the goal is clear, you should persistently pursue it. Second, you must then learn more, increasing your knowledge base. Confucius believed students should study all of the important major subjects in school; in his time, these were propriety, music, poetry, history, and the divination classic the *Book of Changes*. When you study, you must think actively about what you're learning—in other words, you should ask questions and think about its relevance to conduct in the real world. Confucius believed understanding what you're studying is good, being interested in what you're studying is better, and enjoying what you're studying is best. He thought it was delightful to review what you have learned and try your best to practice it in life. Additionally, you should try to put yourself in the place of others before taking action. Finally, self-reflection is necessary in order to know whether or not your behavior has met the standard of *ren*. All of the self-improvement and self-cultivation inherent in becoming *ren* encourages you try to be a better individual than you were before, including expanding your knowledge, mind, heart, and behavior beyond your previous levels.

Confucius also laid out general developmental stages over the course of an individual's lifetime, each marking a certain milestone in terms of their level of understanding and level of cultivation. By 15 years of age, a person should devote themselves to study. By 30 years of age, a person should understand *li* or propriety and be able to stand on their own in society—in other words, hold down a career and successfully manage interpersonal relationships. By 40 years of age, a person should not be perplexed about the world—in other words, one should understand how the real world works. By 50 years of age, a person should understand their destiny—what they were meant to do in life as mandated by the heavens. By 60 years of age, a person should be able to understand anything they hear, and regardless of whether what is said is positive or negative, they should be cultivated enough to discern any possible wisdom or good points in the conversation. By 70 years of age, a person should feel free to follow their heart's desires but also intuitively follow the Confucian principles and not break them. These stages can illustrate the fact that Confucius considered learning and self-cultivation a lifelong process, one that requires persistence. It also demonstrates that, for Confucius, it is not enough to simply understand moral values—you must live them and cultivate yourself, to the point where your thoughts and behaviors are well-integrated and moral behavior is automatic and natural to you.

MENCIUS' AND XUNZI'S PERSPECTIVES ON MORAL EDUCATION

Mencius (372 BC–289 BC) was a famous philosopher in China who was widely regarded as the successor of Confucius and the most important representative of Confucianism after Confucius himself. One of Mencius' contributions is how he expanded the theory of *ren*, which is the basis of Confucianism. Originally, Confucius did not explain where *ren* comes from or what was the basis for establishing *ren* as the basic moral principle. Confucius said that everyone is born similar and should aspire to become a person of *ren*, but since he considered it a lifelong process—and claimed he never became *ren*—it seemed difficult to achieve. Theoretically, Mencius made people more hopeful about becoming a person of *ren* by pointing out that everyone has the potential. Mencius thought that everyone had a basic innate propensity towards becoming *ren* ("Mengzi," n.d.). As an example of this, he mentioned that if people saw a little girl about to fall into a well, everyone will immediately feel compassion for her. Mencius said that this feeling of compassion does not result from a person's desire to be seen publicly as a good person, but simply because it is in their human nature to feel this way.

Mencius considered morality as the defining characteristic of humankind. According to Mencius, one cannot be considered human without four propensities. The first is compassion, which is the origin of *ren* (loving others). The second is a sense of shame towards yourself and a dislike of others' wrongdoing, which is the origin of *yi* (righteousness). The third is to give others precedence out of courtesy and respect, which is the origin of *li* (propriety). The fourth is a sense of right and wrong, which is the origin of *zhi* (wisdom). Mencius believed that people are predisposed to have these four propensities. And these propensities need to be developed into the four corresponding moralities of *ren*, *yi*, *li*, and *zhi*.

Despite the fact that he believed people are inherently good, he thought that this could be influenced by a person's environment—that in a bad environment, goodness can be lost. So he advocated taking active steps to prevent this from happening. Mencius recommended reducing your own desires—as he believed that the more desire you have, the less you will have of the four propensities. He thought that one way to reduce desire was to place yourself in a situation of hardship. He also recommended self-reflection, where you should reflect on yourself and try to find fault in yourself. Mencius also advocated being determined not to change your mind because of personal interest but instead to show determination and courage in life. Eventually, one can become an upstanding individual who would not sacrifice one's own mores for promises of wealth and fame, or be subdued by power in situations where one is asked to do something immoral (Jin, 1995).

Xunzi (about 313 BC–230 BC) was a respected Confucian philosopher at the end of the Warring States Period. Counter to Mencius' view, Xunzi believed people were innately evil and goodness was learned ("Xunzi," n.d.). In his mind, to be considered innately good you needed to be born that way, instead of learning to be a good person. Xunzi believed people are born with needs, desires, and tendencies such as seeking food when hungry and seeking to rest when tired. If the inborn tendencies develop without limits, they will lead to bad consequences, especially to society. To illustrate his point, Xunzi provided the example that people are born with a fondness for their own self-interests. Uncontrolled development of this tendency will lead to conflict, fighting, and a diminished consideration for others. Then the society would be in disorder and people would be poor. Xunzi considered human beings evil in the sense that uncontrolled natural desires will lead to evilness, but desire itself is not evil.

Xunzi believed that the inherent evil in human nature can be changed for the better through education and proper laws and regulations (Zhang, 1995). Education was important to him because he believed people needed to be taught propriety, or *li*, since people are not inherently good. But because not everyone could become good through education, proper laws and regulations are needed to determine what is not proper behavior, and to punish people for it.

Xunzi established *li* or propriety as the foundation for moral education. He believed propriety is a precondition not only for an individual's growth but also for achieving success and societal peace, and he emphasized that propriety was the standard and norm for behaving and managing life. Therefore, for Xunzi, an important task of moral learning is to fully understand propriety.

Xunzi believed the goal of moral education was to cultivate good character. He posited that people could aspire to three different levels of cultivation. For *shi*, or scholars, people cultivate moral character at the most basic level, upholding humaneness and abiding by propriety. Scholars have the most ordinary moral character. *Junzi*, or gentlemen, possess a strong will and have practiced self-cultivation more persistently than scholars; one's speech and conduct are always consistent with the ethical moral principles and free from external constraints such as wealth or desire. The gentleman has a more lofty moral character than the scholar. *Shengren*, or sage, is the highest state of moral cultivation; there is nothing the sage does not understand, suggesting a kind of moral perfection or ideal. Since Xunzi considered people innately evil, we can view these levels on a spectrum where evil is at one end and then, through education and cultivation, one can move away from evil and towards goodness—first to the ordinary scholar, then the lofty gentleman, and finally the ideal sage. Though he differentiated the levels of cultivation in a conceptual sense, this is nevertheless informative because it provides some basic guidance on the stages one might go through to become a sage.

In summary, the heart of Confucianism is the idea of *ren*, or loving others. Confucianism is mainly concerned with morality in interpersonal relationships and behavior, and identifies values that cover a wide range of relationships and behaviors—*ren* (loving others), *li* (propriety), *xiao* (filial piety), *ti* (love and respect among siblings), *zhong* (loyalty), *shu* (tolerance), *yi* (righteousness), *zhi* (wisdom), and *xin* (integrity). The goal of moral education in Confucianism is to cultivate oneself into someone who is *ren*—courteous, courageous, selfless, and loving towards other people. Mencius and Xunzi both expanded our understanding of Confucianism. In seeing people as innately good, Mencius underlined the great moral potential for humans to be better individuals.

Xunzi, however, saw people as innately evil and therefore brought up the necessity for punishment and formal education for guidance. Overall, Confucianism stands out as one of the world's earliest forms of moral and character education.

DAOISM

Brief Introduction to Daoism

Daoism was established at the end of the Spring and Autumn Period (770 BC–476 BC) by its founder Laozi. Like Confucius, Laozi was also troubled by the tumultuous state of the Spring and Autumn Period, with frequent wars, and offered Daoism as a means for people to return to a state of peace and harmony in the world.

Daoism is centered around the Dao, meaning "The Way" (Cihai Bianji Weiyuanhui, 1990). The Dao is the ultimate origin and nature of all things, including heaven, earth, and the entire universe ("Daodejing," n.d.). In Daoism, the Dao is also the principle for how the world works.

Before Laozi, people thought of heaven as the origin of everything and did not consider if there was something that actually created heaven itself (Wang, 1999). Laozi started inquiring into the origins of heaven and later proposed that the Dao was the origin of everything in the universe.

From Laozi's perspective, the Dao follows its own course; the universe follows the Dao; the Earth follows the universe; human beings follow the Earth. In other words, the entire world as we know it follows the Dao, which in another sense is responsible for creating what we often refer to as the laws of nature. These laws affect everything from the changing seasons to the change from night to day to how animals live and even how water flows from mountains to the ocean. Laozi proposed that people should learn the ways of the natural world, and then live their lives in harmony with it.

According to Daoism, the world is made up of opposites—such as night and day, life and death, strength and weakness—referred to as *yinyang* or *yin* and *yang*. These opposites depend on each other and complement one another, as there cannot be day without night or strength without weakness. They can even transform into each other over time, such as how day eventually becomes night or how living things eventually die. If one anticipates such changes and stays focused even in the face of the inevitable changes inherent in life such as aging, one can make the most of every moment and live one's life to the fullest. However, when one deviates from what is considered natural and normal, it will cause a reversion to the opposite and a state that is not natural—for example, exhausting yourself while young will lead to being prematurely old.

While Laozi was the founder of Daoism, Zhuangzi (369 BC–286 BC) carried on and developed Laozi's thoughts. Rulers at the beginning of the Han Dynasty (206 BC–AD 220) espoused Daoism as their guiding philosophy. After Emperor Han Wudi of the Han Dynasty promoted Confucianism as the orthodox state ideology, Daoism lost its official status. Although Daoism was not adopted by the government, it played an important role in the development of ancient Chinese thought. For example, Confucianism during the Wei and Jin period (AD 220–420) and the Song Dynasty (AD 960–1279) adopted some ideas from Daoism. After Buddhism was introduced to China, scholars applied Laozi's and Zhuangzi's thoughts to interpret Buddhist concepts. Daoism is an important part of Chinese culture and has strongly influenced multiple aspects such as ethics, medicine, politics, technology, and art.

The Daoist Perspective on Moral Education

In Daoism, to be moral you should live your life in accordance with the Dao. Daoism suggests that people let go of the knowledge, prejudices, habits, desires, and ego that have distracted them from their own true nature and the true nature of the world around them, and to develop an inner awareness towards the world and oneself.

Daoism considered that being moral is being natural, so naturalness—that things are best in their natural state—is the highest Daoist moral principle. This is symbolized by the idea of *pu*, the unworked or uncarved wood. Such a piece of simple and untouched wood is in its pristine state, like a newborn baby, and stands as an example of the original simplicity that Daoists aspire to. In the natural state, a person's mind is calm and still; like a mirror, the mind can reflect the world without prejudice. Reaching such a state of mind requires a person to first look beyond the kind of knowledge they have acquired through formal education, as such knowledge has from the Daoist perspective distracted people from their natural state. Instead, they should try to see the world more like a newborn infant, which has an inclusive and pristine state of mind and welcomes the entire range of experiences in life without discrimination, judgment, or preconceived notions. To return to the natural state, you should also reduce concern for yourself and reduce your own wants—a kind of simplicity of desire that falls within the Daoist concept of frugality. At the same time, you should live frugally in the sense of economizing your life and not caring about wealth or fame.

Daoism also emphasizes the idea of *wuwei*, effortless action or action without action. This is best symbolized by water. When water flows around rocks, it does not force its way through a rock, but naturally finds its way around it via the path of least resistance, the path that does not require forcing or straining. Water is also soft to the touch and lays as low as possible to the ground, not seeking to be higher than it needs to be. It is selfless in that it provides nourishment to the earth to help other things grow. Therefore, people should aspire to be like water and live in a way that is accommodating, compassionate, selfless, and humble, a way that does not interfere with or meddle with how things naturally are in the world. A philosophical basis for *wuwei* comes from the proposition that the world is made of correlates such as day and night, or young and old. These correlates complement each other and can even naturally transform into each other the way day effortlessly transforms into night or how people effortlessly age. This seamless transition from one correlate to another exemplifies *wuwei*, showing how changes can happen naturally without interference from anything or anyone.

To be consistent with *wuwei*, a person needs to exemplify the Daoist ideas of compassion and humility. The Daoist view of compassion is about being loving and accommodating. As we discussed above in defining the idea of naturalness, it is important that a person is unencumbered by their past knowledge, habits, and prejudices when they face the world, and this is also true in the case of exemplifying Daoist compassion. Our preconceived or taught ideas can cause us to behave in ways that are forced or taught, which may not be natural or in line with the idea of *wuwei*. When we are no longer burdened by such ideas, which might otherwise prejudice us against others (such as thinking of criminals as bad people and thus wanting to treat them badly), we are more able to love and accept everyone, even people who are bad or who we were taught not to care about. For example, a ruler with compassion would make sure to find a place within their community for every single person, even the clumsiest individuals, the criminals, or those without great talents. And as water nourishes all things without demanding rewards, so people should endeavor to help others in a selfless way.

The Daoist idea of humility is that when people have too much of an ego, it can have a coercive or interfering effect in the world. For example, during the Spring and Autumn period when Laozi conceived of Daoism, China was made up of states that were constantly at war because each of them wanted to be the one state that ruled all of China. This desire for power, where war happened frequently, led to instability in society and the suffering of common people. This kind of result, which is arguably coercive by forcing common people to live in a constant state of war and also interfering in the sense that it interfered with common people's ability to live peacefully, is not consistent with *wuwei*. Therefore, Daoism recommends that people should not strive to be first or to be ahead in the world, and instead aim for a humble life—like water, which always flows downward and lays as low as possible.

The ideal character that Daoists promote is the perfected individual or *zhenren* ("Zhuangzi," n.d.). The *zhenren* has returned to their natural state, which allows them to be tranquil and at peace, experiencing every moment without preconceptions. They exemplify frugality, where they lessen their own desires and concern for themselves such that they live a simple and economical life and do not care about money or status. They are like water—showing compassion by being loving and accommodating towards others and the world around them; humble and without ego, preferring to lay as low as possible instead of fighting to be at the top.

While Daoism does not describe a developmental pathway to becoming a *zhenren*, it does advocate a number of approaches for moral cultivation (Ruo, 1999). First, a person must forget everything that is not naturally a part of their own body and mind. Not just the knowledge, prejudices, habits, and anything else that gives them preconceived notions about the world, but also material goods and wealth. Essentially, anything that is man-made should be forgotten or detached from the self. All of these things will tire or worry a person more than is necessary. Forget ego and selfish concerns. Do not seek fame, fortune, or to be ahead of others—do not think about personal gain, in other words. Instead learn to find happiness in simplicity in terms of yourself and your life. After an individual is freed of everything outside of the self as well as ego and selfish concerns, they can become like a blank sheet and face the world like a newborn baby, experiencing it for the first time. In this state, a person has a spacious, open heart that allows them to tolerate and accept anything that happens to them.

In summary, Daoism is a philosophy based on the idea of the Dao, or the Way, which is considered the origin of all things in the universe and the basis for the laws of nature and the universe. In Daoism, to be moral one must be natural, which is why naturalness—the idea that things are best in their natural or original state—is the highest moral principle. Daoism promotes frugality in the sense that you should reduce your ego and desires, and live an economical life without striving for wealth or fame. The Daoist principle of *wuwei*—or effortless action—urges people to behave in a natural way that does not interfere, force things, or meddle in any way. The philosophical basis of *wuwei* comes from the proposition that the world is made of correlates—such as day and night, young and old—which can transform into one another effortlessly. In a moral sense, the idea of *wuwei* promotes being compassionate—as in, a person who is accommodating and loving towards others—and also being humble—as in, selfless and not striving to be ahead or on top. All of these qualities—naturalness, frugality, compassion, and humility—are reflected in the *zhenren*, or perfected individual, which is what Daoists aspire to become.

BUDDHISM

Brief Introduction to Buddhism

Buddhism was said to be established by Sakyamuni, a prince in ancient India during about 600 BC or mid-500 BC. There is no exact consensus as to when Buddhism was introduced to China, but it happened at some time between 2 BC and AD 67. Over time, many schools of Buddhism emerged in China, such as the Discipline School and the Pure Land School, and Buddhism became an important part of Chinese culture (Nan, 1996). The most well-known of those schools, the Chan or Zen School, is seen as a popularized form of Daoism (Ma, 1997). The distinct features of Buddhism in China include simplicity in practice, using the mind as the path to nirvana, becoming a Buddha by gaining sudden insight, and borrowing elements from Confucianism and Daoism into their practice such as filial piety and naturalness (Hong, 2001).

This chapter is focused primarily on introducing Buddhism as it is known in China—not Buddhism as a whole—and discussing its perspectives on moral education. Though Buddhism in China developed its own unique characteristics, it has still retained the original spirit of Buddhism: its emphasis on karma, and the ultimate goal of reaching nirvana—a state of ultimate happiness where one is finally free of suffering—and becoming a Buddha.

Karma refers to any movement or activity which leads to some effect in the world. The idea that goodness brings good karma and evilness brings bad karma is the most typical representation of karma in daily life, and demonstrates the cause-and-effect relation of one's actions to later consequences. Therefore Buddhists aim to make sure that they promote good karma in the world. But to do so, a person must consider not only their behavior but also their mind, as negative thoughts can also lead to bad karma. In the Buddhist path of cultivation, cultivating the mind is the key and a basis for cultivating behavior—ultimately, so that the mind and behavior are consistent.

The Four Noble Truths, which are the Buddha's original teachings, encapsulate the basic tenets of Buddhism (Cihai Bianji Weiyuanhui, 1990). Suffering is the First Noble Truth. While the Buddha described birth, decay, death, and not getting what one wants as the main sufferings in the world, suffering can be seen as primarily originating from the body and the mind. The Second Noble Truth is cause—in other words, the cause of suffering. The Buddha considered desire and ignorance the primary reasons that led to suffering. End is the Third Noble Truth—as in, the end of suffering. This is known as nirvana, the enlightened state where one is free from suffering; nirvana can only be reached after removing the causes of one's suffering. Finally, the Fourth Noble Truth of the *path* points to how one can reach a state of enlightenment, which is detailed in the Eight Noble Paths.

In the Eight Noble Paths, the Buddha laid out a way to end all suffering which covers moral conduct, concentration, and wisdom (Cihai Bianji Weiyuanhui, 1990). The first is Right View, which means one has an understanding of the nature of reality and also the path towards transformation. Right Thought, the second, refers to right intention without thoughts of greed and anger. Then there is Right Speech, where one inhibits any harmful communication and instead aims to speak in a way that is truthful, kind, and useful. In Right Conduct, a person's actions should never harm others. Right Livelihood refers to the fact that people should earn a living in a way that is not exploitative or harmful. People also need to constantly and persistently direct their energies towards the pathway to enlightenment, which is Right Diligence. In Right Mindfulness, a person has an awareness of how things really are in the world and within oneself, without deviant thoughts. Finally, one reaches Right Concentration, where one is not only able to fully concentrate their mind but also has forgotten the self. Buddhists believe an ordinary person can become noble and reach nirvana by successively cultivating oneself through the Eight Noble Paths.

Buddhist Perspectives on Moral Education

In Buddhism, the goal of moral education is to reach nirvana. Nirvana is not just a state where a person is free of suffering; in nirvana, a person is selfless or freed from the idea of self. Self is merely a concept created by humans, and self leads to all problems. Because of this false idea of self, people have desires for the self—such as a desire for material goods or a desire to be ahead of others—and desires can lead to suffering. Ultimately, self is not the nature of reality; in actuality, everyone has a true self within them, the Buddha nature. In order to reach nirvana, people need to see through the pretense of self to their Buddha nature, forgetting the idea of self in the process.

Buddhists believe everything, especially humans, possesses Buddha nature. Buddha nature is the ability to gain understanding and be enlightened. Of course, human intelligence and reflection could be compromised or blocked for various reasons such as subjective prejudices or stubbornness. The difference between a Buddha and the ordinary individual is that one is in an "awakening" state and the other is in a "lost" state. Similarly, educators should believe everyone has the capacity to become a moral person. A task of moral education is to eliminate prejudices or stubbornness and guide individuals out of the "lost" state and into the "awakening" state (Li, 2006).

Because everyone has Buddha nature within them, and therefore has the potential to become enlightened, there is innate goodness in everyone. This is the basis for the principles of loving-kindness and compassion—that if everyone has inherent goodness, then we should treat them well and as equals. That means behaving towards everyone with the same kindness and compassion, regardless of whether they are friends or enemies. Loving-kindness and compassion are fundamental requirements for self-cultivation, because through them one can create good karma and remove suffering in the world. Arguably, karma motivates people to do good in the world, since their actions can affect future consequences for oneself and for others.

In the same vein, Buddhism also gives followers the Five Basic Precepts—namely, no harming of living beings, no stealing, no sexual misconduct, no false speech, and no drinking of alcohol—as a reminder to avoid doing bad, which would lead to bad karma and increase suffering in the world.

Precepts, such as the Five Basic Precepts which exemplify moral conduct, are also considered one of the Three Learnings. The Three Learnings—precepts, concentration, and wisdom—summarize the main methods of cultivation laid out in the Eight Noble Paths. Concentration in this case refers to a state free from external stimuli and internal thoughts or feelings. If a person's mind always changes based on the environment around them, this can lead to negative feelings such as worries, sadness, or anger. At the same time, memories and deviant thoughts can distract a person from the present moment. When one is completely focused on the current moment, this also can lead to another level. In this level, the mind and body become united, and the boundaries between the self and the external environment become blurred such that the whole universe becomes a part of what one usually considers "self." Only when one reaches this level of unity can it be called concentration in the Buddhist sense.

Wisdom is about ridding oneself of suffering. If a person does good but was not rewarded for their good deeds—and subsequently suffers or feels frustrated as a result of not being rewarded—that is not real wisdom. Real wisdom happens at a no-self level. At this level, people do good but not because they hope for some kind of reward; they also are not troubled if other people treat them badly even for their good actions. If a person's wisdom has this selfless quality, then they can equally love all people and be liberated from suffering. To cultivate wisdom, one must read and understand Buddhist sutras and gain experience through practicing the Buddhist principles in daily life. Over time, as a person becomes more cultivated and closer to reaching the goal of nirvana, these teachings and principles will be automatically be integrated into their behavior, such that they no longer need to look for inconsistencies in behavior.

As a summary of the Eight Noble Paths, the Three Learnings can be divided into three different levels—with precepts as the basic level, concentration as the intermediate level, and wisdom as the most advanced level. People who wish to cultivate themselves must first master the precepts, then moving on to concentration and, later, mastering wisdom. Once one reaches a state of enlightenment, with a cultivated mind, everything in daily life—even the most mundane experiences, such as drinking tea or brushing your teeth—can be considered as opportunities for cultivating morality (Foguang Xingyun, 2008).

In summary, Buddhism is a philosophy whose main points are encapsulated in the Four Noble Truths—which state that there is suffering in the world, that suffering has a cause, there is an end to suffering (nirvana), and there are paths to that end. The Eight Paths describe the pathway through which a person can reach the state of nirvana, where they no longer suffer, and these paths cover the areas of moral conduct, concentration, and wisdom. Reaching a state of nirvana is the goal of moral education in Buddhism, and by reaching this state one can forget the self and discover their true self within, the Buddha nature, which is also considered an awakened state. Since everyone has Buddha nature in them and is therefore inherently good, Buddhism encourages people to treat others with loving-kindness and compassion. Such good behavior is also important because it creates good karma, which will lead to good outcomes for the individual. Besides karma, the Five Basic Precepts—which cover moral conduct—encourage people to behave in a moral way. Through good moral conduct, intense concentration that makes one forget the self, and selfless wisdom—the Three Learnings—one can eventually reach an enlightened state.

CONCLUSION

Confucianism, Daoism, and Buddhism are three major thoughts in traditional Chinese culture that dominated education including moral education in China. Confucianism and Daoism first developed locally and Buddhism developed after its introduction from abroad. During over 2,000 years of history, these three traditional teachings expanded into various schools that have had enormous influence in Chinese society and daily life.

Confucianism, Daoism, and Buddhism all care about humanity, but each has a different emphasis. Confucianism emphasizes being involved in the world so that individuals can better promote societal development. Daoism emphasizes forgetting the world, so that individuals can become free from external limitations. Buddhism emphasizes transcending the world, which means to pursue inward happiness. The different emphases and applications of the three traditional Chinese thoughts are represented in the Chinese saying, "Govern the society with Confucianism, manage life with Daoism, and manage the mind with Buddhism."

In terms of morality, Confucianism emphasizes interpersonal relations, becoming a person of *ren* who loves people, has talents, and cares about the society. Daoism advocates that one should become a perfect person who follows the nature, lives in accordance with *wuwei*, and leads a simple life that is free from troubles of fame and wealth. Buddhism emphasizes that one should cultivate the self to reach a state of nirvana, and that everyone is equal and subject to the cause-and-effect law of karma that motivates people to do good in their lives. Overall, these three philosophies could be valuable resources for moral education in terms of nurturing humanity in modern societies, and could offer inspiration to those individuals seeking alternatives to Western approaches.

REFERENCES

Analects. (n.d.). Retrieved from http://ctext.org/analects/zhs.

Cihai Bianji Weiyuanhui. (1990). *Cihai* (1989 ed.). Shanghai, China: Shanghai Lexicographical Publishing House.

Daodejing. (n.d.). Retrieved from http://ctext.org/dao-de-jing/zhs.

Feng, Y. (1989). Duiyu Kongzi suojiang de ren de jinyibu lijie he tihui [Further understanding of Confucius' concept of ren]. *Confucius Studies, 4* (3), 3–4.

Foguang Xingyun. (2008). *Fojiao, shisu* [Buddhism and the secular]. Shanghai, China: Shanghai Lexicographical Publishing House.

Hong, X. (2001). Shilun zhongguo fojiao sixiang de zhuyao tedian jiqi renwen jingshen [A discussion on the essential characteristics and the humanitarian spirit of Chinese Buddhist thought]. *Journal of Nanjing University, 38* (3), 64–72.

Jin, L. (1995). *Mengzi yizhu* [Mencius interpreted]. Shanghai, China: Shanghai Ancient Books Press.

Li, Y. (2006). *Rudaofo yu zhongguo chuantong wenhua jiaoyu* [Confucianism, Daoism, and Buddhism and education on traditional Chinese culture]. Wuhan, Hubei Province, China: Wuhan University Press.

Ma, T. (1997). *Zhongguo chanzong sixiang fazhan shi* [A history of Chinese Chan Buddhism]. Changsha, Hunan Province, China: Hunan Educational Publishing House.

Mengzi. (n.d.). Retrieved from http://ctext.org/mengzi/zh.

Nan, H. (1996). *Zhongguo fojiao fazhan shilue* [A brief history of Buddhism in China]. Shanghai, China: Fudan University Press.

Ruo, S. (1999). Zhuangzi zhenren lun [Zhuangzi's zhenren theory]. *Qinghai Shehui Kexue* [*Qinghai Social Sciences*], *20* (2), 70–74.

Tang, K., & Zhang, H. (1999). *Chengren yu chengsheng: Rujia daode lunli jingcui* [Becoming a person and becoming a sage: Essentials of Confucian morality and ethics]. Changsha, Hunan Province, China: Hunan University Press.

Wang, Z. (1999). *Ziran yu daode: Dujia lunli daode jingcui* [Nature and morality: Essentials of Daoist ethics and morality]. Changsha, Hunan Province, China: Hunan University Press.

Xunzi. (n.d.). Retrieved from http://ctext.org/xunzi/zhs.

Zhang, J. (1995). *Xunzi yizhu* [Xunzi interpreted]. Shanghai, China: Shanghai Ancient Books Press.

Zhu, R. (Ed.). (2006). *Fojiao chengyu* [Buddhist idioms]. Shanghai, China: Hanyu dacidian chubanshe.

Zhuangzi. (n.d.). Retrieved from http://ctext.org/zhuangzi/zhs.

4

TRADITIONAL APPROACHES TO CHARACTER EDUCATION IN BRITAIN AND AMERICA

James Arthur

The formation of character could be said to be the aim that all general education has historically set out to achieve. It is an aim that has often not been explicitly stated, instead it has simply been assumed. Most traditional approaches to character education emphasize the role of habit, imitation, modeling, instruction, rewards and punishments, and authority in the formation of character and regularly invoke Aristotelian ethics in justification. Some of these educational approaches have been interpreted as both coercive and teacher-centered and are seen in sharp contrast to the advocates of child-centered approaches based on moral developmental research which is characterized by a belief in the child's ability to gradually bring their "behaviour under the explicit guidance of rational deliberation" (Narvaez & Lapsley, 2005, p. 141).[1] Therefore, to enter on a discussion about character and, even more, about character education is to enter a minefield of conflicting definition and ideology. It is an educational theme about which there is much fundamental disagreement and division. The disagreement is about whether traditional character education is a legitimate aim of schooling. Can there be said to exist such a thing as a regular and fixed set of habitual actions in a person that constitutes his or her character? In order to begin an answer to this question we must start with the early Greek and Christian ideas of character.

GREEK ORIGINS

Character education is ultimately about what kind of person a child will grow up to be and the early Greek idea of character suggests that moral goodness is essentially a prediction of persons and not acts. It also implies that this goodness of persons is not automatic, but must be acquired and cultivated. Character education is inherently a multi-disciplinary endeavor, which requires its adherents and critics to ask divergent questions and employ disparate methods in approaching the subject. Plato's *Republic* was the first major work on the philosophy of education which argued that to have or to

43

form a good character is also to become fully human. Both the *Republic* and Aristotle's *Ethics* concern themselves with the question of how a good person should live.[2] They are also about how society should structure itself to make this type of life attainable.

In modern discussions about moral character most writers tend to cast the respective views of Plato and Aristotle as polar opposites. They argue that, in Plato's case, a truly good character will be one that understands the good and therefore does what is good. Plato held that a person who *knows* what is good will therefore *do* it. He did not think that anyone *willingly* acted immorally, and explained that if they did so act then it could only be through ignorance of the good. In contrast, Plato's pupil, Aristotle, took a different view. Where Plato had taught that a prior intellectual understanding of the good alone makes moral excellence attainable, Aristotle argued rather that a person *becomes* good by learning first what it is to *do* good. He also recognized, in contrast to Plato, that a person may have the ability to think about the good without having the disposition to implement it.

Aristotle says we become good by practising good actions. From Plato there is the idea that moral education is about improving thinking skills, whilst in Aristotle it is primarily about practising right behavior. In one there is an emphasis on moral reasoning without moral action, in the other, conformity without inner conviction. This is to overstate their differences. Both believed that character must be actively cultivated in the young. Both were concerned about whether ethical behavior could be taught. They debated mainly in terms of virtue and the virtuous, and morality for them was not about rules or principles, but the cultivation of character. Conformity to a set of moral rules was not their aim in the development of this character, but rather character development involved *being* a certain kind of person and not merely *doing* certain kinds of things.

In Aristotle's writings, right moral conduct was not a matter for explicit teaching in terms of a subject on the school curriculum, although he did recommend mentors who guide the individual until he or she is able to cultivate his or her own virtues. Aristotle believed that there is rationality in every moral choice and this cannot be omitted from the process through which virtue is formed. The focus is not on the formation of prescribed habits, but rather on the intentions of the child. Habits are not simply passively learnt through repetition of behavior, but contain a cognitive element—they presuppose a capacity for decision-making and are done for the right reason in the right place. Whilst children must eventually decide voluntarily how to act in a certain way, this behavior is achieved gradually as they become more autonomous and make their own decisions. According to Aristotle, virtues are developed by an individual over time and signify a specific excellence in them of some kind. He recognized that a person may have the ability to think about the good without having the disposition to implement it. This Aristotelian notion of education is also about setting someone free, whilst demonstrating a consistent pattern of behavior.

Aristotle gave more specific attention to the process of education than did Plato. He suggested that there are clear developmental stages in education. The first stage is the training of the body; the second is the training of character; and lastly comes the training of the intellect. He observed that intellect appears later in the child. Only after they have built certain good habits within the second stage can children reasonably move to the stage of comprehension. There is a paradox here: students who already have virtuous characters through their actions are to be taught how to think about moral decisions. And yet Aristotle says that unless you already have skills to think correctly about moral decisions then you cannot be virtuous.

CHRISTIAN DEVELOPMENTS

Greek Patristic thought aimed at the formation of the *anima Christiana*, the Christian, and the child was to be formed after the likeness of Christ—Christ-loving or Christ-minded. This language articulated a unique kind of pedagogy and it is clear that these early Christians would have thought in terms of *paideia* which is a much broader meaning than the word *moral*. *Paideia* is a word that has been lost to modern educational discourse. *Paideia* is the total development of the human person: body, mind, heart, will, senses, passions, judgments, instincts, aimed at what the Greeks called *arête*, excellence in living. Early Greek Christians believed that morality cannot simply be taught as part of schooling: moral character was seen as a firm disposition for the good, for moral excellence, for all that is best in human existence and required the educative force of a Christian community for these things to flourish. This was understood from within the Christian faith which taught that moral character is rooted in intellectual insight and rational judgment and is the outcome of deliberate choice. The early Christians clearly built upon the classical understandings of character.

Much later Aquinas laid great emphasis upon the importance of using reason to make moral choices. Aristotle had taught that becoming virtuous involved using one's powers of reasoning to shape virtues that are innate in each individual and that it was this inherent condition or potential that produced a natural impulse to desire the good (see Porter, 1990). Aquinas combined this natural impulse with the power of rational thought and claimed that together they allow human beings to reach an understanding of what is morally right. In other words, Aquinas develops a more sophisticated sense of the natural law which he says allows us to grasp God's moral laws through our own reasoning powers. In regard to moral character Aquinas insisted upon the relation between reason and faith as the one sustained the other (*Summa Theologiae* 1a 2ae.94.2). Aquinas does not advocate the pursuance of mechanical actions without reflection as he emphasizes again and again that virtuous actions must be the product of liberty.

For the Christian, character formation is not independent of religious faith. Both reason and revelation are required for ethical decisions and actions. The task of Christian ethics is to discover what God is enabling and requiring Christians to be and do. Christianity places a high value on altruism and self-sacrifice, but does not see character education as being an end in itself. Christianity is embedded in all kinds of inclinations, feelings, attitudes, interests, habits, lifestyles, decision patterns, and actions. It is based on a teleological concept of the good life that is contained in the Christian revelation and tradition. Two approaches to character education can be discerned from Christian tradition. First, some Christians want to move deductively from scripture and/or doctrine to contemporary moral issues. Second, others wish to work inductively from contemporary empirical data back to scriptural and/or doctrinal affirmations. In practice, many Christians, especially evangelical Protestants, adopted wholly negative views of the child which assumed that a child was born corrupt and evil and that it was the task of education to rectify this through punishment and training in obedience. An obvious weakness of contemporary Christian approaches to character is that they are often abstract and say little to teachers about the pedagogical practices of character formation.

SECULAR INSIGHTS AND NINETEENTH CENTURY EXPERIMENTS

The period of the Enlightenment brought some secular insights into what character was understood to be. Whilst it is accepted that Enlightenment philosophy was not directly connected to traditional forms of character education, a number of philosophers addressed the issue. James Barclay, for instance, urged that teachers should only be selected for the role if they had strong characters as he considered that the example set by them was crucial. As he said: "Example is allowed to be stronger than precept, and children especially are much readier to copy what they see than what they hear" (Hutchison, 1976, pp. 233f.). Another Scot, David Fordyce, spoke of developing the child's imagination in moral matters and wrote that "dull, formal lectures on several virtues and vices" were of no use in the formation of good character. Francis Hutcheson, professor of moral philosophy at the University of Glasgow in 1747, advocated greater study of character. He sought to "search accurately into the constitution of our nature to see what sort of creatures we are" (Hutchison, 1976, pp. 233f.). What was needed, he argued, was an objective study of human nature, particularly motives and behavior. John Locke also believed that character formation was more important than intellectual attainment. There was also a sustained attack on the relation between religion and character during the Enlightenment. In the writings of David Hume and Jeremy Bentham we see how, in their view, the concept of the divine was superfluous to any thesis of morality. Education was about knowledge and was considered value-free whilst religion was about dogma and was value-laden.

English Victorian education had conscious moral purposes, particularly in the economic and religious domain. Indeed, there are clear similarities between the views contained in Plato's *Republic* and Victorian character education. The production of characters suited to the needs of work was one of the principal goals of nineteenth century elementary schools for the poor. Children in these schools were taught the "habits of industry" (Barnard, 1966, p. 6) for they were destined for either the factories or domestic service. Character training formed the core of their schooling and included a form of moral development firmly based on the Ten Commandments and stories from the Bible. The teacher's role in these schools was to inculcate specific social roles typified by a pattern of behavior in children. Children accepted without question the moral training provided and expected to be punished for bad habits. The emphasis was on obedience and duty to all forms of authority in society and absolute conformity to predetermined social roles for the child. The teachers themselves were often not well educated and were selected for their ability to exhibit virtues in and outside of school. They held a restricted outlook on educational matters, which resulted in crude and mechanistic methods of teaching (see Arthur, 2003).

Society in nineteenth century Britain was acutely class conscious and children were viewed as miniature adults to be inducted into the ways of social convention. Character was viewed as a class-based concept which contained within it a judgment regarding an individual's status as much as their good conduct. The growing middle classes realized that money alone would not secure them the coveted status of the "character of a gentleman." Increasingly they sent their sons to the rapidly expanding number of independent schools. There was a marked revival of interest in character formation for middle class children in the 1820s which began first in some reformed public schools (Rotblatt, 1976, pp. 133–134). Teachers overtook wider societal experience to become the main facilitators for this shaping of character. It was considered important that students developed strong characters from which they could take a principled stand, usually in favor of the established virtues of society. Stefan Collini (1985) identifies these Victorian virtues as including: bravery, loyalty, diligence, application, and manners. Thomas Arnold, the Headmaster of Rugby, gave voice to middle class aspirations by emphasizing that the educational ideal should be the production of the "noble character," the "man of character," or more precisely the Christian manly spirit, better known as "muscular Christianity." His aim was no less than the formation of the Christian character in the young through "godliness and good learning."

Supporters of Arnold were strong adherents of character formation. As well as instituting stern disciplinary regimes in their schools, they encouraged reading of selected great authors to discern the essential core of "common" values. There was a strong belief that games developed manliness and inspired, *inter alia*, the virtues of fairness, loyalty, moral and physical courage and co-operation. Games in the private schools were thus constituted as a course in ethics. The public schools also socialized young men into the habit of good manners. In this view character was a form of social and moral capital and the function of the school was to provide the right environment in which the "right" people could, at an early stage, get to know one another. For many, character was not an ideal, but a display of the required manners solely to those they considered their elders and betters. This was an education designed for the social elite and generally for men, it was not the character of a gentleman, but the reputation of gentlemen, and the social advantage that it would bring, that was the goal in educating their children.

The Victorian period was certainly a high point in character education, or perhaps more accurately the use of the language of character. The Victorians meant many things by the use of the word character. The notion of character formation they operated led to much ambiguity and contradiction in behavior. Much more general was the view that character equaled a socialization in good manners and in a particular form of social conduct. Whilst there was a recognition that human nature could be directly shaped by education, the notion of character was largely embodied in laws, institutions, and social expectations. The kinds of character that teachers and educational thinkers espoused and the training methods they used also varied enormously. Schools as a place to train character was not a totally new concept, but it came to distinguish the English private school, and influenced character education in America.

It is important to remember that British society was relatively homogeneous in religious outlook at this time. There was a common set of values derived from scripture and Protestantism. Morality was not a controversial issue for most schoolteachers since the generalized Protestantism which pervaded culture was implicitly accepted by teachers and by those who wrote the school textbooks of the period (Arthur, Deakin Crick, Samuel, Wilson, & McGettrick, 2001, pp. 61f.). Even when a Victorian abandoned religious belief this did not necessarily mean a lowering of ethical standards. Instead, agnostics pursued the moral life as a good in itself. Their enthusiasm for instilling moral character in the masses was often greater than that displayed by some Evangelicals. There is a long history of ill-conceived, ineffective, and failed efforts at character education in Britain.

As the religious basis for morality began to decline by the late nineteenth century, for some the latter became the surrogate of the former and there developed a heightened awareness of ensuring that moral standards in society and in individuals were upheld. This was the secular ethic, which profoundly influenced the progress of character education in schools. Secular character training became an alternative to the moral lessons derived from Bible teaching and those who used the term "character training" were often the progressives in education. They used this language to avoid conflict with religious-based moral education, but it remained an ethic firmly based on puritan foundations. In 1886 the Ethical Union was established in Britain by a group of agnostics with the primary objective of seeking a secular basis for morality. They became interested in the education of character and formed the Moral Instruction League in 1897. The Moral Instruction League was opposed to Bible reading in schools and encouraged parents to withdraw their children from religious lessons. The government's view of character training was expressed in the *Introduction to the Education Code* of 1904 and 1905, in which it was stated that "The purpose of the public elementary school is to form and strengthen the character and to develop intelligence, of the children entrusted to it." The language and the notion of character here is more Greek than Christian in origin; a certain lip-service was paid to Christianity in order to legitimate or strengthen a secular ethic.

The Moral Instruction League comprised many of the leading educational thinkers and philosophers of the time. It aimed: "to substitute systematic non-theological moral instruction for the present religious teaching in all State schools, and to make character the chief aim of school life" (see Hilliard, 1961, p. 53). It further stated:

> The aim of moral instruction is to form the character of the child. With this object in view, the scholar's intellect should be regarded mainly as the channel through which to influence his feelings, purposes, and acts. The teacher must constantly bear this in mind, since knowledge about morality has missed its aim when no moral response is awakened in the child. A moral instruction lesson ought to appeal to the scholar's feelings, and also to affect his habits and his will.
>
> (1961, pp. 53f.)

This was a good definition of character education in its day and whilst the League did not recommend any specific teaching methods it did produce a syllabus for use in schools in 1901. Developments in the US, particularly the Character Education League, produced many curriculum materials with the explicit aim of teaching about and developing in children 31 virtues aimed at establishing an integral virtue called "character." These virtues were almost identical to the Moral Education League's syllabus so there must have been some cross-fertilization of ideas.

CHARACTER EDUCATION IN AMERICA

Character education has deep roots in the American public school system. Virtually every school in the US in the eighteenth and nineteenth centuries was responding in some implicit way to the educational goal of developing character. During the colonial period character education was based on theology, a reflexive Protestantism predominated in society, and the Founding Fathers saw moral education as a way of shaping the young into good citizens. However, in common with the experience in Britain, character education began to drift away from its Christian moorings by the late nineteenth century. Traditional character education approaches continued in the early twentieth century often without explicit reference to Christian ideals. Craig Cunningham provides a critical survey of the history of character education in the US which is an excellent start for those interested in a more detailed historical account (see Lapsley & Power, 2005).

One of the first major empirical research investigations into character development was entitled *The Character Education Enquiry* conducted in America by Hugh Hartshorne and Mark May (1928–1939). This enquiry seemed to deny that there was anything that could be called character, which it defined as the persistent dispositions to act according to moral principle in a variety of situations. The results of their tests of attitude did not consistently predict behavior and their most significant finding was that moral behavior appeared to be situation specific. This enquiry significantly influenced the work of Lawrence Kohlberg and many other moral developmental researchers. However, the research methodology employed was limited. Hartshorne and May took the profile of a morally mature person as their model and asked a series of questions of young people on stealing, cheating, and lying. The conclusions were, first; that there is no correlation between character training and actual behavior. Second, that moral behavior is not consistent in one person from one situation to another. Third, that there is no relationship between what people say about morality and the way that they act, and finally that cheating is distributed, in other words they claim that we all cheat a little. These results presented a challenge to those who sought to directly teach character to children.

By the 1950s cognitive psychology was becoming a discipline and gave great emphasis to Kohlberg's theories helping to make them popular in education. The success of Jean Piaget, Lawrence Kohlberg, and Erik Erikson was due to their themes of development which indicated progress. These themes satisfied the demands of culture at the time. Culture and society had become more pluralistic and therefore schooling became more sensitive to the increasing heterogeneity of children in many schools. These cognitive approaches to moral education—character education—were also more compatible with the liberal traditions of critical thinking rather than a virtues-based approach. Kohlberg (1984) was perhaps the most influential of the developmental theorists and he believed that knowledge of the good was constructed by the individual in a logical-cognitive progress through six stages of development. Each stage represented a qualitatively different mode of moral thinking and that development could stall at any stage. Kohlberg seemed to be dismissive of virtues as important in morality and to focus exclusively on the cognitive structural dimension of the human person's character development. His early research specified no content and after some criticism (Peters, 1979) he sought to address the substantive content of his approach and to differentiate his position from the values clarification methods which gained widespread currency in schools. Kohlberg also differentiated his approach from value relativists, but many of his followers in schools interpreted and applied his ideas in a way that lacked substantive content for moral education. A number of writers have outlined the limits to the application of Kohlberg's moral psychology by raising a number of empirical and conceptual problems (see Lapsley & Power, 2005).

The important work in the US of Peck and Havighurst (1960) on character education helped to revive explicit thinking in the area, even though they concluded that each generation tended to perpetuate its strengths and weaknesses of character and that character formation in the early years was relatively unmodifiable. The 1960s and 1970s were concerned with values clarification and procedural neutrality in the classroom and there was a widespread presumption in favour of moral relativism. It was the reaction against this relativistic thought that has seen the reemergence of more traditional character education approaches.

Cognitive psychologists, until recently, placed much emphasis on the development of structure of moral reasoning which, they claimed, underlies decision-making. Some even claimed universal application for this method, but David Carr (2002) casts doubts on the scientific basis of many of these developmental theories and questions their logical status. He observes that these theories were generally employed in support of progressive approaches to education with their emphasis on choice of lifestyle. This, he claims, ignores the more traditionalist perspectives that are generally concerned with initiating students into the knowledge, values, and virtues of civil society. Progressives, according to Carr, reject traditional perspectives because they do not wish to predetermine the ends and the goals of human development and because they question the worth of received knowledge and values. However, neo-Kohlbergian research finds cross-cultural validity for most of Kohlberg's stages (Rest, Narvaez, Bebeau, & Thoma, 1999) and newer approaches to moral cognition indicate that there is some evidence for universal elements of moral judgment outside of a universal stage sequence. Larry Nucci (2001, p. 122) for example, found in his research that basic moral concerns are shared across the range of human societies and religious groups and that there exists common ground in making moral judgments.

Given the multifarious positions taken in respect of character, it follows that the discussion about character education, and whether it is possible, is equally discordant. The variety of approaches results in a bewildering variety of educational schemes and curricula. This may be seen as a positive phenomenon potentially resulting in concrete classroom solutions, or perhaps as a wasteful overlapping of character education resources. James Leming (1993, p. 35) believes that this diversity of academic opinion hampers effective development of character education as a school subject. He says that: "the current research in the field consists of disparate bits and pieces of sociology, philosophy, child development research, socio-political analysis, and a variety of different programmes of evaluation." It is necessary to say something first of why traditional approaches to character education are increasingly being advocated.

THE LITANY OF ALARM

Those who have advocated character education in America and Britain often present it as a response to a list of ills facing society which originate in the behavior of juveniles (see *British Social Trends*). This list would normally include the following which have all shown a stubborn increase despite many attempts by government, schools, and welfare agencies to address their causes: suicides, especially of young males; teenage pregnancy and abortion; the crime rate, particularly theft by minors; alcohol and drug abuse; sexual activity and sexual abuse; teenage truancy and mental health problems. This teenage dysfunction has to be contextualized and set against a backdrop of family breakdown, domestic violence, poverty, and the provision of an endless diet of violence and sex in the media. Perhaps as a result of this, increasing numbers of children are arriving in early schooling showing symptoms of anxiety, emotional insecurity, and aggressive behavior. They seem devoid of many social skills and suffer low self-esteem. There are many reasons for the existence of these symptoms but they have a common effect in significantly reducing the ability of the school to develop positive character traits.

Thomas Lickona (1996) lists a further set of indicators of youth problems: dishonesty; peer cruelty; disrespect for adults and parents; self-centeredness; self-destructive behavior; and ethical illiteracy. Altruism often appears as the exception whilst self-interest has become the rule. The general moral relativism of society is also routinely blamed by character educators for this litany of social and moral breakdown, which is often referred to as a "crisis in moral education" (see Kilpatrick, 1992, pp. 13f.). This moral relativism, it is claimed, has replaced the belief in personal responsibility with the notion of social causation.

A criticism leveled at promoters of character education by certain commentators is that they do not examine sufficiently the complex issues which underlie many of the social statistics they detail. David Purple (1997, p. 147) makes the point that "Even if there has been a significant increase in teen-age pregnancies there is still a question of why it is considered a moral transgression." He asks which framework character educators use to criticize the degeneration they see around them. For Purple, teenage pregnancy and divorce are not problems at all. Timothy Rusnak (1998, 1) believes that fear is the justification for many character education programs in the US. Others would strongly argue that there has never been a "golden age," that every generation for the past two hundred years have simply produced their own "litany of alarm." Harry McKown (1935, pp. 18–34), writing in America in the 1930s provides his own litany. He bemoans the social break-up of the family (caused by economic pressures as opposed to marital difficulties); he decries the excessive individualism of the age; notes the decline in citizen participation in elections; abhors the "tremendous increase in crime"; is saddened by fewer young people attending Church; is concerned by the negative effect of advertising on the young; and sees the implications for morality in everything from public dancing and smoking to the wearing by young people of "types of close-to-nature clothing and bathing suits."

CRITICISMS OF CHARACTER EDUCATION

Terry McLaughlin and Mark Halstead (1999, p. 136) take issue with contemporary approaches to character education in the US, as do two major critics of the movement in America—David Purple (1997) and Robert Nash (1997). They all claim, rightly, that American character educators generally begin with detailing the social ills of society and then offer character education as a remedy; that these character educators also believe that core values can be identified, justified, and taught. In addition, they claim that character educators seek explicit teaching in the public schools of moral virtues, dispositions, traits, and habits, to be inculcated through content and the example of teachers, together with the ethos of the school and direct teaching and that the success of character education programs should be measured by the changes in the behavior of students. Character educators also, they claim, leave explaining difficult moral concepts until later in the student's development. They then criticize these views by outlining that character education is narrowly concerned with certain virtues, that it is restricted, limited, and focuses on traditional methods of teaching. Also, that there is a limited rationale given for the aims and purposes of character education by those who propose it in schools and that there is also a restricted emphasis on the use of critical faculties in students. McLaughlin and Halstead (1999, p. 139) observe that the character education movement: "lacks a common theoretical perspective and core of practice."

Whilst McLaughlin and Halstead are reasonably sympathetic to character education, they paint a bleak picture of current narrow practices in the US. However, they fail to deal with Nash whose language can often be extreme. Nash (1997) believes that most models of character education are deeply and seriously flawed, authoritarian in approach, too nostalgic, premodern in understanding of the virtues, aligned to reactionary politics, anti-intellectual, antidemocratic, and above all dangerous. He seeks to replace this tradition of character education with one that is not based on any moral authority and one which has an absence of a common moral standard by which to evaluate competing moral vocabularies. If this is what he seeks then McLaughlin and Halstead should have pointed out that he cannot condemn other competing moral vocabularies as he so obviously does from his own postmodern position. It appears that Nash refuses to acknowledge that all education rests on assumptions and beliefs and that a plurality of positions, including character education, can coexist. In the case of Purple (1997, p. 140) they do not answer his claim that character educators are "disingenuous" in their debates about character education and that they are effectively a conservative political movement with a hidden agenda. In any event, there is no necessary connection between a conservative political outlook and character education (see Howard, Berkowitz, & Shaeffer, 2004). A reasonable outline of the limits of the various approaches to traditional character education is provided by Larry Nucci (2001, pp. 129f.).

David Brooks and Frank Goble (1997) in *The Case for Character Education* follow a standard structure of argument used by many who advocate school-based character education. As previously mentioned, Harry McKown (1935) was one of the first to develop a model of writing about character within the context of schooling, a framework which has since been adopted by many others. McKown's book defines character education, presents a 1930s litany of alarm, explains why we should have character education in schools, describes the objectives of such a program, suggests how it should be in the curriculum, through the curriculum, as an extra-curricular activity, how it should be in the home and community, and how it might be assessed.

Brooks and Goble follow the same pattern. They first ask "what is wrong with Kids?" and answer: "they just don't seem to know the difference between right and wrong" (1997, p. 1). They then focus on student crime rates, etc., detailing a litany of alarm. This leads to the conclusion that something needs to be done. They cite a lack of standards as the reason for the problem and they offer character education as the solution. They then attack all the other methods of moral education, ranging from values clarification to cognitive theories of development, and this is then followed by the outlining of a number of teaching methods for character education. A virtue-ethics approach to character education is suggested, but what this would entail for teaching in schools is never explained. These books, whether consciously or not, follow a model which has its origins in McKown's 1935 seminal work and which was revived by Thomas Lickona's publication of *Education for Character* in 1991.

CONTEMPORARY DEFINITIONS OF CHARACTER EDUCATION

It is important to stress that few in America or Britain would consider the school the most important location for character education, even if it remains the main public institution for the formal moral education of children. The mass media, religious communities, youth culture, peer groups, voluntary organizations, and above all parents and siblings, account for significant influences on character formation. It cannot be easily assumed that the school makes more of a difference than any of these. It would be reasonable to assume that certain positive features of the school contribute to character development. Yet it is common in society to hold students responsible, not only for their behavior, but also for their own character, at a time when the burden of character education has inevitably been falling principally on the school. Obviously, some schools have the potential to be more effective than others at influencing character development. Some would argue that the ordinary public or State school has a more limited role in this for it would need to open longer and for many more days in the year to have a greater effect on character formation. However, in defining character education Ryan and Bohlin (1999, p. 190) say that it "is about developing virtues—good habits and dispositions which lead students to responsible and mature adulthood." The difficulty in attempting to define character education is that the concept is more ethically reflected upon than empirically studied which means that it is often defined in terms of its educational practices. Narvaez (2006, pp. 703f.) provides a review of the various definitions employed in current practice.

In reviewing the diverse views of character educators in America Anne Lockwood (1997, p. 179) develops a "tentative" definition of character education. She defines character education as a school-based activity that seeks to systematically shape the behavior of students—as she says: "Character education is defined as any school-instituted program, designed in cooperation with other community institutions, to shape directly and systematically the behaviour of young people by influencing explicitly the non-relativistic values believed directly to bring about that behaviour." She details three central propositions: first; that the goals of moral education can be pursued, not simply left to an uncontrolled hidden curriculum and that these goals should have a fair degree of public support and consensus. Second, that behavioral goals are part of character education. Third, that antisocial behavior on the part of children is a result of an absence of values. There is of course a presumed relation here with values and behavior.

I would add a fourth proposition: that many character educators not only seek to change behavior, but actually seek to produce certain kinds of character; to help form them in some way. The use of the terms "form" and "formation" here is not to be understood passively, but rather as the individual's active and conscious participation in their own formation. Character education holds out the hope of what a person can be as opposed to what they are. Character education is not the same as behavior control, discipline, training, or indoctrination, it is much broader and has much more ambitious goals. Whilst good character and good behavior are similar the former is broader in scope. Character is an inclusive term for the individual as a whole. Consequently, for many character educators "character education" has much more to do with formation and the transformation of a person and includes education in schools, families, and through the individual's participation in society's social networks.

Much that passes for character education in schools is essentially a pluralistic vision of character education that evades explicit directives for practice and lacks for many the forcefulness to be compelling. How is it possible in a heterogeneous society, composed of people who sharply disagree about basic values, to achieve a consensus about what constitutes character education for citizens in a democracy? Can we agree on what constitutes character education, on what its content should be, and how it should be taught? We live in a pluralistic society in which our values appear to be constantly changing and in which children are presented with all kinds of models and exposed to all kinds of opinions about right and wrong. For some, this appears to necessitate a content-based moral education curriculum that many others have rejected as too problematic and even suspicious. Progressive educationalists have long advocated that individual development should not be hindered by "controversial" moral content and they have cast suspicion on the motives of others who propose such explicit content. Consequently, many teachers and academics have sought to construct an implicit character education rationale without subscribing to any particular set of values or content-based moral education. They have found subscribing to any set of values deeply problematic in a pluralistic society and so they often commit themselves to nothing in particular.

CONTEMPORARY APPROACHES TO CHARACTER EDUCATION

The contemporary approach to character education in schools has been to accord the student a say in their own moral education, a degree of self-direction, which has been largely influenced by the cognitive development theorists. At the same time adult direction and authority has suffered from a great deal of criticism. Since the 1960s progressive teaching methods have emphasized child-centered learning, learning through experience, neutrality, and cooperative learning. These ideas in education tend to view the teacher as a professional educator who should not attempt to deliberately stamp character on students. Berkowitz and Bier (2005) have examined a range of empirical research, principally in refereed academic journals, in character education to examine whether character education works. They concluded that it does if "implemented effectively." They also identify 12 recommended and 18 promising practices in character education that include: problem solving, empathy, social skills, conflict resolution, peace making, and life skills. This is clearly a very broad view of what counts as character education and most teachers would not readily associate the term "character education" with these practices as a way to describe their intentions or objectives. Therefore, Berkowitz and Bier (2005) do not say exactly what is distinctive about the content or teaching methods of character education.

Teachers commonly argue that there is little room in the school curriculum to educate for moral character. Many will say that moral character is the responsibility of parents together with faith communities and that in any case in a multicultural society there is no agreed way to determine what is good and bad character. There also appears to be a growing "moral correctness" mindset in education, as teachers do not say things are "immoral" for fear of being branded discriminatory. In fact, teachers are generally non-judgmental in official language about children. However, it may be that talk of indoctrination and brainwashing often excuses the teacher from the really difficult task of thinking what values they might consciously inculcate. Instead of deciding what should be taught suspicion is raised and concern is voiced about values and controversial issues. Carr and Steutel (1999) have argued that character education ought to be grounded in an explicit commitment to virtue ethics. Whilst the virtue-ethics approaches have made inroads in mainstream education, few teachers have been prepared to deal with their complexity. Teachers are, with few exceptions, ill equipped to discuss, far less consciously adopt a virtue ethics approach to character education as they lack the language in virtue-ethics discourse.

Narvaez (2005, pp. 154–155) has argued strongly that character education should be based on psychologically valid research. Her approach offers a promising line of research which has been to integrate the insights from developmental theory and psychological science into character education. To this end she has described a model of character development and education which she calls Integrative Ethical Education (IEE) that sees character as a set of component skills that can be cultivated to a high level of expertise. She has identified the characteristic skills of persons with good character and believes that children move along a continuum from novice to expert in each ethical content domain that is studied. As she says "True ethical expertise requires concurrent competent interaction with the challenge of the environment using a plethora of processes, knowledge and skills" (Narvaez & Lapsley, 2005, pp. 155). This expertise approach to moral character requires a well-structured school environment in which the child is able to understand and develop skills together with opportunities for focused practice. The child learns from a variety of experiences and builds a knowledge base that can be used in authentic practical learning experiences. Narvaez makes clear that this understanding in the child ought to be evident in their practice and action. She makes clear that her approach is not simply about intellectual ability or mere technical competence. It is an attempt to integrate character education with cognitive science.

Traditionalist advocates for character education include the writings of Bennett (1991), Kilpatrick (1992), Ryan (1996), and Wynne and Ryan (1993). These writers are agreed that moral maturity requires character education that exhibits direct teaching and close guidance of the young. Much of what has followed has built upon their work and a range of authors draw inspiration from their writings. For example, Philip Vincent (1999, p. 3) provides some helpful suggestions which he calls "rules and procedures for character education." He suggests that schools should identify the virtues that need to be developed to help form character traits in students. These, he indicates, should be transformed into rules which are the expectations for appropriate behavior and that these should in turn become procedures which are practices needed to develop the habits of following rules and developing good character. So, the virtue of "respect" becomes a rule to treat all human beings with respect which becomes a set of procedures such as not interrupting others whilst they are speaking. Vincent and many others have looked at ways of translating the virtues into practical suggestions for teachers.

Bill Puka (2000, p. 131) in reviewing character education programs identifies six teaching methods. These are: 1) instruction in basic values and virtues; 2) behavioral codes established and enforced; 3) telling stories with moral lessons; 4) modeling desirable traits and values; 5) holding up moral exemplars in history, literature, religion, and extolling their traits; 6) providing in school and community outreach opportunities (service projects) through which students can exercise "good" traits and pursue "good" values. There are a wide variety of character development strategies which include those listed by Puka, but few have been evaluated. There are also certain assumptions of character educators implicitly or explicitly contained in these strategies. Whilst some subscribe to the psychological idea of moral development as developmental progression through stages, some prefer to substitute the word "development" for "formation." Many character educators do not accept that moral values are relative—they generally insist that moral values can be objectively grounded in human nature and experience. Some would also claim that moral action is not simply rational, but involves the affective qualities of a human being, including feelings and emotions (see Nucci, 2001, p. 122). Ryan (1996) and Wynne and Ryan (1993) would reject many models of moral education as inadequate on the basis that they are not comprehensive enough to capture the full complexity of human character.

Kevin Ryan and Thomas Lickona (1987, pp. 20ff.) provide an interesting model of character development that involves three basic elements—knowledge, feeling, and action. Lickona (1991) further developed this model. First, students learn moral content from our heritage. This heritage is not static, but subject to change for it can be altered and added to. The student learns to know the good through informed rational decision-making. Moral reasoning, decision-making, and the ability to gain self-knowledge through reviewing and evaluating behavior are all essential in this dimension of character development. Second, the affective domain, which includes feelings of sympathy, care, and love for others and is considered by Lickona as an essential bridge to moral action. Lickona (1991, pp. 58ff.) refers to this second element as feelings and adds conscience, love, empathy, and humility as important aspects of it. Third, action depends on the will, competence, and habit of a person. Will is meant in the sense that a student must will their way to overcoming their self-interest and any pride or anxiety they have in order to do what they know to be the right action. Students must also develop the competence to do the "good" which involves certain skills and they must freely choose to repeat these good actions as a form of habit. Ryan and Lickona tell us that these three elements of action do not always work together. Their model also states that character development takes place in and through human community. This requires students to be participative in the affairs of the community.

Thomas Lickona (1996) also outlines 11 principles that have been largely adopted by the Character Education Partnership in the US as criteria for planning a character education program and for recognizing the achievements of schools through the conferment of a national award. Whilst he does not consider these principles to be exhaustive, they are:

1. Schools should be committed to core ethical values.
2. Character should be comprehensively defined to include thinking, feeling, and behavior.
3. Schools should be proactive and systematic in teaching character education and not simply wait for opportunities.
4. Schools must develop caring atmospheres and become a microcosm of the caring community.
5. Opportunities to practise moral actions should be varied and available to all.
6. Academic study should be central.
7. Schools need to develop ways of increasing the intrinsic motivation of students who should be committed to the core values.
8. Schools need to work together and share norms for character education.
9. Teachers and students should share in the moral leadership of the school.
10. Parents and community should be partners in character education in the school.
11. Evaluate the effectiveness of character education in both school, staff, and students.

Lapsley and Narvaez (2006, p. 269) offer a useful critique of these principles which they claim appear, at first sight, to be a kind of manifesto for progressive education.

Almost all character educators emphasize the importance of the school ethos in advancing arguments about character education (De Vries, 1998; Grant, 1982; Wynne

& Walberg, 1985). These authors have all claimed that there is a relation between school ethos and educational outcomes concerning moral character. There is of course no such thing as a "value-free" school ethos. The research and writings of Edward Wynne (1982, 1985/1986) also suggest that the school ethos is crucial to an effective character program. Ryan (1996, p. 75) contends that "classroom life is saturated with moral meaning that shapes students' character and moral development." Wynne focuses on the school rather than on the individual student. He believes that the school could teach morality without saying a single word about it. We can see this in the fact that character or moral education is rarely formally recorded in any lesson plans or schemes of work—rather it forms part of the hidden curriculum. No elementary teacher would doubt how the school often acts as a family for many students replicating some of the formative influences of the family environment—warmth, acceptance, caring relationships, love, and positive role models.

The emphasis on school ethos is a relatively new feature within character education. The term "ethos" is an elusive concept and is closely associated with notions of "atmosphere," "climate," "culture," and "ethical environment." Consequently, it is difficult to focus on the specific meaning of "ethos" for the purpose of analysis and discussion. However, there is a strong and widely-held assumption that the ethos of a school influences the formation of quality relationships and even promotes good moral character. There is some emerging evidence to support these assumptions (see Arthur et al., 2001). Nevertheless, greater critical attention is needed to the kinds of educative influence "ethos" might have in its relation to moral character. There is also a greater awareness of the role of the "hidden curriculum" on character development and some believe that the indirect methods of teaching character are perhaps more beneficial than traditional curricula-based approaches.

Schools in a democracy are not total institutions—the home is the primary shaper of character whilst the school is only a secondary shaper. Schools are limited institutions in democratic societies which are only able to support certain values and virtues of homes and society when asked to do so. Teachers are clearly already involved in the formation of character of their students simply by being part of the school community. In practice most teachers view certain kinds of action by students as wrong and it is not unusual to find teachers insisting, for example, that students ought always to tell the truth. In a study of 2,000 student teachers in England (Arthur, 2005) it was found that the overwhelming majority believed that the teacher influenced the character of their students and that this process of influencing moral values was integral to the role of the teacher. However, it was clear that the students experienced no common practice of moral or character education in schools and their training courses were inadequate at preparing them for this role. In another study of 551 students over a two-year period between the ages of 16 and 19 it was found that the quality of relationships between teachers and students is of central importance for character formation in schools, especially teachers modeling values (Arthur et al., 2001).

CONCLUSION

The development of moral character has been a traditional goal of moral education in schools. Traditional character education focuses on the inculcation of virtuous traits of character as the aim of education. Character education is a label or generic term for a wide range of approaches to moral education, but specific programs often lack an explicit definition of what counts as character, they lack solid supporting empirical evidence, and they often lack a specific theory that underlies them. There are also few evaluations of any traditional approaches to character education in schools. Nevertheless, since character refers to that combination of rational and acquired factors which distinguish one individual from another it is clear that certain aspects of character building are beyond the realm of measurement. Another problem concerns the nature of the teaching role—an exemplary teacher will naturally establish a good ethos in their class and will promote good behavior with or without an explicit character education program. Character is not considered to be formed automatically, but is developed through teaching, example, and practice. There are also new approaches that have emerged to character education from cognitive psychology.

We can conclude that different approaches to character education will be viewed more or less favorably by people of different worldviews. However, because of the wide variety of approaches to character education it is difficult to evaluate them *en masse*—it is necessary to look at individual projects. The research to-date tells us that the danger of traditional character education lies in adopting inappropriate teaching techniques for the classroom which include an overtly coercive teacher-dominated approach. That said, character education programs are popular in many schools and the development of character can be effective moral education, especially when integrated into the whole curriculum and school life.

NOTES

1. Lapsley and Narvaez (2006) and Narvaez (2006, p. 703) provide an excellent review of this developmental research tradition over the last five decades.
2. Plato's *Republic* is presented in the form of a dialogue between Socrates and three different interlocutors. It is an enquiry into the notion of a perfect community and the ideal individual within it. Aristotle's *Ethics* converted ethics from a theoretical to a practical science and also introduced psychology into his study of behavior. Aristotle both widens the field of moral philosophy and simultaneously makes it more accessible to anyone who seeks an understanding of human nature. There are many editions of both books and the editions cited in the references are published by Penguin Books in the UK.

REFERENCES

Aquinas, Thomas (1968). *Summa theologia*. Blackfriars 1968 ed. Oxford: Oxford University Press.
Aristotle (1969). *The Nicomachean ethics*, edited by H. Tredennick. London: Penguin Books.
Arthur, J. (2003). *Education with Character: The Moral Economy of Schooling*, London: Routledge.
Arthur, J. (2005). *Character formation in schools and the education of teachers*. Esmee Fairbairn Foundation/Canterbury Christ Church University, www.citized.info.
Arthur, J., Deakin Crick, R., Samuel, E., Wilson, K., & McGettrick, B. (2001). *Character education: The formation of virtues and dispositions in 16–19 year olds*. John Templeton Foundation, Canterbury Christ Church University and the University of Bristol, www.citized.info.
Bennet, W.J. (1991). Moral literacy and the formation of character. In J. Benninga (Ed.), *Moral character and civil education in the elementary school*. New York: Teachers College Press.
Berkovitz, M.V. & Bier, M.C. (2005). *What works in character education?: A research-driven guide for educators*. Washington, D.C.: Character Education Partnership.
Bernard, H.C. (1966). *A history of English education*. London: London University Press.
British Social Trends (2002–2005). Nos. 32–34, London: HMSO.
Brooks, B.D. & Kann, M.E. (1993). What makes character education programs work? *Educational Leadership*, November, 19–21.

Brooks, B.D. & Goble, F.G. (1997). *The case for character education: The role of the school in teaching values and virtue.* Northridge, CA: Studio 4 Productions.

Carr, David (2002). Moral education and the perils of developmentalism. *Journal of Moral Education, 31* (1), 5–19.

Carr, D. & Steutel, J. (Eds.). (1999) *Virtue ethics and moral education.* London: Routledge.

Collini, S. (1985). The idea of character in Victorian political thought. *Transactions of the Royal Historical Society, 35,* 29–54.

De Vries, R. (1998). Implications of Piaget's constructivist theory for character education. *Action in Teacher Education, 20* (4), 39–47.

Grant, G. (1982). The character of education and the education of character. *American Education, 18* (1), 37–46.

Hartshorne, H. & May, M. (1928–1930). *Studies in the nature of character,* 3 vols. New York: Macmillan.

Hilliard, F.H. (1961). The Moral Instruction League 1987–1919. *Durham Research Review, 12* (3), 53–63.

Howard, R.W., Berkowitz, M.V., & Shaeffer, E.F. (2004). Politics of character education. *Educational Policy, 18* (1), 188–215.

Hutchison, H. (1976). An eighteenth-century insight into religious and moral education. *British Journal of Educational Studies, 24,* 233–241.

Kilpatrick, W. (1992). *Why Johnny can't tell right from wrong: Moral literacy and the case for character education.* New York: Simon and Schuster.

Kohlberg, L. (1984). *Essays on moral development: The psychology of moral development,* Vol. II. San Francisco: Harper and Row.

Lapsley, D. & Narvaez, D. (2005). Moral psychology at the crossroads. In D. Lapsley and C. Power (Eds.), *Character psychology and character education* (pp. 18–35). Notre Dame, IN: University of Notre Dame Press.

Lapsley, D.K. & Narvaez, D. (2006). Character education. In Vol. IV (A. Renninger and I. Siegel, Vol. Eds.), *Handbook of child psychology* (W. Damon and R. Lerner, Series Eds.) (pp. 248–296). New York: Wiley.

Lapsley, D.K. & Power, F.C. (2005). *Character psychology and character education.* New York and Notre Dame, IN: Notre Dame University Press.

Leming, J. (1993). *Character education: Lessons from the past, models for the future.* Camden, ME: The Institute of Global Ethics.

Lickona, T. (1991). *Educating for character: How our schools can teach respect and responsibility.* New York: Bantam.

Lickona, T. (1996). Eleven principles of effective character education. *Journal of Moral Education, 25* (1), 93–100.

Lockwood, A. (1997). *Character education: Controversy and consensus.* London: Corwin Press/Sage.

McKown, H.C. (1935). *Character education.* New York and London: McGraw-Hill.

McLaughlin, T. & Halstead, M. (Eds.). (1999). *Education and morality.* London: Routledge.

Narvaez, D. (2005). The neo-Kohlbergian tradition and beyond: Schemas, expertise and character. In G. Carlo and C. Pope-Edwards (Eds.), *Nebraska symposium on motivation, Vol. 51: Moral motivation through the lifespan* (pp. 119–163). Lincoln, NE: University of Nebraska Press.

Narvaez, D. (2006). Integrative ethical education. In M. Killen and J.G. Smetna (Eds.), *Handbook of moral education* (pp. 703–733). New Jersey and London: Lawrence Erlbaum Associates.

Narvaez, D. & Lapsley, D. (2005). The psychological foundations of everyday morality and moral expertise. In D. Lapsley and C. Power (Eds.), *Character psychology and character education* (pp. 140–165). Notre Dame: IN: University of Notre Dame Press.

Nash, R. (1997). *Answering the virtuecrats: A moral conversation on character education.* New York: Teachers College Press.

Nucci, L. (2001). *Education in the moral domain.* Cambridge and New York: Cambridge University Press.

Peck, R.F. & Havighurst, R.J. (1960). *The psychology of character development.* New York: John Wiley.

Peters, R.S. (1979). Virtues and habits in moral education. In D.B. Cochrane, C. Hamm, and A. Kazepides (Eds.), *The domain of moral education.* New York: Paulist Press.

Plato. (2003). *The republic,* London: Penguin Books.

Porter, R. (1990). *The recovery of virtue.* Louisville: Westminster/John Knox Press.

Puka, B. (2000). Inclusive moral education: A critique and integration of competing approaches. In M. Leicester, C. Mogdil, and S. Mogdil (Eds.), *Moral education and pluralism.* London: Falmer Press.

Purple, D. (1997). The politics of character education. In A. Molnar (Ed.), *The construction of children's character.* Chicago: National Society for the Study of Education.

Rest, J.R., Narvaez, D., Bebeau, M., & Thoma, S. (1999). *Postconventional moral thinking: A neo-Kohlbergian approach.* Mahwah, NJ: Erlbaum.

Rotblatt, S. (1976). *Tradition and change in English liberal education.* London: Faber & Faber.

Rusnack, T. (Ed.) *An integrated approach to character education.* London: Corwin Press.

Ryan, K. (1996). Character education in the United States: a status report. *Journal for a Just and Caring Education, 2,* 75–84.

Ryan, K. & Bohlin, K.E. (1999). *Building character in schools.* San Francisco: Jossey-Bass.

Ryan, K. & Lickona, T. (1987). Character education: the challenge and the model. In K. Ryan and G.F. McLean (Eds.), *Character development in schools and beyond.* New York: Praeger.

Vincent, P. (1999). *Developing character in students.* Chapel Hill, NC: Character Development Publishing.

Wynne, E. (1982). *Character policy: an emerging issue.* Lantham, MD: University Press of America.

Wynne, E. (1985/1986). The great traditions in education: transmitting moral values. *Educational Leadership, 45* (5), 4–9.

Wynne, E. & Ryan, K. (1993). *Reclaiming our schools.* New York: Macmillan.

Wynne, E. & Walberg, H. (1985). The complementary goals of character development and academic excellence. *Educational Leadership, 43* (4), 15–18.

5

LAWRENCE KOHLBERG'S REVOLUTIONARY IDEAS

Moral Education in the Cognitive-Developmental Tradition

John Snarey and Peter L. Samuelson

INTRODUCTION

Lawrence Kohlberg's ideas about moral formation and moral education were revolutionary. He made morality a central concern in psychology, and he remains the person most often identified as a founding figure in the field of moral psychology, including moral development and moral education. He understood that children and adolescents, as well as adults, are *developing* moral philosophers, capable of forming their own moral judgments and capable of revising them. Kohlberg is best known for his three models of moral formation (moral stages, types, and atmosphere) and his three methods of moral education (moral exemplars, dilemma discussions, and Just Community schools). Overall, Kohlberg created lasting frameworks for approaching the study of moral cognition and development and inspired educational programs to prepare citizens for living in a participatory democracy.

Kohlberg (1958, 1969), like all revolutionary thinkers, also stands on the shoulders of his predecessors. Kohlberg's approach to moral education is rooted in the theories and methods of Jean Piaget (1896–1980) and Emile Durkheim (1858–1917). The ideas of these two giants in the field of moral development and education are also evident in contemporary approaches to moral and character education. The approach most influenced by Piaget is often called Moral Education. It emphasizes that students participate in moral thought and action through moral dilemma discussions, role-play, collaborative peer interaction, and a democratic classroom and school culture. Another approach more influenced by Durkheim is often called Character Education. It emphasizes the direct teaching of virtues and exemplary character traits, role modeling, and reinforcement of good behavior (Althof & Berkowitz, 2006; Berkowitz, 2012). Kohlberg draws creatively from both traditions in fashioning his approach to moral development and education.

PIAGET'S COGNITIVE-DEVELOPMENTAL APPROACH

Piaget viewed the development of morality through the lens of his "cognitive-developmental" theory. In this view, a series of organized cognitive structures that govern a child's thoughts and actions are transformed in an ordered sequence as the child constructs, through interaction with the environment, increasingly useful and more complex cognitive operations. In *The Moral Judgment of the Child*, Piaget (1932) distinguished two types of moral reasoning, each of which shows a different understanding of respect, fairness, and punishment:

1. *Heteronomous morality.* Initially morality is based on unilateral respect for authorities and the rules they prescribe. Fairness is understood as obedience to authorities and conformity to their "sacred" rules; consequences are understood as concrete, objective damage, which carries more weight than intentions; expiatory punishment is the favored way of making things right.
2. *Autonomous morality.* Morality is based on mutual respect, reciprocity, and equality among peers. Fairness is understood as mutually agreed upon cooperation and reciprocal exchange. Intentionality is understood as relevant; both intentions and consequences can be kept in mind concurrently; punishment by reciprocity is favored.

Piaget saw moral development as the movement from heteronomous morality to autonomous morality and believed that social interactions, especially with peers, would fuel moral development.

Piaget was a strong advocate of democratic educational methods and critiqued what he believed to be Durkheim's position on this point:

> The problem is to know what will best prepare the child for its future task of citizenship…. For ourselves we regard as of the utmost importance the experiments that have been made to introduce democratic methods into schools. We therefore do not at all agree with Durkheim in thinking that it is the master's business to impose or even to "reveal" rules to the child.
>
> (1932, pp. 363–364)

Piaget claimed that educators best promote mature moral reasoning by talking with children as equals in the search for knowledge rather than with indoctrinative authority that promotes the consolidation of childish reasoning. Piaget considered his moral development approach to be the "opposite pole from the Durkheimian pedagogy" (1932, p. 362).

DURKHEIM'S CULTURAL SOCIALIZATION APPROACH

Durkheim's core principles are laid out in his 1902 and 1903 lecture series, published posthumously as *Moral Education: A Study in the Theory and Application of the Sociology of Education* (1925). At the center of Durkheim's approach is collective socialization or cultural transmission, which is the process whereby a person learns society's norms and expectations through instruction and explanation, role models, and group reinforcement. Therefore, education for moral character is primarily about social solidarity, group conformity, and mutual support.

Durkheim maintained that social norms were the most effective means of control, not because they are socially imposed from the outside, but because they are voluntarily internalized and come to function as the society's norms living within its members. He posited three elements of morality:

Spirit of discipline. Morality requires respect for social norms and authority and consistent conduct.

Spirit of altruism. Morality requires that persons be attached to and identified with social groups.

Autonomy or self-determination. Though the society is the final authority for the child, the child must freely choose whether to follow the society's rules.

Durkheim held that collective responsibility, applied with restraint and judgment, is central to moral education. Thus, in the practice of moral education, the school has a crucial and clearly specified function: to create a new being shaped according to the needs of society. Kohlberg, influenced by Piaget's writings on Durkheim, originally saw striking limitations to this method and derisively labeled contemporary attempts at moral socialization as a "bag of virtues" approach:

> Although it may be true that the notion of teaching virtues, such as honesty or integrity, arouses little controversy, it is also true that vague consensus on the goodness of these virtues conceals a great deal of actual disagreement over their definitions. What is one person's "integrity" is another person's "stubbornness," what is one person's honesty in "expressing your true feelings" is another person's insensitivity to the feelings of others.
>
> (Kohlberg, 1981, pp. 9–10)

Kohlberg believed that an enculturation approach leaves one open to ethical relativity, and he did not want to base his approach on socially relative virtues.

Kohlberg eventually realized that Piaget had attacked something of a caricature of Durkheim. Both Piaget and Durkheim agreed, for instance, that moral behavior entails cognitive understanding and the exercise of free will, not just imitating role models or ideals of virtue. As Durkheim was careful to indicate, "To teach morality is neither to preach nor to indoctrinate; it is to explain" (1925, p. 20). Beyond their shared belief in the egoism of the child, both also stressed the importance of groups' social relations for the child's development, and that morality is formed in the context of relationships and role taking experiences (cf. Selman, 1971, 2003). Finally, both viewed a school's classroom dynamics and authority structure as inevitably involved in moral education (cf. Power, 2004).

KOHLBERG'S REFINED DEVELOPMENTAL-SOCIALIZATION APPROACH

Kohlberg's work is primarily identified with the "cognitive-developmental paradigm." His stage theory of moral development, like Piaget's, postulates that moral reasoning proceeds through an invariant sequence of stages toward an increasingly adequate understanding of what is just or fair. In this view, the child is a philosopher who actively constructs and makes sense of his or her world. The educator's aim is to provide the conditions that promote the natural progression of moral judgment by providing ethically enriched and stimulating educational experiences within which a child is allowed to exercise moral choice. Motivated by insights gained during educational efforts, Kohlberg reread and reconsidered Durkheim. He came to see that the unit of education was the group, not simply the individual, and that moral education should change a school's moral culture, not only develop a person's moral reasoning. In one of his first public statements of his revised perspective, Kohlberg said:

> It is not a sufficient guide to the moral educator, who deals with concrete morality in a school world in which value content as well as structure, behavior as well as reasoning, must be dealt with. In this context, an educator must be a socializer, teaching value content and behavior, not merely a Socratic or Rogerian process-facilitator of development. In becoming a socializer and advocate, the teacher moves into "indoctrination," a step that I originally believed to be invalid ... I no longer hold these negative views of indoctrinative moral education.... Now I believe that moral education can be in the form of advocacy or "indoctrination" without violating the child's rights if there is an explicit recognition of shared rights of teachers and students and as long as teacher advocacy is democratic, or subject to the constraints of recognizing student participation in the rule-making and value-upholding process.
>
> (1978, pp. 14–15)

Moral development and education, thus revised, involve a synthesis of both the democratic socialization of moral content and the developmental promotion of moral reasoning. By democratizing Durkheim, Kohlberg hoped to give priority to the power of the collective in a way that also protected the rights of the individual. These two concepts—the cognitive-developmental promotion of moral reasoning and the collective socialization of moral content—form the foundation on which Kohlberg constructed his three models of moral cognition and his three approaches to moral education.

KOHLBERG'S THREE MODELS OF MORAL COGNITION AND DEVELOPMENT

Kohlberg is renowned for his stage model of moral development. Though his basic stage theory had changed little since its inception in his dissertation study (1958, 2008), Kohlberg augmented it with two additional models. Thus, within the paradigm of structuralism, Kohlberg actually created three models: (1) moral stages, (2) moral types, and (3) social-moral atmosphere levels. Together, they provide a fairly comprehensive view of human moral cognition and development.

Moral Stages

Kohlberg believed that moral judgment development progressed through six stages: cognitively structured moral reasoning steps that follow an invariant sequence. What drives moral development is the adequacy or inadequacy of moral thought structures in making sense of experience. The human mind assimilates the environment to existing thought structures and, when this assimilation fails, accommodates by modifying them to more adequately make sense of environmental moral issues. Kohlberg used moral dilemma interviews as his research tool; he presented the equivalent of nine dilemmas to a cohort of 84 adolescent boys and then studied how they reasoned about the dilemmas.

Whereas Piaget primarily saw two thought structures in moral reasoning (outlined above), Kohlberg believed that six age-related thought structures best described his subject's reasoning about the dilemmas. In the moral realm, that is, a person progresses from focusing on the self, in which he or she tries to avoid punishment or maximize gains (pre-conventional stages 1 & 2), to include the perspective of those in close relation to himself or herself, which will eventually include whole systems of relationships expressed in groups, institutions, and society as a whole (conventional stages 3 & 4). According to Kohlberg, a person cannot move from pre-conventional to conventional moral reasoning unless and until he or she can think beyond an egocentric perspective and hold multiple perspectives in mind (one's own, the other's, and the needs and rights of the group) while performing mental operations on a moral issue. The final level (post-conventional stages 5 & 6) involves holding a complex array of perspectives and thoughts about right moral action against a universalizable set of moral values and principles. Kohlberg's (1981, 1984, 1987) six stages are defined in Table 5.1.

Overall, Kohlberg's model of moral stage development illustrates the potential evolution of moral reasoning toward greater complexity and adequacy. Moral stages, for Kohlberg, were not simply moral ideals, ideal types, or virtual models of reasoning, but actual cognitive-developmental stages in the evolving structure of the social-moral brain.

The sweeping nature of his approach received academic acclaim and media attention. Scholars, of course, also subjected his work to intense scrutiny, raised several critical questions, and pointed to the need for further research. High-quality empirical studies were then conducted and, eventually, several decisive reviews of the accumulated research studies were published. These reviews provided support for the following conclusions:

(a) *Stage validity*. Moral stages have been shown to be qualitatively different from each other, and internally integrated structured wholes, which change in an invariant sequence, one stage at a time (Colby & Kohlberg, 1987; Hart, 1992; Kohlberg, 1984; cf. Dawson, 2002). Brain research, using non-invasive functional magnetic resonance imaging (fMRI) scanners, also has documented that distinct areas of neural activation and distinct modes of neural connectivity differentiate lower *versus* higher moral stage reasoning (cf. Caceda, James, Snarey, & Kilts, 2011; Prehn et al., 2008).

(b) *Cross-cultural universality*. The first four stages are found in virtually all cultural groups, and principled reasoning is found to some degree in all complex societies with elaborated systems of education such as India, Japan, and Taiwan (Snarey, 1985). Although the stage sequence is not altered by diverse cultural context, post-conventional or principled reasoning becomes more pluralistic. Although Kohlberg identified a particular form of post-conventional reasoning that he believed was universal, research among non-Western cultural groups and non-European-American racial-ethnic groups reveals a pluralistic array of genuine ethical principles in addition to those addressed by Kohlberg's theory and scoring manual (cf. Siddle-Walker & Snarey, 2004; Snarey & Keljo, 1991).

Table 5.1 Kohlberg's Six Developmental Stages of Justice Reasoning

Stage 1: Obedience and Punishment Orientation

At Stage 1, what is moral is to avoid breaking rules or to comply for obedience's sake, and to avoid doing physical damage to people or property. Moral judgments are self-evident, requiring little or no justification beyond labeling. A person at Stage 1 does not realize that the interests of others may differ from his or her own. Justice is understood as strict, literal equality, with special needs or mitigating circumstances not understood or taken into consideration. In situations in which an authority is involved, justice is defined as respectful obedience to the authority. The justification for moral action or doing what is right includes avoidance of penalties and the superior power of authorities.

Stage 2: Instrumental Purpose and Exchange

What is moral for the person at Stage 2 is to follow the rules when it is in the person's immediate interest to do so, especially in terms of an equal exchange, a good deal. The person now recognizes that other persons may have other interests. Justice involves relating conflicting individual interests through an instrumental exchange of services or marketplace economy: You scratch my back and I'll scratch yours. The justification for being moral is to serve one's own needs in a world where one must recognize that other people also have their own interests, which may conflict with one's own.

Stage 3: Mutual Interpersonal Expectations, Good Relations

A person at Stage 3 is able to coordinate the separate perspectives of individuals into a third-person perspective, which enables interpersonal trust, mutual relationships, loyalty, and shared moral values. What is moral is conforming to what is expected by people close to you or what people generally expect of people in one's role as son, sister, parent, friend, and so on. Justice now can take into consideration a person's worthiness, goodness, and circumstances. The justifications for acting morally focus on the desire to be seen as a good person in one's own eyes and those of others. One should be caring of others because, if you put yourself in the other person's shoes, you would want good behavior from others.

Stage 4: Social System and Conscience Maintenance

The right thing to do is to be a good citizen, uphold the social order, and maintain the society. What is moral involves fulfilling one's duties. Laws are to be upheld, except in extreme cases in which they conflict with other fixed social duties. Justice centers on the notions of impartiality in application of the law; procedural justice first emerges as a central concern at Stage 4. A just decision also should take into consideration a person's contribution to society. This is a social-maintenance, rather than an interpersonal-maintenance, perspective; being moral involves contributing to one's own society, group, or institution. The justifications for being moral are to keep the institution functioning, to maintain self-respect for having met one's defined obligations, and to avoid setting a socially disruptive precedent.

Stage 5: Prior Rights and Social Contract

What is moral is being aware that many values and rules are relative to one's group and subsuming these culturally relative values under fundamental human rights, such as the rights of life and liberty, which are logically prior to society. The person logically organizes rights and values into hierarchies from most to least fundamental. Such non-relative rights are inviolable and should be built into and upheld by any society. Justice now focuses on human rights or social welfare; due process is also a concern. This is a society-creating rather than a society-maintaining point of view. A social system is understood, ideally, as a social contract freely entered into. A person reasoning at Stage 5 justifies upholding the social contract because it preserves one's own rights and the rights of others, ensures impartiality, and promotes the greatest good for the greatest number.

Stage 6: Universal Ethical Principles

Deciding what is moral is guided by universal ethical principles that generate decisions by which human dignity is ensured and persons are treated as ends in themselves rather than simply as means. Particular laws or social agreements are usually valid because they rest on such ethical principles. When laws violate these principles, however, one acts in accordance with the principle. Going beyond the importance of a social contract, Stage 6 also focuses on the process by which a social agreement is reached. This is a moral-justice point of view, involving the deliberate use of justice principles, which centers on the equality of all human beings as free and equal autonomous persons. The justification for being moral is the belief, as that of a human rights and respect for the dignity of all human beings as free and equal autonomous persons. The justification for being moral is the belief, as that of a rational person, in the validity of universal moral principles that all humanity should follow, and because one has made a self-conscious commitment to them.

Source: Siddle-Walker & Snarey (2004), pp. 18–19.

(c) *Moral action applicability.* Moral behavior and moral reasoning are positively and significantly associated. In both laboratory and real-life settings, moral reasoning is a significant predictor of moral action, including altruistic behavior, resistance of temptation, and nondelinquency (Blasi, 1980). Persons at higher moral stages, for instance, are significantly more likely to help a stranger who needs medical attention (Kohlberg, 1984). The literature also shows a well-established relation between moral immaturity and delinquency. A nine-year longitudinal and cross-sectional study, for instance, confirms the reciprocal relation between moral immaturity and delinquency—the higher the moral reasoning score, the lower the rate of delinquency (Raaijamkers, Engles, & Hoof, 2005). Of course, although the association between moral reasoning and moral action is positive and significant, many moderating factors affect the relation (cf. Bebeau, 2002; Kohlberg, Ricks, & Snarey, 1984; Palmer, 2003; Thoma, 1994; Thoma, Rest, & Davison, 1991).

(d) *Gender inclusiveness.* Possible gender differences in moral judgment have been a source of continued criticism and controversy. In her book, *In a Different Voice,* Carol Gilligan (1982) was one of the first to suggest that Kohlberg's model of moral development was biased to a more male-oriented morality of justice at the expense of a morality of care and responsibility that better suits female moral perspectives. Some research has shown that women and girls tend to use more care-related concerns in their moral justifications (Garmon, Basinger, Gregg, & Gibbs, 1996; Jaffe & Hyde, 2000). Nevertheless, a substantial body of empirical evidence indicates that the current standardized scoring system contains no significant bias against women (Brabeck & Shore, 2002; Walker, 1984) and that Rest's Defining Issues scoring system shows a very small but stable gender effect that consistently favors women (Thoma, 1986). Many studies show that women as well as men, and girls as well as boys, use Kohlberg's ethic of justice (e.g., Garrod et al., 2003). Furthermore, any developmental differences found are more situational than a reflection of gender differences across the lifespan (Clopton & Sorell, 1993; Ryan, Reynolds, & Reynolds, 2004; Thoma, 1986).

(e) *Care is not reducible to justice.* Carol Gilligan (1982) also identified a moral orientation of care that was qualitatively different from the orientation of justice and rights that dominates Kohlberg's theory. While Kohlberg contended that his model of justice included care, others concluded that Gilligan's view had enlarged the psychological understanding of morality (cf. Brabeck, 1984). A number of studies offer evidence that an ethic of care, while used by both men and women, is inadequately represented in Kohlberg's theory (Gilligan, 1982), hypothetical-dilemma interview method (Jaffee & Hyde, 2000), and scoring manual (Walker, 1984). Philosophically, justice and care are equally vital and equally irreducible principles in normative moral values (cf. Blum, 1988; Siddle-Walker & Snarey, 2004). Biologically, neuroscience research had demonstrated overlapping but significantly different brain region activations during the neural processing of care *versus* justice moral sensitivity dilemmas (Robertson et al., 2007; Snarey, 2008). In sum, the ethic of care is a separable ethical voice that cannot be simply reduced to an element of an ethic of justice (cf. Brabeck & Ting, 2000; Jorgensen, 2006; Puka, 1991; Sherblom, 2008).

Kohlberg's stage model, despite a number of necessary qualifications and caveats, remains theoretically forceful and pedagogically useful. It continues to generate innovative, and sometimes ground-breaking, research into the nature of moral thought and action, the causes of delinquency and criminal behavior, our nature as human beings, and the understanding of ourselves as moral agents (cf. Gibbs, 2009; Gibbs, Basinger, Grime, and Snarey, 2007; Parke & Clarke-Stewart, 2010).

Moral Types

Kohlberg (1976) and his colleagues (Schrader, Tappan, Kohlberg, & Armon, 1987; Tappan et al., 1987) recognized that moral development stage scores did not account for some important within-stage variations seen in moral judgment interviews. To address this variation, they incorporated Piaget's view of morality as two forms of moral judgment: heteronymous and autonomous. They initially conceived of heteronomy and autonomy as two substages within each of Kohlberg's six stages (Lapsley, 1996). However, the term "substage" was dropped because research showed that the so-called substages did not meet Piaget's criteria for stages (i.e., there was not an invariant sequence from A to B, nor structured wholes).

Kohlberg then adopted from sociologist Max Weber (1949) the concept of "ideal types," that is, abstractions that define the extreme forms of the possible properties of each stage. More specifically, Kohlberg and colleagues defined heteronomy and autonomy as two subtypes (A or B) that may occur within any stage (e.g., Stage 2A and Stage 2B). These subtypes are defined by variations in the content of moral judgments, including notions of freedom from external constraints, ideas about how human rules and laws are constructed, and issues of who is to be included in the moral domain (Kohlberg, 1984). Moral types are, in essence, a way of accounting for some aspects of a person's reasoning that are overlooked when moral stages are assessed.

Type analysis or scoring focuses primarily on the content of moral reasoning, whereas stage analysis focuses primarily on the cognitive structure of moral reasoning. When interviews are scored for moral type, the content of a person's reasoning is considered. Kohlberg and his colleagues looked for criteria to discern these ideal types in the psychological and philosophical works of Piaget and Immanuel Kant. They derived nine "content themes" and used them to discern the moral type of the subject under examination. In the scoring manual for moral type, these theoretical criteria are translated into coding criteria for each of the three standard interview dilemmas. The unit of analysis for coding the moral types is the individual dilemma as a whole. Moral type scores are calculated on the basis of the data that meet the criteria of the Piagetian and Kantian categories that reflect autonomous reasoning in two out of three moral dilemmas (Schrader et al., 1987). The nine criteria that determine moral type are summarized in Table 5.2.

A six-year longitudinal cross-cultural study (Logan, Snarey, & Schrader, 1990) confirmed Kohlberg's previous longitudinal findings from studies in the United States and Turkey that type B reasoning increased with age. Moreover, the study found that the achievement of type B reasoning was positively and significantly associated with moral stage development; that is, subjects who scored at higher stages were more likely to also use type B reasoning. The longitudinal cross-cultural data, however, also showed a trend of one-time shifts (from type A to type B), after which the type tended to remain stable. Nevertheless, consistent with Kohlberg's conceptualization of moral types, reversals from type B to type A occurred, and both types of reasoning were used by some subjects at every moral stage represented in their study (Stage 2 to Stages 4/5).

Kohlberg's moral types also proved to be a strong conceptual tool for clarifying how moral reasoning translates into moral action. In a number of studies analyzed (Kohlberg, 1984), subjects with a type B moral orientation were more likely to act in concordance with their moral judgments and values even when those values conflicted with a prevailing rule or authority. This discovery is exemplified by data from 26 students involved in the Milgram (1974) experiment who were given the Moral Judgment Interview. The Milgram experiment, which was described to subjects as testing the effects of punishment on memory, required the subjects to administer an increasingly powerful electric shock to a victim in the event of a wrong answer, even to the point of rendering the victim unconscious. The victim was an actor who was not actually shocked, but the situation appeared very real, and subjects were forced to choose between obeying the authority of the experimenter (dressed in a white lab coat and encouraging the subject to continue administering the "shock") versus discontinuing the suffering of the victim by ceasing to participate in the experiment. None of the participants who had been assessed as moral type A quit, and only 18% of those scored as "ambiguous" ceased participation in the experiment. In contrast, a full 86% of the participants assessed as moral type B quit the experiment regardless of moral stage (Kohlberg, 1984). Kohlberg explained these results by noting that type B reasoning is characterized by a clear conception of the "right" thing to do in a situation (deontic choice) as well as a sense of responsibility to act, born of a fully developed notion of autonomy (freedom to act according to one's own values regardless of what others expect), reversibility (a desire to treat others as one would want to be treated), and universality (that you would expect your action to be "right" in all similar situations). Deontic choice and responsibility are two judgments that mediate moral action, according to Kohlberg (1984).

Table 5.2 Kohlberg's Distinctions Between Type A and Type B Moral Orientations

Criteria	Type A (Heteronomous)	Type B (Autonomous)
Hierarchy	No clear moral hierarchy, reliance on pragmatic and other concerns	Clear hierarchy of moral values; prescriptive duties are primary
Instrinsicality	Instrumental view of persons	Persons as ends in themselves; respect for autonomy, dignity
Prescriptivity	Moral duty as instrumental or hypothetical	Moral duty as moral obligation
Universality	Judgments uncritically assumed to be held by everyone or based on self-interest	Generalized view; applies to everyone in same situation
Freedom	External bases validate judgments	No reliance on external authority or tradition
Mutual respect	Unilateral obedience	Cooperation among equals
Reversibility	Views the dilemma from only one point of view	Understanding of the other's perspective; reciprocity
Constructivism	Rigid view of rules and laws as fixed	Flexible view of rules and laws as adaptable
Choice	Does not choose or justify choice in terms of fairness or justice	Chooses solution generally seen as just or fair

Source: Logan, Snarey & Schrader (1990), p. 75.

In sum, Kohlberg's type categories expanded his stage theory in three respects: (1) moral types primarily address the content of moral reasoning, whereas moral stages focus on the structure of moral reasoning; (2) either type may occur at any stage and at any age in the lifespan, thus accounting for observed within-stage variability (cf. Schraeder et al., 1987); and (3) moral type helps clarify the connection between moral reasoning and moral action.

Moral Atmosphere

Kohlberg (1980, 1985) and colleagues (Power, Higgins, & Kohlberg, 1989) developed the concept of "moral atmosphere" to refer to a community's shared expectations and normative values. He also referred to the concept as a community's "moral climate" or "moral culture." Kohlberg understood that the group is the primary context for the development of a moral person. At the time when this concept was being developed, his stage theory was being criticized for his emphasis on the individual reasoner and on individual rights, at the expense of the community (cf. Snarey & Keljo, 1991).

Kohlberg's theory of moral atmosphere analysis is a robust answer to his communitarian and Durkheimian critics. Based in part on Durkheim's idea that the group is greater than the sum of its individual members, Kohlberg and his colleagues sought to characterize the added value of groups that would be the most relevant to moral cognition, development, and behavior. Also, drawing on Durkheim's view that the unit of education was the group, Kohlberg concluded that changing the school's moral culture would profoundly affect an individual's moral formation. Kohlberg further specified that the most beneficial group for moral development is a democratically governed group, one that recognizes the rights and responsibilities of each to each other and to the group as a whole. Thus, a simple focus on the developmental promotion of an individual's moral reasoning was not enough; democratic governance would be the kind of collective socialization that would foster moral ideals, goals, and actions as well as promote moral reasoning. In addition, the promotion of moral development had to include the collective socialization of moral content. Kohlberg (1985) came to emphasize that moral development is not only about doing justice; it also includes the social dimension of a person acting in caring relationships with those attached to each other and with the group (cf. McDonough, 2005).

Clark Power and Ann Higgins worked with Kohlberg (1989) to construct an array of complex variables that, taken together, provide a detailed map of a school's moral atmosphere or climate. Three of these variables (levels of institutional valuing, stages of community valuing, and phases of the collective norm) are summarized in Table 5.3. The first two focus on the valuing of the school as a social entity, and the last one focuses on the phases of commitment to the collective norm.

Kohlberg and his colleagues noted that "the two major units in this analysis, the collective norm and the element of institutional value, correspond to two of Durkheim's goals of moral education: discipline and attachment to the group." They continued: "Durkheim's third goal of moral education, autonomy, corresponds most closely to our analysis of the stage of norms and elements" (p. 116). As Kohlberg (1985) states elsewhere, they made use of Durkheim's concept of the "spirit of discipline" as "respect for group norms and rules" and "respect for the group; which makes them" (p. 42), and they made use of his concept of the "spirit of altruism," which arises from attachment to the group, as "the willingness to freely give up the ego's interests, privileges and possessions

Table 5.3 Moral Atmosphere: Levels, Stages, and Phases

Levels of Institutional Valuing	Stages of Community Valuing	Phases of the Collective Norm
Level 0: Rejection The school is not valued.		Phase 0: No collective norm exists or is proposed.
Level 1: Instrumental extrinsic valuing The school is valued as an institution that helps individuals to meet their own needs.		*Collective Norm Proposal* Phase 1: Individuals propose collective norms for group acceptance.
Level 2: Enthusiastic identification The school is valued at special moments when members feel an intense sense of identification with the school.	Stage 2: There is no clear sense of community apart from exchanges among group members. Community denotes a collection of individuals who do favors for each other and rely on each other for protection. Community is valued insofar as it meets the concrete needs of its members.	*Collective Norm Acceptance* Phase 2: Collective norm is accepted as a group ideal but not agreed to. It is not an expectation for behavior. Phase 3: Collective norm is accepted and agreed to, but it is not (yet) an expectation for behavior.
Level 3: Spontaneous community The school is valued as the kind of place in which members feel a sense of closeness to others and an inner motivation to help them and to serve the community as a whole.	Stage 3: The sense of community refers to a set of relationships and sharing among group members. The group is valued for the friendliness of its members. The value of the group is equated with the value of its collective normative expectations.	*Collective Norm Expectation* Phase 4: Collective norm is accepted and expected (naive expectation). Phase 5: Collective norm is expected but not followed (disappointed expectation).
Level 4: Normative community The school as a community is valued for its own sake. Community can obligate its members in special ways, and members can expect others to uphold group norms and responsibilities.	Stage 4: The community is explicitly valued as an entity distinct from the relationships among its members. Community membership is understood in terms of entering into a social contract to respect the norms and ideals of the group. The community is perceived as an organic whole composed of interrelated systems that carry on the functioning of the group.	*Collective Norm Enforcement* Phase 6: Collective norm is expected and upheld through persuasion. Phase 7: Collective norm is expected and upheld through reporting.

Source: Adapted from Power, Higgins, & Kohlberg (1989), pp. 117, 119, 130.

Note

The parallel listing of the three variables is not intended to imply a clear theoretical parallelism between moral atmosphere levels, stages, and phases.

to the group or other members of it" (p. 42). Going beyond Durkheim, however, Kohlberg and colleagues also placed more emphasis on rational "autonomy" to avoid abuses that could result from "immoral use" of the power of the "collectivist model" (1987, p. 116). Furthermore, Kohlberg (1985) supplemented Durkheim's concept of "loyalty" to one's society with "loyalty to universal principles of justice and responsibility as the solution to problems" (p. 41).

The net effect of this work was to broaden Kohlberg's theory to include the concurrent processes of moral judgment development and cultural values socialization, without reducing one to the other. Subsequent empirical research has provided support for the wisdom of this approach (cf. Narvaez, Getz, Rest, & Thoma, 1999). Within this developmental-socialization approach to morality, Kohlberg employed three distinct pedagogical methods.

KOHLBERG'S THREE METHODS OF MORAL EDUCATION

The center of Kohlberg's identity was that of a moral educator. Kohlberg (1987) understood that what promoted a person's structural changes in moral reasoning was having rich experiences in the social-moral realm. Kohlberg's pedagogical methods of moral education promote learning from interaction with adult role models (moral exemplars), peers and friends (dilemma discussions), and the larger school community (Just Community schools).

Moral Exemplars

The least acknowledged of Kohlberg's methods of moral education is his use of moral exemplars to pedagogically support socialization and promote development. He intuitively understood that observing or learning about those who practiced moral principles was a more direct method of teaching than any theory could hope to attain. Kohlberg often demonstrated stage-level reasoning with concrete examples from moral judgment interviews, thus using moral case examples to teach his moral developmental categories. For advanced stages, he used public moral exemplars to embody the uncommon Stage 5 and the mercurial Stage 6. Kohlberg also saw public moral exemplars as a critical factor in public moral education; through their insights and actions, they "draw" our development toward higher stages of moral reasoning. Kohlberg held up such mature examples as moral exemplars.

In *Essays on Moral Development: The Psychology of Moral Development* (1984, pp. 486–490), Kohlberg and chapter co-author Ann Higgins offered a 32-year-old woman named "Joan" as a moral exemplar. Joan's ability to frame the Heinz dilemma as a dialogue of competing claims and her ability to take the role of each person in the dilemma, in turn, appeared to be an example of post-conventional moral reasoning. This was confirmed for Kohlberg by Joan's life story. Joan worked with juvenile wards of the court for a local judge and allowed one of the wards in her care to escape to a better situation in a halfway house in another state, even to the point of providing her with bus money. This action was a clear violation of her responsibilities as outlined by the law, and Joan lost her job. Joan's words and actions suggest a form of reasoning that posits a universal respect for the rights and dignity of persons regardless of the dictates of the law.

Going beyond the individual case study, Kohlberg often used a "roll call of the saints" rhetorical device to list the names of those whom he saw as moral exemplars. Limiting our survey to his two-volume collected works on moral philosophy (1981) and moral psychology (1984), there are six separate such lists with a total of nine moral exemplars. Two persons are included in five of his six lists and were otherwise also cited the most frequently in his writings: Martin Luther King, Jr., and Socrates. One person was included in two of the lists: Abraham Lincoln. The remaining six were included in one of the six lists: Roman humanitarian Marcus Aurelius, pediatrician and Nazi resister Janusz Korczak, Lord Chancellor Thomas More, Quaker mental health worker Andrea Simpson, stoic philosopher Baruch Spinoza, and non-violent civil disobedience advocate Henry David Thoreau. Occasionally, Kohlberg spoke of at least three other individuals in such a way as to suggest membership in his pantheon of moral exemplars: "Joan," Supreme Court Justice William Brennan, and Watergate special prosecutor Archibald Cox.

What made these dozen people worthy of being included in Kohlberg's roll call of moral exemplars and as valuable models for moral educators today? Perhaps most important, in addition to their exemplary moral reasoning and empathic moral emotions, they had taken action to rectify an injustice (e.g., non-violent public dissent, critical speeches, protest marches). These were acts of public moral education. Morality, without works, is dead, Kohlberg seemed to believe. Thus, while Kohlberg admired many philosophers (e.g., Aristotle, Plato, Kant, John Dewey, John Rawls), the only one he elevated to moral sainthood was Socrates. Although he bestows respectful admiration on several theologians (Paul Tillich, Martin Luther King, Jr., Teilhard de Chardin) and four Saints of the Catholic Church (Saint Thomas Aquinas, Saint Augustine, Saint Thomas More, Saint Paul), Kohlberg only spoke of two of these seven as moral exemplars: Thomas More and Martin Luther King, Jr. While discussing the relation between morality, religion, and a hypothetical Stage 7, Kohlberg acknowledged the work of several well-known and charismatic religious leaders, but he only elevated Spinoza, Marcus Aurelius, Andrea Simpson, and Martin Luther King, Jr. as faith-motivated moral exemplars, which suggests that his positive regard for them had little to do with religious charisma and everything to do with how they lived out their moral principles (cf. Hart & Atkins, 2004).

Finally, Kohlberg always understood that moral exemplars were still flawed human beings and products of their time. For example, one of the central undertakings for many of his exemplars was *moral education against racism* (e.g., Abraham Lincoln, Martin Luther King, Jr., Janusz Korczak). Nevertheless, while discussing the Piaget-like phenomena of historical "decalage" on the subject of enlightenment regarding slavery, Kohlberg notes that "Socrates was more accepting of slavery than was Lincoln, who was more accepting of it than King," who was not accepting of it at all (1981, p. 129). Inevitably, of course, a similar historical partiality was engendered in Kohlberg as a product of his own times. In terms of race and gender, his roll call of exemplars included one black man, two white women, and nine white men. Nevertheless, although he exhibited partiality, his primary criteria for being considered an exemplar for moral education rings true because they lived out their mature moral reasoning and empathy through moral behavior and courageous action that threatened the status quo. Consequently, most faced penalties and some died for their moral stance.

Experienced moral educators know that lecture descriptions of moral stages take on new relevance when illustrated with examples "ripped from the headlines," so to speak, or when a moral exemplar makes a guest visit to a class session to talk about why they care (cf. Vozzola, 1996). Publications on moral exemplars also can be useful in moral education. Colby and Damon (1992) provide portraits of 23 contemporary lives of moral commitment and courageous leadership. Siddle-Walker and Snarey (2004) make use of six moral exemplars, three children and three adults, who embody African-American care-and-justice ethics.

Dilemma Discussions

About a decade after Kohlberg (1958) proposed his moral stage model, the first genuine Kohlbergian venture into moral education began with an experiment by Kohlberg's doctoral student, Moshe Blatt, who attempted to facilitate moral stage development among sixth-grade students through weekly classroom discussions of hypothetical moral dilemmas (cf. Blatt & Kohlberg, 1975). Blatt found that over one-third of the students in the experimental group advanced in stage of moral development during the year, whereas few of the students in a control group exhibited any stage change.

Subsequently, Kohlberg and his colleagues implemented this method by integrating dilemma discussions into the curriculum of school classes on the humanities (e.g., literature) and social studies (e.g., history). To prepare teachers, Kohlberg and colleagues held workshops and wrote about how to lead moral dilemma discussions (e.g., Fenton & Kohlberg, 1976; Kohlberg & Lickona, 1987). Some of the questions were quite similar to those used in a standard moral judgment interview; that is, they asked students to clarify their reasoning about "why" they held a certain position. Other questions asked students to make their meaning clear, ensure a shared understanding, or promote peer interaction, especially perspective-taking (cf. Selman, 1971). Additionally, attention was given to questions designed to promote Socratic discussion. Fritz Oser (1992) advanced a more group-centered method of "discourse ethics" and Georg Lind (2007) attended to the importance of the overall structure and organization of a moral dilemma discussion.

The major assumption of promoting moral dilemma discussions in classrooms and peer groups is that "interactive exchanges with peers" will "speed up the natural development of moral judgment" (Rest & Thoma, 1986, p. 59). Samuelson (2007), for instance, demonstrated that a discussion-based curriculum using film clips containing moral dilemmas from popular Hollywood films produced a statistically significant improvement in the degree to which students endorsed higher stage moral reasoning compared to those who did not participate. Beyond statistical significance, however, Kohlberg asked, how psychologically significant are the gains promoted by participation in dilemma discussions? Subsequent comparison studies of approaches to moral education, and several reviews of moral education research and programs using moral dilemmas, have provided decisive evaluations.

The landmark meta-analysis of 55 studies by Schlaefli, Rest, and Thoma (1985) showed that the dilemma discussion approach produces moderate and significant educational effects on moral development, whereas other types of intervention programs produce smaller effects, and individual academic courses in the humanities produce even weaker effects. Higgins' review (1980) drew similar but more qualitative conclusions.

The most powerful interventions for stimulating moral stage change are those that involve discussions of real [rather than hypothetical] problems and situations occurring in natural groups, whether the family or classroom in which all participants are empowered to have a say in the discussion.

(p. 96)

This finding should alert teachers and professors that many unexpected critical incidents in teaching involve a real moral dilemma and often provide an opportunity to engage in a real-life moral dilemma discussion.

Dilemma discussions are also used in formal courses on ethics. DeHaan and colleagues (1997) compared the effectiveness of three approaches to ethics education among high school students by enrolling students in one of four high school classes: an introductory ethics class, a blended economics-ethics class, a role-model ethics class taught by graduate students, and a non-ethics comparison class. The first two classes used dilemma discussions, and all groups were assessed with pre- and post-test measures of moral reasoning, moral emotions, and moral behavior. The clearest positive pattern evident in the data was that the integrated economics-ethics class and the introductory ethics class showed statistically significant gains in socio-moral reflection maturity, principled moral reasoning, and moral behavior. Similar students in the comparison group and the role-model ethics class showed no such advances. These findings again suggest that high school students have the most to gain when teachers explicitly draw their students' attention to the ethical issues inherent in their respective courses and integrate the discussion of relevant moral dilemmas into their current courses.

It is not just the method or experience of moral dilemma discussion that has an impact on its efficacy in moral development, but also the peer context. Kohlberg hypothesized that the ideal situation for advancement in moral reasoning was to be involved in a discussion with another person who reasoned at a level one stage higher (+1) than one's own level. Blatt and Kohlberg (1975) engaged a group whose participants expressed reasoning at various levels in a dilemma discussion. The experimenter then chose the argument that was one stage above the level of most of the participants and supported it, emphasizing its strengths and encouraging participants to engage in thinking along these lines. This method led to significant increases in moral maturity scores. In a review of the effectiveness of moral development interventions using the plus-one strategy with moral dilemma discussions, Enright, Lapsley, Harris, and Schawver (2001) established that most (10 of 13 interventions) produced significant gains in moral reasoning. Those interventions in which a significant difference did not occur tended to be of shorter duration (e.g., one to six sessions). Although the plus-one strategy has good support in the literature, other strategies have also proven effective. Walker's (1982) study of middle school students found a significant effect on moral reasoning with exposure to persons who reasoned two stages above the subjects, whereas Berkowitz, Gibbs, and Broughton's (1980) study of college students found the ideal stage differential was at a third (+1/3) of a stage for dialogues between two peers. Overall, these studies support the general concept of the "zone of proximal development" that posits that children learn best from a person who performs at one level just above the child's level (Walker & Taylor, 1991).

Although most studies of moral development interventions take place in the school setting, much of a child's moral development takes place at home. Walker and Taylor (1991) investigated the role of dilemma discussions between parent and child. They showed that children with significant gains in moral reasoning over time had parents that adjusted their level of moral reasoning to fit the child's. In other words, it is not high moral reasoning in parents that predicts change in the child; rather it is parents who can accommodate their reasoning to the child's level who will have the most effect. They also found that hypothetical dilemmas were not predictive of children's subsequent moral development, but that "real-life" moral dilemmas from the experience of the child had the greatest impact, supporting Higgins' (1980) prior conclusion. Moreover, Walker and Taylor found that the most effective type of communication in moral dilemma discussions was representational, which included such behaviors as restating the child's reasoning, asking for the child's opinion, asking questions of clarification, and checking for understanding. This, combined with presentation of moral reasoning at approximately one stage above the child's pre-intervention stage score, predicted the greatest gains in the child's moral reasoning.

Ann Kruger (1992, 1993), like Piaget, reasoned that the greater symmetry of knowledge and power in the peer dyads compared to the adult/child dyads produced the freedom to entertain multiple perspectives, which resulted in measurable development in moral reasoning. Kruger's (1992) investigation of moral dilemmas included young girls' discussions both with their peers and with their mothers. She showed that peer discussions of moral dilemmas result in greater improvement in moral reasoning than do discussions between children and adults.

From these studies we can draw several conclusions:

1. Dilemma discussion is a useful method for moral development education.
2. Real-life dilemmas, perhaps especially those drawn from personal experience, are more efficacious for moral development than are hypothetical dilemmas.
3. There is a zone of proximal development in which dilemma discussions will most advance moral development.
4. Peers are the best teachers or conversation partners. Dilemma or problem-situation based discussions continue to be the most widely used method of moral education today.

Just Community Schools

In 1973, Kohlberg's thinking about moral education within schools broke new ground when he recognized a limitation of the moral dilemma discussion method. Although it can change students (slowly), it does not take into account the moral atmosphere of the social context. As Kohlberg put it, the school is a context "in which one cannot wait until children reach [Stage 5 of moral development] to deal directly with moral behavior" (1978, p. 15). However, Kohlberg now faced a pedagogical dilemma: how to teach moral values without imposing them on children or compromising their moral autonomy. In addition, because children often reason within one stage of each other and their interaction provides optimal opportunities to advance moral reasoning, the dilemma then becomes how to help children teach each other universal moral values.

Kohlberg had theorized that this dilemma was solvable because the end principles found in higher stages (4, 5, and 6) of reasoning, such as reciprocity, respect, and justice, were present in some elementary form from Stage 1 onwards (Kohlberg, 1980). His plan for developing children's moral maturity was for the teacher to promote the development of the children's native sense of fairness and, in so doing, prepare them to better understand and then appropriate the principle of justice toward which moral development reaches. The goal was to achieve a "balance [of] 'justice' and 'community'; to introduce the powerful appeal of the collective while both protecting the rights of individual students and promoting their moral growth" (Power et al., 1989, p. 53). His bold and daring approach was deceptively simple—a return to the progressive ideal of educational democracy but within a communitarian mode (cf. Dewey, 1916).

Kohlberg founded the first Just Community school in the spring of 1974. He had received funding to train high school teachers in developmental moral education. At the same time in the city of Cambridge, Massachusetts, plans for a new alternative high school were under way and Kohlberg was invited to consult in its planning. Students, parents, teachers, and Kohlberg met together to design the new school. The end result was the Cluster School, which was governed by the following principles:

1. The school would be governed by direct democracy. All major issues would be discussed and decided at a weekly community meeting at which all members (students and teachers) would have one vote.
2. There would be, in addition, a number of standing committees to be filled by students, teachers, and parents.
3. A social contract would be drawn between members which would define every-one's rights and responsibilities.
4. Students and teachers would have the same basic rights, including freedom of expression, respect of others, and freedom from physical or verbal harm.

The keystone of the Just Community approach was the weekly community meeting (aka, Town Meeting), a gathering of students and staff to decide school policies and practices that dealt with issues of fairness and community. The advisor and standing committee groups met on the day before the community meeting. Each advisory group consisted of one of the five teachers and a fifth of the students. These small group meetings set the stage for the larger community meetings as well as provided an opportunity for students and their advisors to get to know each other and share more personal concerns than could be dealt with in the larger meeting. The agenda for the community meeting would be discussed, and the small group would often debate the issues and try to achieve consensus or agreement on majority and minority proposals to bring to the next day's meeting.

All of these meetings functioned as a context for moral discussion and a place to build community. The general aim was for students to achieve a sense of community solidarity—to create a "moral atmosphere"—through the practice of democratic governance (i.e., coming to fair decisions, carrying out these decisions, and, as necessary, to democratically changing their decisions). One aspect of the Just Community educator's role was similar to that of a youth leader, that is, to function both as a socializer, in the manner of Durkheim, and as a facilitator, in the manner of Piaget. The sense of group solidarity allowed the peer group to function as a moral authority for its members' behavior. Direct participatory democracy, furthermore, functions to protect the rights of the student and to limit the power of group solidarity to coerce conformity, in order to maintain the possibility for alternative conceptions of the good to be voiced.

The role of the teacher was perhaps as important as the students' peers. In typical moral dilemma discussions in a regular classroom, teachers primarily functioned as facilitators, but in the new Just Community schools, teachers also had to function as advocates for moral content: justice and community values (Kohlberg & Selman, 1972; Selman, 2003). Thus, the teachers served as moral leaders by advocating their own positions within the constraints of one person, one vote, and by being invested in "what" students decided to do and "why" they decided to do it (Oser & Renold, 2006).

Later Kohlberg and his colleagues applied the Just Community approach at the suburban Scarsdale Alternative High School in Westchester County, New York, an upper- and upper-middle-class school and at the Brookline High School, Brookline, Massachusetts, a semi-urban middle-class school-within-a-school (cf. Mosher, Kenny, & Garrod, 1994). Finally, toward the end of his life, Kohlberg and his colleagues implemented three Just Community programs in New York City; two in one of the five worst city schools and one in an examination school with high-performing students (see Higgins, 1989). Several other schools have adopted the principles of Just Community schools, at least in part, in order to promote moral development (see Howard-Hamilton, 1995).

Reactions to the idea of "the adolescent as citizen" often create the same initial response as the idea of "the child as philosopher." What "kind of quixotic oxymoron" is this? (Mosher, 1992, p. 179). Educational researchers also have asked; does Kohlberg's Just Community approach actually promote the moral reasoning of students and the moral atmosphere of schools? The answer is a qualified "yes," based on a comparative analysis of the first three Just Community schools (cf. Mosher et al., 1994; Power et al., 1989). The students in each of the three Just Community schools (i.e., Cambridge, Brookline, and Scarsdale) scored significantly higher than their contemporaries attending the parallel or parent high schools on all measures of moral atmosphere, including the level of institutional valuing, stage of community valuing, and phase of collective norm. The results on individual moral judgment were also in the expected direction; the average moral stage scores for the students in the Just Community programs were significantly higher than for the students in their companion traditional high schools. The stage gains were smaller than expected, but still respectable (i.e., at two- and three-year longitudinal follow-up interviews, students at the Cluster School showed that they gained, on average, about a half-stage in moral development). It is also noteworthy that the evaluation studies found no statistically significant gender differences in any of the analyses of moral culture or moral stage variables. Nevertheless, it also is clear that future Just Community interventions need to provide for a greater degree of culturally sensitive adaptation and cultural responsiveness when approaching cross-class, cross-race, or cross-cultural school settings, each with its own distinctive sociocultural history, strengths, and needs (cf. Nucci, 2001; Vozzola & Higgins-D'Alessandro, 2000). At the minimum, as Noddings (1992) has noted, "we respond most effectively [as caring persons] when we understand the other's needs and the history of this need" (p. 23).

In sum, the net effect of the Just Community model of moral education was to extend Kohlberg's theory from the moral reasoning of individuals to the moral culture of communities (cf. Oser, Althof, & Higgins-D'Alessandro, 2008). Kohlberg's Just Community approach to moral education incorporates both socialization and developmental perspectives and provides a way for teachers and administrators to embody justice and care in their treatment of students and each other and a way for students to develop these moral values. In the end, the Just Community approach also expanded our understanding of conventional moral reasoning (stages 3 and 4). Students reasoning at so-called conformist levels were shown to be able to "understand moral concepts" in ways that allow them to "scrutinize, critique, resist, or attempt to change the practices, laws, or arrangements of their" high school society (Turiel, 2002, p. 105).

WHAT KOHLBERG TAUGHT US

Kohlberg opened the eyes of psychologists and educators to the fact that people's moral thinking changes as they mature, and that these changes follow predictable stages of development as they grow older. While his stage model is one of his greatest contributions to moral psychology, Kohlberg also contributed models of moral types, as well as moral cultural atmosphere levels, which have made the picture of human moral development more complete. Kohlberg's models of moral development, alone, would have been a remarkable achievement. But he was, at heart, a dedicated educator, committed to seeing theory bear fruit, and so he developed methods of moral education that would promote moral development and mature character. Kohlberg's three-pronged approach to moral education—moral exemplars, moral dilemma discussions, and Just Community schools—collectively transcend the dichotomy of socialization versus development. His groundbreaking approach to moral education, similarly, taught that we must pay equal and concurrent attention to the moral reasoning development of the individual and the moral cultural development of the community. Both play equally important roles in the development of morality.

Additionally, Kohlberg demonstrated a genuine interest in views of his critics and a willingness to engage new approaches to moral cognition, development, and education. His example remains especially relevant today because the cognitive-developmental tradition is currently characterized by a spirit of revisionism. This pluralism is to be valued because we now understand that "moral functioning is inherently multifaceted" (Walker, 2004, p. 547). Taking our cue from Kohlberg's openness, it is likely that we have much to gain from positive engagement with ongoing constructive critiques of the cognitive-developmental tradition. Many of the critics began their theoretical work during Kohlberg's lifetime (1927–1987) but, during the post-Kohlberg decades, theoretical innovations accelerated, alternative measures of theoretical constructs were perfected, and corresponding methods of moral education have been constructed (cf. Arnold, 2000). A number of these alternatives and innovations are reflected in the chapters in this handbook. These innovations demonstrate the field's current spirit of expansion and pluralistic revisionism. Kohlberg would be the first to remind us, of course, that there is room at the table for everyone.

REFERENCES

Althof, W., & Berkowitz, M. W. (2006). Moral education and character education: Their relationship and roles in citizenship education. *Journal of Moral Education, 35* (4), 495–518.

Arnold, M. L. (2000). Stage, sequence, and sequels: Changing conceptions of morality, post-Kohlberg. *Educational Psychology Review, 12* (4), 365–383.

Bebeau, M. (2002). The Defining Issues Test and the four component model. *Journal of Moral Education, 31,* 271–295.

Berkowitz, M. (2012). Moral and character education. In K. R. Harris, S. Graham, & T. Urdan (Eds.), *APA educational psychology handbook* (Vol. 2, pp. 247–264). Washington, DC: American Psychological Association.

Berkowitz, M., Gibbs, J. C., & Broughton, J. M. (1980). The relation of moral judgment stage disparity to developmental effects of peer dialogues. *Merrill-Palmer Quarterly, 22,* 341–357.

Blasi, A. (1980). Bridging moral cognition and moral action: A critical review. *Psychological Bulletin, 88,* 1–45.

Blatt, M., & Kohlberg, L. (1975). The effects of classroom moral discussion upon children's level of moral judgment. *Journal of Moral Education, 4,* 129–161.

Blum, L. (1988). Gilligan and Kohlberg: Implications for moral theory. *Ethics, 98,* 472–491.

Brabeck, M. M. (1984). Review of the book, *In a different voice* by Carol Gilligan. *Pastoral Psychology, 32,* 217–219.

Brabeck, M. M., & Shore, E. L. (2002). Gender differences in intellectual and moral development: The evidence that refutes the claim. *Handbook of adult development* (pp. 351–368). New York: Plenum Press.

Brabeck, M. M., & Ting, K. (2000). Feminist ethics: Lenses for examining psychological practice. In M. M. Brabeck (Ed.), *Practicing feminist ethics in psychology* (pp. 17–35). Washington, D.C.: American Psychological Association.

Caceda, R., James, G. A., Ely, T., Snarey, J., & Kilts, C. (2011). Modes of effective connectivity within a putative neural network differentiates moral cognitions related to care and justice ethics. *PLoS ONE, 6*(2), e14730.

Clopton, N. A., & Sorell, G. T. (1993). Gender differences: Stable or situational? *Psychology of Women Quarterly, 17*, 85–101.

Colby, A., & Damon, W. (1992). *Some do care*. New York: Free Press.

Colby, A., & Kohlberg, L. (1987). *The measurement of moral judgment (Vols. 1 & 2)*. New York: Cambridge University Press.

Dawson, T. L. (2002). New tools, new insights: Kohlberg's moral judgment stages revisited. *International Journal of Behavioral Development, 26*(2), 154–166.

DeHaan, R., Hanford, R., Kinlaw, K., Philler, D., & Snarey, J. (1997). Promoting ethical reasoning, affect, and behavior among high school students. *Journal of Moral Education, 26*(1), 5–20.

Dewey, J. (1916). *Democracy and education*. New York: Macmillan.

Durkheim, E. (1925) *Moral education*. New York: Free Press.

Enright, R. D., Lapsley, D. K., Harris D. J., & Shawver, D. J. (2001). Moral development interventions in early adolescence. *Theory into Practice, 21*(2), 134–144.

Fenton, E., & Kohlberg, L. (Eds.). (1976). *Teacher training in values education*. New York: Guidance Associates.

Garmon, L. C., Basinger, K. S., Gregg, V. R., & Gibbs, J. C. (1996). Gender differences in stage and expression of moral judgment. *Merrill-Palmer Quarterly, 42*, 418–437.

Garrod, A., Beal, C., Jaeger, W., Thomas, J., Davis, J., Leiser, N., & Hodzic, A. (2003). Culture, ethnic conflict, and moral orientation in Bosnian children. *Journal of Moral Education, 32*(2), 131–150.

Gibbs, J. C. (2009). *Moral development and reality*. Old Tappan, NJ: Pearson.

Gibbs, J. C., Basinger, K. S., Grime, R. L., & Snarey, J. (2007). Moral judgment development across cultures: Revisiting Kohlberg's universality claims. *Developmental Review, 27*(4), 443–500.

Gilligan, C. (1982). *In a different voice*. Cambridge, MA: Harvard University Press.

Hart, D. (1992). *Becoming men: The development of aspirations, values, and adaptational styles*. New York: Plenum.

Hart, D., & Atkins, R. (2004). Religious participation and the development of moral identity in adolescence. In T. Thorkildsen & H. Walberg (Eds.), *Nurturing morality* (pp. 157–172). New York: Kluwer.

Higgins, A. (1980). Research and measurement issues in moral educational interventions. In R. Mosher (Ed.), *Moral education: A first generation of research* (pp. 92–107). New York: Praeger.

Higgins, A. (1989). The Just Community educational program: The development of moral role-taking as the expression of justice and care. In M. M. Brabeck (Ed.), *Who cares?: Theory, research, and educational implications of the ethic of care* (pp. 197–215). New York: Praeger.

Howard-Hamilton, M. F. (1995). A just and democratic community approach to moral education. *Elementary School Guidance & Counseling, 30*(2), 118–130.

Jaffe, S., & Hyde, J. S. (2000). Gender differences in moral orientation: A meta-analysis. *Psychological Bulletin, 126*, 703–726.

Jorgensen, G. (2006). Kohlberg and Gilligan: Duet or duel? *Journal of Moral Education, 35*(2), 179–196.

Kohlberg, L. (1958). *The development of modes of thinking and choice in years 10 to 16*. Doctoral dissertation, University of Chicago, IL.

Kohlberg, L. (1969). Stage and sequence: The cognitive-developmental approach to socialization. In D. Goslin (Ed.), *Handbook of socialization theory and research* (pp. 347–480). Chicago: Rand McNally.

Kohlberg, L. (1976). Moral stages and moralization: The cognitive-developmental approach. In T. Lickona (Ed.), *Moral development and behavior* (pp. 31–53). New York: Holt, Rinehart & Winston.

Kohlberg, L. (1978). Moral education reappraised. *The Humanist, 38*, 13–15.

Kohlberg, L. (1980). Exploring the moral atmosphere of institutions. In L. Kohlberg, *The meaning and measurement of moral development* (pp. 35–52). Worcester, MA: Clark University Press.

Kohlberg, L. (1981). *Essays on moral development: Vol. 1, The philosophy of moral development: the nature and validity of moral stages*. San Francisco: Harper & Row Publishers.

Kohlberg, L. (1984). *Essays on moral development: Vol. 2, The psychology of moral development: the nature and validity of moral stages*. San Francisco: Harper & Row Publishers.

Kohlberg, L. (1985). The Just Community approach to moral education in theory and practice. In M. Berkowitz & F. Oser (Eds.), *Moral education: Theory and application* (pp. 27–86). Hillsdale, NJ: Erlbaum.

Kohlberg, L. (1987). *Child psychology and childhood education: A cognitive-developmental view.* New York: Longman.

Kohlberg, L. (2008). The development of children's orientations toward a moral order. I. Sequence in the development of moral thought. *Human Development, 51,* 8–20. (Reprint of *Vita Humana,* 1963, 6, 11–33.)

Kohlberg, L., & Lickona, T. (1987). Moral discussion and the class meeting. In R. DeVries and L. Kohlberg (Eds.), *Programs of early education* (pp. 143–181). New York: Longman.

Kohlberg, L., Ricks, D., & Snarey, J. (1984). Childhood development as a predictor of adaptation in adulthood. *Genetic Psychology Monographs, 110,* 91–172.

Kohlberg, L., & Selman, R. L. (1972). *Preparing school personnel relative to values: A look at moral education in the school.* Washington, D.C.: ERIC Clearinghouse on Teacher Education.

Kruger, A. C. (1992). The effect of peer and adult/child transductive discussions on moral reasoning. *Merrill-Palmer Quarterly, 38* (2), 191–211.

Kruger, A. C. (1993). Peer collaboration: Conflict, cooperation, or both? *Social Development, 2* (3), 165–182.

Lapsley, D. (1996). *Moral psychology.* Boulder, CO: Westview Press.

Lind, G. (2007). *Script for dilemma discussion: The Konstanz method.* www.uni-konstanz.de/ag-moral/moral/dild-isk-e.htm#script.

Logan, R., Snarey, J., & Schrader, D. (1990). Autonomous versus heteronomous moral judgment types: A longitudinal cross-cultural study. *Journal of Cross-Cultural Psychology, 21* (1), 71–89.

McDonough, G. P. (2005). Moral maturity and autonomy. *Journal of Moral Education, 34* (2), 119–213.

Milgram, S. (1974). *Obedience to authority.* New York: Harper & Row.

Mosher, R. (1992). The adolescent as citizen. In A. Garrod (Ed.), *Learning for life* (pp. 179–209). Westport, CT: Praeger.

Mosher, R., Kenny, R., & Garrod, A. (1994). *Preparing for citizenship.* Westport, CT: Praeger.

Narvaez, D., Getz, I., Rest, J., & Thoma, S. (1999). Individual moral judgment and cultural ideologies. *Developmental Psychology, 35* (2), 478–488.

Noddings, N. (1992). *The challenge to care in schools.* New York: Teachers College Press.

Nucci, L. (2001). *Education in the moral domain.* New York: Cambridge University Press.

Oser, F. K. (1992). Morality in professional action: A discourse approach to teaching. Chapter 8 in F. K. Oser, A. Dick, & J.-L. Patry (Eds.), *Effective teaching and responsible teaching: A new synthesis* (pp. 109–138). San Francisco: Jossey-Bass.

Oser, F. K., Althof, W. & Higgins-D'Alessandro, A. (2008). The Just Community approach to moral education: System change or individual change? *Journal of Moral Education, 37* (3), 395–415.

Oser, F. K., & Renold, U. (2006). Modeling teacher competencies: Identifying and measuring standards. In F. K. Oser, F. Achtenhagen, & U. Renold (Eds.), *Competence-oriented teacher training* (pp. 23–48). Rotterdam: Sense Publishers.

Palmer, E. J. (2003). An overview of the relationship between moral reasoning and offending. *Australian Psychologist, 38* (3), 165–174.

Parke, R., & Clarke-Stewart, A. (2010). Morality: Knowing right, doing good. Chapter 11 in R. Parke & A. Clarke-Stewart (Eds.), *Social development* (pp. 357–392). New York: Wiley.

Piaget, J. (1932). *The moral judgment of the child.* New York: Free Press.

Power, F. C. (2004). The moral self in community. In D. Lapsley & D. Narvaez (Eds.), *Moral development, self, and identity* (pp. 47–64). Mahwah, NJ: Erlbaum.

Power, F. C., Higgins, A., & Kohlberg, L. (1989). *Lawrence Kohlberg's approach to moral education,* New York: Columbia University Press.

Prehn, K., Wartenburger, I., Meriau, K., Scheibe, C., Goodenough, O., Villringer, A., van der Meer, E., & Heekeren, H. (2008). Individual differences in moral judgment competence influence neural correlates of socio-normative judgments. *SCAN, 3,* 33–46.

Puka, W. (1991). Interpretive experiments: Probing the care-justice debate in moral development. *Human Development, 34,* 61–80.

Raaijamkers, Q. A. W., Engles, R. C. M. E., & Van Hoof, A. (2005). Delinquency and moral reasoning in adolescence and young adulthood. *International Journal of Behavioral Development, 29* (3), 247–258.

Rest, J. R., & Thoma, S. (1986). Educational programs and interventions. In J. R. Rest (Ed.), *Moral development: Advances in research and theory* (pp. 59–88). New York: Praeger.

Robertson, D., Snarey, J., Ousley, O., Bowman, D., Harenski, K., & Kilts, C. (2007). The neural processing of moral sensitivity to issues of justice and care: An fMRI study. *Neuropsychologia, 45* (4), 755–766.

Ryan, M. K., Reynolds, B. D., & Reynolds, K. J. (2004). Who cares? The effect of gender and context on the self and moral reasoning. *Psychology of Women Quarterly, 28,* 246–255.

Samuelson, P. (2007). *Moral imagination in theory and practice.* Doctoral dissertation, Georgia State University, Atlanta, GA.

Schlaefli, A., Rest, J., & Thoma, S. (1985). Does moral education improve moral judgment? *Review of Educational Research, 55* (3), 319–352.

Schrader, D., Tappan, M., Kohlberg, L., & Armon, C. (1987). Assessing heteronomous and autonomous moral types. In A. Colby and L. Kohlberg (Eds.), *The measurement of moral judgment, Vol. I: Theoretical foundations and research validation* (pp. 909–997). New York: Cambridge University Press.

Selman, R. L. (1971). The relation of role taking to the development of moral judgment in children. *Child Development, 42* (1), 79–91.

Selman, R. L. (2003). *The promotion of social awareness.* New York: Russell Sage.

Sherblom, S. (2008). The legacy of the "care challenge:" Re-envisioning the outcome of the justice-care debate. *Journal of Moral Education, 37* (1), 81–98.

Siddle-Walker, V., & Snarey, J. R. (2004). *Race-ing moral formation.* New York: Teachers College Press.

Snarey, J. (1985). The cross-cultural universality of social-moral development. *Psychological Bulletin, 97,* 202–232.

Snarey, J. (2008). The neural basis of moral cognition. In F. Power, R. Nuzzi, D. Narvaez, D. Lapsley, & T. Hunt (Eds.), *Moral Education: A Handbook* (Vol. 2, pp. 313–316). Westport, CT: Praeger.

Snarey, J., & Keljo, K. (1991). The cross-cultural expansion of moral development theory. In W. M. Kurtines & J. L. Gewirtz (Eds.), *Handbook of moral behavior and development* (Vol. 1, pp. 395–424). Hillsdale, NJ: Erlbaum.

Tappan, M., Kohlberg, L., Schrader, D., Higgins, A., Armon, C., & Lei, T. (1987). Heteronomy and autonomy in moral development: Two types of moral judgment. In A. Colby and L. Kohlberg (Eds.), *The measurement of moral judgment* (Vol. 1, pp. 315–380). New York: Cambridge University Press.

Thoma, S. (1986). Estimating gender differences in the comprehension and preference of moral issues. *Developmental Review, 6,* 165–180.

Thoma, S. (1994). Moral judgments and moral action. In J. Rest & D. Narvaez (Eds.), *Moral development in the professions: Psychology and applied ethics* (pp. 199–211). Hillsdale, NJ: Lawrence Erlbaum.

Thoma, S., Rest, J., & Davison, M. (1991). Describing and testing a moderator of the moral judgment and action relationship. *Journal of Personality and Social Psychology, 61* (4), 659–669.

Turiel, E. (2002). *The culture of morality.* New York: Cambridge University Press.

Vozzola, E. (1996). The Kohlberg paradigm and beyond: A review of *Moral Development: A Compendium* edited by Bill Puka. *New Ideas in Psychology, 14,* 197–206.

Vozzola, E., & Higgins-D'Alessandro, A. (2000). Competing conceptions of justice: Faculty moral reasoning about affirmative action. *Journal of Adult Development, 7,* 137–149.

Walker, L. J. (1982). The sequentiality of Kohlberg's stages of moral development. *Child Development, 53,* 1330–1336.

Walker, L. J. (1984). Sex differences in the development of moral reasoning: A critical review. *Child Development, 55,* 667–691.

Walker, L. J. (2004). Progress and prospects in the psychology of moral development. *Merrill-Palmer Quarterly, 50,* 546–557.

Walker, L. J., & Taylor, J. H. (1991). Family interactions and the development of moral reasoning. *Child Development, 62,* 264–283.

Weber, M. (1949). *The methodology of the social sciences.* New York: Free Press.

6

MORAL SELF-IDENTITY AS THE AIM OF EDUCATION

Daniel Lapsley and Paul C. Stey

INTRODUCTION

The ambitions that most parents have for their children naturally include the development of important moral dispositions. Most parents want to raise children to become persons of a certain kind, persons who possess traits that are desirable and praiseworthy, whose personalities are imbued with a strong ethical compass. In situations of radical choice we hope that our children do the right thing for the right reason, even when faced with strong inclinations to do otherwise. Moreover, other socialization agents and institutions share this goal. For example, the moral formation of children is one of the foundational goals of formal education (Dewey, 1909; Bryk, 1988; Goodlad, 1992; Goodman & Lesnick, 2001; McClellan, 1999) and there is increasing recognition that neighborhoods and communities play critical roles for inducting children into the moral and civic norms that govern human social life (Eccles & Gootman, 2002; Flanagan, Cumsille, Gill & Gallay, 2007).

Yet how are we to understand the moral dimensions of personality? When our aspiration is to raise children of "a certain kind," what does this mean? Historically, the work of developmental and educational scientists has coalesced around two options. One option draws upon Aristotelian resources to assert that moral formation is a matter of character development; it is a matter of developing those dispositions that allow one to live well the life that is good for one to live. We flourish as persons, in other words, when we are in possession of the virtues. A second option draws upon Kantian resources to assert that moral formation is a matter of cognitive development; it is a matter of developing sophisticated deliberative competence to resolve the dilemmatic features of our lives but in a way compatible with the "moral point of view." Our behavior is distinctly moral, under this view, when it conforms to the duties required by the moral law, or, alternatively, when behavior is undertaken for explicit moral reasons.

The character and cognitive developmental options are associated with various educational strategies that are discussed in a number of chapters in this volume and elsewhere (e.g., Lapsley & Narvaez, 2006; Turiel, 2006). In this chapter we describe a third option that attempts to frame the moral qualities of persons in terms of the psychological literatures on selfhood and identity. These constructs have a long history in psychology, and are variously understood by different research paradigms (e.g., Harter, 2012; Leary & Tangney, 2003). Hence their application to the moral domain is by no means straightforward (Blasi, 2004). Yet, for all the peril, these constructs also hold out considerable promise for understanding the dispositional and motivational bases of moral behavior (Blasi, 2005; Hardy & Carlo, 2005). Moreover, an appeal to self and identity opens up the study of moral development and education to the theoretical and methodological resources of other domains of psychological science, thereby increasing the prospect of our improving the aim of moral education with powerful integrative frameworks.

In the next section we attempt to frame the contemporary appeal of moral self-identity by situating it within the problematic of the character and cognitive developmental alternatives noted earlier. As we will see neither alternative has much use for the language of selfhood or identity, at least in their traditional, unvarnished formulation, but that a number of theoretical and empirical advances have converged to raise its profile. Five theoretical approaches to moral self-identity will then be described, followed by an account of their educational implications. We will conclude with a survey of "doubts and futures"—conceptual doubts about the coherence of moral self-identity as a useful construct in moral psychology, and possible futures for a moral self-identity research program.

SITUATING MORAL SELF-IDENTITY

The increasing prominence of moral self-identity in developmental psychology (e.g., Blasi, 1993; Lapsley & Narvaez, 2004a) is reflected also by recent trends in contemporary ethics that draw a close connection between personal and moral considerations (Taylor, 1989). As Taylor put it, "being a self is inseparable from existing in a space of moral issues" (p. 112). Of course, the recent prominence of the moral self should not imply that it was ever completely absent from ethical theory (Bergman, 2005). The Aristotelian ethical tradition, for example, with its emphasis on virtues, is thought particularly friendly to the moral dimensions of selfhood (Punzo, 1996). Moreover, Carr (2001) associates Kant's moral theory with the view that moral agency is crucial to what it means to be a person. As Carr put it, "although there are other senses in which human agents may be regarded as persons, the most *significant* sense in which they are persons is that in which they are moral agents" (p. 82).

THEORIES OF SELF-IDENTITY
Orienting Frameworks

No one has done more than Augusto Blasi to elevate the importance of moral self-identity for understanding moral behavior. According to Blasi (1984), moral self-identity is constructed on the basis of moral commitments. The moral person is one for whom moral categories or moral notions are central, essential, and important to self-understanding. Moral commitments cut deeply to the core of what and who they are as persons. But not everyone constructs the self by reference to moral categories. For some individuals moral considerations do not penetrate their understanding of who they are as persons; nor influence their outlook on important issues; nor "come to mind" when faced with the innumerable transactions of daily life. Some have only a glancing acquaintance with morality but choose to define the self by reference to other priorities; or else incorporate morality into their personality in different degrees; or emphasize some moral considerations ("justice") but not others ("caring").

Hence moral identity is a dimension of individual differences, which is to say, it is a way of talking about personality. One has a moral identity to the extent that moral notions, such as being good, being just, compassionate, or fair, is judged to be central, essential, and important to one's self-understanding. One has a moral identity when one strives to keep faith with identity-defining moral commitments; and when moral claims stake out the very terms of reference for the sort of person one claims to be.

Blasi's (1984) account of moral identity is not far from his Self Model of moral action. For example, if moral considerations are crucial to the essential self, then self-integrity will hinge on whether one is self-consistent in action. And failing to act in a way that is self-consistent with what is central, essential, and important to one's moral identity is to risk self-betrayal. In more recent writings Blasi has reflected on how and why people come to care about the self and its projects and desires (Blasi, 2004). He has also proposed a psychological account of moral character, and outlined some important developmental considerations (Blasi, 2005).

Moral Character. One's moral character presumably is comprised of *virtues*. But it is useful, on Blasi's (2005) view, to distinguish higher- and lower-order virtues. Lower-order virtues are the many specific predispositions that show up in lists of valued traits favored by character educators including, for example, empathy, compassion, fairness, honesty, generosity, kindness, diligence, and so on. Typically these lists describe predispositions to respond in certain ways in highly specific situations. It is easy to generate these "bags of virtue" (as Kohlberg derisively called them). Indeed, as Blasi (2005) put it, "one immediately observes that the lists frequently differ from each other, are invariably long, and can be easily extended, and are largely unsystematic" (p. 70). In contrast, higher-order traits have greater generality and quite possibly apply across many situations.

Two clusters of higher-order traits are distinguished. Blasi (2005) calls one cluster "willpower" (or, alternatively, self-control). Willpower as self-control is a toolbox of skills that permit self-regulation in problem-solving. Breaking down problems, goal-setting, focusing attention, avoiding distractions, resisting temptation, staying on task, persevering with determination and self-discipline—these are the skills of willpower. The second cluster of higher-order traits are organized around the notion of "integrity," which refers to internal self-consistency. Being a person of one's word, being transparent to oneself, being responsible, self-accountable, sincere, resistant to self-deception—these are the dispositions of integrity. Integrity is felt as *responsibility* when we constrain the self with intentional acts of self-control in the pursuit of our moral aims. Integrity is felt as *identity* when we imbue the construction of self-meaning with moral desires. When constructed in this way living out one's moral commitments does not feel like a choice but is felt instead as a matter of self-necessity. It is rather like Martin Luther at the Diet of Worms: "*Here I stand; I can do no other.*"

This suggests that self-control and integrity are morally neutral but take on significance for moral character only when they are attached to moral desires. Our self-control and integrity are *moralized* by our desire to keep faith with morality. Here Blasi (2005) appeals to Frankfurt's (1971) notion of effective will and second-order volitions. To want to have certain moral desires ("second-order desires"), and to have these desires effectively willed for the self ("second-order volitions"), is the hallmark of moral character. Moral character describes *persons* but not *wantons*. But not all persons possess moral character either, unless they will *moral* desires as second-order volitions.

Influence of Blasian Identity. Blasi's writings on moral identity, personality, and character established the terms of reference for a renewed examination of self and identity in the moral domain. His eloquent, meditative defense of the subjective self-as-agent in psychological science, his insistence on the rational, intentional nature of distinctly moral functioning, and his integration of self and identity with moral rationality and responsibility is a singular, influential achievement. Moreover, Blasi has returned long-forgotten concepts to the vocabulary of modern psychology, including desire, will, and volition; and added new concepts, such as self-appropriation and wholeheartedness. Although the most searching of his theoretical claims have yet to be translated into sustained empirical research, there are lines of research that do encourage the general thrust of his work.

For example, moral identity is used to explain the motivation of individuals who sheltered Jews during the Nazi Holocaust (Monroe, 2003). The study of "moral exemplars"—adults whose lives are marked by extraordinary moral commitment—reveal a sense of self that is aligned with moral goals, and moral action undertaken as a matter of felt necessity rather than as a product of effortful deliberation (Colby & Damon, 1992). Similar findings are reported in studies of youth. In one study adolescents who were nominated by community organizations for their uncommon prosocial commitment ("care exemplars") were more likely to include moral goals and moral traits in their self-descriptions than were matched comparison adolescents (Hart & Fegley, 1995; Reimer, 2003). Moral exemplars show more progress in adult identity development (Matsuba & Walker, 2004), and report self-conceptions that are replete with agentic themes, ideological depth and complexity (Matsuba & Walker, 2005). Moreover, identity integration and moral reasoning appear to be strongly correlated constructs (Maclean, Walker, & Matsuba, 2004).

There are, of course, other approaches to moral self-identity. Indeed, the moral exemplar studies trade mostly on Blasi's insight that a self constructed on moral ideals will show a distinctive behavioral profile. Although there is often broad compatibility with Blasi's framework, alternative approaches to moral identity have starting points other than the subjective self-as-agent, and invoke processes that are more social-cognitive (Aquino & Reed, 2002; Lapsley & Narvaez, 2004b), personological (Walker, 1999), communitarian (Power, 2004), and contextual (Hart, 2005; Hart, Atkins, & Ford, 1998). A brief summary of these approaches is in order.

Alternative Approaches to Moral Identity

Moral Self in Community. The construction of the moral self should not be thought of as an individual achievement, but may have strong communitarian features. For example, in a recent study Pratt, Hunsberger, Pancer, and Alistat (2003), showed that community involvement was a strong predictor of young adults' abilities to construct the moral self ideal. In this study, the authors constructed a moral self-ideal index that was based on participants' endorsement of a set of six personal qualities (trustworthy, honest, fair, just, care, shows integrity, good citizen). At age 19, participants who endorsed a high moral self-ideal were also more likely to endorse the "self-transcendent" values of "universalism" and "benevolence." Moreover, endorsement of each of the six moral qualities predicted an index of involvement in community activities.

Yet longitudinal analysis revealed that community involvement led to subsequent endorsement of a moral self-ideal rather than the other way round. Moral self-ideal did not lead to community engagement but was its result. Moral self-ideal is a precipitate of good works and not its cause. It is a dependent variable. If true this suggests that the best way to influence attitudes and values is to *first change behavior*—in this case in the direction of greater community involvement (Pancer & Pratt, 1999). According to Pratt and colleagues (2003) adolescents' community involvement leads to the development of a sense of identity characterized by a greater emphasis on moral and prosocial values.

Power (2004) also argues that the community dimension is essential for understanding the moral self. In his view, "The self does not experience a sense of obligation or responsibility to act in isolation but with others within a cultural setting" (p. 52). Hence moral self-identity is a matter of group identification and shared commitment to its value-laden norms. The moral self identifies with the community by speaking on behalf of its shared norms and by taking on its obligations as binding on the self.

Power (2004) uses Blasi's (1988) account of identity types (identity *observed*, identity *managed*, identity *constructed*) as a template for understanding how a person might identify with a community by speaking on behalf of its norms. In an early phase, one simply acknowledges that one is a member of a group and is bound thereby to group norms (identity observed). Then, one speaks up more actively in defense of a group norm, and in urging the community to abide by its commitments (identity managed). Finally, one takes "legislative responsibility for constructing group norms" (p. 55; identity constructed). Power (2004) argues that the democratic process challenges members to "appropriate" community group membership into one's personal identity.

A "Systems" Model. According to Hart (2005) identity is a crucial construct for at least two reasons. First, it helps us understand not only moral exemplars, but also instances of moral calamity, such as the Rwandan genocide that saw identity used as a lever for the destruction of Tutsis by Hutus (see also Moshman, 2004). Second, it is a bridge construct between philosophical conceptions of the moral life and certain empirical findings of psychological research. For example, it is a commonplace in ethical theory to assert that moral freedom is grounded by our rational capacity to discern options, make decision, and justify actions. On this account a behavior has no particular moral status unless it is motivated by an explicit moral judgment, one that is reached by means of an effortful, deliberative decision-making calculus.

Yet this image of moral agency collides with empirical research that shows that much of human decision-making is not like this at all; and that, indeed, much social behavior is under "nonconscious control" (Bargh, 2005). Hart (2005) asserts that moral psychology cannot evade findings like these, yet the deliberative quality of moral life also cannot be dispensed with. In his view the identity construct is one "in which occasional conscious moral deliberations can be integrated with action plans, emotions and the structures of life" (Hart, 2005, p. 172), which we take to mean are largely outside of consciousness.

According to Hart (2005), identity includes the ability to take oneself as an object of reflection, and to make an emotional investment in some aspects of the self. Identity is also the felt experience of continuity and sameness over time and place; and a sense of integration of self attributes. Identity requires the participation of others. It is forged in the heat of relational commitments, within *webs of interlocution* (Taylor, 1989), where social expectations influence which aspects of the self become important, essential, and central to one's identity. Finally, identity is a moment of *strong evaluation* (Taylor, 1989) that helps us discern answers to the traditional questions of ethics ("What should I do?" "What sort of person should I become?").

But Hart's model is distinctive for its account of the factors that influence moral identity formation. Five factors are noted, arrayed into two groups of influence. The first group is composed of 1) enduring dispositional and 2) social (including family, culture, social class) characteristics that change slowly and are probably beyond the volitional control of the developing child. As Hart (2005, p. 179) put it, "Enduring personality characteristics, one's family, one's culture and location in a social structure, all shape moral life." But these things are beyond the control of the child. Children do not select their personality traits; they do not select their home environments or neighborhood, though these settings will influence the contour of their moral formation. As a result, there is a certain *moral luck* (Nagel, 1979; Williams, 1982) involved in the way one's moral life goes, and a certain *fragility of goodness* (Nussbaum, 1986), too, depending on the favorability of one's ecological circumstances—including the *goodness of fit* between one's enduring personality dispositions and the contextual settings of development.

The second group of influence includes 3) moral judgment and attitudes, 4) the sense of self (including commitment to ideals), and 5) opportunities for moral action. These factors are closer to the volitional control of the agent, and introduce more malleability and plasticity in moral identity formation. Moreover, they are thought to mediate the link between the first group (personality and social) and moral identity formation and other adaptive outcomes.

Hart and his colleagues have reported a number of studies that document key features of the model. One study (Hart, Atkins, & Fegley, 2003) showed that moral identity (as reflected in voluntary community activity) has deep roots in childhood personality. In this study adolescents whose personality profile was judged "resilient" as children were more likely to be engaged in the voluntary community than were teens who had under-controlled or over-controlled personality types as children. Social structure also influences children's and adolescents' voluntary community service. For example, neighborhoods characterized by poverty and child-saturated environments (a large proportion of the population composed of children and adolescents) are associated with depressed levels of volunteering (Hart, Atkins, Markey, & Youniss, 2004).

More recently Hart and Matsuba (2009) documented a relation between the degree of child saturation in a community and the tendency of young adolescents to participate in volunteer activities. In child-saturated communities with high poverty adolescents are less likely to volunteer, but in communities with less poverty child saturation is associated with greater volunteer activities. Thus, level of poverty moderates the relationship between child saturation in a community and volunteer activities.

Hart et al. (2003) have also shown how social opportunities are associated with increased youth participation in community service. In a recent study the presence of social institutional structures (church, community meetings), along with a "helping identity," predicted voluntary community service in a nationally representative sample of adults (Matsuba, Hart, & Atkins, 2007). Indeed, attachment to institutional groups seems to be a powerful way of facilitating youth involvement in community service (Hart et al., 1998), particularly attachment to school (Atkins, Hart, & Donnelly, 2004).

Hart's (2005) model is the closest thing we have to a developmental systems perspective on moral identity formation; and one implication of an ecological systems perspective is the expectation of relative plasticity in development (Lerner, 2006). Not surprisingly, then, Hart's model suggests that there is plasticity in moral identity development. Moral identity is open to revision across the lifecourse, particularly when one is given opportunities for moral action. This underscores the importance of providing youth with opportunities for service learning and community service (Hart, 2005).

Self-Importance of Moral Identity. Aquino and Reed's (2002) account of moral identity shares some features in common with Blasi's model. They assume, for example, that moral identity is a dimension of individual differences. Moral identity may be just one of several social identities that one might value, and there are individual differences in the centrality of morality in people's self-definition. Moreover, they assume that moral identity is a key mechanism by which moral judgments and ideals are translated into action.

But Aquino and Reed (2002) also diverge from Blasi's model in significant ways. For one thing, they avail themselves of the theoretical resources (and experimental methodologies) of social cognitive approaches to personality, an option that Blasi disfavors. Social cognitive theory assumes, for example, that the activation of mental representations of the self is critical for social information-processing. Hence, they define moral identity in terms of the availability and accessibility of moral schemes (following Lapsley and Lasky, 2002). On this view a person with a moral identity is one for whom moral schemas are chronically accessible, readily primed, and easily activated for appraising the social landscape (Aquino, Reed, Thau, & Freeman, 2007).

Aquino and Reed (2002) also adopt a trait-specific approach to moral identity. They define moral identity as a self-conception that is organized around specific moral traits (e.g., caring, compassionate, fair, friendly, generous, helpful, hardworking, honest, kind). These traits then serve as "salience induction stimuli" (in the manner of spreading activation effects) to activate a person's moral identity when rating the self-importance of these traits on a moral identity instrument. Factor analysis of this instrument revealed two factors: a Symbolization factor (the degree to which the traits are reflected in one's public actions); and an Internalization factor (the degree to which these moral traits are central to one's self-concept). In some studies these nine traits are used in an experimental manipulation to prime the accessibility of moral identity.

Research in this paradigm has yielded highly interesting results. For example, Aquino and Reed (2002) showed that both dimensions were significant predictors of spontaneous moral self-concept and self-reported volunteering, but that internalization showed the stronger relation to actual donating behavior and moral reasoning. In subsequent research individuals with a strong internalized moral identity reported a stronger moral obligation to help and share resources with outgroups; to perceive the worthiness of coming to their aid; and to prefer outgroups in actual donating behavior (Reed & Aquino, 2003). Similarly, Reed, Aquino, and Levy (2007) showed that individuals for whom moral identity is very important prefer to donate their personal time for charitable causes rather than donate money. They also showed that while individuals with high organizational status may prefer to donate money to charity than time, this tendency was considerably weaker among individuals with strongly-important moral identity.

In addition, research shows that moral identity appears to neutralize the effectiveness of moral disengagement strategies (mechanisms that allow us to support or perpetrate doing harm to others while protecting our self-image and self-esteem). When the moral self is highly important to one's identity, it undermines the effectiveness of cognitive rationalizations that otherwise allow one to inflict harm on others (Aquino et al., 2007). Similarly, a person with a strong moral identity tends to include more people within his or her circle of moral regard, and is less likely to have a social dominance orientation (Hardy, Bhattacharjee, Reed, & Aquino, 2010). Individuals with moral identity are more empathic (Detert, Trevino, & Sweitzer, 2008), show greater moral attentiveness (Reynolds, 2008), and are less aggressive (Barriga, Morrison, Liau, & Gibbs, 2001).

Moral Identity and Personality. There are now insistent calls to study moral rationality within the broader context of personality (Lapsley & Narvaez, 2004b; Walker & Hennig, 1998). To this end Hill and Roberts (2010) argue that moral personality is a plural construct, that is, there are many ways of being a moral person. In addition, they argue that models of moral personality are not incompatible with models of moral reasoning or with identity theory, and are not limited to trait conceptions of personality. Moreover, the formation and maintenance of moral personality is a lifespan developmental concern, although much of the extant research has focused on adolescence and emerging adulthood.

Walker and his colleagues have attempted to understand the personality of moral exemplars in terms of the Big 5 taxonomy. One study showed, for example, that the personality of moral exemplars was oriented towards conscientiousness and agreeableness (Walker, 1999). Agreeableness also characterized young adult moral exemplars (Matsuba & Walker, 2005). In a study of brave, caring, and just Canadians, Walker and Pitts (1998) found that brave exemplars aligned with a complex of traits associated with extraversion; caring exemplars aligned with agreeableness; and just exemplars with a mixture of conscientiousness, emotional stability, and openness to experience. This pattern was largely replicated by Walker and Hennig (2004).

More recently, Frimer and Walker (2009) argued that moral centrality is "reflected by narratives that are rich in themes of communion and have agentic and communal themes interwoven into the same thought" (p. 1672). In this study life story narratives were elicited from Canadian university students using an interview protocol. Transcripts of the interviews were analyzed for the presence of 10 values derived from the Schwartz Value Survey (1992) using a narrative coding paradigm called VEINs (Values Embedded in Narratives). A *moral centrality index* was constructed to describe the extent to which agentic and communal values were predominant in a single narrative unit. In their view, moral centrality reflects strong communal themes that are interwoven with agency. The results showed that moral centrality predicted a composite measure of morally relevant behaviors. On this basis the authors suggest that what drives the behavior of moral exemplars is the recognition that moral concerns and self-interest can be reconciled, and that the flexible coordination of agency and communion is undoubtedly a developmental achievement.

Whereas Frimer and Walker (2009) examine the centrality of values in life story narratives to describe moral functioning, Lapsley and Narvaez (2004b) appeal to social cognitive theory in their account of the moral personality. Social cognitive theory draws attention to cognitive-affective mechanisms that influence social perception, and serve to create and sustain patterns of individual differences. If schemas are easily primed and readily activated ("chronically accessible"), then they direct our attention selectively to certain features of our experience. This selective framing disposes one to select schema-compatible tasks, goals, and settings that canalize and maintain our dispositional tendencies (Cantor, 1990). We choose environments, in other words, that support or reinforce our schema-relevant interests, which illustrates the reciprocal nature of person-context interactions. Moreover, we tend to develop highly practiced behavioral routines in those areas of our experience that are regulated by chronically accessible schemes. In these areas of our social experience we become "virtual experts," and in these life contexts social cognitive schemas function as "a ready, sometimes automatically available plan of action" (Cantor, 1990, p. 738). In this way chronically accessible schemas function as the cognitive carriers of dispositions.

Social cognitive theory asserts, then, that schema accessibility and conditions of activation are critical for understanding how patterns of individual differences are channeled and maintained. From this perspective Lapsley and Narvaez (2004b) claim that a moral person, or a person who has a moral identity or character, is one for whom moral categories are chronically accessible. If having a moral identity is just when moral notions are central, important, and essential for one's self-understanding, then notions that are central, important, and essential are also those that are chronically accessible for appraising the social landscape. Chronically accessible moral schemas provide a dispositional readiness to discern the moral dimensions of experience, as well as to underwrite the discriminative facility in selecting situationally appropriate behavior.

Recent research has attempted to document the social cognitive dimensions of moral cognition. For example, research shows that conceptions of good character (Lapsley & Lasky, 2001) and of moral, spiritual, and religious persons (Walker & Pitts, 1998) are organized as cognitive prototypes. Moreover, moral chronicity appears to be a dimension of individual differences that influences spontaneous trait inference and text comprehension (Narvaez, Lapsley, Hagele & Lasky, 2006). In two studies Narvaez et al. (2006) showed that moral chronics and non-chronics respond differently to the dispositional and moral implications of social cues.

Educational Implications

The recent enthusiasm for theoretical and empirical analysis of moral self-identity has not yet produced well-articulated plans for making it the aim of education. One impediment is that moral self-identity is often conceptualized from the perspective of adult functioning, and it has proven difficult to work out possible developmental trajectories with enough specificity to yield testable empirical outcomes. This is particularly true for social cognitive accounts of moral self-identity. In the absence of strong developmental models it is often difficult to work out appropriate educational strategies. Without more precise knowledge of developmental mechanisms it is difficult to know just where, when, and how to intervene.

Yet we are not completely helpless, either. Indeed, each of the perspectives on moral self-identity reviewed here yield clues on how to educate the moral self. For example, one implication of Blasi's approach is that children should develop the proper moral desires as second-order volitions; and to master the virtues of self-control and integrity. But how do children develop wholehearted commitment to moral integrity? Blasi (2005) helpfully describes some possible steps towards the development of the moral will. Yet there are additional clues about possible pathways from research on the development of "conscience" in early childhood.

Kochanska (2002) proposed a two-step model of emerging morality that begins with the quality of parent–child attachment. A strong, mutually responsive relationship with caregivers orients the child to be receptive to parental influence. Within the bonds of a secure attachment the child is eager to comply with parental expectations and standards. There is "committed compliance" on the part of the child to the norms and values of caregivers which, in turn, motivates moral internalization and the work of "conscience." Kochanska's model moves, then, from security of attachment to committed compliance to moral internalization. This movement is also expected to influence the child's emerging internal representation of the self. As Kochanska (2002) put it:

> Children with a strong history of committed compliance with the parent are likely gradually to come to view themselves as embracing the parent's values and rules. Such a moral self, in turn, comes to serve as the regulator of future moral conduct and, more generally, of early morality.
>
> (p. 340)

This model would suggest that the source of wholehearted commitment to morality that is characteristic of Blasian moral personality might lie in the mutual, positive affective relationship with caregivers—assuming that Kochanska's "committed compliance" is a developmental precursor to Blasi's "wholehearted commitment."

A recent longitudinal study by Kochanska and colleagues (Kochanska, Koenig, Barry, Kim, & Yoon, 2010) tracked the interplay of conscience development, moral self, and psychosocial competence over the course of the toddler years to early school age. Two dimensions of conscience were assessed at 25, 38, and 52 months of age. One dimension was "out-of-sight" compliance, that is, the extent to which toddlers internalized their mother's and father's rules when the child was left alone. The second dimension was empathic concern toward each parent, as assessed in a simulated distress paradigm. At 67 months the moral self was assessed using a puppet interview; and at 80 months parents and teachers rated the children on various assessments of psychosocial competence that tapped, for example, peer relationships, school engagement, problem and prosocial behavior, oppositional or defiant behavior, the absence of guilt or empathy, and disregard for rules and standards.

Of particular interest was the puppet interview of the moral self. It works this way: Two puppets are anchored on opposite ends of 31 items. The items pertained to dimensions of early conscience (e.g., internalization of rules, empathy, apology). Each item is presented with a brief scenario, with one puppet endorsing one option and the other puppet endorsing a contrary option. For example, in one scenario Puppet 1 would say: "*When I break something, I try to hide it so no one finds out.*" Puppet 2 would declare "*When I break something, I tell someone right away.*" Then the child is asked "*What about you? Do you try to hide something that you broke or do you tell someone right away?*"

The results showed that children who as toddlers and preschoolers had a strong history of internalized out-of-sight compliance with parents' rules were also competent, engaged, and prosocial at early school age, with few antisocial behavioral problems. Similarly, toddlers and preschoolers with a strong history of empathic responding showed a robust profile of psychosocial competence at early school age. Moreover, children's moral self was a strong predictor of future competent behavior as well. Children at 67 months who were "highly moral" were rated at 80 months to be prosocial, highly competent, and well-socialized. What's more, the child's moral self was shown to mediate the relation between out-of-sight compliance with maternal rules and later psychological competence at 80 months.

Indeed, Kochanska et al. (2010) argued that the moral self is the mechanism that at least partly accounts for the relation between early conscience and later evidence of psychosocial competence. A number of possibilities are suggested: Perhaps the moral self is motivated to avoid cognitive dissonance or is better able to anticipate guilty feelings; or perhaps the moral self exercises automatic regulation due to the high accessibility of moral schemas, an explanation that accords with social cognitive approaches to the moral self (Lapsley & Narvaez, 2004b).

Kochanska's model would be scarce comfort to Blasi to the extent that it yields only a morality of internalization or of compliance. Yet, if there is something to it in broad stroke, that is, if the moral self is congealed within a context of positive, secure attachment relations (Reimer, 2003)—and a relational context is unspecified in Blasi's model but could use one—then this underscores the importance of school bonding, caring school communities, and attachment to teachers as a basis for prosocial and moral development (Lapsley & Narvaez, 2006).

For example, the Seattle Longitudinal Project shows that there is a press toward behavior consistent with standards when standards are clear and when students have feelings of commitment and attachment to school (Hawkins, Guo, Hill, Battin-Pearson, & Abbott, 2001). The Child Development Project showed the elementary schoolchildren's sense of community leads them to adhere to the values that are most salient in the classroom (Solomon, Watson, Battistich, Schaps, & Delucchi, 1996). These findings align with Kochanska's model of early conscience development: Secure attachment promotes committed compliance which leads to internalization of norms, values, and standards, suggesting some continuity in the mechanisms by which children appropriate the moral values of their family or classroom community (Lapsley & Narvaez, 2006).

Power's (2004; Power, Higgins, & Kohlberg, 1989) model of the moral self also underscores the importance of school community for inducing commitment to moral ideals and norms. There are specific guidelines on how this should work: classrooms and schools should be just communities that use participatory democratic practices and frequent class meetings. It is attested by a significant literature that documents the efficacy of moral atmosphere for promoting responsibility (Higgins-D'Alessandro & Power, 2005) and for reducing transgressive behavior in schools (e.g., Brugman et al., 2003).

The moral exemplar (e.g., Colby & Damon, 1992) and systems (Hart, 2005) approach to moral self-identity lead to similar educational recommendations. For example, moral exemplar research holds out as a goal the prosocial commitment exhibited by care exemplars. Colby and Damon (1992) nominate social influence as a decisive mechanism. For example, that a friend's prosocial behavior can influence one's own pursuit of moral goals (e.g., to be helpful or cooperative) when the affective relationship is strong and interactions are frequent (Barry & Wentzel, 2006).

Similarly, Hart's (2005) research illustrates the importance of cultivating attachment to organizations that provide social opportunities for young people to engage their communities in prosocial service. Indeed, we have seen how community involvement predicts moral self-ideal in late adolescence (Pratt et al., 2003). There is a significant literature that documents that salutary effect of participation in voluntary organizations and service learning opportunities more generally on prosocial behavior and moral civic identity (C. Flanagan, 2004; Youniss & Yates, 1997, 1999).

One challenge for a social cognitive theory of moral self-identity is to specify the developmental sources of moral chronicity. Lapsley & Narvaez (2004b) suggest that moral chronicity is built on the foundation of generalized event representations that characterize early socio-personality development (Thompson, 1998). These representations have been called the "basic building blocks of cognitive development" (Nelson & Gruendel, 1981, p. 131). They are working models of how social routines unfold and of what one can expect of social experience.

But the key characterological turn of significance for moral psychology is how these early social-cognitive units are transformed from episodic into autobiographical memory. Autobiographical memory is also a social construction elaborated by means of dialogue within a web of interlocution. Parental interrogatives help children organize events into personally relevant autobiographical memories which provide, as part of the self-narrative, action-guiding scripts that become frequently practiced, over-learned, routine, habitual, and automatic. Hence parental interrogatives might also include reference to norms, standards, and values so that the moral ideal-self becomes part of the child's autobiographical narrative. In this way parents help children identify morally relevant features of their experience and encourage the formation of social cognitive schemas that are chronically accessible (Lapsley & Narvaez, 2004b). This suggests, though, that the education of moral self-ideal is not always a matter of pedagogy or curriculum and does not take place primarily in schools.

Doubts and Futures

As we have seen, moral self-identity is an attractive concept and a promising one. It seems to capture something important about the link between personal agency and the construction of moral ideals. It opens up possibilities for engaging other psychological literatures, particularly those regarding personality and cognition, with the goal of deriving robust integrative models of moral functioning. Moreover, implications for educating the moral self seem broadly compatible with developmental insights about qualities of attachment and affective interpersonal experiences at home, school, and neighborhood; and compatible, too, with instructional best practice with respect to the importance of caring classrooms, just communities, service learning, and participation in voluntary organizations at school and in the wider community.

Nucci (2004) raises several objections. First, he generally doubts that anyone would deny the importance of morality for the self. Virtually everyone thinks that morality is important. Although it is possible for people to disagree about how morality might be displayed for given situations and contexts, he notes that "people generally attend to moral social interactions and have common views of prima facie moral obligations" (p. 119). Second, there is ambiguity about just when and where a moral self-identity is evinced. Indeed, current theory on the moral self does not, in his view, come to grips sufficiently with the heterogeneity of the self system. Our self-concepts are highly differentiated and domain specific; and our self-evaluations are similarly specific, flexible, and subject to discounting. Mindful of such complexity, when are we confident in ascribing moral self-identity to an agent?

Current research ascribes a moral self to individuals who volunteer in the community—they are "care exemplars." But what about the leaders of the Weathermen underground who took up action against an immoral war by engaging in violent protest? Was John Brown exercising the prerogatives of moral self-identity at Harpers Ferry? What is the true measure of a man's moral character, when he leads the nation in a heroic struggle for civil rights, or when he has serial extramarital affairs along the way? Most biographical studies of individuals whose lives are marked by extraordinary moral accomplishment also reveal instances of appalling moral failure. This observation is made banal by the uneven manifestation of moral qualities in our own lives let alone the lives of heroic exemplars. Yet the language of moral self-identity seems inadequate to capture this complexity. The construct seems insensate to the demand of situations, underestimates contextual influence, and otherwise neglects the social contexts that interact dynamically with dispositional tendencies (Doris, 2002). Nucci (2004) asks: "Does our moral identity shift with each context? Is it the case that as the self-same person it is the salience of morality that shifts with the context?" (p. 127). As a corrective Nucci (2004) calls for a "contextualist structural theory" of moral cognition to account for when individuals prioritize morality and when they do not.

Four additional problems are noted by Nucci (2004). First, it is reductionist to argue that the motivation for moral action is the desire to maintain consistency between action and moral identity. To do so reduces the contextual complexity of moral situations to the simple judgment of whether to take a certain action is consistent with one's sense of self. Second, self-consistency is not only reductionism but a species of ethical egoism. It reduces questions about fairness, justice, and human welfare to questions about whether actions accord with desires or make one feel good about the self. Following Frankena (1963), Nucci (2004) argues that self-consistency is not a motive for moral action, but rather judgment that it was "the right thing to do." Third, there is very little specification of the developmental features of moral self-identity. Fourth, in some instances, a moral identity is utterly dysfunctional if our identification with a moral framework is so total that we are frozen into moral rigidity or else burn with the crazed indignation of the moral zealot. Moral saints make life unbearable for the rest of us, and you couldn't be friends with one (Wolf, 1982; also, Sorensen, 2004).

There are also compelling criticisms of the orienting philosophical framework(s) that stands behind current work on moral self-identity (e.g., Keba, 2004). For example, the language of "centrality" is used to describe when moral traits are core to self-identity. Yet, as Rorty and Wong (1990) point out, there are at least seven ways for a trait to be central to identity, and there is no necessary connection among them. In addition O. Flanagan (1990) believes it a mistake to align moral identity too closely with strong evaluation and second-order desires because to do so overstates the degree to which effective identity requires reflectiveness, articulacy, and self-comprehension. One can recognize and acknowledge standards and conform behavior to them, "without ever having linguistically formulated the standard and without even possessing the ability to do so when pressed" (p. 53).

Flanagan's (1990) critique does push extant psychological theory in interesting ways. It holds open the possibility that self-comprehension of the second-order type might proceed unreflectively, perhaps automatically and outside of consciousness. It holds out the possibility that psychological theories that require conscious, intentional, and volitional self-appropriation and self-mastery might overestimate the intellectual resources necessary for the development of the moral will; and overestimate the need for articulate reflective judgment of the sort that is envisioned for moral self-identity.

Future research on moral self-identity could surely take up these and other matters with profit. It might ask, for example: What is the nature of second-order desires, and how transparent must they be to articulate self-comprehension? How and where do automaticity and "non-conscious" control intersect with the development of the moral will? What does self-appropriation look like in early development? In addition, future research must specify more precise developmental models. Although it is useful to explore adult forms of the moral self, particularly as these are regarded as endpoints of a developmental process, we must now work back to discern the proper trajectories that yield these adult forms as outcomes.

By far the most glaring deficiency in moral self-identity research is the relative absence of well-attested assessments of the construct. There is no consensus on how best to measure moral self-identity in adulthood; and we are not aware of any systematic attempt to measure it in children, a fact that explains the paucity of developmental research. Nothing will stop the momentum of scholarly interest in moral self-identity more surely than the failure to develop suitable assessments. Indeed, most of the advances in moral psychology research over the last 50 years were made possible by the availability of well-regarded (interview and questionnaire) assessments of moral development and principled reasoning. Clearly the development of such assessments for moral self-identity should be a high priority.

REFERENCES

Aquino, K. & Reed, A., II. (2002). The self-importance of moral identity. *Journal of Personality and Social Psychology, 83*, 1423–1440.

Aquino, K., Reed, A. II, Thau, S., & Freeman, D. (2007). A grotesque and dark beauty: How moral identity and mechanisms of moral disengagement influence cognitive and emotional reactions to war. *Journal of Experimental Social Psychology, 43*, 385–392.

Atkins, R., Hart, D., & Donnelly, T.M. (2004). Moral identity development and school attachment. In D.K. Lapsley & D. Narvaez (Eds.), *Moral development, self and identity* (pp. 47–64). Mahwah, NJ: Lawrence Erlbaum Associates.

Bargh, J.A. (2005). Bypassing the will: Toward demystifying the nonconscious control of social behavior. In R.R. Hassin, J.S. Uelman, & J.A. Bargh (Eds.), *The new unconscious* (pp. 37–60). Oxford, UK: Oxford University Press.

Barriga, A.Q., Morrison, E.M., Liau, A.K., & Gibbs, J.C. (2001). Moral cognition: Explaining the gender difference in antisocial behavior. *Merrill-Palmer Quarterly, 47*, 532–562.

Barry, C.M. & Wentzel, K. (2006). Friends influence prosocial behavior: The role of motivational factors and friendship characteristics. *Developmental Psychology, 42*, 153–163.

Bergman, R. (2005). John Dewey on educating the moral self. *Studies in Education and Philosophy, 24*, 39–62.

Blasi, A. (1984). Moral identity: Its role in moral functioning. In W.M. Kurtines & J.J. Gewirtz (Eds.), *Morality, moral behavior and moral development* (pp. 128–139). New York: John Wiley and Sons.

Blasi, A. (1988). Identity and the development of the self. In D.K Lapsley & F.C. Power (Eds.), *Self, ego and identity: Integrative approaches* (pp. 226–242). New York: Springer-Verlag.

Blasi, A. (1993). The development of identity: Some implications for moral functioning. In G.G. Noam, T.E. Wren, G. Nunner-Winkler, & W. Edelstein (Eds.), *Studies in contemporary German social thought* (pp. 99–122). Cambridge, MA: MIT Press.

Blasi, A. (2004). Neither personality nor cognition: An alternative approach to the nature of the self. In C. Lightfoot, C. Lalonde, & M. Chandler (Eds.), *Changing conceptions of psychological life* (pp. 3–26). Mahwah, NJ: Lawrence Erlbaum Associates.

Blasi, A. (2005). Moral character: A psychological approach. In D.K. Lapsley & F.C. Power (Eds.), *Character psychology and character education* (pp. 18–35). Notre Dame, IN: University of Notre Dame Press.

Brugman, D., Podolskij, A.J., Heymans, P.G., Boom, J., Karabanova, O., & Idobaeva, O. (2003). Perception of moral atmosphere in school and norm transgressive behavior in adolescents: An intervention study. *International Journal of Behavioral Development, 27*, 289–300.

Bryk, A.S. (1988). Musings on the moral life of schools. *American Journal of Education, 96*(2), 256–290.

Cantor, N. (1990). From thought to behavior: "Having" and "doing" in the study of personality and cognition. *American Psychologist, 45*, 735–750.

Carr, D. (2001). Moral and personal identity. *International Journal of Education and Religion, II*(1), 79–97.

Colby, A. & Damon, W. (1992). *Some do care: Contemporary lives of moral commitment.* New York: Free Press.

Detert, J.R., Trevino, L.K., & Sweitzer, V.L. (2008). Moral disengagement in ethical decision making: A study of antecedents and outcomes. *Journal of Applied Psychology, 93*, 374–391.

Doris, J.M. (2002). *Lack of character.* Cambridge: Cambridge University Press.

Eccles, J. & Gootman, J.A. (Eds.). (2002). *Community programs to promote youth development.* Washington, DC. National Academies Press.

Flanagan, C. (2004). Volunteerism, leadership, political socialization and civic engagement. In R. Lerner & L. Steinberg (Eds.), *Handbook of adolescent psychology* (2nd ed., pp. 721–746). Hoboken, NJ: Wiley.

Flanagan, C., Cumsille, P., Gill, S., & Gallay, L.S. (2007). School and community climates and civic commitments: Patterns for ethnic minority and majority students. *Journal of Educational Psychology, 99*, 421–431.

Flanagan, O. (1990). Identity and strong and weak evaluation. In O. Flanagan & A.O. Rorty (Eds.) *Identity, character and morality: Essays in moral psychology* (pp. 37–66). Cambridge, MA: MIT Press.

Frankena, W. (1963). *Ethics.* Englewood Cliffs, NJ: Prentice-Hall.

Frankfurt, H. (1971). Freedom of the will and the concept of a person. *Journal of Philosophy, 68*, 5–20.

Frimer, J.A. & Walker, L.J. (2009). Reconciling the self and morality: An empirical model of moral centrality development. *Developmental Psychology, 45*, 1669–1681.

Goodlad, J. (1992). The moral dimensions of schooling and teacher education. *Journal of Moral Education, 21* (2), 87–98.

Goodman, J.F. & Lesnick, H. (2001). *The moral stake in education: Contested premises and practices.* New York: Longman.

Hardy, S.A., Bhattacharjee, A., Reed, A., & Aquino, K. (2010). Moral identity and psychological distance: The case of adolescent parental socialization. *Journal of Adolescence, 33*, 111–123.

Hardy, S.A. & Carlo, G. (2005). Identity as a source of moral motivation. *Human Development, 48*, 232–256.

Hart, D. (2005). The development of moral identity. *Nebraska Symposium on Motivation, 51*, 165–196.

Hart, D., Atkins, R., & Fegley, S. (2003). Personality and development in childhood: A person-centered approach. *Monographs for the Society for Research in Child Development.* Hillsdale, NJ: Lawrence Erlbaum Associates.

Hart, D., Atkins, R., & Ford, D. (1998). Urban America as a context for the development of moral identity. *Journal of Social Issues, 54*, 513–530.

Hart, D., Atkins, R., Markey, P., & Youniss, J. (2004). Youth bulges in communities: The effects of age structure on adolescent civic knowledge and civic participation. *Psychological Science, 15*, 591–597.

Hart, D. & Fegley, S. (1995). Prosocial behavior and caring in adolescence: Relations to self-understanding and social judgment. *Child Development, 66*, 1346–1359.

Hart, D. & Matsuba, M.K. (2009). Urban neighborhoods as contexts for moral identity. In D. Narvaez & D.K. Lapsley (Eds.), *Personality, identity, and character: Explorations in moral psychology.* New York: Cambridge University Press.

Harter, S. (2012). *The construction of the self.* New York: The Guilford Press.

Hawkins, D.J., Guo, J., Hill, G., Battin-Pearson, S., & Abbott, R.D. (2001). Long-term effects of the Seattle Social Development Project intervention on school bonding trajectories. *Applied Developmental Science, 5*, 225–236.

Higgins-D'Alessandro, A. & Power, F.C. (2005). Character, responsibility and the moral self. In D.K. Lapsley & F.C. Power (Eds.), *Character psychology and character education* (pp. 101–120). Notre Dame, IN: University of Notre Dame Press.

Hill, P.L. & Roberts, B.W. (2010). Propositions for the study of moral personality development. *Current Directions in Psychological Science, 19*, 380–383.

Keba, A. (2004). The concept of self-identity and moral conflicts. *Croatian Political Science Review, 41*, 134.

Kochanska, G. (2002). Committed compliance, moral self, and internalization: A mediational model. *Developmental Psychology, 38*, 339–351.

Kochanska, G., Koenig, J.L., Barry, R.A., Kim, S., & Yoon, J.E. (2010). Children's conscience during the toddler and preschool years, moral self, and a competent, adaptive developmental trajectory. *Developmental Psychology, 46*, 1320–1332.

Lapsley, D.K. & Lasky, B. (2001). Prototypic moral character. *Identity, 1*, 345–363.

Lapsley, D.K. & Narvaez, D. (Eds.). (2004a). *Moral development, self and identity.* Mahwah, NJ: Lawrence Erlbaum Associates.

Lapsley, D.K. & Narvaez, D. (2004b). A social-cognitive approach to the moral personality. In D.K. Lapsley & D. Narvaez (Eds.), *Moral development, self and identity* (pp. 189–212). Mahwah, NJ: Lawrence Erlbaum Associates.

Lapsley, D.K. & Narvaez, D. (2006). Character education. In W. Damon & R. Lerner (Eds.), *Handbook of child psychology* (6th ed., Vol. 4, A. Renniger & I. Siegel, Vol. Eds., *Child psychology in practice*, pp. 248–296). New York: Wiley.

Leary, M.R. & Tangney, J.P. (Eds.). (2003). *Handbook of self and identity.* New York: Guilford.

Lerner, R.M. (2006). Developmental science, developmental systems and contemporary theories of human development. In W. Damon & R.M. Lerner (Eds.), *Handbook of child psychology* (6th ed., Vol. 1, R.M. Lerner, Vol. Ed., *Theoretical models of human development*, pp. 1–17). New York: Wiley.

Maclean, A.M., Walker, L.J., & Matsuba, K. (2004). Transcendence and the moral life: Identity integration, religion and the moral life. *Journal for the Scientific Study of Religion, 43*, 429–437.

Matsuba, K., Hart, D., & Atkins, R. (2007). Psychological and social structural influence on commitment to volunteering. *Journal of Research on Personality, 41*, 889–907.

Matsuba, K. & Walker, L.J. (2004). Extraordinary moral commitment: Young adults in social organizations. *Journal of Personality, 72*, 413–436.

Matsuba, K. & Walker, L.J. (2005). Young adult moral exemplars: The making of self through stories. *Journal of Research on Adolescence, 15*, 275–297.

Monroe, L. (2003). How identity and perspective constrain moral choice. *International Political Science Review, 24*, 405–424.

Moshman, D. (2004). False moral identity: Self-serving denial in the maintenance of moral self-conceptions. In D.K. Lapsley & D. Narvaez (Eds.), *Moral development, self and identity* (pp. 83–110). Mahwah, NJ: Lawrence Erlbaum Associates.

Nagel, T. (1979). *Mortal questions.* Cambridge: Cambridge University Press.

Narvaez, D., Lapsley, D.K., Hagele, S., & Lasky, B. (2006). Moral chronicity and social information processing: Tests of a social cognitive approach to the moral personality. *Journal of Research in Personality, 40*, 966–985.

Nelson, K. & Gruendel, J. (1981). Generalized event representations: Basic building blocks of cognitive development. In M. Lamb & A. Brown (Eds.), *Advances in developmental psychology* (pp. 131–158). Hillsdale, NJ: Lawrence Erlbaum Associates.

Nucci, L. (2004). Reflections on the moral self construct. In D.K. Lapsley & D. Narvaez (Eds.), *Moral development, self and identity* (pp. 111–132). Mahwah, NJ: Lawrence Erlbaum Associates.

Nussbaum, M. (1986). *The fragility of goodness.* Cambridge: Cambridge University Press.

Pancer, S.M. & Pratt, M. (1999). Social and family determinants of community service involvement in Canadian youth. In M. Yates & J. Youniss (Eds.), *Community service and civic engagement in youth: International perspectives* (pp. 32–35). Cambridge: Cambridge University Press.

Power, F.C. (2004). Moral self in community. In D.K. Lapsley & D. Narvaez (Eds.), *Moral development, self and identity* (pp. 47–64). Mahwah, NJ: Lawrence Erlbaum Associates.

Power, F.C., Higgins, A., & Kohlberg, L. (1989). *Lawrence Kohlberg's approach to moral education.* New York: Columbia University Press.

Pratt, M.W., Hunsberger, B., Pancer, M.S., & Alisat, S. (2003). A longitudinal analysis of personal value socialization: Correlates of a moral self-ideal in late adolescence. *Social Development, 12*, 563–585.

Punzo, V.A. (1996). After Kohlberg: Virtue ethics and the recovery of the moral self. *Philosophical Psychology, 9*, 7–24.

Reed, A., II. & Aquino, K. (2003). Moral identity and the expanding circle of moral regard towards outgroups. *Journal of Personality and Social Psychology, 84* 1270–1286.

Reed A., Aquino, R., & Levy, E. (2007). Moral identity and judgments of charitable behaviors. *Journal of Marketing, 71*, 178–193.

Reimer, K. (2003). Committed to caring: Transformation in adolescent moral identity. *Applied Developmental Science, 7*, 129–137.

Reynolds, S.J. (2008). Moral attentiveness: Who pays attention to the moral aspects of life? *Journal of Applied Psychology, 93*, 1027–1041.

Rorty, A.O. & Wong, D. (1990). Aspects of identity and agency. In O. Flanagan & A.O. Rorty (Eds.), *Identity, character and morality: Essays in moral psychology* (pp. 19–36). Cambridge, MA: MIT Press.

Schwartz, S.H. (1992). Universals in the content and structure of values: Theoretical advances and empirical tests in 20 countries. *Advances in Experimental Social Psychology, 25*, 1–65.

Solomon, D., Watson, M., Battistich, V., Schaps, E., & Delucchi, K. (1992). Creating a caring community: Educational practices that promote children's prosocial development. In F.K. Oser, A. Dick, & J.-L. Patry (Eds.), *Effective and responsible teaching: The new synthesis* (pp. 383–396). San Francisco: Jossey-Bass.

Sorensen, K. (2004). The paradox of moral worth (Or why it can be bad to want too much of a good thing). *Journal of Philosophy, 101*, 465–483.

Taylor, C. (1989). *Sources of the self: The making of modern identity.* Cambridge, MA: Harvard University Press.

Thompson, R.A. (1998). Early sociopersonality development. In W. Damon (Editor-in-Chief) & N. Eisenberg (Vol. Ed.), *Handbook of child psychology: Vol. 3. Social, emotional and personality development* (pp. 25–104). New York: Wiley.

Turiel, E. (2006). The development of morality. In W. Damon and R. Lerner (Series Eds.) & N. Eisenberg (Vol. Ed.), *Handbook of child psychology. Vol. 3: Social, emotional, and personality development* (6th ed., pp. 789–857). New York: Wiley.

Walker, L.J. (1999). The perceived personality of moral exemplars. *Journal of Moral Education, 28,* 145–162.

Walker, L.J. & Hennig, K.H. (1998). Moral functioning in the broader context of personality. In S. Hala (Ed.), *The development of social cognition* (pp. 297–327). East Sussex, UK: Psychology Press.

Walker, L.J. & Hennig, K.H. (2004). Differing conceptions of moral exemplarity: Just, brave and caring. *Journal of Personality and Social Psychology, 86,* 629–647.

Walker, L.J. & Pitts, R.C. (1998). Naturalistic conceptions of moral maturity. *Developmental Psychology, 34,* 403–419.

Williams, B. (1982). *Moral luck.* Cambridge: Cambridge University Press.

Wolf, S. (1982). Moral saints. *Journal of Philosophy, 79,* 419–439.

Youniss, J. & Yates, M. (1997). *Community service and social responsibility.* Chicago: University of Chicago Press.

Youniss, J. & Yates, M. (1999). Youth service and moral-civic identity: A case for everyday morality. *Educational Psychology Review, 11,* 361–376.

7

TEACHING ETHICALLY AS A MORAL CONDITION OF PROFESSIONALISM

Elizabeth Campbell

From Alan Tom's initial identification of teaching as a moral craft (1984) to David Hansen's exploration of the moral heart of teaching (2001); from Goodlad, Soder, and Sirotnik's recognition of the moral dimensions of teaching (1990) to empirical studies that vividly reveal these dimensions (Jackson, Boostrom, & Hansen, 1993; Richardson & Fenstermacher, 2001), the academic and professional literature has increasingly illustrated how the moral aspects and complexities of K-12 teaching can be neither separated from the technical elements of instruction nor, worse, ignored as somehow extraneous to the central mission of education. Some connect these moral nuances, embedded in the daily life of classrooms and schools, to the professional role of the teacher and the ethical implications for professionalism more generally in teaching (Bergem, 1993; Campbell, 2003; Carr, 2000; Oser & Althof, 1993; Sockett, 1993; Strike & Soltis, 1992; Strike & Ternasky, 1993). Within a context that integrates consideration of the moral nature of teaching with applied professional ethics in teaching, this chapter explores the concept of teacher professionalism as being inseparable from what I define as the teacher's ethical knowledge. This knowledge relates to both how teachers conduct themselves in morally appropriate ways and how they engage in moral education.

Specifically, the chapter addresses two interrelated areas, presented within discrete sections. The first argues that ethical knowledge can provide the basis of a renewed professionalism in teaching. It defines ethical knowledge and discusses teaching as unique among the professions, not least because of its moral and ethical layers. It further distinguishes ethical knowledge from formalized codes and standards. The second section, which constitutes the dominant part of this chapter, explores ethical practice as a professional imperative. It offers examples of moral agency, which underlies ethical knowledge, as illustrated by the teacher's actions as both a moral practitioner and a moral educator. Conversely, and contentiously, it further presents an argument against the co-opting of moral agency as a kind of politicized and ideological activism.

The overall theoretical framework underpinning this chapter is informed by three key assumptions or orientations to the concept of ethical knowledge that are woven throughout the discussion. First, I use the adjectives "moral" and "ethical" as more or less synonymous or interchangeable terms, a practice that seems to be increasingly defensible in an applied philosophical sense (Beckner, 2004). In either case, the conceptual basis of the terms is the same in that both relate to human virtues in an Aristotelian tradition, grounded in a rejection of moral or ethical relativism. As I have written elsewhere:

> Many philosophers and researchers interested in the moral dimensions of education assume, as part of varying ideological and conceptual frameworks, that at least a basic distinction between ethical right and wrong does not need a detailed defence. In other words, in insisting that a good teacher is neither cruel nor unfair, we need not haggle over why this is essentially a moral imperative, rather than merely a culturally and socially constructed norm reflecting the interests of some over others.
>
> (Campbell, 2003, p. 15)

This position echoes Clark's argument that,

> In the moral domain, however, one opinion is *not* [author's emphasis] as good as any other.... Overarching principles have been agreed on in our society and within the teaching profession—principles dealing with honesty, fairness, protection of the weak, and respect for all people.
>
> (Clark, 1990, p. 252)

It further borrows Fenstermacher's defense when he identifies virtues such as fairness, honesty, courage, and compassion as exemplary; he states,

> I leave open here the very important issue of why these particular traits are to be regarded as virtues, doing so with the philosophically lame but empirically compelling claim that the literature, customs and norms of the vast majority of world cultures hold these traits in high regard.
>
> (Fenstermacher, 2001, pp. 640–641)

This non-relativist support for core virtues and the moral and ethical principles of professional conduct that build on them conforms to others' identification of a range of professional virtues such as fairness, justice, care, integrity, honesty, patience, constancy, responsibility, and various interpretations of the ancient principles of non-maleficence and beneficence (Haynes, 1998; Lovat, 1998; Osguthorpe, 2008; Reitz, 1998; Sockett, 2012; Strike & Ternasky, 1993). It is further reinforced by Nucci's (2001) clear distinction between the moral domain, with its universal set of values and a "basic core of morality" (p. 19), and the social domain that is more focused on conventions and variable preferences.

As a final note in relation to this first theoretical assumption, I acknowledge that I use both the language of virtues, in the spirit of Carr (2000) and Fenstermacher (1990, 2001), and the language of moral and ethical principles, in the tradition of Strike (1995, 1999) and his work with Soltis (1992) and Ternasky (1993). This may seem philosophically confused. However, this chapter is concerned with the applied ethics embedded in the real life practices of teachers, regardless of whether these are guided by virtuous habituation or adherence to overarching principles, rather than with moral and ethical theory. I also take comfort from Colnerud's argument in relation to teacher ethics as a research problem that, "a synthesis of ethics of virtue and ethics of principles might in this case be seen as a way to create a dialogue between the two viewpoints as complementary instead of conflicting positions" (Colnerud, 2006, p. 372).

The second key theoretical orientation informing this chapter concentrates on the intentions and behaviors of teachers, as expressive of their ethical knowledge, rather than on the impact their style and conduct have on students' moral growth and development. As an issue of teacher professionalism, the focus on ethical knowledge revolves around what teachers do or fail to do and why rather than on what students learn from their experience. Obviously, the latter is not inconsequential, and the separation between what teachers do and say and what students take from their actions in terms of moral messages is not so neat. Nonetheless, for the purposes here, the gauge of one's ethical knowledge as a professional imperative prioritizes transmitted virtue in action and intention, not the received impact. This may be just as well given the ambiguity of any relational connection between the teacher's moral character and the student's moral development (Osguthorpe, 2008). As Hansen clarified in his investigation of the moral impact on students that teachers have, by virtue of their style and character, it is doubtful "whether a teacher's moral influence can ever be verified. Such influence may not be a matter of cause and effect in any direct manner, and so may not be measurable in the familiar meaning of that term" (Hansen, 1993a, p. 418). Ultimately, this chapter is considerably less concerned with the philosophical question, "Can virtue be taught?" than with the professional question, "How can teachers conduct their work in schools virtuously?" One may note that this chapter's title is "Teaching Ethically," and not "Teaching Ethics."

The third and last orientation is based on the premise that ethical knowledge is the domain of responsible and professionally accountable individual teachers, working both independently and collectively, rather than the expression of organizational structures, institutional influences, systemic realities, and other forces beyond the control of the individual practitioner. This is not to deny the obvious point that teachers work within systems and administrative structures, and that contextual elements have an evident influence on their daily working lives. Nonetheless, such realities should not obscure the moral responsibility of individuals for their own professional conduct and replace it with a kind of organizational culpability so sharply criticized by Sommers (1984) as the ideology that shifted the traditional "seat of moral responsibility" (p. 387) from being a matter of an individual's personal virtue to society and its various institutions.

When people reminisce about their school days, in both positive and negative respects, they invariably recall, in terms that say much about human character, individual teachers who touched their lives, for better or worse, rather than referencing overall school policies, norms, and systemic forces. In one study, in which students were asked about the strengths and weaknesses of their schools, they uniformly based their answers on their teachers (Weissbourd, 2003). And, as Hansen (2001) reminds us, "Character has to do with how the person [of the teacher] regards and treats others" (p. 29). Similarly, others have concluded that the character of the individual teacher is central to the moral nature of education (Carr, 2000; Higgins, 2011; Luckowski, 1997; Sockett, 2012; Wynne & Ryan, 1997). Ethical knowledge is rooted in the individual teacher's moral sensibility and character, and augmented through experience by communities of professionals sharing and refining this virtue based knowledge as it is reflected daily in schools.

ETHICAL KNOWLEDGE AS THE FOUNDATION OF TEACHER PROFESSIONALISM

The teacher's moral agency is an inevitable state of being that is revealed whenever the teacher, as a moral person, conducts him or herself in schools with honesty, a sense of fairness, integrity, compassion, patience, respect, impartiality, care, dedication, and other such core virtues. It is also demonstrated when the teacher, as a moral educator, encourages students to appreciate such similar virtues and to conduct themselves in ways that honor them. Teachers may reflect this dual concept of moral agency formally or informally, consciously and intentionally or not, and frequently or rarely.

By extension, ethical knowledge is quite simply the heightened awareness that teachers—some more than others—have of their moral agent state of being. It is the focused and self-conscious recognition of how moral agency influences their daily actions and interactions, and it compels their deliberate attentiveness to ensure that these influences are experienced positively in a moral and ethical sense. As Buzzelli and Johnston (2002) explain in their description of the teacher as a moral agent,

> In this view, teaching is an activity involving a deep awareness of the significance of one's choices and how those choices influence the development and well-being of others. An awareness of the moral significance of one's work enlarges the understanding of that work.
>
> (p. 120)

This level of awareness is cultivated when teachers develop the capacity to identify how moral and ethical values and principles are either exemplified or undermined by their own actions, words, choices, and intentions. Such connections are made intellectually, emotionally, intuitively, philosophically, practically, and experientially as teachers engage in individual reflection and collective discussion with peers about the work they do daily. The concept of ethical knowledge assumes, as many sources from the scholarly literature confirm, that teaching is a moral profession with inherently ethical dimensions embedded in its practice and intent (Buzzelli & Johnston, 2002; Campbell, 2003; Colnerud, 1997, 2006; Goodman & Lesnick, 2004; Haynes, 1998; Hostetler, 1997; Huebner, 1996; Jackson et al., 1993; MacMillan, 1993; Richardson & Fenstermacher, 2001; Sanger, 2001; Simon, 2001; Sockett, 1993; Stengel & Tom, 1995; Strike, 1995; Tirri & Husu, 2002).

Ethical knowledge, albeit incomplete and ever evolving, based on the dynamics of new and unpredictable experiences, "illustrates teachers' devotion to living through their actions essential moral and ethical principles descriptive of a human legacy in all its complexities and apparent contradictions" (Campbell, 2003, p. 138). Thus, on one hand, ethical knowledge is honed within school climates rife with dilemmas and tensions as teachers, like anyone else, interpret and prioritize core moral values and principles in divergent ways. They make intuitive decisions based on what Strike (1999) would characterize as "moral pluralism" in ways that are both conflicting and compatible along a wide spectrum of moral goods. And, as Sirotnik (1990) reminds us, in his defense of moral imperatives, "An anti-relativist position, however, does not automatically resolve fundamental questions, dilemmas, and issues" (p. 320). On the other hand, ethical knowledge, while rooted in an individual's sensibility and experience, is also, I would argue, an expression of applied professional ethics in teaching (Carr, 2000; Lovat, 1998; Nash, 1996; Schwartz, 1998; Sockett & LePage, 2002; Strike & Ternasky, 1993), and should ultimately embody a sense of collective professionalism, not individual subjectivity. And, as I have stated before, the extensive knowledge of some teachers, who are quite aware of and attentive to the moral and ethical elements of their practice, is "usable, sharable, and learnable" (Campbell, 2003, p. 139) in ways that may enable more teachers, who may be less aware, to develop it. As a body of knowledge, then, it can form the foundation of renewed professionalism in teaching in a sense that is unique among the professions (Campbell, 2004).

For those who study professional ethics in teaching as well as other disciplines, be it from an applied philosophical perspective (Nash, 1996; Strike & Ternasky, 1993) or a psychology based orientation (Rest & Narvaez, 1994), some level of agreement on relevant ethical positions is a given, whether they are grounded in general core virtues or on related principles associated with the specifics of the profession, or, most likely, on both (MacMillan, 1993; Thompson, 1997). However, unlike in medicine or law, where the ethical principles are applied to the practice of the dominant professional knowledge base, in teaching the professional knowledge base is the ethical knowledge base. It is far more challenging to disentangle the ethics of teaching from the very process, practice, and intent of teaching as "the teacher's conduct, at all times and in all ways, is a moral matter" (Fenstermacher, 1990, p. 133). As Carr (1993) claims,

> The knowledge and understanding which should properly inform the professional consciousness of the competent teacher is … a kind of moral wisdom or judgement which is rooted in rational reflection about educational policies and practices and what is *ethically* [author's emphasis], as well as instrumentally, appropriate to achieve them.
>
> (p. 265)

This ethical judgment is called on every time a teacher strives to balance the fair treatment of an individual student with the fair treatment of the class group, or when the teacher chooses curricular materials and pedagogical strategies with care and sensitivity, or when evaluation is conducted with scrupulous honesty accompanied by a concern for the emotional well being of students, or when kindness tempers discipline. While mastery of subject matter, proficiency in classroom management techniques, skilled understanding of pedagogy, and a comprehensive grasp of evaluation and assessment strategies are integral elements of the competent teacher's repertoire, it is the practical moral wisdom—the ethical knowledge—that is infused into every aspect of such technical abilities and the humanity teachers bring to their practice that distinguish them as professionals.

Furthermore, education as an ethical profession and a "thoroughly moral business" (Sockett, 1996 p. 124), is unique by virtue of the exceptional vulnerability and dependence of the primary "clients"—other people's children—in addition to their non-voluntary presence in schools (Bull, 1993; Colnerud, 2006; Goodlad et al., 1990). As well as having a significant fiduciary duty represented by the public trust in them, teachers are also considered moral exemplars and educators, implicitly and explicitly, and therefore must be concerned with the educative enrichment in ethical terms of their pupils in ways that other professionals need not be.

Ironically, despite its distinctive moral nature as a profession, many have observed that education lacks an "ethical language" (Strike, 1995, p. 33) or a "moral language" that could help teachers recognize, articulate, and communicate with other teachers about the moral and ethical complexities of their work (Colnerud, 2006; Sockett & LePage, 2002). Despite supporting the belief that most teachers generally try to be seriously committed to the well being of students and act with intuitively good judgment, Sockett and LePage (2002) address the lamentable state in the profession due to this lack of a moral vocabulary. They propose in its absence that teachers need a kind of "moral case law" (p. 170) to provide a base for making confident ethical judgments that transcend mere intuition.

Ethical knowledge has its origins in moral sensibility and intuitive perspectives on right and wrong; however, as it intersects with a deliberative awareness of one's own practice, as well as that of others, it moves into the realm of practical moral wisdom (Carr, 2000; Higgins, 2011; Sockett, 2012), a kind of professional virtue-in-action that could resemble moral case law. To be clear, this is quite distinct from formalized ethical codes and standards that idealize principles and virtues, rather than illuminate how they pertain to daily professional life, or focus so narrowly on legal and contractual issues that any moral emphasis is obscured. Traditionally, such adjectives as "platitudinous and perfunctory" (Strike & Ternasky, 1993, p. 2) have been leveled at ethical codes. While they may provide worthwhile inspiration to teachers by their very existence (Beckner, 2004; Campbell, 2000; Freeman, 1998), codes have not been regarded as an effective vehicle to enhance ethical practice or deepen the profession's appreciation of the moral nuances of the role (Campbell, 2000, 2001; Sergiovanni, 1992). Ethical knowledge, not ethical codes, best captures the essence of professionalism in teaching as it enables teachers to appreciate the complexities of their moral agency.

ETHICAL PRACTICE AS A PROFESSIONAL IMPERATIVE

The previous section introduced the notion of moral agency in teaching as the defining characteristic of the role of the teacher. It is the teacher's astute awareness of the nuances and moral complexities of this role and how they are embedded in practice that measures his or her ethical knowledge. It further proposed that this ethical knowledge, as a kind of applied professional ethics, has the potential to provide the knowledge base in teaching to define its professionalism. This section focuses on practices in teaching that exemplify moral agency, first, by depicting them as being rooted in virtues and principles and, second, by presenting an argument against what I judge to be the co-opting of moral agency on the basis of politics, not principles.

Reflecting Moral Agency as Daily Action

Integral to the moral and ethical nature of teaching and schooling is the role of the teacher as a moral agent and moral exemplar (Fenstermacher, 2001; Hansen, 1993b, 2001; Katz, Noddings, & Strike, 1999; Sizer & Sizer, 1999). Closely associated with this role is the teacher's inevitable capacity to be a moral educator (Berkowitz, 2000; Campbell, 1997; Goodman & Lesnick, 2004; Lickona, 1991, 2004; McCadden, 1998; Nash, 1997; Noddings, 2002; Nucci, 2001; Ryan & Bohlin, 1999; Sanger & Osguthorpe, 2005; Wynne & Ryan, 1997). Moral agency is a dual state that encompasses the teacher as a moral person engaged in ethical professional conduct and as a moral educator who teaches to students the same core virtues and principles that he or she strives to uphold in practice. The connection between these two aspects of moral agency is evident as teachers live out through their actions, attitudes, and words the same virtues they hope to instill in their students. As one secondary school teacher explained,

> If I don't want kids to yell at me, then I have to make sure I don't yell at them. It's as simple as that. If I want them to care about each other, then I have to show care towards them; so, sometimes I do things for them. As a simple example, if a kid drops her pen, I'll get it for her. I don't say, 'Well, you dropped your pen, get it yourself.'
> (Campbell, 2003, p. 37)

It is the first characteristic of moral agency that enables the teacher to establish an ethical tone in the classroom that, by extension, models virtuous conduct and cultivates educative environments conducive to the purposes of the second characteristic, moral education (Goodman & Lesnick, 2004; Simon, 2001; Watson, 2003).

Hansen (1993b) wisely noted, "not everything that teachers do *necessarily* [author's emphasis] has moral significance, but any action a teacher takes *can* [author's emphasis] have moral import" (p. 669). In the terms of moral agency and ethical knowledge, what makes teachers' practices morally and ethically meaningful rests on whether core virtues and principles are evidently bound up in their intentions and actions. The ways in which these may be illustrated are as numerous as the teachers, students, and daily interactions in schools themselves. Perhaps they are reflected when a teacher exercises care in selecting and displaying student work, equitably allocating time, attention, privileges, and duties to students, organizing small work groups to ensure fairness to all, enforcing school and classroom rules with consistency, or when the teacher uses caution and wisdom in the choice of sensitive curricular resources or assesses student performance with honesty, fairness, and kindness. One can also hear ethical knowledge in the tone of a teacher's voice, the terms of politeness, respect, and warmth that are used, the distinction between sarcasm and humor, the refusal to embarrass or humiliate individual students in front of others, and the recognition that negative staffroom gossip about students and their families is not professional conduct. Ethical knowledge is also reflected each time a teacher consciously reminds, admonishes, corrects, and instructs students on how their behavior affects others. The teacher's effort to cultivate a civil and caring climate in the classroom represents more than an organizing strategy for an efficient community of learners—it represents a sense of moral agency and moral purpose.

Since the early 1990s, we have been introduced to a variety of teachers through significant classroom based empirical studies whose daily practices, conscious or not, reflect the moral dimensions of teaching (Campbell, 2003; Hansen, 1993a; Jackson et al., 1993; McCadden, 1998; Richardson & Fallona, 2001; Richardson & Fenstermacher, 2001; Sanger, 2001; Simon, 2001; Sockett, 1993). Invariably, these teachers are shown to be fair, caring, honest, respectful, and empathetic, among other virtues. Their actions support a well-reasoned argument that the two ethics of justice and care should temper each other and not act as opposite extremes (Colnerud, 2006; Katz et al., 1999). Fairness or justice, as "the first professional principle" (Bricker, 1989, p. 28) is revealed to be far more complex than one might imagine, as interpretations of what is just and fair differ in varying contexts between equal or differential treatment of students (Colnerud, 1997; Fallona, 2000; Nucci, 2001). These and other virtues are both exemplified and challenged in seemingly mundane decisions the teacher makes from calling on students to take turns answering questions during class and when to allow extensions on assignments to more serious dilemmas involving students who cheat, colleagues whose conduct is potentially harmful to students (Campbell, 1996; Colnerud, 1997; Tirri & Husu, 2002), or involving suspicions of child abuse.

Not surprisingly, teachers cannot be ever cognizant of the moral and ethical implications of everything they do in the course of a day. Teaching is enormously demanding, frequently frustrating, occasionally overwhelming, and always an eclectic mix of planned formality and spontaneous serendipity. And, as Buzzelli and Johnston (2002) point out, teachers do have "blind spots in [their] ability to perceive the moral in situations" (p. 125). Nevertheless, their actions transmit moral messages, and the students are watching, to borrow a phrase from Sizer and Sizer (1999). Consequently, the teacher's role as a moral exemplar and educator extends from this.

As stated at the beginning of the chapter, this discussion of moral agency and ethical knowledge centers on the conduct of the professional teacher rather than on assessing the moral growth of students. So, as moral exemplars and educators, what are teachers' intentions, aspirations, and actions? For one elementary teacher, her responsibilities as a moral educator were defined not only by the immediate need to foster a positive relational climate in her classroom, but also by a larger societal expectation. She explained:

> I see quite a bit of meanness among students, and I'm not going to tolerate it because we're two months into the school year now, and I think they should know right from wrong in a basic sense. Of course, you're going to get more complicated issues where naturally I'll help them through it, but they should know by now that if somebody drops something, you don't kick it. Also, when you keep disrupting you are disrespecting. You are telling the children around you that it doesn't matter to me that I'm stopping the whole class for attention or I'm stopping the whole class from their learning. What matters is that I want attention and I want it now. And, that's an ethical issue because students have to come to some understanding, maybe not at the moment, but eventually, that you can't function in a society like ours if you're constantly speaking out and you're not listening to others.
>
> (elementary school teacher in Campbell, 2003, p. 48)

This is reminiscent of Grant's (1996) claim, in her discussion of hand-raising and taking turns in class conversations, that "teachers are quite self-consciously teaching both verbal skills and social skills during this time. But these social skills require certain moral capacities and qualities of character" (p. 471). In the language of this chapter, teachers' "self-consciousness" of their moral instruction is indicative of their ethical knowledge. Similarly, one secondary school teacher explained her continuous efforts in the classroom to cultivate a sense of empathy for others, patience, tolerance, self-discipline, courage, personal responsibility, mutual respect, and honesty this way:

> I'm planting the seeds, and the seeds will at some point in time in their lives, they'll blossom. Maybe not right now; maybe one student out of the 28 may get it now. Who knows, but I'm optimistic, and if I can reinforce in them the right behaviour, at some point in their lives, they'll get it. They'll understand.
>
> (Campbell, 2003, p. 56)

Like many other teachers, these two were observed reinforcing good behavior by using combinations of the methods to foster moral conduct identified in Richardson and Fenstermacher's "Manner in Teaching Project": constructing classroom communities, didactic instruction, design and execution of academic tasks, calling out for particular conduct, private conversations, and showcasing specific students (Fenstermacher, 2001). Similarly, Jackson et al. (1993) empirically identified several categories of instruction in which moral education occurs both formally and informally, including official curricula, rituals and ceremonies, visual displays of moral content, spontaneous interjections or moral commentary, and rules and regulations. In a similar vein, Berkowitz (2000) includes in his list of "generic moral education" initiatives the promotion of a moral atmosphere, role modeling of good character, discussions of moral issues in class, and curriculum lessons in character. One of the most currently popular and referenced variants of moral education, which will be addressed further in the subsequent section, is "character education" (Lickona, 1991, 2004; Ryan, 1993; Ryan & Bohlin, 1999). Described as "the methodical and deliberate inculcation of moral virtues through a variety of planned lessons and exercises that usually involve a school-wide initiative" (Campbell, 2004, p. 35), character education is dependent entirely on the role of the teacher as a moral agent and exemplar.

The centrality of the teacher as a moral model and a moral educator is further highlighted by Narvaez and Lapsley (2008) in their account of two approaches for preparing pre-service teachers to be "morally adept" (p. 162) as character educators. Similar to Grant's (1996) acknowledgment of self-consciousness and the definition of "ethical knowledge" (Campbell, 2003) as the intentional awareness and conceptualization of ethical values as they permeate professional practice, Narvaez and Lapsley argue that effective moral education requires the conscious and deliberate cultivation of student character that transcends the mere reflection of best practice instruction. In their support of a "maximalist strategy" (p. 156), which advances a five-step framework for developing a "novice-to-expert approach" to skills acquisition, they remind us that, "as in any domain, moral character skills must be practiced in order to be developed. Teachers must be oriented to providing good practice opportunities for students" (Narvaez & Lapsley, 2008, p. 167). They further conclude, "when teachers are intentional and wise in praxis, they provide students with a deliberative, positive influence on their individual and group characters" (p. 169). Qualities of ethical intentionality and, in Aristotelian terms, practical wisdom are at the core of professional teachers' ethical knowledge—their responsible appreciation of the potency of their own moral agency.

Moral agency, as it is discussed in this chapter, is an inevitable result of the teacher's role and professional responsibilities. It is expressed and revealed in the daily practice of teachers who model, self-regulate, instruct, relate, admonish, and engage. It is the illumination of virtues and moral and ethical principles as they are woven through the intricacies of school and classroom life.

Politicizing Moral Agency as Ideological Activism

This chapter frames the discussion of moral agency in terms of the core virtues and ethical principles teachers personally exude or apply to their practice and, similarly, those they teach to students. It is reflective of a legacy of moral education that is historically, philosophically, and professionally defensible. By contrast, there is a significant conceptual distinction between this interpretation of moral agency as a natural extension of what ethical teachers do on a daily basis and some more contemporary trends towards the promotion of political and ideological agenda disguised as moral education and justified by teachers who corrupt their professional role as moral agents to inculcate such agenda in the classroom. Admittedly, this part of the chapter will be the most argumentative and, to some, contentious. However, it is also central to its conceptual foundation of which an underlying assumption is that moral agency, as well as the ethical knowledge teachers cultivate as a result of their awareness of their agency, is about generalized moral and ethical values relating to how human beings should treat one another (e.g., kindly, fairly, truthfully). This is quite distinct from partisan causes deemed to be moral by some because of a political based, rather than a virtue based, conviction or affiliation. By extension, the purpose of moral education is to develop ethical individuals who appreciate the demands of living in a free civil society, who develop empathy for others and a commitment to personal responsibility for one's individual actions. This is in stark contrast to the cultivation of students as moralistic social activists bent on enforcing their political will on others regarding controversial social issues that have not been fully debated, decided, or ultimately accepted within society.

There are many different approaches to teaching that satisfy the mandates of professionalism by honoring the moral agency role of teachers. There are others that, according to the argument explored here, have the potential to "cross the line" beyond professional virtue into the murky domain of indoctrination. This discussion addresses three broad conceptualizations of moral education: character education (Lickona, 1991, 2004; Murphy, 1998; Ryan & Bohlin, 1999; Wynne & Ryan, 1997) and its critics (Kohn, 1997; Nash, 1997), caring as moral education (Noddings, 2002), and social justice/critical democratic orientations (Beyer, 1997). The comparison will not be exhaustive; however, it will focus on the teacher as a moral agent and exemplar. It concludes that while the first two approaches have the potential to lead to the politicization of the classroom, they need not necessarily do so. On the other hand, the third approach, by its own definition and intention most deliberatively politicizes moral agency.

Character education, as the formalized and direct method of instruction in virtues and principles of moral conduct (Lickona, 2004; Wiley, 1998), has been both championed and criticized more than any other approach to moral education in recent years. Grounded in a repudiation of moral relativism and in a philosophical and historical legacy of support for core virtues and universal moral values, its conceptual basis shares much with this chapter's orientation to ethical knowledge. For many, character education is a natural extension of what teachers, as moral agents, do as part of the inevitable function of their role—helping to socialize children to become virtuous individuals capable of living in a society where principles such as honesty, fairness, kindness, respect, tolerance, integrity, and responsibility are widely valued and reflected in the social norms and legal foundations of the society. Studies have concluded that, in this respect, teachers do not necessarily see character education as controversial or politically motivated, but rather view it as a very significant aspect of their professional responsibilities (Jones, Ryan, & Bohlin, 1998; Leming & Yendol-Hoppey, 2004; Mathison, 1998). As these studies note, teachers may differ on their interpretation of what character education means as a pedagogical approach, but they generally do not question the underlying importance of reinforcing good moral values that transcend normative social or cultural differences among us and instead nurture a positive sense of our collective humanity. As one study noted, the "days of value neutrality are over" (Jones et al., 1998, p. 14).

While generally supportive of the theoretical essence of character education, some critics thoughtfully question its methods as a formal program. They focus on aspects of those programs that emphasize extrinsic rewards for good behavior, drill, and unreflective or simplistic acceptance of moral precepts, or use what are seen to be gimmicky and contrived strategies to inculcate virtues, and they regard such elements as indefensible not only in a moral sense but also in a pedagogical one. However, even among such critics, there are those who would not dispute the importance of good moral values (Berkowitz, 1998; Nash, 1997; Noddings, 2002). In this respect, Sockett (1996) has referred to himself as a "sympathetic critic" (p. 124), as has Noddings (2002). Similarly, even in their pointed criticism of character education, Joseph and Efron (2005) refer to its advocates' "good intentions" (p. 532).

Other critics are not at all sympathetic and vilify character education in political terms as a "right wing" attempt to indoctrinate children (Beyer, 1991, 1997; Kohn, 1997). Such critics, often but not exclusively writing from more radical perspectives of the ideological "left," question not simply the methods of character education but mostly the conceptual justification for the support of core virtues as well as the inherent implication that moral responsibility as well as negligence rest largely within the domain of individuals' actions and attitudes rather than in societal structures, systems, and economies. Fundamental differences in perspectives along broad political and ideological lines between these critics and those who support various philosophies of character education have been well documented by, among others, McClellan (1999), Nash (1997), and Smagorinsky and Taxel (2005).

In contrast to such critics, the conceptual basis of this chapter's discussion of moral agency and ethical knowledge in teaching is consistent with the virtues and principles advanced by the character educators, even though it agrees with previously mentioned criticism of some of their instructional methods. Not surprisingly, this line of argument views accusations against character education as a form of political indoctrination to be overstated and arguable. Of course, character educators can politicize the public school classroom just as any other teacher can; and, if modeling and instruction in the virtues lapse instead into one-sided polemics about specific political, cultural, or religious beliefs and causes—for example, pro-life stances and creationism—then the line separating moral agency and ideological activism has been crossed. However, such political motivations do not define character education. A respect for good moral values that have wide support in the mainstream population and are the bedrock of the norms and laws of civil society is what defines it as a kind of moral education inseparable from the teacher's role as moral agent, model, exemplar, and educator.

As mentioned, there are those who share the character educators' non-relativist support for moral values, such as honesty and care, yet believe that they should be explored in a more nuanced sense and "problematized" in the classroom in ways that acknowledge differing and often conflicting contexts and controversies (Noddings, 2002; Simon, 2001; Sockett, 1996). They refer to the cultivation of "caring communities" (Joseph & Efron, 2005) as an alternative approach to moral education that, while contextualizing moral values more than character education does, still similarly emphasizes mutually supportive relationships, respectful and safe discourse, and fair and inclusive interactions. However, as with character education, the priority is on reinforcing morally positive values that enable empathy and responsibility to flourish within school and classroom based communities, and the role of the teacher as a moral agent is central. While politicization of this approach by means of "sermonizing" (Simon, 2001, p. 206) is certainly possible, as it is in character education, it is not its primary intention.

In contrast, the third broad approach to a more obviously politicized version of moral education changes the teacher's professional role from moral agent to social activist. Advocates of this approach are among the harshest critics of character education, and their orientation to moral education is not that its purpose is to cultivate among individuals a dedication to core virtues and moral principles, but rather to engage students in the critical examination of such principles and more importantly of society's authority structures, systems, norms, and practices. Critics of this approach assert that it "fails as an ethical enterprise" (Grant, 1996, p. 472) for its potential to foster moral relativism, dogmatism, and partisanship in the classroom. Its focus is on "ideology and doctrine rather than on personal responsibility and practical decency" (Sommers, 1984, p. 388).

Ideologically reflective of the political left, this broad approach encompasses a range of curricular orientations such as those frequently aligned with issues of equity and social justice (not to be confused with neo-classical virtue theory based equality and justice), critical theory, anti-discriminatory pedagogy, liberationist perspectives, anti-racist and multicultural education, and critical democratic education (Adams, Bell, & Griffin, 2006; Ayers, 2004; Ayers, Quinn, & Stovall, 2009; Chapman & Hobbel, 2010; Slattery & Rapp, 2003). As a term used by many in education, "social justice" has worked its way into the mainstream discourse and is often indistinguishable as a political concept from character educators' and others' virtue based discussions about the need for all students, regardless of differences, to be treated fairly, kindly, with respect and dignity, and so on. Nonetheless, its modern roots lie, at least dominantly, within the political realm of Marxist as well as more general socialist theory and reflect a central emphasis on societal and material inequities (Koschoreck, 2006). In their defense of the ethic of critique (Starratt, 1994), based on critical theory and social justice, Shapiro and Stefkovich (2005) define its origins in "modified Marxian analysis," "Freirian critical pedagogy that views classrooms as political and not only educational locations," (pp. 14–15), and they connect it closely to the call for political activism on the part of educators.

While advocates of this conceptualization tend not to use the language of virtue or moral and civic dispositions (Nash, 1997), they often represent their critique as a moral or ethical stance, and such critique can take many forms in the classroom. For example, in their comprehensive presentation of "seven worlds of moral education," Joseph and Efron (2005) identify three alternatives to character education that clearly emanate from this perspective. First, they describe the "cultural heritage" world that promotes the teaching of "non-mainstream" values from "non-dominant cultures"; ironically, some of the moral values referenced such as "respect for one another," and "empathy" are not unlike the virtues hailed by the character educators.

Second, the article introduces "peace education" that extends the idea of a caring community beyond the classroom, politicizes it along the lines of partisan causes representing varying interests from environmental education, global education, human rights and animal rights activism to peace studies and conflict resolution. Even the authors, who are not opposed to this alternative, note that it is difficult to implement in public schools because of its "potential for conflict with community values" prevalent in mainstream society (Joseph & Efron, 2005, p. 529).

Third, the article identifies "social action" as a desirable form of moral education that focuses on the political nature of society as a whole, challenges examples of perceived privilege and oppression, and works towards the goal of effecting critical social change. By way of example, we are told of a grade 5 History class in Colorado studying the US Civil War and slavery. In order to make "students learn to view themselves as social and political beings" (p. 530), the teachers engaged them in an activity to raise awareness of slavery in the Sudan. "The children raised money to buy freedom for a few slaves … donations came in from around the world, and the class eventually purchased the freedom of more than 1,000 people" (Joseph & Efron, 2005, p. 530). For those of us who view the teacher's moral agency as rooted in the exercising and exemplifying of virtue and ethical principles rather than the crusading for political causes, such an example of "moral education" seems quite appalling. By tugging on the heartstrings of young children, this initiative essentially helps to sustain rather than disrupt the virulent slave trade by playing by its own terms (purchasing freedom) as if they are somehow morally justifiable or expedient rather than abhorrent, and probably did little more for the students than give them a self-satisfied sense of moral righteousness.

Others have addressed ideologically similar social action initiatives that reflect what Berkowitz (1998) has identified approvingly as a "much more expanded interpretation of character education than once conceptualized" (p. 2). Indeed, one may argue that such a redefinition of the term, "character education," not simply expands its scope to include a highly diffuse range of activities, but also, more significantly, redirects its conceptual orientation into a different ideological arena. For example, Donahue (1999) advocates the use of "change-oriented service-learning" in schools as a way for teachers to "challenge social, political, economic structures that allow injustice" (p. 687). Politically motivated and activist in intention, this orientation to service learning is quite distinct from other forms that some character educators support that tend instead to emphasize philanthropy, caring, the cultivation of empathy and other virtues in students, and social responsibility as opposed to social transformation. As Donahue notes, "a teacher's intention behind assigning such a task shapes the way students reflect on the service, directing their learning toward one orientation or the other" (p. 688). He acknowledges the ethical dilemmas confronting teachers who differ over these two quite different orientations to a form of moral education. He favors the social transformation approach and recommends its introduction in pre-service teacher education as a way to prepare future teachers to understand the moral imperatives of their profession (p. 685).

Such a perspective resonates with the work of Beyer (1997) that, like Donahue, promotes the political, cultural, and social contextualization of moral issues within teacher education programs as a way to enable teachers to raise critical questions about schooling and current teaching practices. Beyer applauds the student teacher who has her pupils "critique their own texts" (p. 249) in the search for historical prejudices, and another teacher who represented to her grade 4 students a school rule about silence in the hallways as a political power struggle with an authoritarian school administration rather than a policy designed to respect other classrooms and guard against their disruption. To the teacher, and to Beyer, the rule is seen as politically based, not virtue based, and the moral lesson is to question authority, not to learn about the virtues of respect and consideration for others.

Such examples of "teaching against the grain" (Joseph, 2003, p. 12) represent the moral agency of teachers as deeply connected to wider social and political causes that are invariably controversial in the public sphere (Nord, 2001) and rarely evoke the language of professional *virtue* that is representative of moral agency and ethical knowledge as discussed in this chapter. Hansen (2001) notes that the "big ideals" about social betterment may motivate teachers in ways that are not necessarily bad. However, he also cautions that, "Ideals can become ideological or doctrinaire and can lead teachers away from their educational obligations and cause them to treat their students as a means to an end, whether the latter be political, social, or whatever" (p. 188). In my own critique of social justice education as a potential vehicle of indoctrination (Campbell, 2013), I argue that an emphasis on social justice, so ubiquitous as a curricular priority of contemporary teacher education, distracts teachers from appreciating their moral agency; it redirects their attention away from the conceptualization of practice in clear moral and ethical ways, more representative of the research literature that has documented what Osguthorpe (2008) refers to as "teaching morally" and "teaching morality."

Ethical teachers should be moral agents and moral models, not moralistic activists. Their professional responsibility in this moral sense is an immediate and direct one that honors the public's trust in them and does not stray beyond the boundaries of their mandate. It is simply to hold themselves accountable for how they treat the students in their care and how they cultivate for them schooling experiences and relationships based on time-honored virtues such as fairness, honesty, integrity, civility, compassion, constancy, and responsibility, that are reflected in the best of societal values, norms, and laws and that parallel most parents' reasonable expectations of public schooling. When teachers come to believe that the ethics of their profession relate more to how they can serve wider political agenda as social reconstructionists than to how they should monitor their daily practice and duties to their own students, their moral agency is compromised, and the prospect for the development of a virtue based professional ethics expressive of ethical knowledge in teaching is threatened.

In conclusion, moral agency may be broadly conceived in terms of not only what teachers teach students by direct curricular means, but also more significantly what teachers do themselves as ethical professionals in classrooms and the virtues and moral principles they reflect and, hence, model to students on a daily basis. As Nash (2005) claims:

> The place we call school is an environment of moral interaction and sometimes moral struggle. Children's ability to expand moral sensitivity and ethical reasoning skills will very much depend upon how adults around them model ethical behavior and ethical reasoning. Essentially, a teacher's conduct, at all times and in all ways, is a moral matter.
>
> (p. 4)

While the emphasis of this chapter has been on the teacher's conduct rather than the students' moral growth, the point to be stressed is that teachers are answerable, individually and collectively, for the choices they make in the classroom, the motivations that drive them, the actions they take, and the words they use, regardless of whether the direct effect they may or may not have on students can be empirically proven. As a matter of professionalism, the measure of ethical teaching relies on the intentions of teachers, as much as on their influence. Their awareness of such intentions and their deliberative attention to the specificities of their daily practice, as filtered through the lens of virtues and moral principles, attest to their ethical knowledge. And, ultimately, it is this ethical knowledge that is a defining characteristic of professionalism in teaching.

REFERENCES

Adams, M., Bell, L.A., & Griffin, P. (2006). *Teaching for Diversity and Social Justice, Second Edition*. London and New York: Routledge.

Ayers, W. (2004). *Teaching the Personal and the Political: Essays on Hope and Justice*. New York: Teachers College Press.

Ayers, W., Quinn, T., & Stovall, D. (2009). *Handbook of Social Justice in Education*. New York: Routledge.

Beckner, W. (2004). *Ethics for Educational Leaders*. Boston: Pearson.

Bergem, T. (1993). Examining aspects of professional morality, *Journal of Moral Education, 22*(3), 297–312.

Berkowitz, M.W. (1998). Obstacles to teacher training in character education, *Action in Teacher Education, 20*(4), 1–10.

Berkowitz, M.W. (2000). Civics and moral education, in B. Moon, S. Brown, & M. Ben-Peretz (Eds.), *Routledge International Companion to Education*, pp. 897–909. New York: Routledge.

Beyer, L.E. (1991). Schooling, moral commitment, and the preparation of teachers, *Journal of Teacher Education, 42*(3), 205–215.

Beyer, L.E. (1997). The moral contours of teacher education, *Journal of Teacher Education, 48*(4), 245–254.

Bricker, D.C. (1989). *Classroom Life as Civic Education: Individual Achievement and Student Cooperation in Schools*. New York: Teachers College Press.

Bull, B. (1993). Ethics in the preservice curriculum, in K.A. Strike & P.L. Ternasky (Eds.), *Ethics for Professionals in Education: Perspectives for Preparation and Practice*, pp. 69–83. New York: Teachers College Press.

Buzzelli, C.A., & Johnston, B. (2002). *The Moral Dimensions of Teaching: Language, Power, and Culture in Classroom Interaction*. New York and London: Routledge Falmer.

Campbell, E. (1996). Ethical implications of collegial loyalty as one view of teacher professionalism, *Teachers and Teaching: Theory and Practice, 2*(2), 191–208.

Campbell, E. (1997). Connecting the ethics of teaching and moral education, *Journal of Teacher Education, 48*(4), 255–263.

Campbell, E. (2000). Professional ethics in teaching: towards the development of a code of practice, *Cambridge Journal of Education, 30*(2), 203–221.

Campbell, E. (2001). Let right be done: trying to put ethical standards into practice, *Journal of Educational Policy, 16*(5), 395–411.

Campbell, E. (2003). *The Ethical Teacher*. Maidenhead, UK: Open University Press/ McGraw-Hill.

Campbell, E. (2004). Ethical knowledge and moral agency as the essence of applied professional ethics in teaching, *Professional Studies Review: An Interdisciplinary Journal, 1*(1), 29–38.

Campbell, E. (2013). Ethical teaching and the social justice distraction, in H. Sockett & R. Boostrom (Eds.), *A Moral Critique of Contemporary Education: National Society for the Study of Education Yearbook, 112*(1), 216–237. New York: Teachers College Press.

Carr, D. (1993). Questions of competence, *British Journal of Educational Studies, 41*(3), 253–271.

Carr, D. (2000). *Professionalism and Ethics in Teaching*. London: Routledge.

Chapman, T. K., & Hobbel, N. (2010). *Social Justice Pedagogy across the Curriculum: The Practice of Freedom*. New York: Routledge.

Clark, C.M. (1990). The teacher and the taught: moral transactions in the classroom, in J.I. Goodlad, R. Soder, & K.A. Sirotnik (Eds.), *The Moral Dimensions of Teaching*, pp. 251–265. San Francisco: Jossey-Bass.

Colnerud, G. (1997). Ethical conflicts in teaching, *Teaching and Teacher Education, 13*(6), 627–635.

Colnerud, G. (2006). Teacher ethics as a research problem: syntheses achieved and new issues, *Teachers and Teaching: Theory and Practice, 12*(3), 365–385.

Donahue, D.M. (1999). Service-learning for preservice teachers: ethical dilemmas for practice, *Teaching and Teacher Education, 15*, 685–695.

Fallona, C. (2000). Manner in teaching: a study in observing and interpreting teachers' moral virtues, *Teaching and Teacher Education, 16*, 681–695.

Fenstermacher, G.D. (1990). Some moral considerations on teaching as a profession, in J.I. Goodlad, R. Soder, & K.A. Sirotnik (Eds.), *The Moral Dimensions of Teaching*, pp. 130–151. San Francisco: Jossey-Bass.

Fenstermacher, G.D. (2001). On the concept of manner and its visibility in teaching practice, *The Journal of Curriculum Studies, 33*(6), 639–653.

Freeman, N.K. (1998). Morals and character: the foundations of ethics and professionalism, *The Educational Forum, 63*(1), 30–36.

Goodlad, J.I., Soder, R., & Sirotnik, K.A. (1990). *The Moral Dimensions of Teaching*. San Francisco: Jossey-Bass Publishers.

Goodman, J.F., & Lesnick, H. (2004). *Moral Education: A Teacher-Centered Approach*. Boston: Pearson Education, Inc.

Grant, R.W. (1996). The ethics of talk: classroom conversation and democratic politics, *Teachers College Record, 97*(Spring), 470–482.

Hansen, D.T. (1993a). The moral importance of the teacher's style, *Journal of Curriculum Studies, 25*(5), 397–421.

Hansen, D.T. (1993b). From role to person: the moral layeredness of classroom teaching, *American Educational Research Journal, 30*(4), 651–674.

Hansen, D.T. (2001). *Exploring the Moral Heart of Teaching: Towards a Teacher's Creed.* New York: Teachers College Press.

Haynes, F. (1998). *The Ethical School.* London: Routledge.

Higgins, C. (2011). *The Good Life of Teaching: An Ethics of Professional Practice.* Malden, MA: Wiley-Blackwell.

Hostetler, K.D. (1997). *Ethical Judgment in Teaching.* Boston: Allyn and Bacon.

Huebner, D. (1996). Teaching as a moral activity, *Journal of Curriculum and Supervision, 11*(3), 267–275.

Jackson, P.W., Boostrom, R.E., & Hansen, D.T. (1993). *The Moral Life of Schools.* San Francisco: Jossey-Bass.

Jones, E.N., Ryan, K., & Bohlin, K. (1998). Character education and teacher education: how are prospective teachers being prepared to foster good character in students?, *Action in Teacher Education, 20*(4), 11–28.

Joseph, P.B. (2003). Teaching about the moral classroom: infusing the moral imagination into teacher education, *Asia-Pacific Journal of Teacher Education, 31*(1), 7–20.

Joseph, P.B., & Efron, S. (2005). Seven worlds of moral education, *Phi Delta Kappan,* March, 525–533.

Katz, M.S., Noddings, N., & Strike, K.A. (1999). *Justice and Caring: The Search for Common Ground in Education.* New York: Teachers College Press.

Kohn, A. (1997). How not to teach values, *The Education Digest,* May, 12–17.

Koschoreck, J.W. (2006). Teaching social justice in educational leadership: an interview with James W. Koschoreck, interviewed by Gerardo R. López, *UCEA Review,* Summer, 10–11.

Leming, J.S., & Yendol-Hoppey, D. (2004). Experiencing character education: student and teacher voices, *Journal of Research in Character Education, 2*(1), 1–17.

Lickona, T. (1991). *Educating for Character: How our Schools can Teach Respect and Responsibility.* New York: Bantam Books.

Lickona, T. (2004). *Character Matters: How to Help our Children Develop Good Judgment, Integrity, and other Essential Virtues.* New York: Touchstone.

Lovat, T.J. (1998). Ethics and ethics education: professional and curricular best practice, *Curriculum Perspectives, 18*(1), 1–7.

Luckowski, J.A. (1997). A virtue-centered approach to ethics education, *Journal of Teacher Education, 48*(4), 264–270.

MacMillan, C.J.B. (1993). Ethics and teacher professionalism, in K.A. Strike & P.L. Ternasky (Eds.), *Ethics for Professionals in Education: Perspectives for Preparation and Practice,* pp. 189–201. New York: Teachers College Press.

Mathison, C. (1998). How teachers feel about character education: a descriptive study, *Action in Teacher Education, 20*(4), 29–38.

McCadden, B.M. (1998). *It's Hard to Be Good: Moral Complexity, Construction, and Connection in a Kindergarten Classroom.* New York: Peter Lang.

McClellan, E. (1999). *Moral Education in America: Schools and the Shaping of Character from Colonial Times to the Present.* New York: Teachers College Press.

Murphy, M.M. (1998). *Character Education in America's Blue Ribbon Schools: Best Practices for Meeting the Challenge.* Lancaster, PA: Technomic Publishing Company.

Narvaez, D., & Lapsley, D.K. (2008). Teaching moral character: two alternatives for teacher education, *The Teacher Educator, 43*(2), 156–172.

Nash, R.J. (1996). *"Real World" Ethics: Frameworks for Educators and Human Service Professionals.* New York: Teachers College Press.

Nash, R.J. (1997). *Answering the "VirtueCrats": A Moral Conversation on Character Education.* New York: Teachers College Press.

Nash, R.J. (2005). Foreword in B. Zubay & J.F. Soltis, *Creating the Ethical School: A Book of Case Studies.* New York: Teachers College Press.

Noddings, N. (2002). *Educating Moral People: A Caring Alternative to Character Education.* New York: Teachers College Press.

Nord, W.A. (2001). Moral disagreement, moral education, common ground, in D. Ravitch & J.P. Viteritti (Eds.), *Making Good Citizens: Education and Civil Society,* pp. 142–167. New Haven: Yale University Press.

Nucci, L.P. (2001). *Education in the Moral Domain.* Cambridge: Cambridge University Press.

Oser, F., & Althof, W. (1993). Trust in advance: on the professional morality of teachers, *Journal of Moral Education, 22*(3), 253–275.

Osguthorpe, R.D. (2008). On the reasons we want teachers of good disposition and moral character, *Journal of Teacher Education, 59*(4), 288–299.

Reitz, D.J. (1998). *Moral Crisis in the Schools: What Parents and Teachers Need to Know*. Baltimore, MD: Cathedral Foundation Press.

Rest, J.R., & Narvaez, D. (1994). *Moral Development in the Professions: Psychology and Applied Ethics*. Hillsdale, NJ: Lawrence Erlbaum Associates.

Richardson, V., & Fallona, C. (2001). Classroom management as method and manner, *Journal of Curriculum Studies, 33*(6), 705–728.

Richardson, V., & Fenstermacher, G.D. (2001). Manner in teaching: the study in four parts, *Journal of Curriculum Studies, 33*(6), 631–637.

Ryan, K. (1993). Why a center for the advancement of ethics and character? *Journal of Education, 175*(2), 1–11.

Ryan, K., & Bohlin, K.E. (1999). *Building Character in Schools: Practical Ways to Bring Moral Instruction to Life*. San Francisco: Jossey-Bass.

Sanger, M.G. (2001). Talking to teachers and looking at practice in understanding the moral dimensions of teaching, *The Journal of Curriculum Studies, 33*(6), 683–704.

Sanger, M.N., & Osguthorpe, R.D. (2005). Making sense of approaches to moral education, *Journal of Moral Education, 34*(1), 57–71.

Schwartz, G.E. (1998). Teaching as vocation: enabling ethical practice, *The Educational Forum, 63*(1), 23–29.

Sergiovanni, T.J. (1992). *Moral Leadership: Getting to the Heart of School Improvement*. San Francisco: Jossey-Bass.

Shapiro, J.P., & Stefkovich, J.A. (2005). *Ethical Leadership and Decision-Making in Education: Applying Theoretical Perspectives to Complex Dilemmas, Second Edition*. Mahwah, NJ: Lawrence Erlbaum Associates.

Simon, K.G. (2001). *Moral Questions in the Classroom*. New Haven and London: Yale University Press.

Sirotnik, K.A. (1990). Society, schooling, teaching, and preparing to teach, in J.I. Goodlad, R. Soder, & K.A. Sirotnik (Eds.), *The Moral Dimensions of Teaching*, pp. 296–327. San Francisco: Jossey-Bass.

Sizer, T.R., & Sizer, N.F. (1999). *The Students are Watching: Schools and the Moral Contract*. Boston: Beacon Press.

Slattery, P., & Rapp, D. (2003). *Ethics and the Foundations of Education: Teaching Convictions in a Postmodern World*. Boston: Pearson Education.

Smagorinsky, P., & Taxel, J. (2005). *The Discourse of Character Education: Culture Wars in the Classroom*. Mahwah, NJ: Lawrence Erlbaum Associates.

Sockett, H. (1993). *The Moral Base for Teacher Professionalism*. New York: Teachers College Press.

Sockett, H. (1996). Can virtue be taught?, *The Educational Forum, 60* (Winter), 124–129.

Sockett, H. (2012). *Knowledge and Virtue in Teaching and Learning: The Primacy of Dispositions*. New York: Routledge.

Sockett, H., & LePage, P. (2002). The missing language of the classroom, *Teaching and Teacher Education, 18*, 159–171.

Sommers, C.H. (1984). Ethics without virtue: moral education in America, *The American Scholar, 53*(3), 381–389.

Starratt, R.J. (1994). *Building an Ethical School: A Practical Response to the Moral Crisis in Schools*. London: The Falmer Press.

Stengel, B., & Tom, A. (1995). Taking the moral nature of teaching seriously, *The Educational Forum, 59*(2), 154–163.

Strike, K.A. (1995). Professional ethics and the education of professionals, *educational HORIZONS, 74*(1), 29–36.

Strike, K.A. (1999). Justice, caring, and universality: in defence of moral pluralism, in M.S. Katz, N. Noddings, & K.A. Strike (Eds.), *Justice and Caring: The Search for Common Ground in Education*, pp. 21–36. New York: Teachers College Press.

Strike, K.A., & Soltis, J.F. (1992). *The Ethics of Teaching, Second Edition*. New York: Teachers College Press.

Strike, K.A., & Ternasky, P.L. (1993). *Ethics for Professionals in Education: Perspectives for Preparation and Practice*. New York: Teachers College Press.

Thompson, M. (1997). *Professional Ethics and the Teacher: Towards a General Teaching Council*. Stoke on Trent, UK: Trentham Books.

Tirri, K., & J. Husu (2002). Care and responsibility in "the best interest of the child": relational voices of ethical dilemmas in teaching, *Teachers and Teaching: Theory and Practice, 8*(1), 65–80.

Tom, A.R. (1984). *Teaching as a Moral Craft*. New York: Longman.

Watson, M. (2003). *Learning to Trust*. San Francisco: Jossey-Bass.

Weissbourd, R. (2003). Moral teachers, moral students, *Educational Leadership, 60*(6), 6–11.

Wiley, L.S. (1998). *Comprehensive Character-building Classroom: A Handbook for Teachers*. DeBary, FL: Longwood Communications.

Wynne, E.A., & Ryan, K. (1997). *Reclaiming Our Schools: Teaching Character, Academics, and Discipline, Second Edition*. Upper Saddle River, NJ: Prentice Hall.

Part II
Theory-Based Approaches to Moral and Character Education

8

SOCIAL COGNITIVE DOMAIN THEORY AND MORAL EDUCATION

Larry Nucci and Deborah W. Powers

What is morality in any given time or place? It is what the majority then and there happen to like and immorality is what they dislike.

Alfred North Whitehead

The above quotation by Alfred North Whitehead sardonically expresses the conventional view of morality that has tacitly guided traditional approaches to character education dating back to the seminal work of Emil Durkheim (1925/1961). This conception of morality carries with it an implicit theory of socialization that places morality outside of the child and calls upon agents of socialization such as parents and teachers to imbue the child with "moral values" through role modeling, emotional attachment to groups, and appropriate uses of rewards and consequences. While this inculcation perspective has a long history and continues to have advocates (see Arthur, this volume), it sits in direct contrast with current understandings of educational processes in virtually every academic subject area from reading (Shanahan, 2000) to mathematics (Saxe et al., 2010; Schoenfeld, 1994). Contemporary research-based accounts of learning view the child as an active interpreter of information and general experience, and researchers and many educational practitioners advocate constructivist approaches to teaching. Ironically then, proponents of traditional character education are advising teachers to ignore educational research and engage in practices that contradict methods of teaching that they employ with every other aspect of instruction.

In addition to being at odds with contemporary educational practices, the traditionalist reduction of morality to the acquisition of the norms and conventions of society mischaracterizes morality and the process of moral development. In this chapter, we will present an alternative account of moral development and moral education, referred to as *social cognitive domain theory* (Smetana, in press) that draws a distinction between morality and matters of societal convention and personal choice. Following an overview of basic theory and research, we will describe how domain theory can be applied to educational practice.

DOMAIN THEORY
Morality and Social Convention

Domain theory maintains that social knowledge is constructed within basic conceptual frameworks to account for qualitatively differing aspects of social and psychological experience (Turiel, 1983). Individuals' concepts and judgments about morality center on actions that have an impact upon the welfare of others. Morality is structured by underlying conceptualizations of justice, welfare, and rights (Turiel, 1983, 2002). Morality is distinguished from societal conventions, which are the consensually defined norms of conduct that regulate the social interactions of members within a particular social group. Concepts and judgments about social conventions (e.g., addressing teachers by titles such as Mr. or Mrs.) are structured by underlying understandings of the role of social norms in lending predictability and coordination to social interaction and the structuring social organization (Turiel, 1983, 2002). A basic premise of domain theory is that our understandings of morality and convention form distinct conceptual systems throughout development (Smetana, in press).

The positions taken by domain theory contradict the assumptions of moral development maintained by Piaget (1932) and Kohlberg (1984), for whom moral development entails a progressive differentiation of morality (fairness) out of earlier stages in which morality is defined by social norms and authority. According to these earlier theories, morality supersedes and operates independently of convention only at the more advanced stages of moral autonomy (Piaget, 1932) or post-conventional thinking (Kohlberg, 1984). Numerous studies, however, conducted in a wide range of cultural contexts over the past 35 years have provided evidence that children as young as two-and-a-half years old (Smetana & Braeges, 1990) and adults maintain conceptual distinctions between issues of morality and societal convention (Smetana, in press; Turiel, 2002).

Studies have also examined whether the distinction between morality and convention extends to reasoning about religious norms (Nucci, 1985; Nucci & Turiel, 1993). In those studies, Christian and Jewish children were asked whether actions considered wrong within their religious traditions would be all right if scripture had not included information that God had an objection to the act. Findings from this research revealed that nearly all of the children and adolescents interviewed felt religious restrictions that are similar to secular conventions would be all right if there were no religious rules or biblical injunctions regulating the acts. These actions included such things as working on the Sabbath, a woman leading worship services, Catholic priests marrying, or not wearing head coverings during worship. On the other hand, at least 80% of participants maintained that moral acts such as stealing from another person, unprovoked hitting, slander, or damaging another's property would continue to be wrong even if God or scripture had been silent about the act. The findings of these studies with Catholics, Amish, Dutch Reform Calvinists, and Conservative and Orthodox Jews indicate that concepts of morality do not depend on adherence to a religious faith. They also are important for moral education in liberal democracies because they demonstrate that an educational focus on morality can be achieved in public schools independent of students' religious affiliations.

A basic assumption underlying the proposal that morality and convention emerge as distinct conceptual frameworks is that they account for qualitatively differing and fundamental aspects of social experience (Turiel, 1983). Evidence in support of this proposition has been obtained in observational studies of children's interactions with one another and with adults in preschool (Killen & Smetana, 1999; Much & Shweder, 1978; Nucci & Turiel, 1978; Nucci, Turiel, & Encarnacion-Gawrych, 1983), elementary school (Nucci & Nucci, 1982a), playground activities (Nucci & Nucci, 1982b), and in home settings (Nucci & Weber, 1995; Smetana, 1989). What these studies uncovered is that interactions having to do with morality tend to focus on the effects those actions have upon the welfare of others. In the case of moral events, children experience such interactions as victims, perpetrators, or third person observers. Interactions around societal conventions, in contrast, tend to focus upon the norms or rules that would apply, along with feedback regarding the social organizational function of the norm (e.g., to maintain classroom order).

These domain-related patterns of social interaction are also associated with differing forms of emotional experience and expression (Arsenio & Lover, 1995). Moral transgressions, especially among young children, are often accompanied by strong emotions of anger or sadness as well as empathy for victims. Positive moral interactions such as sharing are associated with emotions of happiness. Social conventions on the other hand arouse little affect among children. This holds for situations in which children both comply with and violate social norms (Arsenio & Lover, 1995). Negative emotional expressions over violations of convention tend to come from adults rather than children.

In recent years, these discoveries of the early emergence of basic moral concepts and their apparent universality has led some scientists to speculate that morality is largely based upon inherent biological tendencies that are the result of our evolutionary history (Krebs, 2011). This basic distinction is maintained even by children suffering from autism (James & Blair, 2005; Leslie, Mallon, & DiCorcia, 2006). There is strong evidence that infants are sensitive to the emotional distress of others (Martin & Clark, 1982) and capable of identifying facial expressions conveying particular emotional states (Ludemann, 1991), all of which is consistent with the view that humans are primed to respond with empathy towards others (Emde, Hewitt, & Kagan, 2001). These early intuitions, however, do not qualify as moral knowledge, and they do not account for the developmental changes in moral reasoning that we see in children and adolescents. This evolutionary priming forms part of the early experience that children employ in constructing moral concepts, and the related emotions and feelings incorporated within early moral schema also undoubtedly play a role in moral motivation (Arsenio & Lover, 1995). Over the course of a lifetime, the cognitions constructed around moral experiences alter or enter into the regulation of affect and the final appraisal of social situations (Pizarro & Bloom, 2003). Moral development and effective moral education incorporate emotion as part of the informational and affective experiences that generate reflection and the construction of moral knowledge and reasoning.

More recently, researchers employing neuroscience methodologies have provided evidence that individuals evoke different cognitive processing for moral and conventional social judgments (Lahat, Helwig, & Zelazo, 2012). These researchers caution, however, against over-interpretation of their findings as indicative of an innate neural substrate for moral or conventional judgments and point instead to the likelihood that implicit cognitive processing, executive functioning, and cognitive load are differentially implicated in moral and social conventional reasoning in distinct domains (Lahat et al., 2012). In sum, the basic finding of a conceptual distinction between morality and convention has proven to be among the most robust phenomena uncovered by psychological research.

The Personal

Within domain theory morality and social convention are further differentiated from judgments about issues that individuals consider to be personal (Nucci, 1996, 2013a). While morality and convention deal with aspects of right and wrong and with interpersonal regulation, concepts of personal issues refer to the private aspects of one's life such as the contents of a diary and issues that are matters of preference and choice (e.g., friends, music, hairstyle). It has been proposed that the establishment of control over the personal emerges from the need to establish boundaries between the self and others and that this need is critical to the establishment of personal autonomy and individual identity (Lagattuta, Nucci, & Bosacki, 2010; Nucci, 2013a). Interview studies have shown that children and adolescents in multiple cultures judge personal issues to be within their jurisdiction regardless of parental decisions. Evidence has also been presented that parents across a wide range of cultures (Assadi, Smetana, Shahmansouri, & Mohammadi, 2011; Lins-Dyer & Nucci, 2007; Nucci & Smetana, 1996; Nucci & Weber, 1995; Yamada, 2004; Yau & Smetana, 2003) provide for a zone of personal discretion and privacy with children as young as three to four years of age (see Nucci, in press a, for a comprehensive review). Justifications that children and their parents provide concerning why behaviors and decisions should be treated as personal and within the children's jurisdiction focus on the role of such choices in developing autonomy, personal identity, and moral rights of the children or adolescents to have such discretion (for reviews see Nucci, in press a; Smetana, 2011).

Observational studies of mothers and young children in American middle class homes have explored the social interactions between parents and young children around personal domain issues (Nucci & Weber, 1995). The research indicates that parents provide opportunities for children to engage in choice around decisions about food, dress, play activities, and playmates. Mothers also tend to negotiate with children in situations involving resistance by the child to maternal commands around issues such as clothing choices that have a substantial personal component. Mothers were observed negotiating with their children over these personal events 51% of the time. However, they only negotiated with the children 1% of the time about moral or conventional issues (Nucci & Weber, 1995). The findings are consistent with the results mentioned above indicating that parents respond differentially to their children's personal, moral, and conventional domain behaviors.

DEVELOPMENT WITHIN DOMAINS

Conceptual development within each of the domains just described follows a distinctive pattern. Development of morality is structured by changes in underlying conceptualizations of justice and human welfare (Damon, 1977; Nucci, in press a; Nucci & Turiel, 2007). Development of convention is structured by underlying conceptualizations of social systems and social organization (Turiel, 1983). Finally, development of concepts about the personal is structured by underlying conceptions of self, identity, and personhood (Nucci, 2001, 2009). It is beyond the scope of this chapter to present a detailed description of each developmental sequence. What follows are descriptions of general patterns for development of morality and convention with references to sources where detailed descriptions can be found.

Moral Development

Morality begins in early childhood with a focus upon issues of harm to the self and others. Davidson, Turiel, and Black (1983) found that, up to about age seven, moral judgment is primarily regulated by concerns for maintaining welfare and avoiding harm and that it is limited to directly accessible acts. Young children's morality is not yet structured by understandings of fairness as reciprocity. Thus, young children have a difficult time making moral judgments when the needs of more than one person are at stake (Damon, 1977). In addition, there is little subtlety in young children's concepts of moral harm and in their moral evaluations of situations involving helping others (Eisenberg, 1986; Nucci & Turiel, 2007). Research on children's distributive and retributive justice reasoning shows that, as they develop, children form increased understandings of benevolence, equality, reciprocity, and equity (Damon, 1977, 1980; Irwin & Moore, 1971; Lapsley, 1982). The pattern of development reflects an increased ability of children to coordinate elements of moral situations within their justice reasoning. In the case of distributive justice, this increased capacity to handle complexity leads to a linear growth pattern of steady incremental changes in moral thinking. When it comes to reasoning about issues of human welfare, however, the developmental pattern is more complex.

Recent studies of children's reasoning about situations involving harm or helping behavior indicate that concepts about moral culpability and obligation follow a U-shaped pattern rather than a linear one. As we saw above, very young children understand that unprovoked hitting and hurting are morally wrong. As one would expect, reasoning about this straightforward moral transgression does not change with age (Nucci, in press a; Nucci & Turiel, 2007). What does change, however, are children's concepts about indirect forms of harm such as not letting another person know that he or she has dropped money and keeping it for oneself instead. When this situation is placed in a real-life context, eight-year-old children and 16-year-old adolescents are more likely to judge keeping the money as wrong than are 13-year-olds. Moreover, 13-year-olds are far more likely to claim that they would have a right to keep the money (Nucci, 2013a; Nucci & Turiel, 2007). Interestingly, 13-year-old children are as likely to return the money as eight- and 16-year-olds when the person who drops the money is described as handicapped. Across ages, nearly all children agree that it would be wrong to keep the money in that case. Thus, the reasoning of the 13-year-olds does not fit a pattern of purely instrumentalist moral thinking. Instead, several factors related to their increased understanding of the social world are converging to make the moral evaluation of the situation more variable. Development allows young adolescents to recognize the moral ambiguity of non-prototypical situations. In this case, the loss of the money did not occur because of an action taken by the observer. Furthermore, in the absence of an observer, the money would have been lost in any case. To quote one of the adolescents in the study, "It's [the money] in never land." Added to this moral ambiguity is the confusion adolescents experience as they sort out the differences in meaning among free will, personal choice (as in the personal domain), and a moral right to do something. For the eight-year-olds, there is no problem; the situation holds no ambiguity. There is a simple line drawn between the money and its owner. By age 16, most of the adolescents in the study had resolved the complexities identified by the 13-year-olds and, after acknowledging the ambiguities inherent in the situation, judged that the act of observing rendered the bystander obligated to return the money.

Similar U-shaped developmental patterns were found for helping behavior in early adolescents (Nucci & Turiel, 2007) and again in young adults (early twenties) (Eisenberg, Cumberland, Guthrie, Murphy, & Shepard, 2005). These fluctuating patterns of development signal periods of increased attention to new elements of moral situations and mark transitions to more complex integrations of moral thought (Gerskoff & Thelen, 2004).

Social Convention

The development of concepts about convention presents an oscillating pattern between periods—phases affirming the importance of convention and phases negating the basis of the affirmations of the prior phase. Seven levels of development have been described from early childhood to early adulthood (Turiel, 1983). Evidence for these levels comes from cross-sectional (Nucci, Becker, & Horn, 2004; Turiel, 1983), cross-cultural (Hollos, Leis, & Turiel, 1986), experimental (Nucci & Weber, 1991), and longitudinal studies (Hollos et al., 1986). Concepts about convention reflect the person's underlying conceptions of social organization. A typical 10-year-old, with a concrete sense of social hierarchy, affirms convention as serving to maintain social order. For example, people in charge of schools make up rules to keep everyone from running in the hallways.

At the next level of development, typical of early adolescence, children enter into a negation phase in which the prior basis for affirming convention becomes viewed through the lens of the arbitrariness of the norms and their status as "simply" the dictates of authority. Later, in middle adolescence, the dismissal of convention is replaced by an understanding that conventions have meaning within a larger framework. Thus, conventions are seen as normative and binding within a social system of fixed roles and obligations. The oscillating pattern of development of convention indicates the difficulty children have in accounting for the function of arbitrary social norms and illustrates the slow process of reflection and construction that precedes the adolescents' view of convention as important to the structuring of social systems.

Personal

Age-related changes in concepts about personal issues reflect shifts in children's and adolescents' understandings of "self" and the role that control over one's personal domain has for constructing and maintaining autonomy and personal identity (Nucci, 1996). With age, children move from views of the personal zone in terms of physical appearance, characteristic activities, and personal friendships to a deepening sense of personal choice and privacy as essential to the establishment of an interiorized "self" comprising one's personal thoughts, preferences, and tastes that are manifested in one's outward appearance, actions, and relationships.

An aspect of development of the personal is the expansion of what children and adolescents consider as personal matters under their own control instead of parental or societal authority (Smetana, 2011). These shifts are primarily around issues of safety or conventions of dress and other forms of personal expression that children and adolescents increasingly view as important to their sense of autonomy and emerging individual identity.

CROSS-DOMAIN INTERACTIONS AND COORDINATIONS

In making decisions in everyday life, people make use of the social knowledge systems that will help them understand problems or situations. Some social behaviors, such as unprovoked hitting of another person, are clear-cut moral situations that require only the application of moral knowledge to make a decision. In a similar way, we could describe situations that would involve the application of knowledge about social convention. Many social situations, however, contain elements that may draw upon one or more conceptual frameworks. This can occur when elements of fairness or human welfare intersect with societal conventions or when conventions impede or regulate what the individual considers a personal matter.

An historical example of domain overlap between morality and convention would be the Jim Crow laws that segregated Whites and Blacks in the United States in the last century. While Jim Crow laws are a part of the past, many examples of domain overlap confront students in contemporary society. For example, issues of peer inclusion and exclusion are very much a part of the everyday life of students. Instances of peer exclusion and harassment draw upon conceptions of peer conventions of dress and behavior, personal domain construals of the selection of personal associations and friendships, and moral concepts of harm and fairness (Horn, 2003; Killen, Lee-Kim, McGlothlin, & Stangor 2002; Killen & Rutland, 2011). According to domain theory, how an individual will reason about such issues of overlap will depend partly upon whether the person subordinates the given situation to a single domain of fairness, social organization, or personal considerations, or whether the person attempts to coordinate the elements of the issue (Turiel & Smetana, 1984). From an educational point of view, what these examples make clear is that facilitating social and moral growth addressing the full complexity of social and moral issues requires attention to a multi-faceted system of social and moral development rather than a single structure of moral judgment (Nucci, 2001).

DOMAIN THEORY: APPLICATION TO MORAL EDUCATION

The application of domain theory to moral education has been continuous with the broader family of developmental and constructivist approaches to education (Nucci, 2001). This includes attention to the social and emotional needs of children through classroom structure and responses to student behavior as well as the integration of moral education through the regular academic curriculum. Domain theory adds to existing developmentally based educational approaches a set of analytic tools for identifying moral and non-moral aspects of educational experiences along with domain appropriate teacher strategies for fostering moral and social development (Nucci, 2009). What follows is an overview of research findings about best practices for establishing a classroom climate of care and trust that are conducive to moral education, about developmental trends in student misbehavior and transgressions in the school-based context, and about domain appropriate teacher responses to student transgressions. The final subsection is a discussion of uses of domain theory to foster social and moral development through the academic curriculum.

Classroom and School Climate, Rules, and Responses to Transgression

Classroom climate. As was outlined above, moral and social knowledge emerges out of the child's interactions in the social world. Applying this basic premise to the classroom means that a fundamental source for students' social development is the social climate of the classroom and school and the approach that teachers and administrators take toward managing student behavior. Research on the emotional correlates of morality by Arsenio and Lover (1995) sustains basic claims of the importance of attention to affective experiences for moral development. In particular, this work points to the centrality of establishing caring classroom environments (Noddings, 2002) that foster construction of a worldview based on "goodwill" characterized by the presumption that social life operates, for the most part, according to basic moral principles of fairness and mutual respect (Arsenio & Lover, 1995).

This is more than providing students with consistent moral messages in an environment of physical safety. As Noddings (2002) explains, critical to the establishment of a caring orientation is the capacity to accept care from others. This requires a school and classroom climate in which students can afford to be emotionally vulnerable and in which that vulnerability extends to the students' willingness to risk engagement in acts of kindness and concern for others (Noddings, 2002). This notion of an ethic of care relates to a more general conceptualization of a school and classroom environment based upon trust (Watson, 2003, this volume). Trust entails affective connections of care regulated by moral reciprocity and continuity. Trust is basic to the construction of an overall sense of community that is one of the primary predictors of prosocial conduct in schools (Battistich, 2008).

One aspect of school culture that impacts the climate of trust is the extent to which students engage in social exclusion. Children's engagement in social exclusion reflects a complex set of social judgments drawing on understandings across all three social cognitive domains. Issues of peer exclusion and harassment (and bullying) call upon conceptions of peer conventions of dress and behavior, personal domain construals of interpersonal associations and friendships, and moral concepts of harm and fairness (Horn, 2003; Killen et al., 2002). Establishing a climate of trust requires an inclusive classroom and school culture. However, focusing only on the fairness or harm involved in social exclusion will not address the motivations and justifications of young persons whose focus is on the importance of peer conventions or their sense of control over personal associations (Killen & Rutland, 2011). Addressing this complexity entails an open climate of dialogue in which children work through the non-moral justifications that are undergirding their willingness to engage in what would otherwise be perceived as an immoral act of interpersonal harm (Killen & Rutland, 2011).

Establishing classrooms and school communities that foster trust and mutual respect should extend beyond the elementary years that Watson (2003, this volume) identifies as a critical period for meeting the attachment needs of young children. Discussed in greater detail below, adolescence is a period of transition with its own emotional vulnerabilities that make establishing an atmosphere of trust important for secondary education as well (Eccles, Wigfield, & Schiefele, 1998). The broader process of establishing trust in school is beyond the scope of this chapter and is covered in several other places in the handbook (see esp. Watson, this volume). We now turn to ways in which attention to social cognitive domain can contribute to an understanding of age-related shifts in student behavior and to the approach that educators might take concerning school rules and classroom management.

Domain Appropriate Responses to Student Transgressions. The emergence of distinct domains of social knowledge corresponds to qualitatively differing social interactions associated with each domain (Turiel, 1983). As one might expect, research demonstrates that children evaluate teacher responses to transgressions in terms of correspondence to the domain of the transgressions (see Nucci, 2001 for a comprehensive review). Interview studies conducted with preschool (Killen, Breton, Ferguson, & Handler, 1994) and elementary and middle school children in grades 2–7 (Nucci, 1984) indicate that students evaluate teacher responses to transgressions in terms of their concordance with the domain-defining features of the actions. Domain concordant responses to violations of conventions, such as being out of line or not raising one's hand before speaking, would consist of teacher statements referring to the governing rules or of statements engaging students to consider the disruptions to classroom organization or social functioning that result from the transgressions. Directing students to consider the consequences of such actions upon the welfare of others, on the other hand, would be responses concordant with moral transgressions. Students across grade levels were found to rate domain concordant responses higher than they rated domain discordant ones (e.g., providing a moral response to a conventional transgression) (Killen et al., 1994; Nucci, 1984). Fifth graders and above extended their evaluations of responses to transgression such that teachers who consistently responded to transgressions in a domain concordant manner were rated more knowledgeable and effective than teachers who consistently provided domain discordant responses (Nucci, 1984).

Observational studies of the relative frequency of rule violations in first- through eighth-grade classrooms have consistently indicated that the vast majority of misconduct is with respect to violations of conventions rather than moral transgressions (Blumenfeld, Pintrich, & Hamilton, 1987; Nucci & Nucci, 1982a). This indicates that attributing all classroom management issues to morality runs the risk of diminishing the force of moral argumentation by using it primarily for issues of convention. This limits the extent to which classroom interactions can be employed to engage students' thinking about convention.

School Rules, Misbehavior, and Periods of Transition. The importance of attending to students' concepts of social convention becomes more apparent when we consider data indicating that the rate at which students engage in violations of classroom convention is associated with students' modal level of development in the conventional domain. Violations of convention in elementary and middle school are highest in grades 3–4 and 7–8, which correspond to ages at which children are respectively at Levels 2 and 4, negation of concepts about convention (Nucci & Nucci, 1982a; see Table 8.1). As one might expect from the developmental literature, early adolescence is an especially challenging period for teachers and administrators because significant changes are occurring in all three domains of social understanding.

With respect to social convention, young adolescents enter a phase (Level 4) in which they question the conventions they upheld during middle childhood (Nucci et al., 2004; Turiel, 1983). The support for conventions of maintaining basic order (e.g., to keep kids from running in the hallways) evaporates as young people reconsider the arbitrariness of conventional regulation and conclude that they are "simply the arbitrary dictates of authority" (Turiel, 1983). In many cases, students at this level of development continue to adhere to conventions to maintain smooth relationships with teachers or to avoid sanctions. However, students at this level are unable to produce a conceptual rationale for the conventions themselves (Nucci et al., 2004). Thus, there is greater tendency for students at this point in development to engage in the violation of school conventions (Geiger & Turiel, 1983; Nucci & Nucci, 1982a).

By middle adolescence, about age 15 or the sophomore year of high school, most American adolescents have moved to Level 5 reasoning about social convention (Nucci et al., 2004). At Level 5, conventions are viewed as constituent elements of the social system structuring hierarchical relations and coordinating interactions among members of a society or a societal institution such as the school (Turiel, 1983). In their longitudinal study, Geiger and Turiel (1983) found that students who had moved to Level 5 in their concepts of convention engaged in significantly fewer violations of school conventions.

Coincident with these developmental shifts in concepts of convention are basic changes in the ways that adolescents draw boundaries between convention and matters of personal prerogative and privacy (Smetana, 2011). Areas where conventions and norms of family and school touch upon personal expression (dress, hairstyle), personal associations (friendships), personal communication (phone, email), access to information (internet), and personal safety (substance use, sexuality) become zones of dispute wherein adolescents lay increasing claims to autonomy and control. Across cultures, family disputes are largely about such issues as adolescents appropriating greater areas of personal jurisdiction from what had previously been areas of parental influence or control (Smetana, 2011). Students also lay claim to zones of personal privacy and prerogative within school settings (Smetana & Bitz, 1996). They are somewhat more willing, however, to accept conventions regulating conduct within the school settings such as public displays of affection (kissing in public) that would be considered personal in non-school contexts (Smetana & Bitz, 1996). Nevertheless, the combined developmental phase of negation of convention with the extension of what is considered personal renders the period of early adolescence a difficult transition.

In discussing educational implications of this period of early adolescent transition, Smetana (2005) refers to the work of Eccles and her colleagues as providing a window into the mismatch that currently exists between school policies and adolescent acceptance of these normative issues. The researchers (Eccles et al., 1993, 1998) have provided evidence that, despite the increased maturity of adolescents, middle and junior high schools emphasize greater teacher control and discipline and offer fewer opportunities for student involvement in decision-making, choice, and self-management than do elementary school classrooms. Accordingly, Eccles and her colleagues (1998) reported that the mismatch between adolescents' efforts to attain greater autonomy and the schools' increased efforts at control result in declines in junior high school students' intrinsic motivation and interest in school.

From a developmental perspective, the typical responses of schools to this period of transition amount to a defensive maneuver while waiting out a passing developmental storm. An alternative approach recommended by Eccles (Eccles et al., 1993, 1998) is that schools include more opportunities for students to have input into the norms governing classroom practices. More specifically, Smetana's (Smetana & Bitz, 1996) research and the observational studies of student transgressions (Geiger & Turiel, 1983; Nucci & Nucci, 1982a) indicate that the focus of such student input and discourse should be around matters of social convention and personal prerogative. Other work exploring the impact of developmental discourse around issues of convention has demonstrated that such discussion can effectively contribute to students' levels of understanding about the social functions of such norms (Nucci & Weber, 1991).

While the majority of adolescent misconduct concerns issues of convention, some of the efforts to establish autonomy and identity entail risk taking and moral transgressions. For example, shoplifting tends to peak between the ages of 12 and 14 years (Wolf, 1992). This corresponds to the transitional period in early adolescent moral reasoning uncovered in our recent work (Nucci, 2013a; Nucci & Turiel, 2007). The Swiss developmentalist Fritz Oser (2005) has argued that educators should view such moral misconduct as an essential component for moral growth and seize upon moral transgressions as an opportunity for what he refers to as "realistic discourse." Oser's position is that "negative morality," like mistakes in math class, comprises the basis from which a genuine moral epistemology and moral orientation arise. His approach to moral misconduct in adolescence is to make it the subject of moral discourse in which students must confront one another's actual misdeeds, interpretations of their motives, and the consequences of their actions (Veugelers & Oser, 2003). Oser's approach builds from prior work done in the Kohlberg tradition on the "just community" (see Oser, this volume). The processes advocated by Oser have been employed with considerable success by others working within the Kohlberg tradition (Blakeney & Blakeney, 1991) to alter the misconduct and recidivism among behaviorally disordered children and adolescents.

Domain Appropriate Uses of the Academic Curriculum

Attending to students' social experiences can contribute much to their social and moral development. However, schools can extend their impact upon moral and social development through the academic curriculum in several ways. First, the academic curriculum contains many instances in the context of literacy and social studies of stories or events that replicate or reinforce social and moral values that students may be addressing in their everyday experiences. Uses of literature employing constructivist teaching methods with attention to children's developmental levels has been shown to impact both social and emotional learning (Elias et al., this volume) as well as moral development (Nucci, 2001, 2009). Second, the formal curriculum moves the students' knowledge base beyond their own historical or cultural framework and has the potential to motivate students to project themselves as members of a global community with responsibilities for the social welfare of persons beyond their immediate experience. Table 8.1 presents an outline of how curricular content in literature and social studies might be matched with domain and developmental level corresponding to grade and approximate ages.

Developmentalists dating back to Kohlberg (Kohlberg & Mayer, 1972) have cast the aims of moral education in progressive terms of enabling individuals to evaluate society and their own behavior from a critical principled moral perspective. For Kohlberg, this aim was to be achieved by stimulating students to move toward principled stages of moral reasoning. From a domain theory perspective, this same progressive aim is strived for by fostering student skills to apply their moral understandings critically to evaluate social norms and personal conduct at all points in development rather than at a developmental end point (Nucci, 2001, 2009). In both cases, the underlying progressive educational ideology has a shared concept of moral education as fostering the capacity of students to act from a critical moral perspective. This social justice potential of schools has received a lot of attention in recent years, some of it quite critical. Critics such as Diane Ravitch (2005) express a concern that attention to moral issues such as social class or racial inequalities competes with the primary academic aims of education. Such criticisms might have merit if attention to moral development came at the cost of academic

Table 8.1 Development Within Domains and Curriculum Implications by Grade Level

Grade/Age	Moral	Conventional	Personal
Kindergarten–Grade 2 5–7 years	Development: Recognize basic obligations for helping, sharing, avoiding harm. Difficulty coordinating needs of more than one person simultaneously. Moral decisions based on salience of moral elements. Curriculum: Reading as context presenting conflicts of interest between two or more characters. Engage students in generating resolutions based on moral reciprocity.	Development: Conventions tied to observed regularities; conform to general patterns. Curriculum: Use stories to identify contextual variations in conventions. *Emphasis in early grades (K–4) on direct experiences with classroom and family norms.*	Development: Control over personal tied to physical aspects of self. Identity and autonomy shown in appearance to others. Autonomy as literal ownership and control over "self." Curriculum: Readings present protagonists engaging in choices about clothing, etc. to illustrate identity. Differentiate contexts in which personal choice and conventions prevail.
Grades 3–4 8–9 years	Development: Direct reciprocity; tit-for-tat mentality; indirect harm same as direct harm; equal distribution is fair. Curriculum: Reading as context for deepening morality based on reciprocity and coordination of needs of two or more people.	Development: Negation of convention based on observed inconsistencies and exceptions to norms. Curriculum: Reading and social studies as contexts for discussions about impact on social order and behavior of altering or eliminating conventions presented in historical or fictional settings.	Development: Transition toward features of grade 5. Curriculum: Reading instruction as context for identifying and discussing role of personal choices of *activities* in establishing identity.
Grades 5–6 10–11 years	Development: Concerns for equity, others' special needs taken into account. Beginnings of attention to non-moral factors adding complexity to moral situations. Curriculum: Reading as context for discussion about equity in fair distribution and opportunities for participation. Discuss fairness of social exclusion (can be linked to personal domain and identity). Use social studies to begin consideration of social equity.	Development: Affirmation and concrete understanding of conventional rules to maintain order and given top-down by social authority figure. Curriculum: Reading and social studies to consider role of conventions in establishing social organization. Social studies make concrete comparisons of the role conventions in different social systems.	Development: Emphasis of self-definition is about child's displayed behaviors, talents, and skills. Control over personal allows behaviors and activities that define self. Curriculum: Reading for discussing relation between personal choice and identity. Discuss connections between proficiency in personal activities and sense of self. Essential to minimize comparisons with others as basis for academic motivation.

	Moral	Conventional	Personal
Grades 7–9 **12–14 years**	Development: Consolidate relations between equity and equality in concepts of fairness; attention to factors of ambiguity and complexity in moral situations. Conflation of personal choice with "rights"; increased non-moral action choices in ambiguous contexts. Curriculum: Literacy – consider indirect, ambiguous harm; evaluate arguments about moral decisions based on self-interest that entail competing interests and ambiguous harm. Use social studies to evaluate historical events with actors engaged in actions entailing moral ambiguity. Begin discussions of moral considerations of social practices and conventions.	Development: Negation of convention as arbitrary dictates of authority; acts evaluated apart from rules. Curriculum: Use social studies for discussion, reflection, and essays about conventions associated with social hierarchy and organization. Consider historical and societal conventions and their role in social systems. Discuss variations on norms for hypothetical social systems; compare with social systems presented in social studies.	Development: Self is described as one's beliefs, values, and thoughts. Control over personal is to maintain "uniqueness" in terms of superficial differences from others. Early adolescent expands activities and decisions considered "personal" and not a matter of parental or other external authority. Curriculum: Use literature to consider relations between personal decisions about dress, friends, activities, etc. in generating individuality. Discussions: What it means to be individual versus "phony"; whether two people can share the same values, beliefs, and preferences and remain individuals.
Grades 10–12 **15–17 years**	Development: Increased ability to coordinate multiple factors in moral situations. Clear differentiation between personal choice and moral rights. Curriculum: Use literacy and history to prompt discussions and essays about situations pitting moral considerations against societal convention and personal interest. Use moral considerations to evaluate the norms and practices of social systems. Emphasis on cross-domain coordinations. Apply moral considerations to personal decisions on global warming, etc.	Development: Systematic concepts of social structure emerge; conventions understood as normative and binding to maintain social systems and reflect social organization and hierarchy; social group members expected to adhere to conventions. Curriculum: Use literature and social studies for comparative examination of societies as normative systems. Connect with moral considerations of respect for cultural differences.	Development: Self now defined in terms of inner essence or "true" self shown by personal decisions and actions. Control over personal allows self-discovery and coordination of what is outside with what is inside the "true" self. Curriculum: Use literature to examine personal choices of characters in forming their identities. Use of history and literature to consider contexts in which it is legitimate to prioritize personal choice and expression over social norms and moral considerations.

success. In fact, there is mounting evidence that attention to social and moral development may enhance academic performance (Berkowitz & Bier, this volume; Durlak & Weissberg, 2007). Finally, encouraging students to employ moral knowledge to improve society is a goal broadly shared by educators, including proponents of mainstream character education (Lickona, 2004).

We have begun to examine the efficacy of attending to social cognitive domain within the context of academic instruction (Nucci, 2009). In one of our studies, we addressed whether attention to the domain of social values makes a difference in the development of children's moral and social conventional concepts addressed in a set of eighth-grade American History and English composition courses (Nucci & Weber, 1991). We identified issues from American history that were primarily moral, social conventional, or mixed domain. For example, moral issues included slavery and the forced removal of Native Americans from their lands; conventional issues included the adjustments in modes of dress, work conventions, and dating patterns that resulted from the influx of immigrants and the shift from an agrarian to an industrial society; and mixed domain issues included changes in laws permitting women to vote.

Students were randomly assigned to one of three instructional conditions: (a) convention, (b) moral, and (c) domain appropriate. Instruction was carried out by an experienced teacher in pullout sessions supplementing their regular classroom activities. Each instructional period included 30 minutes of discussion and an essay homework assignment based upon the questions used to frame each session. Students in the convention condition were provided questions and teacher statements that directed them to focus upon social norms and social organization, in essence treating all issues as if they were matters of convention. Students in the moral condition were directed to treat these same issues in terms of considerations of fairness and social justice. Students in the domain appropriate condition were asked first to consider normative, conventional aspects and then to consider the justice or welfare features of the issue. Students in the domain appropriate condition were also asked to integrate the moral and conventional features of the event. In other words, students were taught to interpret, analyze, and evaluate situations as primarily social, moral, or mixed. Results indicated that attention to domain had an impact on student learning.

Students who received instruction focusing in only one domain (social conventional or moral) advanced in their level of reasoning or understanding in that domain but not in the other. Only the students in the domain appropriate (mixed social conventional and moral) instructional condition developed in both domains. A second noteworthy finding of the study had to do with how students dealt with overlapping issues. Students who had domain appropriate teaching were the only ones to coordinate elements spontaneously from both domains. In contrast, two thirds of the students in the moral instructional condition subordinated mixed domain issues entirely to their moral elements, and a majority of students in the convention instructional condition subordinated mixed domain issues to their conventional elements.

This last set of findings has particular relevance for developing students' capacities for critical moral reflection. Convention condition students were hampered in attending to the moral implications of situations. Moral condition students prioritized the moral elements of the same situations but did not consider the social organizational ramifications. In real life, however, there are always organizational costs to any change in the conventional social structure. For example, a single-minded attention to needs for gender equality in careers leaves unanswered any number of practical questions about how to restructure the conventions of the family, role expectations, and practical duties. The domain appropriate condition students prioritized the moral elements of these situations, but they also acknowledged the ramifications of changing conventional organization and offered suggestions for how those changes might be resolved. Our interpretation of the findings from this study is that instructional conditions that differentially draw attention to social conventional, moral, or mixed-domain components of the same issues can influence students' capacities to coordinate and transfer forms of reasoning through social cognitive domains about multifaceted, value-laden, real-world issues.

Findings from instructional intervention studies such as the study presented above demonstrate how social cognitive domain theory approaches to moral education can inform and enhance teaching practices that build and coordinate conceptual structures. Using these constructed understandings, students reason about social-conventional and moral issues and events in both real life and within the academic curriculum. Social cognitive domain theory provides a 2-for-1 framework that aligns with and adds greater dimension to formative and performance-driven academic standards. It supports instruction that fosters intellectual, social, and moral development simultaneously by building upon higher-order reasoning skills that transfer across academic disciplines (Nucci, 2009). Thus, this approach to moral education addresses the concerns of schools for academic achievement noted by Davidson and Lickona (this volume) while also contributing to students' moral development.

CONCLUSIONS AND FUTURE DIRECTIONS

This chapter provided an overview of research on children's moral and social development indicating that morality forms a developmental system that is distinct from our concepts of societal convention and personal choice and privacy. That research provides the basis for refinements in the developmental approach to moral education that attends to the contextual and experiential origins of students' concepts in each domain rather than subsuming social and moral development within a single developmental system. Observational studies have demonstrated that classroom social interactions differ by social cognitive domain, and interview studies have shown that students evaluate teacher responses to students' social transgressions in terms of their concordance with the domain of the transgression. Finally, intervention studies have demonstrated that attending to social cognitive domain has salutary effects both on students' development within domains and in their tendencies to integrate knowledge from multiple domains when dealing with complex social issues.

In recent work, we have integrated this developmental research into the design of a teacher education program for the preparation of elementary school teachers. That effort has demonstrated that pre-service teachers can acquire the skills to integrate lessons of domain appropriate moral and social values with the regular academic curriculum and their approach to classroom management (Nucci, Drill, Larson, & Browne, 2005; Nucci, 2013b; Nucci & Powers, 2013). We continue to assess the degree to which pre-service teachers trained in the Developmental Teacher Education (DTE) program at the University of California, Berkeley integrate and continue to use methods and guiding concepts of social cognitive domain theory in their classrooms (Nucci & Powers, 2013). We are also currently exploring how urban public middle school history teachers with varying levels of professional experience foster students' development of conventional and moral reasoning. In this ongoing project, teachers plan lessons and deliver instruction guided by a social cognitive domain approach.

Our goal in conducting this research has been to provide educators and educational researchers with insights to improve their developmentally based moral and social education rather than to promote a specific set of practices or curricula. There are undoubtedly many ways in which classroom teachers and school administrators can integrate attention to moral and social development within educational practices that go beyond the suggestions that we have proposed (Nucci, 2009). What is critical from our point of view is that moral education acknowledges the complexity inherent in social and moral decision-making and in the construction of a moral life. What we have learned in the past four decades about children's moral and social development is that moral education requires a variegated approach. Moral development does not move toward an end-point at which moral principle triumphs over non-moral considerations. Nor does moral education result in the establishment of decontextualized virtue. Instead, what we can hope to accomplish is to develop young people capable of handling moral complexity, ambiguity, and contradiction in ways that will help them to lead moral lives and to construct a more moral society.

REFERENCES

Arsenio, W., & Lover, A. (1995). Children's conceptions of socio-moral affect: Happy victimizers, mixed emotions, and other expectancies. In M. Killen & D. Hart (Eds.), *Morality in everyday life* (pp. 87–130). New York, NY: Cambridge University Press.

Assadi, S., Smetana, J., Shahmansouri, N., & Mohammadi, M. (2011). Beliefs about parental authority, parenting styles, and adolescent-parent conflict among Iranian mothers and middle adolescents. *International Journal of Behavioral Development, 35*, 424–431.

Battistich, V. (2008). The child development project: Creating caring school communities. In L. Nucci & D. Narvaez (Eds.), *Handbook of moral and character education* (1st ed., pp. 328–351). New York, NY: Routledge.

Blakeney, C., & Blakeney, R. (1991). Understanding and reforming moral misbehavior among behaviorally disordered children. *Journal of Behavioral Disorders, 16*, 135–143.

Blumenfeld, P.C., Pintrich, P.R., & Hamilton, V.L. (1987). Teacher talk and students' reasoning about morals, conventions, and achievement. *Child Development, 58*, 1389–1401.

Damon, W. (1977). *The social world of the child.* San Francisco, CA: Jossey-Bass.

Damon, W. (1980). Patterns of change in children's social reasoning: A two-year longitudinal study. *Child Development, 51*, 1010–1017.

Davidson, P., Turiel, E., & Black, A. (1983). The effect of stimulus familiarity on the use of criteria and justifications in children's social reasoning. *British Journal of Developmental Psychology, 1*, 46–65.

Durkheim, E. (1961). *Moral education: A study in the theory and application of the sociology of education.* Glencoe, IL: The Free Press. (Original work published 1925).

Durlak, D., & Weissberg, R. (2007). *The impact of after-school programs that promote social and emotional skills.* Chicago, IL: The Collaborative for Social and Emotional Learning.

Eccles, J.S., Midgley, C., Wigfield, A., Buchanan, C.M., Reuman, D., Flanagan, C., & Mac Iver, D. (1993). Development during adolescence: The impact of stage-environment fit on adolescents' experiences in schools and families. *American Psychologist, 48*, 90–101.

Eccles, J.S., Wigfield, A., & Schiefele, U. (1998). Motivation to succeed. In W. Damon (Ed.), N. Eisenberg (Series Ed.), *Handbook of Child Psychology: Vol. 3. Social, emotional, and personality development* (5th ed., pp. 1017–1095). New York, NY: Wiley.

Eisenberg, N. (1986). *Altruistic emotion, cognition and behavior.* Hillsdale, NJ: Erlbaum.

Eisenberg, N., Cumberland, A., Guthrie, I.K., Murphy, B.C., & Shepard, S.A. (2005). Age changes in prosocial responding and moral reasoning in adolescence and early adulthood. *Journal of Research on Adolescence, 15*, 235–260.

Emde, R., Hewitt, J.K., & Kagan, J. (2001). *Infancy to early childhood: Genetic and environmental influences on developmental change.* Oxford, UK: Oxford University Press.

Geiger, K., & Turiel, E. (1983). Disruptive school behavior and concepts of social convention in early adolescence. *Journal of Educational Psychology, 75,* 677–685.

Gerskoff, L., & Thelen, E. (2004). U-shaped changes in behavior: A dynamic systems perspective. *Journal of Cognition and Development, 5,* 11–36.

Hollos, M., Leis, P., & Turiel, E. (1986). Social reasoning in Ijo children and adolescents in Nigerian communities. *Journal of Cross-Cultural Psychology, 17,* 352–376.

Horn, S.S. (2003). Adolescents' reasoning about exclusion from social groups. *Developmental Psychology, 39,* 71–84.

Irwin, D.M., & Moore, S.G. (1971). The young child's understanding of social justice. *Developmental Psychology, 5,* 406–410.

James, R., & Blair, R. (2005). Morality in the autistic child. *Journal of Autism and Developmental Disorders, 26,* 571–579.

Killen, M., Breton, S., Ferguson, H., & Handler, K. (1994). Preschoolers' evaluations of teacher methods of intervention in social transgressions. *Merrill-Palmer Quarterly, 40,* 399–415.

Killen, M., Lee-Kim, J., McGlothlin, H., & Stangor, C. (2002). How children and adolescents evaluate gender and racial exclusion. *Monograph of the Society for Research in Child Development, 67* (4, Serial No. 271).

Killen, M., & Rutland, A. (2011). *Children and social exclusion: Morality, prejudice, and group identity.* Oxford, UK: Wiley-Blackwell.

Killen, M., & Smetana, J. (1999). Social interactions in preschool classrooms and the development of young children's conceptions of the personal. *Child Development, 70,* 486–501.

Kohlberg, L. (1984). *Essays on moral development: Vol 2. The psychology of moral development.* San Francisco, CA: Harper and Row.

Kohlberg, L., & Mayer, R. (1972). Development as the aim of education. *Harvard Educational Review, 42,* 449–496.

Krebs, D. (2011). *The origins of morality: An evolutionary account.* Oxford, UK: Oxford University Press.

Lagattuta, K.H., Nucci, L., & Bosacki, S. (2010). Bridging theory of mind and the personal domain: Children's reasoning about resistance to parental control. *Child Development, 81,* 616–635.

Lahat, A., Helwig, C.C., & Zelazo, P.D. (2012). Age-related changes in cognitive processing of moral and social conventional violations. *Cognitive Development, 27,* 181–194.

Lapsley, D. (1982). *The development of retributive justice in children* (Unpublished doctoral dissertation). University of Wisconsin, Madison, WI.

Leslie, A., Mallon, R., & DiCorcia, J. (2006). Transgressors, victims, and cry babies: Is basic moral judgment spared in autism? *Social Neurosciences, 1,* 270–283.

Lickona, T. (2004). *Character matters: How to help our children develop good judgment, integrity, and other essential virtues.* Carmichael, CA: Touchstone Books.

Lins-Dyer, T., & Nucci, L. (2007). The impact of social class and social cognitive domain on northeastern Brazilian mothers' and daughters' conceptions of parental control. *International Journal of Behavioral Development, 31,* 105–114.

Ludemann, P. (1991). Generalized discrimination of positive facial expressions by 7-month old infants. *Child Development, 62,* 55–67.

Martin, G.B., & Clark, R.D. (1982). Distress crying in newborns: Species and peer specificity. *Developmental Psychology, 18,* 3–9.

Much, N., & Shweder, R.A. (1978). Speaking of rules: The analysis of culture in breach. In W. Damon (Ed.), *New directions for child development: Vol. 2. Moral development.* San Francisco, CA: Jossey-Bass.

Noddings, N. (2002). *Educating moral people: A caring alternative to character.* New York, NY: Teachers College Press.

Nucci, L. (1984). Evaluating teachers as social agents: Students' ratings of domain appropriate and domain-inappropriate teacher responses to transgressions. *American Educational Research Journal, 21,* 367–378.

Nucci, L. (1985). Children's conceptions of morality, societal convention, and religious prescription. In C.G. Harding (Ed.), *Moral dilemmas: Philosophical and psychological issues in the development of moral reasoning* (pp. 137–174). Chicago, IL: Precedent.

Nucci, L. (1996). Morality and the personal sphere of actions. In E. Reed, E. Turiel, & T. Brown (Eds.), *Knowledge and values.* Hillsdale, NJ: Erlbaum.

Nucci, L. (2001). *Education in the moral domain.* Cambridge, UK: Cambridge University Press.

Nucci, L. (2009). *Nice is not enough: Facilitating moral development.* Upper Saddle River, NJ: Pearson.

Nucci, L. (2013a). The personal and the moral. In M. Killen & J. Smetana (Eds.), *Handbook of moral development* (2nd ed.) (pp. 538–558). New York, NY: Routledge.

Nucci, L. (2013b). Reflections on preparing preservice teachers for moral education in urban settings. In M. Sanger & R. Osguthorpe (Eds.), *The moral work of teaching: Preparing and supporting practitioners* (pp. 148–163). New York, NY: Teachers College Press.

Nucci, L., Becker, K., & Horn, S. (2004). *Assessing the development of adolescent concepts of social convention.* Paper presented at the annual meeting of the Jean Piaget Society, Toronto, Canada.

Nucci, L., Drill, K., Larson, C., & Browne, C. (2005). Preparing pre-service teachers for character education in urban elementary schools: The UIC initiative. *Journal for Research in Character Education, 3*(2), 81–96.

Nucci, L., & Nucci, M.S. (1982a). Children's social interactions in the context of moral and conventional transgressions. *Child Development, 53,* 403–412.

Nucci, L., & Nucci, M.S. (1982b). Children's responses to moral and social-conventional transgressions in free-play settings. *Child Development, 53,* 1337–1342.

Nucci, L., & Powers, D.W. (2013, April). *Reflections on preparing preservice teachers for moral education in urban settings.* Paper presented as part of the symposium, The moral work of teaching: Preparing and supporting practitioners, at the annual meeting of the American Educational Research Association, San Francisco, CA.

Nucci, L., & Smetana, J. (1996). Mothers' concepts of young children's areas of personal freedom. *Child Development, 67,* 1870–1886.

Nucci, L., & Turiel, E. (1978). Social interactions and the development of social concepts in pre-school children. *Child Development, 49,* 400–407.

Nucci, L., & Turiel, E. (1993). God's word, religious rules, and their relation to Christian and Jewish children's concepts of morality. *Child Development, 64,* 1475–1491.

Nucci, L., & Turiel, E. (2007). *Development in the moral domain: The role of conflict and relationships in children's and adolescents' welfare and harm judgments.* Paper presented as part of the symposium "Moral development within domain and within context" at the biennial meeting of the Society for Research in Child Development, Boston, MA.

Nucci, L., Turiel, E., & Encarnacion-Gawrych, G. (1983). Children's social interactions and social concepts in the Virgin Islands. *Journal of Cross-Cultural Psychology, 14,* 469–487.

Nucci, L., & Weber, E. (1991). Research on classroom applications of the domain approach to values education. In W. Kurtines & J. Gewirtz (Eds.), *Handbook of moral behavior and development: Vol. 3. Applications* (pp. 251–266). Hillsdale, NJ: Erlbaum.

Nucci, L., & Weber, E.K. (1995). Social interactions in the home and the development of young children's conceptions within the personal domain. *Child Development, 66,* 1438–1452.

Oser, F. (2005). Negative morality and the goals of education. In L. Nucci (Ed.), *Conflict, contradiction and contrarian elements in moral development and education* (pp. 129–153). Mahwah, NJ: Lawrence Erlbaum.

Piaget, J. (1932). *The moral judgment of the child.* New York, NY: Free Press.

Pizzaro, D.A., & Bloom, P. (2003). The intelligence of moral intuitions: Comment on Haidt (2001). *Psychological Review, 110,* 193–196.

Ravitch, D. (2005). Critique of rethinking mathematics. *Wall Street Journal,* June 20, A14.

Saxe, G.B., Earnest, D., Sitabkhan, Y., Haldar, L.C., Lewis, K.E., & Zheng, Y. (2010). Supporting generative thinking about the integer number line in elementary mathematics. *Cognition & Instruction, 28*(4), 433–474.

Schoenfeld, A.H. (Ed.) (1994). *Mathematical thinking and problem solving.* Hillsdale, NJ: Erlbaum.

Shanahan, T. (2000). Synthesizing reading research. In M.L. Kamil, P. Mosenthal, P.D. Pearson, & R. Barr (Eds.), *Handbook of reading research* (Vol. 3). Mahwah, NJ: Erlbaum.

Smetana, J. (1989). Toddler's social interactions in the context of moral and conventional transgressions in the home. *Developmental Psychology, 25,* 499–508.

Smetana, J.G. (2005). Adolescent-parent conflict: Resistance and subversion as developmental process. In L. Nucci (Ed.), *Conflict, contradiction and contrarian elements in moral development and education* (pp. 69–91). Mahwah, NJ: Lawrence Erlbaum.

Smetana, J.G. (2011). *Adolescents, families, and social development: How teens construct their worlds.* West Sussex, UK: Wiley-Blackwell.

Smetana, J.G. (in press). Social cognitive domain theory. In M. Killen & J. Smetana (Eds.), *Handbook of moral development* (2nd ed.). New York, NY: Routledge.

Smetana, J., & Bitz, B. (1996). Adolescents' conceptions of teachers' authority and their relations to rule violations in school. *Child Development, 67,* 1153–1172.

Smetana, J.G., & Braeges, J.L. (1990). The development of toddlers' moral and conventional judgments. *Merrill-Palmer Quarterly, 36,* 329–346.

Turiel, E. (1983). *The development of social knowledge: Morality and convention.* Cambridge UK: Cambridge University Press.

Turiel, E. (2002). *The culture of morality: Social development, context and conflict.* Cambridge, UK: Cambridge University Press.

Turiel, E., & Smetana, J. (1984). Social knowledge and social action. The coordination of domains. In W.M. Kurtines & J.L. Gewirtz (Eds.), *Morality, moral behavior, and moral development: Basic issues in theory and research* (pp. 261–282). New York, NY: Wiley.

Veugelers, W., & Oser, F.K. (2003). *Teaching in moral and democratic education.* New York, NY: Peter Lang.

Watson, M. (2003). *Learning to trust: Transforming difficult elementary classrooms through developmental discipline.* San Francisco, CA: Jossey-Bass.

Wolf, A.E. (1992). *Get out of my life, but first could you drive me and Cheryl to the mall: A parent's guide to the New Teenager.* New York, NY: Farrar, Straus and Giroux.

Yamada, H. (2004). Japanese mothers' views of young children's areas of personal discretion. *Child Development, 75,* 164–179.

Yau, J., & Smetana, J.G. (2003). Adolescent–parent conflict in Hong Kong and Shenzhen: A comparison of youth in two cultural contexts. *International Journal of Behavioral Development, 27,* 201–211.

9

DEVELOPING ETHICAL EXPERTISE AND MORAL PERSONALITIES

Darcia Narvaez and Tonia Bock

The cognitive and neuro-sciences have made great strides in uncovering the nature of human psychobiology in recent years. Moral educators have yet to make much of their findings. The three theories presented here capitalize on recent research that has implications for building moral personalities and cultivating morally-adept citizens (Lapsley & Narvaez, 2004b; Narvaez & Lapsley, 2009).[1] Adaptive Ethical Expertise blends deliberative and intuitive development for ethical expertise development. The Integrative Ethical Education model is a step-by-step model intended for integration into academic instruction at all levels. Triune-Ethics Theory, a more comprehensive theory of moral development rooted in neurobiological processes, has implications for moral education as well. All three theories address the development of moral personhood.

Approaches to education for moral character are typically divided into two opposing views that are rooted in different philosophical paradigms (see Lapsley & Narvaez, 2006; Narvaez, 2006). One philosophical paradigm represents particularist claims regarding virtue with a focus on the agent and the deliberate cultivation of virtues or excellences (MacIntyre, 1981). Of primary concern is the nature of a good life and the characteristics necessary to live a good life (e.g., Anscombe 1958; Hursthouse 1999; McDowell 1997). The individual is mentored in virtue by the community and gradually takes on the responsibility for discovering and cultivating the virtues and values inherent in the self (Urmson, 1988). From this perspective nearly everything in life has moral meaning, from friend selection to leisure activities. Traditional character education emerges from this view (Wynne & Ryan, 1993), although it seems to have misappropriated how virtue is best cultivated (Kohn 1997a, 1997b; Narvaez, 2006), resulting in minimal outcome success (Leming, 1997).

The contrasting view emphasizes universalist claims regarding justice and reasoning (Kant, 1949), addressing what is *the right thing to do* in a particular moral situation (e.g., Hare 1963; Rawls, 1971). Moral conduct is that which accords with applicable principles, derived from reasoning, for a particular situation and only in select slices of life.

In comparison to virtue theory, typically, few demands are made on individuals, leaving many life choices out of the moral realm. Moral obligation is reduced to that which can be formulated with respect to universal moral principles and becomes what is universally applicable (e.g., Kant's Categorical Imperative).

> If what is right for anyone must be right for everyone in relevantly similar circumstances, then what is right must be such as can be recognized and acted upon by persons who possess very little in the way of developed moral character.
>
> (Norton, 1991, p. xi)

Instead, to make moral judgments, one adopts a "moral point of view," a position detached from personal traits and conditions. Although Kohlberg's ideas about the relation between personality and judgment shifted repeatedly, he considered character dispositions inadequate for moral judgment and emphasized reasoning (Kohlberg, 1981). Approaches to moral education rooted in Kohlberg's work typically do the same.

There has been a longstanding assumption adopted from philosophy that moral reasoning drives moral behavior (e.g., Blasi, 1980; Kohlberg, 1981; Piaget, 1932). Most famously, Kohlberg emphasized deliberative moral reasoning and its advancement through moral dilemma discussion (Blatt & Kohlberg, 1975), what can be called *rational* moral education (Narvaez, 2006). The robust findings in moral judgment research notwithstanding (e.g., Rest, Narvaez, Bebeau, & Thoma, 1999), the centrality of deliberative reasoning in behavior is a fading paradigm across psychology. To be sure, extensive reasoned argument has been instrumental in shutting down discriminatory practices, such as slavery, and instituting more equitable practices, such as women's suffrage. Despite the indisputable importance of moral reasoning, there is only a weak link between moral reasoning capacities and moral action (Blasi, 1980; Thoma, 1994). In fact, the disparity between knowing and doing has become increasingly evident across psychological fields, instigating a paradigm shift in mainstream psychology (Lakoff & Johnson, 1999).

In the paradigm new to psychology, unconscious parallel processing becomes dominant whereas conscious, serial processing becomes secondary (Bargh, 1997). Most information processing is automatic (Bargh & Chartrand, 1999); most decisions are made without deliberation (Hammond, 2000); and most activities are governed by preconscious, automatic processes (Bargh & Chartrand, 1999; Bargh & Ferguson, 2000). In other words, humans have two types of "minds" (e.g., Kahneman, 2003). The deliberative mind processes information serially and consciously. The intuitive mind is comprised of multiple non-conscious, parallel-processing systems that learn implicitly from environmental patterns and behaves automatically, often without awareness (Hogarth, 2001). The intuitive mind develops appropriate sensibilities and habitual responses from immersed experience and comprises the "habits" that are valued in traditional character education whereas the conscious mind cultivates the sophisticated moral reasoning valued by rational moral education.

Despite the perceived conflict between these two approaches to moral character education, they can be viewed as complementary (O'Neill, 1996). The Aristotelian emphasis on intuition development evident in traditional character education is more empirically aligned with everyday human behavior. Yet it is deliberative reasoning that facilitates complex understandings of justice. Therefore, character education should not be approached as Either/Or, as a choice between rational moral education and character education, or between deliberative reasoning and intuition development (Lapsley & Narvaez, 2006). Both systems are required for moral agency. The intuitive mind makes decisions and takes actions without conscious awareness most of the time. Yet the deliberative mind is vital for guiding intuition development and countering poor intuitions (Groopman, 2007; Hogarth, 2001). A person without one or the other is missing a critical tool for moral personhood.

In light of the dual nature of the human mind and the importance of both reasoning and intuition, how should we approach moral character education? A perspective that melds the paradigms is moral expertise development.

ADAPTIVE ETHICAL EXPERTISE AS A FRAMEWORK FOR DEVELOPING ETHICAL CHARACTER

The two seemingly opposed approaches to learning and becoming a moral person are brought together in expertise development, which emphasizes the development of appropriate intuitions and sophisticated reasoning. Experts-in-training are immersed in environments that foster good intuitions about the domain while receiving explicit guidance as to how to think about solving problems in the domain. For example, a working chef practices under the watchful eye of the master chef who models, guides, and advises.

What do we mean by expertise? Experts differ from novices in several key ways. They have more and better organized knowledge (e.g., Sternberg, 1998). They have declarative (explicit), procedural (implicit), and conditional knowledge. In short, they know what knowledge to access, which procedures to apply, how to apply them, and when. They perceive the world differently, noticing underlying patterns and discerning necessity where novices see nothing remarkable (Johnson & Mervis, 1997). Expert behavior is often automatic and effortless (Vicente & Wang, 1998). Experts function as more complex adaptive systems in their approaches to solving problems in the domain whereas novices miss the affordances for action available in the circumstance (Hatano & Inagaki, 1986; Neisser, 1976). Experts have highly developed intuitions as well as explicit knowledge. Moreover, experts' sense of self is highly connected to their efficacy. They are motivated for excellence in their domain of expertise.

The proposal here is that we should treat moral virtue or excellence as a type of adaptive expertise (Narvaez, 2006; Narvaez & Lapsley, 2005), much like the ancients did (e.g., Aristotle, 1988; Mencius, 1970). A virtuous person is like an expert who has highly cultivated skills—sets of procedural, declarative, and conditional knowledge—that are applied appropriately in the circumstance. In other words, moral exemplars in the fullest sense demonstrate moral (knowing the good) and practical wisdom (knowing how to carry it out in the situation). Moral expertise is applying the right virtue in the right amount in the right way at the right time.

Expertise is a set of capacities that can be put into action. Moral experts demonstrate holistic orientations (sets of procedural, declarative, and conditional knowledge) in one or more of at least four processes critical to moral behavior: ethical sensitivity, ethical judgment, ethical focus, and ethical action (Narvaez & Rest, 1995; Rest, 1983). See Table 9.1 for a list of skills. Experts in Ethical Sensitivity are better at quickly and accurately discerning the nature of a moral situation and determining the role they might play. They take on multiple perspectives in an effort to be morally responsive to others. Experts in

Table 9.1 Ethical Skills and Suggested Subskills

ETHICAL SENSITIVITY	ETHICAL JUDGMENT
Understand emotional expression	Understand ethical problems
Take the perspectives of others	Using codes & identifying judgment criteria
Connecting to others	Reasoning critically
Responding to diversity	Reasoning ethically
Controlling social bias	Understand consequences
Interpret situations	Reflect on process and outcome
Communicate well	Coping and resiliency
ETHICAL FOCUS	**ETHICAL ACTION**
Respecting others	Resolving conflicts and problems
Cultivate conscience	Assert respectfully
Help others	Taking initiative as a leader
Being a community member	Planning to implement decisions
Finding meaning in life	Cultivate courage
Valuing traditions & institutions	Persevering
Developing ethical identity & integrity	Working hard

Ethical Judgment reason about duty and consequences, and apply personal ethical codes to solve complex problems. Experts in Ethical Focus cultivate self-regulation that leads them to prioritize and deepen commitment to ethical goals. Experts in Ethical Action know how to keep their spirit focused on the moral goal and implement an action plan step by step. They are able to step forward and intervene courageously for the welfare of others. Experts in a particular moral excellence have more and better organized knowledge about it, have highly tuned perceptual skills for it, have deep moral desire for it, and have highly automatized, effortless responses. In short, they have more *content* knowledge and more *process* knowledge, more moral wisdom and more practical wisdom.

As novices in virtually every domain including the moral, children are best taught using novice-to-expert instruction (Bransford, Brown, & Cocking, 1999). Experts-in-training build implicit and explicit understandings about the domain, engaging both the deliberative and intuitive minds. Immersion in the domain occurs at the same time that explanations are presented, thereby cultivating both intuitions and deliberative understanding (Abernathy & Hamm, 1995). Their practice is focused, extensive, and coached through contextualized, situation-based experience. The learning environment is well-structured, providing appropriate and accurate feedback (e.g., the chef-in-training gets feedback both from the physical results of food prepared and from the coach who judges it). Through the course of expertise training, perceptions are fine-tuned and developed into chronically accessed constructs; interpretive frameworks are learned and, with practice, applied automatically; action schemas are honed to high levels of automaticity (Hogarth, 2001). What is painfully rule-based as a novice becomes, with vast experience, automatic and quick for an expert (Dreyfus & Dreyfus, 1990).

Nevertheless, there appear to be vastly different mindsets that influence perception and orientation in moral behavior. Triune-ethics theory seeks to name these disparate orientations and find their roots.

TRIUNE-ETHICS THEORY

Triune-ethics theory (TET; Narvaez, 2008) is derived from psychological, evolutionary, and neuro-sciences. Unlike most moral psychological work which has focused on the neocortex (e.g., deliberate reasoning), TET and its four goals address multiple neural systems including the subcortical, self-regulatory, and motivational structures (for more detail, see Narvaez, 2008, 2012, 2014). First, it emphasizes motivational orientations driven by unconscious emotional systems that predispose one to process information and react to events in particular ways. Second, MET helps explain individual differences in moral functioning. Individuals differ in early emotional experiences that influence personality formation and brain wiring and in turn affect information processing. Third, TET suggests the initial conditions for optimal human moral development, the *evolved developmental niche* (EDN; Narvaez, Gleason et al., 2013). The EDN emerged over 30 million years ago, designed to match up with the maturational needs of young social mammals, and was slightly altered during human evolution (Konner, 2010). The characteristics include: naturalistic childbirth with no interference with timing, separation of mom and baby or induced pain; breastfeeding two to five years; nearly constant touch; responsiveness to the cues of the child; free play; positive social support and multiple adult caregivers. Despite data showing that all these practices positively influence child health and wellbeing for the long term, the EDN is no longer closely followed in the USA (Narvaez, Panksepp, Schore, & Gleason, 2013). Interestingly, these practices also influence moral development (Narvaez & Gleason, 2012; Narvaez, Wang et al., 2013). Fourth, TET offers an explanation for the power of situations in influencing moral responses.

The moral self, moral identity, and moral motivation are areas of increasing interest to researchers (e.g., Hardy & Carlo, 2005, 2011). Blasi has suggested that a person with a moral identity has moral constructs central to the self and that moral identity acts as an important source of motivation for moral action (Blasi, 1983, 1985). TET contrasts with Blasi's view. Focusing on a person's subjective view, the central question is not about the strength of one's *moral* motivation but *what* moral motivation they have at the time of inquiry. All organisms are goal-driven, including humans (Bogdan, 1994). It is the nature of organisms to aim for what they perceive to be good in the moment so that, subjectively, a person feels they are behaving morally (although reflection later may change opinion). Persons select goals they think are the best in the circumstances, never consciously choosing goals they think are evil or bad (although see "selfish goal theory" Huang & Bargh, in press). Even those who behave violently are motivated to right a wrong (i.e., revenge is felt as "good" in the brain; de Quervain et al., 2004). Those who are impulsive feel that their goals are "right" in part because they feel them so strongly. Thus, from the individual's viewpoint in the moment (the subjective perspective), the person is behaving morally. However, from an objective viewpoint, self-centered behavior that harms or mistreats others is generally considered to be less morally defensible. For example, although egoism and selfishness can be touted as moral (see Weiss, 2012), they are usually considered outside of many moral frames. However, TET does not dismiss some mindsets as non-moral but notes different types. The view here is that everyone has a subjective moral identity—one oriented towards the perceived good. What varies, based on experience and situation, is the type of moral identity active at any given moment.

Triune-ethics theory identifies three basic attractors for moral functioning based on brain evolution: Safety, Engagement, and Imagination (MacLean, 1990; Narvaez, 2008, 2014). The three basic orientations represent different global brain states that emerge from the interplay and dominance of different emotion systems or their suppression. As a result, each brain state or mindset differentially affects perception, information processing, affordances (perceived action possibilities), and goals, propelling moral action on an individual or group level. See Figure 9.1 for types and subtypes.

The first mindset, Safety, involves the extrapyramidal action nervous system (MacLean, 1990: "R-complex"; Panksepp, 1998). The Ethic of Safety is based primarily in systems that revolve around survival and thriving in context, instincts shared with all animals and present from birth. The emotion systems of fear, anger, and exploration dominate here along with behaviors such as territoriality, imitation, deception, struggles for power, maintenance of routine, and following precedent. How much these "survival systems" dominate personality depends in part on early life experience because caregiving shapes self-regulatory systems and the capacity of the frontal lobe to control these subcortical systems. Excessive stress in early life can undermine self-regulatory capacities and wire the brain for threat reactivity (Porges, 2011), leading to a greater propensity to use a Safety Ethic in social interactions (Narvaez, 2014).

Like Kohlberg's preconventional stages, the Safety Ethic is concerned with self-preservation and personal gain, although it operates primarily implicitly. Survival systems dominate thought and behavior when the person or ingroup is threatened (MacLean, 1990). When the Safety Ethic is triggered, the brain is mobilized for

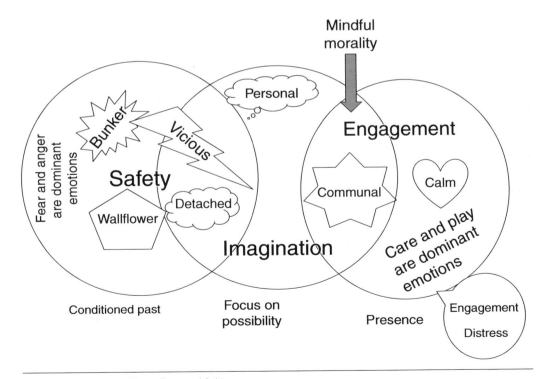

Figure 9.1 Triune-ethics Theory Types and Subtypes.

self—drawing energy away from executive function, hampering higher-order thinking and compassion. Defenses go up, in-group/out-group differences, rivalry, and the pecking order are stressed, and superorganismic (mob) mentality can be set in motion (Bloom, 1995). A moral self that is dominated by the Ethic of Safety may orient to flourishing through the acquisition of wealth, status, and power (Bunker Safety), or submission to hierarchy and order (Wallflower Safety). Perceiving threat easily, it is moral to hold in contempt out-group members or those who violate the moral rules. The virtues of the Safety Ethic are fortitude, loyalty (for protection, not out of love), and obedience.

Providing a safe, secure environment that meets young children's basic needs circumvents establishing the dominance of a Safety Ethic and promotes the ethics systems that better represent human aspirations, Engagement and Imagination. Nevertheless, control systems in the prefrontal cortex are not fully developed until the middle 20s (Giedd et al., 1999) and are easily overtaken by the hindbrain's self-protective impulsivity (Bechara, 2005) so that adults must still offer guidance to youth at least until the brain is fully developed, in the third decade of life.

The Ethic of Engagement involves the emotional systems (care, play) that drive us towards intimacy, identified by Darwin as the locus of human moral sense (Darwin, 1871; Loye, 2002). Although evolution has prepared the human brain for sociality and moral agency, early life care must follow the evolved developmental niche described above for optimal moral development. Proper care during early life is required for normal formation of brain circuitries necessary for successful social engagement, many of which are dominated by the right brain which develops rapidly in the first years of life. With expected care, the foundations of love and trust grow in early life (Narvaez & Gleason, 2012), leading to values of compassion, openness, and tolerance in adulthood (Eisler & Levine, 2002; Greenspan & Shanker, 2004). Figure 9.2 illustrates foundations of sociomoral development provided by the evolved developmental niche, each layer interactively building on prior layers including brain system "wiring" and thresholds for hormones and neurotransmitters. In mammals, poor early care leads to brain-behavioral disorders, evident in poor sociality and greater hostility and aggression towards others (Kruesi et al., 1992; Weaver, Szyf, & Meaney, 2002). The self in the present, in relationship, in emotional context, drives the relational moral orientation towards trust, love, reciprocity, and moral action (Engagement) when a person's brain/body systems are well formed. With poor or misdeveloped self-regulation, personal distress may ensue instead in social situations, undermining moral functioning (see Schore, 1994).

A disposition for Engagement, dominated by right-brain functioning, represents the heart of moral wisdom and virtue. Engagement has a greater capacity for meaningful relationships and a deeper sense of connection to others, a sense of respect and cherishment, and a sense of responsibility for the welfare of others (Oliner & Oliner, 1988; Narvaez, 2014). In fact when the Safety Ethic runs amok, the more humane engagement ethic may provide a counter pressure if awakened, shifting from the Safety Ethic's self-aggrandizement and urge for dominance to compassionate response.

The third ethical mindset, the Ethic of Imagination, uses the recently evolved parts of the brain, the neo- and prefrontal cortices. The Imagination Ethic responds to and coordinates the intuitions and instincts of the Engagement Ethic and the Safety Ethic, as well as sorting out the multiple elements involved in moral decision making (e.g., one's immediate and meta-goals, principles, mood, reactions, and those of others for whom the situation matters). The Imagination Ethic has the ability to countermand instincts and intuitions with "free won't" (Cotterill, 2000), the ability that allows humans through learning and willpower to choose which stimuli are allowed to trigger emotional arousal (Panksepp, 1998). For example, an enraged parent can counter the instinct to beat up a disobedient child. The Imagination Ethic also has the capacity to create narratives to guide behavior or rationalization. The deliberative mind, largely through the brain's "interpreter" (Gazzaniga, 1985), is facile in explaining any behavior, sometimes unaware that it is "making things up." Typically, the interpreter adopts the narratives of a cultural, familial, or affiliative group. The social narrative is further refined into a personal narrative, both of which guide behavior (Grusec, 2002).

Like the brain areas related to the Engagement Ethic, the development of brain areas related to the Ethic of Imagination requires a nurturing environment. The prefrontal cortex and its specialized units take decades to fully develop and are subject to damage from environmental factors (e.g., Anderson, Bechara, Damasio, Tranel, & Damasio, 1999). Underdevelopment of the right brain can lead to a Detached Imagination that makes moral disengagement easy (Bandura, 1999).

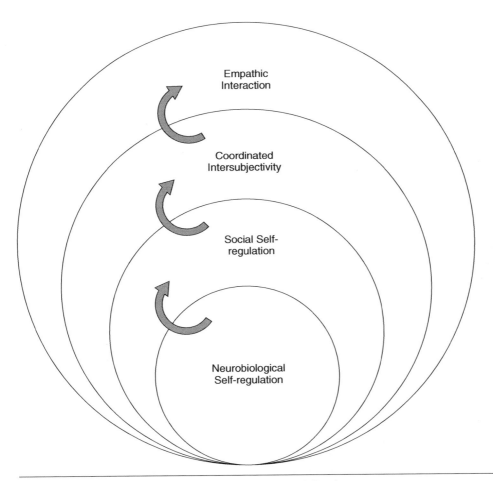

Figure 9.2 Baselines for Virtue Development Co-constructed by Early Experience.

When integrated with the Engagement Ethic, the Imagination becomes Communal Imagination and provides for a greater moral sense than the other ethics. Although humans have evolved to favor face-to-face relationships and have difficulty imagining those not present (such as future generations), the work of the Imagination Ethic provides a means for a sense of community that extends beyond immediate relations. Indeed, a self grounded in the Imagination Ethic is broadly aware of human possibilities, of the power of co-creation of community in the moment. Such a self is broadly reflective, demonstrating exquisite self-command for envisioned goals. The virtues of the Imagination Ethic are the ability to step back from the present moment, take multiple perspectives, and imagine alternative futures. However, when the Imagination Ethic is corralled by the Safety Ethic (e.g., using planning and reasoning skills for aggressive self-protection or emotional detachment), much harm can be perpetrated in the world through Vicious Imagination.

As noted, when the brain capacities for sociality and abstraction are not fully nurtured or damaged, the Safety Ethic becomes the default system, at one or both basic levels (aggressive, Bunker Morality, or passive, Wallflower Morality) or at the elaborated levels (Vicious or Detached Imagination). Although parenting provides the most important context for early brain wiring for engagement and imagination, educators can have an influence on which ethic dominates the classroom. The brain remains plastic so that Engagement and Communal Imagination can be cultivated even in schools. The Integrative Ethical Education model seeks to provide stepwise guidance to nurturing ethical expertise in the engagement and imagination ethics.

STEP-BY-STEP INTEGRATIVE ETHICAL EDUCATION

The Integrative Ethical Education model (IEE; Narvaez, 2006, 2007) provides an intentional, holistic, comprehensive, empirically-derived approach to moral character development. It is informed deeply by both ancient philosophy and current science about what contributes to human flourishing. As Aristotle pointed out, human flourishing necessarily includes individuals and communities, a perspective corroborated by the biological and social sciences. No one survives or flourishes alone. In fact, humans are biologically wired for sociality and love (Maturana & Verden-Zöller, 1996). With the proper care humans are deeply empathic, with ethics of high engagement and imagination (Narvaez, 2013, 2014).

The IEE model is presented in a step-by-step format. Ideally the steps take place simultaneously, but for new teachers, deploying and adding one step at a time is recommended.

Step 1: Establish a caring relationship with each student

Fundamental to any mentoring relationship is establishing a caring connection, the type of relationship that allows mutual influence for mutual benefit. Greenspan and Shanker (2004) describe how parental interaction with infants establishes the cognitive propensities for learning and social being. Ideally, the family home is a source for deep emotional nourishment as pleasurable intimate relationships foster capacities for open communication and growth. But this has become increasingly difficult to maintain, due in part to both parents working and a variety of distracting activities. In a day when children are emotionally malnourished, much rides on the adults they see every day, educators. In fact the most important protective factors against poor outcomes for a child are caring relationships, first, with an adult in the family, and second, with an adult outside the family (Masten, 2003). Why is caring so vital? As mammals, humans are primarily social-emotional creatures, evolutionarily prepared for the rewards of caring, emotionally-engaged relationships. The cool logic of a non-emotional Dr. Spock can be a sign of pathology, not health (Damasio, 1999). It is through caring relationships and supportive climates that teachers nurture motivation and an engagement ethic.

When students have good relationships with their teachers, they are more likely to feel welcome in the classroom and have a greater sense of belonging, which is related to higher motivation and achievement (Klem & Connell, 2004; McNeely, Nonnemaker, & Blum, 2002; Roeser, Midgley, & Urdan, 1996). Teacher caring and support are related to increased student engagement in learning (Libbey, 2004), especially among at-risk students (Connell, Halpern-Felsher, Clifford, Crichlow, & Usinger, 1995; Croninger & Lee, 2001). Teachers can individualize their care for students, like a good parent. Of course, this means getting to know the child, respectfully, as much as possible. Some students with troubled backgrounds require a longer warm-up period before they trust the teacher, requiring teacher persistence and patience (see Watson, 2003, this volume). Establishing a caring relationship is easier with some children than others, and is easier for elementary teachers than high school teachers who see many students relatively briefly. Nevertheless, as long as teachers maintain a humane classroom, students will be more likely to feel safe and engaged in learning, fostering moral character at the same time.

Human minds and hearts are prepared for emotional signaling and emotional motivation (Greenspan & Shanker 2004; Lewis, Amini, & Lannon, 2000; Panksepp, 1998). If these are ignored or mishandled by the educator, then the Safety Ethic may predominate. The student may then spend most energy towards self-protection, leaving little energy for openness to learning. When the educator establishes healthy emotional communication with each student she provides the bridge for communication and influence. Without it, academic motivation is reliant on the residue of family motivation (which may be enough for some students but not others, e.g., Li, 2005; Steinberg, 1996).

Step 2: Establish a climate supportive of achievement and ethical character

In simpler times, children learned morality through direct experience with adults during the basic chores and activities of life at home and in the local community. Today, children's lives are generally divorced from the everyday life of most adults and take place in the artificial learning settings, revolving around the classroom and school. So now it is here they learn how to get along with peers, how to participate in group work and decision making, how to be a citizen, and many other skills they take with them into adulthood. "The only way to prepare for social life is to engage in social life" so schools should be constructed as social institutions that integrate intellectual and moral development through active learning (Dewey, 1909/1975, p. 14).

Organizational climates and cultures shape perceptions and behavior (Power, Higgins, & Kohlberg, 1989; Power & Higgins-D'Alessandro, 2008). In the broad sense, the climate includes the structures of the social environment, the overt and hidden systems of rewards and punishment, the goals and aspirations of the social group, and the general discourse about goals. In the specific sense, climate has to do with how people treat one another, how they work and make decisions together, what feelings and expectations are nurtured.

Considerable research points to the importance of a caring classroom and school climate for optimal student outcomes. When classrooms have climates of mutual respect and caring—when the teacher fosters the Ethics of Engagement in self and students—everyone feels greater physical and psychological safety, leading to a greater sense of belongingness (Anderman, 2003; Ma, 2003). Bonding to school not only increases school engagement and commitment to learning among students (Goodenow, 1993), but also growth in achievement (Libbey, 2004) and healthy development generally (Catalano, Oesterle, Fleming, & Hawkins, 2004; Catalano, Toumbourou, & Hawkins, this volume). Caring classrooms and schools with high expectations for achievement and behavior are related both to high achievement and to moral behavior (Battistich, 2008; Zins, Weissberg, Wang, & Walberg, 2004). According to Solomon, Watson, and Battistich (2002), caring school and classroom communities have the following characteristics:

- Students are able to demonstrate autonomy, self-direction, and influence teacher decisions.
- Students interact positively with one another, collaborating and discussing course content and classroom policies.
- Students are coached on social skills as teachers exhibit warm acceptance of students, providing support and positive modeling.
- The teacher provides multiple opportunities for students to help one another.
- In a caring classroom, discipline is not punishment but is coached character development.

Educators can emphasize both engagement and imagination ethics, asking "who should I be?" as well as "how can we show respect for one another?" and "How can we help one another feel cared for in the classroom?" Schools can establish programs that take up part of the burden for developing empathy and fostering compassion that families are unable to address (e.g., Schonert-Reichl, Smith, Zaidman-Zait, & Hertzman, 2012).

Steps 1 and 2 are integral to best-practice teaching, yet in an era where children are exposed to many negative role models through popular culture, these two steps may no longer be enough to help students develop moral character (Narvaez & Lapsley, 2008). The next three steps identify more intentional cultivation of moral character.

Step 3: Teach ethical skills across the curriculum and extra-curriculum using a novice-to-expert pedagogy

As mentioned above, training for ethical expertise includes developing appropriate intuitions and sophisticated deliberations in at least four areas: Ethical Sensitivity, Ethical Judgment, Ethical Focus and Ethical Action. But what competencies can or should be emphasized in schools? The Integrative Ethical Education model suggests skills and subskills for each of the four processes. These are skills critical for social and emotional intelligence and living a good life generally (see Elias et al., this volume). These skills are also important for active global citizenship. In a multipolar world, educators can help students minimize the Safety Ethic and develop engagement and imagination. See Table 9.1 for the suggested skills for each of the four processes described earlier.

How should moral character education be structured? As in training for expertise, educators should instruct both the deliberative mind and the intuitive mind. The intuitive mind is cultivated through immersion in active environments where skills are practiced and developed. This involves imitation of role models and appropriate feedback from the environment about what works. Social-cognitive moral personality theory suggests that a moral personality is built from social and practical experiences that foster automatized moral schemas (Lapsley & Narvaez, 2004a; Narvaez & Lapsley, 2005; Narvaez, Lapsley, Hagele, & Lasky, 2006).

The deliberative mind can be coached in ways that fine-tune action and in metacognitive skills such as how to select good environments for one's own intuition development. By providing developmentally-sensitive theoretical explanation and dialogue, the deliberative mind builds understanding that coordinates implicit knowledge. Teachers are, first and foremost, role models. They can model a moral orientation to life by thinking aloud about their own moral decisions, telling stories about striving for moral goals, reading stories that develop students' moral imaginations.

Learning involves an active and interactive process of transforming one's conceptual structures through selective attention and by relating new information to prior knowledge (Anderson, 1989). Best-practice instruction provides opportunities for students to develop more accurate and better organized representations and the procedural skills required to use them (Ibid.). In order to do this, children must experience an *expert-in-training pedagogy* for each skill that they learn. Teachers can set up instruction to help students develop appropriate knowledge by designing lessons according to the following four levels of activities (Narvaez, 2005; Narvaez, Bock, Endicott, & Lies, 2004):

Level 1: Immersion in examples and opportunities. Teachers provide models and modeling of the goal, draw student attention to the "big picture" in the subject area, and help the students learn to recognize basic patterns.

Level 2: Attention to facts and skills. As students practice subskills, teachers focus student attention on the elemental concepts in the domain in order to build more elaborate concepts.

Level 3: Practice procedures. The teacher allows the student to try out many skills and ideas throughout the domain to build an understanding of how skills relate and how best to solve problems in the domain.

Level 4: Integrate knowledge and procedures. The student finds numerous mentors and/or seeks out information to continue building concepts and skills. There is a gradual systematic integration and application of skills and knowledge across many situations.

The ethical expertise approach was initially developed in the Minnesota Community Voices and Character Education project. In the final evaluation year, after being familiarized with the framework of skills and pedagogical approach, teacher teams determined which skills their students needed and which academic courses would integrate which skills. Using materials provided by the project designers and teacher-designed lessons, the skills approach had a significant effect on students in schools that implemented broadly over one year's time in contrast to a comparison group and to low implementing schools (see Narvaez et al., 2004; see also Narvaez, 2009, 2012; Narvaez & Bock, 2009; Narvaez & Endicott, 2009; Narvaez & Lies, 2009).[2]

Step 4: Foster student self-authorship and self-regulation

Self-regulation (equilibration) has been a central, driving force of evolution and development within organisms (Darwin, 1871). Self-authorship (autopoeisis) is what living systems do (Varela, Maturana, & Uribe, 1974). Self-authorship requires a coordinated partnership between the different minds (intuition and deliberation) and prosocial ethics (engagement and imagination) in a type of reflective abstraction (Piaget's *prise de conscience*; Gruber & Voneche, 1995). Plato understood human existence to be a problem to the self, "the problem of deciding what to become and endeavoring to become it" (Urmson, 1988, p. 2). In other words, the final responsibility for character development lies with the individual. In their choices and actions, orientations and time allocations, individuals address the question: *Who should I be? Who are my role models and how do I get there?* In an enriched moral environment, students are provided with tools for self-regulation and self-authorship in character formation. As Aristotle pointed out, individuals need mentors for self-regulation and self-development (self-authorship) until they can guide them through the selection of virtuous friends and activities (Urmson, 1988).

Individuals can be coached not only in skills and expertise, as noted previously, but in domain-specific self-regulation (Zimmerman, Bonner, & Kovach, 2002). The most successful students learn to monitor the effectiveness of their problem-solving strategies and, when necessary, alter their strategies for success (Anderson, 1989). Coaching for self-regulation requires enlisting the deliberative mind to select the environments from which the intuitive mind learns effective behaviors, thereby accelerating implicit learning (Hogarth, 2001). For example, different intuitions are developed when reading a good book than when playing violent video games. Teachers thinking aloud about solving challenging problems and their decision making processes provides students with examples of how to monitor progress during goal execution. Students can learn the metacognitive skills that moral experts have, such as noticing moral problems, guiding one's attention away from temptations, self-cheerleading when energy fades, and selecting or redesigning an environment to maximize goal completion (Zimmerman, 1998).

Step 5: Restore the Village: Asset-Building Communities and Coordinated Developmental Systems

It bears emphasizing that the good life is not lived in isolation. One does not flourish alone. IEE is implemented in and with a community. It is the community which establishes, and nourishes, the individual's moral voice, providing a moral anchor, and offering guidance as virtues are cultivated. Indeed, both Plato and Aristotle agreed that a good person is above all a good citizen. Hunter (2000) suggests that we find the answers to our existential questions in the particularities that we bring to a civic dialogue: "Character outside of a lived community, the entanglements of complex social relationships, and their shared story, is impossible" (p. 227). It is in the community that students apply and hone their ethical competencies.

Truly democratic ethical education empowers all involved—educators, community members, and students—as they form a learning community together, developing ethical skills and self-regulation for both individual and community actualization (Rogoff, Turkanis, & Bartlett, 2001). The purpose of ethical behavior is to live a good life *in the community*. Together community members work out basic questions such as: How should we get along in our community? How do we build up our community? How do we help one another flourish? Each individual lives within an active ecological context (Bronfenbrenner, 1979) in which, ideally, the entire community builds ethical skills together.

Overall, we can strengthen the connections among children's life spaces: home, school, and community at various levels. Children who live with coordinated systems are adaptationally advantaged (Benson, Leffert, Scales, & Blyth, 1998). The type of person a child becomes is determined in large part by the dynamic interaction among community, family, and culture. Caring communities with high expectations and involved adults are more likely to raise morally-engaged citizens.

SHAPING MORAL PERCEPTIONS

"[Television is] a cultural environment into which our children are born, and which tells all the stories ... who tells the stories of a culture really governs human behavior. It used to be the parent, the school, the church, the community. Now it's a handful of global conglomerates that have nothing to tell, but a great deal to sell."— George Gerbner.

(Oliver, 2005)

At no time in US history have children's minds been more shaped by non-family members, specifically advertisers who peddle dissatisfaction with self and the need for consuming an endless array of products (Halton, 2008). Neuroscience research shows the effects of popular media on brain maturation, and much of it is worrisome (Kasser, 2002; Quart, 2003). The Ethic of Safety is activated by media from which we develop a "mean world syndrome," desensitization towards violence (it is fun and rewarding) and towards victims of violence, culminating in a general lack of trust in others (Gerbner, 1994). The Ethic of Safety is aggravated when we see what others have that we do not ("affluenza," Hamilton & Denniss, 2005), promoting addictive status seeking. The Ethic of Imagination is hijacked by these artificially-manufactured desires so that virtue is converted into being a good consumer. The Ethic of Engagement, being physiologically "in tune" with others, is experienced less as interaction with others occurs more and more through electronic means (Vandewater, Bickham, & Lee, 2006).

Children learn cultural narrative structures and when to use them through direct experience with stories that provide reasons for action (Narrative Practice Hypothesis, Hutto, 2007). Teachers can foster narratives to counter the hedonism and status-enhancing messages of popular media and instead foster discourse that draws attention to moral issues and the child's social purpose. Teachers can encourage students to construct their own moral goals and moral life story (e.g., *How are you going to make the world a better place for everyone? What skills do you need for it?*). Individuals operate according to the narratives they tell themselves (McAdams, 1993; Schank, 1995). Adults help structure personal narratives by the types of questions they ask (e.g., *How did you help someone in school today? What positive actions did you take over vacation? What positive goals do you have for today?* Nelson & Gruendel, 1981). Teachers (and adults in general) influence children's narratives by what they emphasize, expect, and encourage in the environments they design for children. Teachers can fill children's memories with positive concrete experiences in which they helped others and teachers can remind them of these times.

Providing satisfying social experiences that engage student emotion and motivation can shape not only perceptions and sensibilities but also goals and dreams. By providing a purposeful prosocial narrative, the child internalizes a personal narrative and the deliberative mind's imagination is engaged in activities that bring it about.

CONCLUSION

Educators play a large role in the moral character development of their students. The Integrative Ethical Education model encourages educators to take on an intentional, conscientious approach to cultivating moral character. Specifically, IEE informs educators how they can cultivate their students' expertise in Multi-Ethic Theory's engagement and imagination ethics. IEE's step-by-step, empirically-derived framework is intended to help educators actualize their important responsibility of helping develop their students' moral character.

NOTES

1. Note, we use ethical and moral interchangeably.
2. Earlier versions of these booklets were created under grant #R215V980001 from the US Department of Education Office of Educational Research and Improvement to the Minnesota Department of Children, Families and Learning during 1998–2002 and can be downloaded at http://cee.nd.edu/curriculum/curriculum1.shtml.

REFERENCES

Abernathy, C. M., & Hamm, R. M. (1995). *Surgical intuition.* Philadelphia: Hanley & Belfus.

Anderman, L. H. (2003). Academic and social perceptions as predictors of change in middle school students' sense of school belonging. *Journal of Experimental Education, 72*(1), 5–22.

Anderson, L. M. (1989). Learners and learning. In M. C. Reynolds (Ed.), *Knowledge base for the beginning teacher* (pp. 85–99). Oxford: Pergamon Press.

Anderson, S. W., Bechara, A., Damasio, H., Tranel, D., & Damasio, A. R. (1999). Impairment of social and moral behavior related to early damage in human prefrontal cortex. *Nature Neuroscience, 2*(11), 1032–1037.

Anscombe, G. E. M. (1958). Modern moral philosophy. *Philosophy, 33,* 1–19.

Aristotle (1988). *Nicomachean Ethics* (trans. by W. D. Ross). London: Oxford.

Bandura, A. (1999). Moral disengagement in the perpetration of inhumanities. *Personality and Social Psychology Review, 3*(3), 269–275.

Bargh, J. A. (1997). The automaticity of everyday life. In R. S. Wyer, Jr. (Ed.), *The automaticity of everyday life: Advances in social cognition, Vol. X.* (pp. 1–61). Mahwah, NJ: Lawrence Erlbaum Associates, Publishers.

Bargh, J. A., & Chartrand, T. L. (1999). The unbearable automaticity of being. *American Psychologist, 54,* 462–479.

Bargh, J. A., & Ferguson, M. J. (2000). Beyond behaviorism: On the automaticity of higher mental processes. *Psychological Bulletin, 126,* 925–945.

Battistich, V. A. (2008). The Child Development Project: Creating caring school communities. In L. Nucci & D. Narvaez (Eds.), *Handbook of moral and character education* (1st ed.) (pp. 328–351). Mahwah, NJ: Erlbaum.

Bechara, A. (2005). Decision making, impulse control and loss of willpower to resist drugs: A neurocognitive perspective. *Nature Neuroscience, 8,* 1458–1463.

Benson, P., Leffert, N., Scales, P., & Blyth, D. (1998). Beyond the "village" rhetoric: Creating healthy communities for children and adolescents. *Applied Developmental Science, 2*(3), 138–159.

Blatt, M., & Kohlberg, L. (1975). The effects of classroom discussion upon children's level of moral judgment. *Journal of Moral Education, 4,* 129–161.

Blasi, A. (1980). Bridging moral cognition and moral action: A critical review of the literature. *Psychological Bulletin, 88,* 1–45.

Blasi, A. (1983). Moral cognition and moral action: A theoretical perspective. *Developmental Review, 3*, 178–210.

Blasi, A. (1985). The moral personality: Reflections for social science and education. In M. W. Berkowitz & F. Oser (Eds.), *Moral education: Theory and practice* (pp. 433–444). Hillsdale, NJ: Erlbaum.

Bloom, H. (1995). *The Lucifer principle.* New York: Atlantic Monthly Press.

Bogdan, R. J. (1994). *Grounds for cognition: How goal-guided behavior shapes the mind.* New York: Psychology Press.

Bransford, J. D., Brown, A. L, & Cocking, R. R. (1999). *How people learn: Brain, mind, experience, and school.* Washington, DC: National Academy Press.

Bronfenbrenner, U. (1979). *The ecology of human development.* Cambridge, MA: Harvard University Press.

Catalano, R. F., Oesterle, S., Fleming, C. B., & Hawkins, J. D. (2004). The importance of bonding to school for healthy development: Findings from the Social Development Research Group. *Journal of School Health, 74*, 252–261.

Connell, J. P., Halpern-Felsher, B., Clifford, E., Crichlow, W., & Usinger, P. (1995). Hanging in there: Behavioral, psychological and contextual factors affecting whether African-Americans adolescents stay in school. *Journal of Adolescent Research, 10*(1), 41–63.

Cotterill, R. (2000). *Enchanted looms.* Cambridge, England: Cambridge University Press.

Croninger, R. G., & Lee, V. E. (2001). Social capital and dropping out of high schools: Benefits to at-risk students of teachers' support and guidance. *Teachers College Record, 103*(4), 548–581.

Damasio, A. (1999). *The feeling of what happens.* New York: Harcourt and Brace.

Darwin, C. (1871/1981). *The descent of man.* Princeton, NJ: Princeton University Press.

de Quervain, D. J. F., Fischbacher, U., Treyer, V., Schellhammer, M., Schnyder, U., Buck, A., & Fehr, E. (2004). The neural basis of altruistic punishment. *Science, 305*, 1254–1258.

Dewey, J. (1909/1975). *Moral principles in education.* Carbondale, IL: Southern Illinois University Press.

Dreyfus, H., & Dreyfus, S. (1990). What is morality? A phenomenological account of the development of ethical expertise. In D. Rasmussen (Ed.), *Universalism vs. communitarianism* (pp. 237–266). Cambridge, MA: MIT.

Eisler, R., & Levine, D. S. (2002). Nurture, nature, and caring: We are not prisoners of our genes. *Brain and Mind, 3*, 9–52.

Gazzaniga, M. S. (1985). *The social brain.* New York: Basic Books.

Gerbner, G. (1994). Reclaiming our cultural mythology: Television's global marketing strategy creates a damaging and alienated window on the world. *The Ecology of Justice, 38*, p. 40.

Giedd, J. N., Blumenthal, J., Jeffries, N. O., Castellanos, F. X., Liu, H., Zijdenbos, A. ... Rapoport, J. L. (1999). Brain development during childhood and adolescence: A longitudinal MRI study. *Nature Neuroscience, 2*(10), 861–863.

Goodenow, C. (1993). The psychological sense of school membership among adolescents: Scale development and educational correlates. *Psychology in the Schools, 30*, 79–90.

Greenspan, S. I., & Shanker, S. G. (2004). *The first idea.* Cambridge, MA: Da Capo Press.

Groopman, J. (2007). *How doctors think.* New York: Houghton Mifflin.

Gruber, H. E., & Voneche, J. J. (1995). *The essential Piaget.* New York: Basic Books.

Grusec, J. E. (2002). Parental socialization and children's acquisition of values. In M. H. Bornstein (Ed.), *Handbook of parenting: Vol. 5. Practical issues in parenting* (2nd ed., pp. 143–167). Mahwah, NJ: Erlbaum.

Halton, E. (2008). *The great brain suck.* Chicago: University of Chicago Press.

Hamilton, C., & Denniss, R. (2005). *Affluenza: When too much is never enough.* East Melbourne, Australia: Allen & Unwin.

Hammond, K. R. (2000). *Judgments under stress.* New York: Oxford.

Hardy, S. A., & Carlo, G. (2005). Identity as a source of moral motivation. *Human Development, 48*, 232–256.

Hardy, S. A., & Carlo, G. (2011). Moral identity: What is it, how does it develop, and is it linked to moral action? *Child Development Perspectives, 5*, 212–218.

Hare, R. M. (1963). *Freedom and reason.* New York: Oxford University Press.

Hatano, G., & Inagaki, K. (1986). Two courses of expertise. In H. Stevenson, H. Azuma, & K. Hakuta (Eds.), *Child development and education in Japan* (pp. 262–272). New York, NY: W.H. Freeman & Co.

Hogarth, R. M. (2001). *Educating intuition.* Chicago: University of Chicago Press.

Huang, J. Y., & Bargh, J. A. (in press). The selfish goal: Autonomously operating motivational structures as the proximate cause of human judgment and behavior. *Behavioral and Brain Sciences.*

Hunter, J. D. (2000). *The death of character: Moral education in an age without good or evil.* New York: Basic Books.

Hursthouse, R. (1999). *On virtue ethics,* Oxford: Oxford University Press.

Hutto, D. D. (2007). The Narrative Practice Hypothesis: Origins and applications of folk psychology. In D. D.

Hutto (Ed.), *Narrative and understanding persons* (pp. 43–68). Royal Institute of Philosophy Supplement, no. 60. Cambridge, England: Cambridge University Press.

Johnson, K. E., & Mervis, C. B. (1997). Effects of varying levels of expertise on the basic level of categorization. *Journal of Experimental Psychology: General, 126*(3), 248–277.

Kahneman, D. (2003). A perspective on judgment and choice: Mapping bounded rationality. *American Psychologist, 58*(9), 697–720.

Kant, I. (1949). *Fundamental principles of the metaphysics of morals*. New York: Liberal Arts Press.

Kasser, T. (2002). *The high price of materialism*. Cambridge, MA: MIT Press.

Klem, A. M, & Connell, J. P. (2004). Relationships matter: Linking teacher support to student engagement and achievement. *Journal of School Health, 74*(7), 262–273.

Kohlberg, L. (1981). *Essays in moral development: The philosophy of moral development*.

Kohn, A. (1997a). The trouble with character education. In A. Molnar (Ed.), *The construction of children's character* (pp. 154–162). Chicago: University of Chicago Press.

Kohn, A. (1997b). How not to teach values: A critical look at character education. *Phi Delta Kappan, February*, 429–439.

Konner, M. (2010). *The evolution of childhood*. Cambridge, MA: Belknap.

Kruesi, M. J. P., Hibbs, E. D., Zahn, T. P., Keysor, C. S., Hamburger, S. D., Bartko, J. J., & Rapoport, J. L. (1992). A 2-year prospective follow-up study of children and adolescents with disruptive behavior disorders. *Archives of General Psychiatry, 49*, 429–435.

Lakoff, G., & Johnson, M. (1999). *Philosophy in the flesh: The embodied mind and its challenge to Western thought*. New York: HarperCollins Publishers.

Lapsley, D., & Narvaez, D. (2004a). A social-cognitive view of moral character. In D. Lapsley & D. Narvaez (Eds.), *Moral development: Self and identity* (pp. 189–212). Mahwah, NJ: Erlbaum.

Lapsley, D., & Narvaez, D. (2004b). *Moral development: Self and identity*. Mahwah, NJ: Erlbaum.

Lapsley, D. K., & Narvaez, D. (2006). Character education. In Vol. 4 (A. Renninger & I. Siegel, volume eds.), *Handbook of child psychology* (W. Damon & R. Lerner, Series Eds.) (pp. 248–296). New York: Wiley.

Leming, J. S. (1997). Research and practice in character education: A historical perspective. In A. Molnar (Ed.), *The construction of children's character* (pp. 11–44). Ninety-sixth Yearbook of the National Society for the Study of Education. Chicago: National Society for the Study of Education and the University of Chicago Press.

Lewis, T., Amini, F., & Lannon, R. (2000). *A general theory of love*. New York: Vintage.

Li, J. (2005). Mind or virtue: Western and Chinese beliefs about learning. *Current Directions in Psychological Science, 14*(4), 190–194.

Libbey, H. P. (2004). Measuring student relationships to school: Attachment bonding, connectedness and engagement. *Journal of School Health, 74*(7), 274–283.

Loye, D. (2002). The moral brain. *Brain and Mind, 3*, 133–150.

Ma, X. (2003). Sense of belonging to school: Can schools make a difference? *The Journal of Educational Research, 96*(6), 340–349.

MacIntyre, A. (1981). *After virtue*. London: Duckworth.

MacLean, P. D. (1990). *The triune brain in evolution: Role in paleocerebral functions*. New York: Plenum.

Masten, A. S. (2003). Commentary: Developmental psychopathology as a unifying context for mental health and education models, research and practice in schools. *School Psychology Review, 32*, 169–173.

Maturana, H. R., & Verden-Zöller, G. (1996). Biology of love. In G. Opp & F. Peterander (Eds.), *Focus Heilpadagogik*. Munchen/Basel: Ernst Reinhardt.

McAdams, D. P. (1993). *The stories we live by: Personal myths and the making of the self*. New York: Guilford.

McDowell, J. (1997). Virtues and vices. In R. Crisp & M. Slote (Eds.), *Virtue ethics* (pp. 141–162). Oxford, England: Oxford University Press.

McNeely, C. A., Nonnemaker, J. M., & Blum, R. W. (2002). Promoting school connectedness: Evidence from the national longitudinal study of adolescent health. *Journal of School Health, 72*, 138–146.

Mencius. (1970). *Mencius* (trans. by D. Lau). London: Penguin.

Narvaez, D. (2005). The Neo-Kohlbergian tradition and beyond: Schemas, expertise and character. In G. Carlo & C. Pope-Edwards (Eds.), *Nebraska Symposium on Motivation, Vol. 51: Moral Motivation through the Lifespan* (pp. 119–163). Lincoln, NE: University of Nebraska Press.

Narvaez, D. (2006). Integrative ethical education. In M. Killen & J. Smetana (Eds.), *Handbook of moral development* (pp. 703–733). Mahwah, NJ: Erlbaum.

Narvaez, D. (2007). How cognitive and neurobiological sciences inform values education for creatures like us. In D. Aspin & J. Chapman (Eds.), *Values education and lifelong learning: Philosophy, policy, practices* (pp. 127–159). New York: Springer Press International.

Narvaez, D. (2008). Triune ethics: The neurobiological roots of our multiple moralities. *New Ideas in Psychology, 26*, 95–119.

Narvaez, D. (2009). *Nurturing character in the classroom, EthEx Series, Book 4: Ethical Action.* Notre Dame, IN: ACE Press.

Narvaez, D. (2012). Moral neuroeducation from early life through the lifespan. *Neuroethics, 5*(2), 145–157.

Narvaez, D. (2013). Development and socialization within an evolutionary context: Growing up to become "A good and useful human being." In D. Fry (Ed.), *War, peace and human nature: The convergence of evolutionary and cultural views* (pp. 643–672). New York: Oxford University Press.

Narvaez, D. (2014). *The neurobiology and development of human morality: Evolution, culture and wisdom.* New York: W.W. Norton.

Narvaez, D., & Bock, T. (2009). *Nurturing character in the classroom, EthEx Series, Book 2: Ethical Judgment.* Notre Dame, IN: ACE Press.

Narvaez, D., Bock, T., Endicott, L., & Lies, J. (2004). Minnesota's Community Voices and Character Education Project. *Journal of Research in Character Education, 2*, 89–112.

Narvaez, D., & Endicott, L. (2009). *Nurturing character in the classroom, EthEx Series, Book 1: Ethical Sensitivity.* Notre Dame, IN: ACE Press.

Narvaez, D., & Gleason, T. (2012). Developmental optimization. In D. Narvaez, J., Panksepp, A. Schore, & T. Gleason (Eds.), *Evolution, early experience and human development: From research to practice and policy* (pp. 307–325). New York: Oxford University Press.

Narvaez, D., Gleason, T., Wang, L., Brooks, J., Lefever, J., Cheng, A., & Centers for the Prevention of Child Neglect (2013). The Evolved Development Niche: Longitudinal Effects of Caregiving Practices on Early Childhood Psychosocial Development. *Early Childhood Research Quarterly, 28*(4), 759–773.

Narvaez, D., & Lapsley, D. (2005). The psychological foundations of everyday morality and moral expertise. In D. Lapsley & C. Power (Eds.), *Character psychology and character education* (pp. 140–165). Notre Dame: IN: University of Notre Dame Press.

Narvaez, D., & Lapsley, D. K. (2008). Teaching moral character: Two alternatives for teacher educators. *Teacher Educator, 43*(2), 156–172.

Narvaez, D., & Lapsley, D. K. (Eds.) (2009). *Personality, identity, and character: Explorations in moral psychology.* New York: Cambridge University Press.

Narvaez, D., Lapsley, D., Hagele, S., & Lasky, B. (2006). Moral chronicity and social information processing: Tests of a social cognitive approach to the moral personality. *Journal of Research in Personality, 40*, 966–985.

Narvaez, D. & Lies, J. (2009). *Nurturing character in the classroom, EthEx Series, Book 3: Ethical Motivation.* Notre Dame, IN: ACE Press.

Narvaez, D., Panksepp, J., Schore, A., & Gleason, T. (Eds.) (2013). *Evolution, early experience and human development: From research to practice and policy.* New York: Oxford University Press.

Narvaez, D., & Rest, J. (1995). The four components of acting morally. In W. Kurtines & J. Gewirtz (Eds.), *Moral behavior and moral development: An introduction* (pp. 385–400). New York: McGraw-Hill.

Narvaez, D., Wang, L., Gleason, T., Cheng, A., Lefever, J., & Deng, L. (2013). The Evolved Developmental Niche and sociomoral outcomes in Chinese three-year-olds. *European Journal of Developmental Psychology, 10*(2), 106–127.

Neisser, U. (1976). *Cognition and reality: Principles and implications of cognitive psychology.* New York: W. H. Freeman.

Nelson, K., & Gruendel, J. (1981). Generalized event representations: Basic building blocks of cognitive development. In M. Lamb & A. Brown (Eds.), *Advances in developmental psychology* (pp. 131–158). Hillsdale NJ: Erlbaum.

Norton, D. L. (1991). *Democracy and moral development: A politics of virtue.* Los Angeles, CA: University of California Press.

Oliner, S. P., & Oliner, P. M. (1988). *The altruistic personality: Rescuers of Jews in Nazi Europe.* New York: Free Press.

Oliver, M. (2005). George Gerbner, 86; Educator researched the influence of TV viewing on perceptions. *Los Angeles Times,* December 29.

O'Neill, O. (1996). *Towards justice and virtue: A constructive account of practical reasoning.* Cambridge, England: Cambridge University Press.

Panksepp J. (1998). *Affective neuroscience.* New York: Oxford University Press.

Piaget, J. (1932). *The moral judgment of the child.* London: Routledge & Kegan Paul.

Porges, S. (2011). *The Polyvagal theory: Neurophysiological foundations of emotions, attachment, communication, and self-regulation.* New York: W.W. Norton.

Power, C., Higgins, A., & Kohlberg, L. (1989). *Lawrence Kohlberg's approach to moral education*. New York: Columbia University Press.

Power, F. C., & Higgins-D'Alessandro, A. (2008). The just community approach to moral education and the moral atmosphere of the school. In L. P. Nucci & D. Narvaez (Eds.) *Handbook of moral and character education* (pp. 230–247). New York: Routledge.

Quart, A. (2003). *Branded: The buying and selling of teenagers*. New York: Perseus Books.

Rawls, J. (1971). *A theory of justice*. Cambridge, MA: Harvard University Press.

Rest, J. (1983). Morality. In J. Flavell & E. Markham (Eds.), *Cognitive development*, from P. Mussen (Ed.) *Manual of child psychology, Vol. 3* (pp. 556–629). New York: Wiley.

Rest, J. R., Narvaez, D., Bebeau, M. J., & Thoma, S. J. (1999). *Postconventional moral thinking: A Neo-Kohlbergian approach*. Mahwah, NJ: Erlbaum.

Roeser, R. M., Midgley, C., & Urdan, T. (1996). Perceptions of the psychological environment and early adolescents' psychological and behavioral functioning in school: The mediating role of goals and belonging. *Journal of Educational Psychology, 88*(3), 408–422.

Rogoff, B., Turkanis, C. G., & Bartlett, L. (Eds.). (2001). *Learning together: Children and adults in a school community*. New York: Oxford University Press.

Schank, R. C. (1995). *Tell me a story: Narrative and intelligence*. Evanston, IL: Northwestern University Press.

Schonert-Reichl, K. A., Smith, V., Zaidman-Zait, A., & Hertzman, C. (2012). Promoting children's prosocial behaviors in school: Impact of the "Roots of Empathy" program on the social and emotional competence of school-aged children. *School Mental Health, 4*, 1–21.

Schore, A. (1994). *Affect regulation*. Hillsdale, NJ: Erlbaum.

Solomon, D., Watson, M. S., & Battistich, V. A. (2002). Teaching and school effects on moral/prosocial development. In V. Richardson (Ed.), *Handbook for research on teaching*. Washington, D.C.: American Educational Research Association.

Steinberg, L. (in collaboration with B. Brown & S. Dornbusch) (1996). *Beyond the classroom: Why school reform has failed and what parents need to do*. New York: Simon & Schuster.

Sternberg, R. (1998). Abilities are forms of developing expertise, *Educational Researcher, 3*, 22–35.

Thoma, S. J. (1994). Moral judgment and moral action. In J. R. Rest & D. Narvaez (Eds.), *Moral development in the professions: Psychology and applied ethics* (pp. 199–212). Hillsdale, NJ: Erlbaum.

Urmson, J. O. (1988). *Aristotle's ethics*. Oxford: Blackwell.

Vandewater, E. A., Bickham, D. S., & Lee, J. H. (2006). Time well spent? Relating television use to children's free-time activities. *Pediatrics, 117*(2), e181–e191.

Varela, F., Maturana, H., & Uribe, R. (1974). Autopoiesis: The organization of living systems, its characterization and a model. *Biosystems, 5*, 187–196.

Vicente, K. J., & Wang, J. H. (1998). An ecological theory of expertise effects in memory recall. *Psychological Review, 105*(1), 33–57.

Watson, M. (2003). *Learning to trust*. San Francisco: Jossey-Bass.

Weaver, I. C. G., Szyf, M., & Meaney, M. J. (2002). From maternal care to gene expression: DNA methylation and the maternal programming of stress responses. *Endocrine Research, 28*(4), 699–700.

Weiss, G. (2012). *Ayn Rand nation: The hidden struggle for America's soul*. New York: St. Martin's Press.

Wynne, E. A., & Ryan, K. (1993). *Reclaiming our schools*. New York: Merrill.

Zimmerman, B. J. (1998). Academic studying and the development of personal skill: A self-regulatory perspective. *Educational Psychologist, 33*, 73–86.

Zimmerman, B. J., Bonner, S., & Kovach, R. (2002). *Developing self-regulated learners*. Washington, D.C.: American Psychological Association.

Zins, J. E., Weissberg, R. P., Wang, M. C., & Walberg, H. J. (2004). *Building academic success on social and emotional learning*. New York: Teachers College Press.

10

DEVELOPMENTAL DISCIPLINE AND MORAL EDUCATION

Marilyn Watson

Moral and character educators working from different philosophical perspectives have generally acknowledged a major role in students' moral development of the "hidden curriculum" manifested in the interpersonal environment of schools and classrooms. Dewey (1909/1975), for example, argued that the mode of social life and the nature of the school community were far more important factors in students' moral growth than direct moral instruction. Ryan (1986), from a quite different theoretical perspective, argues that "very little of the moral education that inevitably occurs in the schools is formally recorded in lesson plans, curriculum guides, or behavioral objectives." Rather, students develop their "conceptions of what being a good person entails" from such aspects of schooling as the rules that are or are not enforced, the rituals and procedures of daily classroom life, the expectations for and consequences of their behavior, and their teachers' warnings, advice, and manner (p. 228).

During the first half of the twentieth century, classroom instruction in American schools focused on civic and moral virtues as well as academic competencies (Brophy, 2006). However, by the 1970s, Americans lost interest in instruction in virtues and morals in public education and good classroom management was about efficient control of students to optimize academic learning. The earlier view that classroom management and discipline might also serve to support students' social and moral development had retreated so far into the background that Walter Doyle's chapter on classroom organization and management for the 1986 *Handbook of Research on Teaching* didn't even mention potential social or moral outcomes.

Facing increased pressure for higher levels of academic learning, teachers felt the need for easy and efficient classroom control. Efficient and sometimes elaborate control systems, generally guided by behaviorism's view of children as self-interested and needing to be shaped by extrinsic reinforcers, spread to schools across the country. Lee Cantor's *Assertive Discipline* (1976) is probably the best known and most influential of these approaches. By 1980, the predominant approach to classroom management and discipline in American public schools focused on control of students' behavior by rewards and punishments and traditional citizenship goals had been largely abandoned.

ALTERNATIVE APPROACHES TO CLASSROOM MANAGEMENT

On a parallel track, alternative approaches to managing children's behavior were generated out of clinical psychology (Dreikurs, 1968; Glasser, 1969; Gordon, 1974). These approaches viewed children as having legitimate needs and their misbehavior the result of choosing misguided means for satisfying those needs. Consistent with developmental/constructivist principles, these approaches stress the importance of understanding the reasons behind student misbehavior, but they are not truly developmental. Students are viewed like adults as rational, capable, and socially oriented. Teachers are advised to remain impersonal, as an analyst might, and help students recognize and solve their own problems. For example, Gordon stresses the importance of demonstrating attention to and concern for a student's problem by reflecting the student's statements back, thereby helping the student clarify the problem and find his or her own solution. While respectful of a child's good will and autonomy, he does not make adjustments for children's developmental levels, but rather argues that the methods he advocates "are equally useful and applicable for effective teaching of students of all ages" (1974, p. 13).

Glasser's approach stresses the importance of positive teacher–child relationships and of involving students in class meeting to create class rules and discuss problems. His ten step approach to student misbehavior begins by improving the teacher–student relationship, involves several steps in which the student describes and strives to create a plan to stop the misbehavior, and ends with three successive steps, in-school suspension, home suspension, and finally removal to another institution. Again, there is much in this approach that is consistent with developmental theory—involving students in setting and discussing rules and problems, and allowing students time to think about their behaviors and solve their own problems. However, the lack of a focus on adult guidance is strikingly non-developmental.

The third therapeutic approach developed by Rudolf Dreikurs has a darker view of children and a more controlling role for teachers (Kohn, 1996). Dreikurs stresses four basic goals for student misbehavior; to gain attention, to exert power, to exact revenge, or to gain sympathy by feigning incompetence. Teachers are instructed to build positive relationships in the classroom and to respond to student misbehavior based on one of these four potential causes. Dreikurs believed that students would willingly abandon their inappropriate goals when confronted with them. If they did not, he advised against expiatory punishments, recommending instead what he called natural or logical consequences. However, in Dreikur's own writing and in the application his principles received in schools, natural and logical consequences are often thinly disguised punishments (Kohn, 1996). For example, a child who tips his chair is made to stand throughout a lesson, and a child who forgets lunch money is made to go without lunch (Dreikurs & Grey, 1968).

There is much about these approaches to appeal to developmentalists—the focus on understanding student needs, the respect for student rationality, the idea that students have within them the power to solve their own problems, and for some the idea of controlling behavior using natural or logical consequences. But these approaches lack a developmental perspective—a sense of what the developmental tasks are for children of different ages and the appropriate role of adults in assisting the child's development. Some ideas from these programs have been influential in shaping current developmental approaches to classroom management, for example helping the child understand the causes of his or her misbehavior and problem-solving class meetings (DeVries & Zan, 1994; Kohn, 1996; Power, Higgins, & Kohlberg, 1989; Watson & Ecken, 2003). However, the approaches described above often become punitive, especially when dealing with troubled children from stressful environments (Kohn, 1996). Finally, they place little emphasis on the moral development of students.

EDUCATION FOR MORAL AND CHARACTER DEVELOPMENT

In the 1980s there was a resurgence of interest in the school's role in moral or character education. In response to a Gallup poll, 84% of respondents who had children in public schools favored moral instruction and the United States Secretary of Education called for teachers to help students become good people as well as good students (Ryan, 1986).

The traditional approach to teaching values easily fit with the then predominant direct instruction approach to academic learning and controlling approaches to classroom management (Ryan, 1989). Whether transmitting values or math skills, the educational processes of telling, modeling, practice, and correction would be the same. Likewise, whether motivating learning or good behavior the principles of reward and punishment would apply. Adding character education to the goals of schooling did not require a rethinking of the whole educational endeavor.

Moral educators working in cognitive-developmental or social constructivist paradigms faced many more barriers to implementing their programs in public schools. From the perspective of these educators the mainstream views, 1) of education as the transmission of knowledge, 2) of learning as passive acceptance, and 3) of classroom management and discipline as behavioral control, were wholly unacceptable. Drawing from the work of Piaget (1932/1965), cognitive developmentalists argued that autonomy not obedience and understanding not remembering are the proper aims of education (Copple, Sigel, & Saunders, 1979; DeVries & Zan, 1994; Kamii, 1984; Kohlberg & Meyer, 1972). Also, constructivist educators' view of children as naturally predisposed toward cooperation and learning was directly contrary to the negative view of children as self-interested and work avoidant that predominated in American public education. Moral or character educators applying developmental, constructivist principles needed to create alternative approaches to teaching, classroom management, and discipline and seek alternative venues to hone their approaches.

Kohlberg and his colleagues focused on small, experimental high schools which they organized into "just communities" (Power et al., 1989). Others, for example, Rheta DeVries (DeVries & Zan, 1994), Constance Kamii (1984), and Irving Siegel (Copple et al., 1979), focused on preschool, where the existing views were more compatible. However, the Child Development Project (Brown & Solomon, 1983; Solomon, Battistich, Watson, Schaps, & Lewis, 2000) focused at the elementary level with the goal of working with existing teachers and administrators to craft ways to integrate a moral focus into all aspects of school learning.

THE DEVELOPMENT OF DEVELOPMENTAL DISCIPLINE

During the 1960s and 1970s, social and motivational psychologists working from a variety of theoretical perspectives created a substantial body of research related to children's moral or prosocial development (e.g., Baumrind, 1967; Hoffman, 1975; Kohlberg & Mayer, 1972; Peck & Havighurst, 1960; Pitkanen-Pulkkinen, 1980; Sroufe, 1983; Staub, 1971, 1975; Stayton, Hogan, & Ainsworth, 1971; Zahn-Waxler & Radke-Yarrow, 1979). (See Solomon, Watson, & Battistich 2001 for a review of this research.) This research along with constructivist developmental theory led developmentally oriented educators to create new approaches to classroom management and discipline. All of these approaches have similar assumptions and goals and all stress the necessity of creating a caring or just community as a first principle. (See Watson & Battistich, 2006 for a detailed description of these community approaches to classroom management.)

For example, once the staff of the Child Development Project realized how extensively children's behavior in their elementary schools was controlled by rewards and punishments, they began designing an alternative approach to classroom discipline. They argued this approach would need to fulfill four conditions (Watson, Solomon, Battistich, Schaps, and Solomon, 1989).

1. The teacher–child relationships would need to be warm, supportive, and mutually trusting.
2. The classroom would need to be a caring, democratic community in which each child's needs for competence, autonomy, and belonging are met.
3. Children would need opportunities to discus and refine their understanding of moral values and how they apply to everyday life in the classroom.
4. To help children act in accordance with prosocial values, teachers would need to use both proactive and reactive control techniques that enhance (or at least do not undermine) the above goals.

What Does It Mean To Be Prosocial Or Morally Competent?

To act morally one must act for moral reasons, e.g., to help another or live up to a moral value. Acting to avoid punishment, gain pleasure, emulate a powerful model, or please authority is not moral action. Therefore, a morally supportive management and discipline system must foster students' empathic caring and moral awareness, while minimizing or avoiding the enticement of desirable behavior through praise, rewards, and punishments.

Moral competency also requires that one knows how to carry out the actions that are called for by one's moral values, and have the stamina to act morally in the face of obstacles. Thus, a management and discipline system focused on supporting moral growth will need to focus on teaching the social and emotional competencies required for moral action and help students build moral stamina (Lapsley & Narvaez, 2005). (See Narvaez, 2006 for a description and discussion of a wide range of competencies involved in competent moral action.) Let us turn now to the four necessary components of a developmental approach to classroom management and discipline supportive of moral development.

Warm, Nurturing, and Trusting Teacher–Child Relationships

Arguing for warm, nurturing, trusting teacher–child relationships may seem like arguing for tasty, nutritious school lunches. Who could argue otherwise? However, if one views children as essentially self-interested, a view that undergirds most control oriented management and discipline systems, it would be difficult to feel warm, nurturing, or trusting when children do not behave as we wish. One might feel warm, nurturing, and trusting toward some children, those who behave well, but not toward children who regularly misbehave. As the following comment from a high school student indicates, many classrooms lack warm, nurturing, trusting teacher–child relationships (Watson, 2006).

> Tara: It's like nobody's really pushing us to do our best. If you don't understand … they'll think that you're not understanding on purpose.

Teaching techniques for controlling students is considerably easier than teaching how to build nurturing, trusting relationships. For many teachers, it requires changing their understanding of children, an understanding they have acquired over years of hearing about rewards, reinforcements, and self-interest. However, both developmental theory and research on family socialization practices compel us to undertake this task.

A substantial body of research supports the view that children's moral development is positively related to warm, nurturing, and autonomy supportive parenting styles. Morally mature children were more likely to have been raised in families where their parents were sensitive to their needs and emotionally involved as opposed to distant. These parents trusted their children, involved them in decision making, and allowed reasonable freedom and responsibility (Solomon et al., 2001). If one assumes that the teacher's role as an agent for moral growth should be similar to the parent's role, the research clearly points to the importance of teachers building warm, nurturing, and trusting relationships with students.

The centrality of such relationships to moral development is not only supported by empirical studies. It is consistent with several powerful theoretical perspectives on children's development. For example, care theorists Gilligan (1982), Kerr (1996), and Noddings (2002) argue that a commitment to care is central to morality and that children learn to become caring by being in caring relationships. Attachment theorists argue that when children are reared in an environment in which their caretakers are available and respond sensitively to their needs, "a disposition for obedience—and indeed a disposition to become socialized—tends to develop" (Stayton et al., 1971, p. 1059). This view of children as developing a cooperative stance to the world based on their cooperative interactions with their caregivers is also consistent with Vygotsky's view of the child as an apprentice to the adult and Piaget's view of the role of parent–child cooperation in socialization. For example, in *The Moral Judgment of the Child* (1932/1965) Piaget says:

> There is a spontaneous mutual affection [between parents and children], which from the first prompts the child to acts of generosity, and even of self-sacrifice, to very touching demonstrations which are in no way prescribed. And here no doubt is the starting point for that morality of good…
>
> (p. 195)

From the perspective of Developmental Discipline it is the experience of warm, nurturing, trusting caregiver–child relationships that gives rise to a core aspect of morality, the desire to be caring and cooperative. For many children this desire will already have been kindled in their family. But still, if the classroom is not a caring place, if, for example, students need to compete with each other to obtain teacher attention and favor, then, at the very least, they may find it difficult to behave in caring ways in the classroom. Worse, they may come to think that treating others fairly and kindly applies only at home. They may come to believe that it is justified to shun or tease the students who are less able or who are frequently "disciplined." Even for initially caring or cooperative students an uncaring classroom is unlikely to further and may even hinder moral development.

However, some students arrive at school never having experienced the kind of sensitive, nurturing relationships that allowed them to view others as caring, themselves as worthy of care, and relationships as cooperative (Sroufe, 1988, 1996). These are also the students most likely to cause difficulties in the classroom. Depending on the nature of their earlier experiences, they are likely to have poor social skills, lower impulse control, and greater dependency needs, or to be particularly aggressive and defiant (Cohn, 1990; Howes & Hamilton, 1992; Pianta, Nimetz, & Bennett, 1997; Sroufe, 1983, 1988, 1996; Sroufe & Fleeson, 1986). These children will be mistrustful of their teachers and if teachers view them as capable but self-interested, it will be difficult to like them, let alone form warm, trusting relationships. But without such a relationship these students will not have a basis for building a moral world view—a view of relationships as cooperative and reciprocal.

What's Involved in Forming Caring Teacher–Child Relationships? A caring relationship requires not only that the caregiver be reasonably successful in meeting the legitimate needs of the one cared for, but also that the one cared for perceive the caring intent (Noddings, 2002). With Developmental Discipline teachers are helped to view students as wanting to learn and wanting to have mutually caring relationships, but often needing help in doing so. This will be easier if teachers begin the year with a focus on getting to know each student personally and, because many students will be mistrustful of their teachers, on conveying to each student that they like and care about them. Instead of a focus on being in control or "not smiling 'til Christmas," teachers are advised to do nice things for students, seriously engage their issues and concerns, share their own experiences and stories, and bring fun and humor into the classroom.

Building a Caring, Just, Democratic Learning Community

In addition to a trusting teacher–child relationship, a classroom that supports students' moral development must meet other student needs. Studies of human motivation demonstrate that to flourish children need to experience not only a sense of belonging—that they are loved—but also a sense of competence—that they are capable and seen as capable by others—and a sense of autonomy—that their actions are consistent with what they want or believe they should do (Deci & Ryan, 1985; Nicholls, 1989; White, 1959).

In cognitive developmental theory, the ideal adult–child relationship supportive of moral growth "is characterized by mutual respect and cooperation" in an environment where children have the possibility to interact with one another and to regulate their behavior voluntarily (DeVries, Zan, Hildebrandt, Edmiasto, & Sales, 2002, p. 17). Dewey (1916/1966) and Kohlberg and his colleagues (Power et al., 1989) stress the power of participation in a democratic or just community for fostering moral development and a commitment to democratic ideals. In social-constructivist theory, children are viewed as biologically predisposed to seek cooperative relationships with more accomplished others (adults) around meaningful tasks within their community (Vygotsky, 1968). Through these collaborative interactions "the child acquires the 'plane of consciousness' of the natal society and is socialized, acculturated, made human" (Tharp & Gallimore, 1988, p. 30).

Thus, a constructivist developmental approach to classroom management and discipline needs to involve students in actually creating and maintaining their learning community. They will need ways to influence decisions that affect the community and opportunities to take responsibility for the community. Teachers will need to provide for student choice and explanations for externally imposed rules or requirements. They will need to help students develop the skills of friendship and self-regulation. Thus, Developmental Discipline involves some form of collaborative learning—opportunities for students to learn and work together in fair and caring ways under the guidance of the teacher. It also involves explicit teaching of strategies to resolve conflicts fairly, class meetings for influencing community decisions and life, and class jobs or responsibilities. Teachers are also advised to limit competition, focusing instead on each student's accomplishments while encouraging students to help one another.

Providing Opportunities to Discuss and Think about Moral Values

Developmental theory and research (Berkowitz, Gibbs, & Broughton, 1980; Blatt & Kohlberg, 1975; Nucci, 2001; Oser, 1986) and studies of the family practices of morally mature children (Peck & Havighurst, 1960; Pitkanen-Pulkkinen, 1980; Walker & Taylor, 1991) indicate a positive influence on children's moral development of moral discourse. Care theory also stresses the importance of morally relevant conversations to students' positive development (Noddings, 2005). Such conversations can happen as part of the study of literature and history, in response to individual student actions or questions, and in class meetings to make decisions or reflect on class experiences. For example, in the CDP program such conversations often occur at the beginning and end of collaborative learning activities as students are asked to reflect on and discuss ways to treat one another fairly and kindly and their level of success at doing so (Developmental Studies Center, 1997; Watson, Solomon, Dasho, Shwartz, & Kendzior, 1994).

Ways We Want Our Class to Be. Instead of specific lists of do's and don'ts such as "Keep your hands and feet to yourself" or "Listen when the teacher is talking," most developmental approaches to discipline and classroom management engage students in deciding rules based in moral principles. *Learning to Trust* (Watson & Ecken, 2003) at the elementary level and *Moral Classrooms/Moral Children* (DeVries & Zan, 1994) at the preschool level describe different but related processes for devising class rules through discussion, careful questioning, and guiding by the teacher. In the Just Community (Power et al., 1989) high school students have opportunities for moral discussion in small student advisories and discuss and make all the rules for the school in whole school meetings along with faculty. Teachers can influence the decisions through the power of moral persuasion, but not the power of authority.

Even very young children understand the moral principle of reciprocity and possess such basic moral knowledge as it's wrong to hurt another without reason or to treat people unfairly (Nucci & Turiel, 1978). Thus, they will describe a moral classroom when invited to seriously reflect on how they want their class to be. When children are helped to devise general rules and procedures in these ways, moral concepts such as kindness, fairness, and respect are partly defined by the specific examples and become class guidelines replacing the more traditional lists of specific required behaviors. It becomes clearer to students that when teachers find it necessary to enforce rules, they are exercising moral authority not just the authority of their position.

Control Techniques—Structure, Guidance, and Responses to Misbehavior

In any classroom, sheer numbers of children as well as their levels of immaturity make it necessary for teachers to exert control. While Developmental Discipline is not primarily about control, how teachers achieve control is important and can be a powerful force for moral development. How students respond to their teachers' efforts at control will depend in large part on the quality of the teacher–student relationship—hence Developmental Discipline's initial focus on relationship building. When students view the teacher as responsive to their needs, they are more likely to respond to control efforts in a cooperative spirit. Teachers and students will be able to achieve what Piaget (1932/1965) and others have called a cooperative approach to discipline—an approach that will lead to an autonomous morality (DeVries et.al., 2002; Kamii, 1984). Conversely, how and how much teachers exercise control will affect the student–teacher relationship. In the sections that follow, the principle control techniques consistent with Developmental Discipline are described and discussed.

Indirect Control. Shaping the environment to interfere with potential misbehavior or facilitate desirable behavior can make classroom life easier for everyone. How teachers design the environment will depend on their learning goals and the behaviors they want to facilitate or prevent. For example, seating students in rows makes it harder for them to talk and observe one another's work, while seating students in table groups encourages conversation and work sharing. Assigning partners for group work helps to assure that all students have opportunities to work with and build friendly relationships with one another, while allowing students to choose work partners honors autonomy. Teachers may make these decisions themselves, for example, to help students easily sit in a circle for class meetings a kindergarten teacher might place a circle of tape on the floor or arrange seating such that more distractible students are in areas with fewer distractions. Alternatively, teachers might engage the students in drawing up a set of guidelines that will help the classroom run more smoothly. For example, a second grade teacher might use a series of class meetings to devise and assess the effectiveness of guidelines for leaving the classroom to use the restroom.

Involving students in determining the guidelines and structures that, once established, will exert control is ideal from a developmental perspective. When students are involved in creating structures that facilitate the smooth functioning of the classroom their autonomy is honored and they are helped to understand why the rules and structures are necessary. In *Moral Classroom/Moral Children*, DeVries and Zan (1994), provide several examples of ways to involve students in decisions about nearly all the rules or procedures in preschool classrooms. For example, if a teacher wants to begin the year with a rule limiting the number of students in the block areas, the teacher can alert the students to the problem she is anticipating by asking the students if the whole class can fit in the block center at the same time. Then he or she can guide the students in answering the question, "What guidelines do we need so everyone can have a fair turn with blocks?" (p. 129).

However, for efficiency teachers will often need to take full control in some areas in order to make room for autonomous learning in others. While acknowledging that taking full control, even indirect control, robs students of both autonomy and opportunities to learn, the judicious use of teacher determined structures, rules, and procedures designed to lessen problems and facilitate the teacher's goals and objectives is fully consistent with Developmental Discipline. Fortunately, elementary school children are quite willing to grant teachers the power to regulate a fair number of school and classroom procedures (Nucci, 2001). It is important, however, that teachers offer explanations for the structures if they are questioned, be willing to change them if students present good reasons for so doing, and organize their classrooms to assure that students have meaningful opportunities to act autonomously and solve non-trivial problems on their own.

Hopefully the following examples of teachers' choices in situations in which indirect control might or might not be used illustrate the range of possibilities consistent with a developmental approach to discipline. In the first example, a teacher in an inner-city second–third grade class carefully chooses the children who sit at each of the five tables, changing table groups every month. For academic tasks involving partners, this teacher assigns partners either randomly or based on her judgment of optimal pairings for the given activity. When students groan about not being able to work with their preferred friends or try to trade partners, the teacher acknowledges that they might be disappointed not to get to work with their best friends, but that her goal for the class is for them to learn to work with everybody and to see that everybody in the class is worth getting to know. To facilitate tenuous partnerships, she teaches the students how to greet a partner in a friendly way even if they are disappointed, and works hard to facilitate successful interactions of partnerships when the initial interactions seemed tentative or unfriendly.

Because this is a situation where the students really did mind not having the autonomy to make their own choices, the teacher needed to work hard at establishing this ground rule and used a good deal of humor before the students accepted the teacher's control. The following vignette illustrates one of the humorous ways this teacher made her exercise of control more palatable.

> With some students, if they don't get exactly who they want to work with, they'll say, "I'm not working with them!" So what I've been doing when I introduce a partner activity is to say, "Now, we're going to work with partners in this activity, and I don't care if you get Captain Hook for a partner, If you get Captain Hook, I want you to say, 'I'm glad to be hooked up with you, let's get to work.'" And then I'll go on and say some other goofy stuff. "If you get a boa constrictor for a partner, say, 'Give me a hug, and let's go to work.'"
>
> Well, this week we were going to get new partners for working with the book *Chicken Sunday.* Just as I got ready to name the partners, Rebecca announced, "And remember, Mrs. Ecken, if you get a tiger, say you're glad to be with that tiger and just work with him." And then three or four others piped up with different animals.
>
> (Watson & Ecken, 2003, p. 65)

There is no guarantee that this choice was the right choice for this class. The teacher was guided by her goals—helping her students respect and get along with everyone in the class, creating a caring community, and encouraging respect for individual differences—and her ongoing observations of her students. As the vignette shows, the students did stop resisting and appeared to accept the validity of the teacher's goals. Further confirmation of the teacher's choice came several years later when these students were interviewed in high school. One student attributed his current ability to work with others to his experiences in the class and several others spontaneously recalled their good feelings toward all their classmates.

> John: ...Today I can work with almost anybody. I think it helped me in my life by working with other people in groups.
> Tara: ...Everybody knew everybody.... Everybody was like in one big group because everybody knew each other.

In the second class, a suburban fifth–sixth grade class, the teacher allowed the students to choose with whom they sit and work during collaborative activities. No problems seemed to emerge until January when the class had a meeting to assess how they were doing at creating the kind of classroom they said they wanted—a classroom defined by friendship, kindness, and respect. Midway through the meeting, students began to talk about having their feelings hurt, being teased, and of not being able to trust some of the other students in the class. One student offered the explanation that some of the students don't really know one another that well. Another suggested that the teacher should change seating more often and another threw out a suggestion to the class, saying "Hey, you guys, I've got a suggestion. How about when Mrs. Lewis lets us change our seats, instead of choosing our special friends, we choose someone we don't know that well." The class agreed and the students had solved the problem autonomously.

The heavier as well as the lighter use of control are consistent with Developmental Discipline. Teachers need to make judgments about how much control to exercise based on what they believe about their students' capabilities, the risks and or time involved in not exercising control, and their own particular learning goals. Cognitive developmental and motivation theory and research both point to the importance of autonomy and would seem to imply that less adult control is better. However, as Erikson (1950/1963) argues, it is the adult's role to provide children with "gradual and well-guided experience of the autonomy of free choice" (p. 252). Higher levels of parental control are correlated with moral maturity **if** that control is seen by children as having been in their best interests (Pitkanen-Pulkkinen, 1980) or necessary for safety (Baldwin, Baldwin, & Cole, 1990).

Proactive Control. Proactive control is akin to scaffolding in academics. As students are about to engage in an activity that will place high demands on their social, emotional, or moral skills, the teacher seeks to prime those skills by, for example, reminding students of the skills that will be needed or asking the students to think in advance how they will solve some of the problems likely to arise. CDP's approach to cooperative learning provides a good example of proactive control (Developmental Studies Center, 1997; Watson et al., 1994). Before students set out to work on a collaborative project the teacher either reminds them of the interpersonal problems they might encounter or asks the students to think of potential problems and solutions. If needed, relevant social or moral competencies can be taught before the students begin work.

Alerting students to potential social/moral issues likely to be involved in a given activity and teaching relevant skills is a powerful form of instruction in the social/moral domain. Students have immediate opportunities to practice the skills in the context of authentic learning activities. Such scaffolding can provide students with social/moral success experiences that not only sharpen their skills but also help them see themselves as good people and their classroom as a caring community.

As with indirect control, how much is open to the students to figure out on their own will depend on the teacher's estimate of how much help the students will need to be reasonably successful. One can engage in too much proactive control as well as too little. Too much wastes time, deprives students of the challenge of figuring problems out for themselves, and can imply that the teacher lacks trust in the students' abilities. Too little can cause students to experience unnecessary pain and frustration, undermine class-room relationships, limit learning, and lead students to feel guilty or inept. The goal is not to eliminate all problems, should that even be possible, but to provide enough help to assure that students achieve reasonable success and do not flounder unproductively.

Rewards and Praise. Rewards and praise are frequently used by teachers as a form of proactive control. It's a basic principle of behavioral theory that organisms tend to repeat behaviors that are followed by positive outcomes. One way for teachers to prevent misbe-havior is to reward or praise behaviors that are inconsistent with the undesirable behav-iors they want to eliminate. This sounds like a great form of control, good behaviors are reinforced, misbehaviors are reduced, and nice things happen to students. Numer-ous character education and management approaches have been developed around the "catch them being good" concept.

While developmental educators disagree on whether rewards and praise have any place in a developmental, constructivist approach to classroom management and discipline, there is general agreement that using praise and rewards proactively to encourage good behavior will undermine a teacher's effectiveness as a moral educator. Enticing students to behave in desired ways by the promise of rewards deprives students of the opportunity to act for their own reasons. Because autonomy is a basic human need, manipulative rewards designed to control behavior risk undermining the teacher–student relationship and lessening the desire to perform the rewarded behavior for intrinsic reasons (Kohn, 1993; Lepper & Greene, 1978).

Equally important from the perspective of moral education, such praise deprives stu-dents of the opportunity to behave in positive ways because they understand that those ways are more considerate or fair. Moral actions must be done for moral reasons. Prom-ising rewards undermines autonomy and prevents students from acting for moral or prosocial reasons.

Some developmental educators argue that rewards and praise, even praise that is meant to show appreciation or approval of a student's behavior, have no place in moral education. For example, Kohn (1993, 2005) and DeVries and Zan (1994) both argue that praise is counterproductive because it substitutes an authority's judgment for the student's own. Kohn argues that "what's most striking about a positive judgment is that it's a judgment (2005, p. 155). Similarly, DeVries and Zan (1994) state that when a child does something positive, "the constructivist teacher does not praise the behavior" (p. 32). In the place of praise Kohn (2005) suggests various forms of encouragement such as describing the student's action, pointing out the positive effects of the action on others, and asking the student to reflect on or tell about his or her action or accomplishment.

Other developmentally oriented educators view non-manipulative praise to be con-sistent with developmental theory (Nucci, 2003; Watson & Ecken, 2003). Praise that is meant to validate, inform, or celebrate a child's accomplishment is consistent with a sociocultural view of development in that it can serve to provide children with knowledge of their culture and provide a bonding experience of shared joy.

Desists—Responding to Misbehavior. From a developmental perspective, children naturally want to understand their world and form mutually caring relationships but are still developing the competencies needed to succeed. From this perspective, student misbehaviors are mistakes and mistakes are opportunities for learning. In an appropriate learning environment mistakes indicate the zone of proximal development or ZPD—the area where adult guidance is most likely to help the child advance to a higher plane. It follows from social constructivist theory that teachers' responses to misbehaviors can powerfully affect moral learning.

Research in family socialization also supports the potential for disciplinary responses in moral learning and development (Solomon et al., 2001). Hoffman (2000) offers two reasons why parental disciplinary actions are important for children's moral development: such encounters are frequent, at least for children between two and ten, and they provide parents with highly salient opportunities to teach the misbehaving child how to respond morally in a moral encounter.

In the classroom, teachers can play a similar socialization role. If teachers view discipline desists as primarily about teaching or scaffolding, their responses to student misbehavior can support moral development as well as create order and prevent harm. Good discipline from a developmental perspective involves believing that students want to learn and behave well, understanding the causes of students' failure, providing support based on the presumed causes, and focusing on building student understanding as well as skills. These aspects of good developmental teaching along with the meaning of what it is to be moral have clear implications for how teachers should respond to student misbehavior. The following guidelines for disciplinary interventions follow from or are consistent with developmental theory:

- Because there are many possible causes for misbehavior, **choose desists that address the most likely cause of the misbehavior,** for example, a reminder for momentary inattention; instruction or scaffolding for lack of social/emotional skills; discussion or empathy induction for inconsiderate behavior.
- Because children generally want to learn and do what is right, **attribute to the student(s) the best possible motive consistent with the facts.**
- Because autonomy is a basic human need and moral action must be from internal motives, **minimize the use of power assertion and maximize the autonomy of the misbehaving student(s).**
- Because good teaching requires a caring, cooperative relationship, **minimize negative consequences to the misbehaving student(s) while focusing on solving the problems creating or created by the misbehavior.**
- Because good teaching aims at fostering understanding, **focus on the harmful effects of the misbehavior and engage students in defining the problem and finding a solution.**
- Because children are developing and depend on the help of "more accomplished others," **accept the moral authority and responsibility to insure that students are caring, respectful, and fair.**

Potential Causes of Misbehavior. Sometimes students misbehave because of momentary lapses in self-control, inattention to the needs of others, or forgetting established rules or procedures. If no serious harm has resulted, simply calling the student's attention to what he or she is doing in a tone that implies the student knows better is frequently all that is needed. There is no instruction: the teacher is simply reminding the student to be guided by his or her better self. Such "call outs" are part of just about all discipline systems. The important difference in Developmental Discipline is that these reminders carry no implied negative judgment or threat of impending consequence. In fact, the implied message is one of trust, "I know you wouldn't be doing that if you were thinking about what you are doing." These desists can be quite frequent with some students, particularly in the beginning of the year as relationships and procedures are being established. However, if they continue to be frequent, they may point to a different cause, for example, the demands of the environment may be too high or the student may have a high need for attention.

Sometimes teachers themselves are the cause of student misbehavior (Kohn, 1996). Lessons or class meetings which run longer than the students' ability to attend, academic assignments that are boring or too difficult, competitive classroom structures that pit students against one another, and insufficient support or scaffolding for new or challenging activities will inevitably result in student "misbehavior." In these instances, the corrections need to be taken by the teacher. When teachers are faced with misbehavior by a large number of students, Developmental Discipline suggests teachers analyze their own behavior for the potential cause. When teachers surmise that they are the cause, they can acknowledge the problem, explain what they believe has been causing the problem, seek student input and advice, and make adjustments in order to create a better learning environment.

Sometimes student misbehavior is caused by their lack of acceptance of school or classroom rules or procedures. For example, some schools or teachers disallow hats, running in the halls, or going up the slide, some have strict dress codes and some have neatness or modesty requirements. Students do not view these as moral issues and, especially by early adolescence, may find such regulations unreasonable or personally intrusive (Nucci, 2001). Usually teachers need to enforce such rules, whether they agree with them or not. They can offer reasons for such rules, but students may not accept the reasons. If the teacher–student relationship is positive, and the number of such rules small, students will usually comply.

If students persist in violating a non-moral rule, the teacher may have to use power to force compliance, but not until he or she has tried to cajole the student into cooperating or talked with the student to find a way for the student to live with the rule. The teacher–student relationship is central to enforcing these rules and a sympathetic, light touch in enforcing them will help build student–teacher relationships.

Even in a well orchestrated classroom environment with engaging and appropriate learning activities and few rules that students find unreasonable, students will misbehave. Potential causes for misbehavior abound: failure to understand the teacher's directions or expectations, relative lack of self-control or interpersonal skills; relaxed effort; inability to do the academic work; belief by some students that they have to fight for what they need; strong self-interest conflicting with that of others; an interpersonal style that is rude or aggressive. In any given incident, if a simple request, reminder, or support does not stop the behavior, the teacher's next response needs to be guided by the presumed cause of the misbehavior—explain directions or rules; teach self-control or interpersonal skills; encourage increased effort; provide extra academic help; deny the applicability of their competitive, aggressive world view; help them see the need to balance their self-interest with the needs of others; help them see the problems caused by their poor behavior; and teach more respectful forms of interaction. A complicated set of possibilities, especially given that few misbehaviors come with a sign identifying their cause.

Time is also an important issue in the classroom. Sometimes there is not time in the moment to follow a simple desist with explanation or instruction. Later, it might be important to provide explanation or talk with students to hear their view or simply reconnect. Sometimes, however, the misbehavior does not stop. At such times, Developmental Discipline advocates that teachers stop the misbehavior while conveying respect, minimizing pain, and allowing as much autonomy as possible. The focus is on solving the problem, not on punishing the student. For example, a student who continues to distract his tablemates during reading may be sent to a quiet part of the room to continue reading.

Even disciplinary encounters around non-moral matters—paying attention, walking in the halls—convey moral information. When teachers treat all students with respect, even when they are misbehaving and even those who usually misbehave, they are living and modeling important moral principles of care and respect. When teachers respect the needs and dignity of misbehaving students, they convey the message that moral obligation extends to all. Their behavior says that it is not alright to harm or treat someone badly even if they are behaving badly. They are providing to misbehaving students the consideration, care, and respect they are asking from them. This will not only increase student trust and respect for the teacher, it will increase respect for other students, even those who misbehave. In a climate of mutual respect it will be easier for students to treat one another kindly, fairly, and with respect. At the very least, students will get more practice in being kind and respectful and feel less justified in scapegoating those students who, for whatever reason, more frequently misbehave.

When misbehaviors pose the possibility of or cause harm they offer powerful opportunities for moral learning. Student–student conflict along with behaviors like teasing, excluding, and threatening harm provide teachers with the opportunity to develop many skills involved in moral understanding and behavior. And because the other students are watching, those who have not caused harm are absorbing some of that learning.

The Problem with Punishment. From a developmental perspective, punishment used as an inducement to moral growth is at best ineffective and at worst counterproductive. A punished person may avoid the punished behavior in order to avoid future punishment, but avoiding personal harm is not a moral reason. Thus, the better behavior does not amount to moral growth. Punishment can also cause the punished to focus on the harm done to him or her, lead to resentment of the punisher, and take the focus off of the harm the child caused (Hoffman, 2000). For most children, who generally want to be good but lack the needed skills or understanding, punishment is unnecessary. For oppositional children, those who have little trust and a confrontational stance toward the world, it will likely reinforce their untrusting, defiant stance (Hall & Hall, 2003).

Recognizing that there are times when children's behavior does need to be controlled, many educators have advocated discipline approaches that feature the use of negative consequences that are logically or naturally related to the misbehavior (e.g., Charney,

2002; Dreikurs, Grunwald, & Pepper, 1982). Kohn (1996) calls such approaches "punishment lite." Such consequences may be useful for controlling behaviors that do not cause harm to others, such as forgetting one's lunch money, or not finishing an academic assignment, but letting a child go without lunch or making a student work through recess are not caring. Logical consequences are not inevitable. They are allowed to happen because the authority figure believes they will cause the misbehaving child some discomfort or harm, and thus teach the child that repeating the behavior will result in more unpleasant consequences. Imposing consequences does not join with the student in an effort to solve the problem. Worse, it carries the message that the punisher does not really care for the child. When a teacher causes one student in the classroom to experience a punitive albeit logical consequence, that student and all the others who are watching have one more reason not to trust in the teacher's caring. Students who already believe that the world is uncaring will have their mistaken view confirmed.

So what is a developmentally oriented teacher to do when one student or a group of students misbehaves? While some developmentally oriented educators advocate the use of natural or logical consequences (DeVries & Zan, 1994; Hall & Hall, 2003; Nucci, 2003); most of their examples of logical consequences are actually actions taken to solve the problem created by the misbehavior. Such actions might be unpleasant for the child, but any unpleasantness is the unavoidable consequence of solving the problem. That is, the adult's intention is to solve the problem and sometimes the only way to solve the problem will also cause unpleasantness for the child. For example, Hall and Hall (2003) describe logical consequences as consequences that "restrict privileges only to the extent necessary to protect people's health and safety, to safeguard property, and to ensure the basic rights of others" (2003, p. 131). In the Just Community the purpose of the Discipline Committee

> is to bring students who break rules into a conversation so that they can understand more adequately why their behavior presents a problem for the community and can feel the support of members of the community who genuinely want them to remain a part of the group.
>
> (Power et al., 1989, p. 97)

Nucci (personal communication) offers the following example of an ideal logical consequence. A middle school teacher assigned a student who had teased a student with Down's syndrome to assist in a special education classroom. The special education teacher provided support for the student as he worked with the students. Eventually, the student became an advocate in his school for the handicapped.

From a developmental perspective, for all misbehaviors, the teacher's goals are to preserve the student–teacher relationship and provide whatever support the student needs to stop misbehaving. With a conception of students as generally wanting to learn and wanting to be in mutually caring relationships, the teacher needs to guess at the possible cause of the misbehavior, take action designed to address the potential cause, and judge the effectiveness of her actions.

When misbehavior causes harm, more can and must be done to maintain a caring, moral community. The teacher needs to focus students on the harm they have caused—a true consequence of their behavior—encourage the students' empathic response to the other's distress, and insist that they find a way to repair the harm they caused. As

Oser (2005) argues, truly facing the negative consequences of one's actions can provide a powerful force for moral growth. The following example from a second–third grade classroom illustrates this point.

The teacher, Laura Ecken, had been working hard to build a trusting and supportive relationship with Tralin, a student with many positive characteristics but who had a history of fighting with and teasing classmates. In this incident, the children are getting ready to leave the cafeteria. Tralin shoves another student, Tyrone, out of line so she would be able to stand near her friend, Ella. When Tyrone complained, Laura believed she could simply fix the problem by telling Tralin to give Tyrone back his place in line and proceeded to move the class out of the cafeteria. Here, in the teacher's words, is what happened next.

> Before we could get all the way outside, she [Tralin] was screaming at Tyrone, "Your mom uses crack cocaine! Your mom's a crackhead!"
>
> I asked her to just step aside so we could talk. I asked her why she had called his mother that, and she said, "Because she is and he lied on me and said I pushed him out of the line and I didn't touch him."
>
> I said, "You know, Tralin, you're lying to yourself. I saw you push him out of the line. You wanted to be with Ella and so you shoved him out of the way.
>
> "You know I'm not going to allow that, and I'm not going to allow you to call his mother names. Can you imagine how painful it is for Tyrone to know that about his mother, to suffer all the pain from that, and then to have to be at school and have you make his pain even worse? That's just not right."
>
> I said, "You know, you said some ugly things to Tyrone and I think it'd probably be best to take care of that."
>
> She just looked at me, so I said, "When you have a plan, just find me and let me know, but I think that you should take care of it before the day's over."
>
> About an hour later Tralin came up to me and kind of stood there, so I asked her if she had a plan. She said, "I need to tell him that I'm sorry and that I didn't mean any of it. I was just mad and that's why I said it."
>
> I asked her if she wanted him to come out in the hall so she could tell him that privately, and she said, "Yeah, but first I need a drink."
>
> I told her, "Listen, you go get a drink and I'll tell Tyrone you want to talk to him in the hall."
>
> When Tyrone came back in, he was happy and so was Tralin.
>
> (Watson & Ecken, 2003, pp. 162–163)

In this example, the best possible motives consistent with the facts are none too good. Tralin pushed Tyrone out of line because she wanted to be by Ella and when the teacher did not allow this Tralin was angry and wanted to hurt Tyrone because she blamed him for her plight. When Tralin denies having pushed Tyrone out of line, the teacher tells her that she is lying to herself and confronts her with the consequences of her ugly words to Tyrone. She helps Tralin see Tyrone's perspective and think about how hard his life must be. She calls upon fairness, and then tells Tralin that she should try in some way to repair the harm she has caused. These are real consequences for Tralin, but they are not designed to inflict discomfort on her. They are designed to induce empathy and moral feelings and provide Tralin with a way to right a moral wrong. The teacher also shows respect and confidence in Tralin by letting her figure out a way to make reparation. This is the kind of moral instruction that has both the power to arouse moral desire through the student's empathic response, increase moral sensitivity by helping Tralin really see what she has done, provide moral knowledge by telling her what a moral person who has caused harm does, and allows Tralin to repair her moral standing with Tyrone and the community.

Hoffman (2000) refers to this form of disciplinary response as induction. Induction takes different forms depending on the situation, but essentially it involves empathy, moral reasoning, and moral instruction. It can also be accompanied by genuine moral outrage and power assertion. When students understand that their teacher's goal is to help and protect them, they are more open to learning and less likely to resent the teacher's power assertion or the discomfort they may experience in the process. I had the opportunity to interview Tralin at the end of her sophomore year in high school. When she said that Laura Ecken's class was different from her other classes, I asked her to tell me how it was different. Prominent in her description was the way Laura responded to student misbehavior.

> [In my current classes], You did what you did, you got in trouble ... next day come back, act like nothing happened.... Just start all over again. And Mrs. Ecken, if we got in trouble ... she'll give us a chance to think about it. ... How could we change the situation differently? What could we have done to make it better?

When teachers need to take controlling actions in order to create a caring and productive learning environment, they try to honor the child's good will by providing some autonomy and the message that the student is still part of the community. To help students see such disciplinary actions as efforts to solve problems rather than punishments, teachers can either explain these procedures or ideally generate with the students non-punitive ways teachers can solve problems of student misbehavior (DeVries & Zan, 1994; Nucci, 2003). During calm moments, when their self-interest is not immediately pulling them toward misbehavior, students know they should work hard and be kind and fair and they understand the teacher's responsibility for maintaining order.

THE GOOD ENOUGH TEACHER[1]

A developmental approach to discipline and classroom management is not easy. First, it's not easy to like students who don't work hard, bully other children, defy authority, or continually clamor for attention. It's easier when we view such children as vulnerable and desperately seeking to belong and succeed in a world they perceive as uncaring, but it is still hard. With such children, teachers will need to call upon their capacity for "professional caring," to act as if they liked the students even when they don't (Noddings, 2002). While forming mutually caring relationships with all students is the goal of teachers using Developmental Discipline, it is good enough to treat all students as if we liked them when we cannot make ourselves actually like them.

A developmental approach to discipline requires that teachers balance many needs and goals. It is often difficult to know the best course of action. For example, elementary teacher Donene Polson describes allowing a student freedom to put little effort into a poetry unit, knowing that the student would discover the problem when he displayed his poor work to the class. However, the student's embarrassment at showing his work led Donene to plan "to hold conferences more frequently … to support students in managing their time and responsibilities" (Polson, 2001, p. 126). While treating all students with care is the moral obligation of teachers, the good enough teacher will sometimes make decisions that are not optimal. It is good enough to care enough to reflect and learn from one's mistakes. Consider the following anecdote from another elementary classroom.

> Yolanda and Martin were hitting each other with the pillows. They do that often and I'm just constantly reminding them. I know it was a fun thing, but I said to her "Every single day I need to talk to you both about this. I think that reminding you isn't working, so tomorrow I want you to stay in and we're going to write about why it's important that you just put these cushions away and come right back out when lessons are over." Yolanda got upset about that: I think she saw it as a punishment.
>
> When she got back to her table group I saw her say something to Tyrone. His mouth dropped open and he said "She's gonna get you fired! She's going to the office as soon as the bell rings and tell 'em you've been cussin' at her. We're gonna have a new teacher tomorrow."
>
> I was upset. So, in front of the kids, I said to Yolanda, "No, now we're not going to have threats in the classroom. We're going to walk to the office right now and talk to them about this." I added, "Yolanda, have I ever used a cuss word with you or to you?"
>
> She said "No."
>
> I said, "Well, you know that and the class knows that, so your plan wouldn't work." I probably could have left it at that, but I was concerned with letting these kids know that they can't pull this kind of stuff.
>
> Anyway, after I did all that, I thought later that I was wrong. I asked myself, "Did you wreck your relationship with this child in one incident?"
>
> So, the next day, when she came in I said, "You know, I made a really big mistake with you yesterday. I dragged you off to the office before I really even sat down and talked with you. I'm really sorry about that, and it won't happen again."
>
> And she said, in a second, "I'm really sorry for what I said."
>
> I said, "Yolanda, I know you were upset because I asked you not to go out the next day. I understand that sometimes when we're upset we say things that we shouldn't. And from now on, we're just going to work through things." And she just hugged me.

It is not always possible to do the right thing to best support a student's moral and academic development and maintain a caring, productive, learning community. Good enough teachers genuinely try and when they fail, reflect, apologize, and go on trying.

SUMMARY

Moral and character educators have long understood the influence on moral development of the "hidden curriculum" embodied in teachers' discipline and classroom management systems. The predominant approaches to classroom management and discipline in American public schools rely on adult power to control student behavior through reward and punishment. Developmentally oriented moral educators devised an alternative approach to school and classroom discipline, Developmental Discipline. It differs from traditional discipline in its goals, view of children, methods, and its source of power.

Unlike traditional discipline, Developmental Discipline explicitly aims to foster the moral and social development of students and rather than rewards and punishments, it employs explanation; reflection; reminders; teaching social, emotional, and moral competencies; empathy induction; and reparation. In Developmental Discipline, the source of power comes from the trusting and mutually caring relationship between teacher and children and children's intrinsic desire to learn and form caring relationships.

With its focus on relationship building, explanation and shared control, a well functioning classroom will take longer to establish using Developmental Discipline. In a climate of extreme pressure for rapid academic learning, teachers may find it difficult to devote the needed time. Effective moral or character education requires that they do so.

NOTE

1. This term is a variation on a term "good enough parent" used by Bettleheim (1987) in support of less than perfect parenting.

REFERENCES

Baldwin, A. L., Baldwin, C., & Cole, R. E. (1990). Stress-resistant families and stress-resistant children. In J. Rolf, A. S. Masten, D. Cicchetti, K. H. Nuechterlein, & S. Weintraub (Eds.), *Risk and protective factors in the development of psychopathology* (pp. 257–280). Cambridge, UK: Cambridge University Press.

Baumrind, D. (1967). Child care practices anteceding three patterns of preschool behavior. *Genetic Psychology Monographs, 75,* 43–88.

Berkowitz, M. W., Gibbs, J. C., & Broughton, J. M. (1980). The relation of moral judgment stage disparity to developmental effects of peer dialogues. *Merrill-Palmer Quarterly, 26,* 341–354.

Bettelheim, B. (1987). *A good enough parent.* New York: Random House.

Blatt, M., & Kohlberg, L. (1975). The effects of classroom discussion upon children's level of moral judgment. *Journal of Moral Education, 4,* 129–161.

Brophy, J. (2006). History of research on classroom management. In C. Evertson & C. Weinstein (Eds.), *Handbook of classroom management* (pp. 17–43). Mahwah, NJ: Erlbaum.

Brown, D. & Solomon, D. (1983). A model for prosocial learning: An in-process field study. In D. L. Bridgeman (Ed.), *The nature of prosocial development: Interdisciplinary theories and strategies* (pp. 273–307). New York: Academic Press.

Canter, L. (1976). *Assertive discipline.* Los Angeles: Lee Canter & Associates.

Charney, R. S. (2002). *Teaching children to care: Classroom management for ethical and academic growth, K-8* (revised edition). Greenfield, MA: Northeast Foundation for Children.

Cohn, D. A. (1990). Child-mother attachment of six-year-olds and social competence at school. *Child Development, 61,* 152–162.

Copple, C., Sigel, I., & Saunders, R. (1979). *Educating the young thinker: Classroom strategies for cognitive growth.* New York: Van Nostrand.

Deci, E. L. & Ryan, R. M. (1985). *Intrinsic motivation and self-determination in human behavior.* New York: Plenum Press.

Developmental Studies Center (1997). *Blueprints for a collaborative classroom.* Oakland, CA: Developmental Studies Center.

DeVries, R. & Zan, B. (1994). *Moral classrooms, moral children: Creating a constructivist atmosphere in early education.* New York: Teacher College Press.

DeVries, R., Zan, B., Hildebrandt, C., Edmiaston, R., & Sales, C. (2002). *Developing constructivist early childhood curriculum.* New York: Teachers College Press.

Dewey, J. (1909/1975). *Moral principles in education.* Carbondale, IL: Southern Illinois University Press.

Dewey, J. (1916/1966). *Democracy and education.* New York: The Free Press.

Doyle, W. (1986). Classroom organization and management. In M. Wittrock (Ed.), *Handbook of research on teaching*, 3rd ed. New York: Macmillan.

Dreikurs, R (1968). *Psychology in the classroom*. New York: Harper & Row.

Dreikurs, R. & Grey, L. (1968). *Logical consequences: A new approach to discipline*. Reprinted 1993. New York: Plume.

Dreikurs, R., Grunwald, B., & Pepper, F. (1982). *Maintaining sanity in the classroom: Classroom management techniques*. New York: Harper & Row.

Erikson, E. H. (1950/1963). *Childhood and society*, 2nd ed. New York: Norton.

Gilligan, C. (1982). *In a different voice: Psychological theory and women's development*. Cambridge, MA: Harvard University Press.

Glasser, W. (1969) *Schools without failure*. New York: Harper & Row.

Gordon, T. (1974). *Teacher effectiveness training*. New York: Wyden Inc.

Hall, P. S. & Hall, N. D. (2003). *Educating oppositional and defiant children*. Alexandria, VA: Association for Supervision and Curriculum Development.

Hoffman, M. L. (1975). Moral internalization, parental power, and the nature of parent-child interaction. *Developmental Psychology, 11*, 228–239.

Hoffman, M. L. (2000). *Empathy and moral development: Implications for caring and justice*. New York: Cambridge University Press.

Howes, C. & Hamilton, C. (1992). Children's relationships with child care teachers: Stability and concordance with parental attachments. *Child Development, 63*, 867–878.

Kamii, C. (1984). Autonomy: The aim of education envisioned by Piaget. *Phi Delta Kappan, 65* (6), 410–415.

Kerr, D. (1996). Democracy, nurturance, and community. In R. Soder (Ed.), *Democracy, education, and the schools*. San Francisco: Jossey-Bass.

Kohlberg, L. & Mayer, R. (1972). Development as the aim of education. *Harvard Educational Review, 42* (4), 449–496.

Kohn, A. (1993). *Punished by rewards: The trouble with gold stars, incentive plans, A's, praise, and other bribes*. Boston: Houghton Mifflin.

Kohn, A. (1996). *Beyond discipline: From compliance to community*. Alexandria, VA: Association for Supervision and Curriculum Development.

Kohn, A. (2005). *Unconditional parenting: Moving from rewards and punishments to love and reason*. New York: Atria.

Lapsley, D. & Narvaez, D. (2005). Character education. In W. Damon & R. Lerner (Series Eds.), A. Renninger & I. Siegel (Vol. Eds.), *Handbook of child psychology* (Vol. 4, pp. 248–296). Hoboken, NJ: Wiley.

Lepper, M. & Greene, D. (1978). *The hidden costs of reward*. New York: Wiley.

Narvaez, D. (2006). Integrative ethical education. In M. Killian & J. G. Smetana (Eds.), *Handbook of moral development* (pp.703–733). Mahwah, NJ: Erlbaum.

Nicholls, J. G. (1989). *The competitive ethos and democratic education*. Boston: Harvard University Press.

Noddings, N. (2002). *Educating moral people: A caring alternative to character education*. New York: Teachers College Press.

Noddings, N. (2005). *The challenge to care in schools: An alternative approach to education*. New York: Teachers College Press.

Nucci, L. (2001). *Education in the moral domain*. New York: Cambridge University Press.

Nucci, L. (2003). Classroom management for moral and social development. In C. Evertson & C. Weinstein (Eds.), *Handbook of classroom management* (pp. 711–731). Mahwah, NJ: Erlbaum.

Nucci, L. & Turiel, E. (1978). Social interactions and the development of social concepts in pre-school children. *Child Development, 49*, 400–407.

Oser, F. K. (1986). Moral education and values education: A discourse perspective. In M. C. Wittrock (Ed.), *Handbook of research on teaching*, 3rd ed. (pp. 917–931). New York: Macmillan.

Oser, F. K. (2005). Negative morality and the goals of moral education. In L. Nucci (Ed.), *Conflict, contradiction, and contrarian elements in moral development and education* (pp. 129–153). Mahwah, NJ: Erlbaum.

Peck, R. F. & Havighurst, R. J. (1960). *The psychology of character development*. New York: Wiley.

Piaget, J. (1932/1965). *The moral judgment of the child*. New York: MacMillan.

Pianta, R. C., Nimetz, S. L., & Bennett, E. (1997). Mother-child relationships, teacher-child relationships and adjustment in preschool and kindergarten. *Early Childhood Research Quarterly, 12*, 263–280.

Pitkanen-Pulkkinen, L. (1980). The child in the family. *Nordisk Psykologi, 32* (2), 147–157.

Polson, D. (2001). Helping children learn to make responsible choices. In B. Rogoff, C. G. Turkanis, & L. Bartlett (Eds.), *Learning together: Children and adults in a school community* (pp. 123–129). New York: Oxford University Press.

Power, C., Higgins, A., & Kohlberg, L. (1989). *Lawrence Kohlberg's approach to moral education.* New York: Columbia University Press.

Ryan, K. (1986). The new moral education. *Phi Delta Kappan*, November, 228–233.

Ryan, K. (1989). In defense of character education. In L. Nucci (Ed.), *Moral development and character education: A dialogue.* Berkeley, CA: McCutchan Publishing.

Solomon, D., Battistich, V., Watson, M., Schaps, E., & Lewis, C. (2000). A six district study of educational change: Direct and mediated effects of the Child Development Project. *Social Psychology of Education, 4,* 3–51.

Solomon, D., Watson, M., & Battistich, V. (2001). Teaching and schooling effects on moral/prosocial development. In V. Richardson (Ed.), *Handbook of research on teaching*, 4th ed. (pp. 566–603). Washington, DC: American Educational Research Association.

Sroufe, L. A. (1983). Infant-caregiver attachment and patterns of adaptation in preschool: The roots of maladaptation and competence. In M. Perlmutter (Ed.), *Minnesota Symposia on Child Psychology*, 16, Mahwah, NJ: Erlbaum.

Sroufe, L. A. (1988). The role of infant-caregiver attachment in development. In J. Belsky and T. Nezworski (Eds.), *Clinical implications of attachment.* Mahwah, NJ: Erlbaum.

Sroufe, L. A. (1996). *Emotional development: The organization of emotional life in the early years.* Cambridge, UK: Cambridge University Press.

Sroufe, L. A. & Fleeson, J. (1986). Attachment and the construction of relationships. In W. Hartup & Z. Rubin (Eds.), *Relationships and development.* Mahwah, NJ: Erlbaum.

Staub, E. (1971). A child in distress: The influence of nurturance and modeling on children's attempts to help. *Developmental Psychology, 5,* 124–132.

Staub, E. (1975). To rear a prosocial child: Reasoning, learning by doing, and learning by teaching others. In D. J. DePalma & J. M. Foley (Eds.), *Moral development: Current theory and research* (pp. 113–135). Hillsdale, NJ: Erlbaum.

Stayton, D. J., Hogan, R., & Ainsworth, M. D. S. (1971). Infant obedience and maternal behavior: The origins of socialization reconsidered. *Child Development, 42,* 1057–1069.

Tharp, R. G. & Gallimore, R. (1988). *Rousing minds to life: Teaching, learning, and schooling in social context.* Cambridge, UK: Cambridge University Press.

Vygotsky, L. (1968). *Thought and language.* Cambridge, MA: MIT Press.

Walker, L. J. & Taylor, J. H. (1991). Family interactions and the development of moral reasoning. *Child Development, 62* (2), 264–283.

Watson, M. (2006). Long term effects of moral education in elementary school: In pursuit of mechanisms. *Journal of Research in Character Education, 4* (1&2), 68–82.

Watson, M. & Battistich, V. (2006). Building and sustaining caring communities. In C. Evertson & C. Weinstein (Eds.), *Handbook of classroom management* (pp. 253–279). Mahwah, NJ: Erlbaum.

Watson, M. & Ecken, L. (2003). *Learning to trust.* San Francisco: Jossey-Bass.

Watson, M., Solomon, D., Battistich, V., Schaps, E., & Solomon, J. (1989). The Child Development Project: Combining traditional and developmental approaches to values education. In L. Nucci (Ed.), *Moral development and character education: A dialogue* (pp. 161–182). Berkeley, CA: McCutchan Publishing.

Watson, M. Solomon, D., Dasho, S., Shwartz, P., & Kendzior, S. (1994). CDP cooperative learning: Working together to construct social, ethical, and intellectual understanding. In S. Sharan (Ed.), *Handbook of cooperative learning methods* (pp. 137–156). Westport, CT: Greenwood Publishing Group.

White, R. W. (1959). Motivation reconsidered: The concept of competence. *Psychological Review, 66,* 297–333.

Zahn-Waxler, C. & Radke-Yarrow, M. (1979). Child rearing and children's prosocial initiations toward victims of distress. *Child Development, 50,* 319–330.

11

CONSTRUCTIVIST APPROACHES TO MORAL EDUCATION IN EARLY CHILDHOOD

Carolyn Hildebrandt and Betty Zan

Constructivist approaches to early childhood education focus on developmentally appropriate practices for children from birth to eight years of age (Bredekamp & Copple, 1997). The goal of constructivist education is to promote children's development in all areas of the curriculum (science, mathematics, language and literacy, social studies, and the arts) and in all developmental domains (intellectual, physical, social, emotional, and moral) (DeVries, Zan, Hildebrandt, Edmiaston, & Sales, 2002; Fosnot, 2005).

The term "constructivist," as it will be used in this chapter, comes from Piaget's theory of development. According to Piaget, children *construct* their knowledge and intelligence through interactions with their physical and social worlds (Kamii & Ewing, 1996; Piaget, 1970). Constructivist education is deeply rooted in the progressive education movement and draws inspiration from John Dewey (1909, 1913/1975, 1916, 1938) as well as almost a century of action research in the classroom (DeVries, 2002; Goffin & Wilson, 2001; Mayhew & Edwards, 1936; Read, 1966; Tanner, 1997; Weber, 1984).

In their book, *Moral Classrooms, Moral Children: Creating a Constructivist Atmosphere in Early Education*, DeVries and Zan (2012) state that the first principle of constructivist education is to create a sociomoral atmosphere where mutual respect is continually practiced. "Sociomoral atmosphere" refers to the entire network of interpersonal relations in the classroom—child–child relationships, adult–child relationships, and adult–adult relationships observable by children.

The main goal of constructivist education is for children to become autonomous, life-long learners. Autonomous people do not act through blind obedience. Their thoughts and actions are guided by reason, conviction, and commitment. A major premise of constructivist education is that children cannot become autonomous intellectually or morally in authoritarian relationships with adults. According to Piaget (1932/1965):

> If he [the child] is intellectually passive, he will not know how to be free ethically. Conversely, if his ethics consist exclusively in submission to adult authority, and if

the only exchanges that make up the life of the class are those that bind each student individually to a master holding all power, he will not know how to be intellectually active.

(p. 107)

Similarly, Dewey (1938) writes:

[Teaching] is a co-operative enterprise, not a dictation; development occurs through reciprocal give-and-take, the teacher taking but not being afraid also to give—the essential point is that the purpose grow and take shape through the process of social intelligence.

(p. 72)

In constructivist classrooms opportunities for learning about moral issues and behavior are based, whenever possible, on direct experience. This is consistent with the idea that children must construct their moral understandings from the raw material of their day-to-day social interactions (DeVries & Kohlberg, 1987/1990). The classroom is seen as a community of learners engaged in activity, discourse, interpretation, justification, and reflection (Fosnot, 2005). Constructivist teachers facilitate children's social and moral development by engaging them in resolving their conflicts, making decisions (even decisions about rules), voting, and discussing social and moral issues that are relevant to them. As with other areas of the curriculum, constructivist teachers' aim is to appeal to children's interests and purposes, to promote reasoning, and to foster cooperation between all members of the classroom community.

In this chapter, we begin by providing an overview of the theoretical and historical bases of constructivist moral education. We then turn to a description of the components of constructivist moral education with children aged three to eight years. Next, we review empirical research on the effects of constructivist early education on children's social and moral understandings and behavior. Finally we discuss common misconceptions about constructivist education as well as criticisms of constructivist theory and practice.

THEORETICAL AND HISTORICAL BACKGROUND

Throughout the history of constructivist moral education there has been a dynamic tension between *traditional education*, where instruction is primarily teacher-centered and morality is defined by the rules and dictates of authority, and *progressive education*, where the classroom is primarily child-centered and moral development is seen as the gradual construction and application of principles of justice, equity, and compassion. In this section, we provide an overview of the work of major theorists in the area of constructivist moral education and contrast them with traditional educators of their time.

Piaget's Theory of Moral Development

Piaget believed that social life among children is a necessary context for the development of intelligence, morality, and personality (DeVries, 1997; Piaget, 1948/1973). According to Piaget, all development emerges from action and reflection. Children construct and reconstruct their knowledge of the world in order to make sense of it, eventually arriving at more and more adequate forms of reasoning and behavior.

One of Piaget's most influential works in the area of social and moral development is *The Moral Judgment of the Child.* Written in 1932, between the two world wars, it is a landmark work in the area of developmental psychology. Although not aimed directly at educators, the book provides a strong theoretical basis for current practices in moral education.

The main question of the book is "How do children's moral judgments develop?" Piaget was well aware of the deep social and moral implications of this question, especially for Western Europe at that time. With the rise of fascism and other totalitarian forms of government, it was important to determine how children's moral reasoning and behavior could be nurtured and developed so that the actions of future generations could be based on justice and reason rather than on blind submission to dictatorial rule.

Using naturalistic observations and semi-structured clinical interviews, Piaget studied children's understanding of rules governing childhood games, property damage, lying, stealing, and retributive and distributive justice. He chose these topics because they occur, in one form or another, in all cultures. Following a stage in which the child is unaware of the existence of rules, Piaget found a gradual shift from heteronomy (reliance on rules given by an external authority) to autonomy (understanding that rules can be generated through a process of mutual consent). In this gradual shift from heteronomy to autonomy, children become increasingly capable of taking other people's perspectives into account and making their own judgments about moral issues.

According to Piaget, changes in children's moral reasoning and behavior are due to changes in their cognitive structures. Piaget characterized the thinking of young children as predominantly egocentric. Egocentric thinkers have difficulty coordinating their own views with those of other people. In fact, they may not even realize that other people have thoughts and feelings that differ from their own. In social situations, egocentrism sometimes leads young children to project their own thoughts and feelings onto others. Conversely, it can also lead to a unilateral view of rules and power relations, in which they accept the rules of others without question.

Egocentrism can also lead to various forms of "moral realism," such as "objective responsibility." Objective responsibility can manifest itself in a number of ways, such as valuing the letter of the law above the spirit of the law, or focusing on the consequences of actions rather than the intentions behind them. Moral realism is also associated with a belief in "imminent justice," or the expectation that punishments automatically follow all acts of wrong-doing, either immediately or at some later time. Egocentric children often believe that the amount of punishment should correspond to the amount of damage, regardless of extenuating circumstances or intent. They also have difficulty thinking about the fair distribution of goods and services in terms of equality or equity. The relative powerlessness of young children, coupled with childhood egocentrism leads to a heteronomous orientation toward morality. However, through social interactions with peers and supportive adults, children can construct increasingly autonomous ways of thinking about rules based on general principles of justice, welfare, and the rights of others.

Piaget's findings provided evidence against French sociologist Emile Durkheim's views of moral development and education (Durkheim, 1925/1961). Durkheim, along with Piaget, believed that morality resulted from social interaction and immersion in a group. However, Durkheim believed that moral development is a natural result of an emotional attachment to the group which manifests itself in respect for the symbols, rules, and authority of the group, along with a "spirit of discipline" that helps channel and control behavior. In contrast to Durkheim, Piaget demonstrated that morality was not simply a set of internalized symbols, rules, and norms. He characterized the child's moral development as a progressive construction of increasingly more powerful and inclusive ways of thinking about justice, equity, and respect for persons. He showed that children construct their understanding of morality through struggles to arrive at fair solutions to everyday problems, particularly in the context of interactions with peers.

Piaget advocated a progressive approach to moral education involving cooperative relationships between children and between children and adults. He warned parents and teachers against the use of coercion and indoctrination as a means of moral education, stating that it reinforces the young child's natural tendency toward a heteronomous reliance on external regulation. When adults minimize the exercise of unnecessary authority, it opens up more possibilities for children to construct their own reasons and feelings of necessity about rules and other social relationships.

Piaget emphasized the importance of children's social interactions with peers because social and intellectual equality is often easier to attain in relationships with age-mates than with adults. In particular, Piaget saw clashes with peers as fruitful because they confront children with perspectives other than their own and thus contribute to the overcoming of egocentrism. Piaget concluded that schools should emphasize cooperative decision making and problem solving, and nurture moral development by requiring students to work out common rules based on fairness. Piaget's focus on cooperation and mutual respect continues to be an important component of constructivist early moral education today.

John Dewey's Philosophy of Moral Education

Constructivist early moral education also draws extensively from the work of American philosopher and educator, John Dewey. His goal was to educate children so that they could become productive members of a democratic society (Dewey, 1916). To this end, children "must be educated for leadership as well as for obedience" and "must have the power of self-direction and power of directing others, powers of administration, and ability to assume positions of responsibility" (Dewey, 1909, p. 54).

Dewey emphasized the role of experience, experimentation, purposeful learning, and freedom in education (Dewey, 1938). He saw education as a scientific method by which the individual studies the world, reconstructs knowledge, meanings, and values, and uses these as data for critical study and intelligent living. He believed that activities in early childhood should be familiar, direct, and concrete in character—rather than synthetic, artificial, and symbolic. Moral education should be fully integrated with other areas of the curriculum and should deal with real-life issues that are important to children. In *Democracy and Education*, he writes,

> Moral education is practically hopeless when we set up the development of character as a supreme end, and at the same time treat the acquiring of knowledge and the development of understanding, which of necessity occupy the chief part of school time, as having nothing to do with character.
>
> (Dewey, 1916, p. 411)

Like Piaget, Dewey warned against the use of coercive methods of instruction. Commenting on the enforced quiet and acquiescence demanded by teachers in traditional classrooms, he writes:

> They place a premium upon preserving the outward appearance of attention, decorum, and obedience. And everyone who is acquainted with schools in which this system prevailed well knows that thoughts, imaginations, desires, and sly activities ran their own unchecked course behind this façade.
>
> (Dewey, 1938, p. 62)

According to Dewey (1938), the need for coercion on the part of the traditional teacher is often because "the school [is] not a community held together by participation in common activities" (p. 56). He describes traditional education as "an imposition from above and from outside."

> It imposes adult standards, subject-matter, and methods upon those who are only growing slowly toward maturity. The gap is so great that the required subject-matter, the methods of learning and of behaving are foreign to the existing capacities of the young. They are beyond the reach of the experience the young learners already possess. Consequently, they must be imposed; even though good teachers will use devices of art to cover up the imposition so as to relieve it of obviously brutal features.
>
> (p. 18)

He goes on to write that, "the gulf between the mature or adult products and the experience and abilities of the young is so wide that the very situation forbids much active participation by pupils in the development of what is taught" (pp. 18–19).

In Dewey's Laboratory School at the University of Chicago, moral education permeated every aspect of the curriculum and school life (Tanner, 1997). In an issue of the *Elementary School Record* devoted to kindergarten, Dewey (1900) wrote that the school's primary responsibilities were to teach children to live in cooperative and mutually helpful ways, to use educational activities and games as "foundational stones of educational method," and to reproduce on the children's level "the typical doings and occupations of the larger maturer society" of which they will finally become a part (p. 143). The Laboratory School was organized as an informal community in which each child felt that he or she had a share in the work to do. The spirit of the school was one in which teachers were there to help if a child had a problem, with the aim of guiding the child toward solving his or her own problems in the future. The school sought to develop the kinds of habits that lead children to accept responsibility, cooperate with others, and engage in creative and practical work. Dewey believed that every method that fosters the child's "capacities in construction, production, and creation marks an opportunity to shift the center of ethical gravity from an absorption which is selfish to a service that is social" (1909, p. 26).

Lawrence Kohlberg's Legacy

Among researchers who studied moral development in the twentieth century, perhaps none are more well-known than Lawrence Kohlberg. His landmark research on stages of moral development has profoundly influenced all subsequent work in the field of moral education. Kohlberg extended Piaget's theory by proposing a six-stage sequence of moral development progressing from heteronomous to increasingly more autonomous reasoning and behavior (Kohlberg, 1984). Although Kohlberg's research focused primarily on the development of older children (ages ten and above), it continues to have important implications for early childhood as well.

In addition to his basic research outlining stages of moral reasoning, Kohlberg conducted applied research in the area of moral education, primarily at the high school level (for a summary, see Power, Higgins, & Kohlberg, 1989). Kohlberg's Just Community approach to moral education draws heavily from the work of both Piaget and Dewey. Although Kohlberg's research made use of hypothetical moral dilemmas to draw out and assess individuals' stages of moral reasoning, he maintained that children (and indeed, people of all ages) develop morally through a process of struggling with issues of justice and fairness that arise out of their everyday life experiences. His Just Community approach took advantage of spontaneously-arising situations to engage children in reasoning about what is right and wrong, fair and unfair.

Kohlberg recognized that within every school is a "hidden curriculum"—a system of norms and values that regulates behavior and discipline at the school. Kohlberg's aim was to transform the hidden curriculum into a curriculum based on justice and fairness. Describing Kohlberg's approach, Power et al. write that "to learn 'to understand and feel justice,' students have to be both treated justly and called upon to act justly" (1989, p. 25).

Kohlberg and his colleagues used a small "school-within-a-school" model to create a sense of belonging among members of the group. Regular community meetings were conducted in which moral issues related to school life were discussed and democratically decided, with equal value placed on the voices of both students and teachers. Teachers played a crucial role in guiding group discussions, creating a delicate balance between letting students make their own decisions and advocating higher-level reasoning and behavior. The overall goal was to establish collective norms that were fair to all members of the community.

Although the Just Community approach was designed primarily for high school students, many of the same principles can (and have been) used at the early childhood level (DeVries & Kohlberg, 1987/1990; DeVries & Zan, 2012). Although some constructivist early childhood educators might argue with Kohlberg's characterization of young children's developmental strengths and limitations, few would deny the importance of his work for constructivist early education.

The Domain Approach

Turiel and his colleagues extended Piaget's and Kohlberg's research by distinguishing three domains or developmental systems of knowledge: moral, social conventional, and personal (Smetana, in press; Turiel, 1983). Moral issues are those pertaining to justice, welfare, and the rights of others. Examples of moral issues in a preschool classroom are physical harm (e.g., hitting, pushing), psychological harm (e.g., teasing, name-calling), and justice or fairness (e.g., stealing, destroying others' property, failing to share common goods). Social conventional rules pertain to uniformities or regularities serving functions of social coordination. In a preschool classroom, examples of social conventions might be table manners, forms of greeting, or modes of dress. Personal issues pertain to actions that do not entail inflicting harm or violating fairness or rights, and that are not regulated formally or informally. Examples of personal issues in a preschool classroom might be choices of friends, recreational activities, and other activities designated as "free choice" (Nucci, 1996, 2001, in press). The personal domain, in particular, is important in forming a sense of moral agency or autonomy. Consistent with the work of Piaget and Dewey, domain theorists believe that "personal freedom is not in opposition to morality. A sense of identity and personal agency contributes to the nature of social relationships, including those of reciprocity and cooperation" (Turiel, 2001, p. xiv).

According to domain theory, moral, conventional, and personal concepts form distinct systems of knowledge which follow different developmental trajectories. Domain theory differs from other structural-developmental theories which describe the process of moral development as entailing the gradual differentiation of principles of justice and rights from non-moral concerns with conventions, pragmatics, and prudence (Smetana, in press). Studies in the United States and in other countries show that children, adolescents, and adults judge moral issues to be obligatory, not contingent on authority dictates, rules, or consensus (e.g., the acts would be wrong even if no rule or law exists about it), and not contingent on accepted practices within a group or culture (e.g., the act is wrong even if it were an acceptable practice in another culture). This finding has been demonstrated across a wide range of regions and cultures, including North and South America, Asia, Africa, the Middle East, as well as in urban/rural, and high/low SES settings (Smetana, in press; Wainryb, 2006).

During early childhood, moral concepts focus primarily on concrete physical harm and concerns about welfare. Concepts of psychological harm develop in middle childhood along with concepts of fairness as equality and equal treatment. Concepts of fairness as equity develop in early adolescence along with increased ability to coordinate reasoning within and across domains (for reviews, see Smetana, in press; Turiel, 1998).

Although young children's thinking about moral issues is more limited than that of older children, it is not entirely heteronomous (Nucci & Turiel, 1978; Smetana, 1981, 1985). Smetana and colleagues (2012) showed that young children's understanding of moral transgressions as wrong independent of authority increased over time. In responding to hypothetical stories, young children do not generally accept the legitimacy of an adult's directive to engage in acts judged to violate moral precepts such as commands to steal or cause another harm. Damon (1977) found that with acts entailing theft or physical harm to persons, young children (aged 4–7 years) judge the act itself rather than the status of the authority allowing or forbidding it. Laupa (1994) found that preschoolers (aged 4–6 years) accept peer and adult authorities based on the type of act commanded rather than their position in the school. They accept persons who lack authority attributes as legitimate when they give commands directed toward preventing harm (telling children not to fight), and reject persons who possess authority attributes when they give commands that could lead to harm (allowing children to fight).

As children's ability to make their own moral and social conventional judgments increases, they also begin to judge authorities on the basis of how well they make such judgments. For example, Killen, Breton, Ferguson, and Handler (1994) found that preschool-aged children prefer teachers to use interventions that are consistent with the domain of the transgression (e.g., telling a child who has hit another child, "You shouldn't hit because it hurts the other person") rather than ones that are inconsistent with the domain (e.g., "You shouldn't do that; it's against the rules to hit" or simply saying, "That's not the way a student should act.")

Interpersonal conflicts can stimulate children to take different points of view in order to restore balance in social situations, to produce ideas as to how to coordinate the needs of self and others, and to consider the rights of others—especially claims to ownership and possession of objects. For example, research by Killen and her colleagues (Killen, 1989; Killen & Naigles, 1995; Killen & Nucci, 1995; Killen & Sueyoshi, 1995; Rende & Killen, 1992) have demonstrated that in the absence of adult intervention, young children are often quite capable of addressing social conflicts with peers in ways that take the needs of others into account. In one study, approximately 70% of preschool children's disputes during free play were resolved by the children themselves, either through reconciliation by the instigator or through compromising or bargaining (Killen, 1991). In another study, Eisenberg, Lundy, Shell, and Roth (1985) found that preschool children justified meeting the requests of peers with references to the needs of others and to one's relationships with others while reasons for meeting the requests of adults were justified with references to authority and punishment. This suggests that preschool children are already capable of reciprocity or its precursors in many situations, and supports Piaget's claims that children best develop reciprocity in interactions with peers.

In light of this research, it is clear that children gradually construct moral understandings and convictions along a continuum from egocentrism to reciprocity, from heteronomy to autonomy, and from early intuitions about harm to conceptions of fairness based on moral reciprocity and considerations of equity (Damon, 1977; Nucci, 2001). They do so in the context of both peer and adult interactions, through their own experiences and observations, and through direct teaching from peers and adults. Because young children generate their initial understandings of morality out of direct experiences in social interactions, one of the primary contributions of schools is to help children frame these experiences in moral terms.

Constructivism Compared to Other Approaches

Tension between traditional and progressive approaches to moral education has existed for over 100 years and continues to this day. One of the most vocal proponents of the traditional approach is William Bennett, whose books (*The Book of Virtues* and *The Children's Book of Virtues*) are compilations of stories to be used in children's moral education (Bennett, 1993, 1995). Bennett criticizes constructivist educators who encourage children to judge, examine, and critically evaluate moral matters on their own. He disapproves of such programs because of their emphasis on children's choices, decisions, deliberations, and judgments. Instead, he advocates the use of stories with clear moral lessons. Although most constructivist early educators believe that telling children stories can be useful, they caution that children must be able to actually understand the story and moral principles involved (Narvaez, 2002). Here, again, the debate is over whether the acquisition of morality involves primarily the direct transmission of societal norms and values or whether it is based on children's understandings of justice, rights, and the welfare of others (for a further critique of traditional approaches to moral education, see Turiel, 2001).

Contemporary versions of traditional moral education include programs such as Character Counts. In Character Counts, moral conduct is learned through direct instruction about the Six Pillars of Character: Trustworthiness, Respect, Responsibility, Fairness,

Caring, and Citizenship. Children are presented with examples of good acts associated with each virtue, listen to stories about decision making, and engage in school-wide contests with awards for learning the virtues and applying them to their daily lives. Although there is a balance between rote memorization and the application of reasoning and problem solving, Character Counts is a predominantly "top-down," "teacher-centered" approach to moral education. For a review of several commercially available character education curricula, see Goodman and Lesnick (2004).

In addition to traditional approaches to early moral education, there have been a number of "blended" approaches that combine elements of traditional, adult-centered, or "sociocentric" models of socialization and moral development (e.g., Durkheim, 1925/1961) with the more autonomous developmental emphasis of constructivist theory (Piaget, 1932/1965). For example, the Child Development Project combined constructivist theory, social learning theory, attribution theory, and attachment theory to create a broad, evidence-based approach to children's prosocial development involving classroom, school-wide, and home-school activities (Brunn, this volume). The Character Education Partnership is also a broad-based, blended approach to social and moral development based on 11 principles of effective character education (Lickona, Schaps, & Lewis, 2003).

COMPONENTS OF CURRENT APPROACHES TO CONSTRUCTIVIST
Early Moral Education

The central feature of current approaches to constructivist moral education is the establishment of a sociomoral atmosphere based on mutual respect. This sociomoral atmosphere permeates every aspect of the child's experience at school. Recognizing that children's convictions about fairness and justice develop when they have the opportunity to reflect on social and moral problems in their lives, constructivist teachers strive to provide children with a safe environment in which they can make mistakes, experience the consequences of their actions, and develop their own reasons for behaving in particular ways. Constructivist teachers also recognize the power of the "hidden curriculum." Teachers constantly convey moral messages—messages about what is right and wrong, good and bad—and these messages, conscious or unconscious on the part of the teacher, influence children's moral development in profound ways. Therefore, constructivist teachers recognize that they engage in social and moral education throughout the school day.

According to DeVries and Zan (2012), teachers can create an atmosphere of mutual respect by cooperating with children, minimizing the exercise of external authority to the extent possible and practical, and sharing power with them as appropriate. The components of constructivist education that are most salient to children's moral development include encouraging children to make classroom rules and decisions, providing children with opportunities to play group games, assisting children in resolving (and learning how to resolve) their conflicts, and supporting children in reflecting on social and moral issues in literature and in the classroom.

Minimizing the Exercise of External Authority

One of constructivist teachers' primary aims is for children to become increasingly able to regulate their own behavior in the absence of adult authority. In order to promote autonomy and prevent an overbalance of heteronomy, constructivist teachers consciously monitor their interactions with children. Authoritarian demanding, emotional intimidation, and arbitrary punishments have no place in a constructivist classroom; neither do passive permissiveness or "letting children run wild"—that is, failing to take action when children engage in unsafe, aggressive, or defiant behaviors.

Constructivist teachers strive to support children in constructing internal feelings of necessity about behaving in socially acceptable ways. One way they do this is by refraining from punishing children, and instead looking for opportunities for children to learn from the natural consequences of their actions. For example, when a child splashes water out of the water table, rather than lecturing and/or punishing, a constructivist teacher may point out to the child the problem that the wet floor poses for others in the classroom and require the child to clean up the water.

Young children are not naturally self-regulating, and so the exercise of adult authority is sometimes necessary, especially when children's safety is involved. However, even in these situations, constructivist teachers try to find ways to promote children's autonomy as they exert authority over them. They do this by explaining to children, in language that children can understand, the reasons why they must take certain actions. For example, if a child behaves aggressively on the playground, the teacher may insist that the child play apart from the other children for the remainder of the outside time. The constructivist teacher will take the time to explain to the child that his or her actions hurt other children and that it is the teacher's job to keep all of the children safe; because the child continues to hurt other children, he or she cannot be allowed near them. The teacher will also actively support the child in learning how to take the perspective of others, find alternative ways to negotiate with others, and develop satisfying peer relationships.

Sharing Power: Rule Making and Decision Making

Constructivist teachers consciously seek opportunities for children to exercise authentic power in the classroom. Given the ages of the children they teach, this can sometimes be challenging. Young children lack the knowledge and maturity to make many decisions concerning life in the classroom. Yet, some decisions (such as what to name the class pet, where to go on the next field trip, how to arrange the classroom, what to display on the walls, or what project to undertake as a class) are within children's capabilities. When children are supported in making decisions that affect their common life in the classroom, they gain in experience, maturity, and confidence; they learn that their actions can have a positive effect on their environment; and they gain experience in participatory democracy.

Young children are quite capable of making rules that dictate how they wish to be treated in the classroom. DeVries and Zan (2012) describe several instances of young children suggesting rules for their classroom, such as a rule made by four-year-olds prohibiting name calling—"Call them your name. Don't call them naughty girl or naughty boy" (pp. 150–151)—and rules made by kindergarteners concerning safe treatment of the class guinea pig—"Don't squeeze, drop, or throw him. Hold him gently. Hold him like a baby" (p. 147). DeVries and Zan stress that teachers should assist children in thinking about the reasons for rules, and that they should encourage children to include the reason in the statement of the rule. A teacher at the constructivist laboratory school where DeVries and Zan conducted research reported on a rule made by her first graders one year that stated: "Don't laugh when people pass gas. It might hurt their feelings"

(B. Van Meeteren, personal communication, 2002). This rule reflected an issue that was important to them because many of them had experience with just such an embarrassing situation. When children make rules concerning problems they care about deeply, they tend to remember these rules and insist that others follow them.

Group Games

Group games are a vital part of the constructivist curriculum, both because of the opportunities for academic learning (number, logical reasoning, literacy, etc.) and also because of their implications for moral development. Games provide a unique opportunity for children to voluntarily submit to a system of rules that govern their behavior in a specific context. In order to play a game successfully, children must agree to the rules, abide by the rules, and accept the consequences of the rules. Therefore, even if a game is competitive, children must cooperate in order to play it (Kamii & DeVries, 1980; DeVries, Zan, & Hildebrandt, 2002; Hildebrandt & Zan, 2002; Zan, 1996).

Games also provide opportunities for children to take the perspective of another person. A simple game such as Tic-Tac-Toe includes opportunities to play using both offensive and defensive strategies. In order to do the latter, children must think about where the other player is likely to place the next marker. Card games also provide children opportunities to take the perspective of another. Basic concepts such as keeping one's cards hidden so another cannot see them reflects the ability to understand that if another player sees one's cards, that person will have an advantage (something that is not obvious to the egocentric child).

Games also present unique opportunities for children to learn what happens when someone does not follow the rules. When players cheat, other players become upset and protest. When children consistently cheat at games and find that no one wants to play with them, the teacher takes the time to explain that the other children's reactions (refusing to play the game with them) are due to their cheating, and that if they want other children to play with them, they will have to stop cheating. The teacher also works with the child to overcome the circumstances that lead him or her to feel the need to cheat.

Conflict Resolution

Conflicts are part of the constructivist curriculum and contribute to children's moral education. When children work to resolve their conflicts with others, they develop their ability to take the perspective of another and negotiate with others. Constructivist teachers take an active role in supporting young children in resolving their conflicts. They help children learn how to speak their minds and listen to each other. They sometimes serve as translators, clarifying and stating the problem so that all of the participants have a shared understanding of what happened. They support children in thinking of possible solutions, and when children cannot think of solutions themselves, they make suggestions. Perhaps most importantly, they help children repair broken relationships without forcing children to be insincere (for example, by requiring apologies, no matter how meaningless or unfelt).

Moral Discussion

Discussions of social and moral dilemmas, both real-life and hypothetical, are important means of helping children take the perspectives of others. Each type contributes to children's moral development.

Real-life events in the classroom are valuable because of their relevance to children. Children are very familiar, for example, with how it feels when a group of children takes all of the blocks in the block center and does not allow others to use any of the blocks. A discussion about how it feels, and how they might come up with a fair way to share the blocks, is likely to elicit considerable discussion concerning the rights of others. As children hear others describing how they experience the situation, they have the opportunity to take the perspectives of their friends and classmates and feel empathy for their experiences.

Hypothetical dilemmas also have a role to play. Sometimes real-life events are so highly charged emotionally that children cannot talk about them without falling apart. In such cases, teachers can use fictional situations to explore classroom dilemmas. It is amazing how children can enter into a problem acted out, for example, by the teacher using puppets, and generate ideas concerning how the puppets might feel, what they should do, and why.

Children's literature provides opportunities for children's experiences to be broadened even more. Good literature has the potential to transport children into the lives of others and experience emotions that they might otherwise never experience. For example, hearing books about the experiences of recent immigrants to the United States can give native-born children a chance to understand what it might feel like to look and sound completely different from everyone else in the culture. The Developmental Studies Center (Developmental Studies Center, 1995) has developed an entire curriculum (grades K–8) around the use of literature to support children's ethical development (Brunn, this volume).

RESEARCH ON CONSTRUCTIVIST EARLY MORAL EDUCATION

Research on the effects of constructivist moral education on young children's social and cognitive development is relatively sparse. Studies of most relevance to the evaluation of constructivist education are those that compare constructivist and non-constructivist classrooms, and those that compare democratic and authoritarian teaching styles.

DeVries, Haney, & Zan (1991) and DeVries, Reese-Learned, & Morgan (1991) studied the effects of classroom atmospheres of three kindergarten classrooms—a direct-instruction classroom, a constructivist classroom, and an eclectic classroom—on children's sociomoral development. The teacher in the direct-instruction classroom provided a program of small- and large-group instruction that used primarily recitation, fast-paced drills, and worksheets. Learning centers were never used, and children rarely left their desks. The teacher's interactions with children were highly authoritarian. The teacher used punishment, threats of punishments, and rewards to control children's behavior. The constructivist teacher implemented a program similar to the constructivist approach described above. The curriculum was child-centered and interest-driven. Children engaged in freely chosen activities. Instruction was embedded in learning centers and naturally occurring events. The teacher established a classroom atmosphere based on mutual respect, minimized her own exercise of authority, cooperated with children as much as possible, and engaged children in conflict resolution. She did not use punishments, threats of punishments, or rewards, but instead worked to help children learn how to regulate their own behavior. The eclectic teacher (the label came from her) provided a program that contained elements of both the other two programs, including some direct instruction and some child-centered activities. The sociomoral atmosphere of the eclectic classroom was slightly less authoritarian than the direct instruction classroom, but not as cooperative as the constructivist classroom. The teacher used some punishments and rewards, but her control of the children was not as absolute as that of the direct-instruction teacher.

Analysis of the sociomoral atmospheres of the three classrooms focused on the levels of interpersonal understanding reflected in the teacher–child interactions that occurred during two complete days in each of the three classrooms. Using an adaptation of Selman's (Selman, 1980; Selman and Schultz, 1990) conceptualization of Enacted Interpersonal Understanding, over 20,000 teacher–child interactions were micro-analytically coded from transcripts and video.

Results of the analysis (DeVries, Haney, & Zan, 1991) showed great differences in teachers' enacted interpersonal understanding. The direct instruction teacher's interactions with children were primarily low level, unilateral interactions, with a few higher level reciprocal interactions, and even fewer mutual interactions. The eclectic teacher's interactions were much like those of the direct instruction teacher, predominantly at unilateral level, with a few reciprocal interactions, and fewer mutual interactions. The constructivist teacher had many fewer unilateral interactions and many more reciprocal and mutual interactions. The conclusion was that the sociomoral atmospheres were very different in the three classrooms. The constructivist classroom atmosphere was much more cooperative, and the other two classrooms' atmospheres were much more authoritarian.

The companion study compared the sociomoral development of the children in these three classrooms (DeVries, Reese-Learned, & Morgan, 1991). The results reflected the sociomoral atmospheres of the classroom. Pairs of children (n = 56) were videotaped in two naturalistic situations outside the classroom (playing a board game and dividing up some stickers), and their interactions were coded according to the Selman levels. Results showed that although a predominance of unilateral interactions characterized all three groups and impulsive behavior was about the same for all three groups, children from the direct instruction and eclectic classrooms engaged in less reciprocal behavior than did children from the constructivist classroom. In addition, children from the constructivist classroom resolved significantly more of their conflicts than children from the other two classrooms.

In an earlier study, DeVries and Göncü (1987) used the board game format to compare interpersonal understanding between four-year-old children from constructivist and Montessori classrooms. The pattern of findings was similar to those described above. Children from the constructivist classroom had a significantly higher proportion of reciprocal interactions and resolved a significantly higher proportion of their conflicts than children from the Montessori classroom.

Araujo (1999) conducted a longitudinal study of moral autonomy in 56 six-year-old children in three kindergartens. One center, serving children from low-income families, was constructivist and had a cooperative, democratic classroom climate. The other two centers, one serving children from low-income families and one serving children from middle- or upper-income families, were traditional, and had more authoritarian classroom climates. All children went to traditional authoritarian schools in subsequent years.

Children responded to eight moral dilemmas adapted from Piaget (1932/1965) in 1992 (kindergarten year), 1995, and 1999. Children's responses were categorized as heteronomous, autonomous, or transitional. Results showed that children from the constructivist center expressed higher personal autonomy in 1992 and 1995 than children from the authoritarian centers. In 1999, autonomy scores of the children from the authoritarian centers were higher than children from the constructivist center. The author speculates that this finding is due to "values education" in one of the traditional schools during the last two years of the study period. It may also be that many of the children were reaching a ceiling on the dilemmas.

COMMON MISCONCEPTIONS AND CRITICISMS OF CONSTRUCTIVIST EARLY MORAL EDUCATION

Within the moral domain, we have encountered two common misconceptions about constructivist education: (1) constructivist education is permissive, and (2) constructivist education is spontaneous and unstructured.

Some educators mistakenly believe that constructivist education is permissive, that teachers take an entirely "hands-off" approach to classroom discipline and children do whatever they want to do. This belief has several possible sources. The first is the mistaken belief that Piaget's stages of development are maturational and unfold according to a biologically predetermined plan. According to this view, the teacher's role is to create the least restrictive environment so as to foster children's natural, preordained growth.

The second source of this belief stems from the involvement of children in making classroom rules. Some interpret this to mean that only child-made rules govern the classroom. However, constructivist teachers, like all good early childhood teachers, must make sure children are safe. Based on interviews with constructivist teachers, DeVries and Zan (2012) identified numerous non-negotiable rules that they categorize as safety and health norms (i.e., wearing safety goggles at woodworking, washing hands before cooking, etc.), moral norms (i.e., taking fair turns, not hurting others, etc.), and discretionary norms (i.e., following the daily schedule, wearing a smock at the water table, etc.) (DeVries & Zan, 2012, pp. 158–161).

Finally, some interpret the constructivist emphasis on child initiative and choice as evidence of permissiveness. During activity time, children in constructivist classrooms are free to choose activities that appeal to their interests and purposes. To the uninformed observer, these classrooms may appear chaotic. However, to the informed observer, children's actions occur within a general framework of order, including rules to which everyone has agreed. When conflicts occur, children are encouraged to resolve them, with or without the help of the teacher. If children's engagement with the materials appears to be shallow and unproductive, the teacher redirects the child's attention toward more challenging activities.

Another common misconception is that constructivist education is spontaneous and unsystematic. In the moral realm, there are no lists of character traits to memorize, no "values of the week," and no tangible rewards for good behavior. To an outside observer, the moral curriculum may well appear to be "improvised" based on problems that naturally occur in the classroom. Although there may be standard procedures for conflict resolution (such as rules for the Peace Bench), children are not expected to memorize and follow them exactly. A typical conflict resolution for two four-year-olds might be:

> David: I didn't like it when you hit me.
> Sam: Well, I didn't like it when you took my truck.

After this exchange, the two boys might choose to jump up from the Peace Bench and resume play without any plan for future action. If the children are satisfied with the exchange, the teacher might not interfere, assuming that this is the level of discourse that is developmentally appropriate for them at this time. As children develop, they become better able to engage in conflict resolutions involving higher levels of interpersonal understanding and to make plans for future actions that would benefit themselves as well as the other person.

Whereas it is true that some constructivist teachers' approaches to moral education are more spontaneous and improvised than others, this does not mean that they do not plan for moral lessons. Constructivist teachers' lesson plans often include moral lessons, but they try to keep these plans flexible in case there are "teachable moments" in which children can construct new knowledge within the moral domain.

Criticisms of Constructivist Early Moral Education

A number of criticisms of constructivist early moral education have emerged both from within the ranks of constructivist researchers and educators, and from without. Current tensions revolve around the appropriate amount of direct teaching for children of different ages, the appropriate amount of "discovery learning," what actions should be considered negotiable and non-negotiable, and the amount of coercion coming from the teacher.

In an exchange between DeVries and her colleagues (DeVries, Hildebrandt, & Zan, 2000; DeVries et al., 2002) and Goodman (2000, 2002), Goodman lodged several criticisms against constructivist moral education. According to Goodman, many examples of constructivist early education are developmentally inappropriate for most preoperational children because they are egocentric and incapable of moral reflection. Goodman advocates that teachers should "exploit the child's natural heteronomy by advancing clear rules" (Goodman, 2000, p. 49). According to Goodman, young children are not ready to make their own rules. Goodman explains that "Encouraging premature autonomous thinking is analogous to giving premature reading instruction—you may get decoding but not understanding" (Goodman, 2000, p. 48).

It is possible that one source of Goodman's criticism of DeVries's approach to constructivist moral education rests not in its tenets but rather in Goodman's understanding of the capabilities of very young children. In fact, some of the practices advocated by Goodman closely resemble DeVries and Zan's principles of teaching. For example, Goodman and Lesnick, in their book *Moral Education: A Teacher-Centered Approach* (2004), state that moral education programs "should provide opportunities for student participation and student decision making. This participation must be developmentally staged: less for the younger child, in whom the cultivation of habits and compassion takes center stage; more for the older child" (p. 188). Goodman's criticism of DeVries and Zan's approach seems to be rooted in part in an underestimation of just how much moral reasoning and deliberation young children are capable of engaging in. DeVries and Zan (1994, 2012) describe numerous examples of preschool-aged children reasoning about fairness, justice, and compassion in their own words. If the moral issues that teachers bring to young children are selected carefully for their ease of understanding, young children are remarkably capable of engaging with them.

In the social domain, where children are notoriously egocentric, incipient decentering can often be found in the classroom. Research shows that young children do not suddenly overcome egocentrism. It is overcome little by little, in thousands of small decentrations that eventually lead to reciprocity (Flavell & Miller, 1998; Wellman & Gelman, 1998). A large body of research by Turiel and his colleagues has shown that young children do understand the intrinsic negative consequences of hurting others, especially when the harm is concrete and physical (Nucci, 1996; Smetana, in press; Turiel, 1998). Whereas questions concerning justice are understood later in development than welfare, certain issues concerning justice can also be addressed from an early age (e.g., turn-taking). Thus, from a constructivist perspective, the notion of a continuum from egocentrism to reciprocity guides teachers' thinking about children's development. In contrast to the waiting approach (laissez faire), or the tell-them-what-to-do approach (authoritarian), constructivist teachers strive to create the kinds of situations in which children gradually come to feel a necessity to treat others in moral ways. Constructivist education offers strategies teachers can use to help children begin to overcome egocentrism and become more reflective, decentered, and autonomous thinkers. These strategies are detailed in DeVries & Zan (2012) and summarized in DeVries et al. (2000).

Piaget argued that authorities' injunctions (such as not to lie) simply cover up and conceal the child's egocentric misunderstanding and do not help to change it. Simply enforcing rules when children do not understand them is not likely to change their thinking. Teachers need to make an effort to help children begin to understand why certain behaviors are wrong in terms of the effects of the behaviors on others and on relationships. Children do not need to be concrete operational to begin to understand the reciprocity of sharing, turn-taking, and perspective-taking. It is true that even for some five-year-olds sharing may mean "getting" or "giving up" something. However, in an environment where the adult emphasizes the feelings and rights of others, children even at age three begin to understand the reciprocity involved in sharing and turn-taking and to take the perspectives of others. The constructivist strategy is to create situations in which children will be confronted with the differing ideas and desires of others, and to encourage them to decenter and consider the others' point of view. It is through these processes that egocentrism is gradually overcome.

Need for Further Research

Creating an optimum balance between direct instruction and discovery learning, spontaneous and planned activities, and actions that are negotiable and non-negotiable is an ongoing challenge for constructivist teachers. Since teaching is both an art and a science, we expect that further refinements of constructivist methods will be developed for many years to come.

Many of these problems are best addressed through systematic research. In this chapter, we reviewed research comparing constructivist with other types of classrooms. There is also a growing body of research conducted exclusively in constructivist classrooms (for example, Zan & Hildebrandt, 2003, 2005). Much more research is needed in order to test and refine constructivist early moral education for all children, regardless of culture and socioeconomic status.

REFERENCES

Araujo. U. (1999). A longitudinal approach to the relations between the "cooperative school environment" and children's moral judgment. Unicamp/Brasil. (Unpublished paper). Cited in DeVries (2002).

Bennett, W. J. (1993). *The book of virtues.* New York: Simon and Schuster.

Bennett, W. J. (1995). *The children's book of virtues.* New York: Simon and Schuster.

Bredekamp, S. & Copple, C. (1997). *Developmentally appropriate practice in early childhood programs.* Washington, D.C.: National Association for the Education of Young Children.

Damon, W. (1977). *The social world of the child.* San Francisco: Jossey-Bass.

Developmental Studies Center (1995). *The literature project: Reading for real.* Oakland, CA: Developmental Studies Center.

DeVries, R. (1997). Piaget's social theory. *Educational Researcher, 26,* 4–18.

DeVries, R. (2002). *What does research tell us about effective teaching?* Des Moines, IA: The Iowa Academy of Education, sponsored by the FINE Foundation.

DeVries, R. & Göncü, A. (1987). Interpersonal relations between four-year-olds in dyads from constructivist and Montessori programs. *Journal of Applied Developmental Psychology, 8,* 481–501.

DeVries, R., Haney, J., & Zan, B. (1991). Sociomoral atmosphere in direct-instruction, eclectic, and constructivist kindergarten programs: A study of teachers' enacted interpersonal understanding. *Early Childhood Research Quarterly, 6,* 449–471.

DeVries, R., Hildebrandt, C. & Zan, B. (2000). Constructivist early education for moral development. *Early Education and Development, 11,* 5–35.

DeVries, R., & Kohlberg, L. (1987/1990). *Constructivist early education: Overview and comparison with other programs.* Washington, D.C.: National Association for the Education of Young Children.

DeVries, R., Reese-Learned, H., & Morgan, P. (1991). Sociomoral development in direct-instruction, eclectic, and constructivist programs: A study of children's enacted interpersonal understanding. *Early Childhood Research Quarterly, 6,* 473–517.

DeVries, R. & Zan, B. (1994). *Moral classrooms, moral children: Creating a constructivist moral atmosphere in early childhood* (1st ed.). New York: Teachers College Press.

DeVries, R. & Zan, B. (2012). *Moral classrooms, moral children: Creating a constructivist moral atmosphere in early childhood* (2nd ed.). New York: Teachers College Press.

DeVries, R., Zan, B., & Hildebrandt, C. (2002). Issues in constructivist early moral education. *Early Education and Development, 3,* 313–343.

DeVries, R., Zan, B., Hildebrandt, C., Edmiaston, R., & Sales, C. (Eds.). (2002). *Developing constructivist early childhood curriculum: Practical principles and activities.* New York: Teachers College Press.

Dewey, J. (1900). Froebel's educational principles. *Elementary School Record, 1,* 143–151.

Dewey, J. (1909). *Moral principles in education.* Boston: Houghton Mifflin.

Dewey, J. (1913/1975). *Interest and effort in education.* New York: Free Press.

Dewey, J. (1916). *Democracy and education.* New York: McMillan.

Dewey, J. (1938). *Experience and education.* New York: McMillan.

Durkheim, E. (1925/1961). *Moral education.* Glencoe, IL: The Free Press.

Eisenberg, N., Lundy, T., Shell, R., & Roth, K. (1985). Children's justifications for their adult and peer-directed compliant (prosocial and nonprosocial) behaviors. *Developmental Psychology, 21,* 325–331.

Flavell, J. & Miller, P. (1998). Social cognition. In W. Damon (Series Ed.), D. Kuhn, & R. Siegler (Vol. Eds.), *Handbook of child psychology: Vol. 2. Cognition, perception, and language* (5th ed., pp. 851–898). New York: John Wiley & Sons.

Fosnot, C. T. (2005). *Constructivism: Theory, perspectives, & practice.* New York: Teachers College Press.

Goffin, S. G. & Wilson, C. S. (2001). *Curriculum models and early childhood education: Appraising the relationship* (2nd ed.). Upper Saddle River, NJ: Prentice-Hall.

Goodman, J. F. (2000). Moral education in early childhood: The limits of constructivism. *Early Education and Development, 11,* 37–54.

Goodman, J. F. (2002). Objective truths and the leading of children: A response to Rheta DeVries, Betty Zan, and Carolyn Hildebrandt. *Early Education and Development, 13,* 345–349.

Goodman, J. F. & Lesnick, H. (2004). *Moral education: A teacher-centered approach.* Boston, MA: Pearson.

Hildebrandt, C. & Zan, B. (2002). Using group games to teach mathematics. In R. DeVries, B. Zan, C. Hildebrandt, R. Edmiaston, & C. Sales (Eds.). *Developing constructivist early childhood curriculum: Practical principles and activities.* New York: Teachers College Press.

Kamii, C. & DeVries, R. (1980). *Group games in early education: Implications of Piaget's theory.* Washington, D.C.: National Association for the Education of Young Children.

Kamii, C. & Ewing, J. K. (1996). Basing teaching on Piaget's constructivism. *Childhood Education, 72,* 260–264.

Killen, M. (1989). Context, conflict, and coordination in early social development. In L. Winegar (Ed.), *Social interaction and the development of children's understanding* (pp. 114–136). Norwood, NJ: Ablex.

Killen, M. (1991). Children's evaluations of morality in the context of peer, teacher-child and familiar relations. *Journal of Genetic Psychology, 151,* 395–410.

Killen, M. Breten, S., Ferguson, H., & Handler, K. (1994). Preschoolers' evaluations of teacher methods of intervention in social transgressions. *Merrill-Palmer Quarterly, 40,* 399–415.

Killen, M. & Naigles, L. (1995). Preschool children pay attention to their addresses: The effects of gender composition on peer disputes. *Discourse Processes, 19,* 329–346.

Killen, M. & Nucci, L. (1995). Morality, autonomy, and social conflict. In M. Killen & D. Hart (Eds.), *Morality and everyday life: Developmental perspectives* (pp. 52–86). Cambridge, UK: Cambridge University Press.

Killen, M. & Sueyoshi, L. (1995). Conflict resolution in Japanese social interactions. *Early Education and Development, 6*, 313–330.

Kohlberg, L. (1984). *Essays on moral development. Vol. 2, The psychology of moral development.* San Francisco: Harper & Row.

Laupa, M. (1994). "Who's in charge?" Preschool children's concepts of authority. *Child Development, 57*, 412–415.

Lickona, T., Schaps, E., & Lewis, C. (2003). *CEP's eleven principles of effective character education.* Washington, D.C: Character Education Partnership.

Mayhew, K. & Edwards, A. (1936). *The Dewey school.* New York: Appleton-Century.

Narvaez, D. (2002). Does reading moral stories build character? *Educational Psychology Review, 14*, 155–171.

Nucci, L. (1996). Morality and the personal sphere of actions. In E. Reed, E. Turiel, & T. Brown (Eds.), *Knowledge and values.* Hillsdale, NJ: Erlbaum.

Nucci, L. P. (2001). *Education in the moral domain.* Cambridge, UK: Cambridge University Press.

Nucci, L. (in press). The personal and the moral. In M. Killen & J. Smetana (Eds.). *Handbook of moral development* (2nd ed.). Mahwah, NJ: Erlbaum.

Nucci, L. & Turiel, E. (1978). Social interactions in the home and the development of young children's conceptions of the personal. *Child Development, 66*, 1438–1452.

Piaget, J. (1932/1965). *The moral judgment of the child.* London: Free Press.

Piaget, J. (1948/1973). *To understand is to invent.* New York: Grossman. (First published in *Prospects,* UNESCO Quarterly Review of Education.)

Piaget, J. (1970). Piaget's theory. In *Carmichael's manual of child psychology* (3rd ed.). New York: John Wiley & Sons.

Power, C., Higgins, A., & Kohlberg, L. (1989). *Lawrence Kohlberg's approach to moral education.* New York: Columbia University Press.

Read, K. (1966). *The nursery school: A human development laboratory.* Philadelphia: Saunders.

Rende, R. & Killen, M. (1992). Social interactional antecedents of object conflict. *Early Education Research Quarterly, 1*, 551–563.

Selman, R. (1980). *The growth of interpersonal understanding.* New York: Academic Press.

Selman, R. & Schultz, L. (1990). *Making a friend in youth: Developmental theory and pair therapy.* Chicago: University of Chicago Press.

Smetana, J. (1981). Preschool conceptions of moral and social rules. *Child Development, 52*, 1333–1336.

Smetana, J. (1985). Preschool children's conceptions of transgressions: Effects of varying moral and conventional domain-related attributes. *Developmental Psychology, 21*, 18–21.

Smetana, J. G. (in press). Moral development: The social domain theory view. In P. D. Zelazo (Ed.), *The Oxford handbook of developmental psychology. Vol. 1* (pp. 832–863). Oxford University Press.

Smetana, J. G., Rote, W., Jambon, M., Tasopoulos-Chan, M., Villalobos, M., & Comer, J. (2012). Developmental changes and individual differences in young children's moral judgments. *Child Development, 83*, 683–696.

Tanner, L. (1997). *Dewey's laboratory school: Lessons for today.* New York: Teachers College Press.

Turiel, E. (1983). *The development of social knowledge: Morality and social convention.* Cambridge, UK: Cambridge University Press.

Turiel, E. (1998). The development of morality. In W. Damon & N. Eisenberg (Eds.), *Handbook of child psychology. Vol. 3* (pp. 863–932). New York: John Wiley & Sons.

Turiel, E. (2001). Foreword. In L. Nucci, *Education in the moral domain.* Cambridge, UK: Cambridge University Press.

Wainryb, C. (2006). Moral development and culture: Diversity, tolerance, and justice. In M. Killen & J. G. Smetana (Eds.), *Handbook of moral development* (pp. 185–210). Mahwah, NJ: Erlbaum.

Weber, E. (1984). *Ideas influencing early childhood education: A theoretical analysis.* New York: Teachers College Press.

Wellman, H. & Gelman, S. (1998). Knowledge acquisition in foundational domains. In W. Damon (Series Ed.), D. Kuhn & R. Siegler (Vol. Eds.), *Handbook of child psychology: Vol. 2, Cognition, perception, and language* (5th ed., pp. 863–932). New York: Wiley.

Zan, B. (1996). Interpersonal understanding among friends: A case study of two young boys playing checkers. *Journal of Research in Childhood Education, 10*, 114–122.

Zan, B. & Hildebrandt, C. (2003). First graders' interpersonal understanding during cooperative and competitive games. *Early Education and Development, 14*, 397–410.

Zan, B. & Hildebrandt, C. (2005). Cooperative and competitive games in constructivist classrooms. *The Constructivist, 16*, 1–13.

12

TOWARD A THEORY OF THE JUST COMMUNITY APPROACH

Effects of Collective Moral, Civic, and Social Education

Fritz K. Oser

This chapter expands upon the concept of Kohlberg's just community (JC) approach for moral education. It is intended as a follow-up to the material provided by Power and Higgins-D'Alessandro (2008) in their chapter for the first edition of the *Handbook of Moral and Character Education*. Based upon precursors, experiences and research results, I will discuss suggestions for enlarging the basic idea of a just community with respect to elements of civic, pro-social, systemic, and participation-oriented beliefs. This is followed by accounts of basic functional parts of a JC, a more detailed analysis of resistance to JC schools, accounts of practical examples, and advice on making JC schools work. The final section of the chapter proposes how to expand the theory of just community schools so that moral and social education become the basis for academic learning.

ENLARGING THE BASIC IDEA

"The just community approach has two major aims: (1) to promote students' moral development, and (2) to transform the moral atmosphere of the school into a moral community" (Power & Higgins-D'Alessandro, 2008, p. 231). Although this statement is correct and relates fully to Kohlberg's conception (see Kohlberg, 1985), it is not fully differentiated and does not include enough of the following: (a) a theory of civic education, (b) a theory of school functioning, (c) a theory of social beliefs and social learning, and (d) a theory of complex morality. Having guided several just community schools in Germany and Switzerland, it seems to me that empowerment of students through the process of building up such a just community (JC) school has implications that go beyond moral development and moral atmosphere. Since the JC approach is a comprehensive enterprise, it includes theoretically and practically more than positive non-indoctrinative morality. It also encompasses systemic and collective dangers, fragilities, and inevitable mistakes—factors mostly not taken into consideration in descriptions of the JC approach. Enlarging the basic concept of Kohlberg's idea and its implementation during his time may help in understanding resistances of many teachers and principals to involving themselves more profoundly into the realization of such an idealistic vision today.

ON THE RESISTANCE TO CHANGE

It is not self-evident that most learning processes within the construction of a JC are often seen as "painful" from students' points of view once the "newness bias" of the installation of such a school-form is gone. Since learning involves overcoming resistant forces, it becomes immediately apparent that changing attitudes, beliefs, convictions—and even knowledge bases—is often rough going. If we learn that we must change, we like to resist, especially if the goal toward this change is not seen as worthy enough compared to other learning goals such as, for example, building knowledge in computer programming. Here is an illustrative example. Joining about 250 other students between 12 and 15 years of age for a JC meeting, a tall boy in the last year of compulsory schooling said to me:

> Dr. Oser, do we have to decide on school issues again? This takes from us so much thinking and accountability work. Look, if you, you alone, decide, that is much easier for us. You are an adult person at the university, and we believe that you do the right thing. We do what you want us to do. Why shall we be concerned about others? We are friendly; we prepare for life; and we will be honest. That is all we need. To be moral doesn't give you an apprenticeship position later in an important firm. And to learn democracy has no value for this.

This 15-year-old philosopher fully understood what we were doing. He knew that participation means to be responsible and accountable, but after a year of hard work, he did not see the value of it—even worse, he could see the value, but he did not want to be involved in it. We may add an even more gripping example. Althof (1998), who founded and scaffolded many JC schools, experienced the following situation in a teacher training university in which he had created a JC approach a couple of months previously with these young adults. At a meeting that he could not attend because of illness, some students amazingly proposed to give up this whole concept. Although no action was taken subsequently, they won the vote. This was a clear sign that some of these adults understood that, for the system to survive, school reform demands a total engagement: availability, responsibility, and care. And they were well aware of the JC system's fragility.

I present this rather problematic account because authors are, in general, too enthusiastic about the JC approach; some of them see it as a means for solving a lot of school problems, a technique like "give an I message" (e.g., "*I* see your point about…; however, *I* believe that, as a group, we feel that your message…") and everything will be solved. Others conceive it as a great hope for a better learning climate, and they feel especially that this could be a chance for learning what a positive democracy could be. However, without destroying these hopes, we distinguish the JC approach primarily as a means for learning what we think is a social good for students or primarily as an endpoint for living in a world that could indeed be a better one than we currently experience in most schools. The JC approach as an endpoint is an imposition for all the participants: for the students, but especially for the teachers and principals. They have to exercise what we call the "presupposition of autonomy" (see the paragraph on the teachers' role), meaning that teachers have to act as if students already have autonomy in order to develop it—this is hard pedagogical work.

However, before continuing with the case for an expanded theory of the just community approach, I wish to enlarge the context with a history of related endeavors and a history of just community implementations.

PRECURSORS

Pestalozzi

For Europeans, to speak about the JC approach inevitably invokes a connection with Heinrich Pestalozzi. In the years 1798 and 1799, when French troops entered the so-called old Swiss cantons, soldiers focused particular attention to one of the founding cantons, Schwyz. The result was terrible poverty, broken families, orphans, sicknesses, etc. Pestalozzi received the task from the new central government of Switzerland to care for the lost children of Schwyz, spawning the mythos of Pestalozzi as father of orphans. When he describes the children's poverty, their hunger, and lack of access to rooms and beds—all within the tension between Catholics and Protestants against a background of occupying French troops (see Pestalozzi, 1799/1965, the letter of Stans)—his discussion amounts to a prescription for how to educate for a humane orientation in difficult times. This experience led him to found a children's community based upon the core assumption that children's moral development would emerge from fulfilling the demands of daily living and work.

The daily work element consisted of three stages. The first was to develop a moral mood (a kind of basic trust) through the fulfillment of the fundamental needs of the child. From this core of basic trust, the child then learned to engage in doing the good; to act so that the good becomes habituated. Finally, in the third stage, the child learned about evaluating both the good and the bad. For this latter phase, Pestalozzi introduced ethical constructs, rules, and notions to explain to the children reasons for being good. In this concept the feeling (heart) presupposes the acting (hand), which was followed by reasoning (mind or head). Pestalozzi's personal connectedness to the children was a kind of educational guarantee for stimulating these processes. Thus, Pestalozzi introduced the radical notion for the time period, that moral education emerged from a quasi-family structure that formed the context within which children experienced the good feelings, and responsibilities for action guided by moral judgment that were the basis of children's moral growth.

Makarenko

In many of my courses, I present the following story—by Anton Makarenko (1938, pp. 124ff.) to teachers and educational psychologists who know about Kohlberg's JC approach:

> There was a young man, a commander and quasi-leader, who was responsible for the entire community. He was engaged in cultural work as a member of a theater group. He was a good worker, and enjoyed the esteem and the respect of all—including me. He was one of the older, neglected young persons that I had discovered. He had already experienced a lot of delinquency and vagabond behavior before coming to us (Makarenko, 1976, p. 124). One day a new radio was stolen; it disappeared from the sleeping room. It belonged to a boy who had done hard work to get the money to

purchase it. The young group leader organized a community meeting and proposed an investigation. Later, one of the other boys found the radio in a hidden theater room, and he and others subsequently took turns observing this place to watch for who would come and use the radio. After a while, it was precisely the boy who served as group commander who entered the room looking for the radio. The observing students thus discovered that it was he who was the thief. In the following community meetings, they decided, after long debates, to dismiss the boy from his post and have him move out of the home. Makarenko, the founder and leader of the home, resisted the dismissal. He called on an upper committee to overrule the students' decision, proposed other forms of penance for the young offender, and otherwise fought for a different decision. Finally and painfully, however, he had to accept it.

Teachers and researchers that hear this story generally think that it depicts a typical Kohlbergian dilemma from the Bronx JC school or from the Niantic correction JC system. But the story stems from Makarenko's collective education home. In the story I just omitted words such as "kosomolse," "communards," and "tetchiest" that would remind one of the soviet style of collective working colonies for young orphans, street-children, criminal youth groups, and similar outcasts.

Makarenko had, about 50 years earlier than Kohlberg, similar goals and ideas—namely, to educate morally through the building of communities that were self-governing and to develop high moral standards. In his so-called Gorki-colony (1920–1928) and later in the Dzerzinskij community (1927–1935), he tried to build up a system of rules through a special concept of discipline with a strong human face. Makarenko is often misunderstood and dismissed by American readers as a communist. He was, of course, influenced by the ideas of the Russian Revolution, but his writings are about how to build up resilience for poor children and adolescents in wartime and terrible political chaos. His positions are not political cant, but are indeed serious educational reflections.

For him, similar to Durkheim (1961), discipline produces feelings of security and leads to freedom of thinking and doing the right thing. Interestingly, Makarenko developed three stages of internalization of this freedom-producing discipline: stage 1, to ask for its realization and set norms with great conviction and authority; stage 2, to build groups that share this demand and see the advantages of living with a common discipline; and stage 3, to transform the demand for moral norms into a common-sense community value. He described the dangers and pitfalls of each stage, and he posited that the task of the leader is to give, in each decision-making situation, a face of understanding for these weaknesses. Lastly, Makarenko engaged himself in building these communities for helping disadvantaged children and adolescents to survive—quite similar to what Pestalozzi did.

Korczak

One of the most impressive forefathers of the JC approach is Janusz Korczak (1967), the so-called Polish Pestalozzi. With Stepha Wilczynska, he installed a parliamentary form of his orphan home containing between 200 and 300 children from the streets between three and 14 years of age. Korczak's biography is impressive. He was born into a well-settled Jewish family in Poland. After becoming a well-known medical doctor and participating in World War I on the Russian front, he gave up his medical career to take over a first and then a second home for orphans. Writing under the pseudonym Janusz Korczak, he contributed articles to educational journals and developed the first concept of children's rights. Accompanying 300 deported children, he died in the Treblinka concentration camp in 1942. His greatest idea (and its decisive realization) was a kind of JC approach in a very special sense. He installed in his home a parliamentary concept in which all children were fully involved.

The elements of this system were as follows:

- plenary student meetings for deciding on all important life issues of the home;
- the friendship or comrade court to deal with the task of treating children's and adolescents' infractions of rules in a fair but decisive way;
- a library with books that also included Korczak's diary describing the development of each child so that the children could read what he was thinking about them and thus to be able to ask for changes when they felt misinterpreted;
- a blackboard in the entrance hall for information sharing.

The most important component was the plenary assembly mentioned above and the friendship court elected regularly by the full parliament. Since Korczak knew that children could judge other children harshly, he developed a comprehensive body of regulations to stimulate a basic sensitivity for forgiveness. The first 100 rules included elements of forgiveness. All of the subsequent rules were numbered in 100s (200, 300, etc.) to convey the notion that these referred to serious infractions associated with severe punishment and should be invoked rarely—or as in the case of rule 1000 practically never. Let us look at some examples.

Rule 1: The court declares that the complaint against A has been withdrawn.
Rule 30: The court declares that A could not have acted differently.
Rule 67: The court forgives A for the bad thing done without reflection.
Rule 94: The court forgives A because someone imploringly asks for it (a friend or a relative, etc.).

Then come the big and heavy stones.

Rule 100: The court states without forgiveness that A did act negatively.
Rule 600: The court declares that A did act badly. This judgment has to be made public in the house newspaper and on the blackboard.
Rule 1000: The court dismisses A from the home. This judgment has to be published in the newspaper.

All this was a sensitivity process in which the delinquent behaviors that kids and adolescents committed were thoroughly investigated. Korczak (1967) wanted students to become reflective not only about their own behavior but also about the behavior of the others. Korczak used this experience to develop the universal rights for children adopted by the United Nations in 1949. He declared, for example, that the child has a right to keep a secret, a right to personal belongings, a right to be loved, and, especially, a right to full human respect. Human respect had three faces: (a) the right to live in this day and age, (b) the right to be oneself, and (c) the right to one's own death, which means to take risks, to explore the world, to receive presupposed responsibility for discovering new and challenging situations.

It is quite interesting that Korczak's home community includes the same elements as Kohlberg's JC approach. There was a regular community meeting, a fairness committee (friendship court), a preparation group elected by the plenary community, and the possibility of always demanding a plenary get-together (a real JC meeting). The differences are also quite obvious. First, Korczak's concept of a warm parliamentary interchange is a life concept and not a school form. The children in Korczak's home lived there for their existence whereas Kohlberg's JC approach is a structure implanted into the school. In the JC school, children and adolescents return home afterwards; in Korczak's home, the children leave the parliamentary home for visiting the classical school, outside in the city, which at that time had no democratic roots. Another difference is that Korczak had no developmental theory of growth, but in his famous book *How to Love a Child* (1967), he developed a theory of moral sensibility in the context of norm and rule induction. It is of great historical interest that Lawrence Kohlberg learned about Korczak in 1980, relatively late in his life. In his last chapter of *Essays on Moral Development, Volume One*, he describes Korczak as an example of stage six or even stage seven (Kohlberg, 1981).

Kibbutz Life

In several places when Kohlberg introduces us to the JC approach, he refers to the kibbutzim spirit (e.g., in Kohlberg, 1980, 1985; see also Snarey and Samuelson this volume). But a kibbutz, even with its concept of community education, does not fit well into the concept of the JC approach. A kibbutz is a total life-sharing enterprise with the purpose of survival, with special conceptions of early childhood education, with income sharing, and a special work and survival spirit—traits embedded after the 1948 Arab–Israeli War in the growing of the state of Israel.

A JC is a school transformational concept of power sharing with children and adolescents to learn how to become moral, to be socially engaged, work hard, and develop civility. Here, work and money are not shared, but common norms and self-generated rules are. The JC is a playground democracy, a place for learning and simulating a better togetherness, and a change of the norm-genesis process normally done by the teacher alone and now given to the whole community. A kibbutz, on the other hand, consists of a higher degree of existential communitarian sharedness that includes work, child care, religious belief, traditions and signs of passages but with less formal behavioral codes such as those in a school. Nevertheless, the spirit of a kibbutz in its best form can influence our teachers who engage in the JC approach.

THE JUST COMMUNITY APPROACH: A BRIEF HISTORY

The first JC schools were founded by L. Kohlberg, E. Wassermann, E. Fenton, D. Speicher-Dubin, and R. Mosher. The Cambridge Cluster School, Scarsdale Alternative School, and Brookline High School (School within a School) were places where the idea first received fruition. The book edited by R. Mosher (1980) *Moral Education* is an important account of these beginnings. While enacting his vision within schools, Kohlberg also chartered the concept of the JC approach in prisons in Niantic and other correctional institutes (Hickey & Scharf, 1980).

The second generation of JC schools guided primarily by Higgins and Power (Power & Higgins-D'Alessandro, 2008) continued Kohlberg's work after his death. Additional JC enterprises emerged that were connected to other reform tasks.

Whereas in the USA some highly committed persons continue practicing the JC approach, more commonly it has been incorporated into other approaches. For instance, the Community of Caring school reform program that initially focused on risk prevention broadened its scope to promoting the development of all students through school culture change and an array of student activities including service learning.

(Oser, Althof, & Higgins-D'Alessandro, 2008, p. 400)

The European version of the JC emerged in 1984 when Kohlberg and Higgins visited Germany, and three JC schools in Nordrheine-Westfalia were founded by Oser and Lind (Lind, 1987; Lind & Althof, 1992). In the 1990s, Switzerland started several just communities within schools, often connected with other goals like conflict negotiation or civic education (Luterbacher, 2009). In Germany, this has been expressed more recently in efforts at democratic education (Edelstein & Fauser, 2001; see also Edelstein and Krettenauer this volume).

ADDRESSING A PERCEIVED DEFICIT: KOHLBERG'S VISION OF SCHOOLS

The just community approach founded by Kohlberg in the 1970s and 1980s (Kohlberg, 1985) is, as mentioned, an effort to reform a difficult to change system—a whole school. The beginning of such an expansive intention is felt a fundamental deficit of school functioning and also a deficit with respect to the level of moral judgments, prosocial actions, and moral-caring sensibilities of the individual members of such a community. "Our first two efforts at using the Dewey-Piaget democracy and Durkheimian collective moral education, like the kibbutz experiment, focused heavily on remedial moral education for pre-conventional adolescents and young adults" (Kohlberg, 1985, p. 44). The word "remedial" is important: A just community school starts mostly with evidence and stories of such things as students breaking rules, failing to help others, using drugs, hurting peers, being unmotivated to study, etc. These events can be clustered into the realms of morality, community-oriented values, politics, social issues, and systemic issues—each demanding different reworking strategies. These events lead students to a felt disequilibrium with respect to a caring and positive school climate. They feel a missing state of shared community values and deep disappointment regarding a lack of mutual respect between teachers and students and among students themselves. Even if these negative experiences are often not measured through instruments (scales), principals, teachers, school helpers, parents, and often students talk about them, feel them, and indeed become seriously concerned about them. As the philosopher N. Hartmann (1957) states, "Only negatively can humans get a notion of happiness" (p. 141). From a teleological point of view, a JC system is an instrument for overcoming these deficits. From a deontological framing, however, it is of course an educational enterprise with humanistic goals and values (Veugelers, 2011).

Kohlberg's vision was, nevertheless, not directed at systemic change so much as it was intended to stimulate development within each individual with respect to three fundamental goals, namely:

(a) to develop moral judgment through deliberative discourse whereby the contents are not artificial but real-life or school dilemmas;

(b) to bridge moral judgment and moral agency;
(c) to develop shared norms with a subtle sense of community and central aspects of solidarity.

Although, Kohlberg's 1985 article "The just community approach to moral education in theory and practice" is a masterful foundation for a new reform stream with respect to changing persons within a school, his analysis presents a limited vision focused solely on moral education. To put it differently, the "just community" approach amounts "solely," in the view of John Dewey's conception, as a means for moral education. I would argue that the issue has to be reconsidered under the heading of what we call a *comprehensive domain-specific transformation of the person–system relationship*.

Kohlberg (1985) begins by making it clear that most psychologists use a one-way concept to transfer psychological theory into praxis, and this way can never be fully functional. He states: "The one-way street model of relating theory to practice rests on what I have called the 'psychologist's fallacy', i.e., to believe that what is important for developmental psychology research is what is important for practitioners in the classroom" (p. 33), and, in his bottom-up approach, he explains why the teacher is not just a facilitator of learning but "an advocate for certain moral content" (advocacy approach). If the teacher shows high respect for the student, this allows a participatory democracy in the classroom and, at the same time, advocates certain values without being indoctrinative. The issue then is how to link justice to a small political community based on equal political rights. The notion of a community and the notion of justice are brought together through the concept of collectivity within a communitarian context. However, this always entails a structure in which the teacher has a double role; namely, to set conditions for participation and to participate (without a pseudo-participatory attitude; see below). The importance of membership, the sense of community, the primary negative sanctions of the group's criticism, the basic trust and the conflict between the solidarity of friends versus the solidarity toward the community as a whole—these are all taken into newly developed phases of collective norms, stages of collective normative values, stages of a sense of community-valuing, and degrees of collectiveness of norms. Examples from one of the first just community schools, the Scarsdale Alternative School, help clarify aspects of what is called a moral atmosphere, moral courage (civil disobedience), the difference between an immoral behavior such as stealing (which concerns each student) and cheating (which concerns mainly only one student and the respective teachers). What is especially interesting—what happens often in democracies—is that a new rule (e.g., against cheating) is voted in by unanimous agreement, but the enforcement of the new rule is decided upon with extreme controversy. This construction of a moral atmosphere, which is by no means just an emotional wellbeing factor but is instead a content-specific amount of intensity of the collectiveness of norms, is apparent in the justification structures within JC meetings. In fact, this is a Durkheimian concept because of its discipline and socialization orientation (Durkheim, 1961).

Thus, to sum up:

In Just-Community school meetings students, teachers, staff-members and principals come together on a regular basis in order to thoroughly discuss and democratically decide upon issues relevant to life in school—Special community projects are planned, conflict solutions are generated and rules and policies are established that reflect shared norms and values of the school community.

(Oser et al., 2008, p. 395)

In a parliamentary way, a whole community decides together on: (a) rules that shape their daily school-life; (b) goals for positive togetherness and high solidarity of all members (on issues of a positive school climate and on prosocial engagements in the school); (c) proposed solutions to conflicts, upholding rules, and rule enforcing processes); and (d) special community programs. Participation is at the core of this search for new moral and social learning directions and new school pathways, and, with the belief that in participating in common decision making, students learn to be socially competent first and develop shared norms second (see Figure 12.1).

A NEW WORLD: THE CORE IDEA OF THE JC APPROACH

To find out what happens beyond moral developmental or collective norm oriented tendencies in the Kohlbergian sense, we need to analyze the missing dimensions mentioned above. The following account (edited for length) of a JC meeting at a middle-sized Swiss school reveals these.

Figure 12.1 Example of a Voting Process in a Swiss Just Community Meeting (Photo taken by W. Althof).

It is Monday, 11 o'clock. More than 300 persons (all the secondary students in grades 7 to 9, all the teachers, all the staff members) come together to decide a very difficult case: Three times the last week, somebody entered the girls' restrooms, dirtied them terribly, and destroyed whatever could be destroyed, leaving the restrooms smelling awful. In the first meeting, the planning committee presented the case. Many of the female students stood up and expressed feelings of indignation, injustice, and mistrust—sometimes along with some very embarrassing facts. There followed a general discussion in which many hypothesized about who could do such a terrible thing: someone from inside the school or someone from outside the school.

Many of the students wanted to say something about their understanding of the case: for example, "this is certainly a person who is frustrated about the school as a whole"; "this person must be punished harshly"; or "we need a new rule of observation." One boy offered to let the girls use the boys' restroom on the first floor until the girls' restroom was repaired; the boys would use the restroom in the basement. Afterwards, the planning committee presented three solution proposals: first, install a hidden camera so that the "criminal" could be caught; second, students from the upper classes—taking turns—would go through the corridors every 15 minutes with an alarm clock looking for possible perpetrators; and third, there would be a huge flyer in front of the restrooms saying with huge letters, "Don't do this again. You hurt people."

Then students formed into small groups in the big hall and intensely discussed the propositions. Some developed propositions such as engaging a policeman or father of one of the students who had time to look at things. Another proposition was just to trust that the wrongdoer, probably an upper classman, would have an insight that this was a misguided approach for getting rid of frustration. Then the students came back to the mean assembly, and a representative of each group argued for one or another solution. After a long discussion, the planning committee proposed progressive solutions in four steps: first a flyer; second a hidden camera; third student control; and fourth police control. After a final serious discussion of pros and cons, the meeting came to an end with a vote. By a tiny majority, the planning committee accepted proposition three—the flyer in front of the restroom.

At the end, the school principal gave a small, convincing talk saying that this school is a "good school," not only because it has a good climate, good teachers, and wonderful students, but also because this school brings things out in the open and solves problems itself. Afterwards teacher and student groups stood around the main floor of the school and discussed the issue. The teachers were especially involved deeply in self-criticism, fearing that a negative light would be shed on the school. In a teachers' meeting later in the afternoon, some teachers criticized the solution that was adopted. The principal defended the outcome from the position that to make things open and let the students participate in an open discourse is better than hiding things because the students learn to see what accountability means. Then the principal, a very clever woman, invited a journalist to the school and asked him to write about such a wonderful democratic school where the students take on high responsibility, etc. Only one father, a lawyer, tried to bother the principal afterwards. All in all, after posting the agreed-upon flyer, there was no more dirtying of the girls' restrooms.

Althof (2008) reports that many teachers and parents—but also principals and educational politicians—ask if it would be necessary to spend so much time and the energy of so many people to resolve a case like this. He also reports that many parents feared that students cannot really take responsibility for such situations, that they suffer from them, or that the burden would be too high for them. Some teachers also had the opinion that the school principal should regulate such problems. We call this "a regulation syndrome."

Looking from an educational standpoint, it is obvious that very interesting and intensive learning processes were at stake here. To name some:

- A school-wide organization at a time during the week when everybody has to leave the classroom and to be at this "agora."
- A case is made public within (and only within) the clear borders of a system so that everybody in the system shares the same knowledge and concerns.
- There is public debate in which everyone can make suggestions, take a stance, and share the indignation.
- There is concern expressed about respectful treatment of girls.
- There is apparently a mixture of argumentation levels or stages that stimulates the next higher stage.
- There is a lobbying mode that consists of convincing others from their own convictions.
- The preparation group has a process employing parliamentary solutions that have to be analyzed and valued, first in small groups and then in full parliament.
- There is voting preparation and a process in which the result is taken seriously, even if "philosopher kings" would never accept this solution.
- Most of the time, the minority voters accept the majority decision, but the majority learns to respect the opinion of the minority.
- Because all members of the school make the decision, responsibility and implementation are shared.
- This leads to what we call "system identity"—important also for workplaces, institutes, and similar organizations.

These elements show that a JC school operates in a concrete situation, in a specific time frame, with a concrete problem to solve, and with a sense of necessity for morally problematic issues. Although these elements are initially described above without having been framed by theory, we can begin by taking them into consideration in order to understand what happens in a more comprehensive manner. We stated that the JC approach is missing (a) a theory of civic education, (b) a theory of school functioning, (c) a theory of social beliefs and social learning, and (d) a theory of complex morality. These would be considered alongside the Kohlberg-introduced functions of stimulating moral development and the enhancement of community-related convictions and social bonding.

THE MISSING ELEMENTS

Civic Education and a View of the Whole School

In the above account of a JC meeting, the political and civic dimensions of a meeting become obvious. On one hand, the democracy becomes visible (one person, one vote). On the other hand, students experience and come to understand the consequences of public opinion produced by a process (they participate in a public decision-making process, participate in a voting process, and accept and submit themselves to a majority/minority situation). These are civic issues, not primarily moral-domain issues. Questions of freedom to speak while having respect for others, learning political tolerance, and being aware of the power of the preparation group are political issues. In addition, students learn how helpless and impotent we are in the face of heavy and populist arguments, how much we feel misunderstood if we think that someone is lobbying behind our backs, how decisions of the leading group can be manipulated and nondemocratic, and how to be "neutral" in developing and deciding upon a new rule. The learning of politics thus is embedded in the empowerment of each school member, and the whole system to trust the reason and legitimating capacity of each student and teacher.

"Politics" here has several meanings: to influence the power structure of a system, to argue freely, to understand the process of rule genesis, and to decide by voting or to elect freely in a participative process. And "civic" means to participate in a political community. "Certainly such participation entails interaction with the state (school) and its institutions, but it also includes activities undertaken with fellow community members about matters of shared concern" (Rogers, Mediratta, & Shah, 2012, p. 44). Here students learn to understand that a community, besides consisting of shared feelings and atmosphere, is first of all a system of rules and a sharing of ruling (Gutmann, 1987; Moses & Saenz, 2012). Again, this does not touch on morality directly—only indirectly, like every act in human life.

The school-theoretical perspective is completely different. The school, as a system within a bigger, regulative system of a state, has its own basic and educationally justifiable structure. Because the school is totally coercive (a student must learn a given curriculum, *must* do homework, *must* behave according to rules, *must* listen to a teacher, etc.), and even if all its "musts" are subordinate to a positive human respect, this coerciveness cannot be overlooked or even destroyed. Because the functions of every school in the world are (a) to build knowledge, (b) to test and select students according to their competencies, (c) to allocate life resources, and (e) socialize students into the adult life (see Fend, 2007), it is obvious that the basic functions of schools cannot be subordinated to the JC approach. It rather must be taken into a socially supporting body of mutually supporting individuals within this mentioned coercive structure. Kohlberg did not have many sociologically relevant reflections about the school as a system. His idea was that development to higher stages and shared norms were the basic elements for changing a school. We believe that this idea is a very important part of the JC approach, but it is not all. There are two more elements: First, we must consider the conditions for a school-system change toward a JC approach, and, second, we have to ask how students of different ages conceive of their school as a system.

On a first point, consider the work of Leithwood, Harris, & Strauss (2010) titled *Leading School Turnaround*. It is a top-down concept in which, influenced by the corporate world, the basic goal is to dismiss weak teachers in order to enhance math and reading performances, to control children, and to implement rules and enforce them. In order to prevent schools from failing, turnaround leaders support the high performance of teachers, and try to stimulate the success reflections on their colleagues' professional skills and knowledge. They model desirable practices; redesign schools according to discipline and respect of others; and buffer staff change across fit-in-criteria. The respective strategies are: building productive relationships, building achievement targets, and getting funds for evaluation in order to fit the school into the highest national bench-marks. Even without considering competition, single incentives, and sanctions, we find a similar approach in Darling-Hammonds' concept of educational reform with the elements: standards of assessment, systemic thinking, instructional quality, creation of collegial incentives, and external revisions (Darling-Hammond, 2012).

A different concept is taken in other books like *School Effectiveness for Whom* (Slee, Weiner, & Tomlinson, 1998), and here at least a positive criticism prevails. The editors say in the beginning:

> We maintain that while reporting to be inclusive and comprehensive, school effec-tiveness research is riddled with errors: it is excluding (of children with special needs, black boys, so-called clever girls), it is normative and regulatory (operating mainly within narrow sets of performance indicators), it is bureaucratic and disempow-ering. It focuses exclusively on the processes and internal constructs of schooling, apparently disconnected from educations' social end—adulthood. School effective-ness seems to be neither interested nor very effective in preparing children for cit-izenship, parenthood or work.
>
> (p. 5)

Of course these are two extreme conceptions (one showing a full top-down approach, the other referring to criticism with respect to one-sided reforms), but they are helpful for locating what we mean by carrying out a reform like the JC approach from the bottom up. The self-governing style of a JC school is somehow much more complex, human, and fragile. On one hand, we refer to the empowerment of the children's embeddedness in a just community that is not only well felt but also oriented to just decision making. This has to do with the parliamentary part of the JC approach. Of course, in the JC schools, effectiveness in academics is also related to the moral and social climate. In an environment where children and adolescents protect each other, learning becomes meaningful and purposeful.

We cannot cite research on how students of different ages conceive of systems like schools, states, firms, etc. From our own research, we know that for an eight-year-old child, the system is seen as the persons in it: The school principal is the system; the teacher and a few kids are the system—thus expressing close relationships or powerful positions. For children of this age, the system is what they see. For an adolescent, the system renders you helpless because they do not understand how and why power is there. Adolescents test the system (for example, by breaking rules) in order get a sense of it, to test the power, and to find limits. Young adults, however, see the system as a necessary instrument to keep control. For them, only through the system can humans guarantee justice, trust, and security. They functionalize the system (see Biedermann & Oser, 2010). As stated above, there is no developmental research on students' conceptions of the func-tion of the schools in society. However, our hypothesis is that in a JC school the develop-ment with respect to such issues is more successful than in normal state schools.

A Theory of Social Beliefs and Complex Morality

The third element in my listing of components missing from accounts of the JC is the lack of a theory of social beliefs and social learning. In every school, these processes are obvious. Students and teachers are interacting, communicating, playing, working, and often celebrating together. Students are asking for help, looking for friendship, and are keen on being accepted and socially involved. They are involved in daily discourses and conflict management and its respective solutions—all of which is embedded in automatized symbolic activities. A JC approach thus cannot exist without understanding these basic social processes. They are inextricably embedded in an already present ocean of billions of interactive actions and reactions. In many studies, Nucci and his group (see Nucci, 2001, 2009; Nucci & Powers this volume) convinced us that the development of concepts about societal convention and social sensitivity are distinct aspects of human development that should be distinguished from the moral domain. Whereas the societal domain and norms of social convention consists of unnecessary duties according to Kant, the moral domain is fixed and much less flexible. In one of our studies, we report that parents discuss moral aspects much less than social aspects or personal issues (see Oser, Hattersley, & Spychiger, 2008). The reason for this rests in the absolute necessity of the fairness norms compared to only a wished-for necessity of social engagement. In the story of a JC meeting presented above, social issues come up when a boy offered the boys' restroom on one floor of the building. Social aspects are shown with respect to dignity for human intimacy, and, of course, social aspects involve taking the role of others in the given situation.

When we state that we should offer a more complex moral theory, we mean that more than stages of moral judgment should be our concern. We should also attend to the interactions of morality with societal conventions and personal considerations (Nucci, 2001, 2009), and also take into account moral memory, moral sensibility, moral centrality, moral motivation, moral rule enforcement, moral respect, and, thus, well justified moral acts (on this complexity, see Heinrichs, Oser, & Lovat, 2013).

Functional Conditions: Minimal Elements of a Transparent JC Structure

The enterprise of building a JC school entails the following steps and conditions. In addition this process requires extensive engagement with outside experts trained in the development of the JC within schools.

CONVINCING THE STAFF

The school principal and all the teachers must be convinced of the value and effectiveness of the approach. This requires introductions to theoretical information, and workshops on the model in all its facets. The work of convincing the staff is difficult, but without their compliance there is little reason to attempt engagement in the program. The most difficult part is that teachers have to learn that every negative event is fertile ground for a positive outcome. Without learning from negative events, as the above example of the restrooms illustrates, no progress is possible. We have needed at minimum four days of workshops with teachers and principals before they would agree to participate in forming a JC school. In one case, I convinced the teachers who voted unanimously to adopt the project. However, the principal did not want it in his school, and the project failed. Such rejection is generally attributable to the program requirements for teachers and staff that appear to be impositions upon the existing way the school is run.

Generally the model is initiated and implemented by the principal and the community of teachers and, like a well-organized squall, imposed upon and applied to the students. In other words, the first step is almost never a democratic act.

The basic structure for a JC community is depicted in Figure 12.2. To implement this structure entails an external analysis of the best way of introducing it and a study of the consequences of each step. What is most important is that the system maintains its basic equilibrium and that a lot of coordination is done, structurally and informally.

This central element of the figure contains a community meeting that represents the parliamentary ring for all important decision making. This ring has many necessary elements such as a mix of different student groups, and the physical distribution of teachers such that they do not sit together. There are also some basic rules presented by teachers that establish norms for discussion: for example, not applauding statements of other students, not hurting others by overly criticizing their statements, and listening well to prevent repeating stated positions.

PREPARATION

The second central element is the preparation group that also functions as an agenda committee. Its task is to structure the meeting so that every proposition is directed to an action decision to ensure that issues are resolved and that everyone is quickly informed. This is accomplished by insuring that the central problem is visualized (sometimes through a play or a film sequence), that the agenda is transparent, and that the voting procedure is just. Membership on this committee is representative of each class and the group has a short term of office.

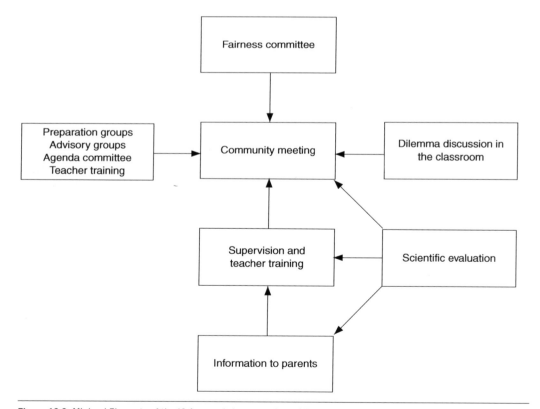

Figure 12.2 Minimal Elements of the JC Approach (source: adapted from Oser & Althof, 1992, p. 365).

THE FAIRNESS COMMITTEE

The third central element is called the friendship or fairness committee. Its task is to deal with all cases of discipline and violations of rules. Members of this committee are elected by the community meeting on the basis of their status as persons displaying trust and fairness. Their tasks are to articulate important school problems and refer them to the preparation group, and most importantly to serve as a friendly court when members of the community do not stick to rules and commitments. This committee bridges the judgment–action gap in every domain: social, moral, personal, and civic.

DISCUSSION PROCEDURES

Generally, following a just community plenary meeting, it is highly desirable to share outcomes with involved teachers and elicit any differences in conceptions of action directions taken within the meeting. A mentor of the JC approach would generally frame the discussion within theoretical elements of the developmental educational theories that guide JC structures and activities. It may also be useful to bring in additional theoretical frames. For example, after introducing the concept of helping behavior in different situations, it may be of relevance to discuss some of the following: a theory of social development (Selman, 1980), self-efficacy belief (Bandura, 2000), social purpose (Damon, 2008), moral necessity theory (Oser & Heinzer, 2010), or the learned helplessness syndrome (Seligman, 1975).

In addition to the structural elements just described the JC approach impacts discourse more broadly across the curriculum. Classroom intervention procedures (dilemma and value discussion, moral storytelling, moral sensibility training or other character education approaches, and conflict mediation on the level of students in the classroom) may have a special didactical focus and be measured separately from the JC meetings. The effect of such classroom moral-education work influences the overall JC approach.

PARENTAL INVOLVEMENT

Providing information to parents is central to success of the JC school. Parents must come to understand that the JC approach is, on one hand, a goal in itself (to develop moral, social, and civic competences in students) and on the other hand, contributes to a climate for better academic school performance. However, parents are not direct participants in the JC activities within the school. Their role is as supporters or friendly external helpers.

SHARED VALUES, SHARED NORMS

Understanding what happens beyond the classroom to changes within the school at large leads to questions regarding how norms and values are perceived of as components of the JC approach. There are two ways in which this issue is relevant to conceptualizing the impact of the JC school. First, is the impact this approach has on the developmental level of students' understandings of the norms; and second is the communal basis of norms, the so-called sharedness of norms.

Early in the history of the JC approach Reimer and Power (1980) proposed a series of seven phases of collective norms ranging from an absence of common norms to broad acceptance and commitment to collective norms among students to account for shifts they perceived as resulting from the institution of the JC. These phases representing developmental shifts in the collective moral orientation of students were reported to be associated within the Cluster School to such behavioral issues as respect for property, drug usage, and school attendance. Reimer and Power (1980) reported that as with individual moral stage development, most JC clusters stayed within midlevel phases of development (see also Power & Higgins-D'Allessandro, 2008). Thus, without blaming the staff, the teachers, or the principal the authors state:

> Community, especially democratic community, represents a social ideal. Few in our culture have grown up or been educated for living in community. We may have a vision of what the ideal should entail, but when we move to realize the vision in a particular social context, we discover that neither vision nor commitment alone can create a community.

And later they state:

> As soon as educators move from teaching about values of democratic and communal living to trying to realize these values in a social world, they become involved in developing new patterns of action for which there are few available models in either the students' or the educators' experience.
>
> (Reimer & Power, 1980, p. 319)

The authors probably did not see it this way, but what emerged from their work was the creation of a new social psychological paradigm for thinking about school community. If one reviews the literature on the social climate of schools, one finds a series of scales on affective ties to the community: perceived sense of community connectedness (Flanagan, Gallay, Gill, Galleay, & Nti, 2005), sense of happiness (Seligman, 2002), trust in a particular system (Levi & Stocker, 2000), or similar ties. In the *Handbook on Educational Psychology* of 2008, Götz, Frenzel, and Pekrun (2008) present the social climate as school, class, or educational norm integration with the aspects of (a) social and performance pressure, (b) student centrality, (c) cohesion, and (d) discipline.

In contrast with these affective approaches Reimer and Power dealt with the concrete content of what defines the community—a set of norms that must be accepted internally by the individual and, in addition, must be bought into and accepted by the group as a whole. This concept is quite novel, and it is also less connected to Kohlberg's construct of formal morality. In this tradition, we find a similar frame to the one Korte (1987) developed from the work of Power. In a more developmental context, stages are related to Kohlberg's tradition and are interpreted with respect to the group-life and the respective group cohesion. A person at stage 2 does not value group life; a person between stages 2 and 3 sees the group as an organization; a person between stages 3 and 4 values the quality of the relationship in the group and a person at stage 4 values the cohesion of the group and values the group as a unit which takes part in a society.

In sum, one central goal within a JC approach is to develop shared norms and values. The process of its genesis is not an easy thing. The process goes through controversial discussion, important decision making, and, later, reinforcing what is decided in the context of the whole school. Finally, this work has resulted in excellent measurement instruments oriented to content, phases, and stages for the understanding of growth with respect to this goal (see Power & Higgins-D'Allesandro, 2008).

THE PSYCHOLOGY OF PARTICIPATION

Discussions of *participation* usually carry positive connotations because it is believed that participation: (a) reflects a democratic principle, (b) motivates engagement, (c) distributes responsibility, and, finally, (d) produces identification with the respective system and its actions (working, learning, or deciding). A JC is a system in which participation around certain issues is granted but controlled. This is a very important restriction. Even if interpreted positively, it is not the same thing to participate in a JC meeting as it is to participate in common things such as the owning of a house or the running of a firm. Moreover, we tend to be too superficial when speaking about what participation really means. To illustrate, consider the participation involved in voting on an important issue facing a community or nation, such as is done in Switzerland's direct democracy system. Even here, only a minority of citizens ends up going to the polls most of the time. Can we conclude from this that the majority who did not vote are not participants in a democratic community? Before drawing parallels to the JC, however, it is necessary to make some important differentiations.

In the "playground democracy" of a JC system, students and the plenary meeting can only decide on a few issues that affect all or most of the community. Examples of such issues include: the moral atmosphere of the school, prosocial engagement (e.g., helping, caring, and sharing behaviors), behavior and discipline rules, signs of trust and trustworthiness, distribution of playground use, consequences of immoral and unjust behavior, and issues in a similar vein. Other decisive issues of the school rest in the hand of the principal, the teachers, or the administrators. In normative terms, the more cases of particular issues being discussed and decided upon in a JC meeting, the greater the attractiveness and deeper the shared interest in these issues become.

Oser and Spychiger (2005) and Althof (2008) were among the first to introduce the JC approach into secondary 1 (middle school) and primary classes (third to six grades). From this experience, Althof stressed that student learning occurs through participation experiences that include two necessary elements. The first is that students must be aware that things begin to be much harder after every student-based group decision than if the teacher had made the decision. He states: "The essential work, however, only began with the decision. Potential problems had to be considered like who could be bothered by what?"(Althof, 2008, p. 146). The second learning component accompanying recognition of the responsibility for carrying out the precepts and enduring the consequences of decisions is the actual activity of these participation experiences. Students' social, political, moral, and civic learning gets stimulated through *doing*.

As in the case of a national democracy, not all students participate in JC meetings with the same intensity. Relying on Milbrath (1972), we can compare political activity with a Roman cirque in which some persons are gladiators, others organizers, and others rule guardians —yet, most of the people are spectators (see Reichenbach, 2000). Even the persons who refuse to participate are thereby expressing disaffection and are, nonetheless, politically involved. Only the small group of apathetic persons, the ones who never participate in any political discourse whatsoever, are problematic because they hand away decisions to people that do not represent their interests. A few years ago we developed a hierarchy of participatory validity. Figure 12.3 presents its basic features. As shown, full participation with total sharing of responsibility seldom occurs.

Participation hierarchy

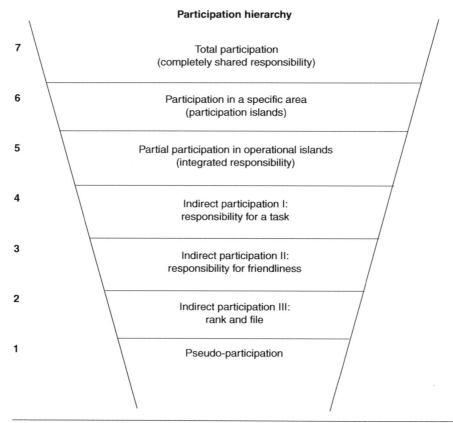

Figure 12.3 Levels of Participation: a Participation Hierarchy (source: adapted from Biedermann & Oser, 2006, p. 35; in Biedermann & Oser, 2010).

In a JC setting, students must accept that although the range of responsibility is small the decisions made have major consequences. This is why taking a full role with responsibilities in such settings is a central issue. In contrast "pseudo-participation" is what students mostly experience in educational settings. Typically, parents say to their children: "Listen, we must talk to each other" or "We must discuss with each other." These sorts of statements are, in fact, a hidden way of providing parental directives. Thus, in a JC setting the most important consideration is that whatever kind of decision is made through student deliberations (within a framework of fairness) must be honored by the teachers and enacted.

What then is the educational effectiveness of JC participation with respect to transfer beyond the school setting? Does someone who participates in a JC school also participate in community service activities or become actively involved in dealing with civic and political issues? The answer is no. In general, we expect too many positive effects to come from just the fact that someone participates, period. There is no correlation between political activity and activity in a different domain. Biedermann (2006) in his dissertation and my colleagues and I in similar research projects (Oser & Spychiger, 2005) found, for example, that social work activities do not correlate with political activities. (For an alternative perspective see Hart, Matsuba, & Atkins this volume.)

THE TEACHERS' ROLE

Every JC endeavor begins with an intensive knowledge- and action-based workshop. From there, teachers learn about the function, goals, and methods of the whole approach. They see film vignettes about other schools having been through the same intellectual and educational journey by seeing examples of JC meetings, teacher discussions, what the principals do, and how they engage their schools. Through the workshops, these teachers also learn about the concepts of participation, authenticity, and that, by losing authority, they actually win student respect and esteem. However, the most unfamiliar things that teachers need to know are evidence-based information about (a) the concept of "Development as the Aim of Education" (Kohlberg, 1981), (b) the concept of the process of parliamentary course of a JC meeting, and (c) the reference view of dealing with the negative behavior of students, which means not to measure the results of the processes of a JC prematurely before learning the way in which it is implemented and functions. Teachers thus need two central inputs, namely: 1) to see education as pedagogical presupposition, the most important common vision; and 2) to develop shared collective pedagogical norms among JC colleagues as a necessary reset of their own pedagogical thinking. These two central interventions for teachers are further defined and explained below.

A Pedagogical Presupposition

We call this educational power "trust in advance." It is a central and archetypical pedagogical practice, treated in many different theoretical concepts such as Vygotsky's "zone of proximal development" or Turiel's "plus 1-convention" or Garz's (1989) and Aufenanger's (1989) pedagogical presupposition. It consists in the belief that educators and teachers have to act as if the child or the learner already can do something or knows something or has already experienced something. They do this knowing full well that it is not the case. A good example is a young mother talking to her baby as if it were an adult, knowing that the child cannot speak and does not fully understand what she is saying. Giving responsibility to students in a JC meeting is another example: The student gets power, and we believe and act as if he or she knows how to deal with it. The reason children and adolescents learn or develop higher moral judgment or participate fully is precisely because the teachers do believe and are totally convinced that they can do it. This is of course, psychologically speaking, a form of expectation effect. It works in the sense of a self-fulfilling prophecy, meaning that teachers bring about students' participation, responsibility, and caring, etc. by presupposing that they have the ability. Not presupposing this results in students without belief in themselves, without motivation, without care, and without responsibility. Although it is perhaps an unwelcomed imposition on teachers, they must learn to presuppose and believe that all of what has to be learned later is possible for the learners. That is, they must trust in advance.

Shared Collective Norms Among JC Colleagues

We have already discussed the notion of shared norms among students within the JC (Power, 1979). A totally different construct refers to what we call "shared norms of teachers." Wehrlin (2009) looked at what a shared norm of teachers really can be. She found that a shared norm is not just a statistical mean of the acceptance of a rule. It is what we call the intensity of a teacher's belief—that another teacher holds the same pedagogical belief and that the respective norm behind the belief is as important to the other teacher as it is to the self. "Shared" means a mechanism of how teachers shape each other's reasoning about what should be kept as a steering maxim for the school. The beginning of questioning of what we call a shared norm is always a social event that affects every teacher in a school. The professional members of a group demonstrate, through a common judging procedure, that they hold as important the same methods, or the same envisioned results. Wehrlin (2009) compared six teacher teams with respect to the scales "teachers' social climate," "teachers' cooperation," "felt common professional self-efficacy," and "professional satisfaction." She found (a) that schools differ enormously and (b) that technical and content-specific sharedness is significantly higher than educational sharedness. In addition, she demonstrated that the more a school is affected with discipline or learning problems, the higher teachers' cooperation is. Shared cooperation norms also lead to higher collective self-efficacy, but not to individual self-efficacy. Higher general cooperation norms also lead to higher professional satisfaction. All this is a sign for what Althof and Oser found with respect to teachers' engagement in a JC project, namely that, even though they work harder and longer workdays, they feel significantly more supported by the principal and by their colleagues, need less formal authority, have more time for informal discussions with students, see more positive relationships among students, show higher trust in students, and have to engage less in conflicts between students.

In summary, besides the theoretical and practical knowledge and all the didactical developmental competences a founding teacher group must have, trust in advance and shared pedagogical norms are core elements for the functioning of a JC school (see also Murrell, Diez, Feinamn-Nemser, & Schussler, 2010).

SOME RESEARCH RESULTS

Having provided a framework for understanding the JC, let's turn now to some representative research results. In an initial study, Kohlberg (1985) contrasted three traditional schools (Brookline, Cambridge, Scarsdale) with their JC counterparts. Independent variables were perceived prosocial choice, prosocial behavior, degree of collectiveness, mean stage of collective norms, and mean phase of collective norms. In all these dimensions, the project schools obtained significantly higher scores.

However, a recently completed research report on a secondary 1 (middle school) JS school in Switzerland (see Luterbacher & Oser, 2013) makes it clear that contemporary applications of the JC face a formidable challenge. Schools are less likely to engage for a full three years in such an enterprise. Instead, they tend to treat a JC project as one of many school "reforms" and generally expect immediate, significant change from a few school meetings. The school in our study had only six school meetings a year. However, the teachers, even those very well guided in workshops and discussions, did not wait to observe for long-term educational effects. They expected rapid change and control of all problems of the school (e.g., vandalism, tardiness, boys' disrespect toward girls). The result was that, from the 17 scales used for measuring student participation, social climate, and personality development such as self-efficacy, belief, and trust in advance, only a few elicited significant change compared with the control group. Thus, we found significant teacher effects on shared values, student effects on a more critical discourse orientation, less group pressure, and more community orientation.

However, there were also negative effects such as attitude toward critical thinking, lack of moral sensitivity, lack of perspective taking, and poor sensitivity toward the justice motive.

We interpret this negative effect to so-called sensibility shock, which refers to the fact that, through pedagogical stimulation, the repeated measure may no longer be valid. For example, if we ask students in a pretest about the amount of participation in school decision making, we will get a score at a middle level. When we introduce the JC approach with many participative decision-making meetings, the students begin to be aware of what real participation means. In this case, they began to estimate their participation possibility as much less intensive. This effect often appears when a new approach is introduced that brings awareness to what is implicitly there but not yet consciously realized.

A third reason for such weak effects is the choice of instruments. Influenced by personality measures of so many large-scale comparison studies like ICCS, TEDs, IGLU, PISA, we forgot the beautiful work of the Kohlberg group in using instruments with much higher-fitting validity. As mentioned in his 1985 article, when Kohlberg compared traditional schools with JC schools, no personality traits were measured, only the frequency of perceived prosocial choice for others, the frequency of predicted prosocial behavior of others, the modal degree of moral collectiveness, the mean stage of collective norms, and a kind of mean-phase of shared norms. These variables captured the intervention more accurately than constructs we included such as constructivism versus instructionism, openness toward reform, or moral courage.

TOWARD A THEORY OF A JUST COMMUNITY SCHOOL

Despite a long experience with the JC movement, we still are lacking a "just community theory." After so many studies and so many reported practical experiences, perhaps we can suggest what is needed to construct one. First, we need a vision of school that is socially, morally, and democratically of high quality. Schools are mostly evaluated and judged by achievement performances, even though this is a secondary consideration for a JC vision. Second, we need an understanding of how children and adolescents perceive systems like schools, and continued research on how they develop morally, politically, socially, and religiously, and the probable conditions for such sensitive changes. Third, more specifically, we need more knowledge about the phases of a JC meeting. Although we have made progress in identifying JC meeting phases and processes they have not been systematically investigated. Research on these variables is central for understanding the JC and its impact. Fourth, we need systematic professional development of the above described competence profiles of the staff and, herein, the development of belief in "trust in advance" and in shared professional norms. Fifth, we need systemic multi-level measurement of all important aspects mentioned in this paper (e.g., elements of justice, civics, morality, strategic and nonstrategic discourse; school-based system elements: participation-oriented caring and prosocial acts on both sides—teachers and students). The moral-atmosphere questionnaire developed by Power and Higgins-D'Alessandro (2008, pp. 241–244) is a first step. However, future work aims for developing a measure for democracy (participation and transformation that is moral, social, and civic) that can be used to capture its quality in any school. This will lead to learning more about an authentic stimulation of the good. There is a lack of measures in many JC fields; for example, there is not yet evidence with respect to the parallelism of changes in the domains within the JC approach. Since the implementation of a JC is a controlled intervention, we also should measure the positive (or inhibiting) influence of social, moral, and civic growth on academic performances in general. And finally, we should acquire knowledge of how the JC approach in its many facets works as an inclusive power for each single child and each staff member (see Biesta, 2009).

These five areas can form the basis for a theory of a "just community." In addition, the school administrators and staff being hierarchically organized must learn that growth in morality and caring is a long-term project and that changes in students' social and moral sensibility means engaging fully in what can be called a bottom-up concept. A JC is not a problem-solving think-tank. Instead, it uses problems and the so-called "social waste" of each school for long-term change and long-term development of its socio-moral climate and management. Teachers must learn that the beginning and ongoing processes of the JC approach are always responses to negative events (Oser & Spychiger, 2005). Janusz Korczak (1967) states it like this: "A child who never stole, lied, did unjust things, misbehaved can never become a moral person"; this is a key to the JC approach. And one day, we may learn even how much of it, in which situations, is necessary. Thus, in a JC school, the negative is the fruitful soil for the growth of civic, caring, and moral persons. At the core of a JC school is the question of how we want to see each other and how we want our school to be, precisely in the face of the negative aspects that have been discussed. Here the turnaround concept is different from that of a classical turnaround school; here developmental moral and social discipline become a basis for the academic learning discipline, and not vice versa. The theory of "development as the aim of a community" implicitly means that knowledge building and immediate growth, like learning mathematics, are not the key motor for change. Development is the result of intensive and often repeated community discourse and the resulting service-learning of students in the school.

Last but not least, we should not forget the contribution the JC approach makes toward students' development of civility. Because the Kohlberg tradition emphasized movement toward principled morality, the contribution of convention to social life was miscast as an inferior form of morality (see Nucci, 2001, 2009). Civility is the coordination of an appreciation of the role of convention for directing our interactions as members of a particular social group with our moral valuation of persons as worthy of respect. Thus, such things as the use of polite language and the everyday small acts of kindness such as holding the door open for someone or giving up a seat to an elderly person are aspects of social life defined by the conventions of each community, but that nonetheless contribute to the overall morality of social existence. Participation within a JC is quintessentially an experience in civility.

REFERENCES

Althof, W. (1998). Designing schools as just and caring communities: Ideas from a school project (orig. German). *Revue Interdialogos, 1* (1), 41–45.

Althof, W. (2008). The just community approach to democratic education: Some affinities. In K. Tiri (Ed.), *Educating moral sensibilities in urban schools* (pp. 145–176). Rotterdam, The Netherlands: Sense.

Aufenanger, S. (1989). *Entwicklungpädagogik: Die soziogenetische Perspektive.* Mainz, Germany: Manuskript.

Bandura, A. (2000). Self-efficacy: The foundation of agency. In W. J. Perrig & A. Grob (Eds.), *Control of human behaviour, mental processes and consciousness* (pp. 17–33). Mahwak, NJ: Erlbaum.

Biedermann, H. (2006). *Young people on the passage of political autonomy* (orig. German). Münster, Germany: Waxmann.

Biedermann H., & Oser, F. (2006). Participation and identity: Young people between sequasity and co-responsibility (orig. German). In C. Quesel & F. Oser (Eds.), *Teilnehmen, Mitteilen, Miteinscheiden: Probleme und Chancen er Partizipation von Kindern und Jugendlichen* (pp. 95–135). Zürich, Switzerland: Rüegger.

Biedermann, H., & Oser, F. (2010). Political autonomy through school participation: On the demystification of the belief of the effectiveness of participation (orig. German). *Journal für politische Bildung, 1* (10), 28–44.

Biesta, G. (2009). Sporadic democracy: Education, democracy, and the question of inclusion. In M. S. Katz, S. Verducci, & G. Biesta (Eds.). *Education, democracy, and the moral life* (pp. 101–112). Dordrecht, The Netherlands/Boston, MA: Springer.

Damon, W. (2008). *The path to purpose: Helping children find their calling in life.* New York, NY: Free Press.

Darling-Hammond, L. (2012). Two futures of educational reform: What strategies will improve teaching and learning. *Schweizerische Zeitschrift für Bildungswissen, 34* (1), 21–38.

Dewey, J. (1916). *Democracy and education.* New York, NY: MacMillan Free.

Durkheim, E. (1961). *Moral education: A study in the theory and application in the sociology of education.* New York, NY: Free Press.

Edelstein, W., & Fauser, P. (2001). *Report on the program "Learning and living democracy"* (Orig. German). *Gutachten zum Programm "Demokratie lernen und leben": Materialien zur Bildungsplanung und zur Forschungsförderung.* Bonn, Germany: Bund-Länder-Kommission zur Bildungsplanung und Forschungsförderung.

Fend, H. (2007). *A new theory of the school* (orig. German). Wiesbaden: VS Verlag.

Flanagan, C. A., Gallay, L. S., Gill, S., Galleay, E., & Nti, N. (2005). What does democracy mean? Correlates of adolescents' views. *Journal of Adolescent Research, 20* (2), 193–218.

Garz, D. (1989). *Social psychological theories of development: From Meas, Piaget, and Kohlberg until today* (orig. German). Opladen, Germany: Westdeutscher Verlag.

Götz, T., Frenzel A. C., & Pekrun, R. (2008). Social climate in schools (orig. German). In W. Schneider & M. Haselhorn (Eds.). *Handbuch der Pädagogische Psychologie* (pp. 504–514). Göttingen, Germany: Hogrefe.

Gutmann, A. (1987). *Democratic education.* Princeton, NJ: Princeton University Press.

Hartmann, N. (1957). *Der philosophische Gedanke und seine Geschichte. Aufsätze.* Stuttgart, Germany: Reclam.

Heinrichs, K., Oser, F., & Lovat, T. (Eds.) (2013). *Handbook on moral motivation.* Rotterdam, The Netherlands: Sense.

Hickey, J. E., & Scharf, P. L. (1980). *Toward a just correctional system.* San Francisco, CA: Jossey-Bass.

Kohlberg, L. (1980). High school democracy and educating for a just society. In R. Mosher (Ed.), *Moral education: A first generation of research and development* (pp. 20–57). New York, NY: Praeger.

Kohlberg, L. (1981). *Essays on moral development.* San Francisco, CA: Harper & Row.

Kohlberg, L. (1985). The just community approach to moral education in theory and practice. In M. W. Berkowitz & F. Oser (Eds.), *Moral education: Theory and application* (pp. 27–88). Hillsdale, NJ: L. Erlbaum.

Korczak, J. (1967). *How to love a child* (8th ed., orig. German). Göttingen, Germany: Vandenheck.

Korte, M. (1987). *The development of the moral atmosphere in a home for adolescent with special needs: An intervention study* (title translated by Oser). Frankfurt, Germany: Lang.

Leithwood K., Harris, A., & Strauss, T. (2010). *Leading school turnaround.* San Francisco, CA: Jossey-Bass.

Levi, M., & Stocker, L. (2000). Political trust and trustworthiness. *Annual Review of Political Science, 3,* 475–508.

Lind, G. (1987). Elements and results of the "Just-Community-school" (orig. German). *Die Deutsche Schule, 79* (1), 13–27.

Lind, G., & Althof, W. (1992). Does the just community experience make a difference? Measuring and evaluating the effect of the DES Project. *Moral Education Forum, 17* (2), 19–28.

Luterbacher, M. (2009). "Together is better": Die Entwicklung einr just community-Schule auf der Sekundarstufe 1. *Lehren und Lernen, 35* (7), 19–24.

Luterbacher, M., & Oser, F. (2013). *"Together is better." Evaluation eines just community—Programms auf der Sekundarstufe I.* Luzern, Switzerland: Reprt PHZ.

Makarenko, A. S. (1938). Second lecture on Problems of the Soviet School Education. In H. Wittig (1976) *Pedagogical texts* (orig. German). Paderborn, Germany: Schöningh UTB.

Makarenko, A. S. (1976). *Pedagogical texts* (orig. German, selected and edited by H. E. Wittig). Paderborn, Germany: Schöningh UTB.

Milbrath, L. (1972). *Political participation: Why people get involved in politics.* Chicago, IL: Rand McNally College.

Moses, M. S., & Saenz, L. P. (2012). When the majority rules: Ballot initiatives, race-conscious, education policy and the public good. *Review of Research in Education,* 113–138.

Mosher, R. (Ed.) (1980). *Moral education: A first generation of research and development.* New York, NY: Praeger.

Murrell, P. C., Diez, M. E., Feinamn-Nemser, S., & Schussler, D. L. (Eds.) (2010). *Teaching as a moral practice.* Cambridge, MA: Harvard Education Press.

Nucci, L. (2001). *Education in the moral domain.* Cambridge, UK: Cambridge University Press.

Nucci, L. P. (2009). *Nice is not enough: Facilitating moral development.* Merrill/Prentice Hall.

Oser, F. & Althof, W. (1992). *Moralische Selbstbestimmung* (Moral self-determination). Stuttgart: Klett.

Oser, F., Althof, W., & Higgins-D'Alessandro, A. (2008). The just community approach to moral education: System change or individual change? *Journal of Moral Education, 37* (3), 395–415.

Oser, F., & Biedermann, H. (2003). *Youth without politics* (orig. German). Zürich, Switzerland: Rüegger.

Oser, F., Hattersley, L., & Spychiger, M. (2008). *Culture of mistakes and negative knowledge in the family* (orig. German). University of Fribourg, Switzerland: Report for the National Foundations.

Oser, F., & Heinzer, S. (2010). "Sense of necessity": Modeling the concept of pedagogical necessity as quality criteria for teachers' professionalism (orig. German). In *Lehrerbildung auf dem Prüfstand. Sonderheft,* 148–195372.

Oser, F., & Spychiger, M. (2005). *Learning is painful: Towards a theory of negative knowledge and a practice of a mistake-culture* (orig. German). Weinheim, Germany: Beltz.

Pestalozzi, H. (1965). *Letter to a friend on his stay in Stans* (orig. German). Stuttgart, Germany: Körner, 237–269. (Original work published 1799).

Power, F. C. (1979). *The moral atmosphere of a just community high school: A four-year longitudinal study.* (Doctoral dissertation.) Harvard Graduate School of Education, Cambridge, MA.

Power, F. C., & Higgins-D'Alessandro, A. (2008). The just community approach to moral education and the moral atmosphere of the school. In L. P. Nucci & D. Narvaez (Eds.), *Handbook of moral education* (pp. 230–247). New York, NY: Routledge.

Reichenbach, R. (2000). The irony of political education (orig. German). In R. Reichenbach, & F. Oser (Eds.), *Between pathos and disillusion. On the state of the civic education in Switzerland* (orig. German) (pp. 118–130). [Zwischen Pathos und Ernüchterung. Zur Lage der Politischen Bildung in der Schweiz/ Entre pathos et désillusion. La situation de la formation politique en Suisse.] Freiburg, Switzerland: Universitätsverlag.

Reimer, J., & Power, C. (1980). Educating for democratic community: Some unresolved dilemmas. In R. Mosher (Ed.), *Moral education: A first generation of research and development* (pp. 303–320). New York, NY: Praeger.

Rogers, J., Mediratta, K., & Shah, S. (2012). Building power, learning democracy: Youth organizing as a site of civic development. *Review of Research in Education,* AERA, 43–66.

Seligman, M. (1975). *Helplessness: On depression, development, and death.* San Francisco, CA: W. H. Freeman.

Seligman, M. E. P. (2002). *Authentic happiness: Using the new positive psychology to realize your potential for lasting fulfilment.* New York: Free Press (in German, 2006).

Selman, R. L. (1980). *The growth of interpersonal understanding.* New York: Academic Press (in German 1984).

Slee, R., Weiner, G., & Tomlinson, S. (Eds.) (1998). *School effectiveness for whom? Challenges to the school effectiveness and school improvement movements.* London, England: Falmer.

Veugelers, W. (2011). *Education and humanism.* Rotterdam, The Netherlands: Sense.

Weber, W. G., Unterrainer, C., & Schmid, B. E. (2009). The influence of organizational democracy on employees' sociomoral climate and prosocial behavioral orientations. *Journal of Organizational Behavior.* Online in Wiley InterScience.

Wehrlin, J. (2009). *Shared cooperation: On the amount and the meaning of shared cooperation norms of teachers in primary schools.* (Masters dissertation.) University of Fribourg, Switzerland.

13

CONTEMPLATIVE EDUCATION

Cultivating Ethical Development through Mindfulness Training

Robert W. Roeser, David R. Vago, Cristi Pinela, Laurel S. Morris, Cynthia Taylor, and Jessica Harrison

Alertness is the hidden discipline of familiarity.

David Whyte

DEFINING CONTEMPLATIVE EDUCATION

The purpose of this chapter is to introduce *Contemplative Education*—an emerging, practical, and applied scientific approach to the cultivation of positive mental skills and social-emotional dispositions that we hypothesize are relevant to individuals' ethical development. (Mind and Life Educational Research Network [MLERN], 2012; Roeser & Peck, 2009). The key question of this chapter is how might developmentally appropriate secular mindfulness training contribute to the ethical development of young people and their parents and teachers?

Contemplative, from the Latin root *contemplatio*, refers to the marking out of a space for the cultivation of attentiveness to the fullness of life—including oneself, other people, and the sociocultural and natural worlds (Zajonc, in press). Education, from the Latin root *educare*, can be defined as the "drawing forth" of children's intrinsic potentials—somatic, emotional, imaginative, cognitive, and attentional in nature—and the guiding of these qualities towards fruitful personal and societal ends (Dewey, 1900). Given these etymologies, we can say that as an applied, practical approach, Contemplative Education (CE) aims to draw forth and cultivate children's intrinsic self-regulatory skills and social-emotional dispositions in the directions of focused attention, mindful awareness, and altruistic motivation and action through joint activity, mentorship, and sustained practice.

At the heart of Contemplative Education as a practical approach is *mindfulness training* (MT). MT refers to secularized teaching approaches and practices aimed at cultivating focused attention and a calm, clear, and non-reactive/non-judgmental awareness of what is occurring moment by moment (Kabat-Zinn, 2003). By cultivating a healthy mind, MT is hypothesized to have implications for ethical development, leading to the development, for instance, of individuals who "know what is good and spontaneously do it" in their daily lives (Varela, 1999, p. 4). How is this so? As an applied scientific discipline, CE aims to answer these questions.

CONTEMPORARY APPROACHES TO ETHICS IN EDUCATION

The need for ethics in education is particularly urgent in a world that is increasingly flat, hot, and crowded (Friedman, 2008), and where ethical lapses among individuals in high positions of governance, finance, sports, and even public education seem all too common today (Dalai Lama, 2012; Sachs, 2011). Paradoxically, given these pressing cultural needs, moral or character development now appears to take a back seat to academic skill development as a top educational priority (White House, 2000). Nevertheless, American parents continue to place high value on having their children learn moral-behavioral skills in school such as communicating emotions, taking turns and sharing, being fair and caring, and being able to pay attention (Phi Delta Kappan, 2012).

Challenges in offering effective programs that impart these kinds of ethical skills and dispositions have existed for decades. In a review of such efforts, however, Nucci and Turiel (2009) concluded that

> the general picture suggests that formal efforts to engage in moral education have not translated into gains in student socialization beyond what is obtained though widely recognized "best teaching" practices ... that emphasize classroom community, student intellectual autonomy, and high levels of academic instruction.
>
> (p. 151)

Over the past several decades, various new programmatic initiatives have focused on the cultivation of the social, emotional, and ethical development of the child as part of an expanded vision in our nation's public schools of what it means to become a fully educated citizen beyond the mastery of the traditional three Rs. Evaluation research on programs such as social-emotional learning (SEL), service learning, and conflict resolution has shown that these programs are effective. Evidence supports the notion that social and emotional learning programs can reduce antisocial behavior (Wilson, Gottfredson, and Najaka, 2001) and increase school attendance and achievement (Durlak, Weissberg, Taylor, Dymnicki, & Schellinger, 2011). Similarly, meta-analyses suggest that the school-wide use of conflict resolution and peer remediation programs reduces antisocial behavior, especially during adolescence (Burrell, Zirbel, & Allen, 2003; Garrard & Lipsey, 2007). Finally, research on service learning has shown it is associated with reduced academic and behavior problems and increased learning and prosocial behavior, especially when reflection on offering service is a central feature of the program (Conway, Amel, & Gerwien, 2009; Hart, Matsuba, & Atkins, this volume). We believe that these kinds of programs work because they all incorporate a focus on community, emotion and emotion regulation, and prosocial attitudes and behavior (e.g., Mahoney, Larson, & Eccles, 2005). A focus on training attention in the service of emotion regulation, self-awareness, awareness of others, and prosociality in a supportive community is also central to contemplative education as a practical endeavor.

DEFINING THE CONTEMPLATIVE SCIENCE PROJECT (CSP)

As an applied scientific endeavor, Contemplative Education is a subfield of the Contemplative Science Project (CSP). The CSP is a trans-disciplinary effort to describe and explain the effects of engagement with contemplative practices on the mind, brain, body, and social relationships within and across different periods in the lifespan (Roeser & Zelazo, 2012; Wallace, 2007). As a meeting of the so-called East and West around mind-body issues, the CSP has rich historical roots that date back centuries (Harrington, 2008). The disciplines involved in the CSP today include psychological, social and developmental science; biology, neuroscience and developmental neuroscience; and the humanities and contemplative studies (see Figure 13.1). Contemplative studies refers to a discipline of study and is populated by individuals who are conversant with the philosophies at the heart of contemplative traditions; and who also have extensive first-person experience in engaging in the contemplative practices of such traditions.

Meta-theoretical Assumptions of CSP. The meta-theoretical assumptive framework of the CSP diverges from classical Cartesian dualistic approaches to mind-body phenomena and ways of conceptualizing human development (see Overton & Reese, 1977). Specifically, the CSP is grounded in a dialectic rather than dualistic meta-model of human development. In Figure 13.2, the ying-yang symbol provides a visual representation of two guiding assumptions regarding the process of human development from a dialectic vantage point (Sameroff, 2010): (a) the unity of apparent opposites (e.g., mind

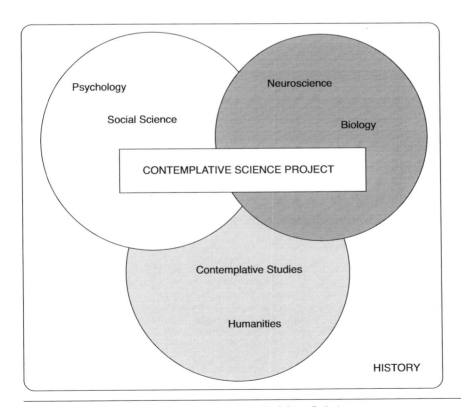

Figure 13.1 Trans-disciplinary Nature of the Contemplative Science Project.

and body) and (b) the interpenetration of apparent opposites (e.g., genes and environments). According to Lerner and Overton (2008):

> Today, the cutting edge of the study of the human life span is framed by a developmental systems theoretical model, one that is informed by a post positivist, relational metatheory that moves beyond classical Cartesian dichotomies, "avoids all splits," and transforms fundamental antinomies into co-equal and indissociable complementarities (Overton, 2006).

> Throughout its history, the study of human development has been the captive of numerous fundamental antinomies (Overton, 1998, 2006). Whereas the original Cartesian splits were between mind and body or subject and object, the most prominent of contemporary split conceptions has been, of course, between nature and nurture or variants of this split, such as maturation versus experience or innate versus acquired ... the central emphasis in contemporary developmental science is on mutually influential, individual-context relations.
>
> (Lerner & Overton, 2008, pp. 245–246)

A dialectic metatheory of human development, including ethical development, assumes that (a) there are continuities between human and primate evolution and development; (b) that mutually influential, individual-context relations are fundamental in shaping development; (c) that the mind is embodied; and (d) that cognition and emotion are intrinsically interdependent processes that can best be described to

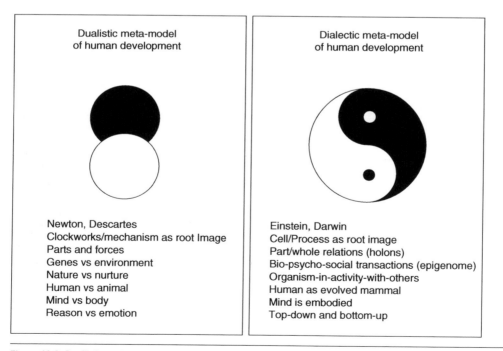

Figure 13.2 Dualistic vs. Dialectical Meta-models of Human Development.

operate in "top-down" and "bottom-up" fashions, respectively (de Waal, 2009; Varela, Thompson, & Rosch, 1991; Zelazo & Carlson, 2012).

In a similar vein, Haidt and colleagues (Haidt, 2007; Haidt & Joseph, 2007) outlined a new synthesis in moral psychology that attempts to move the field beyond dualistic and towards dialectic assumptions. Such assumptions include (a) the view that ethics are grounded in long-evolved emotions characteristic of mammalian social life and are "bequeathed by our biological nature as animals that survive and thrive only in an environment of concern, affection and warm-heartedness—or in a single word, compassion" (Dalai Lama, 2012, p. xi); (b) that emotional intuitions and actions (bottom-up) precede reasoned cognitions (top-down) in regulating ethical behavior; (c) that ethical emotions, actions, and cognitions are transformed in ontogenetic time through culture and social interaction; and (d) that ethics safeguard the welfare of individuals and groups by balancing self-interests with the interests of others. Thus, both the CSP and contemporary moral psychology posit that a moral sense exists from very early in development in the forms of emotional intuitions and actions that are extended and transformed through development into spontaneous ethical dispositions to act in particular ways (Varela, 1999).

Two additional assumptions of the CSP that are important for understanding ethical development are that (a) the brain is an inherently adaptive organ, evolved to change in response to experience and intentional training and education (e.g., mindfulness training) through the processes of neuroplasticity (see MLERN, 2012); and (b) that contemplative practices such as MT are specialized forms of mental training that, when practiced for an extended period of time, significantly alter cognitive, emotional and motor processes and the underlying neural substrates of what are classically called "skills" (e.g., Bransford, Brown, & Cocking, 1999; Ericsson & Charness, 1994). Through sustained training over time, newly acquired skills become automatized and "second nature" (see Figure 13.5).

These two assumptions form the foundation of a secular account, based in the Learning Sciences, of ethical development as the learning and gradual automatization of ethical skills and know-how (e.g., Varela, 1999). Such an account is compatible with new directions in moral psychology (e.g., Narvaez, 2013), and provides a means of understanding what Gandhi may have meant when he suggested we must "be the change we wish to see in the world" and what Mencius may have meant when he said that the virtuous person is "one who knows what is good and spontaneously does it."

Scientific Goals of CSP. The goals of the CSP are threefold (Baltes, Reese, & Nesselroade, 1977): (a) to **describe** the developmental effects of engagement in contemplative practices on body, brain, mind, and social relationships; (2) to **explain** contemplative practice effects at neurophysiological, psychological, and social levels of analysis; and (3) to use descriptive and explanatory findings to **optimize** human development through the introduction of contemplative practice-based interventions in families, schools, clinics, and communities in ways attuned to the needs and requirements of culture, developmental stage, and historical age (see Figure 13.1). During the past decade, the number of peer-refereed journal articles and nationally funded research grants on the use of MT for a variety of health and wellbeing outcomes has risen dramatically (see Roeser & Zelazo, 2012). Relatively few studies have adopted a *developmental* perspective to date regarding these aims, however. Thus, the question of how mindfulness may contribute to the ethical development of children and adolescents remains new and uncharted territory.

owing. In order to achieve these scientific goals, the CSP draws on dialogue collaboration between individuals representing the three broad sets of dis- ted in Figure 13.1. Through transdisciplinary collaboration, the CSP aims _h quality studies that coordinate first-, second-, and third-person accounts of how various forms of contemplative training may affect human development. First-person accounts refer to data gathered through phenomenological/self reports; second-person accounts refer to data gathered from expert observers of target individuals—for instance, parental ratings of children; third-person accounts refer to data collected from non-subjective sources, for example, brain scans (de Wit, 1991; Varela & Shear, 1999).

MINDFULNESS TRAINING AND ETHICAL DEVELOPMENT

Given this basic assumptive framework, we are now in a position to address the question: How might mindfulness training support the ethical development of children, adolescents, and their caregivers such that they become people who know what is good and spontaneously do it?

Contemplative Perspectives. From Buddhist perspectives, the training of attention and emotion is central to ethical development and can be understood in relation to progressions in motivation and behavior from self-interest to selflessness (altruism; Dalai Lama, 2012; Ekman, Davidson, Ricard, & Wallace, 2005). Through training, an individual is assisted in developing three sets of ethics (Dalai Lama, 2012) (1) the ethic of restraint or self-control over afflictive emotions (e.g., fear, greed, jealousy, hatred) and the actions that they motivate; (2) the ethic of virtue or prosocial emotions (e.g., kindness, joy) and the actions these motivate (e.g., consideration of others' needs alongside or even before our own; and (3) the ethic of altruism or selfless altruistic motivations involving expanded feelings of love and kindness for all beings and the actions these motivate. These three ethics can be conceptualized as a path of ethical development (see Table 13.1).

Table 13.1 Preliminary Taxonomy of Ethical Aims of Contemplative Education

Child Quality	Moral Emotions[1]	Moral Motivation	Self-System Target[2]	Type of Ethic[3]	Locus of Moral Responsibility[4]
Calm	Anger, Fear, Desire, Embarrassment, Guilt, Shame, Disgust, Relief	Self-Control	Self-Regulation	Ethic of Restraint	Personal Responsibility for Actions
Mindful and Empathic	Empathy, Joy, Sympathetic Joy	Prosociality	Self-Awareness	Ethic of Virtue	Social Responsibility to Others
Kind	Compassion, Love	Altruism	Self-Transcendence	Ethic of Altruism	Global Responsibility to All

Notes
1 Nucci (2001).
2 Roeser & Peck (2009); Vago and Silbersweig (2012).
3 Dalai Lama (2012).
4 Eccles & Roeser (2010).

Scientific Perspectives. To provide a scientific grounding of these contemplative ideas on attention and emotion training in ethics, we develop four basic issues. These include (a) the role of attention in emotional self-control; (b) the role of attention and emotion in the perception of the "ethical" in social interactions; (c) the role of attention and emotion in the extension of the ethical in the directions of the Golden Rule and Great Compassion; and (d) the role of attention and emotion regulation in remaining calm and practicing "spontaneous virtuous action" in situations where another or oneself is under stress.

Attention and Emotion Regulation

Through the training of attention, the ability to regulate emotion generally, and to inhibit impulsive, dominant response tendencies specifically (i.e., self-control), is enhanced. This is due to the fact that the circuitry of emotion regulation overlaps considerably with the circuitry of executive function/self control in the brain (MLERN, 2012; Zelazo & Carlson, 2012). Moffitt et al. (2011) have recently reported that self-control during childhood predicts physical health, substance dependence, personal finances, and criminal offenses in young adulthood in a cohort of 1,000 children followed from birth to age 32 years. Thus, to the extent MT increases self-control in children, it has the potential to exert long-term consequences on children's ethical development and wellbeing.

Attention, Emotion, and the Perception of the "Ethical"

The training of emotion is also central to ethics, but what is the role of emotion in ethical development? Nucci and Turiel (1978) empirically demonstrated that the ethical domain is distinct from the domains of social-conventions and personal preferences as sources of norms and rules for behavior. Children as young as 4–5 years of age intuitively understand that unprovoked harm of another, or failing to help another in need, are acts that are intrinsically wrong (because they violate fairness and reciprocity). By definition, young children do not need to be socialized to understand this, or come to a personal choice about such matters. Rather, the perception of moral virtue and transgressions are theorized to be *intrinsic* to the events and people in question (Nucci & Turiel, 2009). How?

As one example, consider someone observing someone else physically striking another person in an unprovoked manner. In this case, the perceived consequences to the victim (i.e., the perceived consequences of being struck) have intrinsic meaning, and it is this intrinsic meaning, rather than societal prescription, that is hypothesized to determine whether the event is judged as morally right or wrong (see Nucci & Turiel, 2009). It is plausible that the "intrinsic meaning" that young children derive from such an act is given in significant part by the emotions aroused in actors and observers of the situation (e.g., "That was wrong because it frightened and hurt that person and no-one wishes to be scared or harmed and everyone has the right not to be"). From a dialectic perspective, emotions can be understood as relational, thematic evaluations regarding the current state of person–person or person–environment relations and related action readiness (Lazarus, 1991). From this perspective, one knows something is wrong initially, perceptually, because it feels that way in the body.

Consistent with these views, the ethical domain, in contrast to the conventional or personal domain of norms or rules for behavior, arises early in development and is marked by its emotionally "hot" nature (Nucci, 2001). Ethical issues activate strong emotions even in young children, whereas social-conventional rules or personal preferences

io, 1988; Arsenio & Lover, 1995). For instance, 5-, 8- and ten-year-olds
a recipient, perpetrator, and an observer would feel positive emotion in
tuations of distributive justice (sharing, being fair) or prosocial behavior
g helped). On the other hand, children also reported that recipients and
observers of selfish behavior (harming, being unfair) would feel negative emotions such
as sadness, anger, and fear (Arsenio, 1988).[1] Other work is beginning to establish seeming
ethical preferences in even younger children. Aknin, Hamlin, & Dunn (2012) found, for
instance, that young children (around two years of age) expressed greater positive affect
in behavior when giving treats to others than when receiving treats themselves (which
was also associated with positive affect), even if this act of giving involved a cost to self.
Consistent with a dialectic perspective on emotion and development, the authors speculate that acts of kindness and generosity (giving and receiving gifts) may have long evolutionary roots that cause such acts to be experienced emotionally as intrinsically "good/
liked" and worthy of emulation and extension to others.

A basic assumption in ancient Eastern and Western worlds is that the training of
attention is invaluable in ethical development because it improves an individual's capacity to mindfully perceive and feel the non-virtuous and virtuous in daily life more
clearly (Dalai Lama, 2012; Varela, 1999). To the extent MT can help caregivers, children,
and adolescents to stabilize attention and calm emotional reactivity, the clarity of their
awareness and representations of social interactions may be enhanced in ways that foster
their ethical development.

Attention, Emotion, and the Extension of the Ethical

Enhanced awareness allows young people to directly observe the positive and negative
consequences of particular mind states and behaviors in themselves and other people
clearly and to learn from them (Dalai Lama, 2012). As a consequence of this enhanced
perception, we hypothesize that mindfulness training also supports the capacity of caregivers, children, and adolescents to extend basic ethical intuitions regarding harm and
care to others near and far.

We assume that basic emotions involving the avoidance of harm (e.g., Nucci & Turiel,
1978) and the approach of care (Eisenberg, 1998; Gilligan, 1982) form the basis of moral
motivation. Through socialization, we hypothesize that most children learn to extend
these basic emotions to others along the lines of the Golden Rule and the concept of
moral reversibility (Nucci, 2001). This transformation is hypothesized to occur within
the contexts of average-expectable attachment relationships, authoritative parenting and
teaching practices, and supportive sibling and peer relationships (Nucci, 2001). Through
MT, we propose, the extension of non-harm and care can be widened further in the
directions of "Great Compassion" (Dalai Lama, 1999) to include unfamiliar and even
unknown others. The notion of extension is presented in Figure 13.3.

We propose that the stabilization of attention affected through attuned caregiving
and joint-attention, and the noting and labeling of significant features of emotionally-
charged social experiences (e.g., feelings, feeling–action linkages), enhances the ability
of young people to clearly perceive and develop rich cognitive-affective representations
regarding ethical dilemmas they experience in daily life (e.g., Tharp & Gallimore, 1988).
Enriched perceptions and representations, in turn, enhance children's ability to accurately extend their moral understandings to situations and encounters that share cor-
respondences and affinities with previously encountered ones—from the known to the

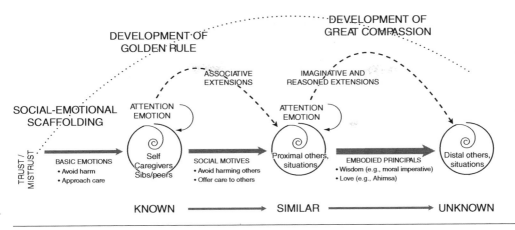

Figure 13.3 Hypothesized Model of the Extension of Basic Moral Emotions to Embodied Moral Principles Through Social-Emotional Scaffolding.

similar (Varela, 1999). As discussed below, ethical enhancement practices that form a key part of MT aim to increase this sphere of ethical extension beyond the known and similar to the unknown and dissimilar (see Figure 13.3). This was the view of Mencius, who posited, "truly virtuous people attend to their nature sufficiently well to understand an event in terms of their experience and thus ensure that appropriate extension follows easily" (Varela, 1999, p. 29).

Attention, Emotion Regulation, and Prosocial Behavior

In addition to clear awareness, another key factor in the cultivation and extension of prosocial behavior is emotion regulation and the ability to maintain a calm mind and body in distressing situations (Eisenberg & Eggum, 2009). Batson and his colleagues (1999) differentiated between empathy and personal distress as motivators of prosocial behavior. In this work, empathy is defined as the capacity to understand and respond to the affective experiences of others and is associated with an other-oriented, altruistic motivational aim (assist the other person). In contrast, personal distress is defined as a self-focused, aversive, affective reaction to another's emotion distress and is associated with an egoistic or self-oriented motivational aim (e.g., to relieve one's own distress). Prosocial responding in the presence of another's distress can be motivated by either altruism or egoism (Batson, Anderson, & Collins, 2005).

Evidence suggests that under conditions of high empathic arousal due to the apprehension of another's distress, emotion regulation is necessary if altruistically motivated responding is to occur (see Eisenberg & Eggum, 2009). By definition, empathic arousal in the presence of another's distress leads to personal feelings of distress (i.e., affective resonance). Effective emotion regulation in the presence of another's distress reduces the probability that feelings of personal distress will cascade into empathic over-arousal and the consequent activation of withdrawal behavior or ego-motivated helping. Empathic over-arousal is especially likely in stressful situations for individuals who are high in dispositional negative affect, high in susceptibility to vicarious negative affect, and who have poor emotion regulation skills (Eisenberg, Fabes, &

Spinrad, 2006). Effective regulation of empathic arousal allows for the activation and implementation of altruistic intentions aimed at helping the other. In other words, as depicted in Figure 13.4, attention leads to empathic awareness, and emotion regulation allows for that awareness to lead to the activation of altruistic intentions or compassion—a strong desire to do something to reduce the suffering of others (Halifax, 2012). Social neuroscientific findings provide support for this set of hypotheses regarding the interconnections of empathy, emotion regulation, and altruistic responding to others (Decety & Howard, 2013).

In summary, social interactions often activate strong emotions with intrinsic meanings. With appropriate mindfulness and emotion regulation, these meanings can be clearly perceived and can inform subsequent ethical behavior through the process of extension. Clearly, the processes of ethical perception, extension and altruistic motivation require mindfulness and compassion on the part of caregivers (parents, teachers) who are role models for and key socializers of children and adolescents. Therefore, assisting adults to become experts in the mental skills and social-emotional dispositions that underlie ethical development (calmness, mental clarity, disposition of kindness) is critically important. A growing body of evidence with adults suggests that MT affects basic processes of attention, sensation-perception, emotion, and social cognition that underlie ethical development (see Vago & Silbersweig, 2012).

EVIDENCE FOR EFFECTS OF MINDFULNESS TRAINING WITH ADULTS

Attention. From the contemplative traditions in which MT originated, training of sustained focused attention is thought to promote tranquility of the mind, an essential step for ethical development. Improving the efficiency and stability of attention also affords powerful forms of behavioral and cognitive regulation (see Ochsner & Gross, 2005). Studies show that MT improves adults' ability to direct and sustain attention and to monitor the focus of attention in a conscious way (Jha, Krompinger, & Baime, 2007), even in the presence of "hot" emotionally charged, but irrelevant, distractors (Ortner, Kilner, & Zelazo, 2007). Research also shows that MT changes the underlying neural substrates for these attentional abilities, with studies of individuals with 10,000 hours or more of formal meditation practice (e.g., experts in meditation) showing enduring changes in the neural circuits of attention (Davidson & Lutz, 2008).

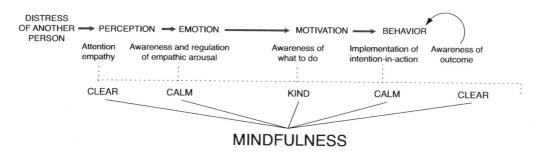

Figure 13.4 Hypothesized Example of How Mindfulness Can Facilitate Altruistic Behavior in the Presence of Another's Distress.

Sensory-Perception. The development of focused attention and a calm, tranquil mind is also critical to developing clearer perceptions of one's surroundings, one's relationships with others, and the causes and consequences of one's behavior. Research shows that MT in adults is associated with enhanced sensory-perceptual clarity and reduced reliance on information-processing biases (Cahn and Polich, 2009; Kerr et al., 2008; Lutz, Slagter, Dunne, & Davidson, 2008; Lutz, Greischar, Perlman, & Davidson, 2009; MacLean et al., 2010). Lutz and colleagues (2008), for instance, found that long-term meditators describe subjective states of attention and awareness with more accuracy than novices, and that their first-person reports are strongly correlated with simultaneously measured brain activity.

Awareness and Regulation of Emotion. Research shows that MT enhances the clarity of awareness of emotions as they manifest in the body and mind (e.g., Nielsen and Kaszniak, 2006), as well as individuals' ability to regulate emotion (Baer, 2009). Noting and labeling of mental experience is often taught in mindfulness-based practice as a way to become more aware of one's emotions. One study has demonstrated that trait mindfulness is correlated with accurately labeling emotions and the corresponding inhibitory influence of the frontal cortex over the amygdala due to such labeling (Creswell, Way, Eisenberger, & Lieberman, 2007).

Empathy and Prosociality. Prosocial motivation has been defined as the expressed wish to help others in need (Batson et al., 1999) whereas prosocial behavior is "behavior that benefits other people" (Staub, 1979, p. 2). Prosocial motivation is critically dependent upon multiple facets of empathic processes, such as mutual concern, perspective taking, experience sharing, neural resonance, emotional contagion, and emotion regulation (Zaki & Ochsner, 2012). Research shows that MT enhances the neural circuits underlying these empathic processes and awareness of others generally (Singer & Lamm, 2009). In a fMRI study of experts and novices, Lutz, Brefczynski-Lewis, Johnstone, and Davidson (2008) found that expertise in the form of 10,000 hours or more of a form of compassion meditation sensitizes the activation of neural circuits linked to empathy and theory of mind. Similarly, in another study, Lutz et al. (2009) found that compassion meditation enhances the emotional and somatosensory brain representations of others' emotions, and that this effect is modulated by expertise. It appears that as expertise in compassion increases, the threshold for the activation of perception–emotion–action links in prosocial directions is diminished and compassionate responding becomes "second nature" or spontaneous. In a recent social psychology experiment with emerging adults, for example, Condon, Desbordes, Miller, and DeSteno (2013) showed that MT was associated with actual prosocial helping behavior. Research on loving-kindness meditation (LKM) practices with adults also shows relevant changes in emotional processing, empathy, psychological wellbeing, and immune function in adults (Hofmann, Grossman, & Hinton, 2011). In one randomized control trial, LKM was found to increase feelings of implicit and explicit social connection towards novel other people (Hutcherson, Seppala, & Gross, 2008).

MINDFULNESS TRAINING SPECIFICALLY FOR PARENTS AND TEACHERS

Based on this work, MT programs for both parents and teachers have been developed. We believe it is critically important to offer MT to caregivers to provide them with a set of tools for personal stress-management that ultimately will improve their ability to be calm, clear, and kind in their caregiving or teaching activities. In addition, the embodiment of virtue on the part of adults provides a powerful, implicit means of socializing these same qualities in young people.

Research with Parents. Duncan, Coatsworth, and Greenberg (2009) proposed that MT impacts basic dimensions of parenting such as attentive listening, emotional awareness, self-regulation, non-judgmental acceptance of self and the child, and compassion for self and child. At this time, only a few studies of mindful parenting have been conducted.

One randomized control trial (RCT) examined the effects of randomization to a parenting program that included MT on parenting outcomes in 64 families in which one of the parents was on methadone maintenance. The 10–12 week program included one 60–120 minute in-home session per week. Results showed that parents receiving the MT-infused program showed significantly reduced parental stress, rigid parenting attitudes, and child behavior problems compared to others receiving a brief intervention or treatment-as-usual (TAU); as well as significantly reduced child abuse potential compared to those in TAU (Dawe & Harnett, 2007). Results were maintained at three- and six-month follow-up.

A second RCT on mindfulness and parenting was done by Coatsworth, Duncan, Greenberg, and Nix (2010). In a sample of 65 families with an early adolescent, researchers examined the effects of randomization to either a parent intervention (Strengthening Families Program) infused with mindfulness practices, the parent-intervention as usual, or a waitlist control condition. The MT-infused program taught both parents and their adolescents (children ages 11–14) very brief exercises using mindfulness. Results showed that while both intervention programs improved child management practices, the mindfulness-infused parenting intervention saw significant improvements in the use of mindful parenting strategies, use of effective management practices, and in the affective relationship between parent and child. Mindful parenting mediated the relationship between MT and improved affective relationship quality.

In a third RCT, Benn, Akiva, Arel, and Roeser (2012) found that parents of special needs children randomized to a five-week MT reported greater increases in empathic concern and tendency to forgive than parents in the waitlist control condition. In a series of small-scale clinical case studies of parents of special needs children, Singh and colleagues (2006, 2007, 2010) found that MT for parents of special needs children was associated with improvements in parents' satisfaction with their parenting skills and interactions with their children, increases in their children's social skills and a reduction in child non-compliance (refusal by child to comply with instructions or requests made by the mother within the time parameters set by the mother).

Research with Teachers. Similarly, only a handful of studies of MT with teachers have been published to date. In an early pilot RCT, Winzelberg and Luskin (1999) examined the effects of MT on teachers' job stress. The four-week program included one 45-minute session per week. The meditation technique taught used sound as a focusing device followed by one of the following practices: mantra repetition (silent repetition of a word or phrase), slowing down (the deliberate practice of slowing down one's actions), and one-pointed attention (the deliberate practice of focusing attention on one thing at a time). Results showed that teachers randomized to MT showed greater reductions in self-reported somatic, emotional, and behavioral manifestations of stress compared to controls.

Franco and colleagues (2010) conducted an RCT for public school teachers that compared a mindfulness intervention to an active control group on the reduction of psychological distress. Teachers were randomly assigned to either a 10-week mindfulness intervention or a 10-week psychomotor therapy program. Mindfulness practices included body scans, focused attention on the breath in conjunction with a word or sound, group discussion of practice, and presentation of metaphors and exercises to explain mindfulness. The psychomotor intervention involved playing games and doing exercises with large balls, rings, music, etc. Results showed that teachers who were randomized to MT showed significantly greater reductions in self-reported psychological distress (especially somatization) after the program and at four-month follow-up compared to those in the psychomotor group.

In an uncontrolled pilot study, Jennings, Snowberg, Coccia, and Greenberg (2011) examined the effects of a teacher MT designed to reduce stress and burnout. The program took place over four to five weeks and included four day-long sessions. Program activities involved teaching of emotion skills and mindful listening, and mindfulness practices like focused attention on the breath and body scans. The program was assessed in two samples: in-service teachers in a lower SES urban setting, and pre-service student-teachers in a university, suburban setting with results showing increases in self-reported mindfulness among the in-service teachers.

In an RCT, Kemeny and her colleagues (2012) evaluated the effects of a mindfulness intervention on the wellbeing of teachers. Eighty-two female public school teachers took part in an eight-week, 42-hour meditation/emotion regulation training. Program activities included focused attention on the breath meditation, open-monitoring meditation, LKM, training in emotion skills, mindful movement, and didactic instruction on emotions and life purposes. Results showed that teachers randomized to MT reported greater increases in self-reported mindfulness, greater improvements on a behavioral task requiring recognition of emotions, and greater reductions in self-reported rumination and symptoms of depression and anxiety, as well as increases in positive affect compared to waitlist controls.

In an RCT with educators and parents of special needs students, Benn et al. (2012) examined the effects of MT on stress, distress, and teaching and parenting practices. The program included ten two and a half hour sessions over five weeks and two six-hour retreats. MT program activities included body scans, focused attention on the breath meditation, open monitoring meditation, LKM, forgiveness meditation, and didactic instruction regarding emotion, forgiveness, and stress reactivity. Results showed that teachers and parents randomized to MT showed greater increases in self-reported mindfulness, self-compassion, forgiveness of others, and empathic concern for others; and greater declines in stress, negative affect, anxiety, and depression at the end of the program and at follow-up two months later compared to waitlist controls.

In two RCTs of the same MT as in Benn et al. (2012), Roeser and his colleagues (2013) examined effects of randomization to MT on Canadian and American public school teachers' mindfulness and stress reduction. The eight-week program included 11 sessions for a total of 36 hours of MT. Results showed that teachers randomized to MT showed greater increases in self-reported mindfulness and occupational self-compassion, greater improvements on a behavioral task requiring focused attention and working memory; and greater reductions in occupational stress and burnout at post-program and follow-up compared to waitlist controls. Results also showed that group differences in mindfulness and occupational self-compassion at post-program mediated longer-term reductions in occupational stress, burnout, anxiety, and depression.

Summary. The emerging research on mindfulness-based contemplative practice with adults—particularly those who are parents or teachers, as well as our emerging understanding of the plasticity of the brain across development (e.g., Decety & Howard, 2013; Giedd, 2008; Zelazo & Lyons, 2012), provide scientific warrants for a careful exploration of MT with school-aged children and adolescents (MLERN, 2012).

MINDFULNESS TRAINING WITH CHILDREN AND ADOLESCENTS

Similar to work with parents and teachers, research on MT for children and adolescents in clinical and community settings is only beginning. Early efforts have focused primarily on adapting practices for use with children and adolescents, and on examining the self-regulatory and stress reduction effects of such practices. There exist almost no studies to date examining the prosocial outcomes of MT (Greenberg & Harris, 2012; Zelazo & Lyons, 2012).

Two randomized control trial studies have examined the effects of a developmentally appropriate MT (Kaiser-Greenland, 2010) for pre-school and elementary school children on executive function and self-regulation, respectively. The program included focused attention on the breath as well as games and activities promoting awareness and attention regulation. In pre-school aged children, randomization to a five-week long version of the MT was associated with improvements in sustained attention and perspective-taking compared to controls (Johnson, Forston, Gunnar, & Zelazo, 2011). For children with poor executive function in grades 2–3, Flook and colleagues (2010) found that an eight-week MT program was associated with increases in parent- and teacher-ratings of students' ability to direct, sustain, and monitor attention at post-test compared to controls.

Napoli, Krech, and Holley (2005) examined the effects of randomization to a 24-week MT program on attention and anxiety levels in first to third grade students. The primary activities included focused attention on the breath and the body, in which attention is gradually guided through each part of the body to increase somatic/emotional awareness; and a mindful movement activity to bring together focused attention and motor behavior. Results indicated that students receiving the MT demonstrated decreases in teacher-rated attentional problems, decreases in self-reported test anxiety, and increases in a behavioral measure of selective visual attention, compared to those in the control condition.

Mendelson et al. (2010) examined the effects of randomization to a 12-week mindful yoga program on involuntary stress responses, mental health, and social adjustment for inner-city elementary school students in grades 4–5. Children were taught yoga-inspired postures and movement series that were selected to enhance muscle tone and flexibility, as well as the health benefits of the poses. At the end of each class the instructors guided children through a mindfulness practice, which involved attending to a specific focus for several minutes, such as paying attention to each breath or sending kind thoughts to others. Results showed that children in the mindful yoga program self-reported greater decreases in rumination, intrusive thoughts, and involuntary emotional arousal to stressful events compared to controls.

In a quasi-experimental study with elementary school students in grades 4–7 of what would become the *MindUp* program (Hawn Foundation, 2011), Schonert-Reichl and Lawlor (2010) examined the effects of a 10-week MT on students' social-emotional wellbeing and socially-responsible behavior compared to controls. The central mindfulness practice in this program was a focused attention meditation done three times per day for three minutes throughout the duration of the program. Results showed that teachers rated students who received MT as less aggressive and less oppositional, better able to focus attention, and more likely to act prosocially towards others compared to teacher ratings of students in the control group. In addition, students receiving MT reported greater wellbeing (optimism, positive mood).

A recent school-based randomized-control trial by Raes, Griffith, Gucht, and Williams (2013) with 408 adolescents and emerging adults aged 13–20 in Flanders, Belgium examined the effects of MT on reducing and preventing depression. Results showed that students randomized to MT reported a greater decrease in symptoms of depression post-MT and at a one-year follow-up compared to controls. Similar results in RCTs with clinically-referred adolescents have been obtained in the USA (Biegel, Brown, Shapiro, & Schubert, 2009).

In a non-randomized study with a control group involving 150 high school students in grades 11–12, Broderick and Metz (2009) examined the preliminary efficacy of a five-week MT for adolescents (Broderick and Jennings, 2012) on mental health outcomes. Each session included a short introduction of the topic (e.g., body awareness, understanding and working with feelings, reducing harmful self-judgments), several activities for group participation and discussion to engage students in the lesson, and an opportunity for in-class mindfulness meditation practice. Mindfulness practices included focused attention on the breath and body, open-monitoring meditation, and LKM. Results showed a significant reduction in negative affect and a significant increase in feelings of relaxation and self-acceptance among adolescent girls receiving MT compared to controls.

Finally, two RCTs have been done looking at the stress-reduction effects of mindful yoga with high school students. The secular yoga program included four key elements: physical exercises and postures, breathing exercises, deep relaxation, and meditation. The majority of yoga postures were simple and adaptable for all physical fitness levels. First, Noggle and colleagues (2012) examined the effects of randomization to a 10-week yoga versus physical education class as usual on 11th and 12th grade high school students' self-reported self-regulation and wellbeing. Results showed that students randomized to yoga showed greater reductions in negative affect and anxiety. Also investigating the program's effects on 11th and 12th grade students, Khalsa and colleagues (2012) found that randomization to an 11-week mindful yoga program versus physical education was associated with students' self-reported increases in anger regulation and the ability to bounce back from stressful events, as well as decreases in fatigue.

In sum, preliminary evidence regarding how developmentally-appropriate MT can stabilize attention, calm the mind, and reduce negative affect among children and adolescents exists; and there is some preliminary evidence that MT might improve students' social adjustment as well. Overall, there exists a need to increase the rigor of research in future studies of MT in education (randomization, active control groups, blinded studies, non-self-report measures), and to examine the effects of MT and yoga not just on self-regulation and stress reduction, but also on self-awareness and empathy, kindness, and altruism (see Table 13.1). Summarizing this emerging body of research, Greenberg and Harris (2012) concluded "meditation and yoga may be associated with beneficial outcomes for children and youth, but the generally limited quality of research tempers the allowable conclusions" (p. 161).

NEUROCOGNITIVE MODELS OF THE EFFECTS OF SPECIFIC CONTEMPLATIVE PRACTICES

The question of how particular mindfulness practices shape these basic processes of attention, sensation-perception, empathy, and compassion at the levels of mental skills and underlying neural substrates is also an intense focus of research currently. Vago and Silbersweig (2012) developed a series of process models of the four main contemplative practices used in MT programs for children, adolescents, and adults today. These practices include three types of formal meditation (focused attention, open monitoring, ethical enhancements) and mindful movement practices (mindful yoga). Models are presented in Figure 13.5.

Focused Attention Meditation (FA). A foundational form of mindfulness practice called focused attention meditation aims to cultivate vivid forms of attention on an object (e.g., the breath, external sound, an image) for sustained periods of time, as well as meta-awareness with regard to whether one's attention is focused on the object of attention or not (see Lutz, Dunne, & Davidson, 2007). FA meditation "exercises" top-down attentional control in the forms of response inhibition, set shifting, sustained attention, and monitoring (Zelazo & Carlson, 2012); and results in the calming of the mind and body (Wallace, 2007). The ability to stay calm and clear in stressful or distressing situations is clearly central to ethical development as discussed earlier (see Figure 13.4). Such practices, through use of props to help direct attention to the body, feelings, and the breath, are used even with young children (Kaiser-Greenland, 2010). A process model of this practice and its putative training effects is presented in Figure 13.5a.

Open-Monitoring Meditation (OM). A second form of practice called receptive or open-monitoring (OM) meditation is characterized by the absence of a focus on a particular object. Instead, attention is directed towards any sensations, feelings, images, and thoughts that arise while maintaining awareness of the phenomenal field of awareness as a non-attached observer (see Lutz et al., 2007). Novices begin by actively monitoring and labeling sensations, feelings, images, and thoughts. Verbal labeling increases awareness of these sensory-affect states and forms of thinking. Although distraction and discursive thinking may arise often in novices practicing OM meditation, the practitioner is encouraged to continually rest in awareness of moment to moment experience and avoid any cognitive forms of appraisals/judgments. Distraction and mind-wandering are also typically associated with the arousal of negative affect. Thus, the practice affords both attentional and emotion training through de-centering and self-compassion. De-centering is the ability to create psychological distance between one's perception and response. De-centering with respect to the activated phenomena in the stream of consciousness from moment to moment is described as a critical self-regulatory capacity that emerges from OM meditation (Vago & Silbersweig, 2012).

Eventually, through training, the active noting of mental contents moment to moment (e.g., thinking, feelings, visualizing, perceiving) can cease, and the process of mental noting becomes effortless. At the point in which mental noting becomes effortless, non-conscious, embodied forms of conditioning have increased the efficiency of substrates within the attentional system, resulting in decreased allotment of attentional resources towards any particular feeling, image, or thought. Perception is clarified, emotional reactivity is reduced, and attention efficiency is increased. The ethical implications of such outcomes seem self-evident. Figure 13.5b illustrates a process model for open-monitoring practice. Given the metacognitive demands of this kind of practice, it is usually introduced in adolescence and beyond (e.g., Broderick, 2013).

Ethical Enhancement Practices (EE). A third kind of practice being explored in secular settings is what we call Ethical Enhancement Practices (EE; see Figure 13.5c). Such practices involve explicit instructions for visualization (imagining others), emotion cultivation (love, forgiveness), and extension of that feeling to the imagined others (Varela, 1999). The cultivation of loving-kindness (Pali; *metta*) is an example of an EE practice, and is based on the idea that all beings wish to be happy (Ricard 2003; Salzberg & Bush, 1999). This practice is characterized by progressively cultivating loving-kindness towards oneself, a good friend, a neutral person, a difficult person, all four of the above equally, and then gradually the entire universe. For a "neutral" person, the practitioner is encouraged to choose someone they may come into contact with every day, but who does not give rise to strong emotions. For a "difficult" person, the practitioner is encouraged to choose someone strongly disliked. Furthermore, the practitioner is encouraged to break down the barriers between self and others by practicing loving-kindness repeatedly, achieving mental detachment and impartiality towards the four persons, including him/herself, the close friend, the neutral person, and the hostile person. EE practices are unique from the others in that they recruit positive forms of reappraisal (Garland, Gaylord, and Park, 2009), in which there is secondary appraisal of stressor stimuli (e.g., difficult person) that allows for reframing with positive emotion. Most other mindfulness-based practices do not reframe any experience as positive, but rather label valence with a neutral attitude—as a form of acceptance and non-judgment. A process model of EE practices is presented in Figure 13.5c. Loving-kindness meditation has the effect of engaging the social cognitive network, a network of brain areas responsible for perspective taking, theory of mind (ToM), and empathic concern. Such practices can be modified for even young children (e.g., Kaiser-Greenland, 2010).

Mindful Movement (MM). Finally, and perhaps most importantly for considering the needs of children and youth, contemplative practices involving mindful movement (e.g., yoga, tai-chi) are very popular. Mindful movement practices train attention through a focus on the whole body and increase awareness of bodily states and sensations. In this way, a "gross object" that is concrete and tangible (the body) becomes the focus of attention, and training in how to "transfer" mindfulness to action in the world is fostered. In adults, mindful movement practices show some of the strongest effects on outcome variables compared to the formal sitting practices (Carmody and Baer, 2008). A process model of EE practices is presented in Figure 5d. The critical mechanisms by which movement practices exert their putative effects include parasympathetic activation (e.g., de-activating the stress response), aerobic fitness, musculoskeletal strength and flexibility, and embodiment of a calm, clear, and focused mind. These practices are adaptable for any age.

CONCLUSIONS

We began this chapter by introducing Contemplative Education as a newly emerging approach to holistic and ethical education, anchored in insights from deep in the history of both Western and Eastern culture. Perhaps the two guiding pillars of Contemplative Education are those of our shared humanity—that we all aspire for happiness and freedom from suffering; and interdependence—that no person is an island, each a part of the main called humanity. Through a supportive community, mentorship, and practices that train attention and emotion, we suggested that Contemplative Education aims at the

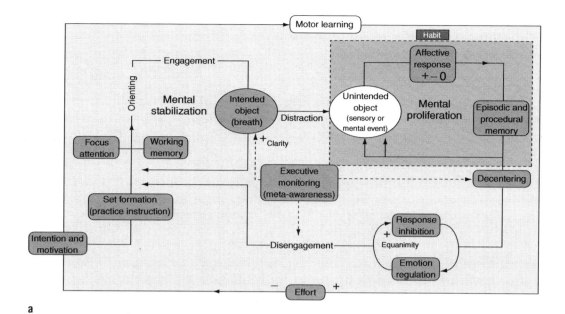

Figure 13.5a/b/c/d Four Theoretical Models of the Neural-Psychological Processes Recruited During Contemplative Practices.

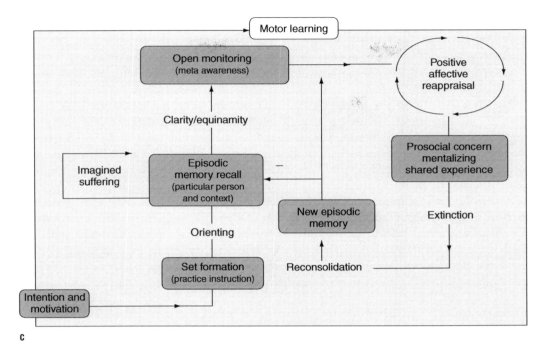

c

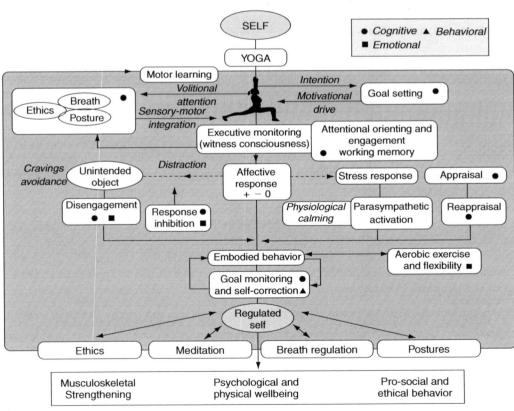

d

cultivation of calm bodies, attentive minds, and empathic and caring hearts (see Table 13.1). We also discussed how secularized mindfulness training is a core practice in Contemplative Education. MT represents one way of training attention, emotion, sensation and perception, and empathy in ways that support the ethical development of children, adolescents, and adults.

We then described the Contemplative Science Project, and noted its aims are to describe and understand efforts at mindfulness training in families, schools, and community settings with children, adolescents, and the adults who raise them. We suggested that the CSP is pursuing questions about the ethical development of children and adolescents that are similar to several new directions in moral psychology, moral education, and character development today (e.g., Narvaez, 2013). These include a focus on: (a) the differential roles of conscious cognitive and non-conscious emotional processes in ethical action, and educational approaches to cultivating each; (b) the development of ethical dispositions and character as forms of expertise; (c) the neurobiology underlying ethical development; and (d) the central roles that sensation-perception, attention, and the emotions play in ethical perception and action.

We then proposed how MT might contribute to the ethical development of children and adolescents by (a) helping them to develop skills and dispositions associated with abstentions from destructive motivations and actions (i.e., those marked by selfishness that fails to account for the rights and welfare of others), and the cultivation of virtuous motivations and actions (e.g., those marked either by "wise selfishness" in which self-pursuits are balanced with needs of others, or those marked by "compassion/altruism" in which one dedicates one's efforts to selflessly serving others (Dalai Lama, 2012). By cultivating self-control and emotional regulation, focused attention, clearer perception, and greater empathy, we suggested that MT affects the fundamental processes underlying ethical development. We then reviewed the nascent research base on the effects of MT on adult caregivers as well as children and youth. We noted that although this work is just beginning, there are some promising indications of the efficacy of MT programs.

Although we see this as an exciting new area of study and practice in ethical development, clearly more research and practical innovation is needed before definitive insights into the feasibility, efficacy, and effectiveness of MT in education can be ascertained. In addition, future work needs to focus on the kinds of outcomes of interest to those in this handbook: How might MT shape the ethical development of individuals? In closing, we want to reiterate that we believe the greatest gift MT may offer in the fields of moral and character education is a way of teaching skills and dispositions with which, through their application in their own lives, young people can discover the intrinsic value of virtue for themselves through their own embodied experience. Such a process of ethical self-discovery through the use of MT does not require belief or faith in any religion. As the 14th Dalai Lama (1999) put it:

> Our own heart, our own mind is the temple. The doctrine is compassion. Love for others and respect for their rights and dignity, no matter who or what they are: ultimately these are all we need. So long as we practice these in our daily lives, then no matter if we are learned or unlearned, whether we believe in Buddha or God, or follow some other religion or none at all, as long as we have compassion for others and conduct ourselves with restraint out of a sense of responsibility, there is no doubt we will be happy.

NOTE

1. It turns out that until adolescence, children tend to see victimizers as "happy" and do not see that it is often unhappiness and suffering that leads individuals to act in unethical ways (see Nucci, 2001). This suggests that scaffolding this kind of awareness through noting and labeling is a key aspect of disrupting hostile attributions to others who act out in antisocial ways. Training students to have compassion for bullies is implicated here.

REFERENCES

Aknin, L. B., Hamlin, J. K., & Dunn, E. W. (2012). Giving leads to happiness in young children. *PLoS ONE, 7*(6): e39211. doi:10.1371/journal.pone.0039211.

Arsenio, W. (1988). Children's conceptions of the situational affective consequences of sociomoral events. *Child Development, 59,* 1611–1622.

Arsenio, W., & Lover, A. (1995). Children's conceptions of sociomoral affect: Happy victimizers, mixed emotions and other experiences. In M. Killen & D. Hart (Eds.), *Morality in everyday life: Developmental perspectives* (pp. 87–128). Cambridge, England: Cambridge University Press.

Baer, R. A. (2009). Self-focused attention and mechanisms of change in mindfulness-based treatment. *Cognitive Behavior Therapy, 38*(1), 15–20.

Baltes, P. B., Reese, H. W., & Nesselroade, J. R. (1977). *Life-span developmental psychology: Introduction to research methods.* Monterey, CA: Brooks/Cole Publishing Company.

Batson, C. D., Ahmad, N., Yin, J., Bedell, S. J., Johnson, J. W., & Templin, C. M. (1999). Two threats to the common good: Self-interested egoism and empathy-induced altruism. *Personality and Social Psychology Bulletin, 25*(1), 3–16.

Batson, C. D., Anderson, S. L., & Collins, E. (2005). Personal religion and prosocial motivation. In M. L. Maher & S. A. Karabenick (Eds.), *Motivation and religion (special issue). Advances in motivation and achievement* (vol. 14, pp. 151–185). Greenwich, CT: JAI Press.

Benn, R., Akiva, T., Arel, S., & Roeser, R. W. (2012). Mindfulness training effects for parents and educators of children with special needs. *Developmental Psychology, 48,* 1476–1487.

Biegel, G. M., Brown, K. W., Shapiro, S. L., & Schubert, C. M. (2009). Mindfulness-based stress reduction for the treatment of adolescent psychiatric outpatients: A randomized clinical trial. *Journal of Consulting and Clinical Psychology, 77,* 855–866.

Bransford, J. D., Brown, A. L., & Cocking, R. R. (Eds.). (1999). *How people learn: Brain, mind, experience, and school.* Washington, DC: National Academy Press.

Broderick, P. C., & Jennings, P. A. (2012). Mindfulness for adolescents: A promising approach to supporting emotion regulation and preventing risky behavior. *New Directions for Youth Development, 2012*(136), 111–126.

Broderick, P. T. (2013) *Learning to breathe.* Oakland, CA: New Harbinger.

Broderick, P., & Metz, S. (2009). Learning to BREATHE: A pilot trial of a mindfulness curriculum for adolescents. *Advances in School Mental Health Promotion, 2*(1), 35–43.

Burrell, N. A., Zirbel, C. S., & Allen, M. (2003). Evaluating peer mediation outcomes in educational settings: A meta-analytic review. *Conflict Resolution Quarterly, 21,* 7–26.

Cahn, B. R., & Polich, J. (2009). Meditation (Vipassana) and the P3a event-related brain potential. *International Journal of Psychophysiology, 72*(1), 51–60.

Carmody, J., & Baer, R. A. (2008). Relationships between mindfulness practice and levels of mindfulness, medical and psychological symptoms and well-being in a mindfulness-based stress reduction program. *Journal of Behavioral Medicine, 31,* 23–33.

Coatsworth, J. D., Duncan, L. G., Greenberg, M. T., & Nix, R. L. (2010). Changing parent's mindfulness, child management skills and relationship quality with their youth: Results from a randomized pilot intervention trial. *Journal of Child and Family Studies, 19*(2), 203–217.

Condon, P., Desbordes, G., Miller, W. B., & DeSteno, D. (2013). Meditation increases compassionate responses to suffering. *Psychological Science, 24,* 2125–2127.

Conway, J. M., Amel, E. L., & Gerwien, D. P. (2009). Teaching and learning in the social context: A meta-analysis of service learning's effects on academic, personal, social, and citizenship outcomes. *Teaching of Psychology, 36*(4), 233–245.

Creswell, J. D., Way, B. M., Eisenberger, N. I., & Lieberman, M. D. (2007). Neural correlates of dispositional mindfulness during affect labeling. *Psychosomatic Medicine, 69*(6), 560–565.

Dalai Lama. (1999). *Ethics for a new millennium.* New York: Penguin Putnam.

Dalai Lama. (2012). *Beyond religion: Ethics for a whole world*. New York: Houghton-Mifflin.

Davidson, R. J., & Lutz, A. (2008). Buddha's brain: Neuroplasticity and meditation. *Signal Processing Magazine, IEEE, 25*, 172–176.

Dawe, S., & Harnett, P. (2007). Reducing potential for child abuse among methadone-maintained parents: Results from a randomized controlled trial. *Journal of Substance Abuse Treatment, 32*, 381–390.

Decety, J., & Howard, L. H. (2013). The role of affect in the neurodevelopment of morality. *Child Development Perspectives, 7*, 49–54.

De Waal, F. (2009). *Primates and philosophers: How morality evolved*. S. Macedo & J. Ober (Eds.). Oxfordshire: Princeton University Press.

Dewey, J. (1900/1990). *The school and society*. Chicago: University of Chicago Press.

De Wit, H. F. (1991). *Contemplative psychology*. Pittsburgh: Duquesne University Press.

Duncan, L. G., Coatsworth, J. D., & Greenberg, M. T. (2009). A model of mindful parenting: Implications for parent–child relationships and prevention research. *Clinical Child and Family Psychology Review, 12*(3), 255–270.

Durlak, J. A., Weissberg, R. P., Dymnicki, A. B., Taylor, R. D., & Schellinger, K. B. (2011). The impact of enhancing students' social and emotional learning: A meta-analysis of school-based universal interventions. *Child Development, 82*, 405–432.

Eccles, J. S., & Roeser, R. W. (2010). School and community influences on human development. In M. H. Boorstein & M. E. Lamb (Eds.), *Developmental psychology: An advanced textbook* (6th ed.). Hillsdale, NJ: Erlbaum.

Eisenberg, N. (1998). Prosocial development. In W. Damon (Ed.) & N. Eisenberg (Volume Ed.), *Handbook of child psychology* (pp. 701–778). New York: John Wiley & Sons, Inc.

Eisenberg, N., & Eggum, N. D. (2009). Empathic responding: sympathy and personal distress. In J. Decety & W. J. Ickes (Eds.) *The Social Neuroscience of Empathy* (pp. 71–83). Cambridge, MA: Massachusetts Institute of Technology Press.

Eisenberg, N., Fabes, R. A., & Spinrad, T. L. (2006). Prosocial development. In N. Eisenberg (Vol. Ed.) & W. Damon & R. M. Lerner (Series Eds.), *Handbook of child psychology: Vol. 3. Social, emotional, personality development* (6th ed., pp. 646–718). Hoboken, NJ: Wiley.

Ekman, P., Davidson, R. J., Ricard, M., & Wallace, B. A. (2005). Buddhist and psychological perspectives on emotions and well-being. *Current Directions in Psychological Science, 14*(2), 59–63.

Ericsson, K. A., & Charness, N. (1994). Expert performance: Its structure and acquisition. *American Psychologist, 8*, 725–747.

Flook, L., Smalley, S. L., Kitil, M. J., Galla, B. M., Kaiser-Greenland, S., Locke, J.,... Kasari, C. (2010). Effects of mindful awareness practices on executive functions in elementary school children. *Journal of Applied School Psychology, 26*(1), 70–95.

Franco, C., Manas, I., Cangas, A. J., Moreno, E., & Gallego, J. (2010). Reducing teachers' psychological distress through a mindfulness training program. *The Spanish Journal of Psychology, 13*, 655–666.

Friedman, T. L. (2008). *Hot, flat and crowded: Why we need a green revolution—and how it can renew America*. New York: Farrar, Straus and Giroux.

Garland, E., Gaylord, S., & Park, J. (2009). The role of mindfulness in positive reappraisal. *Explore: The Journal of Science and Healing, 5*(1), 37–44.

Garrard, W. M., & Lipsey, M. W. (2007). Conflict resolution education and antisocial behavior in US schools: A meta-analysis. *Conflict Resolution Quarterly, 25*, 9–38.

Giedd, J. N. (2008). The teen brain: Insights from neuroimaging. *Journal of Adolescent Health, 42*, 335–343.

Gilligan, C. (1982). *In a different voice: Psychological theory and women's development*. Cambridge: Harvard University Press.

Greenberg, M. T., & Harris, A. R. (2012). Nurturing mindfulness in children and youth: Current state of research. *Child Development Perspectives, 0*, 1–6.

Haidt, J. (2007). The new synthesis in moral psychology. *Science, 316*(5827), 998–1002.

Haidt, J., & Joseph, C. (2007). The moral mind: How five sets of innate intuitions guide the development of many culture-specific virtues, and perhaps even modules. *The Innate Mind, 3*, 367–392.

Halifax, J. (2012). A heuristic model of enactive compassion. *Current Opinion in Supportive & Palliative Care, 6*(2), 228–235.

Harrington, A. (2008). *The cure within: A history of mind-body medicine*. New York: W.W. Norton & Company.

Hawn Foundation (2011). *The MindUp curriculum: Brain-focused strategies for learning and living*. New York: Scholastic.

Hofmann, S. G., Grossman, P., & Hinton, D. E. (2011). Loving-kindness and compassion meditation: Potential for psychological interventions. *Clinical Psychology Review, 31*(7), 1126–1132.

Hutcherson, C. A., Seppala, E. M., & Gross, J. J. (2008). Loving-kindness meditation increases social connectedness. *Emotion, 8*(5), 720–724.

Jennings, P. A., Snowberg, K. E., Coccia, M. A., & Greenberg, M. T. (2011). Improving classroom learning environments by cultivating awareness and resilience in education (CARE): Results of two pilot studies. *Journal of Classroom Interaction, 46*(1), 37–48.

Jha, A. P., Krompinger, J., & Baime, M. J. (2007). Mindfulness training modifies subsystems of attention. *Cognitive, Affective, & Behavioral Neuroscience, 7*(2), 109–119.

Johnson, A. E., Forston, J. L., Gunnar, M. R., & Zelazo, P. D. (2011, April). *A randomized controlled trial of mindfulness meditation training in preschool children.* Poster presented at the biennial meeting of the Society for Research in Child Development, Montreal, Quebec.

Kabat-Zinn, J. (2003). Mindfulness-based interventions in context: Past, present and future. *Clinical Psychology Science and Practice, 10,* 144–156.

Kaiser-Greenland, S. (2010). *The mindful child.* New York: Simon & Schuster.

Kemeny, M. E., Foltz, C., Cullen, M., Jennings, P., Gillath, O., Wallace, B. A., . . . Ekman, P. (2012). Contemplative/emotion training reduces negative emotional behavior and promotes prosocial responses. *Emotion, 12,* 338–350.

Kerr, C. E., Shaw, J. R., Wasserman, R. H., Chen, V. W., Kanojia, A., Bayer, T., & Kelley, J. M. (2008). Tactile acuity in experienced Tai Chi practitioners: Evidence for use dependent plasticity as an effect of sensory-attentional training. *Experimental Brain Research, 188*(2), 317–322.

Khalsa, S. B., Hickey-Schultz, L., Cohen, D., Steiner, N., & Cope, S. (2012). Evaluation of the mental health benefits of yoga in a secondary school: A preliminary randomized controlled trial. *Journal of Behavioral Health Services and Research, 39,* 80–90.

Lazarus, R. S. (1991). Progress on a cognitive-motivational-relational theory of emotion. *American Psychologist, 46*(8), 819.

Lerner, R. M., & Overton, W. F. (2008). Exemplifying the integrations of the relational developmental system: Synthesizing theory, research, and application to promote positive development and social justice. *Journal of Adolescent Research, 23*(3), 245–255.

Lutz, A., Brefczynski-Lewis, J., Johnstone, T., & Davidson, R. J. (2008). Regulation of the neural circuitry of emotion by compassion meditation: Effects of meditative expertise. *PLoS ONE, 3*(3): e1897. doi:10.1371/journal.pone.0001897.

Lutz, A., Dunne, J. D., & Davidson, R. J. (2007). Meditation and the neuroscience of consciousness. In P. Zelazo, M. Moscovitch, & E. Thompson (Eds.) *Cambridge Handbook of Consciousness* (pp. 499–555). New York: Cambridge University Press.

Lutz, A., Greischar, L. L., Perlman, D. M., & Davidson, R. J. (2009). BOLD signal in insula is differentially related to cardiac function during compassion meditation in experts vs. novices. *Neuroimage, 47*(3), 1038–1046.

Lutz, A., Slagter, H. A., Dunne, J. D., & Davidson, R. J. (2008). Attention regulation and monitoring in meditation. *Trends in Cognitive Sciences, 12*(4), 163–169.

MacLean, K. A., Ferrer, E., Aichele, S. R., Bridwell, D. A., Zanesco, A. P., Jacobs, T. L., . . . Saron, C. D. (2010). Intensive meditation training improves perceptual discrimination and sustained attention. *Psychological Science, 21*(6), 829–839.

Mahoney, J. L., Larson, R. W., & Eccles, J. S. (Eds.). (2005). *Organized activities as contexts of development: Extracurricular activities, after school and community programs.* Mahwah, NJ: Lawrence Erlbaum Associates, Inc.

Mendelson, T., Greenberg, M. T., Dariotis, J. K., Gould, L. F., Rhoades, B. L., & Leaf, P. J. (2010). Feasibility and preliminary outcomes of a school-based mindfulness intervention for urban youth. *Journal of Abnormal Child Psychology, 39,* 985–994.

Mind and Life Education Research Network (MLERN). (2012). Contemplative practices and mental training: Prospects for American education. *Child Development Perspectives, 6,* 146–153.

Moffitt, T. E., Arseneault, L., Belsky, D., Dickson, N., Hancox, R. J., Harrington, H., . . . Caspi, A. (2011). A gradient of childhood self-control predicts health, wealth, and public safety. *Proceedings of the National Academy of Sciences, 108,* 2693–2698.

Napoli, M., Krech, P. R., & Holley, L. C. (2005). Mindfulness training for elementary school students: The attention academy. *Journal of Applied School Psychology, 21*(1), 99–125.

Narvaez, D. (2013). The future of research in moral development and education. *Journal of Moral Education, 42,* 1–11.

Nielsen, L., & Kaszniak, A. W. (2006). Awareness of subtle emotional feelings: A comparison of long-term meditators and nonmeditators. *Emotion, 6*(3), 392–405.

Noggle, J. J., Steiner, N. J., Minami, T., & Khalsa, S. B. S. (2012). Benefits of yoga for psychosocial well-being in a US high school curriculum: A preliminary randomized controlled trial. *Journal of Developmental & Behavioral Pediatrics, 33,* 193–201.

Nucci, L. P. (2001). *Education in the moral domain.* Cambridge: Cambridge University Press.

Nucci, L. P., & Turiel, E. (1978). Social interactions and the development of social concepts in preschool children. *Child Development, 49,* 400–407.

Nucci, L. P., & Turiel, E. (2009). Capturing the complexity of moral development and education. *Mind, Brain and Education, 3*(3), 151–159.

Ochsner, K. N., & Gross, J. J. (2005). The cognitive control of emotion. *Trends in Cognitive Science, 9*(5), 242–249.

Ortner, C. N. M., Kilner, S. J., & Zelazo, P. D. (2007). Mindfulness meditation and reduced emotional interference on a cognitive task. *Motivation and Emotion, 31,* 271–283.

Overton, W. F., & Reese, H. W. (1977). General models for man-environment relations. In H. McGurk (Ed.). *Ecological Factors in Human Development* (pp. 11–19). Amsterdam: North Holland.

Phi Delta Kappan (2012). Retrieved from www.pdkintl.org/poll/docs/2012-Gallup-poll-full-report.pdf, June 6, 2012.

Raes, F., Griffith, J. W., Van der Gucht, K., & Williams, J. M. G. (2013). School-based prevention and reduction of depression in adolescents: A cluster-randomized controlled trial of a mindfulness group program. *Mindfulness,* 1–10.

Ricard, M. (2003). *Happiness.* New York: Little, Brown & Company.

Roeser, R. W., & Peck, S. C. (2009). An education in awareness: Self, motivation and self-regulation in contemplative perspective. *Educational Psychologist, 44,* 119–136.

Roeser, R. W., Schonert-Reichl, K. A., Jha, A., Cullen, M., Wallace, L., Wilensky, R., Oberle, E., Thomson, K., Taylor, C., & Harrison, J. (2013). Mindfulness training and reductions in teacher stress and burnout: Results from two randomized, waitlist-control field trials. *Journal of Educational Psychology.* Advance online publication: doi: 10.1037/a0032093.

Roeser, R. W., & Zelazo, P. D. R. (2012). Contemplative science, education and child development: Introduction to the Special Section. *Child Development Perspectives, 6,* 143–145.

Sachs, J. D. (2011). *The price of civilization.* New York: Random House.

Salzberg, S., & Bush, M. (1999). *Voices of insight.* Boston, Shambala Publications, Inc.

Sameroff, A. (2010). A unified theory of development: A dialectic integration of nature and nurture. *Child Development, 81*(1), 6–22.

Schonert-Reichl, K. A., & Lawlor, M. S. (2010). The effects of a mindfulness-based education program on pre- and adolescents' well-being and social and emotional competence. *Mindfulness,* DOI 10.1007/s12671–010–0011–8.

Singer, T., & Lamm, C. (2009). The social neuroscience of empathy. *Annals of the New York Academy of Science 2009,* 81–96.

Singh, N. N., Lancioni, G. E., Winton, A. S., Fisher, B. C., Wahler, R. G., McAleavey, K., … Sabaawi, M. (2006). Mindful parenting decreases aggression, noncompliance, and self-injury in children with autism. *Journal of Emotional and Behavioral Disorders, 14*(3), 169–177.

Singh, N. N., Lancioni, G. E., Winton, A. S., Singh, J., Curtis, W. J., Wahler, R. G., & McAleavey, K. M. (2007). Mindful parenting decreases aggression and increases social behavior in children with developmental disabilities. *Behavior Modification, 31*(6), 749–771.

Singh, N. N., Lancioni, G. E., Winton, A. S., Singh, J., Singh, A. N., Adkins, A. D., & Wahler, R. G. (2010). Training in mindful caregiving transfers to parent–child interactions. *Journal of Child and Family Studies, 19*(2), 167–174.

Staub, E. (1979). *Positive social behavior and morality, Volume 2.* New York: Academic Press.

Tharp, R. G., & Gallimore, R. (1988). *Rousing minds to life: Teaching, learning and schooling in social context.* New York: Cambridge University Press.

Vago, D. R., & Silbersweig, D. A. (2012). Self-awareness, self-regulation, and self-transcendence (S-ART): A framework for understanding the neurobiological mechanisms of mindfulness. *Frontiers in Human Neuroscience, 6,* 1–30.

Varela, F. J. (1999). *Ethical know-how: Action, wisdom, and cognition.* California: Stanford University Press.

Varela, F. J., & Shear, J. (1999). First-person methodologies: What, why, how. *Journal of Consciousness Studies, 6*(2–3), 1–14.

Varela, F. J., Thompson, E. T., & Rosch, E. (1991). *The embodied mind: Cognitive science and human experience.* Cambridge, MA: Massachusetts Institute of Technology Press.

Wallace, B. A. (2007). *Contemplative science: Where Buddhism and neuroscience converge.* New York: Columbia University Press.

White House (2000). Race to the top. Retrieved from www.whitehouse.gov/issues/education/k-12/race-to-the-top.

Wilson, D. B., Gottfredson, D. C., & Najaka, S. S. (2001). School-based prevention of problem behaviors: A meta-analysis. *Journal of Quantitative Criminology, 17*(3), 247–272.

Winzelberg, A. J., & Luskin, F. M. (1999). The effect of a meditation training in stress levels in secondary school teachers. *Stress and Health, 15*(2), 69–77.

Zajonc, A. (in press). Contemplation in Education. To appear in K. Schonert-Reichl & R. W. Roeser (Eds.)., *Handbook of Mindfulness in Education.* Netherlands: Springer.

Zaki, J., & Ochsner, K. (2012). The neuroscience of empathy: Progress, pitfalls, and promise. *Nature Neuroscience, 15*(5), 675–680.

Zelazo, P. D., & Carlson, S. M. (2012). Hot and cool executive function in childhood and adolescence: Development and plasticity. *Child Development Perspectives, 6*(4), 354–360.

Zelazo, P. D., & Lyons, K. E. (2012). The potential benefits of mindfulness training in early childhood: A developmental social cognitive neuroscience perspective. *Child Development Perspectives, 6*, 154–160.

14

RESEARCH-BASED FUNDAMENTALS OF THE EFFECTIVE PROMOTION OF CHARACTER DEVELOPMENT IN SCHOOLS

Marvin W. Berkowitz and Melinda C. Bier*

The intentional promotion of positive development in youth is an age-old project, probably a human enterprise since the earliest forms of human community. No society can endure if it does not take seriously the fundamental project of socializing subsequent generations. Translation of two Sumerian tablets give us evidence that this inclination was evident over 4,000 years ago:

> My son, let me give you instructions. Pay attention to them! Do not beat a farmer's son, or he will break your irrigation canal.... When you are drunk, do not judge.... Do not break into a house.... Do not speak with a girl when you are married, the [likelihood of] slander is strong.... Do not allow your sheep to graze in untested grazing grounds.... Submit to strength. Bow down to the mighty man.
>
> (A Sumerian Father Gives Advice to his Son, about 2300 BCE)

> Why do you idle about? Go to school, recite your assignment, open your schoolbag, write your tablet, let your "big brother" write your new tablet for you. Be humble and show fear before your apprentice teacher. When you show terror, he will like you.... Never in my life did I make you carry reeds to the canebrake. I never said to you "Follow my caravans." I never sent you to work as a laborer. "Go, work and support me," I never in my life said that to you. Others like you support their parents by working.... Compared to them you are not a man at all. Night and day you waste in pleasures.... Among all craftsmen that live in the land, no work is more difficult than that of a scribe. [But] it is in accordance with the fate decreed by [the god] Enlil that a man should follow his father's work.
>
> (A Sumerian Father Wants His Teen-Ager To Be A Scribe, about 2000 BCE)

Over the ensuing four millennia, the body of literature describing how to raise and educate children and adolescents continued to grow, so that now it is a massive collection of advice, unfortunately often conflicting, and more importantly for this discussion, frequently not based in scientific evidence and theory. This is just as true regardless of whether one examines the literature on parenting for character development or the literature on educating for character development.

In this chapter, a more scientific approach will be brought to bear on just this question: What do we know scientifically about best practices in fostering moral and character development in general, and particularly in schools?

THE SEMANTIC MINEFIELD

Before we can reap the lessons of the research, however, we need to turn to one of the obstacles in describing the research: the problem of language and definition. This has proved to be a rather intractable problem (Berkowitz, 1997; Smagorinsky & Taxel, 2005), and it only seems to be getting more complex. The authors currently work mostly under the rubric of "character education" but have all also done similar work under other names; for example, moral education, values education, child development, social-emotional learning, primary prevention, positive youth development, and youth empowerment. Many colleagues have worked under still other rubrics for the same or similar work, such as service learning, citizenship education, and science technology and society (STS).

Defining each term so that it is clear is difficult enough, but defining them so that they are clearly distinct from each other appears impossible because of the remarkable overlap between most of them. We will not attempt to create a taxonomy of the disparate terms and fields that intersect when one attempts to promote healthy and positive development of youth in educational settings, because (1) it is beyond the purview of this chapter; (2) we have made some attempts to do this elsewhere (Berkowitz & Bier, 2005a; Berkowitz, Sherblom, Bier, & Battistich, 2006); and (3) it may ultimately be impossible because of the ill-defined boundaries of many of these fields, as well as the polarizing and projective nature of the promotion of "goodness."

Instead we will simply carve out our turf by trying to define what we include when we talk about character education. Character education occurs in educational settings. Whereas there are many educational settings, for practical purposes more than for any other reason, we try to limit our scope to pre-kindergarten through 12th grade schools, or what many other cultures refer to as primary and secondary schools. We also try to limit our scope to what happens during the regular school day, thus avoiding after-school programs and extracurricular programs that occur outside of regular school hours, although they may be bundled with school day implementation strategies. Certainly these are artificial lines we have drawn, but when one focuses on intentional efforts to promote positive character in youth, one has to draw lines because so much (albeit not enough) of a society's efforts are directed toward this fundamental human project. This is not to devalue the other spheres of influence (certainly families and more particularly parenting are the primary "character educators" and we have become increasingly concerned about the powerful impact of the media on youth character as they have become more ubiquitous, ambiguous, and graphic); rather it is intended to focus on a developmental sphere of influence that is significant, common, and more readily accessed for intervention. Furthermore, as we have learned (Berkowitz, 2012a; Berkowitz & Grych, 1998, 2000), the fundamental principles of what promotes character development remain much the same across different domains of influence. Child development is impacted by the same fundamental forces and strategies, regardless of the source (e.g., parents vs. teachers).

Within those educational settings, we focus on those activities and processes that should influence student character development. That in itself is rife with difficulties. By what basis *should* they have such an influence? Must we individually justify each process and practice we examine? While one could argue affirmatively to the latter question, we will take the authors' prerogative and allow ourselves some slack here. As experts in the field, we will use our professional judgments to decide what can reasonably be included in the domain of character education, knowing full well that there is extensive disagreement about this.

But another issue about the selection of variables of influence has to do with intentionality. While we would prefer to examine only intentionally targeted influences, given the nascent state of this field, some fishing is warranted. For instance, we believe a powerful, even critical, variable in the effectiveness of character education is the nature of school leadership, especially the degree to which leadership understands deep school reform-based character education, is committed to it, and can serve as an instructional leader for it (Berkowitz, 2011; Berkowitz, Pelster, & Johnston, 2012). Yet little is known about the impact of school leadership and rarely is it an intentionally targeted aspect of character education (Devaney, O'Brien, Resnik, Keister, & Weissberg, 2006; Kam, Greenberg, & Walls, 2003). An even stronger but related argument can be made for the nature of the adult culture in schools (Berkowitz, 2012a), another variable for which there is little research (cf. Bryk & Schneider, 2002). In one sense this is a moot argument, as we can only report on that which has been studied thus far, and these unintentional variables almost by definition are not typically studied. However, as we also want to address what needs to be known, it is worth making this point.

The final piece of the definitional puzzle has to do with outcome variables. Up to this point we have really focused on the second word in the term "character education"; that is, education. We defined it as pre-K to 12th grade, during the school day, and expected to impact student character development. However, that still leaves the first word, "character." If, for us, character education is the set of practices and programs during the pre-K to 12th grade school day that should influence student character development, what is this student character that we expect to develop? Here we will simply rely on a definition that we have been using for a while: Character is the set of psychological characteristics that motivate and enable an individual to function as a competent moral agent. In other words, it is those aspects of one's psychological makeup that impact whether one does the right thing, whether that entails telling the truth, helping an unpopular student who is in jeopardy, resisting the temptation to cheat or steal, or some other matter of moral functioning.

These characteristics span a range of psychological domains. One common shorthand for this range has been adopted by the Character Education Partnership in their definition of character as "understanding, caring about, and acting upon core ethical values" (www.character.org). This tri-partite definition incorporates aspects of the cognitive, affective/motivational, and behavioral domains of psychological functioning and development (for a fuller explication see Berkowitz, 2012b). "Of course, this still leaves open the question of what is moral, but we will not attempt to define this other than to rely on the millennia old wisdom of philosophers and simply refer the reader back to them" (cf. Berkowitz, 2012b).

WHAT IS NEEDED

Years of consultation with, training of, and observation of educators grappling with how to effectively promote character development has led to the recognition of the main obstacles to successful moral and character education. Educators typically need assistance with the following:

1. Understanding the nature of character and how it develops; i.e., what it is and what impacts its development;
2. Authentically allowing themselves to give priority to moral and character education (often in the face of countervailing historical, political, cultural, and economic forces);
3. Thinking sociologically (e.g., understanding character education as, in large part, fundamentally organizational/institutional reform), and not just pedagogically and psychologically;
4. Acquiring the often complex knowledge and developing the often equally complex pedagogical competencies required to be an effective moral and character educator.

This chapter will present what is empirically known about effective moral and character development in an attempt to address all four of these needs, but will focus most extensively on those aspects of needs 1, 3, and 4 that directly deal with evidence-based moral and character education practice. Most centrally, however, the focus will be on what research tells us about effective character education practice.

MAJOR SOURCES OF EMPIRICAL FINDINGS

Over a decade ago, the authors began to survey what was empirically known about school-based character education (Berkowitz & Bier, 2005a), and were then surprised to uncover 69 scientifically sound studies of relevance. More recently, in a meta-analysis of studies of social-emotional learning, Durlak, Weissberg, Dymnicki, Taylor, & Schellinger (2011) identified 213 studies of relevance. Whereas SEL is not identical with character education, they are largely overlapping domains. In other words, there is a growing and substantial body of relevant literature upon which to draw in order to address the question of effective practice in this domain. Hence, we have elected to look at a set of meta-analyses and reviews rather than to try to examine all the individual existing studies. An important note is that our focus is on empirically identified "best practices" and most studies and reviews do not include implementation strategies as independent or moderator variables. For example, the one meta-analysis of specifically character education programs that we could find, an unpublished master's thesis, only looked at outcomes of character education and did not examine differences in implementation methods (Berg, 2003).

Furthermore, triggered by an aphorism we often invoke during professional development with educators, "good character education is good education," we will examine reviews of the impact of educational strategies on academic achievement in order to look for such pedagogical similarities.

The character education reviews utilized here are Berkowitz and Bier's (2005a) *What Works in Character Education (WWCE)*, Lovat, Toomey, Dally, and Clement's (2009) review of values education, and Durlak et al.'s (2011) meta-analysis of social-emotional learning, along with Berkowitz's (2011) updating of WWCE.

The civic/citizenship domain will be represented by the EPPI (2005) systematic review of citizenship education. While this study focused on academic outcomes, it was a comprehensive review of outcome research and looked at implementation strategies.

The reviews focusing more broadly on academically successfully educational practices are the cluster of work by Marzano (2003a, 2003b, 2007) and Hattie's (2009) extensive review of over 800 meta-analyses.

FRAMING WITH PRIME

In order to organize the results of the review of reviews, it is helpful to adopt a conceptual model of major character education strategies. Berkowitz (2009; cf. Berkowitz & Bustamante, 2013) has proposed a five component model of optimal character education implementation, called PRIME. The term refers to:

- **P**rioritization of character education in the educational setting. This emphasis must be authentic, and ideally begins with the organizational leader (principal, superintendent, etc.) and is school-wide.
- **R**elationships are the essential building blocks of character development and optimal education (Berkowitz & Bier, 2005b; Watson, 2003). They should be proactively and strategically nurtured and this applies within and across all stakeholder groups in the school or district.
- **I**ntrinsic motivation should be the primary motivational and developmental target of character education (Althof & Berkowitz, 2013). Conversely, modes of extrinsic motivation should be minimized if not eliminated.
- **M**odels of character should surround students. Primarily all adults in the educational setting should model the character they want to see developing in students.
- **E**mpowerment of all stakeholders should be emphasized and strategically supported. Flattening governance structures, increasing democratic processes, and generally making space for "voices" to be elicited, heard, and honored are core aspects of this element.

The effective methods identified in the review will therefore, where appropriate, be clustered under these five concepts. Additionally, where appropriate, aspects of the Character Education Partnership's *Eleven Principles of Effective Character Education* (Lickona, Schaps, & Lewis, 2010) will be identified and related to specific elements described below.

EFFECTIVE METHODS

Table 14.1 presents all the methods for which any of the seven reviews/meta-analyses report empirical support. It also clusters them according to the five PRIME meta-strategies.

Table 14.1 Research-based Practices

METHODS		WWCE	WWCE+	Lovat	CASEL	EPPI	Hattie	Marzano
Reviews	Outcome	Char/Acad	Character	Values	SEL/Academic	Academic	Academic	Academic
	Input	Character	Character	Values	SEL	Citizenship	Mixed	Academic
PRIORITIZATION	Professional Development	✓	✓				✓	
	Common Language			✓				
	School-wide	✓	✓	✓			✓	✓
	Implementation							
RELATIONSHIPS	Interactive pedagogy	✓	✓	✓	✓	✓	✓	✓
	Family/Community Partic.	✓	✓	✓				✓
	Building Trust	✓	✓					✓
	Focus on relationships							✓
	Nurturance	✓	✓					✓
INTRINSIC MOTIVATION	Real/Relevant curriculum					✓		
	Service to others	✓	✓	✓	✓			✓
	Progressive Beh Mgmt.	✓	✓	✓				
MODELING	Modeling	✓	✓	✓				
EMPOWERMENT	Empowerment	✓	✓	✓	✓			✓
	Direct instruction			✓				✓
OTHER	Inquiry-based education		✓					✓
	Recognition						✓	✓
	High expectations						✓	✓
	Safe Schools						✓	✓
	Reflection			✓				

Notes
WWC: Berkowitz & Bier (2005a); WWCE: Berkowitz (2011); LOVAT: Lovat et al. (2009); EPPI: EPPI (2005); HATTIE: Hattie (2009); CASEL: Durlak et al. (2011); MARZANO (2003a, 2003b, 2007).

Prioritization

The importance of authentic prioritization of character education is represented by three research-supported practices:

- professional development;
- common language;
- school-wide emphasis.

Professional development. Professional development was reported as a research-based practice by Berkowitz (2011), Berkowitz and Bier (2005a), and Hattie (2009). Berkowitz and Bier reported that all 33 effective character education programs they identified included professional development either as a mandatory component or as an option. Hattie reports a meta-analysis by Timperley et al. (2007) which identified seven characteristics of professional development that leads to student change, including sustained training, training by outside experts, challenges to teachers' current concepts and language, teachers talking to teachers, and leadership support.

Common language. Lovat et al. (2009) were the only ones to specifically cite common language as a best practice, "the use by teachers, students and often parents of this common language not only led to greater understanding of the targeted values but also provided a positive focus for reflecting on and redirecting children's inappropriate behaviour" (p. 33). Anecdotally schools frequently report a lack of common language as an impediment to optimal implementation, or the development of shared language as a tipping point in moving their initiative forward. Many research-supported programs include their own terminology, often including a list of character outcomes. The Character Education Partnership (Beland, 2003; Character Education Partnership, 2010) strongly encourages schools/districts to identify a set of core ethical values as the framework and language upon which to build a comprehensive character education initiative. The first two principles focus almost exclusively on this approach.

School-wide emphasis. Making character education an organizational priority includes implementing across the entire organization, rather than a single curricular strand, for only some students, or in other ways as an isolated strategy. School-wide implementation was reported by Berkowitz (2011), Berkowitz and Bier (2005a), Lovat et al. (2009), Hattie (2009), and Marzano (2003a, 2003b, 2007). Lovat et al. (2009) actually identified a set of school-wide variables including incorporation in school policy and discussion of values at school-wide assemblies. The Character Education Partnership's (2010) third principle emphasizes the comprehensive implementation of character education across all school elements. Some effective character education programs explicitly include school-wide implementation emphasis (e.g., Caring School Community, Developmental Studies Center, 1994). Berkowitz (2011; Berkowitz et al., 2012) has further emphasized the critical role of school leadership in effective implementation.

Relationships

The promotion of relationships is an element in five evidence-based strategies:

- interactive pedagogy
- family and/or community participation
- promoting trust

- directly targeting relationships
- nurturance.

Interactive pedagogy. Berkowitz and Bier (2005a) identified this cluster of pedagogical strategies to be very common in effective character education programs. Such methods focus on learning and development promoted through predominantly student-to-student interactions. Interactive strategies include peer tutoring, cross-age initiatives, cooperative learning, peer tutoring, etc. In fact, this was the only strategy identified in all seven reviews. Durlak et al. (2011) focused on active learning, EPPI (2005) on engagement and discussion, Lovat et al. (2009) on relational learning, Hattie (2009) on relational learning and cooperative learning, and Marzano (2003a, 2003b, 2007) on relational learning, class meetings, and cooperative learning. Berkowitz and Bier also identified a large set of studies demonstrating the impact of moral dilemma discussion on the development of moral reasoning competencies.

Family and/or community participation. Applying a character education initiative beyond the typical stakeholders in a school or district expands relationship-building to a broader range of individuals and groups. Most commonly these are family members, most notably parents of students, and other related community members (e.g., law enforcement, local government, local businesses, etc.). Strategically encouraging such extra-school relationships was identified as an effective practice by Berkowitz (2011), Berkowitz and Bier (2005a), Lovat et al. (2009), and Marzano (2003a, 2007). In particular, Lovat et al. emphasized communication with families and Marzano emphasized recognition of community members and inclusion of families in behavior management. The Character Education Partnership's (2010) 10th Principle supports engaging "families and community members as partners." Parental involvement in particular can be implemented at many levels, from parent as audience to parent as client to the more desirable parent as partner (Berkowitz & Bier, 2005c). In the latter case, parents partner with the school in designing, implementing, and/or evaluating character education. Santiago, Ferrara, and Quinn (2012) offer an excellent model of comprehensive community-school partnership combined with character education.

Trust. Whereas an intentional focus on building trust per se was identified only by Berkowitz (2011), it has been a major focus of a set of disparate educational models of relevance. It has been invoked as a critical element in school leadership in particular (Tschannen-Moran, 2004) and the adult culture of a school (Bryk & Schneider, 2002) as well as foundational for developmental discipline (Howes & Ritchie, 2002; Watson, 2003).

Relationship-building. Marzano (2003b) directly cites the strategic intentional fostering of healthy relationships between student and teacher as one of the three aspects of effective classroom management (along with rules/procedures and disciplinary interventions). Watson (2003) also includes this (along with student–student relationships and using behavior incidents as opportunities for growth and learning) as the foundation of developmental discipline. One rather unique and effective character education program, Roots of Empathy, incorporates relationships at multiple levels by bringing a mother and her infant, with a trained facilitator, to classrooms (Gordon, 2005), thereby studying parent–infant relationships but also developing a relationship between the students and visitors over repeated visits/lessons.

Nurturance. Despite the foundational importance of love/care in child development, it is not widely studied in educational research. Berkowitz and Grych (1998,

2000) found it to be a key element in both parenting and teaching for character. Other researchers have found this to be true in elementary school (Howe & Ritchie, 2003), middle school (Wentzel, 2002) and high school (Gregory et al., 2010). A growing body of educational theory and philosophy has also focused on an ethic of caring (e.g., Noddings, 1992). Nevertheless, it was only cited in two of the reviews (Berkowitz, 2011; Marzano, 2007). Marzano specifically encourages "behaviors that indicate affection for each student" (p. 155) such as greeting students at the door (cf. Urban, 2008).

Intrinsic Motivation

The internalization of motivation (Althof & Berkowitz, 2013; Streight, 2013) is a central goal of developmental education, particularly developmental education focusing on the development of pro-social characteristics. The Character Education Partnership's (2010) 7th Principle is to foster self-motivation in students. This focus was manifested in the reviews in three research-supported strategies:

- Real and relevant education
- Service to others
- Progressive behavior management.

Real and relevant education. One way to promote the internalization of values and motives is to make education personally meaningful for students. This strategy was identified by both EPPI (2005) and Marzano (2003a, 2007).

Service to others. Another way to increase the likelihood that students will internalize pro-social values is to provide for them the opportunity to serve others, something that is common in character education. Service was identified by Berkowitz (2011), Berkowitz and Bier (2005a), Durlak et al. (2011), and Lovat et al. (2009). It is also the Character Education Partnership's (2010) 5th Principle. Service learning, in particular, links service to others with the school's curriculum, and this has been shown to impact both character development and academic achievement (Billig, 2002).

Progressive behavior management. The concept of character education naturally invokes student behavior, especially misbehavior, and hence interfaces frequently with the challenge of managing student misbehavior in school settings. Despite the wealth of data on ineffective behavior management techniques, most of which are based on an extrinsic theory of behavior change (cf. Deci & Ryan, 2002), educators persist in relying on such approaches (Berkowitz, 2012a; Streight, 2013), rather than on more progressive approaches such as developmental discipline (Bear, 2005; Danforth & Smith, 2005; Watson, 2003). Three of the reviews identified more progressive, developmental, and intrinsically-based behavior management as an effective practice (Berkowitz, 2011; Berkowitz & Bier, 2005a; Marzano, 2003a, 2003b, 2007).

Modeling

Developmental research has long supported the power of imitation and modeling in child development. Three reviews reinforced this emphasis (Berkowitz, 2011; Berkowitz & Bier, 2005a; Lovat et al., 2009). Ideally models are those with whom students have healthy relationships (e.g., teachers). However, there may also be others in the community, historical figures, or even fictional characters in the literature curriculum.

Empowerment

Given that a fundamental purpose of schooling, in democratic societies in particular, is the socialization of youth as future citizens, creating schools that embody democratic practices and principles is critical (Dewey, 1944). Berkowitz (2011, 2012b) has labeled the general focus on empowering educational practices as a "pedagogy of empowerment" and it applies to all stakeholders in a school (administrators, teachers, support staff, students, parents, etc.). Nonetheless, empowerment was identified only by Berkowitz (2011) and Marzano (2003a, 2003b, 2007) as an effective practice. Marzano (2007), for example, identified student voice in setting learning goals and designing educational tasks. Education tends toward hierarchical, authoritarian (albeit benevolent) approaches and tends to strain against the authentic empowerment of stakeholders and the flattening of governance structures (Berkowitz, 2012b).

Beyond PRIME

Six additional strategies that do not fit clearly in any of the PRIME components were also identified as research-supported practices.

Direct Instruction. It is not surprising that education for character includes teaching about character. This tends to focus on teaching character concepts, such as virtues and values that are often the most salient aspect of a school's initiative. It may also focus on examples (e.g., exemplars, role models) in the curriculum or supplemental to the curriculum. Four of the reviews identified some form of direct instruction as an effective practice. This approach was either direct instruction about character (Berkowitz, 2011; Berkowitz & Bier, 2005a) or values (Lovat et al., 2009) or instruction in social-emotional competencies (Berkowitz, 2011; Durlak et al., 2011).

Inquiry-based Learning. The two reviews of specifically academic-focused strategies (Hattie, 2009; Marzano, 2007) both identified inquiry-based learning as an effective practice. While such approaches have been used effectively in character education (e.g., Berger, 2003), they tend not to be included in research studies of character education programs and methods.

Recognition. Marzano (2003a, 2003b, 2007) explicitly recommends recognition of achievement as an effective strategy.

Expectations. Setting high expectations is a core element of both parenting for (Berkowitz & Grych, 1998) and educating for (Berkowitz & Grych, 2000; Wentzel, 2002) character development, but it is not studied widely in the literature and hence was only identified by Berkowitz (2011) and Marzano (2003a, 2003b, 2007). Merely setting high expectations, however, is not likely to be adequate, as supportive conditions need to be in place along with pedagogies that scaffold students' underdeveloped competencies to allow them to achieve excellent performance (Berger, 2003; Turner & Berkowitz, 2005; Urban, 2008). This includes setting clear expectations, checking in on progress, allowing multiple attempts at success, offering constructive feedback, allowing play relevant to the task, etc.

Safe Schools. Despite all the emphasis on school safety (e.g., bullying, violence prevention) and the fact that the major US Department of Education division charged with character, civics, and social emotional learning is the Office of Safe and Drug Free Schools, only one review identified school safety as a best practice, and it was not one of the character-focused reviews, but rather Marzano's (2003a) review of best academic practices. In a study of academic outcomes of character education, Benninga, Berkowitz, Kuehn, and Smith (2003) found safe and clean schools to be a clear predictor of academic achievement.

Reflection. Reflection is an excellent means of promoting and sustaining understanding and retention, and this applies to both academic learning (Marzano, 2003a, 2003b, 2007) and character development (Lovat et al., 2009).

ACADEMIC VS. CHARACTER/VALUES/CIVICS PRACTICES

One of the more frequently asked questions is whether those reviews that focused on academic achievement (EPPI, 2005; Hattie, 2009; Marzano, 2003a, 2003b, 2007) identified different effective practices than did those focusing specifically on character, values, social-emotional, or citizenship outcomes (Berkowitz, 2011; Berkowitz & Bier, 2005a; Durlak et al., 2011; Lovat et al., 2009). It is important to note that this dichotomy is far from pure. Berkowitz and Bier included academic achievement as an outcome variable, Durlak et al. focused heavily on academic outcome variables, EPPI examined citizenship programs but only looked at academic outcomes, and Hattie's review of meta-analyses included character and related programs (see Table 14.1). Nonetheless, the emphases are distinguishable and the studies reviewed varied widely depending on the primary emphasis of the review.

Despite the differential emphasis on academic versus developmental outcomes, the vast majority of practices were cited in both academic-focused and character-focused studies. It was our belief that "good character education is good education" that led to the initial inclusion of those academic reviews in this analysis. This intuition was vindicated by the results. Of the 19 practices identified (see Table 14.1), 12 were cited in both academic-focused and character-focused reviews. Given the fact that three of the reviews were more academic in focus and four were more character-focused, it is not surprising that more of the non-overlapping practices were cited by the character reviews.

There were six practices that were cited only by one or more of the character reviews: direct teaching; setting learning goals; using common language; modeling; service; trust. Interestingly, the first two could be argued to be more academic in focus, yet they were only cited by character-focused reviews. In a similarly counter-intuitive fashion, only one practice was cited only by academic-focused reviews. Marzano (2003a), the most purely academic-focused review, was the only study to cite safe schools, which can be argued to be more closely aligned with character concepts (Benninga et al., 2003).

CONCLUSION

Sufficient research has been amassed to allow for the examination of best practices in character education, and related fields such as values, citizenship, and social-emotional learning. Furthermore, the overlap in these domains of outcomes and methods with studies of best academic achievement practices allows for the examination of an even larger body of research. In so doing, this review has looked at seven research reviews/meta-analyses of relevance and has identified 19 research-based practices for both promoting academic achievement and character development.

Interestingly, the practices that promote academic achievement and character education are predominantly overlapping, and when they are not, the differences are both counter-intuitive and probably artifactual of the variables of focus in particular studies or areas of research.

This set of practices provides a broad-based and research-driven foundation for building effective schools, districts, and classrooms for both the promotion of academic achievement and for fostering the development of character, values, citizenship, and social-emotional maturity.

NOTES

* The authors would like to thank the John Templeton Foundation, SD Bechtel Foundation, and Harry S. Singer Foundation for their support of this work.

REFERENCES

Althof, W., & Berkowitz, M.W. (2013). Character and civic education as a source or moral motivation. In K. Heinrichs, F. Oser, & T. Lovat (Eds.), *Handbook of moral motivation*. Boston: Sense Publishers.

Bear, G.G. (2005). *Developing self-discipline and preventing and correcting misbehavior*. Boston: Allyn & Bacon.

Beland, K. (2003). *Eleven principles sourcebook: How to achieve quality character education in K-12 schools*. Washington, D.C.: Character Education Partnership.

Benninga, J.S., Berkowitz, M.W., Kuehn, P., & Smith, K. (2003). The relationship of character education implementation and academic achievement in elementary schools. *Journal of Research in Character Education, 1*, 19–32.

Berg, H.K.M. (2003). *Values-based character education: A meta-analysis of program effects on student knowledge, attitudes, and behaviors*. Unpublished master's thesis, California State University, Fresno.

Berger, R. (2003). *An ethic of excellence: Building a culture of craftsmanship with students*. Portsmouth, NH: Heinemann.

Berkowitz, M.W. (1997). The complete moral person: Anatomy and formation. In J.M. Dubois (Ed.), *Moral issues in psychology: Personalist contributions to selected problems* (pp. 11–41). Lanham, MD: University Press of America.

Berkowitz, M.W. (2009). Teaching in your PRIME. In D. Streight (Ed.), *Good things to do: Expert suggestions for fostering goodness in kids* (pp. 9–14). Portland: Council for Spiritual and Ethical Education Publications.

Berkowitz, M.W. (2011). Leading schools of character. In A.M. Blankstein & P.D. Houston (Eds.), *The soul of educational leadership series. Vol. 9. Leadership for social justice and democracy in our schools* (pp. 93–121). Thousand Oaks, CA: Corwin.

Berkowitz, M.W. (2012a). *You can't teach through a rat: And other epiphanies for educators*. Chapel Hill, NC: Character Development Publishing.

Berkowitz, M.W. (2012b). Moral and character education. In K.R. Harris, S. Graham, & T. Urdan (Eds.), *APA educational psychology handbook: Vol. 2. Individual differences, cultural variations, and contextual factors in educational psychology* (pp. 247–264). Washington, DC: American Psychological Association.

Berkowitz, M.W., & Bier, M.C. (2005a). *What works in character education: A research-driven guide for educators*. Washington, DC: Character Education Partnership.

Berkowitz, M.W., & Bier, M.C. (2005b). The interpersonal roots of character education. In D.K. Lapsley & F.C. Power (Eds.), *Character psychology and character education* (pp. 268–285). Notre Dame, IN: University of Notre Dame Press.

Berkowitz, M.W., & Bier, M.C. (2005c). Character education: Parents as partners. *Educational Leadership, 63*, 64–69.

Berkowitz, M.W., & Bustamante, A. (2013). Prioritizing the promotion of student flourishing in schools. *Korean Journal of Educational Policy, 2013*, 7–20.

Berkowitz, M.W., & Grych, J. (1998). Fostering goodness: Teaching parents to facilitate children's moral development. *Journal of Moral Education, 27*, 371–391.

Berkowitz, M.W., & Grych, J.H. (2000). Early character development and education. *Early Education and Development, 11*, 55–72.

Berkowitz, M.W., Pelster, K., & Johnston, A. (2012). Leading in the middle: A tale of pro-social education reform in two principals and two middle schools. In P. Brown, M. Corrigan, & A. Higgins-D'Alessandro (Eds.), *The handbook of prosocial education: Vol. 2* (pp. 619–626). Lanham, MD: Rowman & Littlefield.

Berkowitz, M.W., Sherblom, S.A., Bier, M.C., & Battistich, V. (2006). Educating for positive youth development.

In M. Killen & J.G. Smetana (Eds.), *Handbook of moral development* (pp. 683–701). Mahwah, NJ: Lawrence Erlbaum & Associates.

Billig, S.H. (2002). Support for K-12 service-learning practice: A brief review of the research. *Educational Horizons, Summer,* 184–189.

Bryk, A., & Schneider, B.L. (2002). *Trust in schools: A core resource for improvement.* New York: Russell Sage Foundation.

Character Education Partnership (2010). *11 principles of effective character education: A framework for success.* Washington, DC: Character Education Partnership.

Danforth, S., & Smith, T.J. (2005). *Engaging troubling students: A constructivist approach.* Thousand Oaks, CA: Corwin Press.

Deci, E.L., & Ryan, R.M. (Eds.). (2002). *Handbook of self-determination theory.* Rochester, NY: University of Rochester Press.

Devaney, E., O'Brien, M.U., Resnik, H., Keister, S., & Weissberg, R.P. (2006). *Sustainable schoolwide social and emotional learning (SEL).* Chicago: Collaborative for Academic, Social and Emotional Learning.

Developmental Studies Center (1994). *At home in our schools: A guide to schoolwide activities that build community.* Oakland, CA: Developmental Studies Center.

Dewey, J. (1944). *Democracy and education.* New York: Free Press.

Durlak, J.A., Weissberg, R.P., Dymnicki, A.B., Taylor, R.D., & Schellinger, K.B. (2011). The impact of enhancing students' social and emotional learning: A meta-analysis of school-based universal interventions. *Child Development, 82,* 405–432.

EPPI (2005). *A systematic review of the impact of citizenship education on student learning and achievement.* EPPI-Centre, University of London (England).

Gordon, M. (2005). *Roots of empathy: Changing the world child by child.* Toronto: Thomas Allen Publishers.

Gregory, A., Cornell, D. Fan, X., Sheras, P., Shih, T., & Huang, F. (2010). Authoritative school discipline: High school practices associated with lower bullying and victimization. *Journal of Educational Psychology, 102,* 483–496.

Hattie, J. (2009). *Visible learning: A synthesis of over 800 meta-analyses relating to achievement.* New York: Routledge.

Howes, C., & Richie, S. (2002). *A matter of trust: Connecting teachers and learners in early childhood classrooms.* New York: Teachers College Press.

Kam, C.M., Greenberg, M.T., & Walls, C.T. (2003). Examining the role of implementation quality in school-based prevention using the PATHS curriculum. *Prevention Science, 4,* 55–62.

Lickona, T., Schaps, E., & Lewis, C. (2010). *CEP's eleven principles of effective character education.* Washington, D.C.: Character Education Partnership.

Lovat, T., Toomey, R., Dally, K., & Clement, N. (2009). *Project to test and measure the impact of values education on student effects.* Newcastle, Australia: University of Newcastle.

Marzano, R.J. (2003a). *What works in schools: Translating research into action.* Alexandria, VA: Association for Supervision and Curriculum Development.

Marzano, R.J. (2003b). *Classroom management that works: Research-based strategies for every teacher.* Alexandria, VA: Association for Supervision and Curriculum Development.

Marzano, R.J. (2007). *The art and science of teaching: A comprehensive framework for effective instruction.* Alexandria, VA: Association for Supervision and Curriculum Development.

Noddings, N. (1992). *The challenge to care in schools.* New York: Teachers College Press.

Santiago, E., Ferrara, J., & Quinn, J. (2012). *Whole child, whole school: Applying theory to practice in a community school.* Lanham, MD: Rowan Littlefield.

Smagorinsky, P., & Taxel, J. (2005). *The discourse of character education: Culture wars in the classroom.* Mahwah, NJ: Lawrence Erlbaum.

Streight, D. (2013). *Breaking into the heart of character: Self-determined moral action and academic motivation.* Portland OR: The Center for Spiritual and Ethical Education.

Tschannen-Moran, M. (2004). *Trust matters: Leadership for successful schools.* San Francisco: Jossey-Bass.

Turner, V.D., & Berkowitz, M.W. (2005). Scaffolding morality: Positioning a socio-cultural construct. *New Ideas in Psychology, 23,* 174–184.

Urban, H. (2008). *Lessons from the classroom: 20 things good teachers do.* Redwood, CA: Great Lessons Press.

Watson, M. (2003). *Learning to trust.* San Francisco: Jossey-Bass.

Wentzel, K.R. (2002). Are effective teachers like good parents? Teaching styles and student adjustment in early adolescence. *Child Development, 73,* 287–301.

Part III

Schools-Based Best Practices

15

PEDAGOGY FOR THE WHOLE CHILD

The Developmental Studies Center's Approach to Academic, Moral, and Character Education

Peter Brunn

> The most reliable way to improve schools is to improve curriculum and instruction and to improve the conditions in which teachers work and children learn, rather than endlessly squabbling over how school systems should be organized, managed, and controlled.
>
> (Ravitch, 2010)

In many ways it seems as if we have been arguing about what and how teachers should teach since the turn of the last century (Kleibard, 1995). Today, we are dealing with the effects of the past decade of the No Child Left Behind legislation while diving headfirst into the age of the Common Core State Standards. We hear politicians bark, see districts react, and feel the impact of teachers and children left in the middle trying to figure out how to make sense of it all. At the Developmental Studies Center (DSC), we have spent the past 33 years struggling with how to help schools navigate these turbulent waters. We researched how to best support the academic, social, and ethical development of our young people. We investigated how to foster children into the principled, thoughtful, engaged adults we hope them to become.

In the first edition of this book, my late colleague Vic Battistich described the origins and evolution of the Child Development Project (CDP), DSC's first endeavor to support student's positive social, moral, and academic development. (Battistich, 2008). This chapter picks up where Vic left off by tracing the pedagogical development of DSC into a broader and more expansive model of instruction. What we have developed as a result of this journey represents a path schools can take to support the full needs—academic, social, and emotional—of the children they serve.

A PORTRAIT OF OUR STUDENTS

At the writing of this chapter, 45 states have adopted the Common Core State Standards (CCSS) (National Governors Association Center for Best Practices & Council of Chief State School Officers, 2010). With so many states adopting, and with such high stakes tied to their implementation, any discussion of teaching and learning must certainly include mention of them. While controversy surrounds how these standards will be implemented and assessed, one of the helpful elements they provide is a compelling portrait of the learner who is college and career ready. The standards state that, "As students advance through the grades and master the standards in reading, writing, speaking, listening, and language, they are able to exhibit with increasing fullness and regularity these capacities of the literate individual" (National Governors Association Center for Best Practices & Council of Chief State School Officers, 2010). Through mastery of the standards students:

- Demonstrate independence;
- Build strong content knowledge;
- Respond to the varying demands of audience, task, purpose, and discipline;
- Comprehend as well as critique;
- Value evidence;
- Use technology and digital media strategically and capably;
- Come to understand other perspectives and cultures.

While these are certainly valuable skills that are necessary for twenty-first century jobs, this portrait seems incomplete if we are to truly support our children as they grow into adults. To capture a more comprehensive portrait of our students, my colleagues and I often begin our work with teachers with a visualization activity. We have them picture the young girl jumping rope in the schoolyard, or the boy who comes in to class a few minutes late every day. We then ask them to project that image forward 15 years or so and try to see that student as a community member, neighbor, soldier, manager, lawyer, health worker, politician, and parent. Then we ask them to create a picture of the skills, qualities, and traits that student needs to possess, in order to be ready to tackle the myriad roles and responsibilities they will inhabit. The list often contains words from the CCSS portrait above, but it also contains words such as, empathetic, caring, resourceful, engaged, principled, focused, passionate, gritty, creative, reflective, hard working, problem solver, resilient, etc. This picture represents a more complete hope-filled representation of our future. This image serves as a beacon keeping the work we do in schools focused on the ultimate outcomes we desire.

Teachers are ultimately responsible for both images from above. They need to ensure students master the rigorous academic standards, but they also need to help them develop, the other, what the author Paul Tough calls "non-cognitive" skills (Tough, 2012). Moreover, these skills are essential for students' eventual success in life. Our emotions, skills, experiences, and knowledge all work together in one package. Unfortunately, in many settings these non-cognitive skills are not nurtured together but seen as separate discrete things. This is problematic because it is not like students leave their emotions on the shelf above the coat rack outside the classroom. Instead, they come into our rooms as whole bodies possessing full hearts and minds. Supporting and nourishing the whole child must therefore be at the heart of the work of schools. Since its inceptions, the Developmental Studies Center has focused our research, teacher professional development, and curriculum development on this mission—fostering students' academic, social, and ethical development.

NOURISHING THE HEART AND MIND

This concept of educating the "Whole Child" is not a new one. John Dewey was arguing for something similar in the early stages of the last century (Dewey, 1938). More recently, the influential non-profit organization ASCD launched the Whole Child Initiative in 2007. This ambitious initiative defines this work as, "Each child, in each school, in each of our communities deserves to be healthy, safe, engaged, supported, and challenged. That's what a whole child approach to learning, teaching, and community engagement really is" (ASCD, n.d., "The Whole Child"). Due to ASCD's efforts there are signs that policy makers are beginning to lend their support for this effort. In Arkansas, for example, the governor recently signed a bill into law promoting Whole Child Education (ASCD, n.d., "Arkansas Governor Beebe Signs...").

In addition to the work above, there is also a growing body of research demonstrating that expanding schools' focus to include social and emotional learning greatly benefits student development (Thapa, Cohen, Guffey, & Higgins-D'Alessandro, 2013). Indeed there is evidence that students actually increase academic achievement because of this implementation of SEL programs (Durlak, Weissberg, Dymnicki, Taylor, & Schellinger, 2011).

The difficult thing for schools is not deciding whether or not to include social and emotional learning with the academic curriculum. The challenge is trying to figure out how to do it.

PEDAGOGY FOR THE WHOLE CHILD

DSC's pedagogy, which integrates academic and social development into curricula for teachers, was formed over the past 33 years of research and experience in schools. It has its roots in DSC's first program the Child Development Project (CDP) but has evolved greatly since then. This evolution of our pedagogy comes from close analysis of our own work in schools as well as the context schools are working under.

As we examined the data from our six-district study of CDP for example (Solomon, Battistich, Watson, Schaps, & Lewis, 2000), we learned that while there were positive program effects in the high change schools, effects that persisted even into middle school (Battistich, Schaps, & Wilson, 2004), we were still frustrated that the program was not more fully implemented by all of the schools in the study. Additionally because of the pressures of testing and of high stakes accountability (especially after the 2001 passage of the No Child Left Behind Legislation) we have seen a reduction of class time for anything other than what is tested (Darling-Hammond, 2010; Ravitch, 2010). Thus, in many schools teachers don't feel they have the license to focus on the social and emotional development of children.

A review of our own research by DSC's founder Eric Schaps led us to believe we needed to revise our current offerings and expand programming into the most focused upon academic subject area of schooling—literacy. In his review Dr. Schaps found that a revised CDP program, with its expanded reading-skills instruction, will be more responsive to students' academic needs and more feasible for a wide range of schools to implement. And we believe it will continue to enhance students' sense of community in school and to yield the wide-ranging, enduring benefits that follow from such a focus.

(Schaps, Battistich, & Solomon, 2004)

Because of this and other analyses, DSC revised CDP and created new reading and writing programs.

Our current programming now includes a reading comprehension program *Making Meaning: Strategies that Build Comprehension and Community* (Developmental Studies Center, 2008); a writing program, *Being a Writer: Craft, Conventions and Community* (Developmental Studies Center, 2007), and a classroom and schoolwide community building program, *Caring School Community* (Developmental Studies Center, 2009) (this is a revised version of CDP). Taken together these programs illuminate a path schools can take to focus on educating the whole child. The core principles of the pedagogy (which is contained in the programs above) provide schools with a blueprint for deepening academic learning while supporting students' prosocial development. These core principles are:

- A caring, safe, and supportive learning community;
- Academic instruction is integrated with social and ethical learning;
- Students are intrinsically motivated;
- Learning situations are organized for students to do the thinking.

A Caring, Safe, and Supportive Learning Community

There is much evidence that creating a safe and supportive community provides enormous benefits for children both socially and academically (Durlak et al., 2011; Schaps, 2005; Zins, Bloodworth, Weissberg, & Walberg, 2004). School climate also plays a critical role in why some schools are more successful than others (Voight, Austin, & Hanson, 2013). When students experience school as a safe and supportive place they reap some powerful outcomes including:

- Reduced aggressiveness, violence, delinquency, and drug and alcohol use;
- Increased social competence and positive behavior;
- More concern for others;
- Stronger connection to school and higher educational aspirations;
- Increased academic motivation and achievement.

(Learning First Alliance, 2001)

An evaluation of DSC's community building program *Caring School Community* (Marshall & Caldwell, 2007) found similar results. In that study the program schools showed:

- Safer learning communities
- Increased staff collaboration
- Improved classroom strategies

- Improved student discipline
- Improved academic achievement.

In our work with schools DSC builds caring safe and supportive environments through the following ways.

Teambuilding Activities—Each year begins with teambuilding activities that get students talking and interacting with one another. These activities are designed to help students get to know each other, bring students together around a common purpose, and start the process for building a caring community. Activities help students:

- Learn each other's names
- Get to know one another
- Stay connected with one another.

Teambuilders might be done after long breaks, when new students arrive in the classroom, or when seating arrangements change.

Class Meetings—This is the core component of the program. Through class meetings students can plan for upcoming events or make decisions on how certain classroom activities might be run. They are also valuable places for students to solve problems and handle conflict. Class meeting topics might include but are not limited to:

- Preparing for a new student or a guest teacher
- Planning a study trip
- Setting classroom norms
- Discussing bullying, teasing, and fighting
- Discussing playground challenges.

Cross-Age Buddies Program—Our buddies program helps build caring relationships across a school. These may be academic or recreational activities. The activity helps older and younger students take a responsibility for their role in the relationship and teaches them valuable interaction skills.

Homeside Activities—This collection of activities is designed to stimulate conversations between the students and their family and to connect home and school. Every activity begins in the classroom, continues at home, and then ends back in the classroom. The activities are designed to give students an opportunity to share their school lives with their family and their family life with the school.

Schoolwide Community Building Activities—This component helps link the students, parents, teachers, and other adults in the school. The activities focus on building relationships and reinventing traditional schoolwide activities.

Taken together, these program components help teachers establish a caring climate for their students. They also provide the opportunity for students to learn valuable social skills necessary to grow and interact with one another.

Academic Instruction is Integrated with Social and Ethical Learning

DSC's curriculum is designed around the idea that social and academic development are interconnected. In a typical day in school, students have to negotiate with each other in a wide variety of circumstances. They work together constructing a science experiment, sharing math manipulatives, discussing books with partners, and growing new ideas for their writing. All of these subject areas lend themselves to explicit teaching of social skills and are full of opportunities for reflection on behavior. Moreover, integrating social and academic development provides students with the opportunity to develop their social skills in the context of their academic work. This provides authentic reasons to teach, reinforce, and reflect on the social skills students need to work in groups, in pairs, and to share their thinking in whole class settings. The researchers Stephanie Jones and Suzanne Bouffard have postulated that social and emotional learning done in isolation only has had generally modest effects. Integrating social and emotional learning into the academic curricula may be necessary in order for SEL to have a significant impact on student development (Jones & Bouffard, 2012).

Integrating this work, however, needs careful planning in order to be thoughtfully integrated into the curriculum (Brunn, 2010). In our lessons we suggest teachers do this in three key ways:

- **Ensure lessons have both social and academic goals**—Most programs contain learning objectives. These are essential to planning effective instruction. We take this a step further. In addition to having academic objectives, our lessons also include social objectives. In a reading lesson, for example, an academic objective students have might be using evidence from the text to justify their opinions about what was read. The social focus for the same lesson might involve students using prompts to learn to agree and disagree respectfully.
- **Add partner work and group work when appropriate for the academic activity**— Not every lesson has places for students to interact or opportunities for them to work on social skills. If we want students to see the efficacy of the social skills they are learning, then they need authentic opportunities to use them. In the example above, the teacher knows that if students are learning to justify opinions using textual evidence, then there will be opportunities for students to challenge each other's thinking. This text talk provides the opportunity to not only deepen the academic learning, but also provides a real context to learn how to agree and disagree respectfully.
- **Structure lessons to include social skill instruction and reflection**—Having a predictable time in each lesson to teach or reinforce a social skill ensures that social and emotional learning does not get pushed out of the curriculum. With so much content to cover, teachers feel pressed to get the entire curriculum covered causing social development to be left out (Jones & Bouffard, 2012). We structure our lessons so that the first part of every lesson either introduces a social skill or reinforces a skill that has already been taught. At the conclusion of each lesson, the teacher then asks students to reflect on how it went that day (Schaps & Brunn, 2008). So if they are working on the social objective agreeing or disagreeing respectfully, the teacher might ask, "What was challenging about having a different opinion than the group (or their partner)." Or, they might ask, "What worked today when we tried using our prompts?"

Having intentional social goals allows us to scaffold students learning over time. We can introduce the appropriate social skills when they are most relevant in the curriculum. Students see the utility of using the skills instead of de-contextualized skills learned in isolation.

Intrinsically Motivated Students

Anyone who has ever assigned a piece of writing to students knows how important intrinsic motivation is. The writing of a student who is simply going through the motions, just to comply with the teacher's requirement looks much different than the writing from a student who is committed to expressing her idea and actively trying to move the reader. Intrinsic motivation is therefore an essential part of DSC's work in schools. It is critical because, as Larry Ferlazzo relates, "This kind of motivation drives students to put effort into learning because they see that it will help them achieve their personal goals" (Ferlazzo, 2013, p. 3).

It can be tough for teachers to embrace the idea that, no matter how good their lessons are; the student decides what, when, and if, they will learn the desired content. The learning happens within the child. Intrinsic motivation has a great deal to do with this. Luckily, there is much schools can do to impact the level of their students' internal motivation. We have learned that when students' basic needs for autonomy, belonging, and competence are met their level of engagement rises (Deci, Vallerand, Pelletier, & Ryan, 1991; Schaps et al., 2004). At DSC we attempt to meet these needs in the following ways:

- Autonomy—In reading, for example, students get to choose books by favorite authors and in genres they have strong interest in reading. In writing, students learn to choose their own topic, formulate their unique opinions, and get to share their writing in meaningful purposeful ways. In DSC classrooms, students also have a voice in solving classroom problems while getting opportunities to plan key events and making decisions on classroom procedures.
- Belonging—Through teambuilding, class meetings, buddies activities, and lots of opportunities to interact with classmates in academic lessons, students develop a sense of connectedness to school.
- Competence—By providing an engaging and developmentally appropriate curriculum, students get opportunities to develop skills, and to challenge themselves.

Learning Situation Organized For Students to do the Thinking

John Dewey once asked, "How many students, for example, were rendered callous to ideas, and how many lost the impetus to learn because of the way in which learning was experienced by them?" (Dewey, 1938, p. 15). Even though he wrote this almost 75 years ago, the question seems appropriate even for today's students. The fact still remains that how students experience the instruction in our classrooms makes an enormous difference in their engagement and in their learning.

If we are to shift students from the passive role of receiver of information, and toward an active role of investigator, then teachers must shift their teaching "stance" (Brunn, 2010, p. 72). This shift in stance involves moving into the role of facilitator of student thinking. When student thinking is put at the center of our instruction, it means that teachers talk less and students talk, write, and do more. The facilitator's role involves doing the following:

- Listening carefully to student thinking
- Asking open-ended questions
- Using cooperative structures
- Probing student thinking
- Utilizing wait time
- Using non-judgmental responses.

In addition to the points above, supporting student thinking means valuing mistakes. If we are doing our job as facilitators, we are presenting many challenging and complex problems and ideas for students to wrestle with. This means that they will make lots of mistakes. These mistakes are essential for student success in school. As Eleanor Duckworth says, "What you do about what you don't know is, in the final analysis, what determines what you will ultimately know" (Duckworth E., 1987, p. 68).

The challenge, however, is that most students do not value mistakes. In most schools only right answers count. Many of us suffer from this fixed mindset and carry with us the notion that making mistakes is somehow wrong (Dweck, 2006). If, however, we are to put student thinking at the center of our lessons, then we must change this paradigm in our classrooms. We need to set up experiences where students struggle and have to work through that struggle. There is evidence that students benefit greatly from persevering through difficult mistakes and working on a problem over time. Staying with a difficult task may be what separates students who excel and those who don't. Angela Duckworth calls this trait "grit" (Duckworth, Peterson, Matthews, & Kelly, 2007).

The programs at DSC are designed to support teachers in shifting into the stance of a facilitator. We have found that with scaffolded materials support along with in-classroom professional development, teachers can put student thinking at the center of their instruction.

CONCLUSION

Since 1980, the Developmental Studies Center has developed programs, and conducted professional development in schools across the country in order to better foster students' academic, social, and ethical development. We know that attending to the needs of the whole child is an essential yet difficult task in the tempest of today's educational climate. But, as we have shown in this chapter, there is overwhelming evidence that creating safe and supportive environments, and integrating social and emotional development into academic instruction, significantly benefits students. We have also shown that there are concrete steps schools can take to do this work.

We know this will be challenging. This is especially true as districts develop and implement new teacher evaluation systems, and as they implement the new Common Core State Standards assessments. In order to best meet the needs of their students it will be imperative that school leaders stay the course outlined here and not marginalize social and emotional learning.

This can be done through the careful selection of educational materials and continued support of job-embedded professional development for teachers. Through the use of reflective, teacher-led models of professional development, school systems can empower teachers to be more responsive to their students and better prepared to support their social and academic development.

REFERENCES

ASCD. (n.d.). *Arkansas Governor Beebe Signs Education Reform Law Supporting the Whole Child.* Retrieved from ASCD Website: www.ascd.org/news-media/Press-Room/News-Releases/Arkansas-Governor-Signs-Law-Supporting-Whole-Child.aspx.

ASCD. (n.d.). *The Whole Child.* Retrieved from ASCD Whole Child Initiative Website: www.wholechildeducation.org/.

Battistich, V. (2008). The Child Development Project: Creating Caring School Communities. In L. P. Nucci & D. Narvaez (Eds.), *The Handbook of Moral and Character Education* (pp. 328–351). New York: Routledge.

Battistich, V., Schaps, E., & Wilson, N. (2004). *Journal of Primary Prevention, 24* (3), 243–262.

Brunn, P. (2010). *The Lesson Planning Handbook: Essential Strategies that Inspire Student Thinking and Learning.* New York: Scholastic.

Darling-Hammond, L. (2010). *The Flat World and Education: How America's Commitment to Equity Will Determine Our Future.* New York: Teachers College Press.

Deci, E., Vallerand, R., Pelletier, L., & Ryan, R. (1991). Motivation and Education: The Self-Determination Perspective. *Educational Psychologist, 26,* 325–346.

Developmental Studies Center. (2007). *Being a Writer: Craft, Conventions, Community.* Oakland, CA: Developmental Studies Center.

Developmental Studies Center. (2008). *Making Meaning: Strategies that Build Comprehension and Community.* Oakland, CA: Developmental Studies Center.

Developmental Studies Center. (2009). *Caring School Community.* Oakland, CA: Developmental Studies Center.

Dewey, J. (1938). *Experience and Education.* New York: Touchstone.

Duckworth, A., Peterson, C., Matthews, M., & Kelly, D. (2007). Grit: Perseverance and Passion for Long-term Goals. *Journal of Personality and Social Psychology, 92* (6), 1087–1101.

Duckworth, E. (1987). *The Having of Wonderful Ideas: And Other Essays on Teaching and Learning.* New York: Teachers College Press.

Durlak, J. A., Weissberg, R. P., Dymnicki, A. B., Taylor, R. D., & Schellinger, K. B. (2011). The Impact of Enhancing Students' Social and Emotional Learning: A Meta-Analysis of School Based Universal Interventions. *Child Development, 82* (1), 405–432.

Dweck, C. (2006). *Mindset: The New Psychology of Success.* New York: Ballantine Books.

Ferlazzo, L. (2013). *Self-Driven Learning: Teaching Strategies for Student Motivation.* Larchmont, NY: Eye On Education.

Johnson, P. H. (2012). *Opening Minds: Using Language to Change Lives.* Portland, ME: Stenhouse.

Jones, S., & Bouffard, S. (2012). Social and Emotional Learning in Schools: From Programs to Strategies. *Social Policy Report, 26* (4), 3–22.

Kleibard, H. M. (1995). *The Struggle for the American Curriculum.* New York: Routledge.

Learning First Alliance. (2001). *Every Child Learning: Safe and Supportive Schools.* Washington DC: Learning First Alliance.

Marshall, J. C., & Caldwell, S. D. (2007). *Caring School Community Implementation Study.* St. Louis: Cooperating School Districts.

National Governors Association Center for Best Practices & Council of Chief State School Officers. (2010). *Common Core State Standards for English Language Arts and Literacy in History/Social Studies, Science, and Technical Subjects.* Washington DC: National Governors Association Center for Best Practices & Council of Chief State School Officers.

Ravitch, D. (2010). *The Death and Life of the Great American School System.* New York: Basic Books.

Schaps, E. (2005). *The Role of Supportive School Environments in Promoting Academic Success.* Sacramento: California Department of Education, Healthy Kids Program Office.

Schaps, E., Battistich, V., & Solomon, D. (2004). Community in School as Key to Student Growth: Findings from the Child Development Project. In J. E. Zins, R. P. Weissberg, M. C. Wang, & H. J. Walberg (Eds.), *Building Academic Success on Social and Emotional Learning* (pp. 189–205). New York: Teachers College Press.

Schaps, E., & Brunn, P. (2008). They Taste With Their Feet: A Week in the Life of Mrs. Tonge's Fourth Grade Class. *Journal of Research in Character Education, 6* (1), 67–72.

Solomon, D., Battistich, V., Watson, M., Schaps, E., & Lewis, C. (2000). A Six-District Study of Educational Change: Direct and Mediated Effects of the Child Development Project. *Social Psychology of Education, 4* (1), 3–51.

Thapa, A., Cohen, J., Guffey, S., & Higgins-D'Alessandro, A. (2013, April 19). *Review of Educational Research.* Retrieved May 23, 2013, from Sage Journals: http://rer.sagepub.com/content/early/2013/04/18/0034654313483907.

Tough, P. (2012). *How Children Succeed.* New York, NY: Houghton Mifflin Harcourt.

Voight, A., Austin, G., & Hanson, T. (2013). *A Climate for Academic Success: How School Climate Distinguishes Schools that Are Beating the Achievement Odds (Full Report).* San Francisco: WestEd.

Zins, J. E., Bloodworth, M. R., Weissberg, R. P., & Walberg, H. J. (2004). The Scientific Base Linking Social and Emotional Learning to School Success. In J. E. Zins, R. P. Weissberg, M. C. Wang, & H. J. Walberg (Eds.), *Building Academic Success on Social and Emotional Learning* (pp. 3–22). New York: Teachers College Press.

16

THE COMPLEMENTARY PERSPECTIVES OF SOCIAL AND EMOTIONAL LEARNING, MORAL EDUCATION, AND CHARACTER EDUCATION

Maurice J. Elias, Amy Kranzler, Sarah J. Parker, V. Megan Kash, and Roger P. Weissberg

Anyone can become angry—that is easy. But to be angry with the right person, to the right degree, at the right time, for the right purpose, and in the right way—this is not easy.

Aristotle, *The Nicomachean Ethics, Book IV, Section 5*

Aristotle's words suggest that humans have long been interested in how best to manage their emotional and social lives. Most recognize that their emotional reactions to events have significant impact on their social interactions and effectiveness. Many have considered the question of how individuals or groups of individuals might acquire more effective ways of regulating their emotional responses and/or social relations. Others prefer to frame the question in terms of how individuals or groups learn to guide their behavior in correct or virtuous ways. Many have looked to traditional educational environments as places to make progress towards these aims. Indeed, as one of the primary cultural institutions responsible for transmitting information and values from one generation to the next, schools have typically been involved in attending to the social-emotional well being and moral direction of their students, in addition to their intellectual achievements.

Not surprisingly, moral education (along with its close cousin, character education) and social-emotional learning (SEL) have emerged as two prominent formal approaches used in schools to provide guidance for students' behavior. Moral education focuses on values and social-emotional learning focuses on the skills and attitudes needed to function in relevant social environments. Pedagogically, the two approaches have come to differ more in practice than in their deeper conceptualizations. Moral education has focused more on the power of "right thinking" and "knowing the good," and social-emotional learning has focused more on the power of problem solving (Elias et al., 1997; Huitt, 2004). Both, however, in their most discerning theorists and practitioners, have recognized the role of affect (Lemerise & Arsenio, 2000; Nucci, 2001). Now that research has caught up with this observational and intuitive understanding, both approaches are converging toward a central pedagogy involving the coordination of affect, behavior, and cognition and the role of the ecological-developmental context.

Paradoxically, moral education and social-emotional learning are values-neutral approaches to aspects of socialization. Acknowledging the role of context brings to visibility the elephant in the room in discussions of moral education, which is the source of moral authority or direction. This is an arena in which individuals and groups are going to disagree. However, from the perspective of America's public, secular education system in a nation committed to democratic principles, there are sets of values and moral principles that can be seen as consensual. Dewey has written about these with particular eloquence. And Nucci (2001) has found that even among religious children of different denominations, there is a consensus about moral values that transcend religion and degree of belief (e.g., most children would believe that stealing is wrong even if G-d commanded people to steal).

Yet, as it is said, the devil is in the details. What exactly constitutes "stealing"? Taking a friend's pencil and not returning it? Grabbing an apple from an open marketplace to bring home to your siblings when your family is hungry? Copying from a neighbor's test paper? More difficult in many cases is defining the positive value. What is "honesty"? Always saying the truth, all the time? Telling a hospitalized person how lousy they look? Pointing out to a classmate who has a problem with an activity in gym that he has not succeeded on 10 consecutive trials? Walking into class and telling the teacher you did not do the assigned reading?

Gather a group of educators or parents into groups and ask each member of each group to think about one child they know well. Ask the first group to think about a child who is highly responsible. Ask the next one to think about a child who is respectful. Have members of the third group think about one who is honest. Have the final group think about a young person that they would say is an exemplary citizen in their school or community (or if you are able to explain this without "giving away the answer," family). Ask them to picture the child they are thinking about and then write down and/or discuss what is it about that child that has earned the label of responsible, respectful, and so on, in their eyes. Tell them that you are not interested in an abstract list, but things specific to the child they are envisioning. And then have each group come up with a consensus statement containing their observations.

When one leads a discussion and puts each group's responses on pieces of newsprint (yes, we will be honest, we really mean large sheets of post-it pad paper) for all to see, a pattern invariably emerges and participants realize that to enact any of these cherished values and attributes, one needs a large number of skills. Responsibility involves time and task management and tracking and organization; respect involves empathy and social approach behaviors; honesty involves self-awareness and communication skills; good citizenship involves problem solving, decision-making, and conflict resolution, as well as group and teamwork skills. And many of the skills cross-cut areas, such as the need for clear communication in citizenship and interpersonal sensitivity in responsibility. Indeed, there are instances in which children will "want to do the right thing" but either will not know how or do not believe they can do so successfully.

Efforts at moral and character education, however their objectives may be defined, are designed to inform behavior. Enacting their principles requires skills (Berkowitz &

Bier, 2005). Berman (1997) has framed this by defining skills that he believes are essential for the development of social consciousness necessary to live effectively as an engaged citizen in the modern world; Dalton, Wandersman, and Elias (2007) have identified a similar set of cross-cultural "participatory competencies." These are the specific cognitive, behavioral, and affective skills needed to effectively enact key roles in a given social context. Lickona and Davidson (2005) have made explicit what has been implicit, or at least not featured, within character education, by articulating a distinction between moral and performance character. It is their way of codifying that "doing the good" does not follow automatically from "knowing the good." Most current writings about moral education and social-emotional learning are aligned with these prevailing notions.

As moral and character education and social-emotional learning move toward what we believe is an inexorable and long-overdue convergence, having a sense of the trajectory of the SEL side should help practitioners, theorists, and researchers appreciate and put to better use the assets and limitations of the field. Because much has been written about the evolution of moral and character education (e.g., Lickona, 1976, 1991; Nucci, 1989; Wynne & Ryan, 1997; this volume), the following will emphasize the development of SEL and elucidate its underlying bases. Again, it must be noted that in contexts with differing sources of moral authority, focal values and requisite social-emotional skills might vary from those that will be the implicit focus here. The considerations we present are relevant across particular sets of moral principles or interpersonal skills. In subsequent sections, we present thoughts about the implications of this background for linkages with moral and character education.

THE EVOLUTION OF SOCIAL AND EMOTIONAL LEARNING (SEL)

Traditional views of the development and evaluation of SEL point to some of the first known writings about social and emotional skills (e.g., Aristotle's *The Nicomachean Ethics* [Goleman, 1995], as quoted above) and the increasing amount of interest and research on social and/or emotional intelligences over the past 150 years. They typically begin with Darwin's exploration of the importance of emotion in evolution, in *The Expression of the Emotions in Man and Animals* (Goleman, 1995; Mayer, 2001). They also usually cite Thorndike's proposal of a "social intelligence" component—an ability to comprehend others and relate to them effectively—to overall intelligence (Elias, 2001), although proponents did not find much subsequent support for Thorndike's ideas. Sternberg's work (1985) on what he then referred to as "practical intelligence" found more empirical support for such a concept, and Gardner's research (1993) on multiple intelligences delineated and supported two distinct and related components relevant to our discussion—intrapersonal (emotional) and interpersonal (social) intelligences. The Consortium on the School-based Promotion of Social Competence (1994) emphasized the importance of integrating cognition, affect, and behavior to address developmental and contextual challenges and tasks. Prior to this point, the study of intelligence, emotion, and social relations tended to be separate; with Sternberg and Gardner's work, it became clear that these phenomena were related to one another (Mayer, 2001), although others (e.g., Piaget and Dewey) had noted these interrelationships much earlier.

By the late 1980s, much evidence supported the idea of integrated social and emotional skills. Mayer and Salovey played a seminal role in rigorously defining and finding empirical support for "emotional intelligence," as it is understood currently. In the first half of the 1990s, they produced a series of reviews and studies that presented support for emotional intelligence, provided a strict definition for the construct and a measure for assessing it, and demonstrated its validity and reliability as an intelligence (Mayer, 2001). Goleman popularized the concept and added some social components to the definition in his book, *Emotional Intelligence* (1995). Shortly thereafter, Reuven Bar-On's (Bar-On, Maree, & Elias, 2007) extensive work in defining and assessing emotional intelligence came to prominence. Table 16.1 contains a summary of the way in which these founders of SEL defined the key skills and attitudes comprising the construct.

In a parallel track, educators were becoming increasingly interested in applying the ideas of social and emotional intelligence in educational environments. John Dewey (1933) was among the first to propose that empathy and effective interpersonal management are important skills to be conveyed and practiced in the educational environment. It was not until the early 1990s, however—contemporaneous with the work of Mayer and Salovey—that the Collaborative for Academic, Social, and Emotional Learning (CASEL) (2005) was founded to apply the construct of emotional intelligence and its related theory, research, and practice to schools and education.

As Zins, Elias, and Greenberg (2007) explain, the term "social-emotional learning" was derived from a journey that has been driven by concepts, research, and practice. It began with a shift in thinking from prevention of mental illness, behavioral-emotional disorders, and problem behaviors as a goal and moved toward the broader goal of promoting social competence. Looking at the prior literature on social competence, the skills needed for sound functioning in schools, and at the emerging research on the importance of emotions, CASEL drew on Goleman's (1995) formulation of key SEL skill clusters and expanded them (Table 16.1). Indeed, in selecting the name, "social and emotional learning," CASEL recognized that it was essential to capture the aspect of education that links academic achievement with the skills necessary for succeeding in school, in the family, in the community, in the workplace, and in life in general. Equipped with such skills, attitudes, and beliefs, young people are more likely to make healthy, caring, ethical, and responsible decisions, and to avoid engaging in behaviors with negative consequences such as interpersonal violence, substance abuse, and bullying (Elias et al. 1997; Lemerise & Arsenio, 2000).

Such learning is important to students because emotions affect how and what they learn, and caring relationships provide a foundation for deep, lasting learning (Elias et al. 1997). In a climate of ever-growing concern about academic achievement, attending to emotions was emerging as a matter of at least as great an emphasis as cognition and behavior. In a landmark book that brought together the research evidence about SEL and academic success from all fields, Zins, Weissberg, Wang, and Walberg (2004) concluded that successful academic performance by students depends on (a) students' social-emotional skills for participatory competence, (b) their approaching education with a sense of positive purpose, and (c) the presence of safe, supportive classroom and school climates that foster respectful, challenging, and engaging learning communities. It is the totality of these conditions and the processes they imply that are now best referred to collectively as social-emotional learning, rather than continuing to view SEL as linked entirely, or even mainly, to a set of skills.

The logic model behind this view, in simplified form, is that (a) students become open to learning in environments that are respectful, orderly, safe, academically challenging, caring, involving/engaging, and well-managed, (b) effective SEL-related programs

Table 16.1 Primary Conceptualizations of Social-Emotional Learning/Emotional Intelligence Skills

The Salovey and Mayer (Brackett and Geher, 2006) approach to emotional intelligence:
1. Accurately perceive emotions in oneself and others and in one's ambient context.
2. Use emotions to facilitate thinking or that might inhibit clear thinking and task performance.
3. Understand emotional meanings and how emotional reactions change over time and in response to other emotions.
4. Effectively manage emotions in themselves and in others ("social management").

Bar-On et al.'s five key components (2007):
1. Be aware of, understand, and express our emotions and feelings non-destructively.
2. Understand how others feel and to use this information to relate with them.
3. Manage and control emotions so they work for us and not against us.
4. Manage change, and adapt and solve problems of a personal and interpersonal nature.
5. Generate positive affect to be self-motivated.

Goleman (1998) and CASEL's (2005) five clusters of SEL, each of which is linked to a collection of skills:
1. Self-awareness.
2. Social awareness.
3. Self-management.
4. Responsible decision-making.
5. Relationship management.

CASEL's Elaboration of Social and Emotional Learning/Emotional Intelligence Skills (Kress & Elias, 2006):
1. Self-Awareness
   • Recognizing and naming one's emotions
   • Understanding the reasons and circumstances for feeling as one does
   • Recognizing and naming others' emotions
   • Recognizing strengths in, and mobilizing positive feelings about, self, school, family, and support networks
   • Knowing one's needs and values
   • Perceiving oneself accurately
   • Believing in personal efficacy
   • Having a sense of spirituality
2. Social Awareness
   • Appreciating diversity
   • Showing respect to others
   • Listening carefully and accurately
   • Increasing empathy and sensitivity to others' feelings
   • Understanding others' perspectives, points of view, and feelings
3. Self-Management and Organization
   • Verbalizing and coping with anxiety, anger, and depression
   • Controlling impulses, aggression, and self-destructive, antisocial behavior
   • Managing personal and interpersonal stress
   • Focusing on tasks at hand
   • Setting short- and long-term goals
   • Planning thoughtfully and thoroughly
   • Modifying performance in light of feedback
   • Mobilizing positive motivation
   • Activating hope and optimism
   • Working toward optimal performance states

4. Responsible Decision-Making
   - Analyzing situations perceptively and identifying problems clearly
   - Exercising social decision-making and problem-solving skills
   - Responding constructively and in a problem-solving manner to interpersonal obstacles
   - Engaging in self-evaluation and reflection
   - Conducting oneself with personal, moral, and ethical responsibility
5. Relationship Management
   - Managing emotions in relationships, harmonizing diverse feelings and viewpoints
   - Showing sensitivity to social-emotional cues
   - Expressing emotions effectively
   - Communicating clearly
   - Engaging others in social situations
   - Building relationships
   - Working cooperatively
   - Exercising assertiveness, leadership, and persuasion
   - Managing conflict, negotiation, refusal
   - Providing, seeking help

---

emphasize, impart, and develop key attitudes and skills that are essential for reducing emotional barriers to learning and successful interpersonal interactions, and (c) reducing emotional barriers to effective learning and interaction is essential for low performing students to learn academic content and skills deeply and for all students to reach their potential and apply what they learn in school to life inside and out of school.

CASEL's research (CASEL, 2005; Durlak, Weissberg, Dymnicki, Taylor, & Schellinger, 2011; Elias & Arnold, 2006; Elias et al., 1997; Greenberg et al., 2003) has continued to show that schools of social, emotional, and academic excellence generally share five main characteristics:

1. A school climate that articulates specific themes, character elements, or values, such as respect, responsibility, fairness, and honesty, and conveys an overall sense of purpose for attending school;
2. Explicit instruction and practice in skills for participatory competence;
3. Developmentally appropriate instruction in ways to promote health and prevent problems;
4. Services and systems that enhance students' coping skills and provide social support for handling transitions, crises, and conflicts; and
5. Widespread, systematic opportunities for positive, contributory service.

These schools send messages about character, about how students should conduct themselves as learners and members of common school communities, about the respectful ways staff members should conduct themselves as educators, and about how staff and parents should conduct themselves as supporters of learning. In other words, SEL competencies are developed and reinforced not by programs but rather in the context of supportive environments, which lead to asset-building, risk reduction, enhanced health behaviors, and greater attachment to and engagement in school.

In CASEL's definition of SEL, one can see that the theoretical understanding of how children learn key social competencies has become more sophisticated than earlier views of social skills acquisition. First, there is recognition that social performance involves the coordination of affect, cognition, and behavior, and that these areas, as well as their coordination, develop over time. Second, skill acquisition is the ongoing outcome of processes that depends on nurturance, support, and appreciation in various environmental contexts. Third, much is now realized about the many accumulating influences on students, not all of which are consistent with the development of SEL skills. There is pressure and modeling in the mass culture for impulsive behavior, quick decision-making, short-term goal setting, extreme emotions, and violent problem solving. Students' acquisition and internalization of life skills occurs in a maelstrom of many competing forces of socialization and development.

Research has gone beyond showing that SEL is fundamental to children's health, ethical development, citizenship, academic learning, and motivation to achieve (Zins, Weissberg et al., 2004). It has also demonstrated the impact of systematic attempts to improve children's SEL. As they have evolved in the last decades of the twentieth century and the early twenty-first century, these interventions have focused on fostering students' social and emotional development.

Generally, they are premised on the understanding that students experience the educational process as a social one; learning is facilitated (or hindered) by relationships and interactions with teachers and/or peers. In general, a student who has more developed social "intelligence" will have improved abilities to navigate the challenges and processes of learning than one who does not. For example, a child who has poor understanding of how to effectively manage human relationships may be unable to communicate her needs to teachers or to others in the classroom environment; this will likely impede her learning. SEL curricula are also based on the growing body of evidence that students' emotional experiences affect their learning and their demonstration of that learning (Patti & Tobin, 2003). This is most effectively illustrated by contrasting the differences in information acquisition between a child who is enthusiastic about a topic and one who is not, or the differences in test results between a child who can channel her anxiety about an exam into better information recall and a child who is overwhelmed by his fear of assessment. Similarly, self-regulation skills such as delay of gratification can be a more robust predictor of academic performance than IQ (Duckworth & Seligman, 2005).

Although SEL programs seek to develop social and emotional "intelligences," these aspects are not viewed as fixed traits in that field. Instead, SEL programs aim to help students develop a set of skills that can help them better manage their own emotional state and their interactions with other people in the educational environment in order to maximize their learning experiences (Elias, Kress, & Hunter, 2006). Progress toward these goals is made most quickly and enduringly when programs adopt a two-pronged approach to SEL: intervention components aimed at individual students *and* at the overall school climate. Yet, while individual students learn about, practice, and regularly perform new thinking and behavior patterns in their everyday interactions at school, it is equally important that SEL programs help teachers and administrators develop their own social and emotional skills and incorporate SEL paradigms and techniques on a broad level throughout the school (e.g., within the disciplinary and evaluative structure) (Elias, 2001; Elias, O'Brien, & Weissberg, 2006; Elias et al., 1997). As these processes take hold, the classroom and school become places where social and emotional matters are openly discussed, valued, and practiced. When the educational culture changes this way, it is much more likely that any new skills being attempted by students will be noticed and reinforced.

Research suggests that SEL curricula designed in such a way have demonstrated positive effects not only on school-related attitudes and behavior, but also on students' academic achievement and test scores (Zins, Bloodworth, Weissberg, & Walberg, 2004). Durlak et al.'s (2011) meta-analysis of 213 school-based SEL programs found that they had a significant impact on social and emotional skills, attitudes, and behavior, as well as academic performance, with improvements reflecting an 11-percentile-point gain in achievement. Across SEL programs, the overall mean effect size for improvements in test scores and grades was 0.27 and 0.33, respectively, and these effects were sustained through a follow-up period (mean = 150 weeks).

Perhaps most salient in the current education climate is that SEL-related after-school programs yielded improvements in standardized test scores at a magnitude which is more than twice as large as that found in a meta-analysis of academically-related after-school programs (Durlak, Weissberg, & Pachan, 2010).

Such a history hints at but obscures the contributions of three streams of influence on the definition of SEL, its implementation in school-based contexts, and its connection to moral and character education. Understanding this aspect of SEL's background is important for seeing the converging and, we believe, intertwining pathways that will increasingly define these fields.

SOCIAL LEARNING THEORY AND THE COGNITIVE REVOLUTION

Social Learning Theory (SLT) (e.g., Bandura, 1973; Rotter, 1954) had enormous impact on the methods and techniques of SEL programs. It was derived from work in clinical and personality psychology and an appreciation of how cognitive factors led to the persistence of behaviors that appeared on the surface to be undesirable and even counterproductive. Rotter, a seminal theorist in this field, studied under Alfred Adler and was highly influenced by his work with children. "Striving for superiority," "style of life," and "fictional finalism" are all essentially cognitive schema that presage much of the later work in cognitive-behavioral theory. Bandura, in particular, observed how traditional, purely behavioral learning theories were unable to explain how humans acquired novel, unrehearsed, and unreinforced behavior from watching other individuals' actions (Bandura, 1973). SLT therefore focused not only on the impact of modeling and observation but also the way in which individuals draw from their experiences to create expectancies about interactions with others. These expectancies, in turn, exercise strong influence on behavior.

Generalization, in SLT, is a function of creating an expectancy about the likely desirable outcome of a behavior and its value. For this reason, the overall climate of the classroom and school (i.e., the normative structure) is important to sustaining prosocial behavior. Behaviors must reach a certain threshold of repetition, reinforcement, and salience if they are to be internalized. As more influences in the environment provide messages contrary to the program, the "dosage" of whatever an SEL (or moral or character education program) wishes to convey in attitudes and skills will have to be higher before an intervention's message is received and remembered. Hence, SLT recognized the powerful role presented by the ecological environment while also keeping in focus that it is the individual's interpretations of the environmental contingencies (i.e., expectancies) that would ultimately be the most powerful influence on behavior.

Cognitive-behavioral Therapy

Many intervention approaches within SEL draw on cognitive-behavioral therapy (CBT) as the basis of their pedagogy. It was a short road from SLT's focus on expectancies and the role of modeling to the observation of Meichenbaum (1977) and others that these expectancies were in consciousness and therefore likely to be "kept in mind" and influence behavior through the process of self-talk. Behavior founded on faulty premises—misunderstandings of the social environment, extreme thinking about how the world works or one's role in the world, or strong but misplaced emotions, such as depression due to pessimism (all of which can be found in Adler's theories)—is likely to be categorized as maladaptive or pathological.

One area of CBT, social problem solving (Chang, D'Zurilla, & Sanna, 2004) captures best the two main strands of CBT that have contributed to SEL. First, problem solving is at the foundation of the vast majority of SEL approaches (CASEL, 2005). The common features involve a process of identifying a problematic situation, addressing the feelings related to it, putting a problem into words, defining a goal, generating multiple options, analyzing their potential consequences for short- and long-term implications for self and others, making a choice, planning and rehearsing how to carry out that choice, taking the necessary action, and reflecting on what happened and what can be learned from it. Spivack and Shure (1974) were pioneers in recognizing that what they called "interpersonal-cognitive problem solving" need not be taught only to individuals in clinical settings. Rather, a preventive effect could be achieved by building these skills on a universal basis, in the regular context of school and family life.

SEL pedagogy and CBT pedagogy have many points of convergence. Both emphasize the use of real-life problems but also recognize the benefits of thinking through how to handle hypothetical situations before dealing with affectively-charged present situations. Both emphasize the processes of brainstorming, goal-setting, observation/modeling and practice/rehearsal of new behaviors, anticipation of potential obstacles and planning for them, reflection on experiences, and the use of prompts and cues as an aide to generalization. It is essential, from an SEL point of view, to recognize that generalization is viewed as occurring through skill application and repeated mastery, in a large number of contexts, and over a long period of time.

There are powerful implications of this from an intervention point of view. Effective SEL requires congruence between any school-based program and the overall climate and environment and norms of the school. Interventions confined to one class period once or twice per week for even a whole year are not likely to be as effective as approaches that are coordinated across aspects of the school day, carried out and prompted continuously, and continued across multiple years to have a cumulative effect.

The Role of Affect

SEL as a movement grew out of the growing interest in emotional intelligence popularized by Daniel Goleman (1995), although, as noted, the term preceded his usage of it. Nevertheless, Goleman's work placed a strong focus on the role of emotion, or affect, in everyday behavior—reasoning, decision-making, and the like. Others had preceded him. Significantly, Piaget, in his relatively under-noticed work, *Intelligence and Affectivity* (1981), spoke clearly about the integration of affect and cognition and was pessimistic about attempts to disentangle them. He saw emotions as having directive and energizing functions, among others, and as vital for the implementation of intelligent action in the world. Therefore Goleman's emphasis was not new, but his renewal of it was accompanied by a resurgence of research in the area and a strong interest in emotion research on the part of significant funders.

The work of Carolyn Saarni (2007) has illuminated our understanding of the role of affect in everyday life. Saarni focused on the development of emotional competence well before "emotional intelligence" became defined, and her work is an essential part of that field's development. Her view of the eight skills of emotional competence takes a sophisticated developmental/transactional perspective (Saarni, 2007):

1. Awareness of emotional states, including the possibility of experiencing multiple emotions at levels we may not be aware of consciously at all times.
2. Skill in discerning and understanding the emotions of others, based on situational and expressive cues that have a degree of cultural consensus as to their emotional meaning.
3. Skill in using the vocabulary of emotion available in one's subculture and the link of emotional with social roles.
4. Capacity for empathic involvement in others' emotional experiences.
5. Skill in understanding that inner emotional states need not correspond to outer expression, both in ourselves and others, and how our emotional expression may impact on others.
6. Skill in adaptive coping with aversive emotions and distressing circumstances by using self-regulatory strategies and by employing effective problem-solving strategies for dealing with problematic situations.
7. Awareness that relationships are largely defined by how emotions are communicated within the relationships.
8. Capacity for emotional self-efficacy, including viewing our emotional experience as justified and in accord with our moral beliefs.

As one can see, Saarni's view of emotional competence contains bridges to social problem solving and other cognitive skills, much as problem solving can contain bridges to the affective domain. Her final skill contains a link to the moral domain, recognizing the directive and contextual influence that moral beliefs provide.

Indeed, researchers such as Adolphs and Damasio (2001) now view our emotional capacities as being among the earliest human capacities to develop and essential for sound decision-making and relationship formation. In a recent study, Wyland and Forgas (2010) demonstrated the influence of emotion on interpersonal judgments and processing styles and other studies show how positive emotions are associated with increased trust and likelihood to believe that the facial expressions of others are genuine (Forgas & East, 2008a, 2008b). Feelings are not external to how we function and are best relied upon as both internal and external guides to empathy, to understanding the perspective and feelings of others, and to our decisions and their impact on self and others (Damasio, 1994). This point of view has not been lost on those who are concerned about moral and character education and the process by which students make moral decisions and take corresponding action.

Nucci (2001), for example, advocates for a better understanding of how emotion is integrated into moral judgments. "Affect is part and parcel of adaptive intelligence" (p. 109); he argues that it is not useful to see it as somehow having any primacy. He notes that, from an evolutionary psychology point of view, basic emotional schema and quick, automatic responses have a place in interpersonal relationships, especially during infancy and early childhood, but become less adaptive in the typical social environments one encounters later in life. Gradually, the developmental challenge involves the integration of affect into cognitive systems.

Building emotional competence has been a standard part of SEL approaches for many years (and increasingly reflected in moral and character education practices), anticipating the findings derived from neurobiology. However, for the introduction of efforts into mainstream socialization practices of schools, considerations beyond those at the individual level are clearly necessary (Dalton et al., 2007); these are provided by another theoretical perspective, that of community psychology and social ecology.

A Community Psychology–Social Ecological Perspective

SEL theorists and researchers have come to agree that SEL interventions seek to change not only direct, immediate reinforcement contingencies that maintain antisocial behavior, but also aim to alter entire systems through interventions that target classrooms—teachers and students alike—as well as schools, districts, and communities. This understanding began in part with Lewin's field theory and his interest in examining the enormous variety of psychological processes that operate within a particular situation at a given time, and how an individual sits in the midst of an incredibly complex system of interactions between forces at multiple levels (Lewin, 1951). Lewin was among the first to assert that behavior was at least as strongly influenced by context as by individual predilections. This view was expanded by a community psychology/social-ecology perspective, which sought to define the multiple, interactive, and dynamic levels of systems within which individuals develop and adapt (Belsky, 1984; Bronfenbrenner, 1979; Dalton et al., 2007).

Children's social-emotional skills (and moral values) emerge out of an interaction with parents and other caregivers and family members, educators, medical personnel, and others whose responsibilities include navigating children through the socialization process. However, these interactions are framed by the nature of the formal and informal groups and organizations in which these interactions occur, the neighborhoods and communities within which they reside, and the overall zeitgeist that is communicated through the mass media. While social ecology theory is clear that small group interactions are the most powerful development influence, the way in which digital media invade lives of families means that elements of the zeitgeist have greater potency than when events seemed more distant (Dalton et al., 2007). The implications of this are that the influence of SEL programs must be placed in a larger ecological frame. Interventions must be more encompassing and their impact will be related to their congruence with messages being imparted by other sources of influence.

Consider several simple examples. Programs teaching skills in delay of gratification must contend with social influences urging individuals to "just do it" and to take quick, and often violent, action. Pressures to be best or first will balance the skill of waiting one's turn. In an example that intersects both SEL and moral education, the discipline and skills needed for studying for a test are too often offset by an almost desperate need to succeed, and hence to cheat. In summary, the community psychology/social ecology perspective has led SEL researchers to embrace the understanding that lasting SEL skill acquisition and concomitant significant improvements in student behavior and academic achievement will be greatest to the extent that entire systems of psychological and social forces are addressed by particular interventions in sustained ways (Elias & Clabby, 1992; Zins, Bloodworth et al., 2004).

Our understanding of the background of SEL shows its progression toward an ecological, developmental, and systemic conceptualization of how skills are acquired and maintained and the nexus within with interventions work. We now proceed to examine ways to understand the current and potential pathways of convergence between SEL and moral and character education.

AREAS OF CONVERGENCE BETWEEN MORAL AND CHARACTER EDUCATION AND SEL

In recent years, formal organizations have developed to help codify and promulgate theory, research, and practice in moral and character education and SEL. The Association for Moral Education, founded in 1976, was the first of these (www.amenetwork. org/about.html, retrieved 9/11/12). The Character Education Partnership was founded in 1993 for the purpose of advancing the field in schools (www.character.org/about/vision-and-mission/, retrieved 9/11/12). And as noted earlier CASEL was founded in 1993 to bring SEL into schools (www.CASEL.org). That said, the time has clearly arrived when the advocacy aspect of these organizations must give way to convergence in the interest of children and advancing their common agendas, as well as the common aspects of their science and practice.

Huitt (2004) points out that fundamental to many approaches to moral and character education, and a criticism of some of Kohlberg's (1984) work, is a reliance on "right thinking" as leading to "right behavior." This has led to a pedagogical emphasis on values clarification/analysis/inculcation. These methods have not found strong empirical support. However, in more recent years, as the field has coalesced under the banner of character education in the context of schools, the connections between "right thinking" and proper behavior have been given greater attention. As noted earlier, this has culminated conceptually in Lickona and Davidson's (2005) distinction between moral character and performance character. They have urged that an emphasis on moral values is necessary but not sufficient to influence behavior and yield enactments that would allow one to be seen as having "good character." The latter, more often than not, is a result of one's actions. Clearly, this requires some theoretical and practical position regarding what behaviors are important for these enactments. As our exercise earlier about thinking of persons who embody different aspects of admirable character implied, such a perspective leads to greater convergence between SEL and moral/character education. SEL, as a set of basic interpersonal competencies, can be used for good or ill; but to be used for good, they must be mastered well—responsibility, respect, honesty, and other desirable aspects of character all require sound SEL competencies; hence, the latter are participatory competencies in the fullest sense of that concept.

In a recent position paper set forth by the Character Education Partnership, this expanded view of character education is further described, highlighting the interdependent importance of both performance character and moral character (www.character.org/uploads/PDFs/White_Papers/Performance_Values.pdf, retrieved 9/11/12). The paper expands the vision of character education, describing a broader goal of helping children both be their best, and do their best. To accomplish this, they urge, schools must teach children to care about both the purpose and the quality of their work, cultivating "craftsmen" whose contributions to the world will be both meaningful and effective.

This position paper describes specific practices that have been used by teachers and schools to develop performance character, many of which also foster moral character development. For example, the importance of co-curricular activities is highlighted as a central component in the development of both moral and performance character. By creating diverse opportunities for youth to recognize that they are capable of excellence, co-curricular activities help foster a "culture of excellence," that serves to transform the self-image of youth and enhance future performance. Similarly, by fostering "growth mindsets" that emphasize the importance of effort, and encouraging feedback and revisions until mastery is achieved, youth learn to value the growth and achievement as a *process*, rather than just an end goal. This mindset has clear implications for moral character development as well, particularly as mounting pressure to achieve has increased the rates of cheating among today's youth. Also noted as important for the development of performance character is creating safe and supportive learning environments that foster school connectedness, providing models of excellence, using rubrics to help students take responsibility of their work, preparing students to make public presentations of their work, and assigning work that matters. In these ways, schools can help foster the performance character that will enable youth to successfully act upon their moral principles.

We wish to conclude by positing areas that we believe lie at the intersection of moral and character education and SEL. We do this by sharing observations based on a number of schools recognized as exemplary in SEL, character education, and related domains. In doing so, we attempt to align ourselves with others in the field whose past observations have been confirmed subsequently by replicated research.

How to Create Stronger Moral Sensibilities and Morally-Guided Action in Youth

At the end of *Democracy and Education*, Dewey (1916) provides a trenchant and prescient view of moral education in saying that

> The most important problem of moral education in the school concerns the relationship of knowledge and conduct ... the school becomes itself a form of social life, a miniature community and one in close interaction with other modes of associated experience beyond school walls. All education which develops power to share effectively in social life is moral.
>
> (www.worldwideschool.org/library/books/socl/education/ DemocracyandEducation/chap26.html, retrieved 10/26/13)

Dewey's observations implicitly speak to the convergence and synergy of SEL and moral and character education, Here, we wish to move toward some modest, pragmatic suggestions that may be thought of as first steps at fostering integrative approaches.

A current individual with Dewey-an insights, James Comer (2003), has made the point that children cannot be taught character, but rather "catch" it from the adults around them and the nature of the interactions they directly and indirectly experience. That said, it is not obvious exactly what children need to be exposed to, or for how long and in what ways, if they are to become "infected" with sound character. Perhaps some readers can recall parents bringing their children to spend time with friends who had measles or chicken pox in the hope that they would get these diseases then, rather than just prior to a family vacation time. Sometimes it worked, but more often, it did not. How, then, can we maximize the likelihood that parents and teachers can expose children to the conditions that are more likely to lead to a strong moral compass and the fortitude to follow the directions being pointed to? SEL has a great deal to say about how well an individual will be able to pick up the cues and experiences being provided by the environmental context. However, even if the skills are functioning well, the question remains about what kinds of experiences are necessary, or desirable, to create a strong moral sense and a commitment to act on that sense.

As noted earlier, difficult questions must be faced, such as the perceived source of moral authority. Different religions provide different moral codes, although with a strong degree of overlap. What seems true in studies of modern religious identity development is that moral education is best thought of as a comprehensive system of socialization, as opposed to creating religious identity or adherence to a set of values by simply exposing students to a set of individual moral principles. Without a nomological net to connect the moral principles in some way, it is very likely that an individual will deal with morality in a highly pragmatic and contextual manner rather than having an enduring set of guiding principles as the basis for his or her decisions and actions. We believe it is for this reason that Dewey forged such a strong link between democracy (as an organizing principle for morality) and education (as one potent source of moral experiences) and why character education approaches have implicitly or explicitly used frameworks drawn from religious observance as an organizing principle for sets or pillars of values/morals (Peterson & Seligman, 2004).

In their *Values in Action (VIA) Classification of Strengths*, Peterson and Seligman attempt an organization of universal human strengths and values. To accomplish this, they conducted a thorough study of the world's dominant religions and traditions (Dahlsgaard, Peterson, & Seligman, 2005). Results from their literature review revealed a surprising degree of agreement across cultures, indicating "a historical and cross-cultural convergence of six core virtues" including: courage, justice, humanity, temperance, wisdom, and transcendence. The *Classification of Strengths* divides these six virtues into 24 human characteristics, which were determined to be strengths of character, reflected in thoughts, feelings, and behavior. These character strengths have been associated with a range of positive outcomes in adolescence including increased mental health and well being (Gillham et al., 2011) and a reduction of problems such as substance use, alcohol abuse, smoking, and violence (Park, 2004).

Based on the work of Peterson and Seligman, the KIPP (Knowledge is Power Program) schools have integrated a structured and measurable approach to character development within their network of charter schools (www.kipp.org). In partnership with University of Pennsylvania researcher, Angela Duckworth, KIPP schools focus on the integration of seven character strengths: zest, grit, self-control, optimism, gratitude, social intelligence, and curiosity. The KIPP model employs seven steps for the integration of these character strengths into schools: believe and model them, name them (provide labels for values that foster discussion and awareness of them), "find it" or provide real-world and fictional examples of character strengths, "feel it" or help youth feel the positive effects by developing their own strengths, integrate character education into curricula, encourage strength by providing growth mindset praise, and track improvements in character growth by recording and discussing progress towards character goals (www. kipp.org/our-approach/character-and-academics, retrieved 10/26/13). This last step is accomplished through the development of a "character report card," which grants students a CPA (character-point average) that tracks character growth in a systematic and tangible way, conveying to students that success in this domain is of equal importance as academic success (Tough, 2012).

In contemporary society, the print and digital media bring many moral situations to individuals' attention in the comfort of their homes. Often, these take the form of tragedies of hunger and disease, horrors of violence, ravages of natural disasters. In the vast majority of instances, we are not moved to act, though we have a moral objection to what we are seeing and hearing. Brendtro, Brokenleg, and Van Bockern (2002) view children as having sympathy, empathy, and compassion for others. Sympathy refers to the capacity to understand what is happening to others and to take the perspective of being in their shoes. Empathy adds to this an emotional attunement so that one not only understands but also shares the emotions of the others in their situation. Compassion brings in a behavioral component, such that one understands, feels, and is moved to act in a situation. While the distinction between these three emotions is not precise, they serve to underscore that moral action requires something "extra" on the part of an individual and does not follow automatically from being empathic. Moving children toward this "extra" requires the adults in their lives to provide children with a balance of Appreciation, Belonging, Opportunities and Support for Competencies, and Contributions in their lives, and by adults consistently reinforcing SEL behavior and positive values and actions across both the home and school contexts (Albright & Weissberg, 2010; Elias, Tobias, & Friedlander, 2002; Kessler, 2000).

A Culminating Discussion: SEL and Moral and Character Education Are Complementary Perspectives

From at least the time of the Bible and Aristotle, people have wondered about humankind's potential to learn more effective ways of managing emotional experiences and social relationships; an integration of SEL and moral and character education offers a possible route to achieve this goal. Proponents of SEL have acknowledged that skills require direction and that maladaptive direction, such as might come from extremist or criminal ideologies, can be pursued effectively through SEL competencies. Moral and character educators are recognizing that it takes more than volition and intention to act with sound character. SEL is a parallel movement to moral education in that it is more about the *process* of learning than the *content* of learning. That is, the focus is on educating *for* morality and educating for social-emotional competence, as opposed to educating *about* morality and about social-emotional competence. These competencies are not neutral, however; they are aligned with fundamental, common values and attributes of good character and sound moral development. Proponents of both views now see the need to go beyond a focus on programs and content and look at the way in which individuals develop in the context of their ecological environment over time and how that environment can be modified to impart skills and values that can lead children toward productive futures.

The education system has the responsibility of preparing children for citizenship in a democracy and for leading a morally-guided life. Schools contribute to this most effectively when the culture and climate of the school require students to "live" their social-emotional competencies in contexts of moral character with high aspirations. When students are in schools that communicate ambiguous or negative moral messages, students' views of the consequences of their actions become skewed and they use their skills in ways that might be quite harmful to them in the long term.

SEL and moral and character education converge by providing a deep and visceral understanding of moral character by organizing schools as moral, caring communities of character with clear values reflective of strongest cultural convergence, and ensuring that all children are given opportunities and competences to enact their moral character in deep and meaningful ways by becoming active participants in the everyday life of the school. The school becomes a primary context for students' social-emotional and character development. Thus imprinted, children will be strengthened in their desire to seek out such communities as places to live and work and worship, and bring these same influences into how they make their homes into places to raise children of character and competence. This is the promise of ensuring that SEL, moral, and character education are connected, contained in this abbreviated logic model: caring and civil schools, engaged students, prepared and participatory citizens of character.

REFERENCES

Adolphs, R., & Damasio, A. R. (2001). The interaction of affect and cognition: A neuro-biological perspective. In J. P. Forgas (Ed.), *The handbook of affect and social cognition* (pp. 27–49). Mahwah, NJ: Erlbaum.

Albright, M. I., & Weissberg, R. P. (2010). School-family partnerships to promote social and emotional learning. In S. Christenson & A. L. Reschly (Eds.), *Handbook of school-family partnerships* (pp. 246–265). New York: Routledge.

Bandura, A. (1973). *Aggression: A social learning analysis.* Englewood Cliffs, NJ: Prentice-Hall, Inc.

Bar-On, R., Maree, J. G., & Elias, M. J. (Eds.). (2007). *Educating people to be emotionally intelligent.* Westport, CT: Praeger.

Belsky, J. (1984). The determinants of parenting. A process model. *Child Development, 55,* 83–96.

Berkowitz, M. W., & Bier, M. C. (2005). *What works in character education: A research-driven guide for educators.* Washington, D.C.: Character Education Partnership.

Berman, S. (1997). *Children's social consciousness and the development of social responsibility.* SUNY Series: Democracy and Education.

Brackett, M. A., & Geher, G. (2006). Measuring emotional intelligence: Paradigmatic shifts and common ground. In J. Ciarrochi, J. P. Forgas, & J. D. Mayer (Eds.), *Emotional intelligence and everyday life* (2nd ed.) (pp. 27–50). New York: Psychology Press.

Brendtro, L., Brokenleg, M., & Van Bockern, S. (2002). *Reclaiming youth at risk: Our hope for the future* (Rev. ed.). Bloomington, IN: Solution Tree.

Bronfenbrenner, U. (1979). *The ecology of human development.* Cambridge, MA: Harvard University Press.

Chang, E., D'Zurilla, T., & Sanna, L. (Eds.). (2004). *Social problem solving: Theory, research, and training.* Washington, D.C.: American Psychological Association.

Character Education Partnership. (2008). *Performance values: Why they matter and what schools can do to foster their development: A Position Paper of the Character Education Partnership.* Retrieved September 11, 2012, from www.character.org.

Collaborative for Academic, Social, and Emotional Learning [CASEL]. (2005). *Safe and sound: An educational leader's guide to evidence-based social and emotional learning programs—Illinois edition.* Retrieved January 10, 2007, from www.casel.org.

Comer, J. (2003). Transforming the lives of children. In M. J. Elias, H. Arnold, & C. Steiger-Hussey (Eds.), *EQ+IQ: Best practices in leadership for caring and successful schools* (pp. 11–22). Thousand Oaks, CA: Corwin Press.

Consortium on the School-Based Promotion of Social Competence. (1994). The promotion of social competence: Theory, research, practice, and policy. In R. J. Haggerty, L. Sherrod, N. Garmezy, & M. Rutter (Eds.), *Stress, risk, resilience in children and adolescents: Processes, mechanisms, and interaction* (pp. 268–316). New York: Cambridge University Press.

Dahlsgaard, K., Peterson, C., & Seligman, M. E. P. (2005). Shared virtue: The convergence of valued human strengths across culture and history. *Review of General Psychology, 9* (3) 203–213.

Dalton, J. H., Wandersman, A., & Elias, M. J. (2007). *Community psychology: Linking individuals and communities* (2nd ed.). Belmont, CA: Wadsworth.

Damasio, A. R. (1994). *Descartes' error: Emotion, reasoning, and the human brain.* New York: Grosset/Putnam.

Dewey, J. (1916). *Democracy and education.* New York: Macmillan.

Dewey, J. (1933). *How we think.* Lexington, MA: Heath.

Duckworth, A. L., & Seligman, M. E. P. (2005). Self-discipline outdoes IQ in predicting academic performance of adolescents. *Psychological Science, 16* (12), 939–944.

Durlak, J. A., Weissberg, R. P., Dymnicki, A. B., Taylor, R. D., & Schellinger, K. B. (2011). The impact of enhancing students' social and emotional learning: A meta-analysis of school-based universal interventions. *Child Development, 82* (1), 405–432.

Durlak, J. A., Weissberg, R. P., & Pachan, M. (2010). A meta-analysis of after-school programs that seek to promote personal and social skills in children and adolescents. *American Journal of Community Psychology, 45,* 294–309.

Elias, M. J. (2001). Prepare children for the tests of life, not a life of tests. *Education Week, 21* (4), 40.

Elias, M. J., & Arnold, H. A. (Eds.). (2006). *The educator's guide to emotional intelligence and academic achievement: Social-emotional learning in the classroom.* Thousand Oaks, CA: Corwin Press.

Elias, M. J., & Clabby, J. F. (1992). *Building social problem-solving skills.* San Francisco: Jossey-Bass.

Elias, M. J., Kress, J. S., & Hunter, L. (2006). Emotional intelligence and the crisis in education. In J. Ciarrochi, J. P. Forgas, & J. D. Mayer (Eds.), *Emotional intelligence in everyday life* (2nd ed.) (pp. 166–186). Philadelphia, PA: Taylor & Francis.

Elias, M. J., O'Brien, M. U., & Weissberg, R. P. (2006). Transformative leadership for social-emotional learning. *Principal Leadership, 7* (4), 10–13.

Elias, M. J., Tobias, S. E., & Friedlander, B. S. (2002). *Raising emotionally intelligent teenagers.* New York: Three Rivers Press/Random House.

Elias, M. J., Zins, J. E., Weissberg, R. P., Frey, K. S., Greenberg, M. T., Haynes, N. M. et al. (1997). *Promoting social and emotional learning: Guidelines for educators.* Alexandria, VA: Association for Supervision and Curriculum Development.

Forgas, J. P., & East, R. (2008a). On being happy and gullible: Mood effects on skepticism and the detection of deception. *Journal of Experimental Social Psychology, 44* (5), 1362–1367.

Forgas, J. P., & East, R. (2008b). How real is that smile? Mood effects on accepting or rejecting the veracity of emotional facial expressions. *Journal of Nonverbal Behavior, 32* (3), 157–170.

Gardner, H. (1993). *Multiple intelligences: The theory in practice.* New York: Basic Books.

Gillham, J., Adams-Deutsch, Z., Werner, J., Reivich, K., Coulter-Heindl, V., Linkins, M. et al. (2011). Character strengths predict subjective well-being during adolescence. *Journal of Positive Psychology, 6* (1), 31–44.

Goleman, D. (1995). *Emotional intelligence.* New York: Bantam.

Goleman, D. (1998). *Working with emotional intelligence.* New York: Bantam.

Greenberg, M. T., Weissberg, R. P., O'Brien, M. U., Zins, J. E., Fredericks, L., Resnik, H., & Elias, M. J. (2003). Enhancing school-based prevention and youth development through coordinated social, emotional, and academic learning. *American Psychologist, 58,* 466–474.

Huitt, W. (2004). Moral and character development. *Educational Psychology Interactive.* Valdosta, GA: Valdosta State University. Retrieved 2/24/06 from http://chiron.valdosta.edu/whuitt/col/morchr/morchr.html.

Kessler, R. (2000). *The soul of education.* Alexandria, VA: ASCD.

Kohlberg, L. (1984). *The psychology of moral development.* San Francisco: Harper & Row.

Kress, J. S., & Elias, M. J. (2006). Implementing school-based social and emotional learning programs: Navigating developmental crossroads. In I. Sigel & A. Renninger (Eds.), *Handbook of child psychology* (Rev. ed.) (pp. 592–618). New York: Wiley.

Lemerise, E. A., & Arsenio, W. F. (2000). An integrated model of emotion processes and cognition in social information processing. *Child Development, 71,* 107–118.

Lewin, K. (1951). *Field theory in social science.* New York: Harper & Brothers.

Lickona, T. (Ed.). (1976). *Moral development and behavior: Theory, research and social issues.* New York: Holt, Rinehart and Winston.

Lickona, T. (1991). *Educating for character: How our schools can teach respect and responsibility.* New York: Bantam.

Lickona, T., & Davidson, M. (2005). *Smart & good high schools: Integrating excellence and ethics for success in school, work, and beyond.* Cortland, NY: Center for the 4th and 5th Rs (Respect and Responsibility)/Washington, D.C.: Character Education Partnership.

Mayer, J. D. (2001). A field guide to emotional intelligence. In J. Ciarrochi, J. P. Forgas, & J. D. Mayer (Eds.), *Emotional intelligence in everyday life* (pp. 3–24). Philadelphia, PA: Taylor & Francis.

Meichenbaum, D. (1977). *Cognitive behavior modification.* New York: Plenum.

Nucci, L. (Ed.). (1989). *Moral development and character education: A dialogue.* Berkley, CA: McCutchan.

Nucci, L. (2001). *Education in the moral domain.* New York: Cambridge University Press.

Park, N. (2004). Character strengths and positive youth development. *The Annals of the American Academy of Political and Social Science, 591,* 40–54.

Patti, J., & Tobin, J. (2003). *Smart school leaders: Leading with emotional intelligence.* Iowa: Kendall Hunt.

Peterson, C., & Seligman, M. E. P. (2004). *Character strengths and virtues: A handbook and classification.* Washington, D.C.: American Psychological Association.

Piaget, J. (1981). *Intelligence and affectivity: Their relationship during child development.* Palo Alto, CA: Annual Reviews.

Rotter, J. B. (1954). *Social learning and clinical psychology.* Englewood Cliffs, NJ: Prentice-Hall.

Saarni, C. (2007). The development of emotional competence: Pathways for helping children to become emotionally intelligent. In R. Bar-On, J. G. Maree, & M. J. Elias (Eds.), *Educating people to be emotionally intelligent* (pp. 15–36). Westport, CT: Praeger.

Spivack, G., & Shure, M. B. (1974). *Social adjustment of young children: A cognitive approach to solving real life problems.* San Francisco: Jossey-Bass.

Sternberg, R. J. (1985). *Beyond IQ.* New York: Cambridge University Press.

Tough, P. (2012). *How children succeed: Grit, curiosity, and the hidden power of character.* New York: Houghton Mifflin.

Wyland, C. L., & Forgas, J. P. (2010). Here's looking at you kid: Mood effects on processing eye gaze as a heuristic cue. *Social Cognition, 28* (1), 133–144.

Wynne, E., & Ryan, K. (1997). *Reclaiming our schools: A handbook on teaching character, academics, and discipline* (2nd ed.). New York: Merrill.

Zins, J. E., Bloodworth, M. R., Weissberg, R. P., & Walberg, H. J. (2004). The scientific base linking social and emotional learning to school success. In J. E. Zins, R. P. Weissberg, M. C. Wang, & H. J. Walberg (Eds.), *Building academic success on social and emotional learning: What does the research say?* (pp. 3–22). New York: Teachers College Press.

Zins, J. E., Elias, M. J., & Greenberg, M. (2007). School practices to build social-emotional competence as the foundation of academic and life success. In R. Bar-On, J. G. Maree, & M. J. Elias (Eds.), *Educating people to be emotionally intelligent* (pp. 79–94). Westport, CT: Praeger.

Zins, J. E., Weissberg, R. P., Wang, M. L., & Walberg, H. J. (Eds.). (2004). *Building school success through social and emotional learning: Implications for practice and research.* New York: Teachers College Press.

17

SMART & GOOD SCHOOLS

A New Paradigm for High School Character Education

Matthew Davidson, Thomas Lickona, and Vladimir Khmelkov

Writing in the *Journal of Research in Character Education*, character education researcher and historian James Leming (2006) points out a paradox: On the one hand, a "motivating rationale" for contemporary character education has been adolescent behavior such as "suicide rates, teen violence, declining academic performance, increasing drug usage, and precocious sexual activity"; on the other hand, "to date general character education efforts have been primarily focused on elementary and middle school levels" (p. 83). Although character-related challenges are perceived to be greatest at the high school level, character education interventions have primarily targeted the elementary and middle developmental levels. Leming's assessment that character education efforts "have made few inroads in high schools" (2006, p. 84) is corroborated by Berkowitz and Bier's (2006) *What Works in Character Education*. In this monograph, 33 character education programs or strategies are identified that have demonstrated empirical effectiveness; the great majority of these approaches, they note, were developed for the elementary or middle school levels (Berkowitz & Bier, 2006).

If high schools do in fact have less interest in character education than elementary and middle schools, that phenomenon cannot be explained by lack of interest in school improvement. On the contrary, for more than a decade, strengthening high schools has been at the forefront of the national school reform debate. At least a dozen educational organizations are dedicated to promoting one or another high school reform model (cf. National Research Council and the Institute of Medicine, 2004). Philanthropic groups such as the Bill and Melinda Gates Foundation have poured extensive resources into promoting small learning communities, school connectedness, and other efforts to increase high school academic achievement, especially among historically underserved students (Vander Ark, 2005).

If problems such as underachievement, drop-outs, academic dishonesty, violence, drugs, and sexual activity are most pronounced in the high school years, why, then, have high schools not embraced character education as a central school improvement strategy? Leming offers as one reason the fact that

> high school teachers tend to identify themselves as subject matter specialists and give less emphasis to character development than in elementary and middle schools. High school teachers, when asked to define their professional focus, tend to say, "I teach History" or some other subject area.
>
> (Leming, 2006, pp. 83–84)

This tendency of high school educators to define their role as subject matter specialists is reinforced by the high-stakes testing environment (cf. Berliner & Nichols, 2007). The upshot of all this: If academic achievement is the focus of high schools, they are likely to see character education as relevant only to the extent that it supports the academic mission, narrowly defined as teaching and learning the formal curriculum.

In the past, character educators have argued that by helping to create a safe, caring, and orderly school environment, character education creates the conditions conducive to teaching and learning and in that indirect way fosters academic achievement (e.g., Beland, 2003; Lickona, 2004; Schwartz, Beatty, & Dachnowicz, 2006). In fact, research by the Developmental Studies Center at the elementary level (Schaps, Watson, & Lewis, 1996) indicates that students' sense of the school as a caring community is a mediating variable in a diverse range of important school outcomes, including reading comprehension and other academic indicators. However, once teachers have established a safe, caring, and orderly classroom, is there any other, more direct role for character development in fostering academic achievement? Do character strengths, for example, have an ongoing role in helping a student succeed at math, science, and writing, and if so, how? In our experience, high school teachers typically do not see character as contributing directly to academic learning because they tend to equate character education with "discussing ethics" or with "touchy-feely" social and emotional activities, which they view as peripheral to the demands of the academic curriculum. As one chemistry teacher told us, "I teach chemistry; I don't teach character. Occasionally, I might touch on an ethical issue, but I don't have a lot of time for that" (Lickona & Davidson, 2005, p. 27).

OUR TWO-YEAR STUDY OF HIGH SCHOOLS

Our interest in how high school educators think about character education, what they currently do and don't do (intentionally or unintentionally) to develop character, and what can be done to promote the wider implementation of character development practices in the adolescent years led us to undertake a two-year study of high school character education, *Smart & Good High Schools* (Lickona & Davidson, 2005). We began with the belief that the development of character is a worthy pursuit in its own right, not simply for the other desired outcomes it can bring to a school (e.g., academic achievement, school retention, etc.). We believe in the importance of character in all phases of life. From this perspective, the most important goal of character education is to prepare all young people to lead a flourishing life. The work of the Search Institute (Scales, Benson, Leffert, Scales, & Blyth, 1998), and more recently the positive psychology movement (Peterson & Seligman, 2004) has emphasized the value of "asset-building," identifying and developing those human strengths that enable us to become all we are capable of being. It was this broad purpose of character education—to help all young people maximize their potential for meaningful, fulfilling lives—that most deeply informed our study.

However, we also recognize a second legitimate purpose of character education: to help reduce the negative behaviors by which young people hurt themselves and society. Booker T. Washington asserted that "character is power"; we see character and culture as a largely untapped power source that can help to address a range of acute challenges facing schools and society. Indeed, character educators (e.g., Lickona, 1991, 2004; Lickona & Davidson, 2005) have long argued that the troubling behaviors we observe in young people—and in many of the adults who set the example for youth—have a common core: namely, the absence of good character. Developing good character offers the hope of striking at the root of anti-social or self-destructive behaviors and thereby helping to correct and prevent them. This line of argument has sometimes been referred to as the "instrumental" case for character education because it is being offered as a means of ameliorating social ills. But we view this as a legitimate and eminently practical purpose of character education at all developmental levels and especially in high schools, when problematic behaviors such as a lack of responsibility toward schoolwork, academic dishonesty, bullying, substance abuse, and sexual activity typically reach higher levels, as Leming (2006) has pointed out.

Research methodology. In carrying out our two-year study of "promising practices" in high school character education, we conducted a "grounded theory" research methodology (Glaser & Strauss, 1967; Strauss & Corbin, 1994): (1) assembling a database of more than 1,400 books, research studies, reports, and other materials on adolescent development, character education, and high school reform; (2) full-day site visits to each of 24 diverse, award-winning high schools—18 public and six private—in every geographical region of the country; (3) input and feedback from a National Experts Panel (32 authorities on different aspects of adolescent development, character education, and high school reform) and a National Student Leaders Panel (one boy and one girl nominated by each school studied); and (4) supplemental interviews with other high school educators, parents, coaches, community members, and leaders of youth development programs. We established three criteria by which a practice could be considered "promising": (1) research validation (for example, experimental research has found the practice to be effective, or to be related to a variable—such as sense of community—that has been shown to mediate positive character outcomes); (2) relevance to important adolescent outcomes (e.g., development as an ethical thinker) and/or important school outcomes (e.g., reduced discipline problems); and (3) the testimony of credible sources (e.g., an award for excellence from a credible educational organization such as the US Department of Education or the Character Education Partnership). Most of the practices we identified as promising met the first of these criteria (research validation) in that they were directly or indirectly linked to a research base.

In the remainder of this chapter, we lay out some of the core constructs, relevant research, and illustrative practices that define our Smart & Good Schools framework. Our beginning premise is that throughout history, education rightly conceived has had two great goals—to help students become smart (in the multidimensional sense of intelligence) and to help them become good (in the multidimensional sense of moral maturity)—and that they need character for both.

A NEW DEFINITION OF CHARACTER

The first major construct of our Smart & Good Schools model is its conception of human character as having two major parts: performance character and moral character. Our research has led us to propose a paradigm shift in the way we think about character and character education. We came to realize that character isn't just about "doing the right thing" in an ethical sense; it is also about doing our best work. If that is true, then character education isn't just about helping kids get along; it is also about teaching them to work hard, develop their talents, and aspire to excellence in every area of endeavor.

However, this broader conception of character education—as fostering best work as well as best ethical behavior—tends not to be reflected in media accounts of character education. For example, a newspaper article appeared in the *Minneapolis Star Tribune* about character education under the headline, "Don't lie, don't cheat, be on time" (Draper, 2006). The article quoted a state senator as saying, "I would call this 'golden rule education'" (Draper, 2006). The headline and the article conveyed the message that character is about doing the right thing ethically and *not* doing the wrong thing ethically. However, we would ask: Is it enough if students simply don't lie, cheat, and show up late? Is that enough to render character relevant to every high school in America? Is this vision of character a vision of human flourishing? What about the role of character in helping students to do their best work—to give their best effort in the classroom, on the athletic field, in the workplace, and in every area of their lives?

An expanded conception of character education as fostering best work as well as best ethical conduct requires an expanded conception of character. Based on our high school research, we propose a definition of character as having two essential and interconnected parts: *performance character* and *moral character* (depicted in Figure 17.1 below).

We describe performance character as a "mastery orientation." It consists of those qualities—including but not limited to diligence, perseverance, a strong work ethic, a positive attitude, ingenuity, and self-discipline—needed to realize one's potential for excellence in any performance environment, such as academics, extracurricular activities,

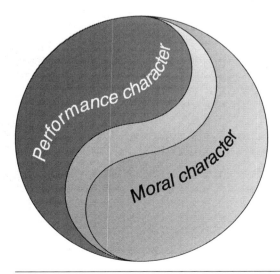

Figure 17.1 Moral and Performance Character Heuristic.

the workplace, and throughout life. Moral character is a "relational orientation." It consists of those qualities— including but not limited to integrity, justice, caring, respect, and cooperation—needed for successful interpersonal relationships and ethical conduct. Moral character enables us to treat others—and ourselves—with respect and care and to act with integrity in our ethical lives. Moral character also has the important job of moderating our performance goals to honor the interests of others, to ensure that we do not violate moral values such as fairness, honesty, and caring in the pursuit of high performance.

RESEARCH RELEVANT TO PERFORMANCE CHARACTER AND MORAL CHARACTER

Support for the importance of performance character and moral character comes from four sources: (1) research on lives of character; (2) research on talent development; (3) research on academic performance; and (4) the voices of teachers and students.

Research on lives of character. If we examine lives of character, we invariably find both strong performance character and strong moral character at work. In their book, *Some Do Care: Contemporary Lives of Moral Commitment,* Colby and Damon (1992) profile 23 men and women of exemplary character, including religious leaders of different faiths, business leaders, physicians, teachers, heads of nonprofit organizations, and leaders of social movements. Their contributions spanned civil rights, the fight against poverty, medical care, education, philanthropy, the environment, peace, and religious freedom. Viewing these portraits of character through the lens of the performance character and moral character construct, one sees, again and again, the interplay of these two sides of character: high ethical goals combined with diligence and determination in the pursuit of those goals.

To take just one example: Colby and Damon describe the work of Cabel Brand, who as a businessman over three decades developed a small family company into a multimillion dollar corporation. Brand launched a social action program called Total Action Against Poverty (TAP). TAP initiated one of the nation's first Head Start programs; developed programs for high school drop-outs, the elderly, ex-offenders, drug addicts, and the homeless; and created a food bank, a program to bring running water to rural people, economic development programs for impoverished urban areas, and community cultural centers. Brand's combination of drive, expertise, organizational skills, and concern for the welfare of others typifies the exemplars in this study. Colby and Damon's book could have been titled, *Some Do Care—And Those Who Care Most Effectively Are Very Good At What They Do.* None of the noble accomplishments of these exemplars would have been possible without the synergistic contributions of performance character and moral character.

Research on talent development. Studies of talent development show that performance character qualities such as self-discipline and good work habits are essential for developing innate ability. In their book *Talented Teenagers,* a five-year longitudinal study of 200 talented adolescents, Csikszentmihalyi, Rathunde, and Whalen (1993) begin by noting that underachievement on the part of talented youth is quite common in fields as varied as athletics, art, science, mathematics, and music. Why do some talented teens develop their potential while other equally gifted peers do not? This study found that adolescents who were more successful in developing their talents were characterized by a stronger "achievement and endurance orientation" and habits conducive to talent development—

such as focusing on goals whether doing talent-related work or general schoolwork, being able to spend time alone, and, when they did spend time with friends, collaborating on hobbies and studying instead of simply "hanging out." Strong performance character was the distinguishing mark of teens who made the most of their talent potential.

Similarly, Ericsson (Ericsson, Charness, Feltovich, & Hoffman, 2006) investigated the origins of expert performance, utilizing performance statistics, biographical details, and their own laboratory experiments with high achievers. Based on their research, they argue that talent is generally overrated as a predictor of excellence, whereas deliberative practice (defined as setting specific goals, obtaining immediate feedback, and concentrating as much on technique as on outcome) is a much more powerful predictor. They assert that across a diverse sampling of fields, "stars"—expert performers—are made, not born. In other words, it is performance character, not simply talent that leads to expert performance. Narvaez and Lapsley (2005) reach parallel conclusions in their work on expertise.

Research on academic performance. Given their focus on academic achievement, high schools will be especially interested in evidence that improvement in students' performance character leads to improved academic performance. For example, Duckworth and Seligman (2006) sought to understand why throughout elementary, middle, and high school, girls earn higher grades than boys in all major subjects, in spite of the fact that boys outperform girls on measures of achievement (e.g., SAT, ACT, AP) and IQ. Previously this performance difference was explained by gender differences favoring boys in these tests. However, using student measures of delayed gratification and self-report, as well as teacher and parent ratings, Duckworth and Seligman's research (2006) identifies the character strength of self-discipline as giving girls the performance edge over boys.

There are multiple theoretical grounds for predicting this positive relation between performance character (e.g., self-discipline) and higher academic performance. Educational, sociological, and social psychological theories of the learning process have long recognized student effort as central to student learning (e.g., Sørensen & Hallinan, 1977; Yair, 2000). In their book *Classroom Instruction That Works*, Marzano, Pickering, and Pollock (2001) report that students who believe that achievement is something they earn through effort, and not primarily the result of innate abilities, do best in school. Tough (2012) presents research on the power of character strengths such as grit and curiosity as a powerful predictor of student success. Students' academic effort and achievement are, in turn, enhanced by a school climate focused on excellence (Bryk, Lee, & Holland, 1993; Shouse, 1996). High school students who become more oriented toward excellence are more likely to choose advanced courses, which are likely to result in skills and credentials that students need to achieve success in college and in the labor market (Davenport et al., 1998; Kerckhoff, 1993). The kinds of courses students take do in fact predict academic achievement and college matriculation (Lukas, 1999; Stevenson, Schiller, & Schneider, 1994).

Moreover, when students' development of performance character leads to their improved effort and quality of work, the classroom conditions for learning and teaching also improve. With more students focused on work and fewer distractions, teachers are able to devote more time to teaching content and working with individual students. A reciprocal expectations-obligations relationship tends to emerge between students and educators, with both sides feeling a stronger commitment to higher quality of teaching and learning (Coleman, 1988, 1990; Khmelkov & Power, 2000; Portes, 1998).

To summarize our conceptualization of performance character and moral character, we offer the following propositions:

A person of character embodies both performance character and moral character. Washington State University historian Richard Hooker (1996) notes that the Greek notion of *arête* is often translated as "virtue" but is actually better translated as "being the best you can be" or "reaching your highest human potential." To become a person of character is to become the best person we can be—to develop our full human potential. Clearly, being the best person we can be includes doing our best work (performance character) as well as doing the right thing in our relationships (moral character).

Performance character and moral character both carry obligation. Performance character, like moral character, has an ethical dimension; it is a moral failure, for example, when we do shoddy work. Green (1999) refers to this moral notion of performance as "conscience of craft." He states: "To possess a conscience of craft is to have acquired the capacity for self-congratulation or deep self-satisfaction at something well done, shame at slovenly work, and even embarrassment at carelessness" (1999, p. 62). All of us have a responsibility to develop our talents, use them to enhance the lives of others, and give our best effort as we perform the large and small tasks of life (performance character). We have this obligation for two reasons: (1) respect for ourselves requires us not to waste our talents but to use them to develop as persons and to perform to the best of our ability in whatever we undertake; and (2) caring about others requires us to do our work well, since the quality of our work, especially in the world beyond school, affects the quality of other people's lives. When we do our work well—whether as a parent, teacher, mechanic, or doctor—other people typically benefit; when we do it poorly, other people suffer. In a similar way, we have a responsibility to be our best ethical self (moral character)—both out of self-respect and because our ethical conduct affects the lives of those around us. If we treat others with respect and caring, we contribute to their welfare and happiness; if we do the opposite, we demean them and subtract from the quality of their lives.

In a person of character, performance character and moral character support each other in an integrated way. In a person of character, the two sides of character are interdependent; each needs the other. Consider what can happen if we have performance character without moral character. We might choose selfish goals (such as making a lot of money that we spend only on ourselves) or even evil goals (such as blowing up innocent people). Or we might choose a good goal (such as doing well in school or fighting terrorism) but corrupt our pursuit of that goal by using unethical means to achieve it (such as plagiarizing papers or employing inhumane methods to interrogate suspected terrorists). Moral character is what motivates us to choose moral goals and then pursue them in a fully ethical way. Or, consider what happens if we have moral character without performance character. We might have good intentions but poor ability to execute. We might want to help others—through a community service project, for example—but lack the confidence, organization, ingenuity, and perseverance to carry that out effectively. In this vision of the interdependence of performance character and moral character, excellence and ethics harmonize to make possible an act—or a life—of character.

WHAT IS THE ROLE OF CHARACTER IN ACADEMICS?

Having argued the case for a concept of character that gives a central role to both performance character and moral character, we return to the question that has until now been difficult for character educators to answer: "What is the connection between character and academics?" We believe this question is easier to answer if we apply our expanded definition of character as comprised of performance character and moral character. From this theoretical perspective, one can identify four important roles for character in academic life (and work in general):

1. Students *need* performance character (work ethic, self-discipline, perseverance, initiative, teamwork, etc.) in order to do their best academic work.
2. Students *develop* their performance character (the ability to work hard, overcome obstacles, find joy in a job well done, etc.) from their schoolwork.
3. Students *need* moral character (respect, fairness, kindness, honesty, etc.) in order to create the classroom relationships that make for a positive learning environment.
4. Students *develop* moral character from their schoolwork (e.g., by helping their peers to do their best work through a "culture of critique" that offers constructive feedback, by studying ethical issues in the curriculum, and by using their curricular learning in service projects that help solve real-world problems).

In short, both performance character and moral character are *needed for* and *developed from* every area of academic work. Character is no longer the "other side of the report card" (i.e., "the ethical" or "social-emotional side"); it is "the whole report card" in that character is a foundation for, and a critical outcome of, all academic and ethical endeavors. The ethical and social-emotional outcomes of character education are not replaced or de-emphasized; instead in this new paradigm, character is wrapped around every element of the formal and informal curriculum. Schools no longer need to talk about "balancing academics and character" as if there were a tension between the two. In the Smart & Good School paradigm, teaching academics and developing character are opposite sides of the same coin. Done effectively, they occur simultaneously in mutually supportive ways.

EIGHT STRENGTHS OF CHARACTER (DEVELOPMENTAL OUTCOMES)

Although performance character and moral character increase character education's relevance to the school's academic mission, we believe these two major parts of character will be more practically useful to educators if they are defined in terms of specific strengths of character that can serve as target developmental outcomes. Our Smart & Good Schools framework proposes eight such strengths of character as the crucial outcomes of schooling: (1) lifelong learner and critical thinker, (2) diligent and capable performer, (3) socially and emotionally skilled person, (4) ethical thinker, (5) respectful and responsible moral agent, (6) self-disciplined person who pursues a healthy lifestyle, (7) contributing community member and democratic citizen, and (8) spiritual person engaged in crafting a life of noble purpose (defined inclusively to encompass non-religious as well as religious world views and to focus on universally important existential questions such as "What is the meaning of life?" and "What is authentic happiness?").

We see these Eight Strengths of Character not as narrow "traits" but rather as a broad heuristic of psychological assets needed for a flourishing life. (Table 17.1 describes each of these eight strengths in terms of what we see as their sub-components.)

Table 17.1 Eight Strengths of Character: Assets Needed for a Flourishing Life

1. Lifelong learner and critical thinker
   - Strives to acquire the knowledge that characterizes an educated person
   - Approaches learning as a lifelong process
   - Demonstrates skills of critical analysis
   - Takes seriously the perspectives of others
   - Seeks expert opinion and credible evidence
   - Makes connections and integrates knowledge
   - Generates alternative solutions
   - Demonstrates willingness to admit error and modify thinking

2. Diligent and capable performer
   - Strives for excellence; gives best effort
   - Demonstrates initiative and self-discipline
   - Knows standards of quality and creates high-quality products; takes pride in work
   - Sets personal goals and assesses progress
   - Perseveres in the face of difficulty

3. Socially and emotionally skilled person
   - Possesses a healthy self-confidence and a positive attitude
   - Demonstrates basic courtesy in social situations
   - Develops positive interpersonal relationships that include sensitivity to the feelings of others and the capacity for "confrontation"
   - Communicates effectively
   - Works well with others
   - Resolves conflicts fairly
   - Demonstrates emotional intelligence, including self-knowledge and the ability to manage emotions

4. Ethical thinker
   - Possesses moral discernment, including good judgment, moral reasoning, and ethical wisdom
   - Has a well-formed conscience, including a sense of obligation to do the right thing
   - Has a strong moral identity that is defined by one's moral commitments
   - Possesses the moral competence, or "know how," needed to translate discernment, conscience, and identity into effective moral behavior.

5. Respectful and responsible moral agent committed to consistent moral action
   - Respects the rights and dignity of all persons
   - Understands that respect includes the right of conscience to disagree respectfully with others' beliefs or behaviors
   - Possesses a strong sense of personal efficacy and responsibility to do what's right
   - Takes responsibility for mistakes
   - Accepts responsibility for setting a good example and being a positive influence
   - Develops and exercises capacity for moral leadership

6. Self-disciplined person who pursues a healthy lifestyle
   - Demonstrates self-control across a wide range of situations
   - Pursues physical, emotional, and mental health
   - Makes responsible personal choices that contribute to continuous self-development, a healthy lifestyle, and a positive future.

7. Contributing community member and democratic citizen
   - Contributes to family, classroom, school, and community
   - Demonstrates civic virtues and skills needed for participation in democratic processes
   - Appreciates the nation's democratic heritage and democratic values
   - Demonstrates awareness of interdependence and a sense of responsibility to humanity

8. Spiritual person crafting a life of noble purpose
   • Considers existential questions ("What is the meaning of life?", "What is happiness?", "What is the purpose of *my* life?")
   • Seeks a life of noble purpose
   • Formulates life goals and ways to pursue them
   • Cultivates an appreciation of transcendent values such as truth, beauty, and goodness
   • Pursues authentic happiness
   • Possesses a rich inner life
   • Pursues deep, meaningful connections—e.g., to others, nature, or a higher power

---

Our Eight Strengths of Character heuristic is built from cross-cultural research on character, notably Peterson's and Seligman's *Character Strengths and Virtues* (2004); classical conceptions of a meaningful life (e.g., Frankel, 1959); positive psychology (Seligman, 2002); moral psychology (e.g., Blasi, 2004; Kohlberg, 1976; Lapsley, 1996); research on social-emotional learning (e.g., CASEL, 2003; Elias et al., 1997; Goleman, 1995); educational research (e.g., Marzano et al., 2001; Pallas, 2000); work on the development of purpose (e.g., Damon, Memon, & Bronk, 2003) and the role of spirituality in education (e.g., Kessler, 2000; Palmer, 1999); research on service learning (e.g., Billig, 2000); theory and research on intellectual character (e.g., Ritchhart, 2002; Sternberg, 1997); the input of our Experts Panel and Student Leaders Panel; and our own grounded theory research.

Just as we see performance character and moral character as mutually supportive, we also see the Eight Strengths of Character as interdependent, each needed for the optimal functioning of the others. Being a diligent and capable performer, for example, affects how hard we work at developing all the other strengths of character. Consider, for example, the hard, persevering work it takes to become a socially and emotionally skilled person who listens well to others and can solve conflicts effectively. Being an ethical thinker—bringing discerning moral judgment to bear on every situation—guides how we live out all the other strengths. Being a self-disciplined person who pursues a healthy lifestyle will clearly affect our ability to actualize all the other strengths of character. As we grow as spiritual persons, deepening our sense of purpose in life, that brings new energy and resolve to the development of the other strengths. And so on.

The Eight Strengths of Character heuristic represents what we think is a needed expansion of character education theory, especially if it wishes to address the real-world challenges faced by high schools. Most previous approaches have defined desired character outcomes more narrowly. Moral education has focused on ethical thinking as the central developmental outcome at the high school level. The social and emotional learning field has viewed social and emotional skills as the major desired outcome. Civic education and service learning have seen democratic citizenship as the central goal, and so on. In reality, however, the varied academic and behavioral challenges faced by high schools and the short- and long-term outcomes desired by society from high schools, require a more comprehensive character theory with a broader set of character outcomes. Without an adequate vision of end-goals, character education gets chopped into such small pieces as to have limited relevance to the array of acute challenges confronting high schools and society. We offer the Eight Strengths of Character as a framework of developmental outcomes that we think are more commensurate with the need.

FOUR KEY STRATEGIES FOR DEVELOPMENT OF PERFORMANCE CHARACTER, MORAL CHARACTER, AND THE EIGHT STRENGTHS OF CHARACTER

In a Smart & Good School, how are performance character, moral character, and the Eight Strengths of Character developed? Most of our 227-page *Smart & Good High Schools* report (Lickona & Davidson, 2005) is devoted to describing nearly a hundred promising practices, culled from our research, for developing these outcomes. In our ongoing efforts to implement this model, however, we have found a simpler "master strategy" emerging that can be applied to any of the Eight Strengths of Character and across different subject areas, co-curricular activities, advisories, remedial assistance, school and classroom discipline, and any other aspect of schooling. We call this overarching strategy the "4 KEYS for Developing Performance Character and Moral Character" (4 KEYS for short). The 4 KEYS are:

1. *The Ethical Learning Community (ELC)*—developing a community (classroom, advisory group, team, whole school) that both supports and challenges and whose members pursue the realization of their own potential for excellence and ethics *and* seek to bring out the best in every other person.
2. *Self-Study*—engaging students in assessing their strengths and areas for growth in performance character and moral character, setting goals for improvement, and monitoring their progress.
3. *Other-Study*—learning from exemplars of performance character and moral character by analyzing and emulating their pathways to success.
4. *Public Performance/Presentation*—using public performances and presentations as experiential learning and authentic assessment of students' performance character and moral character.

Let us illustrate each of these 4 KEYS to show their supporting research, diverse practical applications, and examples of how high schools and teachers have actually used them.

   The Ethical Learning Community (ELC). The first of the 4 KEYS, the Ethical Learning Community, recognizes that character develops in and through community, and that the norms of a community are a potent force in shaping character. Creating an Ethical Learning Community seeks to take character education beyond its focus on the psychological assets of the individual to the assets of the culture in which the individual lives and dwells, the location where the psychological assets are developed. Focusing on creating an Ethical Learning Community fulfills Kohlberg's exhortation to "change the life of the school as well as the development of the individual" (Power, Higgins, & Kohlberg, 1989). As Power and colleagues (Power et al., 1989) argue,

> The teaching of justice, as the teaching of reading or arithmetic, is set in a context of a classroom and a school, and how the students experience the life of the classroom and school will have a shaping effect on what they learn from what the teacher teaches.
>
> (p. 20)

In attempting to map the human ecological system, Garbarino (1990) argues that the habitat of youth includes "family, friends, neighborhood, church, and school, as well as less immediate forces that constitute the social geography and climate (e.g., laws, institutions, and values), and the physical environment" (p. 78). In its largest dimensions, the Ethical Learning Community is an ecological system comprised of all the stakeholder groups that affect the culture of the school and the character development of its members. Those stakeholder groups include faculty and staff, students, parents, and the wider community. The ideal of an Ethical Learning Community is that all four of these groups will support and challenge each other in doing their best work (performance character) and being their best ethical selves (moral character). No one is exempt from the norms of excellence and ethics.

However, this "macro-ELC" is made up of many "micro-ELCs," such as individual classrooms, advisory groups, clubs, teams, and other groups. Any group, whatever its size, will maximize its potential for excellence and ethics if it functions as an Ethical Learning Community. In defining an Ethical Learning Community as a community that supports and challenges, we are advocating an environment where participation in the community means not simply "passing the put-up" (the "warm-fuzzy" stereotype of character education held by many high school educators) but constantly challenging each other to be the best person we can be. In many ways, the Ethical Learning Community seeks to create what Vygotsky (1978) called a zone of proximal development, defined as "the distance between the actual developmental level as determined by independent problem solving and level of potential development as determined through problem solving under adult guidance or in collaboration with more capable peers" (p. 86). An Ethical Learning Community is a place where we intentionally and proactively structure opportunities for individuals to pursue their personal best through the assistance of teachers, parents, or peers.

Our theoretical model of the Ethical Learning Community (Lickona & Davidson, 2005) is supported by our first-hand observation of award-winning high schools and also by relevant theory and/or research (Lickona & Davidson, 2005), including research on "school connectedness" as a predictor of adolescent flourishing (Resnick et al., 1997); research on the experience of democratic school community as a predictor of adolescents' use of their highest available moral reasoning (Power, Higgins, & Kohlberg, 1989), reduced discipline problems (Freiberg, 1989), and civic participation after high school (Grady, 1994); and research showing the power of positive peer pressure to influence the behavior even of previously anti-social youth, especially when coupled with direct instruction in perspective-taking and communication skills (e.g., Gibbs, 2003).

Self-Study. The second of the 4 KEYS is Self-Study. In the Self-Study process, we are engaging students in assessing their strengths and areas for growth in performance character and moral character, setting goals for improvement, and monitoring their progress. Terman and Oden (1959) found that intellectually gifted high school students who learned to set and pursue goals went on to achieve higher levels of success than equally gifted students who did not learn to set goals. The goal of Self-Study as a pedagogical strategy is student engagement and personalization; it seeks to move the locus of control from outside of the individual to inside the individual. With Self-Study we attempt to take the character words "off the wall" and to put them inside students' hearts and minds. Through Self-Study, students have direct access to plan, monitor, and change their own behaviors.

In Csikszentmihalyi's *Flow: The Psychology of Optimal Experience* (1990), he provides insight into the importance of Self-Study. He describes "flow" as "deep concentration, high and balanced challenges and skills, a sense of control and satisfaction." He describes the requirements for flow as:

1. Setting an overall goal and as many sub-goals as realistically feasible;
2. Finding ways of measuring progress in terms of goals chosen;
3. Keeping concentrating on what one is doing to keep making finer and finer distinctions in the challenges involved in the activity;
4. Developing the skills necessary to interact with the opportunities available;
5. Raising the stakes if the activity becomes boring.

The steps to "flow" is a Self-Study template, a way to assist students in the development of a task orientation (Duda & Nicholls, 1992; Nicholls, 1984, 1992). Like Csikzentmihalyi's flow theory, the literature on achievement motivation helps us understand self-study and in particular the relation of self to others. This research suggests that an ego (or performance) orientation is one where a person is motivated to show competence in relation to others by showing superiority (e.g., by winning, getting the most right, being able to list the most kind things done to others), whereas with a task (or learning) orientation, the person competes against self-referenced personal achievement (e.g., a better time than before, more right on this test than last time, fewer unnecessary interruptions of the class today than yesterday). In addition to facilitating numerous positive performance outcomes (academic, athletic, and other), a task orientation tends to promote self-reflection and awareness, to support strong intrinsic motivation, and to reduce helpless response to failure (Duda & Nicholls, 1992; Nicholls, 1984, 1992).

Other-Study. Our third "Key" is "Other-Study." With Other-Study we have students study people and products that exemplify performance character and moral character. From Other-Study, students learn the skills of analyzing and emulating the pathways to success. Other-Study builds upon social-cognitive learning theory (Bandura, 1977, 1991). "Growing out of behaviorism, social learning theory focuses on the ways in which individuals learn from others and their surroundings—including the mechanisms of modeling, imitation, and social reinforcement" (Lapsley, 1996, p. 193). The Other-Study process helps students understand, internalize, and master the requisite skills for reproducing high levels of excellence and ethics in their own lives. As Green states: "We encounter the conscience of craft being formed whenever we observe the novice coming to adopt the standards of some craft as his or her own" (Green, 1999, p. 61).

Other-Study isn't just a strategy for studying people as models; it also serves as a powerful model for studying products of excellence and ethics. For example, Berger (2003) argues for providing students with examples of beautiful, powerful, important work created by their fellow students or by professionals. He sees these models as providing inspiration for students—a standard to strive for. He states:

When my class begins a new project, a new venture, we begin with a taste of excellence…. We sit and we admire. We critique and discuss what makes the work powerful: what makes a piece of a creative writing compelling and exciting; what makes a scientific or historical research project significant and stirring; what makes a novel mathematical solution so breath-taking.

(Berger, 2003, p. 31)

As a strategy for promoting excellence, studying products of excellence challenges students to ask: What does excellence look like, where does it come from, what does it take to create excellence in your own work? Questions like these have the potential to help students understand better how to develop their own performance character.

Current events are a rich source of both positive and negative examples of character. Virtue in Action, an online current events resource (www.virtueinaction.org), offers compelling in-the-news examples of integrity, compassion, and courage as well as instances of greed, disrespect, violence, and dishonesty. One Virtue in Action lesson, for example, featured Shirin Ebadi, the first Muslim woman and the first person from Iran to win the Nobel Peace Prize. After presenting a character exemplar such as Shirin Ebadi, the teacher would have students reflect on questions such as the following:

1. What strengths of character enabled this person to do what he or she did?
2. What obstacles did this person have to overcome?
3. What is one character strength possessed by this person that you would like to develop to a higher degree? Make a plan.

Contemporary and historical examples of man's inhumanity to man can offer equally compelling forms of Other-Study. *Facing History and Ourselves* (www.facing.org) is one of the 33 programs identified as having research validation by *What Works in Character Education* (Berkowitz & Bier, 2006). An evaluation of this curriculum showed gains in students' moral reasoning and relationship maturity as well as reduced fighting and racist attitudes. Kohlberg argued, "The main experiential determinants of moral development seem to be amount and variety of social experience, the opportunity to take a number of roles and to encounter other perspectives" (1973, p. 96). Other-Study programs like *Facing History* clearly provide students opportunities for new roles and perspectives.

Regarding the influence of modeling, Lapsley (1996) argues that the "literature leaves little question that observing prosocial models can have powerful effects on children" (p. 193). He argues that prosocial models have been shown to enhance altruistic behavior, generosity, and resistance to temptation; further, he argues that the effects of modeling endure over time.

Public Performance/Presentation. The last of the 4 KEYS is public performance or presentation. Public performance/presentation functions pedagogically for us as both experiential learning (Kolb, 1983) and authentic assessment (Darling-Hammond, 1993; Wiggins & McTighe, 1998) of students' performance character and moral character. For example, service learning provides a public performance activity that provides students a chance to "exercise" moral character as they serve others. It gives them an opportunity to practice moral character "in the real world." A ten-year compilation of research on the impact of service learning indicates that it helps develop students' sense of civic and social responsibility and citizenship skills, improves school climate, increases respect between teachers and students, and improves the interpersonal development and ability to relate to diverse groups (Billig, 2000).

In his book, *An Ethic of Excellence: Creating a Culture of Craftsmanship with Students*, master teacher and part-time carpenter Ron Berger (2003) makes a strong case for the motivational power of presenting one's work publicly. He points out that for most students, the audience for their work is an audience of one—the teacher. For many students, that is not audience enough; they don't care if the teacher gives them a bad grade. More powerful, Berger says, is a classroom culture where students have to regularly present your work to their peers and where their peers expect them to do their best. Every student wants to fit in, and if the peer norm is to do your best work, students will strive to fit in to that culture.

Essential to creating this kind of classroom is what Berger calls "a culture of critique." Students regularly share their work with the whole class, with the teacher guiding the process. There are rules for critique: "Be kind; be specific; be helpful." Students presenting a piece of work first explain their ideas or goals and state what they are seeking help with. Classmates begin with positive comments and phrase suggestions as questions: "Would you consider [e.g., adding X, deleting Y, changing Y, etc.]…?" The teacher uses the critique session as the optimal opportunity for teaching necessary concepts and skills. Following critique sessions, students have the opportunity to use the group feedback to do revisions, sometimes many revisions. Berger laments that in most schools, students turn in first drafts—work that doesn't represent their best effort and that is typically discarded after it has been graded and returned. By contrast, in the workplace, where the quality of one's work really matters, one almost never submits a first draft. An ethic of excellence requires revision.

Following revision, students present their work to a wider audience. *Every* final draft students complete is done for some kind of an outside audience—whether a class of kindergartners, parents, the whole school, the wider community, or the local or state government. In this kind of classroom, the teacher's role is not as the sole judge of their work but rather similar to that of a sports coach or play director—helping them get their work ready for the public eye.

CONCLUSION

We conclude our chapter with two quotes. The first is from Martin Luther King, Jr. On the evening of his assassination, King addressed the striking sanitation workers of Montgomery, Alabama, with these words:

> You must discover what you are made for, and you must work indefatigably to achieve excellence in your field of endeavor. If you are called to be a street sweeper, you should sweep streets even as Michelangelo painted, or Beethoven composed music, or Shakespeare wrote poetry. You should sweep streets so well that all the hosts of heaven will pause to say, here lived a great street sweeper who did his job well.

The second quote is from one of the high school teachers in our *Smart & Good High Schools* study. He commented:

> Students today are growing up in a world where it seems okay to cheat to get ahead. When I find out about an incident of cheating in my class, I give a little talk to my students:

> "There are two roads in life: a high road and a low road. The high road is harder, but it takes you somewhere worth going. The low road is easy, but it's circular—you eventually find yourself back where you started. If you cheat now, you'll cheat later. Your life won't get better—and *you* won't get better—on the low road."

There are certainly many forces, in human nature and in society, that can influence young people to take the low road. But we believe that deep within every young person, there is also a desire to lead a flourishing life. It falls to us as parents and teachers to point out—and make accessible—the high road of character as the reliable pathway to a flourishing life. That high road includes both the summons to excellence of which King spoke and the call to ethical integrity of which the high school teacher spoke.

To prepare our young to lead flourishing lives, we therefore need a broader vision of character education than the one that has thus far guided the field. To date, the field has focused on ethics (moral character) while neglecting excellence (performance character). We need to view character education as the *intentional integration of excellence and ethics*—the systematic effort to develop performance character, moral character, and the Eight Strengths of Character through every phase of school life. The academic curriculum, school routines, rituals and traditions, discipline, co-curricular activities, service learning, and teachable moments all become opportunities to develop the full range of assets needed for an ethical, productive, and fulfilling life.

This broader definition of character education represents, we think, a paradigm shift for the field. It is, we think, an essential paradigm shift for character education in high schools—because it makes character education directly relevant to the school's central mission of teaching and learning.

REFERENCES

Bandura, A. (1977). *Social learning theory.* New York: General Learning Press.

Bandura, A. (1991). Social cognitive theory of moral thought and action. In W.M. Kurtines & J.L. Gewirtz (Eds.), *Handbook of moral behavior and development: Volume 1: Theory* (pp. 45–103). Hillsdale, NJ: Lawrence Erlbaum Associates.

Beland, K. (Ed.). (2003). *Eleven principles sourcebook: How to achieve quality character education in your school or district.* Washington, DC: Character Education Partnership.

Benson, P.L., Leffert, N., Scales, P.C., & Blyth, D.A. (1998). Beyond the "village" rhetoric: Creating healthy communities for children and adolescents. *Applied Developmental Science, 2,* 138–159.

Berger, R. (2003). *An ethic of excellence.* Portsmouth, NH: Heinemann.

Berkowitz, M., & Bier, M. (2006). *What works in character education: A research-driven guide for educators.* Washington, DC: Character Education Partnership.

Berliner, D.C., & Nichols, S.L. (2007). High-stakes testing is putting the nation at risk. *Education Week, 26*(27), 36, 48.

Billig, S. (2000). *Service-learning impacts on youth, schools and communities: Research on k-12 school-based service learning, 1990–1999.* Denver, CO: RMC Research Corporation.

Blasi, A. (2004). Moral functioning and moral personality. In D.K. Lapsley & D. Narvaez (Eds.), *Moral development, self, and identity* (pp. 335–347). Mahwah, NJ: Lawrence Erlbaum Associates.

Bryk, A.S. Lee, V.E., & Holland, P.B. (1993). *Catholic schools and the common good.* Cambridge, MA: Harvard University Press.

Character Education Partnership. (2005). *2005 National School of Character: Award-Winning Practices.* Washington, DC: Character Education Partnership.

Character Education Partnership. (2006). *2006 National School of Character: Award-Winning Practices.* Washington, DC: Character Education Partnership.

Colby, A., & Damon, W. (1992). *Some do care.* New York: Free Press.

Coleman, J.S. (1988). Social capital in the creation of human capital. *American Journal of Sociology, 94,* S95–120.

Coleman, J.S. (1990). *Foundations of social theory.* Cambridge, MA: Belknap Press of Harvard University Press.

Collaborative for Academic, Social, and Emotional Learning (CASEL). (2003). *Safe and sound: An educational leader's guide to evidence-based social and emotional learning programs.* Chicago: CASEL.

Csíkszentmihalyi, M. (1990). *Flow: The psychology of optimal experience.* New York: Harper and Row.

Csíkszentmihalyi, M., Ratunde, K., & Whalen, S. (1993). *Talented teenagers: The roots of success and failure.* New York: Cambridge University Press.

Damon, W., Memon, J., & Bronk, K.C. (2003). The development of purpose during adolescence. *Applied Developmental Science, 7*(3), 119–123.

Darling-Hammond, L. (1993). Setting standards for students: The case for authentic assessment. *NAASP Bulletin, 77,* 18–26.

Davenport, E.C. Jr., Davison, M.L., Kuang, H., Ding, S., Se-Kang, K., & Kwak, N. (1998). High school mathematics course-taking by gender and ethnicity. *American Educational Research Journal, 35,* 497–514.

Draper, N. (2006). Don't lie, don't cheat, be on time. *The Star Tribune,* June 6.

Duckworth, A.L., & Seligman, M.E.P. (2006). Self-discipline gives girls the edge: Gender in self-discipline, grades, and achievement test scores. *Journal of Educational Psychology, 98*(1), 198–208.

Duda, J.L., & Nicholls, J.G. (1992). Dimensions of achievement motivation in schoolwork and sport. *Journal of Educational Psychology, 84*(3), 290–299.

Elias, M.J., Zins, J.E., Weissberg, R.P. et al. (1997). *Promoting social and emotional learning: Guidelines for educators.* Alexandria, VA: Association for Supervision and Curriculum Development.

Ericsson, K.A., Charness, N., Feltovich, P.J., & Hoffman, R.R. (2006). *The Cambridge handbook of expertise and expert performance.* Cambridge: Cambridge University Press.

Frankel, V. (1959). *Man's search for meaning.* Boston: Beacon.

Freiberg, H.J. (1989). Turning around at-risk schools through consistency management. *Journal of Negro Education, 58,* 372–382.

Garbarino, J. (1990). Youth in dangerous environments: Coping with the consequences. In K. Hurrelman & F. Losel (Eds.), *Health hazards in adolescence* (pp. 193–218). New York: Walter de Gruyter.

Gibbs, J.C. (2003). *Moral development and reality.* Thousand Oaks, CA: Sage Publications.

Goleman, D. (1995). *Emotional intelligence.* New York: Bantam.

Glaser, B.G., & Strauss, A.L. (1967). *The discovery of grounded theory: Strategies for qualitative research.* New York: Aldine De Gruyter.

Grady, E.A. (1994). After cluster school: A study of the impact in adulthood of a moral education intervention project. Unpublished doctoral dissertation, Harvard University.

Green, T.F. (1999). *Voices: The educational formation of conscience.* South Bend, IN: University of Notre Dame Press.

Hooker, Richard. (1996). World civilizations: About world civilizations. Retrieved April 19, 2007, from the World Wide Web: www.wsu.edu:8080/~dee/WORLD.HTM.

Kerckhoff, A.C. (1993). *Diverging pathways: Social structure and career deflections.* Cambridge, England: Cambridge University Press.

Kessler, R. (2000). *The soul of education: Helping students find connection, compassion, and character at school.* Alexandria, VA: Association for Supervision and Curriculum Development.

Khmelkov, V.T., & Power, A.M. (2000). Examining the relationship between teacher-student social ties and math achievement. Paper presented at the annual meeting of the American Educational Research Association, New Orleans.

Kohlberg, L. (1973). *Collected papers on moral development and education.* Harvard University: Center for Moral Education.

Kohlberg, L. (1976). Moral stages and moralization: The cognitive-developmental approach. In T. Lickona (Ed.). *Moral development and behavior: Theory, research, and social issues* (pp. 31–53). New York: Holt, Rinehart, and Winston.

Kolb, D.A. (1983). *Experiential learning: Experience as the source of learning and development.* New York: Prentice Hall.

Lapsley, D.K. (1996). *Moral psychology.* Boulder, CO: Westview Press.

Leming, J. (2006). Smart & good high schools: Integrating excellence and ethics for success in school, work, and beyond. *Journal of Research in Character Education, 4,* 83–91.

Lickona, T. (1991). *Educating for character: How our schools can teach respect and responsibility.* New York: Bantam.

Lickona, T. (2004). *Character matters: How to help our children develop good judgment, integrity, and other essential virtues.* New York: Simon & Schuster.

Lickona, T., & Davidson, M. (2005). *Smart & good high schools: Integrating excellence and ethics for success in school, work, and beyond.* Cortland, NY: Center for the 4th and 5th Rs (Respect and Responsibility)/Washington, DC: Character Education Partnership.

Lukas, S.R. (1999). *Tracking inequality: Stratification and mobility in American high schools.* New York: Teachers College Press.

Marzano, R., Pickering, D., & Pollock, J.E. (2001). *Classroom instruction that works: Research-based strategies for increasing student achievement.* Alexandria, VA: Association for Supervision & Curriculum Development.

National Research Council and the Institute of Medicine. (2004). *Engaging schools: Fostering high school students' motivations to learn.* Washington, DC: The National Academies Press.

Narvaez, D., & Lapsley, D.K. (2005). The psychological foundation of moral expertise. In D.K. Lapsley & F.C. Power (Eds.), *Character psychology and character education* (pp. 140–165). Notre Dame, IN: University of Notre Dame Press.

Nicholls, J.G. (1984). Achievement motivation: Conceptions of ability, subjective experience, task choice, and performance. *Psychological Review, 91,* 328–346.

Nicholls, J.G. (1992). The general and the specific in the development and expression of achievement motivation. In G. Roberts (Ed.), *Motivation in sport and exercise.* Champaign, IL: Human Kinetics.

Pallas, A.M. (2000). The effects of schooling on individual lives. In M.T. Hallinan (Ed.), *Handbook of the sociology of education* (pp. 499–525). New York: Kluwer Academic/Plenum Publishers.

Palmer, P. (1999). Evoking the spirit in public education. *Educational Leadership, 56*(4), 6–11.

Peterson, C., & Seligman, M. (2004). *Character strengths and virtues: A handbook and classification.* New York: Oxford University Press.

Portes, A. (1998). Social capital: Its origins and applications in modern sociology. *Annual Review of Sociology, 24,* 1–24.

Power, F.C., Higgins, A., & Kohlberg, L. (1989). *Lawrence Kohlberg's approach to moral education.* New York: Columbia University Press.

Resnick, M.D., Bearman, P.S., Blum, R.W. et al. (1997). Protecting adolescents from harm: Findings from the National Longitudinal Study on Adolescent Health. *JAMA, 278,* 823–832.

Ritchhart, R. (2002). *Intellectual character.* San Francisco: Jossey-Bass.

Scales, P.C., Benson, P.L., Leffert, N., & Blyth, D.A. (2000). The contribution of developmental assets to the prediction of thriving outcomes among adolescents. *Applied Developmental Science, 4*(1), 27–46.

Schaps, E., Watson, M., & Lewis, C. (1996). A sense of community is key to effectiveness in fostering character education. *Journal of Staff Development, 17*(2), 42–47.

Schwartz. M.J., Beatty, A., & Dachnowicz, E. (2006). Character education: Frill or foundation? *Principal Leadership, 7*(4).

Seligman, M.E. (2002). *Authentic happiness: Using the new positive psychology to realize your potential for lasting fulfillment.* New York: Free Press.

Shouse, R.C. (1996). Academic press and sense of community: Conflict, congruence, and implications for student achievement. *Social Psychology of Education, 1,* 47–68.

Sørensen, A.B., & Hallinan, M.T. (1977). A reconceptualization of school effects. *Sociology of Education, 50*(4), 273–289.

Sternberg, R. (1997). *Successful intelligence: How practical and creative intelligence determine success in life.* New York: Penguin.

Stevenson, D.L., Schiller, K.S., & Schneider, B. (1994). Sequences of opportunities for learning. *Sociology of Education, 67,* 184–198.

Strauss, A.L., & Corbin, J. (1994). Grounded theory methodology: An overview. In N.K. Denzin & Y.S. Lincoln (Eds.), *Handbook of qualitative research.* Thousand Oaks, CA: Sage Publications.

Terman, L.M. & Oden, M.H. (1959). *The gifted group at mid-life: Thirty-five years' follow-up of the superior child.* Stanford, CA: Stanford University Press.

Tough, P. (2012). *How children succeed: Grit, curiosity, and the hidden power of character.* New York: Houghton Mifflin Harcourt Publishing Company.

Vander Ark, T. (2005). Lessons from high school reform: Achieving "success at scale." *Education Week, 24*(41), 46–47, 56.

Vygotsky, L. (1978). *Mind in society: The development of higher psychological processes.* Cambridge: Harvard University Press.

Wiggins G., & McTighe, J. (1998). *Understanding by design.* Alexandria, VA: Association for Supervision and Curriculum Development.

Yair, G. (2000). Reforming motivation: How the structure of instruction affects students' learning experiences. *British Educational Journal, 26*(2), 191–210.

18

AN APPLICATION OF KOHLBERG'S THEORY OF MORAL DILEMMA DISCUSSION TO THE JAPANESE CLASSROOM AND ITS EFFECT ON MORAL DEVELOPMENT OF JAPANESE STUDENTS

Noriyuki Araki

The goal of this chapter is to share what we have learned from our efforts to transform and update moral education within public schools in Japan. Much criticism has been directed toward the present Japanese method of moral education for its inculcative and indoctrinaire nature that ignores students' autonomous reasoning. The students often express frustration that moral education classes are simply boring and uninteresting, or that the conclusions to be drawn from the classes are easily predictable (Mase, 1987; Sano,1985).

Given such criticisms, we have so far attempted:

1. To sustain the original objective of traditional moral education to foster the growth of "good" people, while also breaking down the long-held myth that indoctrination of certain moral values is almost unavoidable in any effort to attain that goal.
2. From the perspectives of cognitive development, to help students develop their own views and thoughts from which moral judgments can be drawn.
3. To create a classroom environment where the students can feel free to relate their own life experiences in the discussion of moral problems, rather than moving toward predetermined conclusions for hypothetical and abstract situations established by the curriculum.

In short, we have applied Kohlberg's (Power, Higgins, & Kohlberg, 1989) method of moral education to make classroom moral discussion more interesting and fruitful, and to enable the students to think and analyze according to their autonomous reasoning. It is our fundamental principle to try to avoid the imposition of values so that the students can truly enjoy the class and develop their own intellectual skills (Araki, 1987, 1988a, 1990b, 1990c, 1993a, 1993b, 1996a, 1996b, 1997, 2002a, 2002b, 2005a, 2005b, 2012, 2013).

In order to apply Kohlberg's approach to moral education in Japan, we formed "The Society for the Study of Moral Education" in 1982. We changed the name of our organization to "The Society for the Study of Moral Development" in 1984 and to "The Japan Society for Studies of Educational Practices on Moral Development" in 2001. This year is the 30th anniversary of our founding. Throughout this period, we have tried to review and develop our methods to effectively incorporate Kohlberg's method into the Japanese educational context.

As is well-known and discussed in this handbook (see chapter by Snarey and Samuelson) Kohlberg (1969) proposed a cognitive-developmental theory of moral growth, following the philosophy of John Dewey who stated the goal of education as to have children develop. Such factors as the experience of discussing moral and cognitive dilemmas and opportunities for role-taking were thought to be very important for moral development. On the basis of this view, we conducted a series of classes, in which students were given stories with moral dilemmas in them, and allowed to participate in open-ended moral discussion. Many of these classroom practices proved to be effective (Araki, 1988a; Inoue, 1985; Ohnshi, Tokunaga, Sugimoto, Araki, & Naito, 1990; Sakurai, 1992; Tateishi, 1986). For more detailed descriptions of the research activities, and a critical review of the classroom applications, see also Fujita (1985), Morioka (1987, 1992), Naito (1987), Sano (1985), Yamagishi (1985a, 1985b), and Yamauchi (1986). This chapter reviews this work. It describes the structure of moral dilemma classes and the moral dilemmas that were employed, and the results of analyses on the effects on student moral growth. The effects discussed include the degree to which students developed their moral reasoning, and their ability to perform expected social roles after they had participated in the class. Three statistical methods were employed to measure the effects: meta-analysis (Imae, 1985; Iwawaki, 1986); pre-post scores in relation to classroom participation; and assessments of teaching.

MORAL EDUCATION IN JAPAN

Moral education in Japan is largely based on a set of top-down mandates that apply to the entire educational system. Moral education today is conducted within classes specifically designated for this purpose as well as occasionally within selected subject matter classes (e.g., foreign language activity, the period for integrated studies and special activities). The designated "moral education" classes are specially set up to provide discrete training for 1 hour per week (45 hours per year). The aim of the class is for students to increase moral sensitivity, improve moral judgment, and improve motivation and attitudes towards moral practices in order to facilitate their engagement in moral action (Ministry of Education, Culture, Sports, Science and Technology, 2008).

In 1987, Fujita introduced "character education" as practiced in the US as an example of educational practice that encourages "internal consciousness about moral values," and argued that moral education in primary and junior high schools in Japan should adopt this approach. While making this proposal Fujita (1987) also admitted that a central goal of character education is "to transfer a moral inheritance" and that there is a risk of falling into indoctrination (a forcing of values). Fujita further argued that a character education approach is limited by an "arbitrariness of the value content intended to teach to children, and a teaching method which does not secure rediscovery of the value by a child" (pp. 106–135). Thus, the character education approach amounts to practices that he ultimately criticized as emblematic of the practices already widespread in Japanese schools. Araki (1990a) concurred with Fujita's views and provided a critical analysis of the traditional Japanese approach to moral education that shared many of the same assumptions and practices being touted by proponents of the adoption of US based forms of character education. He identified five characteristic practices of traditional Japanese moral education:

1. Show a normative model and tell children that it is to be followed.
2. Tell children the necessity of particular moral values and make sure the students can recall them.
3. Make children choose a given value from the set of values that are accepted by the adults.
4. Control children by rules, and discipline them to accept such rules without thinking.
5. Control children's behavior so that the feeling of a guilty conscience may work against any violation of regulations.

Araki then summarized the downsides of these characteristics when embedded within typical applications in the Japanese classroom from the learner's point of view. First, the focus of such lessons conducted from a classical approach to moral education constituting a "forcing of value" do not connect with the concerns or interests of children. Such abstract approaches to values do not touch upon how the children live, how they spend time with their friends, and what they want to be and so on. According to Araki, it is these concerns that should be the center of attention in moral education. However, as practiced in Japan, the students simply make a confession, give the appearance of reflection, and then listen to a sermon. Children in this educational framework are surely in a defensive position, and while there might be a teacher's turn in this framework, there is no turn for the children (Araki, 1990a). Second, children often already understand the value which they are presumably to learn from the beginning of the lesson, or they just think "this has nothing to do with me." As a result the responses from the children become stereotypical, public, or idealistic, and the lesson is therefore pointless. Third, during a lesson, active interaction between children and between teacher and children is nonexistent. Instead, children are watching out for the teacher's mood and try to align themselves with the teacher's aim and expectations.

Not surprisingly, there has been a lot of criticism from school teachers directed at the character education and traditional moral pedagogy since the advent of moral education in postwar Japan when it became educational policy beginning in 1958. Criticisms include: "teaching materials are dominated by feelings and attitudes towards morality"; "the contents are too hypocritical and heart-warming"; "it does not fit with their usual way of life"; "it tends to become forcing of value"; and teachers were not positively concerned with moral education. Furthermore, children reported that moral education class was "tedious," "not fun," and "answers are already known." In these circumstances, the normative consciousness of children is weakened and rich human relationships are lost; there are continuous problematic behaviors such as school truancy, school bullying, and violence among children in Japanese primary and junior high schools in the twenty-first century.

THE DEVELOPMENTAL ALTERNATIVE FOR MORAL EDUCATION AS APPLIED IN JAPAN

Classroom Models: Procedures and Materials

The Japan Society for Studies of Educational Practices on Moral Development provided an alternative intended to address the limitations of the traditional approach to moral education. In considering how to plan our approach to moral education we reviewed the guidance for conducting moral dilemma discussions provided by Kohlberg and his colleagues in several sources (e.g., Beyer, 1976; Galbraith & Jones, 1975; Kohlberg, Colby, Fenton, Speicher-Dubin, & Lieberman, 1975). However, the procedures described were by and large intended for use in one-hour time segments at the junior high school and senior high school level. When we examined them to see if they could be applied to the schools that we worked with in Japan, we identified various limitations. A central concern was that the time allotted for issue discussions was judged to be too short for a typical Japanese classroom (comprising 40 students) to share an understanding of the dilemma or to discuss and focus on the point at issue (Araki, 1985). Therefore, we designed an approach to classroom moral discussion that focused upon a single theme over a two-hour time-frame (see Table 18.1). In the first hour, students are engaged in an initial effort to understand the basic issues being presented in the situation, and to form some tentative decisions about what to do. The instructors employ these emerging student-identified themes to shape the ensuing discussion. The focus of the second hour is the moral discussion, through which students are asked to consider the competing moral values or concerns that are involved, and in what ways the students might resolve the problem, while trying to take into account the various roles of the people engaged in the situations.

The procedure described in Table 18.1 is for middle and upper grade elementary school students and may also be used with students at the junior and senior high school levels. For the lower elementary grades, the class procedure is compressed into a one-hour framework and students are not required to write down their judgments in notebooks. Instead they are asked to form groups of those who have come to the same judgments, and to express themselves through action or role-taking, rather than through simple verbal discussions. In this way younger children are better able to visualize and grasp their differences in viewpoints than would be achieved through standard discussion formats.

We provided the following general guidelines to teachers to help them conduct these discussions.

1. Reduce or eliminate if possible elements of the classroom atmosphere that would convey to students the notion that the positions they express are being evaluated by their teachers, or that the objective of the discussion is to arrive at the "right answer" consistent with the viewpoint being presented by teachers.

2. Arrange desks and chairs so that students can see and hear one another very well.

3. Listen to students' voluntary statements, and respect the trend of their discussion, without restricting discourse to a preset plan made by the teacher in advance.

Table 18.1 A Model of Classroom Moral Dilemma Discussion Process

Period	Times	Guidance Process	Contents	Thought
1st hour	10–35 mins	Presentation of moral dilemma (reading of materials)	Teacher clarifies characters and contents of dilemma and helps pupils sympathize with the protagonist	Individual
		Length of talking depends on the reading (mutual understanding of the situation)	Students talk to one another to promote self-involvement (empathy), and also to avoid misunderstanding of the situations	Group
	10–25 mins	Judgments/reasoning for the first hour	Pupils are asked to write on cards answers to questions like "What should he/she do?" "Why? For what reason?"	Individual

Things the teacher does after completing period 1:
· Classify the reasoning cards of part 1 and prepare them for period 2.
· Check the guiding questions to be asked in period 2.
· Make instruction plan for period 2.

Period	Times	Guidance Process	Contents	Thought
2nd hour	5–10 mins	Recheck the moral dilemma	At the beginning of the second hour students share their understanding of the situation. They confirm points at issue in mutual understanding	Group
	7–10 mins	Write down questions/opinions on the judgment/ reasoning cards of other pupils	On the cards in which reasonings of all classmates are listed and classified makes students aware of reasoning from different viewpoints	Individual
	7–15 mins	Criticize/evaluate one's own judgment and that of other classmates (Discussion 1)	Discuss among classmates different judgments drawn from various points of view and clarify the conflicting points in opinions (to be done in classroom/group discussion)	Group
	10–15 mins	Synthesize one's own opinions with those of others (Discussion 2)	Depending on their own notes they mutually criticize/examine different reasoning derived from different positions. In the exchange of views they bring points of discussion to a focus	Group
	5–8 mins	Judgments/reasoning for the second hour	To think about once again what the story character should (must) do with the dilemmas she/he faces and choose the most convincing reasoning for the final judgment	Individual

4. Respect communication among students, especially promoting the exchange of views between students who are within one developmental stage of each other, bearing in mind the limitations of reliance upon this "plus-one" strategy identified in prior research (Berkowitz & Gibbs, 1983).

5. Finally, develop the necessary skills and abilities needed to conduct effective classroom discussions (for example, to establish rules relating to how students should pose questions, opinions, counterarguments) and the skills to introduce additional comments and picking up of supporting arguments. Develop a warm, accepting classroom atmosphere.

Within the broad framework just outlined, the process for moral discussion was comprised of four different stages or phases. In the first phase at the very beginning of instruction, the teacher's primary responsibility is to insure that each student clearly understands the core elements of the focal dilemma. Not all students can be expected to immediately comprehend or identify the dilemmas contained in a given story or situation. Some students may show a clear sign of immediate comprehension but others may take much longer. In addition some students may avoid addressing the moral conflict and try to come up with a pragmatic solution to the given problem. Therefore, the instructor is responsible for fostering students' understandings of the moral dilemma confronted by the main characters of the story. Slow and careful reading of the story, making repeated pauses and reviews whenever appropriate, are some well-known strategies teachers may employ to reduce incorrect and arbitrary interpretations. In addition, teachers may pose questions to students that (1) check for story comprehension, (2) ask students to relate their life experience to the story, and (3) center around particular elements of the situation that the teacher anticipates will be challenging for the students to comprehend or recognize as critical to the situation.

In the second stage in the discourse process the focus of the teacher is on supporting students' efforts at expressing their initial reactions or responses to the focal moral dilemma. The teacher's role is to help students to arrive at and clarify their own positions. Teachers pose clarifying questions and direct students to consider the opinions of their classmates.

The third stage involves actual moral discussion which constitutes the core of the class. What must be done at this stage is to enable the students to clarify the reasoning process from which their moral judgments are to be drawn. It is also important to expose the students to forms of moral argument that will cause them to experience the cognitive conflict that will generate a shift in their own moral reasoning structures. As was mentioned above the teacher's role is to create a classroom climate that will ensure frank exchange of the opinions among students, which can eventually move toward the final student resolution or judgments. To generate cognitive imbalance and hopefully foster growth in students' moral development, teachers are encouraged to pose several types of questions. First are questions that expose the students to higher stage reasoning than they currently use. Second are questions that help students to engage in appropriate role-taking for each story character. Third are questions that make them speculate about the general consequences that one particular action might generate in the lives of others.

In the final stage, the students are directed to draw final moral judgments. The teacher in this phase of the lesson summarizes and coordinates the differing views and conclusions being offered so that each student may take into account the whole range of diverse opinions to determine his/her own final position.

Moral Dilemma Materials

In order to develop children's morality, we need to have them experience moral disequilibrium or moral value conflict (Power et al., 1989). The materials employed to generate cognitive conflict present situations that are characterized by competing values or competing needs of protagonists such that resolution is perceived as difficult by students due to the situational ambiguity about what is morally right. A morally "unbalanced" state evokes children's awareness of the necessity of seeking out a resolution, motivates them to figure out the resolution, and promotes their efforts to restore equilibrium (Araki, 1984, 2010; Araki & Noguchi, 1987; Araki & Tokunaga et al., 1989). Altogether Araki and colleagues (2008) constructed 182 moral dilemma situations for use in primary and secondary Japanese classrooms with accompanying guides (Araki, 2012, 2013).

As noted above, a story that has moral value conflicts is presented at the beginning of a lesson. There are two types, depending on the complexity of the dilemma structure.

As shown in Figure 18.1, for lower grade students, the material deals with a value conflict with a single value (Type I). For instance, in the moral dilemma story named "corn harvest" constructed by Forita Yashunaga, the issue focuses on how to distribute harvested corn among the friends who helped grow the corn. In this story, different ways of distribution should be examined from the perspective of what is most equitable to each of the individual contributors. This story deals with the moral value of "fairness and justice" (Araki, 1993a).

For higher grade students, the moral material deals with conflicts among multiple values (Type II). For example, in the material titled "Kira in Southern Island" constructed by Matsuo Hirofumi, the two values of "loving one's hometown" and "awareness of roles and responsibility" are pitted against one another:

> Kira, a village mayor, has been dreaming about establishing new industry on Kaura island which has suffered from depopulation. A good offer for new development has come in, but if accepted, Kaura's rich natural environment will suffer and be drastically damaged. Kira is distressed about making this decision.

We should note here that the stories do not deal with conflicts between value and counter-value such as "strong and weak" will or "good and evil," such as in the case of whether a person should walk a dog while he wants to play with the computer (Araki, 1996a).

EVALUATION OF THE MORAL DILEMMA CLASSROOM

Meta-Analytical Evaluations

There are six published research papers that report the outcomes of the approach to moral education employing the instructional model described above (Aragaki, 1990; Hara, 1991; Matuo, 1991; Noguchi, 1987; Suzuki, 1988; Yaegashi, 1985). In this section of the chapter we report on the results of a meta-analysis combining the effects of these individual studies. The research reported by Yaegashi (1985) analyzed a series of moral dilemma classes conducted for fifth grade pupils over a one year period. In this project,

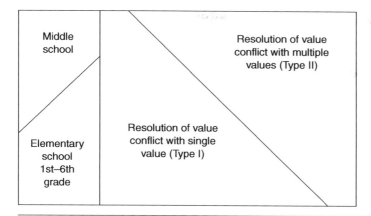

Figure 18.1 Two Types of Moral Dilemma.

Tokunaga taught the experimental group (dilemma discussion) classes of 12 hours with six different topics based on Kohlberg's theory. During the same period, he also conducted a series of comparison group classes that employed the traditional type of moral education common to Japan (similar to character education in the US). In these classes she allocated one class hour for one moral topic.

Suzuki (1988) compared the outcomes of a fifth grade experimental group taught under his own instruction (eight hours for four topics) employing Kohlberg's theory, along with a control classroom of the same grade taught by a traditional method at a school of equal size. Aragaki (1990) made a similar comparative analysis comparing two months of dilemma based instruction to an experimental group of sixth grade (eight hours for four topics) and a control group at another school employing traditional character education teaching methods. The Hara (1991) study compared an experimental group of fifth grade children he had instructed for two months using Kohlberg's method (eight class hours with four moral topics), with a control group of the same grade children also taught by Hara for the same instructional but using the traditional method. In both classes, the same moral topics were discussed.

Still another comparative study was conducted by Noguchi (1987) who measured outcomes with two groups at the junior high school level. Noguchi taught the moral dilemma based lessons for the experimental group. The classes for this experimental group were conducted over two extended sessions: one of which lasted three months with five class hours allocated for three different topics, and the other that lasted five months with eight class hours allocated for five topics. The control group for this study was taught by the eighth grade homeroom teacher with traditional methods. Instruction for the eighth grade students in the former group was initially provided by Noguchi himself but was later taken over by the homeroom teacher.

Finally, Matsuo's (1991) comparative research compared the outcomes from two experimental instructional conditions with a traditional approach to moral/character education. In one of these experimental conditions instruction focused upon the use of role play to enact the moral issues and conflicts within given situations. The second experimental classroom employed discussion of moral situations or dilemmas. Each class lasted two months and was allocated over six class hours for three moral topics.

Analyses explored the outcomes on moral reasoning and perspective-taking of the two experimental and the control classroom.

The above studies all used a pre- and post-test design examining the impact of instruction on several messages. These were (1) the Japanese Version of Moral Judgment Test (MJT) (Araki, Yaegashi, & Maeda, 1986), (2) the Japanese Version of Role Taking Ability Test (Selman Type Test) (Araki, 1988b), and (3) Social-Perspective Test for Junior High School students. In the Yaegashi (1985) and Noguchi (1987) classes, the Role Taking Test was omitted. In order to express the observed effect of the Kohlberg based method employed in each experimental group, we calculated an Effect Size (ES, *1). The mean figures provided in Tables 18.2 and 18.3 correspond to the collective average of students' moral stage in each class (i.e., point 1 is granted to the class that collectively represents moral stage 1, and one extra point is added as each class moves up one moral stage). The standard deviation has been calculated from these figures. Table 18.2 represents the ES of the Moral Judgment Test while Table 18.3 shows that of the Role Taking Ability Test.

From the numbers shown in Table 18.2, we can calculate that the arithmetic average of all the control groups among the fifth grade children is 1.64. That of the sixth grade children is 1.78, 2.57 for the seventh grade, and 2.85 for the eighth grade accordingly. These figures indicate that moral stage is accelerated as the students' age and learning experience increase. Development of the students' role-taking ability also shows a similar trend. The fifth grade children on average are rated as stage 1.66 and the sixth grade and the seventh grade 1.86 and 2.62 respectively. Increase in age affects role-taking ability just as it does in the case of moral judgment. It was also observed that the development of the students' role-taking ability occurs in earlier ages than that of their moral judgment.

Table 18.2 indicates that out of the nine classes surveyed, all but one class showed positive ES figures on the development of students' moral stage. The average ES figure of all nine classes is 0.38 with its standard deviation 0.19. From this data, we can conclude that interventions produced moderate effects in the classes where it was employed. The effect on the development of students' role-taking ability is more considerable. Table 18.3 shows that the average ES figure of all five classes surveyed is 0.71 with its standard deviation 0.22. Suzuki's class obtained a considerably higher figure of 1.1. Matsuo who took up Role-Taking itself as the experimental variables discovered that while the ES

Table 18.2 Effects of Dilemma Discussion Method on Students' Moral Development

	Elementary School								Junior High School								
	Yaegashi (Grade 5)		Suzuki (Grade 5)		Hara (Grade 5)		Aragaki (Grade 6)		Noguchi (Grade 7)		Noguchi (Grade 8)		Noguchi (Grade 9)		Matsuo (Grade 7)		
	EG	CG	EG	CG	EG	CG	EG	CG	EG	CG	EG	CG	EG	CG	EG1	CG	EG2
N	27	24	14	32	32	32	41	37	28	33	35	35	39	40	34	34	32
M	1.96	1.75	2.14	1.81	1.66	1.38	2.07	1.78	2.78	2.60	2.74	2.57	2.82	2.85	2.61	2.26	2.50
SD	0.74	0.60	0.52	0.63	0.59	0.54	0.60	0.62	0.41	0.64	0.49	0.59	0.54	0.47	0.72	0.55	0.55
ES	0.35		0.52		0.52		0.47		0.28		0.29		−0.06		0.64		0.44

Notes
EG = Experimental Group; CG = Control Group.
N, M, SD, and ES are averages of moral developmental stages measured by the MJT.

Table 18.3 Effects of Dilemma Discussion Method on Development of Students' Role-taking Ability

	Suzuki (Grade 5)		Hara (Grade 5)		Aragaki (Grade 6)		Matsuo (Grade 7)		
	EG	CG	EG	CG	EG	CG	EG1	CG	EG2
N	14	32	32	32	41	37	34	31	32
M	2.50	1.81	1.78	1.50	2.27	1.86	2.94	2.90	2.62
SD	0.50	0.63	0.60	0.61	0.70	0.58	0.59	0.53	0.48
ES	1.1		0.46		0.74		0.67		0.58

figure in the class focused on group discussion exercise is 0.58, the class focused on the role-taking exercise obtained a very high figure of 0.67.

From the survey of results of the meta-analysis presented above, it can be concluded that Kohlberg's method produced a greater effect on the students' moral development than the traditional method, and that its effect was considerable especially on the development of students' role-taking ability.

Outcomes of evaluations employing pre- and post-test designs

In the field of educational research in general, we often conduct comparative tests, experiments, or surveys in order to determine whether a certain type of educational plan is effective or not. This is usually done by observing the change in students' performance after relevant educational treatment is given, or by comparing the scores they have obtained before and after such a treatment. This kind of method is frequently employed as a way of measuring the effect of a certain educational model, since under this method there is no need to set up a control group for the statistical purpose. Having discussed in the previous section nine studies conducted by the meta-statistical method, I would like in this section to analyze the results of two additional studies employing pre- and post-test assessments Horita (1992) and Ueda (1992) without the inclusion of control groups.

These studies examined the impact of eight class hours of moral discussion with fourth and fifth grade students. The effect of these two classes is examined by comparing the scores of the Moral Judgment Test obtained by the students in these classes (experimental groups only) and those obtained by the nine experimental groups together with the eight control groups shown in Table 18.2. To see the comparative difference or effect after Kohlberg's method is introduced in class, both pre-test scores (before the relevant educational treatment is given) and post-test scores (after the relevant educational treatment is given) are compared. In the same way, the pre-class and post-class scores on the Role Taking Ability Test are also compared. The scores have been obtained by the two experimental groups of Horita and Ueda, and by the seven experimental groups as well as four control groups cited in Table 18.3.

The score distributions of the entire number of students on the Moral Judgment Test and Role Taking Ability Test are shown in Table 18.4 and 18.5 respectively. Although most students' moral judgment scores remained the same, a score increase is more prominent among the experimental groups than the control groups. Regarding Role Taking Ability, there was no significant score change observed among the control groups, while a majority in the experimental groups showed some increase.

In order to determine whether or not these results truly indicate any statistical significance on moral stage growth, the effect figures of both the experimental and control groups were recalculated by adopting the following method. If, after the class, the group moved two moral stages higher than before the class, two points were granted to the group score. Likewise, if it moves one stage higher, one point is given, and no point is given if the group remains in the same stage. Following the same manner, negative points of −1 and −2 were given if the group shows the decrease in its moral stage. The mean figures and standard deviation of both the Moral Judgment Test and Role Taking Ability Test have been calculated by this method for both the experimental and control groups. Our analyses revealed that the control group had obtained the average effect score of 0.05 on both tests, which indicates no significant increase in moral stages at all. On the other hand, the experimental group had obtained the effect score of 0.34 on the Moral Judgment Test, which indicates an average increase of one-third moral stage, and on the Role Taking Ability Test, as well, the score they had obtained is 0.4, which is equivalent to an average increase of the two-fifths moral stage. These gaps in the effect scores between the two groups are statistically significant. The relevant statistical figures of the Moral Judgment Test are; $t(604) = 6.118$, $p < 0.001$ and those of the Role Taking Ability Test are; $t(340) = 6.601$, $p < 0.001$. The discovery of an average increase of one-third moral stage on the moral judgment test, which owes to the use of Kohlberg's method, is consistent with the conclusion of the research conducted by Blatt and Kohlberg (1975), in which an average

Table 18.4 Pre- to Post-test Changes in Moral Stage Across Studies

Moral Stage (Pre-Test)	Moral Stage (Post-Test)				
	I	II	III	IV	Total
I	41 (48)	58 (16)	6 (0)	0 (0)	105 (64)
II	2 (6)	87 (85)	55 (20)	0 (0)	144 (111)
III	1 (2)	15 (15)	64 (71)	8 (3)	88 (91)
IV	0 (0)	0 (0)	0 (0)	2 (1)	2 (1)
Total	44 (56)	160 (116)	125 (91)	10 (4)	339 (267)

Note
Numbers in parentheses represent control groups.

Table 18.5 Pre- to Post-test Changes in Role-taking Ability Across Studies

Role-Taking (Pre-Test)	Role-Taking (Post-Test)				
	I	II	III	IV	Total
I	26 (33)	32 (9)	4 (0)	0 (0)	62 (42)
II	1 (4)	61 (53)	37 (8)	0 (0)	99 (65)
III	0 (0)	0 (3)	40 (22)	8 (0)	48 (25)
IV	0 (0)	0 (1)	0 (0)	0 (1)	2 (1)
Total	27 (37)	93 (66)	81 (30)	8 (0)	209 (133)

Note
Numbers in parentheses represent control groups.

increase of one-third moral stage was found among experimental groups after 12 hours of moral discussion classes over a period of 12 weeks. The fact that the repeated application of Kohlberg's method has enhanced moral development (moral reasoning and role-taking) of the students strongly supports Kohlberg's (1969) fundamental belief that the essential objective of moral education should be to promote students' moral judgment ability.

EVIDENCE OF FACTORS THAT SUPPORT EFFECTIVE MORAL DILEMMA CLASSROOMS

The work described above indicates that the use of discussion techniques proposed by Kohlberg and his colleagues (Power et al., 1989) some time ago continues to have relevance within Japanese classrooms. Moreover, the work that our colleagues have conducted has amply demonstrated that the introduction of discourse methods contributes to our students' growth and development in ways that are not achieved through traditional classroom pedagogy. What we have been working on more recently are ways to characterize or capture the impact of such pedagogy from the perspectives of the participating children. We have organized the process of lessons centering on moral discussion on the assumption that the moral dilemma method is one that engages students directly in their own activity of problem-solving directed at solutions to open-ended moral problems. In this educational approach, we expected children to take the lead in lessons as a result of increasing intrinsic motivation for resolving moral-value conflicts. Araki (1990a) summarized feedback from 33 children who participated for the first time in a moral dilemma classroom into the following five categories: (1) the lesson was fun; (2) there is no regular answer; (3) I could express my thoughts firmly; (4) I could hear different ideas from different people; and (5) it took two hours to finish a lesson. With the exception of the final observation about the length of the class, the focus of student reactions was on elements of the class that connected directly to their own experiences of engagement and intellectual stimulation.

Observational data and analyses of classroom interactions in the context of moral issue discussions are also collected. We have integrated three methods: (1) Category Analysis System using "Interaction Analysis Categories" (Flanders, 1970); (2) Categories for the Analysis of "Small Group Interaction" (Bales, 1950); and (3) S-T analysis (Fujita and Yoshimoto, 1980). Here, I will focus on (1) and (3). Flanders' Interaction Analysis Categories (FIAC) method is one of the most popular and most widely used methods for class improvement in Japan. However, there are only two out of 10 categories in Flanders' (1970) system regarding children. Therefore, we employed a modified version that includes codes for children's actions in our work examining the characteristics of successful moral discussion classrooms. The work I will focus upon here employed the "Face Diagram" modification of Flanders' coding developed by the Okayama Education Centre. This Okayama method uses 15 categories for analysis including seven categories of teacher's expression (nod, compliment, question, lecture, order, criticism, and so on), and five categories of children's expression (simple response, autonomy response, adding, question, and counterview), and three categories (silence, teacher's operation, and children's operation). The category analysis of the expression of a teacher and a student is conducted every four seconds. A "face diagram" analysis (Chernoff, 1973) is conducted based on this result.

Flanders' Observational Coding and "Face Diagram" Analysis

A face diagram is a drawing of a student's face in which aspects of the face graphically represent components of student engagement and overall motivation for learning. Each portion of a face corresponds to an item assessed as a "stage point," and by assigning points to a given aspect of the face diagram we could know instantly how the class was functioning. For example, an opening and inclination of eyes expresses a Pupil Initiation Rate (PIR), and an opening of a mouth expresses the Pupil Talk Rate (PT). In other words, if the eyes are opened and inclined, and mouth is opened, it shows that children in the classroom are expressing ideas actively and articulately. Furthermore, the size of an ear expresses a teacher talk rate, and the more remarks of teachers and corresponding "listenings" of students in the class there are, the bigger the ear is. Finally, the wrinkles on the forehead express a student's confusion and silence, and the width of a nostril express the receptive attitudes of teachers towards students' remarks. Thus as explained so far, the "face diagram" helps us to visually understand the characteristics of a classroom.

Araki, Morimoto, and Suzuki (2011) reported the results of the face diagram analysis of three moral dilemma classrooms for fifth graders of primary schools using CNR (Category Number Recorder) interaction analysis software. Common features of the face diagram among the first hours of three lessons were as follows. (1) Almost no silence and children are engaged in the lesson without displaying signs of confusion. (2) Many mutual utterances among children and high motivation for learning were observed. Since the eyes are opening up a little, the children are taking the lesson positively. The common features of face diagrams in the second hour of three lessons were as follows. (1) As the length of an ear is quite short and the width of an ear is quite large, the teacher's utterances are quite few whereas children's listening is rather long. (2) Almost no silence and children are engaged in the lessons without being puzzled. Many mutual utterances among children, and high motivation for learning were seen. (3) Since the width of a nostril is standard, the teacher has responded with a receptive attitude to children's remarks, and the children have attended to the lesson in comfort. (4) Since the bridge of the nose is a little elevated, the children seemed to be working for an extended time, and thus achieved a sense of accomplishment and assurance.

In the first hours of the lesson, a number of problems can be pointed out from the profile such as the time for the children to listen to the teachers was too long, and the students' remarks were rather sporadic. However, from the viewpoint of primary characteristics of moral dilemma lessons where pupils need to cultivate a shared understanding of moral dilemma, and make decisions by connecting the dilemma with their everyday lives within the first hours of the lesson, this face diagram well-represented such characteristics of introduction to the moral dilemma content. The second hour of the lesson is, on the other hand, expected to unfold using moral discussion as a core feature. In particular, children are expected to lead the lesson on their own by using a mutual nomination method. The role of the teacher turns into that of a catalyst, engaging in actions such as smoothing the discussion or introducing the opportunity of role acquisition and attention to contradictory viewpoints. The face diagram obtained at this point in the lesson was considered to be reflecting those points.

S-T Analysis of Classroom Engagement

S-T analysis is a method employed to critically analyze whether a lesson is performed under the active talk led by the students, or developed by the lead of teachers. This is done by focusing on the teaching-learning process of a lesson and analyzing the emerging pattern of a teacher's actions (T-activity) and a student's action (S-activity) taking place during the lesson. Beginning with the lesson onset the subject of a given action is recorded either as student (S) or a teacher (T) at 30 second intervals. Actions recorded as T-activity include exposition, suggestion, writing on the blackboard, questions, and criticism, and so on. Actions recorded as S-activity include thinking, expression, presentation, experiment, operation, acting, choral speaking, and so on. In this study, six moral dilemma lessons conducted among a class of fifth graders were analyzed (Araki, 1987). Table 18.6 shows the activities, occupancy, and conversion ratios of the first half hour and the second half hour of each of six lessons (total of 12 analysing points).

An average number of activities within 12 analysing points were 37.4 times for teachers, and 53.1 times for students, and the average number of activities of students were significantly higher than that of teachers ($F_{(1,20)} = 7.10$, $p < 0.05$), and this was more pronounced for the second half than the first half of an hour ($t_{(10)} = 2.9$, $p < 0.05$). Regarding the activity occupancy based on S-T analysis, students' were significantly higher than teachers' ($F = 532.77$, $p < 0.001$), and there was significant main effect of interaction between the first half and the second half of lessons ($F = 5.71$, $p < 0.05$). Regarding the conversion ratio, the average was 0.21 for both the first half and the second half that is rather low. According to the S-T binary time-series data, the lesson was advanced consistently by active talk centering on a student in a free atmosphere.

The results of these observational analyses of classroom interactions indicate that the outcomes associated with the introduction of dilemma discussion were associated with classroom practices that fostered student engagement and student dialogue. Thus, we can conclude that the activities that took place within the classrooms affiliated with efforts to

Table 18.6 Characteristics of Moral Dilemma Class by S-T Analysis

Moral Dilemma	Class Practice	Frequency of Behavior		Occupation Rate		Turn Rate
		Teachers	Students	Teachers	Students	
What to do leader	1st half-hour	72	71	0.27	0.73	0.23
	2nd half-hour	39	80	0.25	0.75	0.28
Michiko's doll	1st half-hour	51	60	0.27	0.73	0.19
	2nd half-hour	37	54	0.16	0.84	0.19
Flawed vase	1st half-hour	47	81	0.29	0.71	0.24
	2nd half-hour	40	55	0.16	0.84	0.23
Let's make a symbol	1st half-hour	41	45	0.10	0.90	0.18
	2nd half-hour	19	47	0.08	0.92	0.16
Marathon meet	1st half-hour	28	37	0.26	0.74	0.23
	2nd half-hour	16	40	0.17	0.83	0.21
Fun and games	1st half-hour	32	31	0.25	0.74	0.18
	2nd half-hour	27	36	0.25	0.83	0.19
M (SD)	1st half-hour	45.2 (14.4)	54.2 (18,0)	0.24 (0.06)	0.76 (0.06)	0.21 (0.03)
M (SD)	2nd half-hour	29.5 (9.6)	52.0 (14.2)	0.17 (0.05)	0.82 (0.06)	0.21 (0.04)

change the nature of moral education were consistent with the goals set for instructional practices. Moreover, observational data indicate that these effects were accomplished without any loss of student discipline or increase in student disruptive conduct. On the contrary, the evidence suggests that the approach we have advocated for moral education was embraced by the students, and had salutatory effects on classroom climate and moral growth.

CONCLUSION

In this chapter I began by criticizing traditional moral education in Japan. As an alternative, I introduced the use of moral dilemma discussion (Kohlberg, 1969), altered for the Japanese context. The approach was extended to two-hour classes with middle school and high school students focused upon a single theme. The work has produced extensive curriculum materials and guidelines for use of dilemma discussion in Japan. Extensive evaluation of the outcomes used standardized assessments of moral judgment and role-taking and applied observational methods. These evaluations demonstrate that the dilemma approach to moral education bears significant results. For example, while no changes in moral development were observed in control classrooms employing traditional moral education, consistent and sustained moral growth in the moral dilemma classes was observed. Furthermore, pupils seemed to participate in moral dilemma classes more actively and enthusiastically compared with traditional classes.

The use of moral dilemma classes has been accepted, particularly among young teachers, and has become more widely implemented in Japan. In fact, the materials for moral dilemma classes were recently found to be used to the same extent as the standard materials for traditional moral education developed and published by the Ministry of Education (23.6% cf. 32.0%; Ministry of Education, Culture, Sports, Science and Technology, 2013). Other evidence demonstrating a high interest in the adoption of moral dilemma classes is the number of reprints of related books. We have published more than 10 books on the topic, and all of these have been reprinted (and one of these has actually been reprinted 28 times). This recent success has overcome earlier criticisms of moral dilemma classes such as 1) they inhibit a child's emotional growth and make students intellectually biased, 2) consideration of alternative judgments restricts student thinking, and 3) it does not make students feel that they must engage in moral education classes, and so on. However, we have demonstrated that each of these criticisms was unfounded.

In looking ahead I would like to point to the importance of embedding the moral dilemma class within a school environment that aims at moral development with democracy as its backdrop (see Oser, this volume). This will take additional time to achieve within Japan. However, my colleagues and I are committed to this effort to extend our approach to infuse the whole school with an educational climate with justice and consideration toward the just community just as Kohlberg tried.

REFERENCES

Aragaki, C. (1990). Practice and effects of moral education based on Kohlberg's Theory. Unpublished Master's thesis, Hyogo University of Teacher Education, Hyogo, Japan. (Written in Japanese.)

Araki, N. (1984). On the development of "moral dilemma" teaching materials for moral discussions. Studies on the Development of Teaching Materials and Unfolding of Instruction by Educational Engineering Skills (Special Research Supported by the Ministry of Education). Hyogo University of Teacher Education, Hyogo, Japan. 23–68.

Araki, N. (1985). Research Note: The Kohlberg Theory and the process of moral class. *Journal of Teaching and Assessment, 6.* T. Mizukoshi & E. Kajit (Eds.), Tokyo: Meiji Publishing Corporation. 145–153. (Written in Japanese.)

Araki, N. (1987). Moral classrooms in primary and secondary schools based on Kohlberg's Theory and their effects on the morality of students. *Moral education (East & West); tradition and innovation: International conference on moral education.* 330–335. (Written in Japanese.)

Araki, N. (1988a). Kohlberg's theory on moral development. Ch. 2 in N. Araki (Ed.), *You can make moral education more interesting in this way—Kohlberg theory and its educational practice.* Kyoto: Kitaooji Publishing Corporation. 12–25. (Written in Japanese.)

Araki, N. (1988b). *Role-taking test & its manual.* Fukuoka: Toyo Physical Corporation. (Written in Japanese.)

Araki, N. (1990a). *The improvement of moral education using dilemma story—Kohlberg theory and its educational practice.* Tokyo: Meiji Publishing Corporation. (Written in Japanese.)

Araki, N. (Ed.). (1990b). *Moral dilemma materials and curriculum—elementary school.* Tokyo: Meiji Publishing Corporation. (Written in Japanese.)

Araki, N. (Ed.). (1990c). *Moral dilemma materials and curriculum—middle school.* Tokyo: Meiji Publishing Corporation. (Written in Japanese.)

Araki, N. (Ed.). (1993a). *Instruction method of moral dilemma education with moral dilemma materials.* Tokyo: Meiji Publishing Corporation. (Written in Japanese.)

Araki, N. (Ed.). (1993b). *New ways in moral education using the assessment and measurement of morality.* Tokyo: Meiji Publishing Corporation. (Written in Japanese.)

Araki, N. (1996a). *Materials development for moral dilemma education.* Tokyo: Meiji Publishing Corporation. 96–103. (Written in Japanese.)

Araki, N. (1996b). Moral education. Ch. 6 in H. Hashiguchi, K. Inagaki, M. Sasaki, K. Takahashi, N. Uchida, & T. Yukawa (Eds.), *Annual review of Japanese child psychology.* 129–156. Tokyo: Kaneko Publishing Corporation. (Written in Japanese.)

Araki, N. (Ed.). (1997). *You can make moral education more interesting in this way—Kohlberg theory and its educational practice.* Kyoto: Kitaooji Publishing Corporation. (Written in Japanese.)

Araki, N. (Ed.). (2002a). *Instruction with moral dilemma discussion—elementary school.* Tokyo: Meiji Publishing Corporation. (Written in Japanese.)

Araki, N. (Ed.). (2002b). *Instruction with moral dilemma discussion—middle school.* Tokyo: Meiji Publishing Corporation. (Written in Japanese.)

Araki, N. (Ed.). (2005a). *Moral dilemma materials and curriculum—elementary school Vol. 2.* Tokyo: Meiji Publishing Corporation. (Written in Japanese.)

Araki, N. (Ed.). (2005b). *Moral dilemma materials and curriculum—middle school Vol. 2.* Tokyo: Meiji Publishing Corporation. (Written in Japanese.)

Araki, N. (2010). The moral dilemma made by the Study Group for Moral Development. *The Japanese Journal of Educational Practices on Moral Development, 5* (1), 1–19. (Written in Japanese.)

Araki, N. (Ed.). (2012). *Heated moral discussion with dilemma materials—elementary school.* Tokyo: Meiji Publishing Corporation. (Written in Japanese.)

Araki, N. (Ed.). (2013). *Heated moral discussion with dilemma materials—middle school.* Tokyo: Meiji Publishing Corporation. (Written in Japanese.)

Araki, N. & Noguchi, H. (1987) Moral discussion model and moral dilemma story in junior high school. *Bulletin of Hyogo University of Teacher Education, 7,* 55–86. (Written in Japanese.)

Araki, N., Morimoto, R., & Suzuki, T. (2011). Assessment of moral dilemma classroom by the Face Diagram Method. *The Japanese Journal of Educational Practices on Moral Development, 6* (1), 27–37. (Written in Japanese.)

Araki, N., Nakaue, M., & Yamane, K. (2008). Practices in Japan of the moral dilemma education on Kohlberg's theories. The development and practice of moral dilemma educational materials. 34th Annual Conference of Association for Moral Education.

Araki, N., Yaegashi, S., & Maeda, K. (1986). Assessments of school children's moral judgments using a Norm-Element Method. *Bulletin of Hyogo University of Teacher Education, 6,* 97–137. (Written in Japanese.)

Araki, N., Tokunaga, E., Yamamoto, E., Aragaki, T., Okada, T., Katou, K., Nagata, K., Hino, M., Noguchi, H., Hata, K., Matumoto, A., & Yoshida, S. (1989). Practice of moral education in elementary and junior high schools based on Kohlberg's Theory: Meaning and structure of dilemma materials and teaching plans. *Bulletin of Hyogo University of Teacher Education, 1,* 105–133. (Written in Japanese.)

Bales, R.F. (1950). The set of categories for analysis of small group interaction. *American Sociological Review, 15* (2, April), 257–263.

Berkowitz, M. & Gibbs, J. (1983). Measuring the developmental features of moral discussions. *Merrill Palmer Quarterly, 24,* 399-410.

Beyer, B.K. (1976). Conducting moral discussion in the classroom. *Social Education, April,* 194–202.

Blatt, M.M. & Kohlberg, L. (1975). The effects of classroom moral discussion upon children's level of moral judgment. *Journal of Moral Education, 4,* 129–161.

Chernoff, H. (1973). The use of faces to represent points in K-dimensional space graphically. *Journal of the American Statistical Association, 68,* 361–368.

Flanders, N.A. (1970). *Analyzing teaching behavior.* Reading, MA: Addison Wesley.

Fujita, M. (1985). *History, present situation and problems of moral education.* Tokyo: The Ehdel Institute. (Written in Japanese.)

Fujita, M. (1987). Various approaches to moral education and their relations. *Moral education (East & West); tradition and innovation: International conference on moral education.* 453–460.

Fujita, H. & Yoshimoto, H. (1980). Using Binary representation of data in analysis of instruction for purposes of teacher training—S-T Instruction analysis. *Japanese Journal of Education Technology, 15* (3), 119–128.

Galbraith, R.E. & Jones, T.M. (1975). Teaching strategies for moral dilemma. *Social Education, 39* (1), 16–22.

Hara, K. (1991). Practice and effects of moral education based on Kohlberg's Theory—in comparison with traditional moral education. Unpublished Master's thesis, Hyogo University of Teacher Education, Hyogo, Japan. (Written in Japanese.)

Horita, Y. (1992). Analysis of interactions in moral education based on Kohlberg's Theory. Unpublished Master's thesis, Hyogo University of Teacher Education, Hyogo, Japan. (Written in Japanese.)

Imae, K. (1985). The meta-analysis of research on effects of instruction. In T. Umemoto (Ed.), *Advance in educational psychology.* Tokyo: Shinyosha. 145–152. (Written in Japanese.)

Inoue, J. (1985). The trends of the studies of moral education in overseas. *Moral Education, 299.* Tokyo: Meiji Publishing Corporation. 112–119. (Written in Japanese.)

Iwawaki, M. (1986). *The method of research in educational psychology.* Kyoto: Kitaooji Publishing Corporation. 13–14. (Written in Japanese.)

Kohlberg, L. (1969). Stage and sequence: The cognitive-developmental approach to socialization. In D.A. Goslin (Ed.), *Handbook of socialization theory and research* (pp. 347–480). Chicago: Rand Macnally.

Kohlberg, L., Colby, A., Fenton, E., Speicher-Dubin, B., & Lieberman, M. (1975). Secondary school moral discussion programs led by social studies teachers. In L. Kohlberg (Ed.), *Collected papers.* Cambridge, MA: Harvard Graduate School of Education.

Mase, M. (1987). Moral education in Japan. *Moral education (East & West); Tradition and innovation: International conference on moral education.* 1–4. (Written in Japanese.)

Matuo, H. (1991). Practice and effects of moral education in junior high school based on Kohlberg's Theory. Unpublished Master's thesis, Hyogo University of Teacher Education, Hyogo, Japan. (Written in Japanese.)

Ministry of Education, Culture, Sports, Science and Technology. (2008). *The new course of study in Japan.* (Written in Japanese.)

Ministry of Education, Culture, Sports, Science and Technology. (2013). *The outline of the result of actual condition survey of moral education in 2012 Japan. "What sort of materials did you use in teaching moral education?"* (Written in Japanese.)

Morioka, T. (1987). Special attention on use of the dilemma material of Kohlberg type. *Moral Education. 315.* Tokyo: Meiji Publishing Corporation. 116–123. (Written in Japanese.)

Morioka, T. (1992). A study of having adapted Kohlberg to the Japanese classroom. *Bulletin of Osaka University of Teacher Education, 40* (2), 187–198. (Written in Japanese.)

Naito, T. (1987). Moral education. Progress of child psychology, 1987 year. Ch. 7 in H. Hashiguchi, K. Inagaki, M. Sasaki, K. Takahashi, N. Uchida, & T. Yukawa (Eds.), *Annual review of Japanese child psychology.* Tokyo: Kaneko Publishing Corporation. 145–169. (Written in Japanese.)

Noguchi, H. (1987). Positive study of moral development based on Kohlberg Theory on the continuing effects of open-ended discussion using moral dilemma materials on junior high school students. Unpublished Master's thesis, Hyogo University of Teacher Education, Hyogo, Japan. (Written in Japanese.)

Ohnishi, I.F., Tokunaga, E., Sugimoto, K., Araki, N., & Naito, T. (1990). Voluntary symposium. Paper read at the 34th General Meeting of Japan Society of Education, S32. (Written in Japanese.)

Power, F.C., Higgins, A., & Kohlberg, L. (1989). *Lawrence Kohlberg's approach to moral education.* New York: Columbia University Press.

Sakurai, I. (1992) . The effectiveness of the development theory in the moral education. Papers read at the 34th General Meeting of Japan Society of Educational Psychology. J10.

Sano, Y. (1985). *Foundation of moral education: Development of morality.* Kyoto: Mineruba-shobo. 225–252. (Written in Japanese.)

Suzuki, T. (1988). The study of role-taking opportunities on moral development. Unpublished Master's thesis, Hyogo University of Teacher Education, Hyogo, Japan. (Written in Japanese.)

Tateishi, Y. (1986). Classroom practice based on Kohlberg's Theory. *Moral Education, 1.* Tokyo: Meiji Publishing Corporation. 61–70. (Written in Japanese.)

Ueda, K. (1992). Practice and effects of moral education in the elementary school based on Kohlberg's Theory. Unpublished Master's thesis, Hyogo University of Teacher Education, Hyogo, Japan. (Written in Japanese.)

Yaegashi, S. (1985). A study of moral education based on Kohlberg's Theory: Application of moral discussions for classroom. Unpublished Master's thesis, Hyogo University of Teacher Education, Hyogo, Japan. (Written in Japanese.)

Yamagishi, A. (1985a). Development of moral judgment in Japan. In S. Nagano (Ed.), *Moral development and education.* Tokyo: Shinyosha. 243–267. (Written in Japanese.)

Yamagishi, A. (1985b). The development of Kohlberg's Theory. In S. Nagano (Ed.), *Moral development and education.* Tokyo: Shinyo-sha. 193–222. (Written in Japanese.)

Yamauchi, M. (1986). General view, progress of child psychology 1986 year. Ch. 1 in H. Hashiguchi, K. Inagaki, M. Sasaki, K. Takahashi, N. Uchida, & T. Yukawa (Eds.), *Annual review of Japanese child psychology.* Tokyo: Kaneko Publishing Corporation. 9–12. (Written in Japanese.)

19

MORAL AND CHARACTER EDUCATION IN KOREA

In Jae Lee

INTRODUCTION

Throughout history across the world, moral development and character formation have been considered to be among the most important goals of school-based education (Lee, 2002; Lickona, 1991; Molnar, 1997; Nucci, 1989; Park & Chu, 1996; Ryan & Bohlin, 1999; The Korean Association of Education, 1997). Although the structure, content, and educational practices of moral and character education approaches differ across countries as a function of their respective traditional, religious, societal, and cultural backgrounds they share similar educational aims to help students grow into well-established and functioning members of society. This chapter will take up these issues as they play out within moral and character education in Korea.

Moral and character education for youth varies in structure based on who is being taught (the students), where they are being taught (the setting), and in what form instruction occurs (differing curriculums, such as specific programs or following an example in everyday settings). Within Korea, moral and character education is closely related to one another, with "moral subject education" and "character education" comprising two complementary components within the educational system as a whole. However, the more common and typical form is the curriculum-based moral education—"moral education as a curriculum."

Let us begin with a look at the key terms used in Korean moral education, their definitions, and their relation to one another. First is "moral education" and "moral education as a curriculum"—hereafter mentioned as MEC. The ultimate goals of these two forms of education do not differ, but the time periods, objects, and the settings in which each form of education occurs are different. "Moral education" is a broader concept that encompasses the formal and informal learning of morals in common settings such as home, schools, and society. MEC is an official and systematic interaction between the teacher and student that takes place in a classroom setting that helps students learn knowledge, values, behaviors, and other skills needed to understand and habituate the expected moral lifestyle of a functioning adult in Korean society. The Moral Education Curriculum presents general guidance for how to teach the characteristics, goals, and content of moral education as a nation-wide standardized subject in Korean elementary and middle schools.

A second key distinction is the differentiation between MEC and character education (hereafter referred to as CE). These two terms are similar with respect to general goals, but each approach reaches its goals with different methods and emphasizes different aspects of the topic. Historically, MEC was the central point of moral education following the first introduction of moral education in all levels of schooling in South Korea in 1973. However, over time increasing attitudes of rudeness, self-centeredness, physical violence, and bullying accompanied the competition of students trying to get into higher-ranking schools. As a result of these broader effects of the educational environment, MEC was criticized as a knowledge-based curriculum that students "know of but do not put into practice." As a consequence, CE was promoted as an effective plan to overcome this problem.

The issues thought to be addressed by CE are larger than those of MEC. Good character, which is the goal of CE, is demonstrated in people's lifestyles as a whole and is influenced by their school, home, and society. In Korea, there are two types of academic activities—curriculum-based activities and extracurricular activities, with CE belonging to the latter type (Korea Institute for Curriculum and Evaluation, 2011). In Korea, on May 31st, 1995, the concept of CE was made public via a written report, "The Agenda of Education Reform for the Establishment of a New Educational System." It was produced by an Ad hoc Committee of Education Reform and basically states that education needs to change in such a way that it positively enhances the development of sound moral character and creativeness in students. To this end, "Practical CE" needs to be strengthened throughout all educational activities in the school. This became the case that would "reinforce practical character education" through extracurricular activities such as discussion (debates), experiences, and community service in 1995 (K. C. Heo, Jo, Kim, Yu, & Lee, 1994; S. H. Heo, 1998; Kang et al., 2008; Lee, 2002).

However, CE has expanded to become more curriculum-based in recent years, and has been integrated with MEC. This is because, despite the attention that was directed toward CE, the effects of CE have not been evident. The assumption is that this ineffectiveness was because CE has not been integrated within curriculum-based activities that take up the majority of school hours. In March 2012, the national curriculum was reformed under "Project based character education"—a plan that was created in response to the significant amount of violence among students. Each school level came up with goals that reflect core values, and students were encouraged to initiate, explore, experience, and put these values into practice. Referring to this event, it was declared that MEC is to become the "central curriculum for character education," and it was said that "Considering the role and mission that schools hold in CE today, MEC is to become its core, supervising curriculum" (2012 Revised National Curriculum, Notification No. 2012–14, Ministry of Education, Science, and Technology). This led to an increased emphasis on the significance of MEC in the school curriculum.

Whereas MEC typically focuses on teaching students to understand moral values and develop a sense of moral judgment, and, in addition, encourage them to put these teachings into practice as its main goal within the classroom setting, CE encourages a comprehensive approach to improving character and virtue through curriculum-based activities (including MEC), creative extracurricular or experiential activities, and optimistic climate building through the modeling of good deeds within the student body. Therefore, the knowledge about moral values taught in MEC can be put into practice more easily through extracurricular activities or experiential activities in the bigger subject field of CE.

The remainder of this paper focuses upon the specific systems and the practices of moral education as a curriculum and its relation to character education. Together these components comprise the approach to moral education in Korea.

MORAL EDUCATION AS A CURRICULUM: SYSTEM AND CHARACTERISTICS

Korea's idea of national curriculum is a general and common standard that serves as the foundation of educational policy for elementary and middle schools. The national curriculum helps to standardize how goals are to be achieved and with what content, methods, and evaluations (2009 Revised National Curriculum, Notification No. 2009–41, Ministry of Education, Science, and Technology). There have been 10 reforms of education policies at a national level since the emancipation of Korea in 1945. Of most significance to this topic of discussion was the third national curriculum reform that took place in 1973. This third reform was the one that introduced and established "Morals" as a normal subject within the school system. Since then, whenever the national curriculum has been revised, moral education as a curriculum has altered focusing on MEC's substantiality, students' character building, and society's demands. Korea's current moral education curriculum was codified according to the national curriculum policy which was introduced in 2009 and revised in August 2011. It was based on "the curriculum for fulfillment of Project Based Character Education" that emphasized the role of character education to fit society's demands for school violence prevention. According to this curriculum, several subjects related to students' character formation must teach students through various projects that would help students put into practice what they learn in the classroom.

In much of Korea's history, the idea that "education means moral education" has continued, emphasizing the idea that character cultivation is needed for a humanistic life. In the Joseon Dynasty, due to the heavy influence of Confucianism, the only education that was taught was moral education. This culture carries on into today's policies where there is an academic subject set apart for morals studies. It is true that throughout the years there have been pros and cons to MEC and its results, but setting MEC apart as a subject proper reflects the cultural and educational background of Korea and accommodates society's current situation well (Jo, 2000).

Moral education as a curriculum refers to a normal subject, in other words, an independent subject for moral education in elementary, middle, and high school levels of education in which students and teachers interact to promote character building. As seen in Table 19.1 below, first to second graders learn "Proper Lifestyle" and third to ninth graders learn "Morals," with tenth to twelfth graders learning "Lifestyle Ethics" and "Ethics and Thoughts." All students in elementary and middle school are required to take "Proper Lifestyle" and "Morals" while "Lifestyle Ethics" and "Ethics and Thoughts" in high school are optional courses.

Table 19.1 Course Listing for Elementary, Middle, and High Schools

School Level	Elementary School		Middle School	High School
Grade Level	1st & 2nd grade	3rd–6th grade	7th–9th grade	10th–12th grade
Curriculum	Proper Lifestyle	Morals		Morals
Subject	Proper Lifestyle	Morals		Lifestyle Ethics
				Ethics and Thoughts
Features	Mandatory for all students that fall under the National Common Basic Curriculum			Optional

Concisely speaking, elementary and middle school MEC is taught from textbooks. The textbooks present not only the systematic accumulation of information regarding concepts of morality recognized in everyday behavior but also the ideal moral citizen that we pursue today. The primary objective in MEC is to learn moral concepts and to practice them—in other words, use ethical concepts to understand different behaviors from a moralistic aspect (Lim, Yu, & Lee, 1998).

The following are characteristics of the courses that students study in MEC, starting from elementary school until high school.

- First, "Proper Lifestyle" is an integrated course for first and second graders—a course for the lower grades in elementary school. This main focus of this course is to teach students standard learning habits and lifestyle customs, such as basic societal norms and recognizing expected roles in society, along with fundamental moral concerns such as honesty, keeping promises, and treating others with kindness. Finally this course engages students in the initial phases of the development of self-awareness as a social and moral being.

- Second, MEC for third to ninth graders expands students' moral concerns for fairness and human welfare as well as norms of etiquette and understandings of roles and responsibilities of interpersonal relationships. Students at this level extend their moral and social orientations to include the broader society, nature, and the supernatural. Students are taught to develop their personal standard of morality, be aware of diverse moral issues, and to develop knowledge about dealing with or judging situations, putting into practice these skills in distinguishing moral issues, helping them to become better citizens in Korean society as well as to enact progress of the world (2012 Revised National Curriculum, Notification No. 2012–14, Ministry of Education, Science, and Technology).

- Third, MEC for tenth to twelfth graders, "Lifestyle Ethics," focuses on developing skills, attitudes, and ethical awareness including dealing with current ethical problems in a righteous and reasonable way by re-examining Korean ancestors' ethical lives from a current point of view and understanding the characteristics of ethical problems in various aspects of contemporary life.

- Fourth, MEC for tenth to twelfth graders, "Ethics and Thoughts," teaches students about the system of morals in not only Korea, but in both the Eastern and Western worlds. By studying morals from different parts of the world and their various societies, students can develop an autonomous definition of morality and develop the skills necessary to properly deal with and overcome ethical problems in current times.

Korea's youth learn basic lifestyle habits and basic learning habits in first and second grade through the "Proper Lifestyle" course. Students deepen their knowledge and understanding of the content in third grade to ninth grade through "Morals" and set up the foundation to learn more extensively in high school through "Ethics and Thoughts" as well as "Lifestyle Ethics." "Morals" taught to third through sixth graders places its main focus on having students internalize typical lifestyle norms, understand values and virtues, foster a sense of moral judgment, and form a routine of practicing this knowledge in real life. On the other hand, "Morals" taught to seventh through ninth graders puts an emphasis on deepening the knowledge that was learned in the previous half of the course, challenging students to think more extensively about values and virtues, assess situations according to moral principles, and come to an autonomous sense of morality. "Morals" in elementary school focuses on habituation of basic lifestyle and etiquette, while "Morals" in middle school focuses on the advanced understanding of virtues and the engagement of moral judgment based on moral principle.

MORAL EDUCATION AS A CURRICULUM: GOALS AND CONTENT

The goals of moral education as a curriculum have two important aspects: One is that it clearly illuminates an educational direction in fostering students to become a "good citizen" through the moral education curriculum. The other is that it provides a standard that sets up the subject's content selection and organization, teaching methods, evaluations, and a variety of other educational activities. These goals of this MEC are set to reflect the characteristics of MEC for nourishing the four desired character traits that the national curriculum pursues.

In the current Korean education system, four desired character traits are presented in order to foster "the creative and talented people" that Korea's future society needs—a self-directed person, a creative person, a cultivated person, and a global-minded person. The following describes each of the four types (2009 Revised National Curriculum, Notification No. 2009–41, Ministry of Education, Science, and Technology):

1. Self-Directed Person: Intelligence, internal character, and physical health are well-developed all around. He/she pioneers his/her individualistic path of development.
2. Creative Person: Comes up with innovative ideas and creative challenges to build upon the basic foundation of knowledge he/she already possesses.
3. Cultivated Person: Leads a dignified life grounded in the acknowledgment and appreciation of cultural qualities and pluralistic values.
4. Global-Minded Person: Exercises caring and sharing in order to take part in a common development for all as one who recognizes himself/herself as a part of a bigger world.

The goal of MEC is to cultivate a good character or moral development of students in order to achieve these four desired character traits that the national curriculum pursues. In other words, its goal is to harmoniously develop moral knowledge, moral emotions, and moral behaviors together. The main focus of moral education is to foster different levels of moral development, with the formation of basic lifestyle norms in the lower levels and the cultivation of autonomic characters with increasing ability to think and judge situations appropriately.

A. Elementary school: The objectives of Proper Lifestyle
   Developing necessary lifestyle habits that our households, schools, and communities require of us. Forming habits to learn properly from households and schools. Learning basic skills by putting the learned material into practice.

B. Elementary and middle school: The objectives of Morals
   Learning how to respectfully maintain relationships with self, others, society, nation, world, nature, and the supernatural. Increasing awareness of various morality-related problems that arise in different aspects of life by developing cognitive skills, emotions, virtues, and putting them into practice in order to progress into a more autonomous being.

C. High school: The objectives of Lifestyle Ethics
   Learning how to explore and reflect the various ethical problems that arise in current times in light of understanding, judgment, and decision-making skills cultivated from studying ethics. Building character to produce functioning members of society.

D. High school: The objectives of Ethics and Thoughts
   Acquiring thoughts from the East (including Korea) and the West to come to better understandings, reflections, and effective responses to various ethical problems present in different aspects of life today.

At the center of EMC content are core values and virtues. The concept of core values and virtues is a combination of the traditional values that underlie Korean history and the expectations that the current society puts on its citizens to be a sound and participating member. The content of MEC has been reformed time and time again under the influences of moral education theorists' research findings as well as the opinions of teachers and parents alike (Cha & Yun, 2002; Yun, Chu, & Jeong, 2009).

In moral curriculum, we apply "the principle of Expansion of Value Relationships" as a criterion to select and organize the contents to be taught. And taking into account the level of moral development and the range of moral experiences of the students, we integrated the virtue-centered contents and the moral issue-centered (theme) contents. Human beings live within a moral community which is filled with questions that challenge what "ought to be" the norm according to moral sense. In such a moral space, we reflect on our own and the world's ways of dealing with morals. The reflection means that "I" as a subject of reflection direct the object of thought and am aware of it. At this time the relationship between the moral subject and thinking object is defined by the "moral values" and the moral subject and thinking object are built through the value relationship interconnecting through moral values.

There are four types of central value relationships in a person's life—the relationship to the self as moral subject; the relationship between self and we/others; the relationship between self and society, nation, and the global world; and the relationship between self and natural and supernatural beings. The Principle of Expansion of Value Relationships refers to the idea that as one progresses through the level of value relationships, the area that contains the subject to be reflected grows larger in size. As Figure 19.1 below shows, as direction (A) moves along the different levels of relationships, the relative area

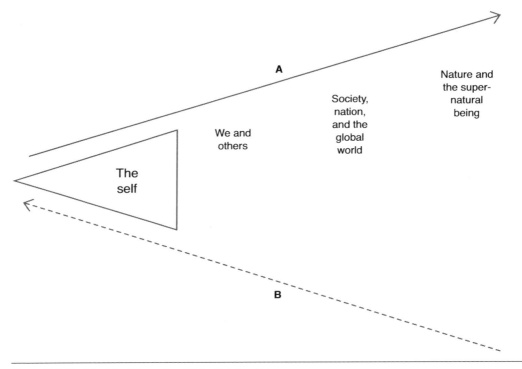

Figure 19.1 The Principle of Expansion of Value Relationships.

of the reflected subject increases. In the same way, as you move down direction (B), the influence the relationship has on the individual increases as well. Therefore, it is not only important to put significance on knowing about the differences in relative area for various levels of relationships, but it is also important to consider which moral values are placed in each of the relationships.

Following the Principle of Expansion of Value Relationships, the core values and virtues that must be taught from the third grade to the ninth grade through MEC have been separated into two types. You can see them in Table 19.2. Holistic-domain orientation values and virtues (respect, responsibility, justice, caring) must be taught in all domains without domain distinction. But domain-specific orientation values and virtues must be taught with three to four values and virtues in each domain.

On one hand, the contents of "Lifestyle Ethics" and "Ethics and Thoughts" in high school curricula are as described in Table 19.3 and Table 19.4. Unlike elementary and middle school, these contents were organized focusing on moral issues (themes), which all students should understand, explore, and practice in their everyday lives.

MORAL AND CHARACTER EDUCATION METHODS AND CHARACTER EDUCATION PROGRAM BASED ON EXPERIENCES

No one can deny that it is good to foster respectable character in students. As an integrated character education emphasizes, one who has good character is a person who possesses the moral virtues as integrated aspects of the self, and acts on the basis

Table 19.2 Elementary and Middle School MEC System and Contents According to the Principle of Expansion of Value Relationships

Domain	Core Values and Virtues		Main Topics
	Holistic-Domain Orientation	Domain-Specific Orientation	
The self as a moral subject • The ego is established through subjectively based moral values	Respect, Responsibility, Justice, Caring	Autonomy, Sincerity, Self-control	• Human and morals • The objective of life and morals • Autonomous morality • Moral exploration and reflection
The relationship between self we/others • Values and virtues of interpersonal relationships		Filial piety, Etiquette, Cooperation	• Family ethics • Mannerisms within neighboring relations • Morals in school life • Youth and morals
The relationship between self and society, nation, and the global world • Responsibilities, duties, social justice of a citizen to its society, nation, global world		Compliance, Public interest, Nationalism, Will of reunification, Humanity	• Social justice and social ethics • National ethics • Unification and ethics • Global ethics
The relationship between self and natural and supernatural beings • Enhancement of values placed on nature and the supernatural		Love for nature, Respect for life, Peace	• Environmental ethics • Scientific ethics • Cultural ethics • Religion ethics

Table 19.3 Contents of High School Curricula: Lifestyle Ethics

Domain	Topic	The Related Applied Ethics
Modern Life Application Ethics	• Necessity of applicable modern life ethics • Exploration and practice of ethical problems • Varying methods to resolve ethical problems	Application Ethics
Life and Sex and Family Ethics	• Life and death ethics • Life science ethics • Sex and love ethics • Family relationships ethics • Friend and acquaintance relationships ethics	Life Ethics Sex Ethics Family
Scientific Technology, Environmental, and Information Ethics	• Science and technology ethics • Human and nature's relationship • Ethical concern regarding environmental issues • Information age and ethics	Scientific Technology Ethics Environmental Ethics Information Ethics
Societal Ethics and Work Ethics	• Societal moral norms and ethics • Social justice and a just society • Human rights and an equal society • Significance of work and its ethical responsibilities	Societal Ethics Work Ethics
Culture Ethics	• Aesthetic values and ethical values • Religious ethics • Food, clothing, and shelter ethics • Multi-cultural ethics	Art Ethics Religious Ethics Basic Needs Ethics Multi-cultural Ethics
Peace Ethics	• National Integration and Ethical Issues • Global Ethical Situation and Issues	Nation Ethics Global Ethics

Table 19.4 Contents of High School Curricula: Ethics and Thoughts

Domain	Topics	Remarks
Significance of Ethical Thoughts and Societal Thoughts	• Life and ethical thoughts • Ideal society's fulfillment and societal thought • Exploration of ethical thoughts and societal thoughts	Life, ethical, and societal thoughts
Asian and Korean Ethical Thoughts	• Asian and Korean ethical thoughts' characteristics and flow • Confucianist thought's origin and development • Characteristics of Confucianist ethical thought • Korean Confucianism's characteristics and significance • Buddhist thought's origin and development • Characteristics of Buddhist ethical thought • Korean Buddhism's characteristics and significance • Taoist thought's origin and development • Characteristics of Taoist ethical thought • Korean Taoism's characteristics and significance • Korea's unique origin, characteristics, and significance	Asian and Korean ethics' flow Confucianist ethical thoughts Buddhist ethical thoughts Taoist ethical thoughts Korea's unique ethical thoughts
Western Ethical Thoughts	• Western ethical thought's characteristics and flow • Relativism and absolutism • Idealism and realism • Hedonism and asceticism • Christian ethics • Empiricist and rationalism • Consequentialist ethics and Utilitarianism • Deontological ethics and Kantian thought • Pragmatic ethics and existentialism	Western ethical thought flow Happiness ethics Faith and ethics Obligation ethics Modern ethical thoughts
Societal Thoughts	• The individual and autonomy • Community and solidarity • Nation and ethics • Democratic Society's ethics • Social justice • Capitalist society's ethics • Socialist society's ethical implications	Individual, common, and national ethics Democracy and justice Capitalism and socialism

of them rather than merely possessing an awareness of the virtues as abstract qualities. A person of good character is someone who attends to the moral implications of actions and acts in accordance with what is moral in all but the most extreme of circumstance (Nucci, 2000). In other words, we can say a person of good character is a "morally mature person" with equal development in moral judgment, moral emotion, and moral behavior. It means that a "morally mature person" is able to understand and judge what is the right thing or value and signifies this understanding with enthusiasm by putting moral principles into practice (Lee, 2001). In conclusion, the concept of a "morally mature person" is in accordance with Lickona's (1991) concept of "a good character." According to Lickona, character is composed of active value, and it is constituted by values that can be seen through one's behavior. If a value becomes a virtue—a reliable inner inclination that acts to the situation in a moral way—then his character is developed. And a good character is constructed of moral knowing, moral feeling, and moral behavior all co-related with one another. These three things are really necessary means to lead a moral life, and eventually it allows a person to be mature (Lickona, 1991; Lee, Park, Sim, & Jo, 2000).

In concert with the definition of character presented above, Lickona (1991) emphasizes the need for a comprehensive, intentional, and proactive approach to character education. In Korea, the approach to CE has likewise been intentionally directed toward impacting the following three elements: moral knowing, moral feeling, and moral behavior in harmony. Efforts at CE have been directed toward precise sequencing and planning of the curriculum and activities that are sustained over time. The approach has been to grasp natural tendencies of students with respect to CE, confirm the organic cooperation of these tendencies through educational practices, to encourage students to practice it continuously, and to reinforce activity with feedback and adequate evaluation. In order to get maximum efficiency out of moral and character education, the moral education curriculum needs to combine different aspects of traditional and modern Eastern and Western methods that have been effective in the past. The goal is to extract from these diverse methods ways to impact students' growth in three components that make up morality—moral knowledge, moral emotion, and moral behavior.

In order to accomplish this in the overall time period spent in schools, and to continue the process of "living" character beyond the classroom, each of the different elements of school, family, and community are envisioned as components within an integrated approach. Korean moral and character education's integrated approach is as shown in Figure 19.2.

Figure 19.2 presents components of a comprehensive moral and character education framework. This broader conceptual frame reflects our recognition that fully impacting moral development and character formation goes beyond the confines of classrooms and schools (Lee, 2000, 2001). Having said that let us turn now to a focused discussion of the components of moral and character education as they are carried out within school setting. In elementary, middle, and high schools, teachers basically utilize the teaching and learning methods of moral and character education presented by the national moral curriculum in order to achieve the goal of moral and character education (2012 Revised National Curriculum, Notification No. 2012–14, Ministry of Education, Science, and Technology). In each school level, however, teachers choose and apply adequately various teaching and learning methods while considering the goals and contents of the moral

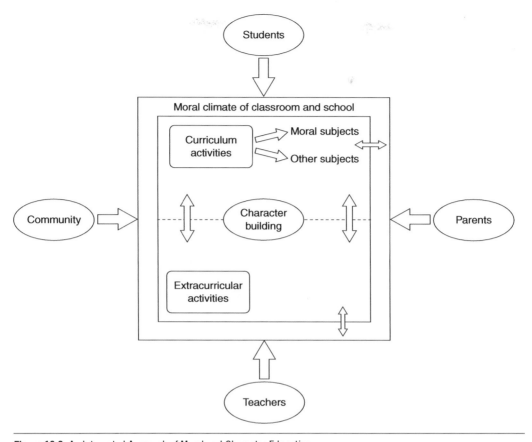

Figure 19.2 An Integrated Approach of Moral and Character Education.

education curriculum and the levels and characteristics of students' cognitive and moral development.

The most commonly used methods for MEC and CE within the Korean school system can be separated into the following types:

1. *Following the example of role-models of respectable character*
   Students possess a developmental characteristic that makes them want to be more like the moral exemplars they witness in their lives. One of Korea's oldest methods of moral and character education is encouraging students to follow morally-righteous behavior of people in their daily lives—their parents, teachers, friends, neighbors, or notable historical figures or characters from literature (Do, 2011; Park & Chu, 1996). This method typically involves two approaches (Lee, 1998, 1999, 2000).

   First, teachers can carry out deeds that inspire students to follow in his/her footsteps. When students recognize that teachers actually live according to the moral values and norms they teach, they will voluntarily take their teachers' lifestyles and deeds as a model to follow. Koreans strongly believe that a teacher's esteemed character is a learning environment and educational value in itself, and consider it to be one of the most effective methods of moral and character education. Therefore teachers, knowing they are objects of identification for students, demonstrate honesty, kindness, fairness, consideration, responsibility, adherence to laws and regulations, justice, love, and other qualities in their daily lifestyle so that students may follow properly.

Second, teachers can present various literature or moral stories that have characters with admirable traits, inspiring the students to be moved by the heroes' deeds and follow in the characters' footsteps. Moral stories demonstrate morally valuable and virtuous characteristics including how a person should act when facing adversity or moral conflict. In order to help students reflect on morality in their own lives, teachers suggest that students make up and explore within their own moral stories. Teachers construct moral stories to use during moral education (Lee, 1999) by collecting a variety of hypothetical and/or real moral stories that exemplify an upright and proper life. These moral stories can usually be found in literature, history, myths, traditional tales, films, soap operas, or newspapers. Teachers then reconfigure the moral stories based on the class's goal and content, the students' level of morality, the appropriate time to teach the material (timings for the introduction, development, and conclusion), functionality (understanding moral values and the concept of norms, practicing in making moral decisions to resolve conflicts, developing empathy, forming a commitment to morality, and habituation), and the method of presenting the material (reading the text content, audio recordings, forms of multimedia, cartoons, and role-playing). Other than the aforementioned, teachers prevent students from falling into an improper way of life by providing a list of accredited books and encouraging students to identify the characters' good deeds and maxims, and wise sayings of famous individuals, and to unravel the meaning, recite, or write a book report about the suggested readings.

2: *Concept exploration and explanation of moral values and norms*

Teachers use concept learning and explanations of moral knowledge in order to help students clearly understand moral values and norms. This method is effective in teaching students moral values, virtues, social norms, and understanding and recognition of what a suitable member of society is and the importance of such things (Yu, 2010). When using this method, teachers encourage students to lead an exploration of moral knowledge in consideration of the students' experiences, their morality's breadth and depth, and their level of concept comprehension. In this way, the teacher is able to provide hypothetical moral situations in which there are conflicting sides of good and evil, right and wrong, and justice and injustice. As students identify moral values and/or norms within these situations through individual or group learning processes, they can explore the significance and meaning behind the values and norms. In order for students to understand the importance of the values and norms, students learn a victim-oriented approach of thinking to help realize how the consequences of not following the standards of morals would affect the students themselves as well as their surroundings.

3. *Discussion or debate through moral dilemmas*

Teachers use discussion or debate to help students develop upright moral thought, judgment, and decision-making ability around specific moral problems that students face. This discussion-based learning is one method of moral teaching and learning with proven effectiveness through many experiences (Oser, Althof, & Higgins-d'Alessandro, 2008). As real or hypothetical moral dilemmas are presented to students, individuals have a chance to imagine themselves as protagonist of the story and take a viewpoint from which they can discuss what they believe and why, so that the students can inclusively come to a conclusion about the best scenario possible. Teachers provide scenarios that are similar to real-life so that students are interested and more willing to participate in these activities. In doing this, teachers can use discussion as a tool for students to learn how to distinguish what is right and expected in a situation, as well as learning the highest moral principles and investigating, judging, and determining the consequences of immoral actions in such scenarios (Frankel, 1977; J. S. Kim, 2006; Yu, 2010).

4. *Peer exchange of moral experiences through narratives*
   Narratives present everyone with a number of decisions around moral dilemmas and give the speaker a chance to reflect on past decisions as they recite before an audience. Narratives are student-centered individual experiences that allow students to become the author of their own life story and give meaning to their moral experiences. In the process, students form and improve their moral authority (H. I. Kim, 2001; Lee, 1999; Tappan & Brown, 1989). Teachers provide an opportunity for students to share their experiences amongst their peers. In story-telling about personal moral experiences, comparing these to others' stories, and reflecting on others' experiences, students can heighten their sense of responsibility about their own thinking, emotion, or actions based on the other students' experiences. In other words, students can become the author of their own lives and tell how they have failed or were successful in various moral dilemmas. Students reflect and see the mistakes they made, and gain a stronger will to put their learning into practice.

   The important point here is that students not only come to a conclusion but also have an understanding of their thinking processes and justifications for having arrived at that conclusion, including the reason why the predicted outcome was different from the actual outcome. By doing this, they are able to share their regrettable or victorious experiences with their peers, and motivate and encourage his/her friends' righteous behavior. In exchanging their moral experiences, they are teaching one another moral values. To achieve this, teachers most frequently use "story-telling" and "writing" to have the students express their moral experiences (Lee, 1999).

5. *Project-based character education*
   Various character education projects have been put into action in order to raise a global twenty-first century generation full of creativity and character. Creativity and character education is an organic combination that produces people with the culture of creativity, the driving force of character education, and the proper judgment founded upon sound morals (Moon, 2010; Moon, Choi, Kwak, & Lee, 2010). The character elements that creativity and character education aims to promote are moral values, virtues, and behavior norms. Core virtues applicable to any school level are interpersonal virtue, honesty, keeping one's appointment, forgiveness, care, responsibility, and ownership. The ideal

virtues of a creative talent are judgment for creative character, moral sensitivity, moral judgment, decision-making skills, and moral behaviors.

In March of 2012, the Ministry of Education, Science, and Technology saw a dire need for a project-based CE that could put knowledge into practice. They started to teach elements of core character competency, such as empathy, communication skills, problem-solving skills, and justice in all school levels in literature, moral education as curriculum, and social studies classes. They reformed the curriculum emphasizes putting these values into practice instead of just accumulating knowledge. The project-based character education is activity- and experience-centered practical character education that moves away from knowledge-based character education. The educational activities foster righteous character and the ability to resolve conflicts that may occur in school settings through various project activities that require the students to resolve on their own through individual or teamwork. In the case of MEC, teachers addressed issues of bullying, dilemmas between friends, youth violence, and the responsibilities and obligations of students through a project approach in which students had a chance to explore and reflect back on the issues.

Instructions for project-based character education for teachers can be separated into four steps as follows. First, as a preparatory step, the students make a plan and prepare what they need according to the requirements of the project. Second, as the starting phase of the project, the students set themes and create a specific list of questions to be explored in the project. Third, as a procedure to put the project into practice, the students prepare to go on-site after coming up with the list of questions, and visit the site to obtain the desired information and solve the inquired tasks. Also, through interviews with experts in that particular field of study, the students explore a more detailed depth regarding the given tasks. Fourth, as the final step of the project, students organize the obtained results after having participated in the project and express their impressions they took away from the experience. And finally the students render the experience and knowledge gained through the activities of the project as their own. At that point, the teacher has students reflect by asking themselves, "How will I live," "What will I live for," "Who am I," and "What is violence and why is it a problem." The MEC teacher's main focus is on guiding, advising, and assisting students.

6. *Creating a moral and caring school community*
Teachers try their best to create a positive and moral climate within a classroom and school. To make a school function well as a democratic and moral community, the school's institution, structure, classroom mood, and scholastic activities must be thriving morally. If this is accomplished, students are able to experience the acceptance of moral values while in school and therefore habituate themselves into a culture of good morals during all the hours they spend at school. To do this, teachers must facilitate different methods and activities to promote an atmosphere in which students respect each other, participate in student governments, uplift one another through conversations, become a Secret Santa (anonymous gifting) for a friend in need, establish and abide by school rules, and participate in a culture of encouragement (Lee, 2001).

7. *Experiencing and practicing moral values first-hand*

Teachers put into practice the core values and virtues learned in school through MEC through first-hand experiences to help students internalize and habituate these values in the following ways:

First, students take part in volunteer services in nursing homes or orphanages in order to foster a sense of caring for the others and social responsibility towards their community. Second, by using the school's classroom for manners, students actually experience various manners and etiquettes such as tea etiquette, the proper way to wear clothes, greeting properly, and making courteous phone calls. Third, while participating in cleanup activities early in the morning with friends and teachers in the classroom and around the school and sharing conversations with them, students raise a sense of industry, cooperation and a sense of service. Fourth, through activities such as raising plants and animals at school and home, students cultivate a bright mind and a sense of respect for life. Fifth, by writing a letter of thanks to their parents and siblings, students feel gratitude and grow a heart of love between family members. Sixth, while praising a friend's strength and talents (relaying compliments) and exchanging encouraging letters of friendship (setting up and running a mailbox of friendship), students uplift a mind to respect and cherish their friends. Seventh, by getting an opportunity to play a role of team leader in the classroom, students take a part in school life rewardingly and learn how to be a responsible leader. Eighth, by operating a school-run mock court, they develop a sense of autonomy and social responsibility. Ninth, using a self-checking accountability system such as "the righteous life practice card," students are able to reflect back on their deeds and make a habit of moral behavior.

8. *School-home-community partnership*

Youth grow in multiple environments—school, home, and community—so it is vital that households and communities utilize each other efficiently as partners in moral education. In order to do this, both establishments must cooperate purposefully. First, teachers encourage parents to help with CE in their children's lives by participating in two ways: by becoming a "helper" in their lives, or by becoming a resourceful person within the community. Second, households as a whole can participate in and/or create programs. The following are some of the after-school programs that are currently implemented: creating family newspapers (learning to appreciate family more), sharing meals together (becoming better communicators), and going out on Saturdays as a designated "family day." On Saturdays, families can go out to experience traditional music, take technology classes together, or go out on a bike ride as a household. Third, students set up and implement a plan to collaborate with the community in order to promote students' character development and perform service. Teachers use programs such as experiential events/camps, where students can volunteer for the less fortunate or other local events that promote good character. This approach is based on the premise that students can internalize their knowledge and put it into practice with the three environments, becoming a "household-like school," a "school-like household," and a "family-like community" (Lee, 2000, 2001).

CONCLUSION

As a result of a self-centered culture that prioritizes academic ranking and lowers the significance of moral education, problems such as lack of sympathy and sharing, incidents of crime and youth violence, and substance abuse are prevalent in Korean society today. Despite a dire need for successful moral education, there are many challenges in Korea today.

First of all, although teachers and parents alike agree that there is a crucial need for character building, they still prioritize subjects like English and Math—so students will have a better chance at getting into top-ranking schools—and therefore limit the amount of time moral education is taught in the classroom. Students do not show interest in the subject so teaching the material becomes harder as students grow older in age. Second, various temporary character-building projects put in place by the government have not been effective, more like applying first aid to an urgent situation without thinking about the long-term effects. Moral education as a curriculum in the scholastic setting is viewed as more of an external response to society's complaints rather an intrinsic value that should be learned and internalized for the sake of improving one's character (Korea Institute for Curriculum and Evaluation, 2011). Third, teachers have little interest, passion, or expertise in the subject matter. The lack of participation on the part of administrators within schools, from both principals and vice principals, also restricts curricula growth. Fourth, there is little cooperation among households, schools, and communities with little shared instruction.

It is not expected that students' character building will happen overnight. CE is a progressive concept with an objective to eventually develop men and women of admirable character. Building character is a composite interaction that requires a linkage among many elements. In order to achieve this, students, parents, and teachers need to practice active participation and acknowledge the necessity of CE. In doing so, it must be known that MEC and CE are mutually dependent curricula that encompass both curricula and extracurricular activities in school, households, and communities and are properly designed to run for long-term periods.

CE, which belongs to a larger category than MEC, had been reduced down to an alternative of MEC because of the critiques of effectiveness following the continued misconduct of youth and their violent behaviors, however, MEC is now recognized as the core of CE. If MEC's role or its significance were to be ignored, the fulfillment of CE's goals would be heavily restricted. In developing admirable character, MEC's unique method of teaching morals and its values, norms, and recognition is necessary in order to promote morality and habituate it into our lives.

REFERENCES

Cha, W. G. & Yun, H. J. (2002). *A study on the goals and contents system of moral subject education (1).* Seoul: Korea Institute for Curriculum and Evaluation.

Do, H. C. (2011). *The narrative, literature and moral education.* Seoul: Ingansarang.

Frankel, J. R. (1977). *How to teach about values: An analytic approach.* Englewood Cliffs, NJ: Prentice-Hall, Inc.

Heo, K. C., Jo, N. S., Kim, Y. G., Yu, G. S., & Lee, S. H. (1994). *School education model development and evaluation for human building* (CR 94–01). Seoul: Korea Educational Development Institute.

Heo, S. H. (1998). The analysis of the character education programs in the elementary school. *The Journal of Elementary Education, 12.*

Jo, N. S. (2000). The developing of moral subject education in the elementary school. *The Moral-Ethics Education, 12.* Seoul: The Korean Society of Moral-Ethics Education.

Kang, S. B., Park, E. S., Kim, G. S., Song, S. J., Jung, Y. K., Kim, Y. R., & Go, M. S. (2008). A foundational study for the vision of education of the human nature for the 21st century. *The Journal of Research in Education, 30*, 1–38.

Kim, H. I. (2001). The elementary moral education through narrative storytelling. *The Journal of Primary Moral Education, 7*, 75–98. Seoul: The Korean Society of Primary Moral Education.

Kim, J. S. (2006). *The understanding of elementary moral subject education.* Seoul: Ulryeok.

Korean Educational Research Association. (1997). *Character education.* Seoul: Munemsa.

Korea Institute for Curriculum and Evaluation. (2011). *The character education vitalization ways through subject education and creative extracurricular activities* (RRC 2011–7–1). Seoul: Korea Institute for Curriculum and Evaluation.

Lee, I. J. (1998). The role of teachers for the integrated character education in the elementary school. *The Journal of Primary Moral Education, 4*, 19–44. Seoul: The Korean Society of Primary Moral Education.

Lee, I. J. (1999). The effective strategies for moral stories used in character education. *The Journal of Primary Moral Education, 5*, 59–87. Seoul: The Korean Society of Primary Moral Education.

Lee, I. J. (2000). Developing effective strategies for character education in the elementary school. *The Journal of Primary Moral Education, 6*, 209–230. Seoul: The Korean Society of Primary Moral Education.

Lee, I. J. (2001). The proper direction and practical ways for character education in the Korean elementary school. *Asia Pacific Education Review, 2* (2), 72–84.

Lee, I. J. (2002). The effects of open character education program on character development in the elementary schools: An ethnographic study. *Journal of Korean Ethics Studies, 50*, 261–318.

Lee, I. J., Park, B. G., Sim S. B., & Jo, K. M. (2000). *The construction of children's character.* Seoul: Ingan Sarang.

Lickona, T. (1991). *Educating for character.* New York: Bantam Books.

Lim, B. D., Yu, H. G., & Lee, H. W. (1998). *The theory of moral subject education in the elementary school.* Seoul: Kyoyook Kwahak SA.

Ministry of Education, Science, and Technology. (2009). *The 2009 Revised National Curriculum* (Notification No. 2009–41). Seoul: Ministry of Education, Science, and Technology.

Ministry of Education, Science, and Technology. (2012). *The 2012 Revised National Curriculum* (Notification No. 2012–14). Seoul: Ministry of Education, Science, and Technology.

Molnar, A. (1997). *The construction of children's character.* Chicago: NSSE.

Moon, Y. R. (2010). It's the proper time to teach creativity and character. *Science and Creativity, 149*, 6–9.

Moon, Y. R., Choi, I. S., Kwak, J. Y., & Lee, H. J. (2010). *A study on the creativity and character education vitalization ways for the building of creative talented persons to practice caring and sharing.* Seoul: The Korea Foundation for the Advancement of Science and Creativity (KOFAC).

Nucci, L. (1989). *Moral development and character education.* Berkeley, CA: McCutchan Publishing Corporation.

Nucci, L. (2000). *Moral education in the information age. The direction of character education in the information age.* Gwangju National University of Education.

Oser, F. K., Althof, W., & Higgins-d'Alessandro (2008). The just community approach to moral education: System change or individual change? *Journal of Moral Education, 37* (3), 395–475.

Park, B. G. & Chu, B. W. (1996). *Ethics and moral education (1),* Seoul: Ingansarang.

Ryan, K. & Bohlin, K. E. (1999). *Building character in schools.* San Francisco: Jossey-Bass Publishers.

Tappan, M. & Brown, L. M. (1989). Stories told and lessons learned: Toward a narrative approach to moral education. *Harvard Education Review, 59*, 182–215.

The Korean Association of Education. (1997). *The character education.* Seoul: Monum SA.

Yu, B. Y. (2010). A study on the basic structure of moral textbook and main activities in elementary moral education. *The Journal of Primary Moral Education, 33*, 61–108. Seoul: The Korean Society of Primary Moral Education.

Yun, H. J., Chu, B. W., & Jeong, C. W. (2009). *A study on the revision of moral subject education contents* (RRC 2009–3–1). Seoul: Korea Institute for Curriculum and Evaluation.

Part IV

Moral Education in Relation to Civic Engagement, Citizenship, and Democracy Education

20

CITIZENSHIP EDUCATION IN THE UNITED STATES

Regime Type, Foundational Questions, and Classroom Practice

Walter C. Parker

Every government degenerates when trusted to the rulers of the people alone. The people themselves therefore are its only safe depositories. And to render them safe their minds must be improved to a certain degree. This is not all that is necessary, though it be essentially necessary. An amendment of our [Virginia] constitution must here come in aid of the public education.

Thomas Jefferson, 1787

INTRODUCTION

Citizenship and citizenship education are two of the oldest ideas in political theory, and scholars are showing new interest in both. Through every era of recorded history, these ideas have been present, linked, and contested. Jefferson's view, summarized here in his plea for public education, is a distillation of centuries of Western writing on the subject—beginning with the Greeks (especially Plato and Aristotle), the Romans (Cicero), and then the daring thinkers of the Renaissance who jettisoned theism (Machiavelli) and of the Enlightenment who constructed reason, rights, and individuals (Locke, Rousseau). This tradition set the precedent for what followed in the United States. When Elizabeth Cady Stanton and her associates met at the Seneca Falls Convention in 1848 and ratified the *Declaration of Sentiments*, or when Martin Luther King, Jr. addressed the crowd at the *March on Washington* more than a century later, they were mobilizing the civil rights principles of the *Declaration of Independence* and the US *Constitution* to advance their own causes. The woman suffragists famously altered the second sentence of the *Declaration of Independence* to read: "We hold these truths to be self-evident: that all men and women are created equal…" (Stanton, Anthony, & Gage, 1889, p. 70). Similarly, King demanded not an alternative to the founding principles of the United States but their fulfillment. "Now is the time to make real the promises of democracy," he said.

We have come to our nation's capital to cash a check. When the architects of our republic wrote the magnificent words of the Constitution and the Declaration of Independence, they were signing a promissory note to which every American was to fall heir.... We have come to cash this check, a check that will give us upon demand the riches of freedom and the security of justice.

(King, 2001, p. 82)

The idea of citizenship is concerned with membership in a political community. Who belongs and who does not? The stakes are high because not only is *citizen* an identity but because rights and benefits come with membership—access to voting and police protection, for example. Criteria become important: Can you access these things simply by being here for an amount of time, or must you be born here? Do you need additional qualifications—blood, language, or religion? And what about educational attainment? To be a member of this political community must you be literate? Must you pass a "citizenship test"?

We can see, then, that *citizenship* is a longstanding idea and still vital today. The idea of citizenship *education* is old and still vital, too. In contemporary US society, it is also called "civic education" and "political education" although the latter is often avoided outside academe, perhaps because it connotes indoctrination. In schools, citizenship education includes formal coursework in government—not government generally but US government in particular and, less frequently offered or taken, comparative government (specifically, *Advanced Placement Comparative Government and Politics*). Citizenship education also occurs formally in US history courses. These are typically offered in grades 5, 8, and 11. Less formally, citizenship education also occurs in student council programs, elections to various school offices, daily recitation of the loyalty oath known as *The Pledge of Allegiance*, and elsewhere.[1]

For a proper understanding of citizenship education in any society, it is necessary to appreciate that it is, in William Galston's (2001) succinct phrase, "relative to regime type" (p. 218). Democratic regimes "require democratic citizens whose specific knowledge, competencies, and character would not be as well suited to nondemocratic politics." *Regime* is no longer a widely used term outside the academy, but it is key to understanding citizenship education in any country. A country's regime is its form of government coupled with its political culture, including its practices and its aspirations. *Patriotism*, whatever its particular meanings, is an idea related to membership in a particular regime. In a democratic regime, the animating idea is that the people themselves are the governors. This is *popular sovereignty* or the idea that "we the people" (the opening words of the US Constitution) create governments to secure their rights, and that we consent to be governed. This is, quoting Lincoln at Gettysburg, "government of, by, and for the people." Citizens need not only comply with authorities, but become authorities; not only obey laws, but make laws; not only abide by judges' rulings, but serve as jurors and deliberate policy with other citizens. As Jefferson implies in this chapter's opening quote, the people cannot rule well if they are a band of unskillful or unthoughtful know-nothings. Their minds "must be improved to a certain degree." Accordingly, he tried to convince fellow Virginians to fund public education. He failed. That innovation came in the middle of the next century in Massachusetts, championed by Horace Mann.

Every regime has an interest in civic education, even non-democracies like contemporary China and Saudi Arabia or 1940 Germany. Nazi Germany had extensive civic education programs, both in school and out, tailored to the cultivation of good Nazis. Youth were taught obedience to state authority, militarism, patriarchy, heterosexism, love of Hitler, hatred of Jews, and racism (Rempel, 1989). Two millennia earlier, Plato had another idea about citizenship education. Unlike the Nazis, he had a fair and just regime in mind, but he doubted citizens' ability to rule. It is easy today to answer affirmatively the question, *should* the people rule? Americans grow up in a cultural surround that believes fervently in popular sovereignty, at least rhetorically and generally. But *can* the people rule? Are they *able*? This is a different question, and probably every reader of this chapter is circumspect about it. Jefferson believed education could compensate for the people's lack of native ability to govern. Plato famously did not. Ordinary citizens mistake their opinions for knowledge, Plato believed, and "democracy" in practice is the tyranny of these opinions multiplied by the number of citizens—the blind leading the blind while confidently believing they can see clearly. This is not a promising situation. And so, in *The Republic*, he presented an education system where children were removed from their mother's care and then educated according to their abilities, with the most able trained to be the governors of the country.

With this introduction to the central ideas of this chapter in hand (citizenship and citizenship education), let me preview what is to come. In the next two sections, I address the current state of scholarship on both concepts. We will see that investigations of each have returned to prominence. Then, I turn to three foundational issues that help to explain some unique political controversies that animate citizenship education in the United States, "unique" because they are specific to the US regime type and its core tension between democratic authority (e.g., a school board) and personal freedom (e.g., religious beliefs). Following this, we will peer into citizenship-education practices in classrooms and schools where we find, first and foremost, inequality in the distribution of effective pedagogies and, again unique to the US regime type, the key role of nongovernmental organizations.

SCHOLARSHIP ON CITIZENSHIP RETURNS

Citizenship and citizenship education, both ancient and much-addressed topics, have not always been foremost on scholarly agendas. Today they are back with gusto.[2] Reasons for this can be found at the juncture of globalization, migration, and the decline in civic engagement in actually-existing democracies. Gershon Shafir (1998), the editor of a leading volume on the subject, suggests that *citizenship* is back because of four contemporary processes: the recent wave of democratization in Eastern Europe and parts of Africa, Latin America, and the Middle East; the rise of ethnic conflicts in the European Union; the associated debate over welfare entitlements (an argument over the rights and benefits of citizenship); and global migration to modern industrial nations. All of these, he notes, have been analyzed through the prism of citizenship.

Anthropologist Aiwa Ong (1999, 2003) examines the buzzing heterogeneity in these global flows. In two studies, she contrasts the affluent transnational citizens of global metropolises—"flexible citizens," she calls them, because they hold multiple passports and properties in, say, Hong Kong and San Francisco—with poor and often desperate migrants seeking low-end work in nearby countries (Indians in Persian Gulf states, Mexicans in the United States), and their ensuing struggles for access to rights and benefits. On the same platform, geographer Katharyne Mitchell (2001) examined the education conflicts that resulted when affluent Chinese, who had migrated from Hong Kong and Taiwan to neighborhoods in and around Vancouver, clashed with their similarly affluent but ethnically different Anglo-Canadian neighbors over curriculum policies in the school district. Deweyan democracy and child-centered pedagogy met Confucian meritocracy and filial piety. The formation of the "good Canadian citizen" was opened to debate.

Also inviting the new scholarship on citizenship is the decline in traditional forms of civic engagement in the United States and other democratic societies. Civic engagement or "political participation" has long been understood to be a leading indicator of the vibrancy of any democratic society. Alexis de Tocqueville (1969), the astute French observer of the early nineteenth century, argued that it was not merely an indicator but a cause. In his chapter in *Democracy in America* called "Causes Which Mitigate the Tyranny of the Majority in the United States," he identified the chief mitigating factor as the dispersal of government power. The dispersion is both across territory (today, the federal government in Washington, D.C. and local governments in the 50 states plus the still more-local municipalities, counties, and school districts that are sanctioned by states) and within governments (legislative, executive, judicial) at both national and local levels. Importantly, this dispersal of power operates cooperatively with a farrago of close-to-home, intermediary institutions. These are mid-range solidarities that range from faith communities and political parties to choirs, bowling leagues, and unions. These networks, known jointly as "civil society," are outside government; yet they are its foundation. This is because they join people together outside their families. "Americans of all ages, all stations in life, and all types of disposition," de Tocqueville wrote,

> are forever forming associations. There are not only commercial and industrial associations in which all take part, but others of a thousand different types—religious, moral, serious, futile, very general and very limited, immensely large and very minute.... Nothing, in my view, deserves more attention than the intellectual and moral associations in America.
>
> (p. 517)[3]

A century and a half later, Robert Putnam (1995) wrote an article on the decline of civic engagement in the United States. He called it "Bowling Alone." His conclusion was that civic decline had reached so far into society that, just as the number of people reading a common newspaper or attending precinct meetings had declined, or going to the Elks Lodge or a weekly card game, so had the number of people joining bowling leagues. The whole system of social networks was declining. His research struck a chord with scholars and pundits and popularized the concept "social capital": these prosaic social networks and the norms of reciprocity and trust that they generate and support.

Of special concern to civic educators today is the decline in civic engagement among youth. Many high school seniors reach voting age before they graduate and, ironically, while they are sitting in the high school government course offered to seniors. But research demonstrates that their political involvement is meager. Flanagan and Levine (2010) provide the details:

> Young adults today are less likely than their counterparts in the 1970s were to exhibit nine out of ten important characteristics of citizenship: belonging to at least one

group, attending religious services at least monthly, belonging to a union, reading newspapers at least once a week, voting, being contacted by a political party, working on a community project, attending club meetings, and believing that people are trustworthy. Only in a tenth form of citizenship—volunteering—are they more likely to participate, probably as a result of deliberate efforts over the past several decades by schools, colleges, and community groups to encourage volunteering. For several of these ten types of engagement—notably voting—rates have risen in the 2000s compared with the 1990s, but not enough to compensate for thirty years of decline.

(p. 161)

Are Americans participating less or differently? And, if less, is the decline more a matter of delay or long-term decline? Difference theorists point to graduates who are reconnecting with lost classmates on Facebook, stay-at-home parents who meet one another on social networking portals such as *Meetup*, the proliferation of book clubs thanks to *Oprah* and fan clubs thanks to the reality television show *American Idol*, and so forth. Delay theorists emphasize that adolescence (a construct dating to approximately 1900 in the United States) is lengthening, which predictably delays civic engagement. This is because civic engagement is related to life-cycle patterns and historical forces. The young adult finishes school, moves out of the parental home, moves into the work force, and starts a new family. These are watersheds that make regular engagement in civic life more likely because the youth is outside the family of origin and spending more time "in public" where she is exposed to diverse ideologies and lifestyles. The young adult is thereby positioned on a social platform where it is easier to see opportunities for civic engagement, plus she is more available for recruitment into community activity (Finlay, Wray-Lake, & Flanagan, 2010). A broadened horizon alongside availability to others—seeing and being seen—is a powerful combination for civic involvement. But, it is easily interrupted, too. The Great Recession of 2008–2012 destabilized the life-cycle transitions of the middle and working classes, and time spent in gated communities has increased the segregation of Americans, thereby narrowing, not broadening, their horizons. The sorting-by-incarceration of Black and Latino males (Alexander, 2010) further entrenches a caste system in America, the civic engagement consequences of which include temporary or, in some states, permanent restrictions on voting rights and an "ex-con's" lasting status as a second-class citizen.[4]

To summarize: citizenship and citizenship education are old ideas and practices, and they are venerable topics of scholarly inquiry. Furthermore, they are relative to regime type and, therefore, hollow topics without the meanings, issues, and power relations found in particular political contexts: Athens in the fifth century BCE, Lexington in 1775, Gettysburg in 1863, Paris in 1789, Berlin in 1933, Birmingham in 1963, Arizona today. Both topics ebb and flow as objects of study depending on historical contingencies, and both are back on the scholarly agenda today thanks to a combination of forces: a decline in civic engagement, the intensification of globalization and migration, and the appearance of new patterns of integration and segregation.

CITIZENSHIP EDUCATION MATTERS

The return of citizenship education to critical study, research, and development in the United States is welcome news. It had been buried from the 1960s through the 1990s under a curious scholarly consensus that believed formal citizenship education in classrooms had no significant effect on civic knowledge or behavior. The study that put the nail in the coffin was "Political Socialization and the High School Civics Curriculum in the United States," by Langton and Jennings (1968) in the *American Political Science Review*. Personally, I began my teaching career in the aftermath of this study. I had just completed a bachelor's degree in political science and was enrolled in the University of Colorado's fine, year-long, post-BA program in teacher education. Along with others who were training to become high school government teachers, I learned of the study and was puzzled not only by its findings but by the way they had been embraced by the political science field. The findings were truly counterintuitive. A maxim of both parenting and educational research is that children stand a better chance of learning something if it is taught than if it is not, and if they study it than if they don't. This is why parents and teachers encourage students to attend rather than skip classes, to pay attention rather than sleep, and to do the homework; and it is why colleges are more likely to admit applicants who have done well in their high school courses than those who have failed them or dropped out.

Thirty years later, political scientists Niemi and Junn (1998) presented evidence and analysis contrary to Langton and Jennings. On Langton and Jennings' survey, civic knowledge had been measured by only six items. Niemi and Junn used the 1998 NAEP Civics Assessment, which had 150 knowledge items. Moreover, these items were tied to actual civics courses that students were likely to take. To show whether civics courses affect civic knowledge, the knowledge measure needs to match the curriculum of the civic courses whose effect is being determined. Niemi and Junn's study did this. Not only did they tie their study to actual civics coursework (vs. general political knowledge), they focused on four aspects of coursework: amount, recency, topics addressed, and inclusion of current events. They found that higher student knowledge was associated with higher amounts and greater recency of civics courses, a greater range of topics, and more discussion of current events.[5]

Niemi and Junn's (1998) study was a watershed that ended the "coursework doesn't matter" consensus and re-opened the gates to research on civics coursework generally and *kinds* of civics coursework in particular (we will come to effective practices later in this chapter). And because the recency of civics coursework had been shown to matter, Niemi and another colleague (Niemi & Smith, 2001) immediately studied the prevalence of the high school government course that students most often take in the twelfth grade. They found that, after a temporary decline during the 1960s and 1970s (a period sometimes described as "curriculum anarchy" [e.g., Taylor & Haas, 1973, p. 83]), enrollment in this course had returned to a high level. By 2001, 75% of high school students were taking the course.

The high school government course deserves critical attention despite its homely façade. It is a "structures and functions" course, its focus being "how government works" in the United States. The subject matter includes the history and ratification of the Constitution, federalism, separation of powers, checks and balances, landmark Supreme Court cases, limited government, legislation, political parties, media, and interest groups. The course is intriguing on the landscape of citizenship education because it is both prevalent and pedestrian. Though its footprint is enormous, it almost escapes detection—lost in plain sight. Most students take it, but its mention in the citizenship education literature is rare and then often derisive, with criticism of boring topics, maintenance of sociopolitical orthodoxies, and unrealistic portrayals of US democracy. Remarkably, its curriculum has been settled for decades, so much so that the course escapes the partisan public wrangling that routinely besets the US history curriculum.[6]

FOUNDATIONAL ISSUES

Yet, citizenship education (like any common endeavor) cannot avoid politics. The dull high school government course may fly beneath the radar screen, but the daily conduct of citizenship education in a democracy is lively and contentious on several fronts. In my judgment, three are central. The first issue is conceptual and concerns the objectives of citizenship education: For what type of democratic regime do we want to educate students in the United States? That is, what kinds of democratic political identity and corresponding virtues should schools try to cultivate? This involves a distinction between liberal and illiberal democracy. The second issue concerns authority over the citizenship education curriculum. In a theocracy or military regime, there is little question as to who is authorized to shape and distribute the education of future citizens: priests or generals. In a democracy, however, there are contending forces and interests, each clamoring for a say. Which group(s) of adults can legitimately decide on the particulars of citizenship education in schools? Parents? Professional educators? Citizens? The third issue stems from the conflicts that arise in liberal-democratic regimes over the meaning of patriotism and the tension between majority rule and personal freedom. Specifically, should students be exposed to a range of beliefs, even those that oppose their parents' beliefs? That is, should they be taught to think for themselves?

The three issues are related. The founders of the United States created a liberal democracy, which guarantees personal freedom and human rights in addition to majority rule. One implication is that parents cannot demand that schools cater to their own ethnic customs, religious beliefs, or political ideologies. At least, they cannot demand this if doing so would harm or interfere with or otherwise burden the customs, beliefs, and ideologies of other families. Citizenship education is particularly interesting from this liberal perspective not only because it aims to shape children into particular kinds of citizens, but because it also aims to shape them into the kind of people who decide for themselves what shape they will take. Accordingly, the teaching of critical thinking and toleration as two hallmarks of good citizenship in a liberal democracy have been challenged on the grounds that they might draw children away from the beliefs of their parents. Should schools be able to interfere in family life in this way, and does liberal-democratic citizenship education demand it? A consideration of the three issues will afford a more robust understanding of the politics of citizenship education in the United States.

Issue 1: Liberal or Illiberal Democracy?

A politician working to restore peace in a genocide-ravaged country today could very well worry that free and fair elections might eventually be held under the banner of "democracy." Her concern is that the men who are thereby elected would be the same racists and separatists who engineered the mass rape, murder, and plunder during the genocide. It would be a democratic government—in Greek *demos* (the many) and *cracy* (rule)—but it would ignore limits on its power and continue to deny civil rights and liberties to members of the despised minority group. This would be an *illiberal* democracy.

Popular sovereignty, made manifest in free and fair elections, is the critical attribute of democracy, but more is required of a *liberal* democracy. As Crick (2008) wrote, liberal democracy is a hybrid—a "fusion of the idea of the power of the people and the idea of legally guaranteed individual rights" (p. 15; also Habermas, 1997).

Any sort of democratic regime—liberal or illiberal—is a rare occurrence historically, so much so that its absence at any time or in any place does not demand attention or explanation. Yet my experience in 40 years of teaching suggests that American students of all ages take democracy for granted, as though it were common and easy rather than rare and difficult. Historians know better. They are surprised when democracies appear, all the more so when they develop and endure. Historians know that tyranny—absolutism—is the historical norm, the most common forms being theocracy, military dictatorship, and absolute monarchy—rule by clergy, colonels, and kings. The third often combines with the first in such a way that the monarch's absolute authority is believed to be supernatural—derived from the heavens (the "divine right of kings"). By the time Aristotle wrote *Politics*, there had been such a variety of political systems that he could classify and evaluate them. Among them were democracies, which he considered feckless: Either they devolved quickly into illiberal mob rule (majority will without constitutional restraint) or oligarchy (an elected but corrupt managerial class).

The founders of US constitutional democracy were also critical of democracy. Having just won independence from the divine-right king of England, and having been avid readers of ancient Greek and Roman and then Renaissance and Enlightenment thinkers, the US founders were convinced that democracy's prospects were bleak. Hamilton wrote in *Federalist No. 9* (1982, p. 44):

> It is impossible to read the history of the petty Republics of Greece and Italy without feeling sensations of horror and disgust at the distractions with which they were continually agitated, and at the rapid succession of revolutions by which they were kept in a state of perpetual vibration between the extremes of tyranny and anarchy.

Democracies usually failed, the founders believed, not for lack of splendid ideals but for an excess of wishful thinking combined with bad planning. They failed because they required "we the people" to be angels, which they are not. On this the historical record needs no elaboration. As Madison (1937) wrote in *Federalist No. 51*, "If men were angels no government would be necessary" (p. 337). Government is necessary because "we the people" easily become an illiberal mob, seduced by demagogues, or a motley of interest groups each blinded by its own passions. Madison wrote, "A dependence on the people is, no doubt, the primary control on the government; but experience has taught mankind the necessity of auxiliary precautions." For this reason, the men who founded the US regime created a constitution that controlled both the people and the government and aimed to constrain or prevent absolutism and oppression or, stated positively, to preserve liberty and rights. ("Liberty is the right to do what the law permits," Montesquieu wrote, summarizing the tension between political freedom and constraint.) Among these precautions were the separation of powers into distinct branches of government, checks and balances that kept one branch from overwhelming the others, a bicameral legislature, federalism, and, eventually, a Bill of Rights. These have become widespread features of liberal democracies ever since.

It is well known that illiberal oppressions based on race, class, and gender were present even as these liberal-democratic innovations were being inscribed in the late eighteenth century. When the US Constitution was ratified in 1787, African Americans were chattel and women were only somewhat better off. Native peoples were in another category still—savages, demons. "We the people" referred to White, male, property-owning citizens of a certain age. Slaves and women *were* property. Liberal democracies fall short of their aspirations (there are no ideal democracies), and this motivates social movements that aim to close the gap between ideals and realities. The framers of the US Constitution may have been the birth parents of liberal democracy on a large scale, but those who were excluded became the adoptive, nurturing parents. That is, the core values of liberal democracy have been pursued not necessarily by those already secured within "we the people" but by those people living at the margins and fighting for inclusion (Okihiro, 1994). The woman's suffrage and civil rights movements noted in the first paragraph of this chapter are the iconic cases in the United States.

Issue 2: Who Has Legitimate Educational Authority?

Who has the legitimate authority in a liberal-democratic regime to decide how the next generation of citizens shall be educated? The US Constitution reserves education policy to the states but does not resolve the matter further. Who or what will fill in the details of curriculum and instruction?

Parents are key players in curricular decision making, of course. As Dewey (1956) wrote, "What the best and wisest parent wants for his own child, that must the community want for all of its children. Any other ideal for our schools is narrow and unlovely; acted upon, it destroys our democracy" (p. 7). This is an appealing assertion of collective responsibility for all children, not just our own children. Yet, Amy Gutmann (1999) noticed its undemocratic contradiction. Where are "we the people" in Dewey's formulation? In other words, where is the *citizenry* working together to create and maintain a free society within the constraints of a constitution? The "enforcement of any moral ideal of education," Gutmann writes, "whether it be ideologically liberal or conservative, without the consent of citizens subverts democracy" (p. 14). A liberal-democratic society, because it values rights and liberties, requires citizens to deliberate collectively about the education of future citizens. Citizens are obliged to negotiate the curriculum of democratic education across plural interests and beliefs just as they negotiate tax rules, gun law, and foreign policy across plural interests and beliefs. The "best and wisest parents" are not of a single voice. They want different goods for their children. *They don't and won't agree.* This pluralism is a fact of life in society, and a liberal-democratic regime embraces it.

Some parents will claim they have a natural right to exclusive educational authority. They will assert this because, first, the children in question are "their" children (the proprietary assumption), and second because parents are naturally concerned to maximize the welfare of their children (the altruistic or evolutionary assumption). But these assumptions are specious, as both educators and citizens are quick to point out. Parents may have given birth to or adopted children, but that does not establish possession. Children could be (and have been) imagined to "belong" to the gods, the state, or the village, for example. The propensity of at least some families to teach racist, ethnocentric, and sexist values that contradict liberal-democratic ideals—particularly the bedrock values of civic equality, popular sovereignty, tolerance, inalienable rights, and liberty—undermines the second assumption, not to mention the frequency of child abuse and neglect. Parents cannot hold their children in a state of what Eamon Callan calls "ethical servility" (1997, p. 152) where they exist only to fulfill their parents' wishes and are never taught to think for themselves. As Walter Lippmann (1993) wrote, curriculum controversies "are among the bitterest political struggles which now divide the nations" (p. 22). But why the bitterness? Why not simply disagreement? He believed the assertion of parental authority is often the cause:

> Wherever two or more groups within a state differ in religion, or in language and in nationality, the immediate concern of each group is to use the schools to preserve its own faith and tradition. For it is in the school that the child is drawn towards or drawn away from the religion and the patriotism of its parents.
>
> (p. 23)

Most parents are far from holding their children in a state of ethical servility, so let us not overstate the liberal-democratic case against parents being the sole authorities for the education of democratic citizens. Still, we must note that neither educators nor democratic citizens are inclined, as parents may be, to claim exclusive educational authority, for that would be patently undemocratic. Rather, both groups claim a seat at the deliberative table *alongside* parents where curricular policy is developed in a democratic society. Gutmann (1999) argues that collective moral argument and decision making (collective deliberation) among the various educational stakeholders is the most democratically justifiable approach to the authority question.[7] In brief, who should decide the curriculum by which the next generation of democrats shall be educated? On Gutmann's analysis, consistent with her political theory of deliberative democracy, the answer is straightforward: All of us together, weighing the alternatives, arguing across differences, and, when needed, voting to decide the issue. After all, the most important thing adults can do together, across their differences, is decide how to educate their children for what will be a shared future. This is not something they can be doing in isolation, not if they aim to have a liberal democracy.

Issue 3: Should Schools Teach Toleration and Critical Thinking?

Some readers will be surprised to learn that a perennial controversy affecting citizenship education in the United States is whether public schools should aim to teach critical thinking and toleration. It is surprising because both are usually considered unremarkable, pedestrian aims that are intuitively fundamental to education, almost defining it (Jefferson's "their minds must be improved to a certain degree"). So accustomed have American citizens become to freely exercising or seeking their rights and liberties that, generally, toleration has become a mundane aim, not a public controversy. Episodes of intolerance, such as hate crimes, are generally reviled.[8] Governors appoint commissions and order flags flown at half-mast; legislatures pass resolutions; vigils are held. As Justice Brennan wrote matter-of-factly in 1989,

> We are not an assimilative, homogeneous society, but a facilitative, pluralistic one, in which we must be willing to abide someone else's unfamiliar or even repellent practice because the same tolerant impulse protects our own idiosyncrasies.

Nevertheless, challenges to the teaching of toleration and critical thinking arise regularly, and there follow court cases and turbulent school board elections. The case of *Mozert v. Hawkins County* served as a bellwether in 1987. Conservative parents claimed that a pro-toleration, multicultural policy by Tennessee public schools was intolerant of their own "born again Christian" world-view and undermined their First Amendment right to freely exercise their religion and pass it along to their children. The school board had unanimously voted to adopt a series of basal reading textbooks that exposed their children to beliefs contrary to their own in several categories. Quoting from the court's decision:

> [A parent] identified passages from stories and poems used in [the publisher's] series that fell into each category. Illustrative is her first category, futuristic supernaturalism, which she defined as teaching "Man As God." Passages that she found offensive described Leonardo da Vinci as the human with a creative mind that "came closest to the divine touch." Similarly, she felt that a passage entitled "Seeing Beneath the Surface" related to an occult theme, by describing the use of imagination as a vehicle for seeing things not discernible through our physical eyes. She interpreted a poem, "Look at Anything," as presenting the idea that by using imagination a child can become part of anything and thus understand it better. [The parent] testified that it is an "occult practice" for children to use imagination beyond the limitation of scriptural authority.

The 6th Circuit Court of Appeals ruled that the citizens of Tennessee had a compelling interest here, which justified the burden being placed on these parents. That interest, quoting the Court, is that "public education must prepare pupils for citizenship in the Republic," which includes exposing children to diverse beliefs and controversial issues.[9]

More recently, the platform of the Texas Republican Party of 2012, following the battle over the state's revised curriculum standards for social studies,[10] contained this plank: "We oppose the teaching of … critical thinking skills and similar programs that … have the purpose of challenging the student's fixed beliefs and undermining parental authority" (p. 12). This statement reveals, again, that citizenship education can conflict with parental authority when the child, per Lippmann's observation earlier, is "drawn away from the religion and the patriotism of its parents."

A number of theorists in addition to Gutmann, notably Brighouse (2000), Callan (1997), and Levinson (2012) argue that a liberal-democratic regime has a morally compelling obligation to educate its citizens both to think critically and to tolerate one another. As we saw in the Mozert case, the courts often agree. The reason is that the US regime type exists to maintain individuals' rights and liberties, which include their freedom to pursue happiness in whatever direction they choose, within the law: a life of faith and family, or not; a life of science and industry, or not; a life of baseball caps or *hijabs*, or neither. This regime type assumes that individuals will differ on conceptions of the good, the true, and the beautiful, and that they have a natural right to do so. *The ensuing freedom leads to further proliferation of diversity in all directions, thus requiring a political culture of tolerant co-existence.* This regime type assumes, further, that these individuals are capable of making the decision to "consent" to be governed, as the Declaration of Independence states.[11] Young children cannot consent, which is one reason why they are in the custody of their parents. But as young people approach their "majority" or "emancipation," as it is called (legal adulthood, independence, and responsibility for conduct), this is precisely what is required: an independent decision to live within the social contract, with rights and liberties both guaranteed by and constrained by law. Consent requires critical thinking or in the language of political philosophy "political autonomy": the capacity to make un-coerced decisions—to develop one's own views without manipulation by others.

Dewey characterized this kind of education—liberal civic education—as a "method of intelligence" or "intelligence in operation." It is a middle way between extremes. The political left and right have different conceptions of the good life, and they often see schools as technologies for realizing them. On the right (e.g., Finn, 2003), students should be taught to serve, succeed in, and preserve the current social order. Patriotism on the right is pride in what has already been accomplished—the status quo—and one's civic duty is to protect and nurture it. On the left (e.g., Counts, 1932), students should be taught to transform the social order so as to realize a more just and vibrant democracy, one that would include the economy rather than leaving it solely in the hands of the market. Patriotism on the left is pride in democratic ideals, and one's civic duty is to help achieve them. Dewey advocated neither of these but carved a middle way: Students should be taught to use their minds well—to think critically and to value and use scientific inquiry. They should not be told to what ends they should use these competencies, however, but left free to determine their own ends and path. It is up to them—well-educated democratic citizens, trained thinkers—to engage in the ongoing work of government of, by, and for the people.[12]

The obligation of schools to teach critical thinking and tolerance does not license them to indoctrinate students into a particular conception of the good life, only to enable students to think for themselves and let others think for themselves. Here, then, is the famous tension: Liberal democracy is neutral as to conceptions of the good life *and* it is committed (not neutral) to the values of liberal democracy. Citizens, therefore, have both freedoms and obligations. Liberty is not independence from the community, but a dimension of community. Quoting Aristotle, "Individuals are so many parts all equally depending on the whole which alone can bring self-sufficiency" (1958, p. 6).

By now it will have occurred to readers that Dewey's middle way wasn't so neutral after all. *The child's character is deliberately formed to meet regime requirements; she is required to become a tolerant, independent, and critical thinker.* And this is why liberal democratic regimes face an enduring role conflict. While parents may and do indoctrinate children into particular beliefs and lifestyles—this is the parent's right—civic educators are obliged to "prepare pupils for citizenship in the Republic" as ruled in Mozert. The regime has a compelling interest in cultivating liberal-democratic character—citizens who are democratically enlightened and politically engaged (Parker, 2008). These are citizens who know and do particular things. They know the historical rarity of democracy and the historically predictable routines by which it descends into demagoguery and autocracy. They know why in the more successful democracies power is divided among "branches" and why the state is neutral (to an extent) and non-interfering as to religion. They do things, too. They vote and serve on juries, for example, and call out intolerance and discrimination where they find them. Importantly, they protect from governmental or popular incursions not only their own group but other groups. They *do* this because they *know* something: Like King (1963) sitting in Birmingham City Jail, they know that "injustice anywhere is a threat to justice everywhere" (p. 77). Moreover, they can and do endeavor to communicate with one another across their differences in ways that make liberal-democratic living possible—Dewey's "mode of associated living, of conjoint communicated experience" (1985, p. 93). This becomes their *common* way of life, a public similarity bridging private difference, to which children are assimilated at the *common* school.

CLASSROOM AND SCHOOL PRACTICE

How can we characterize the practices of classroom and school-based citizenship education in the United States? The aforementioned high school government course plays an important, formal role in the upper grades, but so do the many less formal classroom and school-wide practices at all levels. The daily recitation of the *Pledge of Allegiance*, for example, is required by law in 35 states and practiced by custom in most of them (Piscatelli, 2003). "Citizenship" (comportment) marks are often given in the lower grades along with subject area marks, and homeroom meetings and student councils continue to dot the school landscape. Some elementary school principals convene one council for grades 1–3 and another for grades 4–6. "Our one purpose here," one principal told the children, "is to identify problems and try to solve them" (Parker, 2011a, p. 97). Like the US Senate, each class elects two members to serve on the council. These students may be told they are delegates of their classrooms, not representatives, and consequently must vote at council meetings as instructed by their classmates. Therefore, the elections matter to the class, and class meetings at which delegates are given instructions are an important part of the program. In such a council program, even primary-grade children gain experience with electing and being elected, with majority rule, with the distinction between delegate and representative, and with discussion of issues that are important to them.[13]

Returning to the formal curriculum,[14] the US history curriculum is typically taught across the nation in grades five, eight, and eleven. Not merely historical or historiographic in emphasis, it serves a civic, nation-building purpose (Barton & Levstik, 2004; Epstein, 2009). Nations everywhere create schools to advance national cohesion, a positive story, and a national imaginary, and the US history curriculum follows suit. Its subject matter at all three levels centers on the founding of the nation, the Constitution, its greatest crisis (the Civil War), and the fulfillment, to an extent, of its promise in the Civil Rights Movement. Each of these four eras has one or two events at its center; consequently, a narrative history style ("And then what happened?" and "Who did it?") is both common and popular with old and young students alike. Indeed, the evidentiary historiographic approach is rare: Few history teachers even in the upper grades engage students in historical inquiry where the emphasis is on the creation and evaluation of claims and their warrants. This practice is unfortunate, for as Barton and Levstik (2010) conclude, students are left with

> no way of distinguishing historical claims that are based on evidence from those that aren't—such as myths, legends, or outright lies. The inability to distinguish between a myth and a warranted assertion destroys the foundation for democracy, because students will be susceptible to any outrageous story they may be told.
>
> (pp. 39–40)

With this introduction behind us, let us turn briefly to three dimensions of citizen-ship-education practice in US classrooms and schools: inequality, discussion-oriented pedagogy, and the role of non-governmental organizations.

Inequality

First, classroom and school practices of citizenship education in the United States are variant and unequal. They vary because the national government plays only a small role in citizenship education in schools; school practices are reserved by the Constitu-tion to the 50 states, most of which further devolve authority to local school districts—some 16,000 little ministries of education with an elected school board. Contrast this decentered system to the standardization and uniformity found in many other modern democracies; in Singapore for example, where all students take a common civic educa-tion course using materials produced by the central curriculum office (Sim, 2011), or in England where a new citizenship education program—the first ever in that nation—was instituted nation-wide in 2001 (Kerr & Cleaver, 2009).

But alongside state and local variation in civic education in the United States, which is legitimate in a federalist regime, lies an illegitimate form of variation: inequality. This is the gap between students who receive high and low quality civic education in school. It is called the "civic achievement" or "civic opportunity" or "civic empowerment" gap (e.g., Levinson, 2012). A consensus report in 2003 (Gibson & Levine) and again in 2011 (Campaign for the Civic Mission of Schools) identified six research-supported practices in civic education, each related to higher levels of student civic knowledge, skill, commit-ment, and actual civic involvement. They are:

1. Learning information about local, state, and national government.
2. Opportunities to debate and discuss current events and other issues that matter to students.
3. Service-learning opportunities.
4. Participation in extra-curriculum activities.
5. Opportunities for decision-making and governance experiences.
6. Participation in simulations of civic processes.

These practices are distributed unequally in the United States on the basis of social class, ethnicity, and college-going plans. In a sweeping study of California high school seniors, Kahne and Middaugh (2010) found that African American students were less likely than others to have had participation-oriented government courses, less likely to report having opportunities to participate in school decision making, and less likely to report opportunities for discussions and simulations. Latino students reported fewer opportunities for service than did other students and also fewer experiences with simu-lations. Also, seniors who did not expect to take part in any form of post-secondary education reported significantly fewer opportunities to develop civic skills and com-mitments than seniors with post-secondary plans. The Campaign for the Civic Mission of Schools (2011) concluded that schools exacerbate the civic empowerment gap "by providing poor and nonwhite students fewer and less high-quality learning opportun-ities than they provide to middle class and wealthy white students" (p. 19).[15]

Let us focus first on practice 1—learning about government—and then turn to some of the others. As we saw earlier, most high school students take a US government course.

Additionally, most take a US history course three times, in grades 5, 8, and 11. Each time they likely are exposed, in one form or another, to the core texts of the US regime (the *Declaration of Independence* and the *Constitution of the United States*) and to information about their creation. Because social class remains the strongest predictor of the particular school curriculum and classroom resources to which American students are exposed, and because the rich–poor gap in the United States is widening,[16] it is difficult to determine the number of students who are exposed to additional resources, from *The Federalist Papers* to King's *Letter from Birmingham Jail*. What is surprising to observers from other nations (e.g., Frazer, 2002) is that there is widespread bi-partisan agreement in the United States on these and a handful of additional texts that are considered "core." Accordingly, there is in a kind of "civic canon" alongside a consensus on research-based pedagogies. To summarize, while the distribution of political information, core texts, and best practices is unequal, there is remarkable agreement on what they are.

Discussion-Oriented Pedagogy

We can consider practices 2, 5, and 6 together under the name "discussion-oriented pedagogy." (For reasons of space, we will leave aside practices 3 and 4.[17]) Practices 2, 5, and 6 easily converge in classroom practice—they fit together well—and each involves participatory, active learning and discussion. Practice 2 is teaching and learning about current events and issues. These are not synonyms. Events are happenings in time and space (an election, a natural disaster, an incident in the school building) whereas issues are controversies or dilemmas involving value tensions (What is fair tax policy? Should voting be required?). Neither events nor issues are self-evident; each is a "text" requiring interpretation, and this is best done with others. As Bridges (1979) wrote, the advantage of discussion is "to set alongside one perception of the matter under discussion the several perceptions of other participants, challenging our own view of things with those of others" (p. 50).

Practice 5 involves decision making about community and school problems. Community problems often are current events and issues, it should be noted; school problems are as well, and these can be studied and deliberated in the aforementioned classroom meetings and school councils. Practice 6 is also participatory, for students take roles and, with them, social positions and political perspectives. Discussions are conducted in these roles. The simulated civic process may be a mock trial, election, congressional floor debate, committee hearing, or a moot (already decided) Supreme Court case. The branches of government are involved as are media, political parties, and interest groups. Fourth-grade students may be simulating their community—its politics, businesses, mail and other public services—while seniors in the government course simulate the federal government or city hall, from campaigning to law making and judicial review.

Discussion-oriented pedagogy has always been popular with civic educators but has grown since the 1980s and been subjected to an array of investigations and design experiments (e.g., Beck, 2003; Billings & Fitzgerald, 2002; Hahn, 1998; Haroutunian-Gordon, 2009; Hess, 2009; Larson, 2003; Paley, 1992; Parker et al. 2011, 2013; Power, 1988; Torney-Purta & Wilkenfeld, 2009). The rationale, in brief, is that democratic regimes entail government by discussion. The ability to discuss—to argue and deliberate, to speak and listen to strangers—has been a central strategy for democratic public policy formation at least since Socrates held discussions in the *agora*. It becomes, therefore, a curricular end of schools in democratic regimes, not simply a lively instructional means. As an end, a goal, it is part and parcel to schools' democratic mission.

Discussion-oriented pedagogy takes advantage of powerful assets that prevail at school (Parker, 2003). First, diversity. Schools are not private places like our homes but public places with diverse students. When five-year-olds come to kindergarten, they emerge from the private silos of babyhood, family, and kin into the mixed public arena of acquaintances and strangers. While some schools are more diverse than others, *all schools are diverse to some pedagogically meaningful extent*. The work of cognitive developmentalists has established this (e.g., Finlay et al., 2010; Kohlberg, Levine, & Hewer, 1983). In a public school, furthermore, boys and girls are both there; Jews, Protestants, Catholics, Muslims, Buddhists, and atheists may all be there; there are racial and class differences, and therefore differences in social status and power; and immigrants from the world over may be there. Ideological differences are present, too, and not to be overlooked (Hess, 2009). This variety does not exist at home, church, temple, or mosque.

A second asset that is abundant is schools, thanks to the diversity of students and the tasks of educating them and keeping them safe, is the prevalence of problems. These problems are mutual, collective concerns; they are *public* problems. There are two kinds of problems at school: social and academic. Social problems arise over resources, policies, classroom assignments, injustices, scarcity, safety, and the myriad frictions of social interaction. Academic problems, on the other hand, reside in each discipline. Expertise in a discipline is defined by one's knowledge of its core and emerging problems. Both social and academic problems lend themselves to discursive practices: communication about the nature of the problem (interpretation) and communication about solutions (deliberation). Interpretation and deliberation correspond to discussions of powerful literature and speeches (these are *seminars*) and discussions of controversial issues where a decision is needed as to what course of action to take (e.g., *Structured Academic Controversy*).[18]

Practices 2, 5, and 6 mobilize these assets, which is to say they lend themselves to increasing the variety and frequency of interaction among diverse students around social and academic problems. If the school is homogeneous or if the school is diverse but curriculum tracks keep students apart, then the first asset is impeded. Still, school leaders can capitalize on whatever diversity is present and increase the interaction among students, both in the classroom and in student councils and other governance settings. As Paley (1992) has demonstrated, this discursive pedagogy is perfectly suitable for even the youngest children in kindergarten.

Influential Organizations

Non-governmental organizations (NGOs) understandably play a large role in civic education in a decentralized school system. They produce classroom materials, lesson plans, and professional development opportunities for teachers. They have even helped write curriculum standards, a task reserved for government agencies in most other regimes. The most prominent among these NGOs are those that have networks spanning the 50 states. Here is a sample:

- *iCivics* is the creation of former US Supreme Court Justice Sandra Day O'Connor. It features an innovative website and instructional video games for students.
- *Street Law* developed the leading website for teaching about landmark cases of the Supreme Court. It also brings teachers to the Court for professional development, and across the US it connects law school students with high school classrooms.

- *Close Up* brings middle and high school students on field trips to the nation's capital each year for a close-up experience with US government and politics.
- *Kidsvoting* produces opportunities for experiential learning about voting and elections, including the right to vote and active citizenship.
- The *Center for Civic Education* produces *We The People* and *Project Citizen*, widely successful programs that are practiced in every state. *We The People* concentrates on historical knowledge while *Project Citizen* engages students in community problem solving.
- The *Constitutional Rights Foundation* produces *Deliberating in a Democracy*, in which high school students engage in authentic civic deliberations, and a popular newsletter for history and government classes, *The Bill of Rights in Action*.
- *Facing History and Ourselves* produces lessons and professional development for teaching students to take action against injustice and bigotry of all sorts, especially racism and anti-semitism.
- The College Board's *Advanced Placement* (AP) program is expanding to new groups of students as local superintendents lower the threshold for entry into courses, sometimes even requiring them. Consequently, the number of students taking the AP version of the high school government course is skyrocketing (see Parker et al., 2011, 2013).

CONCLUSION

The five anchoring concepts of this review were *citizenship, citizenship education, regime type, liberal democracy,* and *classroom and school practice*. Citizenship and citizenship education are old ideas, and today they are again at the forefront of scholarship in the social sciences and education. A liberal-democratic regime such as the United States aims to balance individual rights and liberties with a common political culture. In its schools, the regime has to be more or less neutral (impartial) with respect to differences, such as religious belief and political ideology; yet it is obliged also to educate students to value liberal democracy and to possess the knowledge and skills, such as toleration and critical thinking, needed to sustain it. *This is the regime's unique brand of moral and character education.* Accordingly, value neutrality is practiced alongside value commitment, and conflict inevitably arises among parents, educators, and the state. Democratic education cannot be democratic education without this tension; it comes with the territory of liberal democracy and its array of conflicting interests each endeavoring to express the freedom that the regime is established to protect. There are rival and incompatible conceptions of the good life, of god and country, of community and individual freedom. Of course, there are power and history, too, which advantage some conceptions over others and fuel the struggles that attempt to redraw the playing field.

I opened this chapter with a Jefferson quote for two reasons. The first is its substantive meaning: democratic citizens are not born with the knowledge, skills, and character they need. This is the assertion that justifies public education generally and citizenship or civic education in particular. Second, the assertion serves a discursive function, which is to locate this review not in universal verities but in a particular time, place, and political regime: the United States of America, its Constitution, and its political culture. In this particular context, unequal access to effective classroom practice is a paramount problem. Alongside it lies another: illiberal groups that seek to exempt students from exposure to diversity and from learning to think critically and independently. These exemptions are problematic because they undermine democratic education at its root: informing a person's capacity to make an un-coerced decision to consent to be governed and, reciprocally, to govern a diverse society. Present and future attempts to solve the first problem are likely to encounter opposition from groups that seek exemptions, and this ongoing conflict summarizes a key skirmish in citizenship education in the United States today.

AFTERWORD

I want to recommend two other reviews of citizenship education in the United States that will serve as complements to this one: one by Carole L. Hahn (2008) and another by Kathleen Knight-Abowitz and Jason Harnish (2006).

ACKNOWLEDGMENT

My thanks to Carole Hahn, Kathleen Knight-Abowitz, Carol Coe, Regie Routman, Joe Jenkins, and the editors for their helpful reviews of earlier drafts of this chapter.

NOTES

1. I return to the curriculum in the final section of the chapter.
2. Unfortunately their return to *scholarly* interest does not mirror a return to classroom and school practice. Citizenship education and, more broadly, social studies (studies of the social disciplines: history, political science, economics, geography, sociology, psychology, anthropology) of any sort have been pushed in some locales to the margins of the curriculum, particularly in elementary and middle schools. This is due to the frenzied attention now being paid to testing-and-accountability and "STEM" (the "harder" disciplines of science, technology, engineering, and math). This squeezing of citizenship education, it should be noted, has had a disproportionate impact on the most disadvantaged students (Kahne & Middaugh, 2010; Rothstein & Jacobson, 2006). See the "Inequality" section later in this chapter.
3. Historical note: The "tyranny of the majority," from Aristotle onward, is regarded as the primary threat to democracy and the reason why many democracies fail. Madison's project in *The Federalist No. 10* was to solve this problem. Later, it is on de Tocqueville's mind, too, coming as he was from the tyranny of the Jacobin "Terror" of the French Revolution.
4. See Dewey (1985) on the personal and public effects of lives lived segregated, and the education thus afforded as "partial and distorted" (p. 89); also Parker (1996).
5. Both studies have been widely reviewed. See Avery (2000), Galston (2001), and Torney-Purta (1999).
6. See Zimmerman's (2002) history of this contention and McKinley (2010) for a recent example: "Texas Conservatives Win Curriculum Change."
7. Because these are roles, not persons, they overlap. Many parents are citizens, many teachers are parents, etc.
8. Certainly not always (e.g., Nussbaumn, 2012).
9. See Macedo's analysis (1995).
10. The new standards emphasize "the superiority of American capitalism, question the Founding Fathers' commitment to a purely secular government, and present Republican political philosophies in a more positive light" (McKinley, 2010, p. A10).
11. "...life, liberty, and the pursuit of happiness. That to secure these rights, governments are instituted among men, deriving their just powers from the consent of the governed..."
12. I am grateful to William Stanley (2010 and personal communications) for his analysis of the transmission-transformation question.
13. In addition to Parker (2011a) see Howard and Kenny (1992) and Power (1988) on robust forms of student participation in school governance.
14. On civic learning *outside* school, there is a burgeoning literature, e.g., Bennett (2010), and Biesta, Lawy, and Kelly (2009).

15. There are other inequalities, too. See, for example, Dabach's (2012) examination of this intriguing asymmetry: teachers who are legal citizens teaching about citizenship and voting to immigrant students who are not.
16. The United States has the greatest income inequality of any wealthy nation in the world (Wilkinson & Pickett, 2010).
17. But see chapters by Hart and Power, this volume, and Billig, Root, and Jesse, 2005.
18. On this distinction, see Parker 2006, 2010, and 2011b.

REFERENCES

Alexander, M. (2010). *The new Jim Crow: Mass incarceration in the age of colorblindness.* New York: New Press.

Aristotle. (1958). *The politics* (E. Barker, Trans.). New York: Oxford University Press.

Avery, P. (2000). Book review: "Civic Education: What Makes Students Learn?" by R. G. Niemi & J. Junn. *Theory and Research in Social Education, 28,* 290–295.

Barton, K. C., & Levstik, L. S. (2004). *Teaching history for the common good.* Mahwah, NJ: Erlbaum.

Barton, K. C., & Levstik, L. S. (2010). Why don't more history teachers engage students in interpretation? In W. C. Parker (Ed.), *Social studies today: Research and practice* (pp. 35–42). New York: Routledge.

Beck, T. A. (2003). "If he murdered someone, he shouldn't get a lawyer": Engaging young children in civics deliberation. *Theory and Research in Social Education, 31*(3), 326–346.

Bennett, W. L. (2010). Civic learning in changing democracies. In P. Dahlgren (Ed.), *Young citizens and new media: Learning for democratic participation.* London: Sage.

Biesta, G., Lawy, R., & Kelly, N. (2009). Understanding young people's citizenship learning in everyday life: The role of contexts, relationships and dispositions. *Education, Citizenship and Social Justice, 4*(1), 5–24.

Billig, S., Root, S., and Jesse, D. (2005). *The impact of participation in service-learning on high school students' civic engagement* (CIRCLE Working Paper 33). Accessed 1/5/13 at www.civicyouth.org/PopUps/WorkingPapers/WP33Billig.pdf.

Billings, L., & Fitzgerald, J. (2002). Dialogic discussion and the Paideia Seminar. *American Educational Research Journal, 39*(4), 907–941.

Brennan, W. J. (1989). Michael H. v. Gerald D., 491 U.S. 110. Dissenting opinion.

Bridges, D. (1979). *Education, democracy, and discussion.* Atlantic Highlands, NJ: Humanities Press.

Brighouse, H. (2000). *School choice and social justice.* New York: Oxford University Press.

Callan, E. (1997). *Creating citizens: Political education and liberal democracy.* Oxford: Clarendon.

Campaign for the Civic Mission of Schools and the Leonore Annenberg Institute for Civics (2011). *Guardian of democracy: The civic mission of the schools.* Washington, DC: Campaign for the Civic Mission of Schools and the Leonore Annenberg Institute for Civics.

Center for Civic Education (1994). *National standards for civics and government.* Calabasas, CA: Center for Civic Education.

Counts, G. S. (1932). *Dare the school build a new social order?* New York: John Day.

Crick, B. (2008). Democracy. In J. Arthur, I. Davies, & C. Hahn (Eds.), *Sage handbook of education for citizenship and democracy* (pp. 13–19). London: Sage.

Dabach, D. B. (2012). *"You can't vote, right?" Questions from an immigrant-origin EL US civics class during the 2008 Obama campaign.* Paper presented at the American Educational Research Association (AERA), Vancouver, April 2012.

Dewey, J. (1956). *The school and society.* Chicago: University of Chicago Press (originally 1899).

Dewey, J. (1985). *Democracy and education.* Carbondale: Southern Illinois University Press (originally 1916).

Epstein, T. (2009). *Interpreting national history: Race, identity, and pedagogy in classrooms and communities.* New York: Routledge.

Finlay, A., Wray-Lake, L., & Flanagan, C. (2010). Civic engagement during the transition to adulthood. In L. R. Sherrod, J. Torney-Purta, & C. A. Flanagan (Eds.), *Handbook of research on civic engagement in youth* (pp. 277–306). Hoboken, NJ: Wiley.

Finn, C. E. (Ed.). (2003). *Terrorists, despots, and democracy: What our children need to know.* Washington, DC: Thomas B. Fordham Foundation.

Flanagan, C., & Levine, P. (2010). Civic engagement and the transition to adulthood. *The future of children, 20*(1), 159–179.

Frazer, E. (2002). Citizenship education: Anti-political culture and political education in Britain. In W. C. Parker (Ed.), *Education for democracy: Contexts, curricula, and assessments* (pp. 27–42). Greenwich, CT: Information Age.

Galston, W. A. (2001). Political knowledge, political engagement, and civic education. *Annual Review of Political Science, 4*(1), 217–234.

Gibson, C., & Levine, P. (2003). *The civic mission of schools*. Washington, DC: Carnegie Corporation of New York.

Gutmann, A. (1999). *Democratic education* (2nd ed.). Princeton: Princeton University Press.

Habermas, J. (1997). *A Berlin republic*. Lincoln: University of Nebraska.

Hahn, C. (1998). *Becoming political*. Albany, NY: State University of New York Press.

Hahn, C. (2008). Education for citizenship and democracy in the United States. In J. Arthur, O. Davies, & C. L. Hahn (Eds.). (2008). *Sage handbook of education for citizenship and democracy* (pp. 263–278). London: Sage.

Hamilton, A. (1982). The Federalist No. 9. In J. Madison, A. Hamilton, & J. Jay (Eds.), *The Federalist Papers* (pp. 44–50). New York: Bantam (originally 1787).

Haroutunian-Gordon, S. (2009). *Learning to teach through discussion: The art of turning the soul*. New Haven: Yale University Press.

Hess, D. E. (2009). *Controversy in the classroom*. New York: Routledge.

Howard, R., & Kenny, R. (1992). Education for democracy: Promoting citizenship and critical reasoning through school governance. In A. Garrod (Ed.), *Learning for life: Moral education theory and practice* (pp. 210–227). Westport, CT: Praeger.

Jefferson, T. (1954). *Notes on the State of Virginia*. W. Peden (Ed.). Chapel Hill: University of North Carolina Press (originally 1787).

Kahne, J., & Middaugh, E. (2010). High quality civic education: What is it and who gets it? In W. C. Parker (Ed.), *Social studies today: Research and practice* (pp. 141–150). New York: Routledge.

Kerr, D., & Cleaver, E. (2009). Strengthening education and democracy in England. In J. Youniss & P. Levine (Eds.), *Engaging young people in civic life* (pp. 235–273). Nashville, TN: Vanderbilt University Press.

King, M. L., Jr. (1963). *Why we can't wait*. New York: Mentor.

King, M. L., Jr. (2001). I have a dream. In C. Carson & K. Shepard (Eds.), *A call to conscience: The landmark speeches of Dr. Martin Luther King, Jr.* (pp. 81–87). New York: Time Warner.

Knight-Abowitz, K., & Harnish, J. (2006). Contemporary discourses of citizenship. *Review of Educational Research, 76*(4), 653–690.

Kohlberg, L., Levine, C., & Hewer, A. (1983). *Moral stages: A current formulation and a response to critics*. New York: Karger.

Langton, K., & Jennings, M. K. (1968). Political socialization and the high school civics curriculum in the United States. *American Political Science Review, 62*, 862–867.

Larson, B. E. (2003). Comparing face-to-face discussion and electronic discussion. *Theory and Research in Social Education, 31*(3), 347–365.

Levinson, M. (2012). *No citizen left behind*. Cambridge, MA: Harvard University Press.

Lippmann, W. (1993). *American inquisitors*. Piscataway, NJ: Transaction Publishers (originally 1928).

Macedo, S. (1995). Liberal civic education and religious fundamentalism. *Ethics, 105*(3), 468–496.

Madison, J. (1937). The Federalist No. 51. In J. Madison, A. Hamilton, & J. Jay (Eds.), *The Federalist* (pp. 335–341). New York: Modern Library (originally 1788).

McKinley, J. C., Jr. (2010, March 13). Texas conservatives win curriculum change. *New York Times*, p. A10.

Mitchell, K. (2001). Education for democratic citizenship: Transnationalism, multiculturalism, and the limits of liberalism. *Harvard Educational Review, 71*(1), 51–78.

Montesquieu, C. (2012). Book XI. *The spirit of laws*. Accessed August 2, 2012 from www.constitution.org (originally 1751).

Mozert v. Hawkins County (TN) Public Schools. 827 F.2d 1058 (6th Cir. 1987).

Niemi, R. G., & Junn, J. (1998). *Civic education: What makes students learn*. New Haven, CT: Yale University Press.

Niemi, R. G., & Smith, J. (2001). Enrollments in high school government classes: Are we short-changing both citizenship and political science training? *PS: Political Science and Politics, 34*(2), 281–287.

Nussbaum, M. C. (2012). *The new religious intolerance*. Cambridge, MA: Belknap Press/Harvard University Press.

Okihiro, G. Y. (1994). *Margins and mainstream*. Seattle: University of Washington Press.

Ong, A. (1999). *Flexible citizenship*. Durham, NC: Duke University Press.

Ong, A. (2003). *Buddha is hiding: Refugees, citizenship, the New America*. Berkeley: University of California Press.

Paley, V. G. (1992). *You can't say you can't play*. Cambridge, MA: Harvard University Press.

Parker, W. C. (Ed.). (1996). Introduction. *Educating the democratic mind*. Albany: State University of New York Press.

Parker, W. C. (2003). *Teaching democracy: Unity and diversity in public life*. New York: Teachers College Press.

Parker, W. C. (2006). Public discourses in schools. *Educational Researcher, 35*(8), 11–18.

Parker, W. C. (2008). Knowing and doing in democratic citizenship education. In L. Levstik & C. A. Tyson (Eds.), *Handbook of research in social studies education* (pp. 65–80). New York: Routledge.

Parker, W. C. (2010). Listening to strangers: Classroom discussion in democratic education. *Teachers College Record, 112*(11), 2815–2832.

Parker, W. C. (2011a). Democratic citizenship education (chapter 3). *Social studies in elementary education* (14th ed.). Boston: Allyn and Bacon.

Parker, W. C. (2011b). Feel free to change your mind. *Democracy & Education, 19*(2), 1–4.

Parker, W. C., Mosborg, S., Bransford, J. D., Vye, N. J., Wilkerson, J., & Abbott, R. (2011). Rethinking advanced high school coursework: Tackling the depth/breadth tension in the AP US Government and Politics course. *Journal of Curriculum Studies, 43*(4), 533–559.

Parker, W., Lo, J., Yeo, A. J., Valencia, S. W., Nguyen, D., Abbott, R. D., Nolen, S. B., Bransford, J. D., & Vye, N. J. (2013). Beyond breadth-speed-test: Toward deeper knowing and engagement in an Advanced Placement course. *American Educational Research Journal,* 50(6), 1424–1459.

Piscatelli, J. (2003, August). Character/citizenship education: Pledge of allegiance. *State Notes.*

Power, C. (1988). The just community approach to moral education. *The Journal of Moral Education, 17*(3), 195–208.

Putnam, R. D. (1995). Bowling alone. *Journal of Democracy, 6*(1), 65–78.

Rempel, G. (1989). *Hitler's children: The Hitler Youth and the SS.* Chapel Hill: University of North Carolina Press.

Rothstein, R., & Jacobsen, R. (2006). The goals of education. *Phi Delta Kappan, 88*(4), 264–272.

Shafir, G. (Ed.). (1998). *The citizenship debates.* Minneapolis: University of Minnesota Press.

Sim, J. B.-Y. (2011). Social studies and citizenship for participation in Singapore. *Oxford Review of Education, 37*(6), 743–761.

Stanley, W. B. (2010). Social studies and the social order: Transmission or transformation? In W. C. Parker (Ed.), *Social studies today: Research and practice* (pp. 17–24). New York: Routledge.

Stanton, E. C., Anthony, S. B., Gage, M. J. (1889). *A history of woman suffrage* (2nd ed., Vol. 1). Rochester, NY: Fowler and Wells.

Taylor, B. L., & Haas, J. D. (1973). *New directions: Social studies curriculum for the 70's.* Boulder, CO: Social Science Education Consortium.

Texas Republican Party Platform. (June 2012). Accessed July 5, 2012 from http://conventiongop.org/.

de Tocqueville, A. (1969). *Democracy in America* (G. Lawrence, Trans.). Garden City, NY: Doubleday (originally 1847).

Torney-Purta, J. (1999). Book review: "Civic Education: What Makes Students Learn?" by R. G. Niemi & J. Junn. *American Journal of Education, 107*(3), 256–260.

Torney-Purta, J., & Wilkenfeld, B. S. (2009). *Paths to 21st century competencies through civic education classrooms.* Silver Springs, MD: ABA Division for Public Education, Campaign for the Civic Mission of Schools.

Wilkinson, R., & Pickett, R. (2010). *The spirit level: Why greater equality makes societies stronger.* London: Penguin.

Zimmerman, J. (2002). *Whose America? Culture wars in the public schools.* Cambridge, MA: Harvard University Press.

21

FOSTERING THE MORAL AND CIVIC DEVELOPMENT OF COLLEGE STUDENTS

Anne Colby

MORAL AND CIVIC DEVELOPMENT AS GOALS OF HIGHER EDUCATION

This chapter takes up the question of what kinds of influence undergraduate education can have on students' development as ethical, committed, and engaged human beings and citizens. The undergraduate years are just one part of a life-long developmental process but, especially if the efforts are intentionally designed with these outcomes in mind, colleges can establish some groundwork that students will later build on, shape the intellectual frameworks and habits of mind they bring to their adult experiences, change the way they understand the responsibilities that are central to their sense of self, teach them to offer and demand evidence and justification for their moral and political positions, and develop wiser judgment in approaching situations and questions that represent potential turning points in their lives.

If a college education is to support the kind of learning graduates need in order to be involved and responsible citizens, its goals must go beyond the development of intellectual and technical skills and beginning mastery of a professional or scholarly domain. They should include the competence to act in the world and the judgment to do so wisely. A full account of competence, including occupational competence, must include consideration of judgment, the appreciation of ends as well as means, and the broad implications and consequences of one's actions and choices. Education is not complete until students not only have acquired knowledge, but can use that knowledge to act responsibly in the world.

The suggestion that colleges and universities ought to educate for moral and civic values, ideals, and standards raises potentially contentious questions about what those values and ideals should be. Fortunately, there are some basic values that form a common ground to guide higher education institutions' efforts to educate their students as responsible citizens of a democracy. Prominent among these core values are intellectual integrity, concern for truth, and academic freedom. By their very nature, it is also important for colleges to foster values such as mutual respect, open-mindedness, a willingness to listen to and take seriously the ideas of others, procedural fairness, and public discussion of contested issues. The academic enterprise would be seriously compromised if these values ceased to guide scholarship, teaching, and learning, however imperfect the guidance may be in practice.

Another important source of a common core of values derives from educational institutions' obligation to educate students for responsible democratic citizenship. Most college and university mission statements—for both private and public institutions—explicitly refer to their responsibility to educate for leadership and contribution to society. This conception of higher education in the United States dates back to the founding of the country and implies the centrality of values that include mutual respect and tolerance, concern for both the rights and the welfare of individuals and the community, recognition that each individual is part of the larger social fabric, critical self-reflection, and a commitment to civil and rational discourse and procedural impartiality (Galston, 1991; Gutmann, 1987; Macedo, 2000).

Beyond this generic set of core values that derive from the intellectual and civic purposes of higher education, some private colleges (and even a few public ones) stand for more specific moral, cultural, or religious values. These institutions' particular missions—and the implications of these missions for the educational programs—are made clear to prospective students and faculty, thus providing the basis for informed choice in deciding whether to join a higher education community that professes particular values along with those that are inherent in the academic enterprise. The most obvious examples are religiously affiliated schools that offer faith-based education. Among public institutions, military academies are mandated to educate military officers, so their values are defined with reference to this goal. There are other public colleges that were established to serve particular populations, such as (American Indian) tribal colleges, which often explicitly acknowledge special values, such as traditional tribal values, in their curricula and programs, and private colleges that serve groups such as women, African-American women, and African-American men, drawing on their relevant histories in order to best serve these populations.

If the values on which there is broad consensus within an institution are taken seriously, they constitute strong guiding principles for programs of moral and civic development in higher education. Even so, they leave open to debate which principles should be given priority when they conflict as well as the application of the principles to many particular situations. Especially in institutions that stand for a commitment to rational public discourse, as higher education must, the most difficult questions of conflicting values are left to public debate and individual discernment. Moral and civic education provides the tools for these discussions and judgments.

KEY DIMENSIONS OF MORAL AND CIVIC LEARNING

Research on human development reveals three major clusters of capacities that are critical to fully mature moral and civic functioning, and all three can continue to develop during the college years, regardless of the age of the students. The first main area is moral and civic understanding. This includes interpretation, judgment, knowledge, understanding of complex issues and institutions, and a sophisticated grasp of ethical and democratic principles.

The second major area has less to do with understanding what is right than motivation to do the right thing. This cluster includes goals and values, interests, commitments, conviction, and perseverance in the face of challenges. It also includes a sense of efficacy and emotions such as compassion, hope, and inspiration. Closely related to these dimensions is the individual's identity, a sense of who she is and what kind of a person she wants to be.

The third broad category is the domain of practice. Fully effective citizenship requires a well-developed capacity for effective communication, including moral and political discourse; many specific skills of political participation; the capacity to work effectively with people, including those who are very different from oneself; and the ability to organize other people for action.

First year college students exhibit a wide range of development in all of these areas. Students who enter college as adults may be more fully developed on many of these dimensions than younger students. But this is not necessarily true, since most studies show developmental variables to be more highly correlated with educational attainment than with age.

Moral and Civic Understanding, Judgment, and Knowledge

Moral Judgment. The ability to think clearly about difficult moral issues is important not only in the domain of personal morality but also in civic and political affairs, since they so often entail moral issues such as balancing the rights and welfare of individuals and groups. In response to research findings and critiques of various kinds, many features of the cognitive approach to moral development have been questioned and revised, and moral judgment has been reconceived as only one component in a complex set of processes. (See, e.g., Snarey & Samuelson, this volume; Turiel, 2008.) Even so, Kohlberg's (1969) description of the increasing sophistication of people's capacity to think about difficult moral issues remains a useful tool for operationalizing the intellectual side of moral growth, a dimension of morality that has obvious relevance for institutions of higher education.

Kohlberg proposed that the underlying logic or structure of individuals' thinking about moral issues can be described independently of the content of their beliefs, and that this logic becomes more sophisticated and functionally adequate as development proceeds. In Kohlberg's scheme, moral judgment moves from simple conceptions of morality grounded in unilateral authority and individual reciprocity to judgments grounded in shared social norms to an appreciation of a more complex social system to a perspective that is capable of evaluating the existing social system in relation to some more fundamental principles of justice. These shifts have important implications for people's understanding of and judgments about a whole range of important issues. Kohlberg's description of development within a framework of justice is particularly important for thinking about the civic goals of American higher education, since justice and human rights are central to US systems of politics and law.

Related Dimensions of Social Cognition. Moral judgment is part of the broader domain of social cognition, which includes a number of other dimensions that have also been framed in cognitive-developmental terms. Investigators studying the development of individuals' understanding of friendship, interpersonal perspective-taking, political understanding, and religious faith have all described trajectories of increasing maturity, which are said to emerge from individuals' attempts to interpret their experience as they interact with other people and social institutions. Although development within an individual can proceed at different rates in the various domains of social cognition, the basic patterns of developmental change within these domains show striking parallels.

Studies of political understanding (Adelson & O'Neil, 1966; Helwig, 1995; Jankowski, 1992; Raaijmakers, Verbogt, & Vollebergh, 1998) have revealed developmental shifts toward increasingly subtle and complex conceptions of social and political institutions. Concepts such as civil liberties, methods of social control, and governance show regular patterns of elaboration as development proceeds. Political thinking has been described as moving from the personal or authoritarian toward greater comprehension of social structures and general principles. For example, younger adolescents are usually insensitive to individual liberties and opt for authoritarian solutions to political problems. At the same time, they are unable to achieve a differentiated view of the social order, and thus cannot grasp the legitimate claim of the community upon the citizen (Adelson & O'Neil, 1966).

Moral Interpretation. Even though the way people think about moral issues is important, this does not mean that morality is always conscious, rational, reflective, and deliberative. Often it is not. It is useful to distinguish between two quite different kinds of moral process, which have been termed "reflective morality" and "habitual or spontaneous morality" (Davidson & Youniss, 1991; Walker, 2000). In daily life, reflective morality, which involves careful evaluation and justification, comes into play relatively infrequently, when the right course of action is not obvious or when one's initial moral response is challenged and there is time to reflect. In contrast, most moral actions—the many unremarkable moral choices and actions that characterize daily life—are not preceded by conscious reflection, but instead are immediate, seemingly intuitive responses. For example, most people do not have to stop and think before paying a blind newspaper salesman, rather than only pretending to pay. This kind of routine honesty is taken for granted. As the name implies, habitual morality is based in repetition over time, not only behavioral repetition, but also repetition of ingrained habits of "reading" or interpreting moral situations.

One reason that moral interpretation is so important is that in real life, moral dilemmas do not come neatly packaged like hypothetical dilemmas, which typically involve a given set of simple facts. In contrast, almost any real moral dilemma or question involves significant ambiguity, and interpretation of the situation can differ from one person to the next. Thus, in order to find meaning amid the moral ambiguity of real-life situations, people must develop habits of moral interpretation and intuition through which they perceive the everyday world. People with different habits of moral interpretation see the world in very different terms and are, therefore, presented with very different opportunities and imperatives for moral action. Through the aggregate of their moral choices in daily life, they actively shape their own moral reality (Walker, 2000).

But even habitual morality has important underlying cognitive elements. Our thinking processes rely on our capacity to recognize patterns in the environment, and this pattern recognition depends on cognitive schemas that derive from many sources. One source is the set of concepts and assumptions represented by cognitive-moral development. Even though it seems clear that people don't deliberate about or argue through every moral situation in a way that mirrors the kinds of moral argumentation elicited in research interviews, different cognitive-moral frameworks (such as Kohlberg's moral judgment stages) represent different sets of assumptions that help inform and shape their reactions to the many small moral decisions of both habitual and reflective morality. In this sense, their conceptual frameworks, including understandings associated with their developmental stage, provide patterns or schemas that shape moral interpretations. The way people understand fairness, for example, will be a backdrop to the way they react to perceived injustices. Concepts such as distributive justice, moral authority, trust, and accountability are central to morality, and the way they are understood plays an important part in shaping individuals' understanding of ambiguous moral situations. Individuals learn what constitutes a meaningful pattern, in part, through interaction with their social environment. As they participate in cultural routines, they acquire habits of interpretation consistent with that culture. The impact of the social context on habits and schemas is part of the broader issue of socialization of values.

Cognitive schemas can influence interpretations, judgments, and behavior without the conscious awareness of the actor, but it is also possible for individuals to reflect on and discuss with others their moral interpretations. These processes can lead to moral growth. In the many brief moments of moral decision we encounter every day, we have the capacity to reflect, and we have some room to choose the interpretation we settle on, over time creating new habits of interpretation that can lead in a different direction. This can involve considering and resolving several conflicting interpretations or questioning one's original interpretation after confronting an uneasy feeling that one's interpretation may be self-serving or biased in other ways. The capacity to override or change one's own habits of interpretation is important, because by doing so we can actively shape our future moral habits. In this view of moral development, people can grow morally by making an effort to become more aware of their own interpretive habits, acknowledging and trying to overcome their biases, and working to understand and take seriously others' interpretations (Walker, 2000).

Development of Moral Judgment and Interpretation during College. In part due to the availability of a measure that is easy to use (James Rest's Defining Issues Test; see Rest, Narvaez, Bebeau, & Thoma, 1999), moral judgment as conceived by Kohlberg has been included in many studies of college student development (Pascarella & Terenzini, 2005). Investigators have found consistently that attending college increases students' scores on this measure, and many studies have found a significant correlation between adults' years of higher education and scores on Kohlberg's Moral Judgment Interview as well. Moral judgment stage is more likely to stop increasing at the end of formal education than at any particular age. In fact, some studies have shown a small negative correlation of DIT scores with age in age-diverse samples of adults (probably a cohort effect) and a larger positive correlation of DIT with educational attainment (Pascarella & Terenzini, 2005).

Given the evidence that higher education contributes to higher levels of moral judgment, it may seem that colleges and universities do not need special programs aimed specifically at fostering moral development. However, the research in this area makes clear that there is significant room for improvement. Most college-educated adults do not achieve the highest level of moral judgment, reasoning instead at Stage 4 or some combination of Stages 3 and 4 (Colby, Kohlberg, Gibbs, & Lieberman, 1983). Because a deep understanding of the American constitution and legal system requires a Stage 5 perspective in which the social system is understood to be grounded in fundamental human rights, the failure of many citizens to achieve that developmental level raises questions about their capacity to fully appreciate the foundations of American democracy.

A large body of research makes it clear that the experience of grappling with challenging moral issues in classroom discussions or in activities that require the resolution of conflicting opinions contributes significantly to the increasing maturity of individuals' moral judgment. This is especially true when the teacher draws attention to important distinctions, assumptions, and contradictions (Pascarella & Terenzini, 2005).

The college experience can also be a powerful opportunity for students to develop more reflective and mature habits of moral interpretation. Students bring their own characteristic habits of interpretation with them when they enter college, but their experiences in college have significant potential to reshape those habits. Much of the positive impact of programs that foster understanding across the diversity of a campus and its environment may reside in the power of those programs to make students aware for the first time of their previously unquestioned interpretive schemes, to bring their biases to light, and to highlight the inherent ambiguity of moral situations that previously appeared clear-cut.

This view of moral change also clarifies the significance of the reflection component that is known to be critical to the success of service-learning courses. Reflection on service activities often includes discussions in which students share with each other their interpretations of the common experience, along with written assignments in which they explore the ways in which the service experience changed their understanding of the people with whom they worked, the social issues their work confronted, and their relationship to those people and issues. This kind of activity is well suited for revealing alternative interpretations of common experiences and helping students see the personal significance of those alternative interpretations through self-examination (Eyler & Giles, 1999).

Moral Relativism. As students begin to question their unexamined assumptions and appreciate the multiplicity of interpretations inherent in any situation, they may conclude that there are no grounds for evaluating the relative validity of different, sometimes conflicting, moral or intellectual interpretations. At least some degree of both epistemological and ethical relativism are part of the predictable developmental sequence that college students go through as they begin to grapple with uncertainty and question the simple absolutes they previously understood as the "right answers" to complex and subtle questions. William Perry (1968) and others (e.g., King and Kitchener, 1994; Knefelkamp, 1974) trace a developmental pattern that shifts gradually from seeing the world in polar terms of right vs. wrong and good vs. bad to a point at which all knowledge and values are seen as contextual and relative, then eventually to a point at which it is possible to orient oneself in a relativistic world through the development of commitment, which is experienced as an ongoing activity through which identity and responsibilities are affirmed. Empirical studies of college students' progression through this sequence reveal that many students move from the initial *dualistic* stage to the more relativistic positions during college, but very few reach the most advanced level—the stage of commitment (Knefelkamp, 1974; Perry, 1968).

In light of consistent findings that college students tend to leave behind absolutistic thinking but generally do not reach a full understanding of grounds for intellectual and moral conviction, it is not surprising that faculty report a great deal of epistemological and ethical relativism among their students. Although we are not aware of any systematic research on how widespread *moral* relativism is among college students (aside from the studies of Perry's stages, which do not distinguish between epistemological and ethical relativism), many faculty and other observers have noted its pervasiveness.

College students' relativism ought to be cause for concern among educators, because beliefs such as "everyone is entitled to his own opinion and there is no way to evaluate the validity of those opinions," prevent students from engaging fully in discussions of ethical issues, learning to articulate and effectively justify their views, and adopting new perspectives when presented with high quality evidence and arguments. In essence, "the stakes drop out of ethical deliberation" and students are less likely to take it seriously (Trosset, 1998).

Knowledge. Even intellectually sophisticated reasoning and judgment cannot be powerful forces for effective action if they are abstract or disembodied. Being deeply knowledgeable about the issues is also essential. In addition to fostering clearer reasoning and more mature judgment, colleges can promote students' moral and civic learning by imparting broad and deep knowledge bearing on civic, political, and moral issues.

At a minimum, foundational knowledge in a range of fields provides support for moral and civic effectiveness. The need for an understanding of basic philosophic concepts, for example, is evident in the phenomenon of student moral relativism discussed above. Students often fail to distinguish between a moral principle of respect and tolerance and the challenges inherent in evaluating the relative validity of moral claims. Insofar as these are developmental issues, it may take time for students to work their way through them. But coursework and classroom discussions focusing directly on these questions can contribute a great deal to clarifying the intellectual issues involved. And developmental research indicates that without foundational knowledge of basic political concepts, it is impossible to understand political stories or assimilate new information about political issues (Stoker, 2000).

Likewise, students need to develop foundational knowledge of democratic principles, as well as an understanding of complex social, legal, and political structures and institutions if they are to be fully prepared as engaged citizens. Research on the context-specificity of expertise suggests that programs fostering generic analytic capacities are not sufficient preparation for effective action. A general grasp of critical thinking and problem-solving that is not specific to the field in question does not suffice.

MOTIVATION FOR MORAL AND CIVIC RESPONSIBILITY

Like understanding, moral and civic motivation is multi-faceted, and includes values and goals; identity or sense of self; a sense of efficacy or empowerment; faith; and various aspects of moral emotion such as hope and optimism, as opposed to alienation and cynicism. Although the connection of higher education with moral and civic motivation may be less obvious than its connection with knowledge and understanding, colleges have great potential to contribute to students' development in this area as well.

Values and Goals. There is a large body of evidence that a college education affects students' values, goals, and attitudes. We know that changes in college students' values depend partly on characteristics of the college they attend and on students' entering characteristics, including gender, religiosity, and their own and their parents' political views.

Even so, ever since the 1940s when research on these questions began to emerge, students in most colleges and universities showed some predictable shifts in their values, including increased socio-political tolerance, greater concern for civil rights and civil liberties, more egalitarian views of gender roles, declines in authoritarianism and dogmatism, and more secular religious attitudes. Higher education is also associated with a modest increase in knowledge of and interest in politics (Pascarella & Terenzini, 2005). Longitudinal studies indicate that most of these changes in attitudes and values are maintained in the years after college (e.g., Newcomb, Koenig, Flacks, & Warwick, 1967).

These changes in values and attitudes, along with documented increases in intellectual dispositions such as interest in and knowledge of cultural and intellectual issues, tolerance for ambiguity, flexibility of thought, rational and critical approaches to problem-solving, and receptivity to further learning, are at the heart of American higher education's espoused mission. The importance of higher education lies as much in these outcomes as in subject matter knowledge and vocational preparation.

However, as in the case of moral judgment, there is still immense room for improvement in college students' moral and civic values. Some of the documented gains, though statistically significant, are small. For example, the impact of higher education on students' social conscience and humanitarian values appears to be very modest (Pascarella, Smart, & Braxton, 1986; Pascarella, Etherington, & Smart, 1988). In addition, some positive shifts during college are not maintained in the post-college years. Sax (1999) reports, for example, that the percentages of students who rate as very important helping others in need, participating in community action, and influencing the political structure show temporary increases over the four years of college, but almost all of these increases disappear in the five years after college graduation. Finally, the rates of political participation among college-educated Americans are higher than among those without a college education, but only a third of the college-educated follow public affairs regularly and less than two-thirds vote regularly in both national and local elections. Participation numbers are significantly lower for the youngest cohorts of college graduates (Galston, 2001; Putnam, 2000).

This is not surprising, since most colleges and universities have only a few programs that specifically address the moral and civic development of their students, and many students do not take part in these programs. For those who do take part, the impact can be dramatic. There is clear evidence that high quality service learning and other pedagogies such as political deliberation or political action and research projects, are highly effective in increasing students' moral, civic, and political motivation, understanding, and skills (Colby, Beaumont, Ehrlich, & Corngold, 2007; Pascarella & Terenzini, 2005; Youniss, McLellan, & Mazer, 2001).

In his book, *Involving Colleges: Successful Approaches to Fostering Student Learning and Development Outside the Classroom*, George Kuh and his colleagues (Kuh, Schuh, & Whitt, 1991) point to the importance of several features of the campus culture that influence students' moral and civic development. These include the institution's history, traditions, language, heroes, sagas, physical setting, and symbols that express unifying assumptions and democratic values. The establishment and enforcement of policies that follow from the institution's core mission and philosophy are also influential, as is the make-up of the student body and resulting peer culture. Although the "involving colleges" Kuh writes about make it clear that they stand for particular values, they also work to maintain open dialogue and sensitivity to student concerns. In an in-depth analysis of 12 colleges and universities that have shown unusual commitment to undergraduate moral and civic education, my colleagues and I saw this same effort to establish a positive and unifying culture around some core values, balanced with opportunities for reflection on and critique of that culture (Colby, Beaumont, Ehrlich, & Stephens, 2003). The importance of settings, stories, rituals, and other practices that we describe in that study are clear parallels of the features of campus culture reported by Kuh.

Students' values and goals can also change through the extra-curricular activities they seek out, the people they encounter in the course of those activities, and the new demands that are made on them as a consequence. Among the most important of these activities for the development of humanitarian social concern and values are leadership programs (Kuh, 1993; Kuh, Douglas, Lund, & Ramin-Gyurnik, 1994) and community service (Youniss & Yates, 1997). Both of these are widespread in higher education in the US.

Moral and Civic Identity. Explanations of the psychological constructs and processes that mediate the relation between moral judgment and moral action have converged on the important role of an individual's sense of moral identity. In this view, moral under-standing acquires motivational power through its integration into the structures of the self (Bergman, 2002; Narvaez & Lapsley, 2009). If identity is understood as the core or essential self, those aspects without which the individual would see himself or herself to be radically different (Erikson, 1968), it follows that people will be motivated to act in ways that are consistent with this core self, to maintain consistency in regard to these essential features of his or her identity. When these essential features of the self include moral beliefs and convictions, there is strong internal pressure to maintain consistency with those beliefs. Of course, sometimes people act morally simply in order to avoid neg-ative consequences. But many people act morally even when sanctions are not involved. In these cases, they do so, in part, because not to would be a violation of their core self; to do otherwise would be to betray one's true self (Bergman, 2002).

Individuals' understanding and experience of the core self develops over time, and the integration of moral convictions into one's core sense of self is one of the most important features of moral development. Damon and Hart (1988) traced the development of self-understanding from childhood through adolescence, finding that younger children tended to focus on physical characteristics, skills, and interests when asked to define and describe who they are. Study participants did not begin to include moral qualities such as honesty or loyalty in their self-definitions until they reached adolescence.

Despite these predictable developmental patterns, both adolescents and adults vary in the degree to which morality is central to their sense of self and in the content of that morality. In "The Moral Self," John Dewey (1998) wrote, "The real moral question is what kind of self is being furthered or formed" (p. 346). This question is central in studies of moral and civic commitment. Daniel Hart and Suzanne Fegley (1995), for example, found that in highly altruistic adolescents, moral concerns were more likely to be central to their current sense of self and their ideal self than in adolescents from a comparison group of normal but not especially altruistic adolescents. Similarly, Colby and Damon (1992) found that a close integration of self and morality formed the basis for the unwavering commitment to the common good exhibited by moral exemplars who had dedicated themselves for decades to fighting against poverty or for peace, civil rights, and other aspects of social justice.

Others have written about the development of political or civic identity in a way that parallels this conception of moral identity (e.g., Flanagan & Sherrod, 1998; Verba, Schloz-man, & Brady, 1995; Youniss & Yates, 1997). For example, Youniss and Yates present data showing that the long-term impact of youth service experience on later political and community involvement can best be explained by the contribution these service experiences make to the creation of an enduring sense of oneself as a politically engaged and socially concerned person. In their view, civic identity—which entails the establishment of individual and collective senses of social agency, responsibility for society, and political-moral awareness—links certain kinds of social participation during adolescence and young adulthood with civic engagement by these same people later.

This question of the development of a civic or political identity may help explain why some changes that take place during the college years last well beyond college while others do not. McAdam (1988) studied adults who as college students had spent a summer taking part in the 1964 Freedom Rides, which sought to integrate interstate bus lines in the south during the Civil Rights Movement. This powerful and dangerous experience had a long-term impact on those who took part, and they followed quite different life trajectories than others who had volunteered to participate but were unable to join the group in the end. The follow-up data showed that the Freedom Riders' lives were permanently altered by the experience, and many went on to be leaders in community organizing for social justice, the movement against the Viet Nam War, the women's movement, and other efforts to promote social change. The Freedom Ride experience had changed their understanding, beliefs, and values in a number of ways, and also seems to have changed the way they understand their own identities. McAdam explains one aspect of the difference between participants and the comparison group this way: "Having defined themselves as activists, a good many of the Mississippi veterans had a strong need to confirm that identity through [further] action" (p. 187).

Identity is one of a number of psychological mechanisms through which culture can have a long-term impact on an individual's behavior. The stories, images, and routines that constitute the cultural context can be incorporated into the participating individuals' sense of self, thus becoming a stable aspect of their orientations to themselves, other people, and the world (Newman, 1996). This can work for good or ill, depending on the cultural messages that are internalized. On some of the campuses my colleagues and I highlighted in our book, *Educating Citizens* (2003), members of the campus community were aware of the positive potential of this phenomenon. For example, at the College of St. Catherine (a Catholic women's college), stories of the courage and resourcefulness of the founding nuns were common knowledge for all students and were understood to mean that "We here at St. Kate's are women of unusual strength and moral courage." Educators at the college hoped and expected that graduates would take with them a sense of self that includes these virtues, and our study showed evidence that many students had internalized the iconic founding narrative of the college.

What are the implications of this work for moral and civic education? We know that identity development takes place in part through identification with admired others (Bandura, 1977, 1986). Hazel Markus (Markus & Nurius, 1986) has described the interplay between people's actual and possible selves, which can include both the selves they hope to become and the selves they are afraid of becoming. Markus and Nurius (1986) argue that the self-construct is not singular but "a system of affective-cognitive structures (also called theories or schemas) about the self that lends structure and coherence to the individual's experiences" (p. 955). They present data suggesting that individuals can reflect on their possible selves, and they understand development as a process of acquiring and then either achieving or resisting certain possible selves.

Experience with people who provide either positive or negative models can contribute to the construction of possible selves and eventually to the individual's actual self. Exposure to faculty members, residence life mentors, members of the community, and other students who represent an inspiring vision of personal ideals can play an important role in fostering the incorporation of moral and civic values into students' sense of who they want to be and eventually who they feel they are. Likewise, awareness of why they do not want to emulate some others with whom they have contact can provide a motivating force through avoidance of a feared possible self.

Undergraduate programs that adopt an outcomes-based approach often include self-understanding and self-reflection among their goals, asking students to think about questions like "What kind of self should I aspire to be?" as well as the perennial college student question, "Who am I?" If reflections on questions like these are to have lasting impact on students' sense of self, they must be of more than theoretical or academic interest. This can happen best when the questions are asked in the context of engagement with complex moral pursuits such as those provided by high quality service-learning, when students are engaged in this work with people who represent inspiring models with whom they can identify, and when the campus culture supports the development of habitual moral schemes that are consistent with important moral values. Both academic and co-curricular activities can contribute to students' awareness of and reflection on what is important to them and to their sense that they can play an active role in determining what kind of people they become (Colby et al., 2003; Colby, Ehrlich, Sullivan, & Dolle, 2011). Pedagogies of active engagement can be especially powerful in linking intellectual work in higher education to its significance for what kind of person the student wants to be.

Political Efficacy and Moral and Civic Emotions. Colleges and universities can also help foster students' sense of efficacy. In order to be civically and politically engaged and active, people have to care about the issues and value this kind of contribution. But socially responsible values alone are not sufficient to motivate action. People also have to believe that it matters what they think and do civically and politically and that it is possible for them to make some kind of difference. This belief is what we mean by having a sense of political efficacy.

Social scientists agree that a sense of political efficacy is critically important in supporting political action. But having a strong sense of efficacy does not mean one believes that political action will necessarily have an impact. In fact, people who are highly engaged may not even ask that question. As former Czechoslovakian president and author Vaclav Havel said:

> When a person behaves in keeping with his conscience, when he tries to speak the truth and when he tries to behave as a citizen even under conditions where citizenship is degraded, it may not lead to anything, yet it might. But what surely will not lead to anything is when a person calculates whether it will lead to something or not.
>
> (as quoted in Meadows, 1991, p. 48)

Likewise, studies of people who have dedicated their lives to serving others and improving their communities have found that these extraordinary individuals rarely asked themselves whether they were making measurable progress toward their goals (Colby &

Damon, 1992). Especially when working to fight poverty, as many were, they would have become discouraged if they had focused on the question of how much progress they were making in relation to the magnitude of the remaining problem.

Others have suggested that promoting students' political interest also requires imparting a sense of passion and even playfulness about politics. Political scientist Wendy Rahn (2000) argues that what students really need to learn about politics is "a love of the game and a sense of sportsmanship." If they do that, the question of whether they are making a difference with each specific act is less central. And yet, fostering this love of the game, which pushes the question of efficacy into the background, is one of the most effective ways to foster a sense of political efficacy.

When one takes on great moral and political causes such as poverty or political reform, immersion in the process of collective action can preserve one's spirits and determination. Thus, a love of the activity for its own sake, passion for the cause, and solidarity with others working toward the same goals can all sustain moral and civic commitment in the face of difficulties that would otherwise be very discouraging. An important question for educators, then, is how to help students achieve this kind of satisfaction in their moral, political, and civic discussions and action (Colby et al., 2007).

Moral emotions play an important role in motivating action (Haidt, 2001; Hoffman, 1981), and many programs of moral and civic education include efforts to elicit some kind of moral emotion, either negative or positive—outrage at injustice, disgust with hypocrisy, compassion for the poor, hope for peace, and inspiration through solidarity. Research indicates that the motivational impact of negative and positive emotions can be quite different. It is important to be aware of this, because many educators rely heavily on eliciting negative emotions as a means to rouse students from self-absorption. Out of concern for social justice, faculty often take a critical stance toward American history, culture, and politics. The goal is to shock students out of their complacency and motivate them to act through a sense of outrage. The irony is that in many cases, this critical approach, instead of solving the apathy problem, *contributes* to the growing sense of alienation and cynicism that students feel, and finally to a lack of conviction that anything can be done about the injustice, which seems so pervasive as to be unavoidable. The belief that corruption, exploitation, and greed are rampant (and perhaps even part of the human condition) can be used to justify a life of self-interest as well as a life of civic commitment.

A study of political advertising helps to illuminate this phenomenon. This experimental study (Rahn & Hirshorn, 1999) looked at the effect of arousing positive or negative feelings about the state of the country and found that both positive and negative feelings can lead to more involvement in community and political action. That is, feeling either more outraged or more inspired and hopeful can lead to more engagement. But the investigators also found an interaction between emotion and sense of efficacy. In this study, positive emotions (hopefulness or inspiration) led to greater interest and engagement among study participants who began with *either* a low or a high sense of political efficacy. In contrast, negative feelings like outrage mobilize those who begin with high efficacy, but demobilize even more those who start with low levels of efficacy.

It is likely that the teachers who create a sense of outrage by focusing very heavily on abuses and injustice have higher political efficacy than their students, so it makes sense that the teachers would feel mobilized by vivid critiques of the status quo and would expect students to be mobilized as well. But students who begin with low levels of efficacy may be immobilized by the apparent hopelessness of the situation. An emerging understanding of this dynamic is contributing to a growing consensus that the most effective approach to civic engagement combines an appreciation of the ideals of one's own democratic system—that democratic ideals are unrealized but not unrealizable—with a realistic sense of where one's country has fallen short of the ideals (Damon, 2011; Gutmann, 1987; Rahn, 1992). This approach avoids both cynicism and naive, uncritical complacency. In practice, this is difficult to achieve. But teachers at all levels need to ask themselves which is the greater challenge (and thus worth the greatest attention and effort)—to make students more realistic or to make than more idealistic (Gutmann, 1987).

CIVIC AND POLITICAL SKILLS OR EXPERTISE

We have said that if we are to educate engaged citizens it is important for students to have a sense of political efficacy. But what about actually *being* efficacious as well as *feeling* efficacious? In addition to understanding and caring about justice, people need to develop the skills and expertise of civic and political practice if they are to be engaged and effective citizens.

Prominent among the needed civic and political capacities are skills of deliberation, communication, and persuasion, including the capacities for compelling moral discourse—how to make a strong case for something, ensure that others understand one's point of view, understand and evaluate others' arguments, compromise without abandoning one's convictions, and work toward consensus (Colby et al., 2007). These capacities go to the heart of moral and civic functioning, because individuals' moral and political concepts are both developed and applied through discourse, communication, and argumentation. Individuals take positions in the context of social interactions or discourse, which helps to shape the way those positions are played out, modified, and reconstructed (Habermas, 1993; Turiel, 1997).

Having these political and civic competencies not only makes effective action possible, it naturally leads to a greater sense of efficacy or empowerment, and leads people to see themselves as politically engaged and thus to be further motivated toward engagement (Colby et al., 2007; Lake, Snell, Perry & Associates, 2002). That is, the development of skills contributes to and interacts with the development of values, understanding, and self-concept. Kuh and colleagues (1991) report, for example, that participation in leadership activities during college is the single most important predictor of students' development of humanitarian social concern and values. The significance of developing these practical competencies is also evident in longitudinal research on civic engagement. In a comprehensive review, Kirlin (2000) found that involvement with organizations that teach adolescents how to participate in society by learning how to form and express opinions and organize people for action is a powerful predictor of adult civic engagement.

GENERAL ARCHITECTURE OF COLLEGE LEVEL MORAL AND CIVIC EDUCATION

There are three main sites of moral and civic education in colleges and universities, and all are important: the curriculum, including both general education and the major; extra-curricular activities and programs; and the campus culture, including honor codes, residence hall life, and spontaneous "teachable moments," as well as various cultural routines and practices—symbols, rituals, socialization practices, shared stories, and the like. Some of the most effective programs integrate learning from at least two of the sites—usually curricular and extra-curricular—and sometimes all three. Institutions that make undergraduate moral and civic education a high priority use a holistic approach in which moral and civic learning takes place in all three major sites and is well aligned and dynamically interconnected across sites (Colby et al., 2003).

The Curriculum

In curricular programs that make moral and civic learning a serious priority, courses intended to serve that purpose are evaluated and screened to ensure that they meet clearly established criteria of focus and quality. When colleges and universities are committed to reaching all or most of their students, they build moral and civic goals into required core courses and into majors in both arts and sciences and vocational fields rather than limiting them to electives that will be chosen only by students who already show a strong interest in ethical concerns or social responsibility. In addition, these institutions encourage faculty to employ a wide array of active pedagogies and provide training and other support in the use of these pedagogies.

Moral and Civic Learning beyond the Classroom

Moral and civic learning beyond the classroom includes both structured extra-curricular programs and activities and many aspects of the environment or culture. Leadership programs, service activities, disciplinary, religious, and political clubs, and programs designed to foster communication and respect across diversity are directly relevant to students' moral and civic growth, but moral and civic learning can be incorporated into virtually any kind of student activity with sensitive guidance and support from faculty and staff advisors.

The campus culture is another important site of moral and civic learning. The culture of any given campus conveys many, often conflicting, messages, however, only some of which support the values the institution wishes to convey. Only by talking directly with students is it possible to identify which of the institution's physical symbols, iconic stories, socialization practices, and widely shared key ideas are salient to them and how they understand the meaning of these cultural practices and artifacts. Institutions that have a vibrant tradition of social contribution, a rich set of public events that explore social and political issues, or a faculty that is especially engaged with the local or national community often highlight and build on these strengths to students' great benefit (Colby et al., 2003).

Within the realm of institutional culture, honor codes are important ways to highlight some of the central values of higher education—honesty, trust, self-restraint, civility, and mutual respect. Research indicates that when honor codes make explicit the links between honorable student behavior and responsible citizenship within the campus and broader communities, enjoy faculty support, involve students in their development and implementation, are enforced fairly and consistently, and are accompanied by discussions of their meaning and rationale, they are highly effective in reducing cheating and fostering a strong sense of intellectual integrity and moral community (Bok, 1990; Cole & Conklin, 1996; McCabe, Treviño, & Butterfield, 1999).

URGENT AGENDA UNDER THREAT

Since the publication of the first edition of this volume in 2008, the traditional purposes of higher education, including cultivation of a life of the mind and the shaping of character, have come under increasing attack (Selingo, 2012; Tugend, 2012). Due mostly to the high cost of college and rising student debt, the pressure for accountability has intensified, and accountability criteria for what is often called the "education *industry*" are more likely to be framed in terms of graduates' raw earning power (Mitchell Stevens, 2012). The popularity of vocational majors continues to rise, swamping arts and sciences majors, especially the humanities. Business is by far the largest undergraduate major in the US, and more than two-thirds of US college students choose to major in vocational fields. Unless faculty and administrative leaders bring to higher education renewed commitment to its formative capacities and creativity in weaving moral and civic learning into every field of study, the growing trends toward efficiency, economic conceptions of accountability, and narrowly defined vocational preparation at the expense of other goals are likely to weaken higher education's capacity to prepare thoughtful, engaged citizens and persons of integrity and moral wisdom.

Studies show that, at the end of college, students who majored in business or engineering rate as significantly lower than other students the importance of developing a meaningful philosophy of life, influencing the political structure, improving their understanding of other countries and cultures, and related outcomes. Correspondingly, students in these majors rate more highly the importance of being very well off financially. Students in vocational majors tend to be more instrumental in their orientation toward learning—asking how each experience will help them get a job—and less interested in thinking about problems from many fundamentally different points of view (Colby et al., 2011).

On the other side of the gulf between vocational and arts and sciences education, the humanities report feeling under assault and are struggling to attract students. Their efforts to increase "rigor" and theoretical grounding for their scholarship often make their fields seem more esoteric and disconnected from the world of non-academic work (Kronman, 2007). Yet the humanities traditionally have been fertile grounds for fostering a wider sense of meaning, reflective exploration, the capacity to imagine alternative life paths that are driven by different sets of values, and the means to make thoughtful choices among those alternative paths. Serious attention to moral and civic learning in college can, therefore, benefit from drawing on the substance and modes of thought represented by the humanities, incorporating these perspectives into whatever fields of study undergraduates choose to pursue.

Although the increasing share of students pursuing vocational majors is, in some ways, a barrier to the widespread adoption of moral and civic learning as serious goals of higher education, this need not be the case. Preparing students for a profession or other vocational field presents many opportunities for teaching about the broader historical, social, cultural, and institutional contexts of that work, its potential impact on society, and the responsibilities of practitioners to consider those impacts and make them as constructive as possible. My colleagues and I have offered some suggestions for accomplishing this in several fields based on research we conducted at the Carnegie Foundation for the Advancement of Teaching (Benner, Sutphen, Leonard, & Day, 2009; Colby et al., 2011; Sheppard, Macatangay, Colby, & Sullivan, 2008).

On a more optimistic note, it seems that faculty interest in active pedagogies has increased (Stanton, Giles, & Cruz, 1999), and many of these pedagogies hold strong potential for influencing not only students' moral and civic understanding but also their motivation and skill. However, engaged pedagogies will contribute to the full range of moral and civic outcomes only if they are designed explicitly to do so (Colby et al., 2007, 2011). Well designed team projects, for example, can teach civic capacities such as collaboration, compromise, persuasion, and sense of responsibility beyond the self. And the more explicitly these goals are built into the demands of the assignment, the more likely students are to achieve the desired outcomes. Similarly, if the project's substance invites consideration of political and policy questions or questions of ethical standards and choices, it will likely contribute to moral and civic learning. If not, the learning may be limited to technical or narrowly academic dimensions of the issues at hand.

Given the serious economic, political, social, and environmental challenges facing the world in the twenty-first century, this is no time to push moral and civic formation to the margins of higher education. Advanced knowledge and technical skill are urgently needed. But if students don't also learn how to wield that knowledge and skill responsibly, they will be unable to meet the great challenges of their times. Higher education is in a strong position to enable students to make sense of the world and their place in it, to prepare them to use knowledge and skills to engage responsibly with the life of their times. In order for it to meet this potential, all of the major sites of moral and civic learning—the curriculum, student life outside the classroom, and the institutional culture—need to be integrated intentionally toward the development of moral and civic understanding, motivation, and skill.

REFERENCES

Adelson, J., & O'Neil, R. P. (1966). Growth of political ideas in adolescence: The sense of community. *Journal of Personality & Social Psychology, 4*(3), 295–306.

Bandura, A. (1977). *Social learning theory.* Englewood Cliffs, NJ: Prentice-Hall.

Bandura, A. (1986). *Social foundations of thought and action.* Englewood Cliffs, NJ: Prentice-Hall.

Benner, P., Sutphen, M., Leonard, V., & Day, L. (2009). *Educating nurses: A call for radical transformation.* San Francisco: Jossey-Bass.

Bergman, R. (2002). Why be moral? A conceptual model from developmental psychology. *Human Development, 45*(2), 104–124.

Bok, D. (1990). *Universities and the future of America.* Durham, NC: Duke University Press.

Colby, A., Beaumont, E., Ehrlich, T., & Corngold, J. (2007). *Educating for democracy.* San Francisco: Jossey-Bass.

Colby, A., Beaumont, E., Ehrlich, T., & Stephens, J. (2003). *Educating citizens: Preparing America's undergraduates for lives of moral and civic responsibility.* San Francisco: Jossey-Bass.

Colby, A., & Damon, W. (1992). *Some do care: Contemporary lives of moral commitment.* New York: Free Press.

Colby, A., Ehrlich, T., Sullivan, W., and Dolle, J. (2011). *Rethinking undergraduate business education: Liberal learning for the profession.* San Francisco: Jossey-Bass.

Colby, A., Kohlberg, L., Gibbs, J., & Lieberman, M. (1983). A longitudinal study of moral judgment. *Monographs of the Society for Research in Child Development, 48*(1–2), 1–96.

Cole, S., & Conklin, D. (1996). Academic integrity policies and procedures: Opportunities to teach students about moral leadership and personal ethics. *College Student Affairs Journal, 15*(2) 30–39.

Damon, W. (2011). *Failing Liberty 101: How we are leaving young Americans unprepared for citizenship in a free society.* Stanford, CA: Hoover Institution Press.

Damon, W., & Hart, D. (1988). *Self-understanding in childhood and adolescence.* New York: Cambridge University Press.

Davidson, P., & Youniss, J. (1991). Which comes first? Morality or identity? In W. Kurtines & J. L. Gewirtz (Eds.), *Handbook of moral development and behavior* (Vol. 1, pp. 105–121). Hillsdale, NJ: Erlbaum.

Dewey, J. (1998). The moral self. From his *Ethics* (1932). In L. A. Hickman & T. M. Alexander (Eds.), *The essential Dewey* (Vol. 2, pp. 321–354). Bloomington: Indiana University Press.

Erikson, E. H. (1968). *Identity: Youth and crisis.* New York: Norton.

Eyler, J., & Giles, D. E. (1999). *Where's the learning in service-learning?* San Francisco: Jossey-Bass.

Flanagan, C. A., & Sherrod, L. R. (1998). Youth political development: An introduction. *Journal of Social Issues, 54*(3), 447–456.

Galston, W. (1991). *Liberal purposes: Goods, virtues, and diversity in the liberal state.* Cambridge, UK: Cambridge University Press.

Galston, W. (2001). Political knowledge, political engagement, and civic education. *Annual Review of Political Science, 4,* 217–234.

Gutmann, A. (1987). Democratic citizenship. In J. Cohen (Ed.), *For love of country* (pp. 66–71). Boston: Beacon Press.

Habermas, J. (1993). *Justification and application: Remarks on discourse ethics* (C. Cronin, Trans.). Cambridge, UK: Polity Press.

Haidt, J. (2001). The emotional dog and its rational tail: A social intuitionist approach to moral judgment. *Psychological Review, 108*(4), 814–834.

Hart, D., & Fegley, S. (1995). Prosocial behavior and caring in adolescence: Relations to self-understanding and social judgment. *Child Development, 66*(5), 1346–1359.

Helwig, C. C. (1995). Adolescents' and young adults' conceptions of civil liberties: Freedom of speech and religion. *Child Development, 66*(1), 152–166.

Hoffman, M. (1981). Is altruism part of human nature? *Journal of Personality and Social Psychology, 40,* 121–137.

Jankowski, T. B. (1992). Ethnic identity and political consciousness in different social orders. In H. Haste & J. Torney-Purta (Eds.), *The development of political understanding: A new perspective* (pp. 79–93). San Francisco: Jossey-Bass.

King, P., & Kitchener, K. (1994). *Developing reflective judgment: Understanding and promoting intellectual growth and critical thinking in adolescents and adults.* San Francisco: Jossey-Bass.

Kirlin, M. K. (2000). *The role of experiential programs in the political socialization of American adolescents.* Paper presented at the meeting of the American Political Science Association, Washington, D.C.

Knefelkamp, L. (1974). Developmental instruction: Fostering intellectual and personal growth in college students. Unpublished doctoral dissertation, University of Minnesota, Minneapolis and St. Paul.

Kohlberg, L. (1969). Stage and sequence: The cognitive developmental approach to socialization. In D. A. Goslin (Ed.), *Handbook of socialization theory and research* (pp. 347–480). Skokie, IL: Rand McNally.

Kronman, A. (2007). *Education's end: Why our colleges and universities have given up on the meaning of life.* New Haven, CT: Yale University Press.

Kuh, G. (1993). In their own words: What students learn outside the classroom. *American Educational Research Journal, 30*(2), 277–304.

Kuh, G., Douglas, K., Lund, J., & Ramin-Gyurnik, J. (1994). *Student learning outside the classroom: Transcending artificial boundaries.* Washington, D.C.: ASHE-ERIC Higher Education Report No. 8.

Kuh, G., Schuh, J. H., & Whitt, E. (1991). *Involving colleges: Successful approaches to fostering student learning and development outside the classroom.* San Francisco: Jossey-Bass.

Lake, Snell, Perry, & Associates (2002). *Short term impacts, long term opportunities: The political and civic engagement of young adults in America* (Analysis and Report for The Center for Information and Research in Civic Learning & Engagement [CIRCLE] and The Center for Democracy & Citizenship and The Partnership for Trust in Government at the Council for Excellence in Government), Washington, DC.

Macedo, S. (2000). *Diversity and distrust: Civic education in a multicultural democracy.* Cambridge, MA: Harvard University Press.

Markus, H., & Nurius, P. (1986). Possible selves. *American Psychologist, 41*(9), 954–969.

McAdam, D. (1988). *Freedom summer.* New York: Oxford University Press.

McCabe, D., Treviño, L., & Butterfield, K. (1999). Academic integrity in honor code and non-honor code environments: A qualitative investigation, *The Journal of Higher Education, 70*(2): 211–234.

Meadows, D. M. (1991). The question of leadership. *In Context, 30,* 48.

Narvaez, D., & Lapsley, K. (2009). *Personality, identity, and character: Explorations in moral psychology.* New York: Cambridge University Press.

Newcomb, T., Koenig, K., Flacks, R., & Warwick, D. (1967). *Persistence and change: Bennington College and its students after 25 years.* New York: John Wiley & Sons.

Newman, K. (1996). *Ethnography, biography, and cultural history: Generational paradigms in human development.* In R. Jessor, A. Colby, & R. A. Shweder (Eds.), *Ethnography and human development: Context and meaning in social inquiry* (pp. 371–393). Chicago: University of Chicago Press.

Pascarella, E., Ethington, C., & Smart, J. (1988). The influence of college on humanitarian/civic involvement values. *Journal of Higher Education, 59*, 412–437.

Pascarella, E., Smart, J., & Braxton, J. (1986). Postsecondary educational attainment and humanitarian and civic values. *Journal of College Student Personnel, 27*, 418–425.

Pascarella, E., & Terenzini, P. (2005). *How college affects students: A third decade of research, Volume 2*. San Francisco: Jossey-Bass.

Perry, W. G., Jr. (1968). *Forms of intellectual and ethical development in the college years: A scheme*. New York: Holt, Rinehart & Winston.

Putnam, R. D. (2000). *Bowling alone: The collapse and revival of American community*. New York: Simon & Schuster.

Raaijmakers, Q. A. W., Verbogt, T. F. M. A., & Vollerbergh, W. A. M. (1998). Moral reasoning and political beliefs of Dutch adolescents and young adults. *Journal of Social Issues, 54*(3), 531–546.

Rahn, W. M. (1992). The decline of national identity among young Americans: Diffuse emotion, commitment, and social trust. Unpublished manuscript, University of Minnesota.

Rahn, W. M. (2000). Panel discussion at the Advisory Board Meeting of the Civic Identity Project, Grand Cayman, Bahamas.

Rahn, W. M., & Hirshorn, R. M. (1999). Political advertising and public mood: A study of children's political orientations. *Political Communication, 16*, 387–407.

Rest, J., Narvaez, D., Bebeau, M. J., & Thoma, S. J. (1999). *Postconventional moral thinking*. Mahwah, NJ: Erlbaum.

Sax, L. J. (1999). Citizenship development and the American college student. In T. Ehrlich (Ed.), *Civic responsibility and higher education* (pp. 3–18). Phoenix, AZ: Oryx Press.

Selingo, J. (2012, June 25). Fixing college. *The New York Times*. Retrieved from www.nytimes.com/2012/06/26/opinion/fixing-college-through-lower-costs-and-better-technology.html.

Sheppard, S., Macatangay, K., Colby, A., & Sullivan, W. (2008). *Educating engineers: Designing for the future of the field*. San Francisco: Jossey-Bass.

Stanton, T., Giles, D., and Cruz, N. (1999). *Service-learning: A movement's pioneers reflect on its origins, practice, and future*. San Francisco: Jossey-Bass.

Stevens, M. L. (2012, May 9). "Whither Accountability? The Second Academic Revolution," presentation at Stanford University, Division of Literatures, Cultures, and Languages.

Stoker, L. (2000). Panel discussion at the Advisory Board Meeting of the Civic Identity Project, Grand Cayman, Bahamas.

Trosset, C. (1998). Obstacles to open discussion and critical thinking: The Grinnell College Study. *Change, 30*(5), 44–49.

Tugend, A. (2012, May 4). Vocation or exploration? Pondering the purpose of college. *New York Times*. Retrieved from www.nytimes.com/2012/05/05/your-money/career-or-deep-learning-pondering-the-purpose-of-college.html?pagewanted=all.

Turiel, E. (1997). The development of morality. In N. Eisenberg (Ed.), *Social, emotional, and personality development* (5th ed., Vol. 3, pp. 863–932). New York: John Wiley & Sons.

Turiel, E. (2008). The development of children's orientations toward moral, social, and personal orders: More than a sequence in development. *Human Development, 51*, 21–39.

Verba, S., Schlozman, K. L., & Brady, H. E. (1995). *Voice and equality: Civic voluntarism in American politics*. Cambridge, MA: Harvard University Press.

Walker, J. S. (2000). Choosing biases, using power and practicing resistance: Moral development in a world without certainty. *Human Development, 43*, 135–156.

Youniss, J., McLellan, J. A., & Mazer, B. (2001). Voluntary service, peer group orientation, and civic engagement. *Journal of Adolescence Research, 16*, 456–468.

Youniss, J., & Yates, M. (1997). *Community service and social responsibility in youth*. Chicago: University of Chicago Press.

22

CITIZENSHIP AND DEMOCRACY EDUCATION IN A DIVERSE EUROPE

Wolfgang Edelstein and Tobias Krettenauer

THE CALL FOR DEMOCRACY EDUCATION IN EUROPE

In the year 2007, the *European Union*, in the understanding laid down in the so called Lisbon Accords, defined democratic citizenship and human rights, together with social cohesion and sustainable economic progress, as fundamental goals of the Union. These goals were to serve as a cornerstone of its ongoing and future development as one of the most advanced regions of the world. Ten years earlier, in 1997, the *Council of Europe*, the agency of political and cultural cooperation of more than 40 European nations, launched a program of citizenship and human rights education designed to support and evolve democratic citizenship education in schools across Europe. Starting with the study of exemplary projects and schools, it continued from 2002 onwards with a program of education for democratic citizenship developing local, national, and transnational initiatives, curricula, and standards, and publishing handbooks and teaching materials (Bîrzéa et al., 2004; Dürr, Ferreira Martins, & Spajic Vrkas, 2001). The program reached a new level of intensity with its *European Year of Citizenship through Education* in 2005. In the wake of this programmatic high point a new phase of the program was launched in 2006 under the heading *Learning and Living Democracy for All*. A center for democratic education, the European Wergeland Center, was established in Oslo with support of the Norwegian government to organize and coordinate European action in the field of democracy education and school-based action for democratic development. In May 2005, the heads of state and governments in Europe agreed upon action according to the so called Warsaw Action Plan to implement the following three lines of action: (1) Education policy development and implementation for democratic citizenship and social inclusion; (2) Democratic governance of educational institutions; (3) New roles and competencies of teachers and other educational staff in a common program enterprise of Education for Democratic Citizenship and Human Rights Education (EDC/HRE).

Finally, in 2010, the Standing Conference of Ministers of Education of the Council of Europe debated and decided on the main goals and objectives of the EDC/HRE program for the coming years, strengthening policy development and policy implementation with special focus on social cohesion, social inclusion, and respect for human rights; with special attention to democratic governance of educational institutions. They called for a special effort to disseminate knowledge and best practice and to foster research in the field to establish a satisfactory knowledge base. and, finally and most importantly, to develop sustainable frameworks and mechanisms that make EDC/HRE part of everyday practices and processes at all levels of society. In May 2010 the Committee of Ministers adopted a Council of Europe *Charter on Education for Democratic Citizenship and Human Rights Education* that sums up the history of the endeavor. This document provides a serious and substantive set of definitions, objectives, and principles as well as detailed policy measures, which are aptly summed up by Section 13 of the Charter under the heading *Skills for promoting social cohesion, valuing diversity and handling differences and conflict.*

> In all areas of education, member states should promote educational approaches and teaching methods which aim at living together in a democratic and multicultural society and at enabling learners to acquire the knowledge and skills to promote cohesion, value diversity and equality, appreciate differences—particularly between different faith and ethnic groups—and settle disagreements and conflicts in a nonviolent manner with respect for each others' rights, as well as to combat all forms of discrimination and violence, especially bullying and harassment.
>
> (Council of Europe, 2010, p. 12)

Evidently, education for democratic citizenship has rapidly moved up in the policy agendas of national and supranational organizations in Europe over the past two decades and is now considered a top priority in many of the European Ministries of education (see also Georgi, 2008; Kerr, 2008). There are plenty of reasons for this increased emphasis on democratic citizenship education. Some of them are global in nature; others are specific to Europe. For a long time, social scientists have been issuing warnings about a decrease in political and civic engagement in particular among youth. Renowned political scientists such as Herfried Münkler in Germany (Münkler & Wassermann, 2008) and Colin Crouch in the UK (Crouch, 2004) have identified serious threats to the very foundation of modern democracies that are manifest in an erosion of trust in political institutions. These long-term threats more or less affect all Western societies and are hardly specific to Europe. They have been associated with excessive *utilitarian individualism* (Durkheim, 1898/1969), which is corrosive of any social bonds beyond economic self-interest, as well as with globalization, which confronts democratically legitimized national institutions with unprecedented challenges on the level of international governance. After the end of the cold war and the fall of the Soviet Regime, Europe had to manage the integration of former communist countries from Central and Eastern Europe into the Union and find appropriate ways to support their fledgling democratic institutions. Although the European Union fared reasonably well in this process (as recognized by the Nobel Peace Prize committee in 2012) many countries faced economic challenges and declines in social-welfare systems that were further exacerbated in the wake of the financial crisis in 2008. As a consequence, even well-established democracies in Western Europe with long-standing traditions of democratic governance have experienced an upsurge of right-wing, xenophobic, and nationalistic movements that threaten immigrants living in these countries and question the process of European integration itself.

All these trends make obvious that a democratically unified Europe which promotes social cohesion, respect for human rights, value diversity, and the peaceful cohabitation of different faith and ethnic groups (as defined in the Lisbon Accords and the Charter of the European Council) cannot be taken for granted but has to be actively promoted and cultivated. Once achieved, democratic forms of governance are not self-sustaining and have to be constantly reinforced. Thus, education for democratic citizenship is no luxury. It is a necessity. This insight led to the strong emphasis in the European Union on Education for Democratic Citizenship. The question then arises, how shall we go about when organizing education for democracy? What are the competencies children and adolescents need to develop for engaging in democratic governance at local, provincial, national, and supranational levels? What are the operational characteristics of the corresponding learning environments? And what are the challenges and barriers for democracy education that thwart the education for democratic citizenship in a unified and diverse Europe? These are the main questions addressed in this chapter. In the following, we will first deal with the importance of schools for democracy education. This focus on schools will be maintained throughout the chapter. This is not to deny the importance of other social institutions for promoting democratic forms of life (e.g., the family, youth organizations). However, schools are in a particularly privileged position for teaching democracy as will become evident in the following section. This privilege defines an important institutional responsibility. In the subsequent sections, after describing key competencies that can be considered essential for participating in democratic forms of life, we will turn to important principles and practices that are suitable for promoting democratic competencies in schools. Finally, we will outline major challenges that Education for Democracy in Europe has been facing in the past and likely will face in the future.

EDUCATION FOR DEMOCRACY—THE IMPORTANCE OF SCHOOLS

At the beginning of this chapter major initiatives of the Council of Europe and the European Commission regarding EDC/HRE were described. Starting in the late 1990s, these political and administrative initiatives were paralleled by increasing efforts to gain empirically based knowledge on civic education in European countries. An important milestone in this development was the IEA Civic Education Study (CIVED99)—a two-phase, cross-national study that involved 90,000 14-year-olds from 28 countries, 24 of which were European. This study, on different levels and by various indicators, documented the particular importance of schools for the process of democracy education. It demonstrated that civic knowledge was the strongest predictor of students' intention to vote as adults. Schools have an important role in democracy education by teaching about political institutions and the processes of democratic decision-making. Traditionally, this has been the prevailing form of citizenship education in the past (Torney-Purta, Lehmann, Oswalk, & Schulz, 2001). Although civic knowledge is necessary for democratic citizenship it is far from being sufficient. In the CIVED99 Study only one out of five students indicated that they intend to participate in conventional political activities (such as writing a letter to a newspaper) apart from voting. In most countries, young people appeared to be only moderately interested in political issues. Thus, active citizenship turned out to be a rare outcome of traditional citizenship education. Those schools that modeled democratic values and practices through encouraging students to discuss issues in the classroom and to take an active role in the school life were more successful in this regard. An open classroom climate and participatory school culture was found to be a positive predictor of students' civic knowledge and political engagement in almost all countries (cf. Torney-Purta et al., 2001). However, for many students this experience was not the norm. Only about one third of the participants in the CIVED99 study agreed that they were often encouraged in their schools to make up their own minds or encouraged to express opinions that differ from those of other students and of the teacher. Thus, even though a democratic school culture was found to be a positive predictor of two main pillars of democratic citizenship (civic knowledge and engagement) only a minority of students were able to benefit from this experience. From this perspective, the CIVED99 study pointed at an enormous untapped potential of schools for contributing to democracy education.

Schools need to teach students civic knowledge and critical thinking abilities. They often do so, more or less effectively (cf. Torney-Purta et al., 2001). However, their potential contribution to democracy education is far greater. Schools are typically the first public institution children enter in their lives. It is in the school that students experience first-hand what it means to live and work in a public institution that has a certain mandate and that is governed by formal rules and role obligations. Second, schools provide a common denominator in children's and adolescents lives. Even if students may have little in common because of increasingly diverse ethnic, cultural, and family backgrounds, they share their school experience. This experience provides a common ground for meaningful cooperation and conflict resolution. Finally, schools are always part of a larger community, as they bring together children *and* their parents, teachers *and* school staff, administrators *and* community members. Schools are not isolated from society. Any initiative that starts on the level of schools has the potential to reach out to the community and to impact society.

As schools are public institutions that are designed for the sake of students' learning, they are in the privileged position of teaching democracy in three different yet interconnected ways. In schools students are able to (a) learn *about* democracy in order to become a knowing and conscious democratic actor in (future) situations of social and political choice and decision (Rawls, 1971); they can (b) learn *through* democracy by the experience of participation in a democratic school community, and thus, through experience, to acquire sustainable democratic habits (Dewey, 1963, 2004); and they can (c) learn *for* democracy by developing democratic forms of life that reach out to local, national, or even transnational contexts (Himmelmann, 2007). Evidently, learning *through* and *for* democracy cannot be achieved simply by adding another school subject to the curriculum. It is the serious business of learning for a life of social solidarity (called social cohesion in the *Charter on Education for Democratic Citizenship and Human Rights Education*). What it aims for is a habitus of peaceful cohabitation, of diversity and participation, in a co-constructive model of social regulation. This is not an isolated skill that can be trained in a time-limited program. It is a cognitive, affective, and behavioral disposition that involves the person as a whole. Thus, learning for democracy requires fostering competencies that are key for participating in democratic forms of life. What are these competencies?

KEY COMPETENCIES FOR PARTICIPATING IN DEMOCRATIC FORMS OF SOCIAL LIFE

At this point it is useful to direct our attention to another voice claiming education for democracy in Europe and beyond, the OECD. Parallel to the Lisbon process and the Council of Europe's policy generating the EDC/HRE program, the OECD's group of educational experts developed their concept of *key competencies* for a successful life and a well-functioning society (Rychen & Salganik, 2003), to become the basic orientation for the OECD's educational policies and performance evaluations (known as the Program of Student Assessment or PISA) across the OECD's member states. These key competencies enable individuals to respond to complex situations and challenges, to navigate in a heterogeneous social space, to deal with differences and contradictions, and to take responsibility for themselves as well as others (Rychen & Salganik, 2001, 2003; Weinert, 2001). Thus they represent promising tools or instrumental capabilities that enable individuals to act according to the norms, and in view of the goals defined by the Council of Europe's Charter: the norms of democracy and human rights. The OECD defined three key competencies that are taken to be instrumental for these goals:

1. *The ability to interact in socially heterogeneous groups*—with integration, networking, partnerships, solidarity, and cooperation the operational constructs most frequently used to define the concrete meaning attached to the process. The ability to interact in socially heterogeneous groups implies the ability to relate to others, to cooperate, and to manage and resolve conflict. It is thus a basic operational capability for action and interaction *in* a democratic process and *for* a democratically structured social world.

2. The second key competence for a successful life and a well-functioning society defined by the OECD working group is *the ability to act autonomously*. This implies that individuals are empowered to navigate in the social space and to manage their lives in meaningful and responsible ways to experience self-efficacy and exercise control over their living and working conditions (Rychen & Salganik, 2003, p. 91). It calls for the ability "to play an active, reflective and responsible part in any given context" (p. 91). It implies the individual's ability to act within the big picture, that is: to think globally and act locally (p. 92), to understand the role one plays as well as the roles played by others. And this again means understanding "the rules of the game," the social norms and moral rules that relate to the context of action.

3. The third key competence is the ability *to use tools interactively*—the more conventional identification of abilities and skills acquired in the course of education-for-competence processes, yet stressing their interactive use *beyond* the tradition: using language, symbols, and texts; information and information technologies interactively and cooperatively.

It is important to note that the three key competences described by the OECD, the ability to interact in socially heterogenous groups, the ability to act autonomously, and the ability to use tools interactively were not initially defined as democratic competencies but as competencies individuals need for leading a successful life in a well-functioning society. At the center of these competencies is the ability of individuals to think independently as an expression of moral and intellectual maturity and to take responsibility for their own learning and their actions. However, as these competencies stress the cooperative and interactive nature of problem-solving they can be easily translated into key competencies for democratic citizenship. The three competences that are key for leading a successful life are equally important for engaging in core democratic activities of deliberation, cooperation, and participation. Students need to learn to deliberate about different viewpoints, norms, ideas, and goals by listening to their counterparts in discussions. They need to deal constructively with diversity and difference and need to be able to solve conflicts in a cooperative and fair way. Finally, they need to be motivated to contribute to processes of democratic decision-making and to seek out meaningful opportunities of political participation. All this requires conceptual, interpretative, and procedural knowledge tools for acting democratically, that is a profound understanding of the various requirements of democratic problem-solving in different social contexts and situations.

The overall message of the OECD definition and selection of key competencies, thus, appears to be a call for a psychologically grounded and socially validated *competence* orientation towards achieving the goal of democracy. These competencies provide the foundation for cognitive-affective dispositions and skills that are necessary for engaging in democratic forms of life. Without these social competencies there will be no deliberation, no cooperation, and no participation as core democratic activities. The question therefore must be: How can schools organize the learning processes required to develop these competencies?

In a variety of ways all relevant skills, practices, and learning processes are experientially linked in learning communities that are embedded in a participatory school culture. Piaget described these processes as early as 1934 in his disquisition on "self-government" of children in the schools (Piaget 1934/1998). In his footsteps, Lawrence Kohlberg developed his concept of schools as Just Communities. Here, in a "scaffolding environment" (Vygotski), under "responsive conditions" ("entgegenkommende Verhältnisse," Habermas), children will encounter "the existential and social experience" that according to John Dewey (1963) grounds a democratic form of life. First of all, this existential experience is the recognition and appreciation experienced by children and adolescents in participation processes. *Self-efficacy* (Bandura, 1994) follows logically and psychologically from the experience of being accepted, recognized, and appreciated. *Responsibility* (for tasks as well as for persons) follows from shared social action towards a common goal. The triple quality: recognition by others, self-efficacy, and responsibility thus is grounded in the participatory processes on which a democratic school culture is based. But none of these *capabilities* (Amartya Sen's term for the competencies unfolding in social action and interaction; Sen, 1993) will develop, unless the school community provides concrete organizational arrangements for the activation of democratic citizenship practices and the social competencies that an activating school environment will typically both rely on and bring about. These include taking the perspective of the other (Selman, 1980) and engaging in discursive practices (Habermas, 1983; Piaget, 1932, 1934/1998). In order to achieve this goal, schools must work towards turning *formal membership* in the *institution* into active and *motivated participation* in a *community*. A collectively shared sense of recognition and responsibility arising from the experience of belonging to a community of purpose will transform the closely regulated life of an educational institution into a *democratic school culture* characterized by reciprocal recognition, by the self-efficacy of motivated actors, and by the shared responsibility of cooperating members—the principles guiding participation in school as a moral community (Althof & Stadelmann, 2009; Kohlberg, 1986).

IDEAS INTO ACTION—SCHOOL PRACTICES FOR PROMOTING DEMOCRATIC COMPETENCIES

There is a broad range of practices that can contribute to the development of the socio-moral resources and capabilities required for the growth of a democratic school culture. Such practices, to be effective, will combine efforts and methodologies conducive to learning *about* democracy, to learning *through* democracy, and to learning *for* democracy. They will construct, in the classroom and across classrooms, the framework for Dewey's "existential and social experience" that is basic to developing democratic skills and habits. Following Frank and Huddleston (2009), the opportunities for active experience of democracy in schools can be grouped into three broad categories according to the communal experience they provide. There is (a) the community of the classroom, (b) the community of the school as a whole, and (c) the wider community of which the school is a part. These three communal spaces define the "social ecology" of democracy learning in schools, similar to what Bronfenbrenner (1979) described as the ecology of human development. That is, the developing person is embedded in several overlapping environmental systems that range from the immediate setting of the classroom to the more remote context of the political culture in a given society. Each system interacts with all others and with the individual to influence the development of democratic competencies. Thus, what happens on the level of classrooms has ramifications for the school community. Creating a democratic school culture, in turn, impacts the culture in the classroom as well as the wider community. Correspondingly, practices designed to foster democratic citizenship in schools can be located on three different levels. They may focus (a) on classroom activities, (b) cut across classrooms and involve the school community as a whole, or they may (c) reach out to the wider community of which the school is a part. Ideally, democratic practices on these various levels do not occur in isolation but are meaningfully orchestrated to promote learning for democracy. Thus, students should be able to benefit from their learning on the level of classroom activities when engaging in school-wide practices, which, in turn, should enable them to participate in democratic forms of social life in their communities.

As mentioned above, a number of successful practices have been identified and described by Frank and Huddleston (2009) in a handbook with the title "Schools for Society: Learning Democracy in Europe." This handbook was fostered by the Initiative for Learning Democracy in Europe (ILDE) of the Network of European Foundations. Support for this initiative came from the Freudenberg Foundation in Germany and the Citizenship Foundation in London within the context of the Council of Europe's program of Democratic Citizenship Education. The handbook consists of 23 case studies that were drawn from 11 different European countries with quite diverse political and cultural histories (Belgium, Bosnia-Herzegovina, England, Estonia, Finland, France, Germany, Italy, Poland, Sweden, Turkey). The projects were arranged in five different topical sections that cut across the three categories of communal experience described above (fostering tolerance and awareness of diversity, developing civic skills and attitudes, involving the whole school community, creating a democratic school culture, engaging schools in their communities). On the level of classroom-based activities, projects included promotion of students' critical thinking abilities and debating skills, improving political literacy as well as cultivating *Classrooms of Difference* that aim at raising self-esteem of students from culturally diverse and socially disadvantaged backgrounds by affirming their sense of identity. On the level of schools, projects ranged from Citizenship Manifestos (crafting a short, public document that sets out a school's vision for citizenship education), through establishing systems of peer mediation, to organizing schools as a democratic republic. In the latter case, students of a school generate a constitution, establish democratic institutions, such as a parliament government and independent courts, and hold elections regularly. Community-wide activities included projects aimed at increasing and strengthening the participatory opportunities of students in their communities, such as integrating service to the community in the school curriculum via service learning or engaging schools with their wider communities through collaborative student projects. In these community-based projects students were encouraged to identify a local problem, research potential remedies, and propose a solution presented to local authorities with the power to implement it (modeled after the US program Project Citizen). These different approaches and projects clearly vary in scope and breadth. Some of them are rather circumscribed; others are far-reaching and require fundamental changes in the administration of schools. Regardless of scope and breadth, the successful implementation of these programs requires careful consideration of the many social, cultural, and historical particularities that serve as the backdrop of any effort to promote democracy learning. Learning for democracy is not cut and dried.

It is beyond the scope of the present chapter to provide a detailed description of the many different approaches that can be taken to promote children's and adolescents' learning for democracy. To further illustrate important principles of democracy learning a few examples will have to suffice. These examples refer to the various communal spaces and levels of democratic activities described above (classroom, school as a whole, the wider community). On the level of classroom activities, we will describe the *Classroom Council* as a prototype of democratic self-governance; on the level of schools we describe *peer mediation* as a vehicle to improve the school culture, on the level of the wider community we will refer to *service learning* and volunteering as an effective way to engage schools in their communities.

Classroom Council. The classroom council (*Klassenrat*) can be considered a prototype of democratic self-governance. It originated as a discursive device developed by the French school reformer Celestin Freinet in the early years of the twentieth century with the purpose of discussing issues of instruction with the class and organizing classroom practice in the homeroom (Freinet, 1946/1979). It can be defined as a particularly effective variety of cooperative self-government as described by Piaget. In a number of schools intent on reform of instruction and pedagogy in Germany, it has since developed into a major example of democratic self-regulation within the classroom (Edelstein, Frank, & Sliwka, 2009; Friedrichs, 2009; Kiper, 1997). The classroom council is the site of collective responsibility for the life of the group. The teacher acts as a coach, rather than as a teacher monitoring the class, while the group practices self-determination regarding life in the classroom and the goals of common action.

Students meet regularly once a week at a fixed time slot to discuss issues that have been collected over the previous week. All students in the class are encouraged to suggest topics for the council meeting. However, students who want to have a particular issue discussed in the group typically need to find seconders. Topics may range from praising classmates for doing an excellent job, to voicing criticism and expressing a desire for changing established rules or practices. One student chairs the classroom council meeting, while other students assist the chair, for instance, by taking minutes or by managing the time. All students in the class are encouraged to take these formal roles for a predefined period of time. In the council meeting students are asked to discuss the issue at hand and to find an appropriate procedure for solving the problem. The classroom council defines rules and regulations for the class, confers about classroom projects, defines the duties of its members, their tasks, and their obligations. Votes are cast, decisions are taken, conflicts are adjudicated, and projects are planned on the basis of discussions. Various roles and tasks are carried out by elected officers or by commissions that report to the plenary assembly about their activities and efforts. Where a school assembly exists, the classroom council elects one or several delegates to represent the class in that assembly. In schools organized along participatory lines, the conference of teachers, the headmaster, and the teacher/parents council will invite student representatives elected by the classroom councils to participate and to share both discussions and responsibilities. The councils thus operate as institutions of self-government and representational bodies that train their members for participation and social responsibility, as well as for collective conflict resolution and representative government. The foundational process for all these functions is the *discursive practice* of the regular classroom council with all members of the class attending as voting members. The council trains participants from early on to speak and to listen; to take the perspective of the other and to assess the power of arguments; to seek and to maintain agreement and to resolve conflict fairly where agreement fails; to negotiate rules and to evaluate these in the light of experience; to plan, and to participate in collective actions and common projects. In schools that are geared to participatory schoolroom practice, the classroom council is the space of choice for instructional and institutional feedback that is likely to enhance both understanding and performance.

The practices of serving learning and social entrepreneurship in social projects can also be organized and carried out under the supervision and with the commitment of the Classroom Council. The same holds true for school-wide practices of peer mediation whose organization may be linked to the classroom councils as the responsible agency within school.

The classroom council was one of the democracy-enhancing methods adopted by the semi-federal German program "Learning and Living Democracy" (BLK-Programm "Demokratie lernen und leben") active in 13 German states between 2002 and 2007. Although, no specific evaluation of this method was implemented to gauge its effectiveness (cf. Abs, Roczen, & Klieme, 2007), a number of publications, narrative accounts, and films have focused on it as a particularly effective device to train for democratic forms of interaction and decision-making in student groups beginning with early grade levels. Few institutional settings could be better suited than schools to develop the socio-moral competencies and individual capabilities for cooperation and reciprocity on which the development of the basic democratic virtues depend (Edelstein, Frank, & Sliwka, 2009; Eikel & de Haan, 2007; Friedrichs, 2009).

We shall now proceed to describe more closely the practices of peer mediation and projects of service learning that can either be parts of the activities of the classroom councils or take place in schools without or beyond such councils.

Peer Mediation. Peer mediation is a process of conflict resolution in which a neutral peer who is uninvolved in the conflict helps the disputing parties to reach a mutually acceptable settlement (see Rademacher, 2009). Peer mediation, as a particular form of peer support (similar to peer counseling and peer tutoring), was established in the US in the 1970s and has extended into many different parts of the world since then. As peer mediation has been widely publicized, the basic setup of this process does not need to be described here (note, however, that there are many different forms of organizing the process of peer mediation in schools; for an overview see Lupton-Smith, 2004). Peer mediation has been mostly discussed as an effective way to reduce aggression, violence, and bullying in schools. It is less known as a means for democracy education. However, conflicts are inevitable in any socially heterogeneous group. The ability to deal with these conflicts cooperatively and constructively is essential for developing and maintaining democratic forms of social life. While classroom and school councils empower students to make decisions about many school-related affairs they do not necessarily transform the power structure between individual students on the level of their everyday interaction. This can be achieved by peer mediation. As pointed out by Cremin (2007), per mediation in schools enables students to engage in "cooperative conflicts" (Coleman, 2000). In situations of cooperative conflict, the dispute is framed as a mutual problem to be solved by both parties. This leads to minimized power differences between the disputants, and to enhanced willingness to work together effectively to achieve shared goals. Peer mediation is a way to let students take responsibility for conflict resolution. By introducing a cooperative and power-sharing approach to conflicts young people learn to engage in the vital practice of effective dispute resolution, thus improving the quality of life in school, and preparing them for life beyond the school gates (Cremin, 2007). Peer mediation can be combined with other forms of self-governance, for instance, by establishing democratic recruitment procedures for mediators, which in turn increases students' sense of responsibility in school.

It has been often documented that peer mediation programs, if properly supported and resourced, can effectively improve the overall school climate and create an atmosphere of mutual trust (cf. Haft & Weiss, 1998). At the same time, it has been stressed that sustained positive effects of peer mediation require a "whole-school approach," where the goal of cooperative conflict resolution is shared by the whole school community, i.e., by students, teachers, headteachers, and parents. Thus, establishing and maintaining a program of peer mediation can provide important incentives for creating a democratic school culture.

Service Learning. We shall now proceed to the third type of educational projects to serve the development of democratic competencies among children and adolescents in school. This form of project is identified by its traditional American name as *service learning*, in spite of the fact that it has undergone noticeable development towards a tool for democratic action in the transfer process, especially to Germany (Sliwka, 2008; Sliwka & Frank, 2004). (Also see chapter by Hart, Matsuba, and Atkins in this volume.) In service learning projects students take responsibility for the common good by addressing a social problem, working on a solution, and responding to a challenge in the community. Generally the focus is upon local problems, but students may also choose to engage in a school project in the third world or join a cooperative network designed to respond to a general environmental need. In the traditional model, service learning projects work on two fronts. On the level of practice they attempt to solve a "social problem," e.g., helping senior citizens to cope with computers, run a soup kitchen for a poor neighborhood, or plant trees in a living quarter while informing citizens about climate change. Simultaneously, the problem will become a topic of instruction, so that the projects combine responsibility in the communal context with social learning in school, and social *action* with a rational discussion of the aim and the context of action. The cooperation of a teacher (or several teachers) is, of course, essential. When this model of service learning is placed in a classroom with a classroom council, the council is recognized as the collective actor pursuing the practice of *social entrepreneurship* in a community context. Successful action of this kind will likely initiate strong reciprocity between the school and the community—certainly both a case of learning through experience, and of developing the socio-moral resources of democracy. The projects call for shared action, negotiation, and agreement on a common goal, rationally planning and conducting action together, a meaningful evaluation and documentation of results, and a subsequent public presentation. In sum, these activities entail participation and cooperation of the entire group. In its developed form, the project productively confronts the group with social reality. The teachers must engage in exchange with the students, by confronting a social problem with the requirements of instruction. This process requires coordination of the flow of project time with the regulated school timetable. Finally, the school is invested in working with the community. When implemented successfully, all of these elements come together as a context for democracy and individual development.

Once service learning goes beyond a specific project it is transformed into what can be called *civic engagement* or civic commitment, and in English may be approximately rendered by *volunteering* or community service. Volunteering may, indeed, be understood to transfer responsibility taken within the school to an arena outside and beyond the school. It clearly has a positive impact on many skills and capabilities that are required for democratic citizenship, in particular when students are encouraged to reflect upon their volunteering experiences (Hart et al., this volume; Krettenauer, 2006; Yates & Youniss, 1999). Obviously, the development of the capability to volunteer in the service of the community is a worthy goal of education in the schools, and training young people for thoughtful commitment to issues of public welfare is a contribution to education for democracy, where action is paired with understanding. When a classroom council engages in this kind of action, it may organize some kind of *public deliberation* about an issue of common concern (Sliwka, 2008). Public deliberation is a hotbed of democracy development, both individual and social. When schools engage systematically in such initiatives of civic engagement they can be seen as educating for active citizenship in the communitarian sense of the term.

We have now described three types of democracy-enhancing activities in schools: (a) the classroom council as an instrument of democratic self-regulation; (b) peer mediation as a means for improving the school culture; and (c) service learning and volunteering as a basis for developing and cultivating the competence required for community organizing and democratic action in the local community. All require, and provide in practice, the socio-cognitive and socio-moral competencies on which democratic forms of social life thrive. In the context of a democratic school culture there is an obvious advantage in granting the classroom council a privileged position as a center of action. This entails organizing and planning the social projects and volunteering initiatives of the class as an exercise in social entrepreneurship where students are trained to cooperatively and discursively practice and develop their social-cognitive and socio-moral competencies in the service of the socially desirable aims of citizenship and democratic empowerment.

CHALLENGES FOR DEMOCRACY EDUCATION

As described at the beginning of this chapter, the need for democracy education has been recognized by many European organizations and institutions. Charters have been adopted, agendas formulated, and many projects were initiated to jump-start democracy education all over Europe. There is no shortage of excellent ideas to be put into action. At this point, the question almost imposes itself: How far has Europe gone in establishing education for democracy in schools as a cornerstone of educational practice? An answer to this question is certainly not straightforward as the educational landscape of Europe is far too diverse for applying a common benchmark to all countries. Moreover, for many European countries the idea of schools as agents of democracy is still relatively new and therefore faces challenges on many different fronts. Traditionally, the school system has been organized in a hierarchical way, where students and parents have little say in running schools, and teachers are told what to teach. As a consequence, adults tend to be suspicious of attempts to develop democratic schools and teachers are reluctant to grant their students the degree of autonomy they have been denied by their school administration. Even if teachers are supportive of democracy education in their school, the existing school curricula impose considerable restrictions on them. In many European countries, the content of the school curriculum and sometimes even the teaching methods are prescribed at a provincial or national level. Training in reading and writing, math, science, computers, etc. takes up most of the time and leaves little room for any cross-curricular activities. Because of the enormous pressure to succeed in nation-wide tests, many principals and teachers feel that democratic education is a luxury they cannot afford. From this perspective, it is not surprising that a systematic study of the implementation of Education for Democratic Citizenship (EDC) policies published in 2004 along with five regional studies (Bîrzéa et al., 2004), stated a massive "compliance or implementation gap" between EDC declarations and the practice in schools. The main support for EDC in many countries was found to be limited to formal school curricula providing a structured framework for teaching civic knowledge. This consists mostly of frontal dissemination and memory directed acquisition of information about formal procedures and the institutional setup of government in a more or less marginal time slot of the timetable in middle classrooms, usually between the ages of 12 and 16. Democracy education through participatory action on the level of classrooms, schools, and in the wider community was the exception, not the rule.

Since the publication of this report in 2004 things have improved as evidenced by the second report on Citizenship Education in Europe published by the Eurydice Network in May 2012 (Eurydice, 2012). This report captures how polities and measures relating to citizenship education in Europe have evolved since 2005, when the first Eurydice study was published (Eurydice, 2005). The study demonstrates that the majority of national curricula of European countries now emphasize citizenship education as a cross-curricular dimension of the curriculum that aims at fostering key competencies for engaging in democratic forms of life. All 31 countries that are part of the Eurydice network (EU Member states plus Iceland, Croatia, Norway, and Turkey) have introduced measures to promote the involvement of students in school governance, and half of these countries have established regulations and official recommendations for the creation of councils at the class level. However, a closer look reveals that students in these councils are mostly confined to taking a consultative or informative role. Thus, students are allowed to voice their opinions on school matters and to inform other students of decisions that are made by the school management, but they do not participate in actual decision-making. In around a third of European countries the involvement of students in citizenship-related activities outside the school is explicitly promoted by national curricula or other recommendations and regulations. When school principals were directly asked about civic engagement of their students in the community, responses suggest that 66.2% of Grade 8 students in European countries had an opportunity to participate in an awareness-raising campaign, and 55% took part in activities related to an environmental issue at the local level. Moreover, almost half of the students had been given the opportunity to be involved in activities related to human rights projects (47.5%) and to help under-privileged people or groups (46.6%). Activities related to improving facilities in the local community were least common in European countries (22%).

Although these numbers suggest that some progress has been made with regard to education for democratic citizenship in European countries, challenges continue to thwart the project. Both Eurydice reports from 2005 and 2012 emphasize the enormous difficulties in assessing, evaluating, and monitoring educational performance with regard to democracy education. The development of assessment methods for students' democratic competencies that go beyond measuring the acquisition of theoretical knowledge has been identified as one of the major challenges in the field of citizenship education (Eurydice, 2005, 2012). A second major challenge is related to preparation, professional development, and support for teachers and school heads. While European countries have reformed their citizenship education curricula in response to the initiatives of the Council of Europe described at the beginning of this chapter, the introduction of related reforms in teacher education and professional development remains the exception. This failure is reflected by another sobering finding reported in the Eurydice study (Eurydice, 2012). When Grade 8 teachers of ordinary school subjects (who were, thus, not specialized on civic education) were asked about the most important aims for civic and citizenship education only 4.4% considered "future political engagement" to be an important goal. In fact, out of a list of 10 goals "future political engagement" ranked last, whereas the more traditional role of "promoting knowledge of citizens' rights and responsibilities" was the front-runner (63% endorsement). Knowledge about rights and responsibilities is a necessary condition for democratic participation. However, as should have become evident throughout this chapter it is far from being sufficient.

CONCLUSION

The school-based institutions and processes described in this chapter appear to be potentially powerful strategies for the construction, among the young, of the socio-moral resources needed to develop and maintain democracy as a normative value and as a functional way of life. By sharing exercises of democratic participation and deliberation young people are enabled to acquire the social competencies needed to engage in democratic and social practice and to develop initiatives of their own—without expecting private profits in return. Social competencies and democratic habits thus are matched with the ability to engage in socially productive practices and commitments which help participants preserve their identities and their self-respect even when faced with the social challenges of poverty and precarious positions on the labor market. Social competencies and democratic habits are the social capital of tomorrow. And they may even contribute importantly to economic capital—as some exceptional economists like George Soros, Mohammed Junus, or Amartya Sen would believe, whose capability approach has been important for the present argument (see Otto & Ziegler, 2010; Walker & Unterhalter, 2007), whose roots, however, derive from concepts of social cognitive development formulated by Piaget, Selman, and Kohlberg.

Democratic self-regulation and democratic projects in schools serve the development of social competencies—the socio-moral resources required for processes of democratic deliberation and decision-making, of conflict resolution, of responsible cooperation and participation. On the other hand, these competencies are essential for maintaining democratic forms of life. Democratic school cultures generate democratic habits among their members, enabling them to participate responsibly in democratic institutions as adults. The classroom council is a central device for the development of a democratic school culture. But besides its aims of preparing a democratic form of future life, the practices that characterize democratic schools improve the present atmosphere of these institutions so as to enhance pupils' motivation and performance, and to generate a sense of belonging and empowerment. It turns out that—almost unintended—these are milestones on the path to more efficient schools.

Democratic schools are inclusive schools that foster social cohesion and successfully integrate poor children into the school community. Inclusive schools work towards integrating children of migrant origin into both the school and the social communities. Democratic schools are the best defense against the transmission of poverty from one generation to the next.

Democratic convictions thrive on *experience*. Nothing will contribute more to the stability of democratic ways of life and institutions than the commitment of the young generation rooted in the experience of active participation and empowerment (cf. Dewey, 1963). Whereas democratic schools are called for on normative grounds as both a consequence and a prerequisite of children's rights, on empirical grounds and based on reliable evidence they also promise to be the better schools. All prize-winning schools selected for the Robert Bosch Foundation's German School Award 2007 turned out to be democratic schools. However, the jury was not awarding a prize for democracy in schools. They were giving a prize for *good practices*, to the *best schools* and these happened to be democratic schools (Beutel & Fauser, 2009).

REFERENCES

Abs, H. J., Roczen, N., & Klieme, E. (2007). *Abschlussbericht zur Evaluation des BLK-Programms "Demokratie lernen und leben."* Frankfurt: Deutsches Institut fuer Internationale Pädagogische Forschung.

Althof, W. & Stadelmann, T. (2009). Demokratische Schulgemeinschaft. In W. Edelstein, S. Frank, & A. Sliwka (Eds.), *Praxisbuch Demokratiepädagogik* (pp. 20–53). Weinheim: Beltz.

Bandura, A. (1994). *Self-efficacy. The exercise of control.* New York: Freeman.

Beutel, W. & Fauser, P. (Eds.). (2009). *Demokratie, Lernqualität und Schulentwicklung.* Schwalbach/Ts.: Wochenschau Verlag.

Bîrzéa, C., Kerr, D., Mikkelsen, R., Froumin, I., Losito, B., et al. (2004). *All-European study on education for democratic citizenship policies.* Strasbourg: Council of Europe.

Bronfenbrenner, U. (1979). *The ecology of human development.* Cambridge, MA: Harvard University Press.

Coleman, P. T. (2000). Power and conflict. In M. Deutsch & P. T. Coleman (Eds.), *The handbook of conflict resolution: Theory and practice.* San Francisco: Jossey-Bass.

Council of Europe (2010). *Council of Europe charter on education for democratic citizenship and human rights education.* Strasbourg: Council of Europe.

Cremin, H. (2007). *Peer mediation: Citizenship and social inclusion revisited.* Maidenhead, UK: Open University Press.

Crouch, C. (2004). *Post-democracy.* Malden, MA: Polity.

Dewey, J. (1963). *Experience and education.* New York: Collier Books.

Dewey, J. (2004). *Democracy and education.* Mineola, NY: Dover Publications.

Dürr, K., Ferreira Martins, I., & Spajic Vrkas, V. (2001). *Demokratie-Lernen in Europa.* Strasbourg: Council for Cultural Cooperation (Project on Education for Democratic Citizenship).

Durkheim, E. (1898/1969). Individualism and the intellectuals. *Political Studies, 17,* 19–30.

Edelstein, W., Frank, S., & Sliwka, A. (Eds.) (2009). *Praxisbuch Demokratiepädagogik.* Weinheim: Beltz.

Eikel, A. & de Haan, G. (Eds.). (2007). *Demokratische Partizipation in der Schule.* Schwalbach/Ts.: Wochenschau Verlag.

Eurydice. (2005). *Citizenship education at school in Europe.* Brussels: Eurydice.

Eurydice. (2012). *Citizenship education in Europe.* Brussels: Eurydice.

Frank, S. & Huddleston, T. (2009). Schools for society. Learning democracy in Europe. In Network of European Foundations (Ed.), *A handbook of ideas for action.* London: Alliance Publishing Trust.

Freinet, C. (1979). *Die moderne französische Schule* (H. Jörg, Trans.). Paderborn: Ferdinand Schöningh. (Original work published 1946.)

Friedrichs, B. (2009). *Praxisbuch Klassenrat. Gemeinschaft fördern, Konflikte lösen.* Weinheim: Beltz.

Georgi, V. B. (2008). Citizens in the making: Youth and citizenship education in Europe. *Child Development Perspectives, 2,* 107–113.

Habermas, J. (1983). *Moralbewusstsein und kommunikatives Handeln.* Frankfurt/Main: Suhrkamp.

Haft, W. S. & Weiss, E. R. (1998). Peer mediation in schools: Expectations and evaluations. *Harvard Negotiations Law Review, 3,* 213–270.

Himmelmann, G. (2007). *Demokratie Lernen als Lebens-, Gesellschafts- und Herrschaftsform. Ein Lehr- und Arbeitsbuch.* 3. Auflage. Schwalbach/Ts.: Wochenschau Verlag.

Kerr, D. (2008). Research on citizenship education in Europe: A survey. In V. B. Georgi (Ed.), *The making of citizens in Europe* (pp. 167–178). Bonn: Bundeszentrale für politische Bildung.

Kiper, H. (1997). *Selbst- und Mitbestimmung in der Schule. Das Beispiel Klassenrat.* Baltmannsweiler: Schneider Verlag Hohengehren.

Kohlberg, L. (1986). Der "Just Community"-Ansatz der Moralerziehung in Theorie und Praxis. In F. Oser, R, Fatke, & O. Höffe (Eds.), *Transformation und Entwicklung* (pp. 21–55). Frankfurt/M.: Suhrkamp.

Krettenauer, T. (2006). Freiwilliges Engagement im Jugendalter: Entwicklungspsychologische Perspektiven [Volunteering in adolescence: Developmental perspectives]. In T. Rauschenbach & W. Düx (Eds.), *Freiwilliges soziales Engagement im Jugendalter* (pp. 93–120). München: Juventa.

Lupton-Smith, H. (2004). Peer mediation. In E. R. Gerler (Ed.). *Handbook of school violence* (pp. 137–159). New York: Haworth Press.

Münkler, H. & Wassermann, F. (2008). Was hält eine Gesellschaft zusammen. Soziomoralische Ressourcen der Demokratie. In Bundesministerium des Innern (Ed.), *Theorie und Praxis gesellschaftlichen Zusammenhalts* (pp. 3–23). Bonn: Bundeszentrale für politische Bildung.

Otto, H.-U. & Ziegler, H. (Eds.). (2010). *Education, welfare and the capabilities approach: A European perspective.* Opladen: Budrich.

Piaget, J. (1932). *The moral judgment of the child.* London: Routledge & Kegan Paul.

Piaget, J. (1934/1998). Remarques psychologiques sur le self-government (1934). In J. Piaget, *De la pédagogie* (pp. 121–138). Paris: Éditions Odile Jacob.

Rademacher, H. (2009). Mediation und konstruktive Konfliktbearbeitung. In W. Edelstein, S. Frank, & A. Sliwka (Eds.), *Praxisbuch Demokratiepädagogik* (pp. 91–113). Weinheim: Beltz.

Rawls, J. (1971). *A theory of justice.* Cambridge, MA: The Belknap Press of Harvard University Press.

Rychen, D. S. & Salganik, L. H. (Eds.). (2001). *Defining and selecting key competencies.* Seattle: Hogrefe & Huber.

Rychen, D. S. & Salganik, L. H. (Eds.) (2003). *Key competencies for a successful life and a well-functioning society.* Cambridge, MA: Hogrefe & Huber.

Selman, R. L. (1980). *The growth of interpersonal understanding.* New York: Academic Press.

Sen, A. (1993). Capability and well-being. In A. Sen & M. Nussbaum (Eds.), *The quality of life* (pp. 30–61). Oxford: Oxford University Press.

Sliwka, A. (2008). *Bürgerbildung: Demokratie beginnt in der Schule.* Weinheim: Beltz.

Sliwka, A. & Frank, S. (2004). *Service-Learning. Verantwortung in Schule und Gemeinde.* Weinheim: Beltz.

Torney-Purta, J., Lehmann, R., Oswald, H., & Schulz, W. (2001). *Citizenship and education in twenty-eight countries: Civic knowledge and engagement at age fourteen.* Amsterdam: IEA.

Walker, M. & Unterhalter, E. (Eds.). (2007). *Amartya Sen's capability approach and social justice in education.* Basingstoke: Palgrave Macmillan.

Weinert, F. E. (2001). Concept of competence: a conceptual clarification. In D. S. Rychen & L. H. Salganik (Eds.), *Defining and selecting key competencies* (pp. 45–65). Seattle: Hogrefe & Huber.

Yates, M. & Youniss, J. (Eds.). (1999). *Roots of civic identity: International perspectives on community service and activism in youth.* New York: Cambridge University Press.

23

DEMOCRATIC MORAL EDUCATION IN CHINA

Sharon To, Shaogang Yang, and Charles C. Helwig

INTRODUCTION

In this chapter, we will look at how moral education in China transformed from a purely political/ideological form of indoctrination to an increasingly more holistic approach designed to meet changing social needs and to address the problems encountered by more traditional moral education efforts. The current moral education curriculum has been implemented since 2003 in primary and secondary schools according to the *Guidelines for Ideology and Morality in Full-time Compulsory Education* (PRCMOE, 2003). This curriculum has generally moved in the direction of the establishment of a democratic classroom where students ideally have input into the classroom discourse and are being treated as unique individuals whose perspectives and views need to be respected and heard. As we will see, these changes in the ideas and practice of moral education are helping to meet not only the economic needs of the rapidly changing Chinese society, but also the psychological and developmental needs of adolescents in China. However, these democratic reforms coexist with the retention of more traditional forms of moral and political or ideological education, often in an uneasy and complex relation. We will argue that the kind of democratic moral education efforts emerging in China is consistent with recent and ongoing psychological theory and research that examines how autonomy support and democratic classroom environments promote adolescents' moral and cognitive development, as well as their psychological well-being. These changes in Chinese moral education programs, however, are also fraught with conflicts, paradoxes, and tensions, as educational systems and schools within China encounter difficulties of various sorts in fully putting these reforms into practice. The issues raised in our review are not wholly unique to China, but have parallels with similar efforts to instantiate a more democratic form of moral education in schools and classrooms in Western societies.

HISTORY OF MORAL EDUCATION IN CHINA

In order to appreciate the current Chinese moral education curriculum, it is necessary to examine the historical, social, and political influences that have molded and shaped its modern form. Throughout most of China's 5,000 years of history, ideological shifts in conceptions of morality were often accompanied by political policy change and reform. For example, Confucianism emerged as a Chinese philosophy during the Spring and Autumn period of Chinese history (771 BC–476 BC), and was then regarded as the orthodoxy since the Han Dynasty (206 BC–AD 220) up to the Communist revolution. During the period following the Communist revolution, Confucianism was dismantled and replaced by socialist ideology based on Marxism-Leninism and Mao Zedong Thought, the official Ideology of the ruling Communist Party of China. After Deng Xiaoping's "reform and opening up" policy at the end of the 1970s, China's economy started booming as capitalist ideas and materialism took its hold on the country. Material gain and the accumulation of personal wealth became the overarching emphasis amongst the population. These changes further brought to light issues of corruption, often popularized in the growing national media, and similar efforts by the ruling Communist Party to address these pervasive social problems. In this atmosphere, many people started questioning the lack of morality in their day-to-day lives and started turning back to the teachings of Confucianism for answers (Ai, 2008; Yu, 2008). Accordingly, we will attempt to understand how social and political changes in various historical periods have also changed and shaped the form and hence the practice of the current moral curriculum in China.

Reform policy scholars have generally divided the development of Chinese moral education into four periods of development: 1) before 1949; 2) between 1949 and 1966, when the first education reform happened after the establishment of the PRC; 3) between 1966 and 1976 when the Cultural Revolution suspended schooling altogether; and 4) after 1976 when the reform and opening up policy was implemented (e.g., M. Li, Taylor, & Yang, 2004; P. Li., Zhong, Lin, & Zhang, 2004). (New educational reforms begun in 2003, i.e., the "Guidelines," to be subsequently described, may be considered extensive enough to have opened up a new chapter in the development of moral education in China.) Since the end of the first historical reference point until current times, China has transformed from a closed, conservative, authoritarian society to a more open, diverse, and modern society. Each of these four periods significantly shaped moral education development in China. During the first period following the establishment of the PRC, moral education, or *deyu*, was a means of political socialization used to uphold the socialist government. Gradually moral education partially delinked itself from politics and currently its focus—at least officially—is to serve the development of students and, by extension, to strengthen society.

Origin of Chinese Moral Education (Zhou Dynasty)

The origins of Chinese moral education can be dated as far back as 3,000 years ago, when Zhou Gong (the Duke of Zhou) initiated the concept of "ruling the country by morality" (P. Li et al., 2004). He is the first person in Chinese history to write a moral text that systematically expounded the ethical interpersonal relationships that should exist between people in a hierarchical society (Yang, 2012). The "Zhou" rite system deals with the basic codes of conduct that govern all aspects of a person's social life. For example, he established "filial piety" as the core ethical code to regulate the relationships within the family and mandate the ethics of "father as the leader" in the family. This relationship framework extended from the father-son relationship to that of monarch-subject. The monarch of the country was regarded as the leader in the political system just as the father was seen as the leader in the family unit. This link between interpersonal relationships and political stability provided the framework for Confucian social morality that was to follow.

Everyone had his/her defining role in society according to his or her respective position in the hierarchy (e.g., parents must provide and children must serve and obey). These hierarchical relationships were mirrored in politics. As a result, few distinctions were made between moral and political principles. This moral system, developed in the Western Zhou Dynasty (eleventh century–776 BC), laid the foundation for Chinese ethical culture/morality and set the tone for moral education that would extend for more than two millennia.

Confucianism and Moral Education

While the concept of filial piety and its conceptual framework of social hierarchy was first laid down by Zhou Gong, it was Confucius and his writings that propelled it into the forefront of Chinese philosophical thought. Confucius was a philosopher during the Spring and Autumn period of Chinese history (771 BC–476 BC). During that time, China was divided into several opposing states. War was rampant as these states battled one another. Strangely enough, this was a golden age for Chinese philosophy that became known as the Hundred Schools of Thought (Roetz, 1993). The rulers of each state sought whatever advantage they could over their opposition. Philosophers, thinkers, and scholars were highly valued as advisers who had the potential to tip the scale in their employer's favor. They gave advice on a myriad of topics including war, diplomacy, economics, etc. Confucian philosophy itself emphasized a variety of moral matters, including governmental morality, correctness of social relationships, and justice and honesty, but it was not particularly influential during his lifetime. Yet his teachings were later translated/interpreted by authoritarian political philosophers into strict guidelines, distilling the complexity of his elaborate system of moral philosophy and political theory into a simple message: obedience (Roetz, 1993). This resulted in a common misconception about the association of Confucianism and immutable hierarchy of authority and unquestioning obedience. In contrast to what many believe, while Confucius prized hierarchy and order, democratic ideals are also present in fundamental Confucian thinking about the ideal state and family (de Bary & Weiming, 1998). Indeed, Confucianism is not only about learning moral values and generally honoring role obligations; it also encourages moral reflection on conventional virtues, and frowns upon blindly following the "right" principles. Confucius believed that blind subservience should not happen within the family or the nation and mere conformity should be avoided (for elaboration of some of these misconceptions, see de Bary & Weiming, 1998; Helwig, 2006a; Roetz, 1993).

During the Han dynasty, Confucianism was adopted by the emperor as the official ideology of the state in order to maintain social stability. Socially conservative interpretations of Confucian teachings were used to achieve this aim. This resulted in a "politicized Confucianism" that dominated the official state ideology of China until it was replaced by the "Three Principles of the People" ideology with the establishment of the Republic of China.

The Establishment of the PRC

In 1949, the People's Republic of China (PRC) was established. It was led by the Communist Party of China (CPC) with Mao Zedong ruling the country as Chairman of the CPC. With the establishment of the PRC also came the first restructuring of education in terms of its goals and focus, its organization, curriculum, and the population it served. Universal access to education implied that moral education was no longer solely granted to the privileged few (e.g., advisors to the monarch), but to all people across the country. The aim of moral education was also modified to serve the revolution and the new "democracy" in building a socialist government. With the highly politically-oriented education content focusing on Marxism-Leninism and Mao Zedong Thought as its guidelines, moral education was often synonymous with ideo-political education. Accordingly, citizenship values, such as patriotism and collectivism, which emphasized the subordination of the individual to the greater interest of the society or the group, were viewed as in accord with national goals and hence were propagandized as part of moral education (Lee & Ho, 2005).

Cultural Revolution

A decade of political, economic, and social turmoil began in 1966 during the socio-political movement known as the Cultural Revolution. In order to impose Maoist orthodoxy within the Party and to enforce Communism to foster social equality in the country, Mao Zedong inaugurated mass mobilization of urban Chinese youth as part of the movement to eliminate differences between town and city, workers and peasants, and mental and manual labor. Schools were closed and students were encouraged/forced to join the Red Guard units, which denunciated and persecuted Chinese teachers and intellectuals, and engaged in widespread book burnings. At that time, moral education became a tool for indoctrination. Emphasis was placed on passivity, conformity, and obedience to authority. These values were guided by Maoist doctrine as they were expounded in *The Little Red Book*, otherwise known as *Quotations of Chairman Mao*, of which every Chinese citizen was issued a copy. The social movement soon turned into violence and resulted in widespread factional conflicts in all walks of life, especially during 1967–1969. The ensuing chaos paralyzed China politically and significantly affected the country economically and socially. Due to the close association that moral education had with these events during the Cultural Revolution, there was a general sense of disdain towards moral education until its next overhaul in the late 1970s.

Implementation of Reform and Opening Up Policy

In the period following the Cultural Revolution, the development of the education system in China mainly has been oriented to the advancement of economic modernization. In the late 1970s, the Chinese government (under the leadership of Deng Xiaoping) implemented the "reform and opening up" policy. By opening the country to the rest of the world, it aimed to move China towards becoming a modern, more democratic, and developed country (Qi & Tang, 2004). Moral education was viewed as the foundation of the Four Modernizations (agriculture, industry, national defense, science and technology) in China at that time, and vocational and technical skills were considered paramount in meeting China's modernization goals. Among the notable initiatives to improve the country was a 1985 plan to reform the education system. Nine years of compulsory education was called for. Aligned with policy change, emphasis was shifted away from politics and towards economic reconstruction. Moral education practices were also shifted/renewed accordingly, to meet this change in policy and social needs. On the other hand, the formation of a market economy in China not only promoted economic growth; it also brought with it an increased exposure to modern ideas, values, and beliefs. Internet and mass media allowed unprecedented levels of communication and promoted the exchange of ideas, especially within urban areas. The rise in popularity of contemporary concepts such as individual rights, freedom, and democracy, interpreted in various ways, was being recognized and revered by many youth. Hence, many of the traditional ideas/values (e.g., hierarchical social system of interpersonal dependence) and politicized moral education were no longer seen as appropriate for the new social arrangements and orientation of values. Instead, modernization called for a reorientation of educational priorities. Emphases were shifted to cultivate personal qualities such as independence, self-motivation, and creativity in students. Moral education was no longer solely a political apparatus. Mottos such as "All we do is for the students and for all of the students" became more common in schools (Qi & Tang, 2004). Taking teacher-student relationships as an example, dialogue and discussion gradually permeated the classroom, replacing the traditional authoritarian and hierarchical classroom (Qi & Tang, 2004). At the same time as the modernization and marketization of the country was underway, there appeared an "ideological vacuum" and a decline in morality. Contemporary problems of corruption and a widening gap between the standard of living of modern, urban centers and rural areas exacerbated the sense of crisis. Neo-conservatives saw the need to turn "back to tradition" and called for reinstating Confucian traditions, especially its sense of social responsibility and focus on moral virtues, as a foundation on which to rebuild Chinese cultural identity (Chen, 1997; Lee & Ho, 2005).

CURRENT CURRICULUM ON MORAL EDUCATION IN CHINA

The rapid modernization, socioeconomic development and globalization, together with increasing implementation and practice of "quality-oriented education" brought about further educational reform (Zhan & Ning, 2004). The latest *Guidelines for Ideology and Morality in full-time compulsory education* (PRCMOE, 2003) were fully implemented nationally in primary schools headed by Prof. Lu Jie and in junior high schools headed by Prof. Zhu Xiaoman in Fall 2006. In this reform, while the collective and social dimensions (ideological and political elements) were still very much upheld, much emphasis also was placed on the development of personal moral qualities and moral judgment abilities, and the psychological health of the students as individuals. These changes addressed the needs of educating young citizens in order to develop personal qualities that would match the features of Chinese market economy. Hence, the focus of moral education shifted from political socialization to the promotion of individual growth. In order to meet these ends, the new curriculum promoted a learning style that was characterized by "autonomy, co-operation, and exploration." It addressed the deficit of the previous curriculum, namely the lack of relevance in students' lives and attempted to increase students' motivation for the subject matter by emphasizing active learning about matters that were practical and pertinent to the students (Lee & Ho, 2005; Zhan & Ning, 2004). Being student-centered was the core concept of the new curriculum. The curriculum also adapted its teaching content according to the students' cognitive and moral development, gradually expanding the consideration of the life world relationships of the students—e.g., from the Growing Self, to the Relations between Self and Others, and then to the Relations between Self, Collective, State, and Society (Zhan & Ning, 2004). These themes were integrated with the four subject areas, namely Mental Health, Morality, Law, and National Conditions Education, and were implemented in every grade.

While *Guidelines* expounded an idealized vision of the new moral education curriculum, turning theory into practice and bringing the essence of the curriculum into play in the classroom is a task with many difficulties and obstacles. This is particularly the case for teachers who have not received training to better understand and utilize the skills that are needed to deliver the new curriculum. Instead, many maintain a traditional teacher's role and continue with an indoctrinating approach that only allows unidirectional knowledge transmission in the classroom (Zhu & Liu, 2004). Moreover, despite the emphasis on balancing knowledge and practice, many teachers keep devoting the majority of their time to textbook knowledge versus real-life practice. There is also a downplaying of moral education by teachers or parents, as the educational system in China is heavily geared toward preparing students for the national standardized examinations that determine students' eligibility for university, and moral education is not part of the subject matter of these exams (Zhan & Ning, 2004). As argued long ago by Dewey (1916), democratic education must be a part of the whole school climate, but attempts by educational innovators to give full life to the democratic spirit of the new curriculum are often greeted with great suspicion. One example is the citizenship training program in Shenzhen Nanshan Affiliated School, which was initiated by the principal, Li Qingming. He pushed for the idea of Equality and Respect, launched an "Election Month" for students to learn about elections, and set up monthly meetings to allow teachers to listen to students' questions/criticisms so that students could have a channel to express their views and learn about public affairs participation in action. However, his approach has been questioned and criticized by many parents and educators (Liu & Lin, 2010). He was publicly known as a controversial person and was often seen by education leaders and colleagues as "strange" (he was often referred to by them as "madman"). One of the criticisms leveled against him was that he did not use his time properly to teach, and instead used it to make things "messy." Parents expressed worries that letting their child participate in these activities (e.g., being a representative in the students' association) would affect their academic performance and hurt their chances of getting into a good university.

An additional issue concerns the enormous complexity of the curriculum, and at times, tensions within parts of the new curriculum itself. The current moral education curriculum is extremely heterogeneous, and draws on both "newer" democratic values as well as more traditional values, sometimes in an uneasy mixture. For example, the new curriculum includes a combination of values drawn from the older ideological approach to moral education (e.g., patriotism, collectivism, and socialism) as well as traditional Chinese moral values of honesty, respect for others, self-discipline, and even "knowing shame" (Fung, 1999), along with "modern" values such as open-mindedness and a pioneering spirit (Zhan & Ning, 2004). According to Zhan & Ning (2004), the goals of the new curriculum are to help students to be "independent and critical in thinking and questioning" and to establish in the classroom a democratic environment in which students can "exchange their own ideas." Yet, in addition, other goals of the new curriculum (Zhan & Ning, 2004) are: to teach students to "cherish the collective interest," to "habitually follow the law," to show "filial piety to parents," and to "increasingly love the Communist Party of China and the motherland" in order to "make them understand that, led by the CPC, the route to socialism with Chinese characteristics will improve people's living standards and make possible personal goals" that are also "in agreement with the common ideal." By any measure, this is a rather tall order for any moral education program to carry, with a lot of potential contradictions to resolve in practice and for a complex and changing social reality as in China today (M. Li, 2011). Cheung and Pan (2006) have described the current situation in China as essentially one of "regulated individualism," in which a much larger space has been granted by the State for individual autonomy in the personal sphere and, as we have seen, in school classrooms, however, "when individuals exercise their autonomy, they are not expected to challenge the social and ideological basis of the collective" (p. 47). Other Chinese educational theorists (P. Li et al., 2004) have noted that moral education remains in a complex and changing relation with the official political ideology and its aim of political indoctrination. How these tensions ultimately may be addressed for China's future social and political development remains to be seen.

Other tensions involve how notions of individual rights and personal freedoms are being incorporated and theorized within the curriculum and elsewhere (e.g., within societal institutional and legal reforms). Within official Communist Party ideology, individual rights and freedoms are seen largely conditionally and in utilitarian or instrumentalist terms, for example, as a means to create citizens who will have the characteristics necessary to strengthen the State and improve the economic development of society (Cheung & Pan, 2006; Peerenboom, 2002). This utilitarian and conditional approach to autonomy, however, may be in tension with the new emphasis in the Chinese moral education curriculum on self-development and psychological health. As we will see later in the chapter, autonomy may be more than an historical or social fact emerging out of changing societal conditions; rather, autonomy may be a universal human need that is importantly related to individuals' psychological health and well-being.

Finally, the official moral education curriculum itself is not the only way in which morality is socialized and taught within the schools (Zhu & Liu, 2004). Extracurricular activities also play a major role, and these activities are often designed to enhance group solidarity and to inculcate associated values, such as patriotism, through means such as routines, modeling, and rewards. For example, Zhu and Liu (2004) describe the morning meeting ritual in Chinese schools in which the national flag is raised every Monday. During this meeting, three students who are believed to have "well-rounded development" are selected to raise the flag. These students announce to other students the reasons they were selected in order to encourage others to behave well so that they may also gain such an honor. Following this, the principal or sometimes another student makes a patriotic speech. In other such activities, student groups, such as the Youth League or Young Pioneers (student Communist Party associations), organize class activities that also have moral and patriotic educative functions, sometimes incorporating rewards, medals, and other honors associated with demonstrations of virtues or desirable characteristics. These approaches, and the social hierarchies they may create, typically involve "heteronomous" moral education methods that, although consistent with the older ideological moral education, may run counter to the principles of equality and critical reflection meant to form the heart of the new, democratic moral education curriculum (P. Li et al., 2004). In reality, Chinese students thus experience a diverse range of moral education efforts in schools, each with varying views of the agent (active versus passive, students as equals versus as subordinates) that may not always be consistent in underlying philosophy or values.

CONFLICTS, TENSIONS, AND HETERODOXY: PARALLELS WITH WESTERN MORAL AND DEMOCRATIC EDUCATION

In the previous section, we have provided an overview of the historical development of moral education philosophies and practices in China from Confucianism through the Maoist Communist era to the more recent period of "opening up" characterized by enormous economic and cultural transformations. The contemporary state of Chinese moral education can be described as one of complexity, heterogeneity, and even contradiction, with more traditional practices and philosophical approaches enduring and coexisting alongside more recent democratic and child-centered educational innovations. Indeed, many parallels may be drawn between this state of affairs and that of contemporary moral and civics education efforts in the West. Western educational theorists have frequently drawn a contrast between character and civics education (e.g., Osborne, 2004; Sears & Hughes, 2006), each having a different perspective on the overall aims of education and on the child as a moral agent in this process. Character education has traditionally been concerned with instilling in the child those traits deemed morally desirable by society, such as honesty, compassion, duty, loyalty, love of country, and a good work ethic. As Osborne (2004, p. 13) states, the character education approach has "equated the good citizen with the good person, the man or woman who helps others, respects other people's rights, obeys the laws, is suitably patriotic, and the like." In accordance with this approach, there is an emphasis on molding citizens to become productive contributors to the workplace, and the emphasis is on duties and responsibilities over rights. The pedagogical model implicit and sometimes explicit in this approach is a top-down emphasis on fixed social traditions and values transmitted to the child through routines, habits, role models, and repetition (Schaps, Shaeffer, & McDonnell, 2001). In contrast, civics education emphasizes the rights and duties of democratic citizenship, with the goal of helping children to become critical and reflective citizens who can contribute to public democratic institutions and themselves help shape social change. Within this perspective, children's own rational autonomy is given center stage, and moral education efforts accordingly stress "open ended" problems, deliberation and debate, and the need for active participation in democratic social life.

Given the democratic political culture of Western societies and the emphasis on personal autonomy and rights, it might be expected that civics education would be the dominant approach in moral education in North America, but many reviews over several decades have suggested otherwise (Helwig & Yang, in press). Berman (1997) has noted that much of what is taught in civics classes in the United States and Canada consists of dry, disembodied facts and definitions, usually centering on the structure and workings of government. Controversial issues and conflicts tend to be downplayed or even avoided, and the role of the citizen is largely relegated to voting (Caroll et al., 1989). In both elementary and secondary schools, lectures followed by recitation or individual work comprise the main form of civics instruction (Berman, 1997). This state of affairs is not limited to North America. Strikingly, a survey of 90,000 students in 28 countries found that only 16% of students stated that their civics teachers *sometimes* allowed class discussions (Torney-Purta, Lehmann, Oswald, & Schultz, 2001). The prevailing approach to civic education in many countries, including Western democracies, appears to be ill-suited to stimulating students' critical thinking and reflection and engaging their actual moral reasoning.

Western educational theorists have cited several reasons for the failure to adopt a more constructivist and democratic form of civics education, and these reasons are strikingly similar to those proffered by Chinese educators in discussing problems with implementing the new moral education curriculum in China (Zhan & Ning, 2004). First, many teachers and administrators themselves may hold a more traditional view of education focusing on the need to prepare students for conformity to adult roles and institutions, rather than instilling a critical or democratic consciousness. Teachers and administrators may fear ceding control of the classroom to students and the ramifications of this for maintaining classroom order. There is also a tendency for teachers to avoid controversial issues because of fear over retribution from parent organizations or administrators (Berman, 1997). Time pressures and a focus on standardized tests and "objective" outcomes may work against implementing more student-centered teaching methods. And finally, many teachers may feel ill-prepared to handle constructivist methods in their classrooms, having little experience or training with such methods themselves (Helwig & Yang, in press).

ILLUMINATING THE TENSIONS: RECENT RESEARCH ON AUTONOMY, DEMOCRATIC CLASSROOMS, AND STUDENTS' PERSPECTIVES IN CHINA AND IN WESTERN CULTURES

These tensions between the different philosophies and approaches to moral education evident in both China and the West probably reflect the inevitable differences among the perspectives of the various stakeholders in educational systems (e.g., teachers, students, administrators, governments). Teachers and authorities may be more concerned with transmitting specific content or with maintaining order, whereas students may be eager to try out their developing sense of autonomy in educational realms, including in engagement with relevant but at times controversial moral or social issues. In support of the latter, research on conceptions of moral education among North American students has found that, beginning in the elementary school years and increasingly with age, students tend to prefer constructivist methods (e.g., class discussions) to top-down or teacher-centered approaches such as lectures (Helwig, Ryerson, & Prencipe, 2008). Furthermore, students who experience more democratic classrooms (those with greater opportunities for student involvement and choice) have been found to have fewer symptoms of anxiety or depression and exhibit less conduct problems than those who are taught in a more authoritarian or traditional manner (Way, Reddy, & Rhodes, 2007).

This process appears to reflect an extension into the educational sphere of a more general developmental phenomenon in which children's desire for autonomy expands in tandem with their developing competencies and abilities (e.g., Erikson, 1968; Helwig, 2006b; Nucci, 2001; Smetana, 2011). Some theorists have proposed that autonomy is a universal and basic psychological need, necessary for optimal human flourishing and functioning (Ryan & Deci, 2011). Autonomy here is meant to involve the exercise of will and choice, along with the autonomous endorsement of the choices one makes, rather than "independence" from others as it is sometimes characterized (Kagitcibasi, 2005). Thus, individuals can be both autonomous (having opportunities to exercise their will and choice) and interdependent and therefore connected with others; indeed, optimal human flourishing and well-being is believed to be associated with the satisfaction of both needs for autonomy and relatedness with others (Ryan & Deci, 2011). When both needs are supported and met in social and institutional settings, the character of interpersonal (including student-teacher) relations becomes more one of mutual respect (Piaget, 1932), a cornerstone of democratic social systems (Dewey, 1916; Helwig & McNeil, 2011). Seen in this way, calls for greater acknowledgment of children's autonomy and participation in moral educational settings voiced by both Chinese and Western educational theorists (and attempts to instantiate it in the new curriculum in China) may be interpreted to reflect an emerging recognition of the importance of children's autonomy by educators and policy makers in diverse cultural settings, and the necessity of coordinating these psychological requirements with complex institutional goals and values.

This conclusion, however, is likely to be at odds with certain popular social scientific theories that have maintained that cultures have widely varying notions of self and morality that may be fundamentally incommensurable (Haidt, 2012; Shweder, Mahapatra, & Miller, 1987). In particular, the cultural universality of autonomy and rights, along with their meaning and implications for social and moral development in diverse cultural settings, have been the subject of recent debates in social scientific circles. For example, some theorists working within a perspective known as "cultural psychology" have emphasized the cultural shaping of human conceptions of self and morality and their concomitant variations across cultures (e.g., Miller, 1994). With regard to autonomy, some have argued that autonomy follows a different developmental pathway in different societies, with individual choice, equality, and personal decision making a hallmark of children's development and socialization in "Western" or "individualistic" societies, whereas in other societies (including non-Western cultures such as China) autonomy is believed to be realized through increasing conformity to received social duties, the dictates of authorities, and the desires of groups to which individuals have strong identifications (Greenfield, Keller, Fuligni, & Maynard, 2003). The conclusion that human autonomy in the form of personal choice is universally valued, for example, has been argued to be a product of a particular focus in psychological research on samples from Western, highly educated, industrialized, rich, and democratic societies (or "WEIRD" peoples, see Henrich, Heine, & Norenzayan, 2010). In contrast, individuals in the rest of the world are believed to prize social harmony, adhering to received social duties and following the group, in accordance with a more sociocentric or interdependent self (Markus & Kitiyama, 1991—but see Miller, Rekha, & Chakravarthy, 2011, for a recent "middle" ground that acknowledges universal needs for autonomy along with cultural variations in how these needs may be expressed). Following this line of thinking, then, the importance of acknowledging and incorporating student voices and the emphasis on student autonomy and rights that underlies constructivist moral educational approaches would be seen as a largely "Western" conception of education that would not be expected to be valued highly in traditional and collectivist societies such as China. If these notions are now being incorporated into Chinese moral education, as we have seen in our historical overview, this may only be due to the external influence of forces of Westernization as China has opened up to the world and (perhaps inadvertently) allowed these ideas to seep into its educational systems.

We do not, however, believe that the conflicts and tensions that we have identified within Chinese moral education can be explained away as merely the incorporation of foreign ideological perspectives ("ideological pollution"). Rather, we believe that they have their source in indigenous conflicts and tensions of the same general sort that underlie similar debates and disagreements in Western educational contexts. First of all, we note that many Chinese students expressed very positive views about the new curriculum in the initial trial experiments conducted by Chinese educational researchers before its general implementation (An, 2004; Zhan & Ning, 2004). Second, as in the West, there remain many conflicting perspectives within China on the new role of students and teachers, with similar reservations about the degree of teacher preparedness and concerns over the inclusion of controversial topics as documented in Western educational settings (Zhu & Liu, 2004). In devising the new curriculum, Chinese educators looked to a variety of societies (Western and Asian), with the goal of taking from each what they felt was useful in addressing perceived problems and deficiencies with the existing Chinese moral educational system. Although student autonomy was expanded and incorporated, often in original and even radical ways, at the same time, indigenous Chinese ideological systems (e.g., Deng Xiaoping and Marxist Communist thought) were retained and also given prominence, especially in regard to political education. Rather than reflecting ideological colonization by Western theorizing, these reforms may be seen as arising from indigenous issues and problems (new and old) that the previous moral educational system was perceived as failing to adequately address.

We believe that this interpretation also is more consistent with the growing body of moral developmental research that has been conducted in China over the past decade or so (see Helwig, Ruck, & Peterson-Badali, 2014, for a review). The picture emerging from this body of research is that Chinese children from a variety of settings within China, in both urban and traditional rural environments, develop ideas about personal autonomy and rights, and use these notions to define the boundaries of legitimate regulation between the individual, authorities, and the group. For instance, Yau and Smetana (2003) examined Chinese adolescents' and their mothers' views about familial conflicts and disputes in Hong Kong and a mainland Chinese city (Shenzhen). Chinese adolescents not only experienced frequent conflicts with parents (often over issues such as schoolwork, chores, and interpersonal relationships) but also differed with parents in their perspectives on these disputes. Chinese adolescents frequently supported their positions with references to the importance of being able to pursue their desires and choices and exercise their freedoms. Parents, on the other hand, frequently appealed to authority or family rules or conventions, or concerns about children's safety (prudence), when justifying their perspectives. These patterns were replicated in a subsequent study (Chen-Gaddini, 2012) that included a sample from a rural Chinese community. In addition, Chen-Gaddini (2012) asked adolescents about how such disputes were settled, and found that adolescents were more likely than parents to report that disputes were settled in a unilateral way, with the parents' views prevailing. When disputes were settled unilaterally (by parental authority), rather than through negotiation and compromise, Chinese adolescents were more likely to judge the resolutions as unfair. Moreover, both studies (Chen-Gaddini, 2012; Yau & Smetana, 2003) found that Chinese adolescents' appeals to autonomy and personal choice increased with age. These studies are consistent with developmental theories (e.g., Erikson, 1968; Nucci, 2001; Smetana, 2011) that suggest that the expansion of autonomy in adolescence is a universal process and that this process is regulated through reciprocal interactions, negotiations, and conflicts with parental or other authority figures. They are not consistent, however, with the view that autonomy takes a different form in "collectivist" or non-Western cultures or that adolescents within these societies simply conform to authority or existing social norms or expectations in an uncritical fashion.

Perhaps most striking in this regard was the finding that appeals to autonomy and personal choice were *greater* in the more traditional rural setting (Chen-Gaddini, 2012). Although rural settings have changed less than urban settings, both economically and culturally, and have much less exposure to Western influences (Tang & Parish, 2000), adolescents within these environments not only develop notions of autonomy based on personal choice and freedom, but appeal to these notions in instances of disputes or conflicts with parents even more than those who are socialized in more modern, urban (and possibly more "Westernized") settings. This finding is consistent with the notion that a heightened sense of autonomy may arise when cultural practices place too many restrictions on people's basic needs for autonomy and personal choice (Helwig, 2006b; Lau, 1992; Lo, Helwig, Chen, Ohashi, & Cheng, 2011). Taken together, these findings suggest that autonomy is not something that is simply absorbed directly from cultural practices but is constructed out of the complex interplay of individual psychological needs and how these needs may be met or thwarted in different societies and in more proximal environments within societies such as the family or school (Chirkov & Ryan, 2001).

As noted, the new curriculum within China reflects the incorporation of greater student choice and involvement, and more room for class discussions, including even over social issues that may be considered controversial. Thus, the form of autonomy instantiated in the new curriculum reflects a recognition of children's "intellectual rights" (Moshman, 1986) to freedom of expression and belief. These particular rights are often characterized as "Western" notions more associated with liberal democratic political systems. However, recent research has shown that Chinese adolescents also understand and apply these rights when reasoning about conflicts with authorities in school and family settings. For example, Lahat, Helwig, Yang, Tan, and Liu (2009) investigated urban and rural Chinese adolescents' conceptions of various "self-determination" rights, such as freedom of speech, freedom of religion, and privacy, as well as other rights associated with children's psychological and physical well-being. With age, Chinese adolescents in both urban and rural settings increasingly affirmed children's self-determination rights to freedom of speech (e.g., whether it would be acceptable for a school principal to prohibit a high school student from publishing an article in the school newspaper critical of the school rules) and freedom of religion (whether a child's parents, who are atheists, could prohibit a child from belonging to a religion of the child's choice). In supporting these rights, Chinese adolescents appealed to individual rights, autonomy, and universal freedoms. These findings show that Chinese adolescents understand personal choice and freedom as extending to freedom of conscience and expression, key foundational concepts for a truly democratic civic and moral education.

Other recent research on Chinese adolescents' concepts of democratic decision making has yielded some interesting findings directly relevant to curricular issues in school settings. In one study (Helwig, Arnold, Tan, & Boyd, 2003), Chinese adolescents from three settings (a rural village, a small city, and a large, modern city) were asked about different ways to make decisions in a variety of settings, including the peer group, family, and school. The specific decisions were varied, and adolescents were asked to evaluate the acceptability of making decisions in a purely authority-based fashion (teachers or parents decide unilaterally), by majority rule (a vote, with children having equal say as adult authorities) or by consensus (everyone, adults and children must agree). One of the decisions concerned whether parents should require a child to take special tutoring on weekends to boost the child's grades in school. This is a common practice in China, where parents are typically highly involved in decisions over academic matters. However, it was found that most Chinese adolescents from all three settings rejected parents making this decision alone. Many of them endorsed consensus because it would require the child's assent. In their reasoning, Chinese adolescents appealed to the child's right to make the decision and to the negative effects of coercion upon the child's motivation, psychological health, and well-being. Here are two examples of characteristic responses (both from senior high school students):

> "Tutoring will only be effective when the child wants to learn. Also, the child has the right to arrange her own time. Parents should give the child the right to veto [if parents make the decision unilaterally]."

> "Many things, such as natural inclination, creativity, and freedom, are strangled because of this."

A second example from this research pertained to how the school curriculum (what the child learns in class) should be decided. Although the curriculum in China is decided centrally (by educational authorities), Chinese adolescents nonetheless tended to prefer democratic decision making (such as by consensus or majority rule) because it would lead to overall agreement and stimulate children's learning and motivation. Many of them explicitly took a critical perspective on curricula decided solely by educational authorities, as reflected in the following examples:

> "Education authorities' decisions are only based on examinations, and make us learn the boring texts. As to today's education, it develops one's interest. No to education authorities' decision!"

> "This [authority decides] will make kids passive in action.... When kids want to learn a subject, they must be interested in it. As it goes, interest is the best teacher. This way [majority decides] will make them learn actively."

This study (Helwig et al., 2003) was conducted before the new moral education curriculum was implemented and was directed at the curriculum in general (not moral education in particular), so we do not know how these adolescents might have responded to the newer educational reforms. However, these studies reveal that Chinese adolescents clearly value their own autonomy and personal choice, recognize the importance of intellectual freedoms such as freedom of expression, and endorse more active, autonomy-supportive forms of teaching over rote memorization or traditional, top-down approaches. These findings also suggest that the curriculum reforms discussed earlier have arisen in response to long-standing issues and problems recognized by stakeholders (e.g., Chinese students themselves) and also by many progressive Chinese educators who are concerned with incorporating students' perspectives and voices (M. Li, 2011; P. Li et al., 2004).

Other research on Chinese children's conceptions of moral education practices used in the family suggests that Chinese children take a critical perspective on more traditional Chinese socialization methods based on shaming or "psychological control" (Barber, 1996). For example, Helwig, To, Wang, Liu, and Yang (in press) examined urban and rural Chinese children's and adolescents' (7–13 years of age) judgments about a variety of hypothetical moral socialization practices used by parents when a child commits a moral transgression (i.e., hits another child and takes the child's possession). Overall, in both urban and rural Chinese settings and in a Canadian comparison sample, children preferred parental use of what Hoffman (2000) has termed "induction" (or parental reasoning accompanied by encouragement of perspective taking and the child's consideration of the consequences of their actions on others) over other socialization practices such as parental shaming involving negative comparisons with other children (e.g., appeals for the child to be more like other children who behave better), appeals to group-based social shame (e.g., the family "losing face"), and love withdrawal (explicit withdrawal of affection), despite the fact that rural Chinese children saw these other types of parental practices (shaming and love withdrawal) as much more commonly used by parents than did Canadian children. Across both settings, when asked to justify their evaluations, children, with age, increasingly viewed shaming and love withdrawal as psychologically harmful forms of discipline and they preferred induction or reasoning because of its perceived ability to stimulate moral reflection, empathy, and understanding. Chinese children did not support the types of shaming practices used and endorsed by parents in ethnographic and observational studies, frequently argued to be a part of traditional Chinese moral socialization (Fung, 1999), although they sometimes recognized that parents used these practices because they might be effective in achieving immediate compliance. These findings illustrate the necessity of tapping into children's own views about different types of moral education (rather than merely "what is done") in order to gain a complete understanding of how cultural practices may be assimilated, evaluated, and sometimes critiqued by those occupying different positions in social hierarchies (Turiel, 2006).

AUTONOMY, DEMOCRATIC ENVIRONMENT, AND PSYCHOLOGICAL WELL-BEING

The research discussed so far has shown that Chinese adolescents develop views about the child as a rational moral agent that need to be adequately incorporated into moral education efforts, whether in the family or the school. Chinese adolescents also endorse and apply democratic concepts such as freedom of expression and active participation in decision making that form the core of a truly democratic education (Dewey, 1916). As noted earlier, research in the West has found that educational environments that incorporate these elements are associated with more positive psychological outcomes in students, such as less depression or anxiety or conduct disorders (Way et al., 2007). Do these relations also apply in a non-Western society such as China, especially in more traditional, rural settings? Recent research suggests that they do (Jia et al., 2009; To, Helwig, & Yang, 2012). For example, To et al. (2012) examined democratic climate, defined as school or family environments that allow for greater opportunities for student involvement in decision making, and authority support for students' freedom of expression and due process rights, and how these perceived features of school classrooms or families relate to a variety of dimensions of adolescent psychological well-being, including anxiety, depression, and overall life satisfaction. Adolescent perceptions of democratic climate in both family and school settings was found to be positively related to adolescents' self-reported psychological well-being (i.e., predicted lower levels of anxiety and depression, and greater overall life satisfaction). Furthermore, these relations between democratic school and family environment and psychological well-being were just as strong (correlations in the range of 0.2–0.4) in the more traditional rural setting (in a Northern and mountainous area of Guangdong Province) as in the large, modern city (Guangzhou), so they could not be accounted for simply by level of modernization or "Westernization."

SOME LESSONS FOR THE WEST FROM CHINA

These findings from cross-cultural research are broadly compatible with the highly positive student survey findings generated by Chinese education researchers who investigated the reception received by the new, more autonomy-supportive moral education curriculum (An, 2004). To be sure, these changes in the Chinese moral education curriculum incorporating student autonomy exist alongside the retention of other, more traditional educational practices, and so the transformation of Chinese moral education is piecemeal and remains in relations of tension with other aspects of the curriculum (and there are undoubtedly local variations in how well teachers have adhered to these changes or in the extent to which they have wholeheartedly put them into practice). We stress, however, that our argument should not be misconstrued to suggest a straightforward, historical progression, with China at an earlier "stage" and now only beginning to incorporate, in fledgling fashion, practices long in use in Western education settings (although this may be true in some instances). Instead, our intention is to argue that the need for student autonomy in moral educational settings is universal (despite divergences in cultural values and historical patterns) and that its actual incorporation into educational practices and settings inevitably will occur in different ways in different societies at different times.

Indeed, China currently may be in a rather unique position as a society with a centralized government heavily invested in the moral education of its citizens and where educators thereby have the resources and opportunities to experiment on a large scale with a greater variety of curricular practices than their counterparts in Western societies. China may even be seen as a hotbed of moral educational theorizing and innovation, when compared to the highly politicized and sometimes even ossified educational climate found in some Western countries. And so there may be many opportunities for Western educational theorists to learn from Chinese moral educational innovations as the democratic values long-prized in the West are tested and evaluated under very different cultural circumstances.

Perhaps strikingly, the new Chinese moral educational curriculum may sometimes incorporate student autonomy, reflection, and democratic processes in ways that may be considered radical or daring even within Western educational systems. As an example, consider the following take-home exercise incorporated in the new Chinese moral education curriculum designed to foster greater understanding and communication between students and their parents (Zhan & Ning, 2004). In this exercise, children and their parents are given different hypothetical types of relationship styles between children and parents to evaluate (e.g., ranging from strictly controlling to democratically negotiating), and they are asked to express agreement or disagreement with one another's choices, to state their reasons, and then to engage in a subsequent discussion about the points of agreement and disagreement. As a moral education exercise embodying constructivist developmental principles, one could hardly imagine a practical application that is more in line with both the spirit and the findings of developmental research conducted in North America on familial discussions and their important role in stimulating moral development (e.g., Walker, Hennig, & Krettenauer, 2000; Walker & Taylor, 1991). But it may be amusing and perhaps even humbling for the Western reader to contemplate the reception (politically, and by local school boards and parent-teacher associations) that such a pedagogical exercise would likely receive were it to be mandated on a national basis and carried out by the public schools within a society such as the United States. The Chinese "experiment" in the new moral educational curriculum may afford an opportunity for Western educational theorists to reflect on the shortcomings of their own social institutions, including ways to remove institutional inertia or other impediments, in order to reinvigorate efforts to foster democratic schools and families in Western societies. The ultimate lesson of these contrasts may be that democracy is something that is lived "in the trenches," within schools and families, in ways that often bring it into tension with authority and received social hierarchies; it is not to be gauged merely by a simple analysis of the contrasting features of political systems (e.g., China versus the US).

CONCLUSIONS

In sum, we argue that human autonomy is a universal psychological need whose instantiation is directly relevant to democratic moral education efforts such as those found in China and elsewhere. At the same time, there are complexities and conflicts inevitably encountered in any attempt to realize this need within diverse educational settings. Although the particulars of the cultural and historical contexts are certainly different, some universal processes appear to be at work in both Chinese and Western moral education efforts, and the parallels here are worth restating. First, conceptions of moral education are naturally heterogeneous as they are often based on incompatible fundamental assumptions about the particular values that should be taught or instilled as well as the process by which moral education is best realized. One approach, associated with traditional moral education in both China and the West, emphasizes inculcation of a particular set of moral values or character traits, such as patriotism or group solidarity, often through mechanisms such as extrinsic rewards and routines (e.g., the recitation of the US Pledge of Allegiance; the Chinese "flag raising ceremony"). The emphasis here is on creating a well-behaved citizen, one who replicates societal values and fits in to the existing social order to lead a productive life (often seen from an economic point of view but also understood as in service of the group or society). The other approach sees moral education as founded on the recognition of student autonomy (expressed in accordance with developmentally appropriate capacities), and prioritizes the cultivation of moral reasoning and reflection capacities. This may involve the formation of a critical consciousness that can be applied by students to help them to navigate a complex and often changing social reality, like that confronted by China today. The latter approach recognizes that students themselves construct their social worlds and are often charged with the difficult task of negotiating, or even resolving, received contradictions in societal values, priorities, and goals. The main purpose of a truly democratic moral education, then, is not to provide students with a particular set of values (although some values may be better suited to this purpose than others), but to give students a set of skills that will enable them to function autonomously in a democratic social order that includes opportunities to exercise their voice to help shape their society (and not just being shaped by it).

Of course, the democratic approach to moral and civic education is never easy to implement, and in diverse cultures (China, North America) it confronts many similar institutional pressures such as standardized testing and an educational system that prioritizes "results" or social utility over student engagement, not to mention educational authorities who themselves may differ in their commitment to democratic education and their willingness to put this model of moral education into practice within their schools or classrooms. As we have seen, these tensions may raise questions over how to cultivate student motivation, and concerns over student perceptions of the relevance or irrelevance of moral education to their lives. Ultimately, students' willingness to accept or to reject the different types of moral education efforts that they experience may rest on how these tensions are resolved. As the emerging research on psychological outcomes suggests, democratic moral education may not only be an ethical imperative valued and endorsed in its own right by many people in diverse cultures. In China as elsewhere, it could well turn out to be an important means of achieving individual—and by extension societal—health and well-being.

REFERENCES

Ai, J. (2008). The refunctioning of Confucianism: The mainland Chinese intellectual response to Confucianism since the 1980s. *Issues and Studies, 44*, 29–78.

An, Y. (2004). Experimental moral education textbook series. *Journal of Moral Education, 33*, 625–629.

Barber, B. K. (1996). Parental psychological control: Revisiting a neglected construct. *Child Development, 67*, 3296–3319.

Berman, S. (1997). *Children's social consciousness and the development of social responsibility.* Albany, NY: SUNY Press.

Carroll, J. D., Broadnax, W., Contreras, G., Mann, T., Ornstein, N., & Stiehm, J. (1989). *We the people: A review of US government and civics textbooks.* Washington, DC: People for the American Way.

Chen, F. (1997). Order and stability in social transition: Neoconservative political thought in post-1989 China. *The China Quarterly, 151*, 595–613.

Chen-Gaddini, M. (2012). Chinese mothers and adolescents' views of authority and autonomy: A study of parent–adolescent conflict in urban and rural China. *Child Development, 83*, 1846–1852.

Cheung, K. W., & Pan, S. (2006). Transition of moral education in China: Towards regulated individualism. *Citizenship Teaching and Learning, 2*, 37–50.

Chirkov, V. I., & Ryan, R. M. (2001). Parent and teacher autonomy-support in Russian and US adolescents: Common effects on well-being and academic motivation. *Journal of Cross-Cultural Psychology, 32*, 618–635.

de Bary, W. T., & Weiming, T. (Eds.). (1998). *Confucianism and human rights.* New York: Columbia University Press.

Dewey, J. (1916). *Democracy and education.* New York: Macmillan.

Erikson, E. (1968). *Identity, youth, and crisis.* New York: W. W. Norton.

Fung, H. (1999). Becoming a moral child: The socialization of shame among young Chinese children. *Ethos, 27*, 180–209.

Greenfield, P. M., Keller, H., Fuligni, A., & Maynard, A. (2003). Cultural pathways through universal development. *Annual Review of Psychology, 54*, 461–490.

Haidt, J. (2012). *The righteous mind: Why good people are divided by politics and religion.* New York: Pantheon.

Helwig, C. C. (2006a). Rights, civil liberties, and democracy across cultures. In M. Killen, & J. G. Smetana (Eds.), *Handbook of moral development* (1st ed., pp. 185–210). Mahwah, NJ: Erlbaum.

Helwig, C. C. (2006b). The development of personal autonomy throughout cultures. *Cognitive Development, 21*, 458–473.

Helwig, C. C., Arnold, M. L., Tan, D., & Boyd, D. (2003). Chinese adolescents' reasoning about democratic and authority-based decision making in peer, family, and school contexts. *Child Development, 74*, 783–800.

Helwig, C. C., & McNeil, J. (2011). The development of conceptions of personal autonomy, rights, and democracy, and their relation to psychological well-being. In V. I. Chirkov, R. M. Ryan, & K. M. Sheldon (Eds.), *Human autonomy in cross-cultural context: Perspectives on the psychology of agency, freedom, and well-being* (pp. 241–256). New York: Springer.

Helwig, C. C., Ruck, M. D., & Peterson-Badali, M. (2014). Rights, civil liberties, and democracy. In M. Killen & J. G. Smetana (Eds.), *Handbook of moral development* (2nd ed, pp. 46–69). New York: Psychology Press.

Helwig, C. C., Ryerson, R., & Prencipe, A. (2008). Children's, adolescents', and adults' judgments and reasoning about different methods of teaching values. *Cognitive Development, 23*, 119–135.

Helwig, C. C., To, S., Wang, Q., Liu, C., & Yang, S. (in press). Judgments and reasoning about parental discipline involving induction and psychological control in China and Canada. Child Development.

Helwig, C. C., & Yang, S. (in press). Toward a truly democratic civics education. In R. Shaffer & K. Durkin (Eds.), *Blackwell handbook of developmental psychology in practice*. Oxford: Blackwell.

Henrich, J., Heine, S. J., & Norenzayan, A. (2010). The weirdest people in the world. *Behavioral and Brain Sciences, 33*, 61–83.

Hoffman, M. L. (2000). *Empathy and moral development: Implications for caring and justice*. New York: Cambridge University Press.

Jia, Y., Way, N., Ling, G., Yoshikawa, H., Chen, X., Hughes, D., Ke, X., & Lu, Z. (2009). The influence of student perceptions of school climate on socioemotional and academic adjustment: A comparison of Chinese and American adolescents. *Child Development, 80*, 1514–1530.

Kagitcibasi, C. (2005). Autonomy and relatedness in cultural context: Implications for self and family. *Journal of Cross-Cultural Psychology, 36*, 403–422.

Lahat, A., Helwig, C. C., Yang, S., Tan, D., & Liu, C. (2009). Mainland Chinese adolescents' judgments and reasoning about self-determination and nurturance rights. *Social Development, 18*, 690–710.

Lau, S. (1992). Collectivism's individualism: Value preference, personal control, and the desire for freedom among Chinese in Mainland China, Hong Kong, and Singapore. *Personality and Individual Differences, 13*, 361–366.

Lee, W. O., & Ho, C. H. (2005). Ideopolitical shifts and changes in moral education policy in China. *Journal of Moral Education, 34*, 413–431.

Li, M. (2011). Changing ideological-political orientations in Chinese moral education: Some personal and professional reflections. *Journal of Moral Education, 40*, 387–395.

Li, M., Taylor, M. J., & Yang, S. (2004). Moral education in Chinese societies: Changes and challenges. *Journal of Moral Education, 33*, 405–428.

Li, P., Zhong, M., Lin, B., & Zhang, H. (2004). Deyu as moral education in modern China: Ideological functions and transformations. *Journal of Moral Education, 33*, 449–464.

Liu, F., & Lin, T. H. (2010, October 16). Yi suo xuexiao de gongmin shiyan [A civics experiment from a school]. Retrieved from http:/blog.sina.com.cn/mengma20100801.

Lo, C., Helwig, C. C., Chen, S. X., Ohashi, M. M., & Cheng, C. M. (2011). A needs-based perspective on cultural differences in identity formation. *Identity, 11*, 211–230.

Markus, H. R., & Kitayama, S. (1991). Culture and the self: Implications for cognition, emotion, and motivation. *Psychological Review, 98*, 224–253.

Miller, J. G. (1994). Cultural diversity in the morality of caring: Individually oriented versus duty-based interpersonal moral codes. *Cross-Cultural Research, 28*, 3–39.

Miller, J. G., Rekha, D., & Chakravarthy, S. (2011). Culture and the role of choice in agency. *Journal of Personality and Social Psychology, 101*, 46–61.

Moshman, D. (1986). Children's intellectual rights: A first amendment analysis. *New Directions for Child and Adolescent Development, 33*, 25–38.

Nucci, L. (2001). *Education in the moral domain*. Cambridge, UK: Cambridge University Press.

Osborne, K. (2004). Political and citizenship education: Teaching for civic engagement. *Education Canada, 45*, 13–16.

Peerenboom, R. (2002). *China's long march toward rule of law*. Cambridge, UK: Cambridge University Press.

People's Republic of China Ministry of Education (2003). Quanrizhi yiwu jiaoyu Sixiang Pinde kecheng biaozhun (Shiyan gao) [Guidelines for Ideology and Morality in full-time compulsory education (Experimental draft)] (pp. 30–33). Beijing, Beijing Normal University Press.

Piaget, J. (1932). *The moral judgment of the child*. London: Routledge & Kegan Paul.

Qi, W., & Tang, H. (2004). The social and cultural background of contemporary moral education in China. *Journal of Moral Education, 33*, 465–480.

Roetz, H. (1993). *Confucian ethics of the axial age.* Albany, NY: SUNY Press.

Ryan, R. M., & Deci, E. L. (2011). A self-determination theory perspective on social institutional, cultural, and economic supports for autonomy and their importance for well-being. In V. Chirkov, R. Ryan, & K. Sheldon (Eds.), *Human autonomy in cultural context: Perspectives on the psychology of agency, freedom, and well-being* (pp. 45–64). New York: Springer.

Schaps, E., Shaeffer, E. F., & McDonnell, S. N. (2001, September 12). What's right and wrong in character education today. *Education Week,* 40–44.

Sears, A., & Hughes, A. (2006). Citizenship: Education or indoctrination? *Citizenship and Teacher Education, 2,* 3–17.

Shweder, R. A., Mahapatra, M., & Miller, J. G. (1987). Culture and moral development. In J. Kagan & S. Lamb (Eds.), *The emergence of morality in young children* (pp. 1–83). Chicago: University of Chicago Press.

Smetana, J. G. (2011). *Adolescents, families, and social development: How teens construct their worlds.* West Sussex, UK: Wiley-Blackwell.

Tang, W., & Parish, W. L. (2000). *Chinese urban life under reform: The changing social contract.* New York: Cambridge University Press.

To, S., Helwig, C. C., & Yang, S. (2012, June). *Does democracy in the family and school promote adolescents' psychological well-being?: Findings from urban and rural China.* Paper presented as part of a symposium entitled "Morality, Socialization, and Culture" at the annual meeting of the Jean Piaget Society, Toronto.

Torney-Purta, J., Lehmann, R., Oswald, H., & Schultz, W. (2001). *Citizenship and education in twenty-eight countries: Civic knowledge and engagement at age fourteen.* Amsterdam: IEA.

Turiel, E. (2006). The development of morality. In W. Damon and R. Lerner (Series Eds.) & N. Eisenberg (Vol. Ed.), *Handbook of child psychology. Vol. 3: Social, emotional, and personality development* (6th ed., pp. 789–857). New York: Wiley.

Walker, L. J., Hennig, K. H., & Krettenauer, T. (2000). Parent and peer contexts for children's moral reasoning development. *Child Development, 71*, 1033–1048.

Walker, L. J., & Taylor, J. H. (1991). Family interactions and the development of moral reasoning. *Child Development, 62*, 264–283.

Way, N., Reddy, R., & Rhodes, J. (2007). Students' perceptions of school climate during the middle school years: Associations with trajectories of psychological and behavioral adjustment. *American Journal of Community Psychology, 40*, 194–213.

Yang, S. (2012). Zhōugōng jī dàn de dàodé xīnlǐ xué sīxiǎng jí qí dāngdài jiědú [Duke of Zhou's thoughts in moral psychology and its contemporary interpretations]. In *Thesis collection from the Second International Conference of the Ethical Culture in Zhou and Qin Dynasties and the Modern Moral Values.* Shanxi: Shaanxi People's Publishing House.

Yau, J., & Smetana, J. G. (2003). Adolescent-parent conflict in Hong Kong and Shenzhen: A comparison of youth in two cultural contexts. *International Journal of Behavioral Development, 27*, 201–211.

Yu, T. (2008). The revival of Confucianism in Chinese schools: A historical-political review. *Asia Pacific Journal of Education, 28*, 113–129.

Zhan, W., & Ning, W. (2004). The moral education curriculum for junior high schools in 21st century China. *Journal of Moral Education, 33*, 511–532.

Zhu, X., & Liu, C. (2004). Teacher training for moral education in China. *Journal of Moral Education, 33*, 481–494.

Part V

Moral and Character Education Beyond the
Classroom

24

POSITIVE YOUTH DEVELOPMENT IN THE UNITED STATES

History, Efficacy, and Links to Moral and Character Education

Richard F. Catalano, John W. Toumbourou, and J. David Hawkins

INTRODUCTION

Positive youth development (PYD) refers in broad scope to childhood and adolescent development experiences that provide optimal life preparation for the attainment of adult potential and well-being. This paper reviews specific conceptual frameworks and focuses on the evidence from evaluations of program applications delivered prior to age 21 that have the common aim of encouraging PYD.

The study of optimal development is relatively new and emerges from research into human growth through the life course. In the twentieth century, childhood and adolescence came to be increasingly regarded as special periods of development in which children were provided extra support to learn and develop. Early in the century, American society assumed an increased sense of responsibility for the care of its young people, including increasing the reach of education, delaying entry into the workforce, and providing supports for families who, historically, had nurtured the development of children. As the century progressed, changes in family socialization created changes in conceptualization of school and community practices to support families to raise successful children (Weissberg & Greenberg, 1997).

Prevention of youth problems in the twentieth century has evolved from earlier treatment and intervention models. Many early prevention efforts were not based on child development theory or research, and most approaches failed to show positive impact on youth problems (Kirby, Harvey, Claussenius, & Novar, 1989; Malvin, Moskowitz, Schaeffer, & Schaps, 1984; Snow, Gilchrist, & Schinke, 1985).

Faced with early failures, prevention program developers became increasingly aligned with the science of behavior development and change, and began designing program elements to address predictors of specific problem behaviors identified in longitudinal and intervention studies of youth. These prevention efforts were often guided by theories about how people make decisions, such as the Theory of Reasoned

Action (Ajzen & Fishbein, 1980; Fishbein & Ajzen, 1975), and the Health Belief Model (Janz & Becker, 1984; Rosenstock, Strecher, & Becker, 1988). In the 1980s these prevention efforts focused on predictors of a single problem behavior and came under increasing criticism for having such a narrow focus. Concerns expressed by prevention practitioners, policymakers, and prevention scientists helped expand the design of prevention programs to include components aimed at promoting positive youth development (Catalano & Hawkins, 2002).

In the 1990s, practitioners, policymakers, and prevention scientists adopted a broader focus for addressing youth issues (Pittman, O'Brien, & Kimball, 1993). In the late 1990s, youth development practitioners, the policy community, and prevention scientists reached similar conclusions about promoting better outcomes for youth. They all called for expanding programs beyond a single problem behavior focus and considering program effects on a range of positive and problem behaviors (Catalano, Hawkins, Berglund, Pollard, & Arthur, 2002; Kirby, Barth, Leland, & Fetro, 1991; National Research Council Institute of Medicine, Chalk, & Phillips, 1996; Pittman, 1991). This convergence in thinking has been recognized in forums on youth development including practitioners, policymakers (Pittman, 1991; Pittman & Fleming, 1991), and prevention scientists (National Research Council Institute of Medicine, 2002; National Research Council Institute of Medicine et al., 1996; O'Connell, Boat, & Warner, 2009) who have advocated that models of healthy development hold the key to both health promotion and prevention of problem behaviors.

POSITIVE YOUTH DEVELOPMENT CONSTRUCTS

In the late 1990s, a review of the literature was conducted to discover the multiple ways PYD constructs appeared in the literature. This review was followed by a consensus building meeting of leading scientists (Catalano, Berglund, Ryan, Lonczak, & Hawkins, 1999) to create an operational definition of positive youth development constructs. This definition was further developed by a meeting of scientists organized by the Annenberg Sunnylands Trust (Seligman et al., 2005). The following section provides a listing followed by a brief description of constructs addressed by youth development programs.

1. Promotes social competence
2. Promotes emotional competence
3. Promotes cognitive competence
4. Promotes behavioral competence
5. Promotes moral competence
6. Fosters self-efficacy
7. Provides opportunities for prosocial involvement
8. Provides recognition for positive behavior
9. Promotes bonding
10. Promotes strength of character
11. Fosters self-determination
12. Fosters clear and positive identity
13. Fosters belief in the future
14. Fosters prosocial norms
15. Fosters spirituality

16. Promotes life satisfaction
17. Fosters positive emotions
18. Fosters resilience

Promotes Competencies

Competence covers five areas of youth functioning: social, emotional, cognitive, behavioral, and moral competencies.

SOCIAL COMPETENCE

Social competence is a range of interpersonal skills that help youth integrate feelings, thinking, and actions in order to achieve specific social and interpersonal goals (Caplan et al., 1992; Weissberg, Caplan, & Sivo, 1989; Zins, Weissberg, Wang, & Walberg, 2004).

EMOTIONAL COMPETENCE

Emotional competence is the ability to identify and respond to feelings and emotional reactions in oneself and others. The W. T. Grant Consortium on the School-Based Promotion of Social Competence (W. T. Grant Consortium 1992, p. 136) list of emotional skills includes: "Identifying and labeling feelings, expressing feelings, assessing the intensity of feelings, managing feelings, delaying gratification, controlling impulses, and reducing stress." Goleman (1995) proposed empathy and hope as components of emotional intelligence.

COGNITIVE COMPETENCE

Cognitive competence includes two overlapping but distinct subconstructs. The first relates to personal skills such as problem solving (W. T. Grant Consortium, 1992, p. 136). The second aspect is related to academic and intellectual achievement.

BEHAVIORAL COMPETENCE

Behavioral competence refers to effective action in three dimensions: nonverbal communication, verbal communication, and taking action (W. T. Grant Consortium 1992, pp. 136–137).

MORAL COMPETENCE

Moral competence is a youth's ability to assess and respond to the ethical, affective, or social justice dimensions of a situation. Nucci and Turiel (Nucci, 1997, 2001; Turiel, 1983) considered fairness and welfare as central concerns for moral judgments.

Fosters Self-Efficacy

Self-efficacy is the perception that one can achieve desired goals within specific domains (e.g., educational attainment) through one's own action (Bandura, 1989, p. 1175). Given that differences in self-efficacy are commonly observed across domains (e.g., school, sport, relationships), to offer PYD benefits, high self-efficacy may need to be maintained across domains that align with valued opportunities.

Provides Opportunities for Prosocial Involvement

Opportunity for prosocial involvement is the presentation of events and activities across different social environments that encourage youths to participate in prosocial actions.

There are links between the emphasis on opportunities in PYD and the United Nations Millennium Development goals that have established a strategy to reduce severe poverty by ensuring basic opportunities (nutrition, education, and rights) for youth internationally (United Nations, 2000, 2005).

Provides Recognition for Positive Behavior

Recognition for positive involvement is the positive response of those in the social environment to desired behaviors by youths. Both external and intrinsic reinforcers are generally agreed to have important influences on behavior (Akers, Krohn, Lanza-Kaduce, & Radosevich, 1979; Bandura, 1973).

Promotes Bonding

Bonding is the emotional attachment and commitment a child makes to social relationships in the family, peer group, school, community, or culture. The importance of bonding reaches far beyond the family. How a child establishes early bonds to caregivers (Bowlby, 1982) will directly affect the manner in which the child later bonds to peers, school, the community, and culture(s) (Catalano, Haggerty, Oesterle, Fleming, & Hawkins, 2004).

Promotes Strength of Character

Positive traits like curiosity, kindness, gratitude, hope, and humor are components of strength of character (Peterson & Seligman, 2004).

Fosters Self-Determination

Self-determination is the ability to think for oneself and to take instrumental action consistent with that thought (Fetterman, Kaftarian, & Wandersman, 1996).

Fosters Clear and Positive Identity

Clear and positive identity is the internal organization of a coherent sense of self. The construct is associated with the theory of identity development emerging from studies of how children establish their identities (Erikson, 1968), including gender and ethnic identity (Josephs, Markus, & Tafarodi, 1992; Phinney, Lochner, & Murphy, 1990).

Fosters Belief in the Future

Belief in the future is the internalization of hope and optimism about possible outcomes (Wyman, Cowen, Work, & Kerley, 1993).

Fosters Prosocial Norms

Prosocial norms are healthy beliefs and clear standards for a variety of positive behaviors and prohibitions against involvement in unhealthy or risky behaviors (J. D. Hawkins, Catalano, & Miller, 1992; J. D. Hawkins et al., 1992).

Fosters Spirituality

To incorporate religiosity and nontraditional forms of applied spiritual practice, spirituality is defined here to include affiliation, belief in a transcendent hierarchy of values, and practice relevant to both formal religion (which considers God-given values to be at the top of the hierarchy of values) and also less formal conceptions of spirituality such as internal reflection and considering a transcendental hierarchy of solely humanistic values (Berube, Jost, Severynse, & Ellis, 1995).

Promotes Life Satisfaction

Life satisfaction is the overall judgment that one's life is a good one (Diener, Emmons, Larsen, & Griffin, 1985).

Fosters Positive Emotions

Emotions like joy, contentment, and love have been linked by research to the broadening and building of psychological skills and abilities (Fredrickson, 2000, 2002).

Fosters Resilience

Resilience is an individual's capacity for adapting to change and stressful events in healthy and flexible ways (Masten, Best, & Garmezy, 1990; Rutter, 1985).

INTERVENTION IMPLICATIONS

Identification of youth development constructs has proven useful in defining targets for intervention, as well as understanding how youth development program components might be structured. For example, the youth development construct of bonding suggests that bonding to family, peers, school, and positive community members is an important process of youth development that could be targeted by youth development interventions.

However, the field must progress beyond a listing of positive youth development constructs. To be most useful as a program development or structuring tool, the ability of the youth development constructs to predict positive and problem behaviors should be examined. Establishing predictive validity of youth development constructs provides a stronger rationale for addressing them through intervention. Consistent, longitudinal evidence across positive and problem behavior has not been generated for the youth development constructs. However, recently a series of reviews has examined the longitudinal evidence for whether youth development constructs predict sexual and reproductive health (Gloppen, David-Ferdon, & Bates, 2010; House, Bates, Markham, & Lesesne, 2010; House, Müller, Reininger, Brown, & Markham, 2010; Markham et al., 2010). This series of reviews found consistent longitudinal evidence for seven (cognitive and social competence, self-efficacy, belief in the future, self-determination, prosocial norms, and spirituality) of the 13 PYD constructs examined (positive emotions, life satisfaction, resilient temperament, strength of character, and behavioral competence were not examined). This suggests that these seven PYD constructs have evidence for being promising targets of PYD interventions to promote adolescent sexual and reproductive health. Further reviews of the ability of the youth development constructs to predict other problem and positive behaviors will assist PYD interventions to target malleable and predictive youth development constructs and provide a firmer basis for PYD program development.

YOUTH DEVELOPMENT THEORY

In addition to establishing whether PYD constructs predict positive and problem behavior, there is a need to tie this long list of youth developmental constructs together through theories of positive youth development (Catalano & Hawkins, 1996; Cichetti & Cohen, 1995; Lerner, 2000; Lopez & McKnight, 2002; Seligman, 2001).

While the field of PYD is characterized by several theories of PYD, no theory predominates. Rather than review theories, we briefly present our theory as an example guide to mechanisms that produce youth development. The social development model (SDM) (Catalano & Hawkins, 1996, 2002) is a theory of human behavior that attempts to provide an explanation of the development of positive and problem behavior. It recognizes that development is a product of an individual's behavior in multiple social environments across development. The SDM is explicitly developmental. Four developmental submodels of the SDM have been specified. The same constructs are included in each submodel, although their specific content is defined differently by individual development and changes in social environments. These developmental periods include preschool, elementary school, middle school, and high school, corresponding to major transitions in socializing environments (Catalano & Hawkins, 1996). The developmentally specific submodels have been constructed as recursive models; however, the SDM hypothesizes reciprocal relationships between constructs across developmental periods.

The model builds on social control theory (Hirschi, 1969), social learning theory (Bandura, 1977; Cressey, 1953), and differential association theory (Cressey, 1953; Matsueda, 1988). Control theory is used to identify causal elements in the etiology of problem and positive behavior. Social learning theory is used to identify processes by which patterns of positive and problem behavior are learned, extinguished, or maintained. Differential association theory is used to identify parallel but separate causal paths for prosocial and antisocial processes. This synthetic theory pays particular attention to resolving competing theoretical assumptions of these different theories (Catalano & Hawkins, 1996). The SDM hypothesizes that children and youth must learn patterns of behavior, whether prosocial or antisocial. These patterns are learned in families, schools, peer groups, and the community. It is hypothesized that socialization follows the same processes of social learning whether it produces positive or problem behavior. Children are socialized through processes involving four constructs: 1) perceived opportunities for involvement in activities and interactions with others, 2) the degree of involvement and interaction, 3) the skills to participate in these involvements and interactions, and 4) the reinforcement they perceive from these involvements and interactions (see Figure 24.1).

When socializing processes are consistent, a social bond develops between the individual and the socializing unit. Once strongly established, the social bond has power to effect behavior independently of the above four social learning processes. The social bond inhibits deviant behaviors through the establishment of an individual's "stake" in conforming to the norms and values of the socializing unit. It is hypothesized that the behavior of the individual will be prosocial or antisocial depending on the relative influence of norms and values held by those to whom the individual is bonded. Social and emotional bonds are only expected to inhibit antisocial behavior if those to whom a child is bonded hold norms clearly opposed to the antisocial behavior. Individuals who develop bonds to antisocial family, peers, or school personnel are expected to be encouraged to engage in antisocial behavior. Thus, two paths are hypothesized with similar socialization processes operating, one a prosocial (protective) path, and one an antisocial (risk) path. Both paths influence positive and antisocial behavior.

This theory weaves together several PYD concepts, including opportunities; social, emotional, behavioral, and cognitive competencies; recognition for involvement;

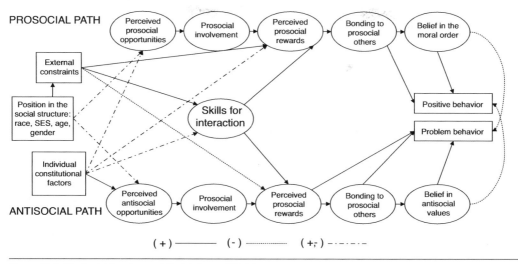

PROSOCIAL PATH

ANTISOCIAL PATH

(+) ———— (-) ·················· (+;̄) –·–·–·–·

Figure 24.1 The Social Development Model: General Model.

bonding; belief in the future; and positive norms. It brings them together in a way that provides mechanistic links among the concepts and provides explanations for both pro-motive and risk paths among these constructs. The latter is particularly important since it provides caution that the PYD concepts might actually promote problem behavior depending on whether the activities, interactions, and beliefs are prosocial or antisocial. This theory thus takes the concepts beyond a list and provides dynamics among the concepts and explanations for how they might work together. This type of theoretical development is needed in the field.

CONSENSUS ON POSITIVE BEHAVIOR OUTCOMES IN ADULTHOOD IS NEEDED

While there has been consensus on problem behaviors and PYD constructs, there is less consensus on positive behavior outcomes in adulthood. Defining a limited number of PYD outcomes would assist the field in both theory and intervention development.

Some work has been completed in defining PYD outcomes. For example, Benson, Hawkins and colleagues (2004), defined eight outcomes in young adulthood, including physical health, psychological and emotional well-being, life skills, ethical behavior, healthy family and social relationships, educational attainment, constructive engagement, and civic engagement. However, one of these outcomes, life skills, overlaps with the PYD competency constructs, thus providing seven unique youth development outcomes.

Another example of work to define positive young adult outcomes has occurred in Australia (M. T. Hawkins, Letcher, Sanson, Smart, & Toumbourou, 2009). In addi-tion to the outcomes identified by Benson et al. (2004), Hawkins and colleagues also include social trust, defined as respect for diversity and key societal institutions. Trust is conceptualized as an important developmental outcome that emerges from the PYD construct of bonding. M. T. Hawkins and colleagues' (2009, 2011) integrative model was found to offer a good fit to data from a young adult Australian cohort. Similar to the work of Benson et al. (2004), their model integrated constructs measuring general life satisfaction and competence (conceived as universal individual indicators of positive development) with constructs from social capital theories that included civic engagement and social trust. Social trust and civic engagement have been conceptualized in social capital theories to be important young adult outcomes that indicate both healthy development at an individual level, but also as collective resources contributing to the success of democratic societies. Their model of positive youth development appeared longitudinally valid in being predicted appropriately by child socialization and PYD indicators (O'Connor et al., 2011) and in predicting subsequent reductions in common young adult problems in areas including mental health and alcohol misuse, while also enhancing intimate peer relationships, physical well-being, and positive development (M. T. Hawkins et al., 2012).

These varied efforts to better define and measure PYD outcomes are important for improving conceptualization of the relation between PYD constructs and positive and problem outcomes in adults. Establishing consensus on positive outcomes can provide a firmer basis for examining the predictive validity of PYD constructs, and assist in designing measures that could be added as outcomes for PYD interventions, in addition to reducing problem behaviors. Further conceptual work needs to be completed to define and gain consensus on PYD young adult outcomes.

POSITIVE YOUTH DEVELOPMENT AND MORAL AND CHARACTER EDUCATION

The constructs included under the umbrella of positive youth development have emerged through consensus meetings involving scientists, practitioners, and policy-makers synthesizing findings across the developmental, evaluation, and behavioral sciences. These efforts have married diverse science and practice across a range of disciplines and achieved an encompassing scope in the characterization of positive youth development such that domains that form the focus in the moral and character education movement have been included. The moral and character education movement shares historical similarities with many areas of positive youth development in the youth domains that have been addressed, the interventions that have been developed and tested, and in the challenges faced in attempting to integrate research and practice (Lapsley & Narvaez, 2006; Leming, 1993). A common starting point evident in the writing of supporters of moral and character education has been the concern that modern socializing institutions have failed to reinforce the moral development of children and young people (Bebeau, Rest, & Narvaez, 1999; Leming, 1993). Although there are efforts to realign with evidence-based approaches (Institute of Education Sciences, 2006; Lapsley & Narvaez, 2006), the moral and character education programs that are most commonly used in American schools do not appear to reflect the diversity of underpinning theory and practice evident in the history of this movement. Many programs utilize school curricula with the aim of encouraging a common code of values, and, in this sense, resemble the ineffective programs developed in the earliest period of the character education movement (Bebeau et al., 1999; Leming, 1993); systematic reviews and evaluations of programs have shown mixed effects, with some programs demonstrating no effects (Institute of Education Sciences, 2006). Bebeau et al. (1999) comment that the implicit theory underpinning a number of curriculum-based programs is that didactic teaching of traditional values, reinforced with a behavioral code reflecting these curriculum values, will be effective in changing both values and behavior.

The review of character education programs conducted by the Institute of Education Sciences (2006) identified four programs that had been submitted to evaluations that at least partly met quality evidence standards. None of the programs evaluated was found to have impacted prosocial behavior and only one program (Building Decision Skills combined with service learning) was found to have had potentially positive effects on attitudes and values (Leming, 2001), while one other program (The Lessons in Character curricula) was found to have potentially positive effects for academic achievement (Devargas, 1999; Dietsch & Bayha, 2005; Dietsch, Bayha, & Zheng, 2005).

The growing emphasis on the evaluation of character and moral education programs reflects the broader emphasis on evidence-based practice. Interest in character education has seeded innovative programming and scientific investigation that has influenced positive youth development programs. The failure of a number of evaluations to find effects for character education programs (Institute of Education Sciences, 2006) has led to calls to better integrate the practice of character education with the lessons from the evaluation of programs that have successfully promoted positive youth development (Lapsley & Narvaez, 2006). One indicator of the need for more research in this area is that the evidence available for inclusion of this approach on the Institute of Education What Works Clearinghouse website remained effectively unchanged between July 2006 and July 2012.

EVALUATIONS OF POSITIVE YOUTH DEVELOPMENT PROGRAMS

Two systematic reviews of the unpublished and published PYD program evaluations were conducted, one published in 2002 (Catalano, Berglund, Ryan, Lonczak, & Hawkins, 2002) and the second in 2010 (Gavin, Catalano, David-Ferdon, Gloppen, & Markham, 2010). To be included, both reviews required that program evaluations met the following criteria:

- Address one or more of the positive youth development constructs.
- Involve a universal sample of youth (not a sample selected because of their need for treatment).
- Address at least one youth development construct in multiple socialization domains, or address multiple youth development constructs in a single socialization domain, or address multiple youth development constructs in multiple domains. Programs that addressed a single youth development construct in a single socialization domain were excluded from these reviews.

The 2002 review included studies that:

- Involved youth between the ages of six and 20 years.

The 2010 review included studies that:

- Involved youth between 0–20 years of age.

In addition to these program criteria, the program's evaluation had to meet the criteria described below. Complete description and operationalization of these inclusion criteria can be found in the two reviews.

- Experimental or quasi-experimental designs without design flaws that affect conclusion validity;
- Adequate description of the research methodologies; ·
- Description of the population served;
- Description of the intervention;
- Description of implementation.

The 2002 study accepted studies with:

- Effects demonstrated on positive or negative behavioral outcomes.

The 2010 study accepted only studies with:

- Effects demonstrated on an adolescent sexual and reproductive health outcome.

A diverse range of programs met these selection criteria, some of which may be described as positive youth development programs, some as health promotion programs, and others as primary prevention programs. In the 2002 review, 30 positive youth development programs met the inclusion criteria and 25 had positive effects on behavioral outcomes with an acceptable standard of statistical proof. In the 2010 review, 30 PYD programs met the inclusion criteria. Fifteen of the 30 programs had evidence of improving at least one adolescent sexual and reproductive health outcome. The two reviews included a number of the same programs.

SUMMARY OF YOUTH DEVELOPMENT PROGRAM OUTCOMES

Program results are briefly summarized in this section, organized by effects on positive and negative outcomes. Illustrative references to articles describing outcomes of these programs are provided when the program is first mentioned. More complete descriptions of the programs, research designs, behavioral outcomes, and complete references for the programs named below are available in the 2002 and 2010 reviews (Catalano, Berglund et al., 2002; Gavin et al., 2010).

Positive outcomes for youth in these programs included a variety of improvements in emotional competence, including greater self-control (PATHS—Greenberg & Kusche, 1997; Bicultural Competence Skills—Schinke, Orlandi, Botvin, Gilchrist, & Locklear, 1988); frustration tolerance (Children of Divorce—Pedro-Carroll & Cowen, 1985); increased empathy (PATHS); and expression of feelings (PATHS; Fast Track—Conduct Problems Prevention Research Group, 2002). Improvements in social competence included interpersonal skills (Children of Divorce; Fast Track; Child Development Project—Battistich, Schaps, Watson, & Solomon, 1996; Life Skills Training—Botvin et al., 2000; Social Competence Promotion Program—Weissberg & Caplan, 1998); greater assertiveness (Bicultural Competence Skills; Children of Divorce); greater self-efficacy with respect to substance use refusal (Project Northland—Perry et al., 1996); healthy and adaptive coping in peer-pressure situations

(Bicultural Competence Skills); improvements in acceptance of authority (Fast Track); and improvements in race relations and perceptions of others from different cultural or ethnic groups (Woodrock Youth Development Project—LoSciuto, Freeman, Harrington, Altman, & Lanphear, 1997). Increases in cognitive competence included decision making (Life Skills Training) and better problem solving (Children of Divorce; PATHS; Social Competence Promotion Program). Increases in behavioral competence included better health practices (Growing Healthy—Smith, Redican, & Olsen, 1992; Know Your Body—Walter, Vaughan, & Wynder, 1989) and greater self-efficacy around contraceptive practices (Reducing the Risk—Kirby et al., 1991). Positive youth development programs were associated with improvements in parental bonding and communication (Reducing the Risk; Seattle Social Development Project—Hawkins, Catalano, Kosterman, Abbott, & Hill, 1999; Hawkins, Kosterman, Catalano, Hill, & Abbott, 2005, 2008; High Scope Perry Preschool—Schweinhart, Barnes, & Weikart, 1993; Schweinhart et al., 2005; Big Brothers/Big Sisters—Tierney, Grossman, & Resch, 1995). Positive outcomes also included increased acceptance of prosocial norms regarding substance use (Life Skills Training; Project ALERT—Ellickson & Bell, 1990). A variety of positive school outcomes were also achieved by some youth development programs, including higher achievement (Big Brothers/Big Sisters; High/Scope Perry Preschool; Seattle Social Development Project; Teen Outreach—Allen, Philliber, Herrling, & Kuperminc, 1997; Abecedarian Project—Campbell, Ramey, Pungello, Sparling, & Miller-Johnson, 2002; Valued Youth Partnerships—Cardenas, Montecel, Supik, & Harris, 1992; Adult Identity Mentoring—Clark et al., 2005; Success for All—Slavin, 1996); higher school attachment (Seattle Social Development Project); increased high school attendance (Big Brothers/Big Sisters; Quantum Opportunities—Hahn, Leavitt, & Aaron, 1994); increased high school graduation (Across Ages—LoSciuto, Rajala, Townsend, & Taylor, 1996, Quantum Opportunities Program; Seattle Social Development Project; Valued Youth Partnerships); increased postsecondary school and college attendance (Quantum Opportunities Program; Seattle Social Development Project); and employment in adulthood (Abecedarian Project; High/Scope Perry Preschool). Other positive youth outcomes included higher levels of voluntary community service (Across Ages) and use of community services when needed (Creating Lasting Connections—Johnson et al., 1996).

Importantly, these programs reduced or prevented problem behaviors. For several programs substance use was lower, including alcohol or drug use (Abecederian Project; Bicultural Competence Skills; Big Brothers/Big Sisters; Child Development Project; High/Scope Perry Preschool; Life Skills Training; Project ALERT; Project Northland; Seattle Social Development Project; Woodrock Youth Development Project; Adolescent Sibling Pregnancy Prevention—East, Kiernan, & Chavez, 2003; Aban Aya—Flay, Graumlich, Segawa, Burns, & Holliday, 2004; Staying Connected with Your Teen—Haggerty, Skinner, MacKenzie, & Catalano, 2007; Gatehouse Project—Patton et al., 2006; Midwestern Prevention Project—Pentz et al., 1994; Familias Unidas—Prado et al., 2007; Wolchik et al., 2007; New Beginnings—Wolchik et al., 2002) and tobacco use (Child Development Project; Growing Healthy; Know Your Body; Life Skills Training; Midwestern Prevention Project; Project ALERT; Project Northland; Woodrock Youth Development Project). Several programs reduced delinquency and aggression (Aban Aya; Adolescent Transitions Program; Big Brothers/Big Sisters; Gatehouse Project; High/Scope Perry Preschool; Fast Track; PATHS; Seattle Social Development Project; Social Competence Promotion Program; Staying Connected with Your Teen; Responding in Peaceful and Positive Ways—Farrell & Meyer, 1997; Metropolitan Area Child Study—Guerra, Eron, Huesmann, Tolan,

& Van Acker, 1997; Reach for Health—O'Donnell et al., 1999; O'Donnell et al., 2002). Youth contraception practices increased, and initiation and prevalence of sexual activity were reduced in multiple programs (Aban Aya; Adult Identity Mentoring; Familias Unidas; Gatehouse Project; Reach for Health; Reducing the Risk; Seattle Social Development Project; Staying Connected with Your Teen; Keepin' it REAL—DiIorio et al., 2006; DiIorio et al., 2002; Adolescent Sibling Pregnancy Prevention—East et al., 2003; CAS-Carrera Program—Philliber, Kaye, Herrling, & West, 2002; Teen Incentives Program—Smith, 1994). Teen pregnancy was reduced by several programs (Abecedarian Project; Adolescent Sibling Pregnancy Prevention; CAS-Carrera Program; High/Scope Perry Preschool; Teen Outreach; Seattle Social Development Project). Negative school outcomes were reduced, including truancy (Adolescent Sibling Pregnancy Prevention; Big Brothers/Big Sisters) and school suspension (Adult Identity Mentoring; Responding in Peaceful and Positive Ways).

CHARACTERISTICS OF EFFECTIVE POSITIVE YOUTH DEVELOPMENT PROGRAMS

Summary of the characteristics of the effective positive youth development programs across the two reviews is instructive.

Youth Development Constructs

Both reviews showed consistency in the youth development constructs addressed by efficacious programs. At least two thirds of the efficacious youth development programs addressed some form of competence, opportunities for prosocial involvement, recognition for positive behavior, and bonding; and at least 40% of the efficacious well-evaluated programs addressed positive identity, self-efficacy, self-determination, belief in the future, and prosocial norms.

Program Frequency and Duration

Twenty (80%) efficacious programs in the 2002 review were delivered over a period of nine months or more and two-thirds of the efficacious programs in the 2010 review had this duration.

Program Implementation and Assurance of Implementation Quality

Fidelity of program implementation is one of the most important topics in the positive youth development field. The efficacious positive youth development programs reviewed here consistently attended to the quality and consistency of program implementation.

POSITIVE YOUTH DEVELOPMENT PROGRAM CONCLUSIONS

We found a wide range of positive youth development approaches that resulted in promoting positive youth behavior outcomes and preventing youth problem behaviors. Thirty-seven programs showed either positive changes in youth behavior, including significant improvements in interpersonal skills, quality of peer and adult relationships, self-control, problem solving, cognitive competencies, self-efficacy, commitment to schooling, and academic achievement; or significant improvements in problem behaviors, including drug and alcohol use, school misbehavior, aggressive behavior, violence, truancy, high-risk sexual behavior, and smoking. This is good news indeed. Promotion and prevention programs that address positive youth development constructs are definitely making a difference in well-evaluated studies.

Although a broad range of strategies produced these results, the themes common to success involved methods to strengthen social, emotional, behavioral, cognitive, and moral competencies; shape messages from family and community about clear standards for youth behavior; increase healthy bonding with adults, peers, and younger children; expand opportunities and recognition for youth; and intervene with youth for nine months or more.

IMPLICATIONS OF EVALUATIONS OF POSITIVE YOUTH DEVELOPMENT PROGRAMS FOR MORAL AND CHARACTER DEVELOPMENT PROGRAMS

The constructs addressed by effective positive youth development programs provide some confirmation of character and moral development program elements as well as some potential extensions. While these youth development constructs were not tested individually, their presence in effective positive youth development programs is suggestive of their importance. It appears that addressing multiple positive youth development constructs was associated with positive program impact. However, for the field to most efficiently develop now, we suggest that a relatively small set of positive outcomes in young adults be agreed upon, and call for more studies demonstrating that these PYD constructs are predictive of a range of positive and negative outcomes. Both directions would assist in progressing the research, program development, and ultimately the effectiveness of PYD programs.

In sum, there is clear evidence from well-conducted trials that positive youth development programs can be effective. Many of the elements of character and moral development have been included in the programs reviewed here. Cross-fertilization of programming and theory could lead to improvements in our understanding of youth development.

REFERENCES

Ajzen, I., & Fishbein, M. (1980). *Understanding attitudes and predicting social behavior.* Englewood Cliffs, NJ: Prentice Hall.

Akers, R. L., Krohn, M., Lanza-Kaduce, L., & Radosevich, M. (1979). Social learning and deviant behavior: A specific test of a general theory. *American Sociological Review, 44,* 636–655.

Allen, J. P., Philliber, S., Herrling, S., & Kuperminc, G. P. (1997). Preventing teen pregnancy and academic failure: Experimental evaluation of a developmentally based approach. *Child Development, 68,* 729–742.

Bandura, A. (1973). *Aggression: A social learning analysis.* Englewood Cliffs, NJ: Prentice Hall.

Bandura, A. (1977). *Social learning theory.* Englewood Cliffs, NJ: Prentice Hall.

Bandura, A. (1989). Human agency in social cognitive theory. *American Psychologist, 14,* 1175–1184.

Battistich, V., Schaps, E., Watson, M., & Solomon, D. (1996). Prevention effects of the Child Development Project: Early findings from an ongoing multisite demonstration trial. *Journal of Adolescent Research, 11,* 12–35.

Bebeau, M. J., Rest, J. R., & Narvaez, D. (1999). Beyond the promise: A perspective on research in moral education. *Educational Researcher, 28,* 18–26.

Benson, P. L., Scales, P. C., Hawkins, J. D., Oesterle, S., & Hill, K. G. (2004). Successful young adult development. A report submitted to The Bill & Melinda Gates Foundation. Retrieved from https://docs.gatesfoundation.org/Documents/SuccessfulDevelopment.pdf

Berube, M. S., Jost, D. A., Severynse, M., & Ellis, K. (Eds.). (1995). *Webster's II new college dictionary.* New York: Houghton-Mifflin.

Botvin, G. J., Griffin, K. W., Diaz, T., Scheier, L. M., Williams, C., & Epstein, J. A. (2000). Preventing illicit drug use in adolescents: Long-term follow-up data from a randomized control trial of a school population. *Addictive Behaviors, 25,* 769–774.

Bowlby, J. (1982). *Attachment. Vol. 1 of Attachment and loss* (2nd ed.). New York: Basic Books.

Campbell, F. A., Ramey, C. T., Pungello, E., Sparling, J., & Miller-Johnson, S. (2002). Early childhood education: Young adult outcomes from the Abecedarian Project. *Applied Developmental Science, 6,* 42–57.

Caplan, M., Weissberg, R. P., Grober, J. S., Sivo, P. J., Grady, K., & Jacoby, C. (1992). Social competence promotion with inner-city and suburban young adolescents: Effects on social adjustment and alcohol use. *Journal of Consulting and Clinical Psychology, 60,* 56–63.

Cardenas, J. A., Montecel, M. R., Supik, J. D., & Harris, R. J. (1992). The Coca-Cola Valued Youth Program. Dropout prevention strategies for at-risk students. *Texas Researcher, 3,* 111–130.

Catalano, R. F., Berglund, M. L., Ryan, J. A. M., Lonczak, H. S., & Hawkins, J. D. (1999). *Positive youth development in the United States. Research findings on evaluations of the positive youth development programs.* Report to the US Department of Health and Human Services, Office of the Assistant Secretary for Planning and Evaluation and National Institute for Child Health and Human Development. Seattle, WA: Social Development Research Group, University of Washington School of Social Work.

Catalano, R. F., Berglund, M. L., Ryan, J. A. M., Lonczak, H. S., & Hawkins, J. D. (2002). Positive youth development in the United States: Research findings on evaluations of positive youth development programs. *Prevention and Treatment, 5(15),* Article 15.

Catalano, R. F., Haggerty, K. P., Oesterle, S., Fleming, C. B., & Hawkins, J. D. (2004). The importance of bonding to school for healthy development: Findings from the Social Development Research Group. *Journal of School Health, 74,* 252–261.

Catalano, R. F., & Hawkins, J. D. (1996). The social development model: A theory of antisocial behavior. In J. D. Hawkins (Ed.), *Delinquency and crime: Current theories* (pp. 149–197). New York: Cambridge University Press.

Catalano, R. F., & Hawkins, J. D. (2002). Response from authors to comments on "Positive Youth Development in the United States: Research findings on evaluations of positive youth development programs." *Prevention and Treatment, 5,* Article 20.

Catalano, R. F., Hawkins, J. D., Berglund, M. L., Pollard, J. A., & Arthur, M. W. (2002). Prevention science and positive youth development: Competitive or cooperative frameworks? *Journal of Adolescent Health, 31,* 230–239.

Cichetti, D., & Cohen, D. J. (1995). *Developmental psychopathology: Vol. 2. Risk, disorder, and adaptation.* New York: Wiley.

Clark, L. F., Miller, K. S., Nagy, S. S., Avery, J., Roth, D. L., Liddon, N. et al. (2005). Adult identity mentoring: reducing sexual risk for African-American seventh grade students. *Journal of Adolescent Health, 37,* 337. e1–337.e10.

Conduct Problems Prevention Research Group. (2002). Evaluation of the first 3 years of the Fast Track prevention trial with children at high risk for adolescent conduct problems. *Journal of Abnormal Child Psychology, 30,* 19–35.

Cressey, D. R. (1953). *Other people's money, a study of the social psychology of embezzlement.* New York: The Free Press.

Devargas, R. C. (1999). A study of "lessons in character": The effect of moral development curriculum upon moral judgment (character education, fifth-grade). *Dissertation Abstracts International, 59(11-A),* 4042. (UMI No. AEH9913706.)

Diener, E., Emmons, R. A., Larsen, R. J., & Griffin, S. (1985). The Satisfaction With Life Scale. *Journal of Personality Assessment, 49,* 71–75.

Dietsch, B., & Bayha, J. L. (2005). *Short-term effects of a literature-based character education program among fourth grade students: Report to the Young People's Press, Inc.* Los Alamitos, CA: WestEd.

Dietsch, B., Bayha, J. L., & Zheng, H. (2005, April). Short-term effects of a character education program among fourth grade students. Presented at the American Educational Research Association annual meeting, Montreal, Quebec, Canada.

DiIorio, C., Resnicow, K., McCarty, F., De, A. K., Dudley, W. N., Wang, D. T. et al. (2006). Keepin' it R.E.A.L.!: Results of a mother-adolescent HIV prevention program. *Nursing Research, 55,* 43–51.

DiIorio, C., Resnicow, K., Thomas, S., Wang, D. T., Dudley, W. N., Van Marter, D. F. et al. (2002). Keepin' it R.E.A.L.!: Program description and results of baseline assessment. *Health Education and Behavior, 29,* 104–123.

East, P., Kiernan, E., & Chavez, G. (2003). An evaluation of California's Adolescent Sibling Pregnancy Prevention Program. *Perspectives on Sexual and Reproductive Health, 35,* 62–70.

Ellickson, P. L., & Bell, R. M. (1990). Drug prevention in junior high: A multi-site longitudinal test. *Science, 247,* 1299–1305.

Erikson, E. H. (1968). *Identity: Youth and crisis.* New York: W. W. Norton.

Farrell, A. D., & Meyer, A. L. (1997). The effectiveness of a school-based curriculum for reducing violence among urban sixth-grade students. *American Journal of Public Health, 87,* 979–984.

Fetterman, D. M., Kaftarian, S. J., & Wandersman, A. (Eds.). (1996). *Empowerment evaluation. Knowledge and tools for self-assessment and accountability.* Newbury Park, CA: Sage.

Fishbein, M., & Ajzen, I. (1975). *Belief, attitude, intention and behavior: An introduction to theory and research.* Reading, MA: Addison-Wesley.

Flay, B. R., Graumlich, S., Segawa, E., Burns, J. L., & Holliday, M. Y. (2004). Effects of 2 prevention programs on high-risk behaviors among African American youth: A randomized trial. *Archives of Pediatrics & Adolescent Medicine, 158,* 377–384.

Fredrickson, B. L. (2000). Cultivating positive emotions to optimize health and well-being. *Prevention and Treatment, 3,* Article 0001a.

Fredrickson, B. L. (2002). Positive emotions. In C. R. Snyder & S. J. Lopez (Eds.), *Handbook of positive psychology* (pp. 120–134). London: Oxford University Press.

Gavin, L., Catalano, R. F., David-Ferdon, C., Gloppen, K., & Markham, C. M. (2010). A review of positive youth development programs that promote adolescent sexual and reproductive health. *Journal of Adolescent Health, 46(3 Suppl. 1),* S75–S91.

Gloppen, K. M., David-Ferdon, C., & Bates, J. (2010). Confidence as a predictor of sexual and reproductive health outcomes for youth. *Journal of Adolescent Health, 46(3 Suppl),* 42–58.

Goleman, D. (1995). *Emotional intelligence.* New York: Bantam Books.

Greenberg, M. T., & Kusche, C. A. (1997, April). Improving children's emotion regulation and social competence: The effects of the PATHS curriculum. Presented at the Annual Meeting of the Society for Research in Child Development, Washington, DC.

Guerra, N. G., Eron, L. D., Huesmann, L., Tolan, P. H., & Van Acker, R. (1997). A cognitive-ecological approach to the prevention and mitigation of violence and aggression in inner-city youth. In D. P. Fry & K. Bjorkqvist (Eds.), *Cultural variation in conflict resolution: Alternatives to violence* (pp. 199–213). Hillsdale, NJ: Lawrence Erlbaum Associates.

Haggerty, K. P., Skinner, M. L., MacKenzie, E. P., & Catalano, R. F. (2007). A randomized trial of Parents Who Care: Effects on key outcomes at 24-month follow-up. *Prevention Science, 8,* 249–260.

Hahn, A., Leavitt, T., & Aaron, P. (1994). *Evaluation of the Quantum Opportunities Program (QOP). Did the program work? A report on the post secondary outcomes and cost-effectiveness of the QOP Program (1989–1993).* Waltham, MA: Brandeis University Heller Graduate School Center for Human Resources.

Hawkins, J. D., Catalano, R. F., Kosterman, R., Abbott, R., & Hill, K. G. (1999). Preventing adolescent health-risk behaviors by strengthening protection during childhood. *Archives of Pediatrics and Adolescent Medicine, 153,* 226–234.

Hawkins, J. D., Catalano, R. F., & Miller, J. Y. (1992). Risk and protective factors for alcohol and other drug problems in adolescence and early adulthood: Implications for substance-abuse prevention. *Psychological Bulletin, 112,* 64–105.

Hawkins, J. D., Catalano, R. F., Morrison, D. M., O'Donnell, J., Abbott, R. D., & Day, L. E. (1992). The Seattle Social Development Project: Effects of the first four years on protective factors and problem behaviors. In J. McCord & R. E. Tremblay (Eds.), *Preventing antisocial behavior: Interventions from birth through adolescence* (pp. 139–161). New York: Guilford Press.

Hawkins, J. D., Kosterman, R., Catalano, R. F., Hill, K. G., & Abbott, R. D. (2005). Promoting positive adult functioning through social development intervention in childhood: Long-term effects from the Seattle Social Development Project. *Archives of Pediatrics and Adolescent Medicine, 159,* 25–31.

Hawkins, J. D., Kosterman, R., Catalano, R. F., Hill, K. G., & Abbott, R. D. (2008). Effects of social development intervention in childhood fifteen years later. *Archives of Pediatrics and Adolescent Medicine, 162,* 1133–1141.

Hawkins, M. T., Letcher, P., Sanson, A., O'Connor, M., Toumbourou, J. W., & Olsson, C. (2011). Stability and change in positive development during young adulthood. *Journal of Youth and Adolescence, 40,* 1436–1452.

Hawkins, M. T., Letcher, P., Sanson, A., Smart, D., & Toumbourou, J. W. (2009). Positive development in emerging adulthood. *Australian Journal of Psychology, 61,* 89–99.

Hawkins, M. T., Villagonzalo, K.-A., Sanson, A. V., Toumbourou, J. W., Letcher, P., & Olsson, C. A. (2012). Associations between positive development in late adolescence and social, health, and behavioral outcomes in young adulthood. *Journal of Adult Development, 19,* 88–99.

Hirschi, T. (1969). *Causes of delinquency.* Berkeley, CA: University of California Press.

House, L. D., Bates, J., Markham, C. M., & Lesesne, C. (2010). Competence as a predictor of sexual and reproductive health outcomes for youth: A systematic review. *Journal of Adolescent Health, 46(3 Suppl),* 7–22.

House, L. D., Müller, T., Reininger, B., Brown, K., & Markham, C. M. (2010). Character as a predictor of reproductive health outcomes for youth: A systematic review. *Journal of Adolescent Health, 46(3 Suppl),* 59–S74.

Institute of Education Sciences. (2006). Review of character education. Retrieved from www.whatworks.ed.gov/.

Janz, N. K., & Becker, M. H. (1984). The health belief model: A decade later. *Health Education Quarterly, 11,* 1–47.

Johnson, K., Bryant, D., Strader, T., Bucholtz, G., Collins, D., & Noe, T. (1996). Reducing alcohol and other drug use by strengthening community, family, and youth resiliency: An evaluation of the Creating Lasting Connections Program. *Journal of Adolescent Research, 11,* 36–67.

Josephs, R. A., Markus, H. R., & Tafarodi, R. W. (1992). Gender and self-esteem. *Journal of Personality and Social Psychology, 63,* 391–402.

Kirby, D., Barth, R. P., Leland, N., & Fetro, J. V. (1991). Reducing the risk: Impact of a new curriculum on sexual risk-taking. *Family Planning Perspectives, 23,* 253–263.

Kirby, D., Harvey, P. D., Claussenius, D., & Novar, M. (1989). A direct mailing to teenage males about condom use: Its impact on knowledge, attitudes and sexual behavior. *Family Planning Perspectives, 21,* 12–18.

Lapsley, D. K., & Narvaez, D. (2006). Character education. In K. A. Renninger, I. E. Sigel, W. Damon, & R. M. Lerner (Eds.), *Handbook of child psychology: Vol 4. Child psychology in practice* (6th ed., pp. 248–296). Hoboken, NJ: John Wiley & Sons.

Leming, J. S. (1993). In search of effective character education. *Educational Leadership, 51(3),* 63–71.

Leming, J. S. (2001). Integrating a structured ethical reflection curriculum into high school community service experiences: Impact on students' sociomoral development. *Adolescence, 36,* 33–45.

Lerner, R. M. (2000). Developing civil society through the promotion of positive youth development. *Journal of Developmental and Behavioral Pediatrics, 21,* 48–49.

Lopez, S. J., & McKnight, C. G. (2002). Moving in a positive direction: Toward increasing the utility of positive youth development efforts. *Prevention & Treatment, 5,* Article 2.

LoSciuto, L., Freeman, M. A., Harrington, E., Altman, B., & Lanphear, A. (1997). An outcome evaluation of the Woodrock Youth Development Project. *Journal of Early Adolescence, 17,* 51–66.

LoSciuto, L., Rajala, A. K., Townsend, T. N., & Taylor, A. S. (1996). An outcome evaluation of Across Ages: An intergenerational mentoring approach to drug prevention. *Journal of Adolescent Research, 11,* 116–129.

Malvin, J. H., Moskowitz, J. M., Schaeffer, G. A., & Schaps, E. (1984). Teacher training in affective education for the primary prevention of adolescent drug abuse. *American Journal of Drug and Alcohol Abuse, 10,* 223–235.

Markham, C. M., Lormand, D., Gloppen, K. M., Peskin, M. F., Flores, B., Low, B. et al. (2010). Connectedness as a predictor of sexual and reproductive health outcomes for youth. *Journal of Adolescent Health, 46(3 Suppl),* 23–41.

Masten, A. S., Best, K. M., & Garmezy, N. (1990). Resilience and development: Contributions from the study of children who overcome adversity. *Development and Psychopathology, 2,* 425–444.

Matsueda, R. L. (1988). The current state of differential association theory. *Crime and Delinquency, 34,* 277–306.

National Research Council Institute of Medicine. (2002). *Community programs to promote youth development.* Committee on Community-Level Programs for Youth. Jacquelynne Eccles & Jennifer Gootman (Eds.), Board on Children, Youth, and Families, Division of Behavioral and Social Sciences and Education. Washington, DC: National Academy Press.

National Research Council Institute of Medicine, Chalk, R., & Phillips, D. A. (Eds.). (1996). *Youth development and neighborhood influences: Challenges and opportunities; summary of a workshop.* Report by the Committee on Youth Development, Board on Children, Youth, and Families, Commission on Behavioral and Social Sciences and Education. Washington, DC: National Academy Press.

Nucci, L. (1997). Moral development and character formation. In H. J. Walberg & G. D. Haertel (Eds.), *Psychology and educational practice* (pp. 127–157). Berkeley, CA: MacCarchan.

Nucci, L. (2001). *Education in the moral domain.* Cambridge: Cambridge University Press.

O'Connell, M. E., Boat, T., & Warner, K. E. (Eds.). (2009). *Preventing mental, emotional, and behavioral disorders among young people: Progress and possibilities.* Washington, DC: The National Academies Press.

O'Connor, M., Sanson, A., Hawkins, M. T., Letcher, P., Toumbourou, J. W., Smart, D. et al. (2011). Predictors of positive development in emerging adulthood. *Journal of Youth and Adolescence, 40,* 860–874.

O'Donnell, L., Stueve, A., Doval, A. S., Duran, R., Haber, D., Atnafou, R. et al. (1999). The effectiveness of the reach for health community youth service learning program in reducing early and unprotected sex among urban middle school students. *American Journal of Public Health, 89,* 176–181.

O'Donnell, L., Stueve, A., O'Donnell, C., Duran, R., San Doval, A., Wilson, R. F. et al. (2002). Long-term reductions in sexual initiation and sexual activity among urban middle schoolers in the reach for health service learning program. *Journal of Adolescent Health, 31*, 93–100.

Patton, G. C., Bond, L., Carlin, J. B., Thomas, L., Butler, H., Glover, S. et al. (2006). Promoting social inclusion in schools: A group-randomized trial of effects on student health risk behavior and well-being. *American Journal of Public Health, 96*, 1582–1587.

Pedro-Carroll, J. L., & Cowen, E. L. (1985). The Children of Divorce Intervention Program: An investigation of the efficacy of a school-based prevention program. *Journal of Consulting and Clinical Psychology, 53*, 603–611.

Pentz, M. A., Dwyer, J. H., Johnson, C. A., Flay, B. R., Hansen, W. B., MacKinnon, D. P. et al. (1994). Long-term follow-up of a multicommunity trial for prevention of tobacco, alcohol, and drug use. Unpublished manuscript.

Perry, C. L., Williams, C. L., Veblen Mortenson, S., Toomey, T. L., Komro, K. A., Anstine, P. S. et al. (1996). Project Northland: Outcomes of a communitywide alcohol use prevention program during early adolescence. *American Journal of Public Health, 86*, 956–965.

Peterson, C., & Seligman, M. E. P. (2004). *Character strengths and virtues: A handbook and classification.* Washington, DC: American Psychological Association.

Philliber, S., Kaye, J. W., Herrling, S., & West, E. (2002). Preventing pregnancy and improving health care access among teenagers: An evaluation of the Children's Aid Society–Carrera program. *Perspectives on Sexual and Reproductive Health, 34*, 244–251.

Phinney, J. S., Lochner, B. T., & Murphy, R. (1990). Ethnic identity development and psychological adjustment in adolescence. In A. R. Stiffman & L. E. Davis (Eds.), *Ethnic issues in adolescent mental health* (pp. 53–72). Thousand Oaks, CA: Sage.

Pittman, K. J. (1991). *Promoting youth development: Strengthening the role of youth-serving and community organizations. Report prepared for The US Department of Agriculture Extension Services.* Washington, DC: Center for Youth Development and Policy Research.

Pittman, K. J., & Fleming, W. E. (1991). *A new vision: Promoting youth development. Written transcript of a live testimony by Karen J. Pittman given before The House Select Committee on Children, Youth and Families.* Washington, DC: Center for Youth Development and Policy Research.

Pittman, K. J., O'Brien, R., & Kimball, M. (1993). *Youth development and resiliency research: Making connections to substance abuse prevention. Report prepared for The Center for Substance Abuse Prevention.* Washington, DC: Center for Youth Development and Policy Research.

Prado, G., Pantin, H., Briones, E., Schwartz, S. J., Feaster, D., Huang, S. et al. (2007). A randomized controlled trial of a parent-centered intervention in preventing substance use and HIV risk behaviors in Hispanic adolescents. *Journal of Consulting and Clinical Psychology, 75*, 914–926.

Rosenstock, I. M., Strecher, V. J., & Becker, M. H. (1988). Social learning theory and the health belief model. *Health Education Quarterly, 15*, 175–183.

Rutter, M. (1985). Resilience in the face of adversity: Protective factors and resistance to psychiatric disorder. *British Journal of Psychiatry, 147*, 598–611.

Schinke, S. P., Orlandi, M. A., Botvin, G. J., Gilchrist, L. D., & Locklear, V. S. (1988). Preventing substance abuse among American-Indian adolescents: A bicultural competence skills approach. *Journal of Counseling Psychology, 35*, 87–90.

Schweinhart, L. J., Barnes, H. V., & Weikart, D. P. (1993). *Significant benefits: The High/Scope Perry Preschool Study through age 27. (Monographs of the High/Scope Educational Research Foundation, 10.)* Ypsilanti, MI: High/Scope Press.

Schweinhart, L. J., Montie, J., Xiang, Z., Barnett, W. S., Belfield, C. R., & Nores, M. (2005). *Lifetime effects: The High/Scope Perry Preschool study through age 40. (Monographs of the High/Scope Educational Research Foundation, 14.)* Ypsilanti, MI: High/Scope Press.

Seligman, M. E. P. (2001). Comment on "Priorities for prevention research at NIMH." *Prevention and Treatment, 4*, Article 24c.

Seligman, M. E. P., Berkowitz, M. W., Catalano, R. F., Damon, W., Eccles, J. S., Gilham, J. E. et al. (2005). The positive perspective on youth development. In D. L. Evans, E. B. Foa, R. E. Gur, H. Hendin, C. P. O'Brien, M. E. P. Seligman & B. T. Walsh (Eds.), *Treating and preventing adolescent mental health disorders: What we know and what we don't know* (pp. 499–529, 762–771). New York: Oxford University Press, The Annenberg Foundation Trust at Sunnylands, and The Annenberg Public Policy Center of the University of Pennsylvania.

Slavin, R. E. (1996). Success for All: A summary of research. *Journal of Education for Students Placed at Risk, 1*, 41–76.

Smith, D. W., Redican, K. J., & Olsen, L. K. (1992). The longevity of growing healthy: An analysis of the eight original sites implementing the School Health Curriculum Project. *Journal of School Health, 62*, 83–37.

Smith, M. A. (1994). Teen Incentives Program: Evaluation of a health promotion model for adolescent pregnancy prevention. *Journal of Health Education, 25*, 24–29.

Snow, W. H., Gilchrist, L. D., & Schinke, S. P. (1985). A critique of progress in adolescent smoking prevention. *Children and Youth Services Review, 7*, 1–19.

Thomas, B. H., Mitchell, A., Devlin, M. C., Goldsmith, C. H., Singer, J., & Watters, D. (1992). Small group sex education at school: The McMaster Teen Program. In B. C. Miller, J. J. Card, R. L. Paikoff, & J. L. Peterson (Eds.), *Preventing adolescent pregnancy: Model programs and evaluations. Sage focus editions, Vol. 140* (pp. 28–52). Thousand Oaks, CA: Sage.

Tierney, J. P., Grossman, J. B., & Resch, N. L. (1995). *Making a difference: An impact study of Big Brothers/Big Sisters.* Philadelphia, PA: Public/Private Ventures.

Turiel, E. (1983). *The development of social knowledge: Morality and convention.* Cambridge: Cambridge University Press.

United Nations. (2000). *Millennium Declaration.* New York: United Nations.

United Nations. (2005). *The Millennium Development goals report.* New York: United Nations.

W. T. Grant Consortium on the School-Based Promotion of Social Competence. (1992). Drug and alcohol prevention curricula. In J. D. Hawkins, R. F. Catalano, Jr. & Associates (Eds.), *Communities That Care. Action for drug abuse prevention* (pp. 129–148). San Francisco: Jossey-Bass.

Walter, H. J., Vaughan, R. D., & Wynder, E. L. (1989). Primary prevention of cancer among children: Changes in cigarette smoking and diet after six years of intervention. *Journal of the National Cancer Institute, 81*, 995–999.

Weissberg, R. P., & Caplan, M. (1998). *Promoting social competence and preventing antisocial behavior in young urban adolescents.* Chicago: University of Illinois at Chicago.

Weissberg, R. P., Caplan, M. Z., & Sivo, P. J. (1989). A new conceptual framework for establishing school-based social competence promotion programs. In L. A. Bond & B. E. Compas (Eds.), *Primary prevention and promotion in the schools* (pp. 255–296). Newbury Park, CA: Sage.

Weissberg, R. P., & Greenberg, M. T. (1997). School and community competence-enhancement and prevention programs. In W. Damon (Ed.), *Handbook of child psychology* (5th ed., Vol. 5, pp. 877–954). New York: John Wiley & Sons.

Wolchik, S. A., Sandler, I. N., Millsap, R. E., Plummer, B. A., Greene, S. M., Anderson, E. R. et al. (2002). Six-year follow-up of preventive interventions for children of divorce: A randomized controlled trial. *JAMA, 288*, 1874–1881.

Wolchik, S. A, Sandler, I., Weiss, L., Winslow, E., Briesmeister, J. M., & Schaefer, C. E. (2007). New Beginnings: An empirically-based program to help divorced mothers promote resilience in their children. In J. M. Briesmeister and C. E. Schaefer (Eds.), *Handbook of parent training: Helping parents prevent and solve problem behaviors* (3rd ed., pp. 25–62). Hoboken, NJ: John Wiley & Sons.

Wyman, P. A., Cowen, E. L., Work, W. C., & Kerley, J. H. (1993). The role of children's future expectations in self-esteem functioning and adjustment to life stress: A prospective study of urban at-risk children. *Development and Psychopathology, 5*, 649–661.

Zins, J., Weissberg, R., Wang, M., & Walberg, H. J. (2004). *Building academic success on social and emotional learning: What does the research say?* New York: Teachers College, Columbia University.

25

COMMUNITY CONTRIBUTION TO MORAL AND CHARACTER DEVELOPMENT

Constance Flanagan, Alisa Pykett, and Erin Gallay

In approaching the topic of community contribution to moral and character development, we begin with the observations of some prominent political scientists who have challenged rational choice models of human behavior (i.e., that people will make decisions in their own self-interest with little regard for the common good). In their book, *Voice and Equality*, Verba, Schlozman, and Brady (1995) note that rational choice theory predicts that few people will be active in community affairs when, in fact, many are. Indeed, people contribute to the common good of their communities because there is a sense of satisfaction from "performing a civic duty or doing one's share to make the community, nation, or world a better place" (p. 10).

In a similar vein, Elinor Ostrom (1998), winner of the 2009 Nobel Prize in economics, challenged the notion that states or markets were better than communities of people in determining how best to manage natural resources. She contested the inevitability of a "tragedy of the commons" which assumed that, driven by self-interest, people would destroy and deplete the natural resources on which their community depended. Rather, Ostrom (2010) and her colleagues demonstrated empirically that communities throughout the world use collective decision-making processes to determine how to sustain environmental resources that are their commons. In her Nobel Prize lecture, she contended that humans have more capability and complex motivation to solve social dilemmas than suggested in rational choice theory. Furthermore, this recognition calls for creating policies and institutions that bring out the best in humans as opposed to policies that force individuals, assumed to be driven by self-interest, into behaviors for the common interest. Aspects of community institutions and policies that enable people to freely choose to act in the interests of the commons include extending the breadth of communication to include all participants, possibilities for collective efficacy and the sense among participants that their contributions have an impact, cooperation and trust among participants, and a long-term horizon.

The focus for our chapter is on the potential of a community as a commons to contribute to moral development. We begin with a discussion of the commons and an argument about the potential of community-based organizations for contributing to moral development. Following that we discuss the *processes* underlying moral development in community-based organizations: Drawing primarily from research on youth, we claim that moral selves form through feelings of membership in and identification with a community of mutual obligations. Further, we argue that moral development benefits when the community extends beyond familiar others and includes a diversity of backgrounds, experiences, and perspectives. In the third section we discuss the moral foundations of environmental action in communities, focusing on such things as interdependence, empathy, and generative concern.

COMMUNITY/THE COMMONS

Often, mention of "the commons" elicits an image of the village green where people brought their sheep to graze—an image that may not appear, on the surface, to hold relevance in current times. However, an updated conceptualization of the commons as the public space where people come together, form relationships and group identities, and develop feelings of social responsibility, is useful for a discussion of moral development in community settings. The commons serves as a symbol for understanding the world as interdependent and the need for people to engage in what Harry Boyte (2011) has called *public work* in order to make it better. Elinor Ostrom's (2010) explanation of the commons distinguished tangible (common pool resources, like fisheries and forests) from intangible public goods such as peace, security, and knowledge. Others have described the modern commons as: the image that stands behind the concept of the common good (Parks, 2000), the "symbolic and material foundations for a shared life" (Boyte, 2011, p. 638), and "a place where the diverse parts of a community could come together and hold a conversation within a shared sense of participation and responsibility" (Daloz, Keen, Keen, & Parks, 1996, p. 2).

The commons is where we build and experience our shared lives. In communities we create something together—with others whose lives and experiences extend beyond the narrower range within one's family and close friends. The very word "community" means the gift of coming together. As moral theorists have argued, it is the coming together in relationships, identifying with a group and its values, and feelings of responsibility for the group that underlies the formation of a moral self (Power, 2004). Youniss (2009) takes the argument a step further: People engage in moral action by working with others in community-based institutions and those organizations have a history, ideology, and professed sets of values that informs the work that they do. Thus, in choosing to work with a particular community organization, people deepen and extend the reach of the values for which that organization stands.

Many moral questions reside in the commons: What are my roles and responsibilities in this complex, diverse, and global commons that is comprised of people like me *and* people very different than me? What is our shared purpose? What might we create together? The commons also contains the practical concerns of managing shared resources, addressing social problems, and making community decisions. People create their public, shared lives in the commons as they learn about each other, support one another, celebrate, struggle, and grieve. Compared to the village green from earlier conceptualizations, the new commons is, as Daloz et al. (1996) have noted, "global in scope, diverse in character, and dauntingly complex" (p. 2).

For this reason alone, moral development nurtured in community groups cannot be construed as teaching young people what is true or how they should think. Rather, in the repeated acts of wrangling with others over how to live in a civil society, youth should gain skills for handling morally complex issues that will be increasingly common in their lives. As Nucci (2008) has noted, with the complexity of moral decision-making and creating a moral life, "what we can hope to accomplish is to develop young people capable of handling moral complexity, ambiguity, and contradiction in ways that will help them to lead moral lives and to construct a better moral society" (p. 305).

Participating in the new commons, or working for the common good, requires an awareness of the interdependencies that are facts of life, from recognizing at a basic level that the piece of trash one throws in the river could kill an animal and, as a result, cause the death of its offspring, to recognizing at a more complex level that the company in one's town—a major employer of, among others, members of one's family—is polluting the river, impacting people who make their living fishing and those eating the fish in towns downstream.

A mature moral identity is capable of recognizing, grappling with, and working with others to identify and address injustice (Blum, 1999; Daloz et al., 1996; Parks, 2000). The commons framework provides a language to discuss morality and responsibility in a shared life without using an exclusive religious language, which would inevitably include some and exclude others in the moral conversation. In fact, unique to the commons or what the philosopher Hannah Arendt referred to as the "public realm" is the fact that it brings everyone, regardless of status, social background, or beliefs, together. Thus, the public realm is a more diverse context for moral identity formation than the more homogeneous settings of family life.

In her book, *The Human Condition*, Arendt (1958) provides several mechanisms whereby activity in the public realm could contribute to moral development: first the term "public" means that things that appear in this realm can be seen and heard by everybody. Consequently, in the public realm there will be diversity in perspectives of what constitutes moral, ethical, virtuous behavior. Although people will choose different ways to live their own private lives, it is in the public realm that a wide range of beliefs on how best to live together in a civil society can be aired and debated.

Second, according to Arendt, the public realm is the common world that gathers us together; when we realize our personal stake in the common good, we are motivated to act in the interests of the whole. Further, the inclusive nature of the public realm should expand our moral community. As theologian Ronald Marstin (1979) has argued,

> issues of social justice are essentially about who is to be cared for and who neglected, who is to be included in our community of concern and who excluded, whose point of view is to be taken seriously and whose ignored.
>
> (p. 37)

As people develop morally and have experiences that broaden their boundaries of community, they can develop a critical consciousness about how some are cared for, included, and taken seriously while others are neglected, excluded, and ignored. For some, this critical consciousness will motivate actions to redress disparities and challenge what they perceive as an unjust system (Marstin, 1979; Watts, Diemer, & Voight, 2011).

Third, action in the common world transcends individual life spans. In fact, Arendt (1958) considered the intergenerational responsibilities in the public realm the very means whereby human beings overcame the fact of their mortality.

> The common world is what we enter when we are born and what we leave behind when we die. It transcends our life span into past and future alike; it was there before we came and will outlast our brief sojourn into it. It is what we have in common not only with those who live with us, but also with those who were here before and with those who will come after us. But such a common world can survive the coming and going of the generations only to the extent that it appears in public. It is the publicity of the public realm which can absorb and make shine through the centuries whatever men may want to save from the natural ruin of time. Through many ages before us—but now not any more—men entered the public realm because they wanted something of their own or something they had in common with others to be more permanent than their earthly lives.
>
> (p. 50)

MINI-POLITIES IN MANAGEABLE FRAMES

A conceptual discussion on the commons, justice, and moral development elicits questions about processes. How do people get initiated into the interdependent commons, feel at home there, value it, and develop an identity as a member, especially in an American society that stresses individualist values? The answers lie in processes of wrangling in real life communities.

Dewey addressed such questions in *The Public and Its Problems* (1927) where he argued that the concept of democracy and community is utopian and consequently meaningless, until people define it through communication and actions with one another in concrete (and not neat and tidy) community settings:

> Only when we start from a community as a fact, grasp the fact in thought so as to clarify and enhance its constituent elements, can we reach an idea of democracy which is not utopian. The conceptions and shibboleths which are traditionally associated with the idea of democracy take on a veridical and directive meaning only when they are construed as marks and traits of an association which realizes the defining characteristics of a community. Fraternity, liberty, and equality isolated from communal life are hopeless abstractions.
>
> (p. 142)

In other words, democracy itself and the ideals of liberty and equality are utopian—abstract and meaningless—until people give them definition through the commitments they form on the ground. Dewey argues that it is through communication, through getting to know and bond with one another, that we create a sense of the public and transform local community experiences into what he called the "Great Community." He writes, "Without such communication the Public will remain in eclipse. Communication can alone create a great community" (p. 142).

In line with Dewey's emphasis on the constituent elements of real world communities, we emphasize that young people's understanding of society and of their rights and responsibilities as citizens of societies are interpreted and filtered through what we have referred to as mediating institutions (schools; extracurricular activities; faith-based, cultural, and other community-based organizations). These mediating institutions provide people with an opportunity to experience and participate in the commons in what Parks (2000) calls *manageable frames*—concrete entry-points to the abstract notion of the commons. In other work we have referred to these spaces as mini-polities to emphasize the fact that it is through the experiences and relationships they forge in these local, proximal contexts that teens formulate ideas about their membership, rights, and obligations as citizens in the broader polity (Flanagan, 2013). Other scholars have used terms such as the micro experience of the commons (Parks, 2000) or the "mini-publics" of deliberative democracy processes (Fung, 2003). Whatever terms we use the main point is that people's (and we emphasize youths') concepts of themselves as citizens, as members of the body politic, are built up via their memberships in groups and institutions— peer groups, schools, community-based institutions—spaces where they enact what it means to be part of a group, that is, exercise the prerogatives and assume the responsibilities of membership in the group.

PROCESSES OF MORAL DEVELOPMENT IN COMMUNITY-BASED ORGANIZATIONS

In general, research has not specifically focused on the potential of youth participation in extracurricular or community-based programs for moral or character education. However, reviews of an extensive body of work confirm strong positive associations between such participation and developmental outcomes including psychological adjustment, lower rates of smoking and drug use, and higher quantity and quality of interactions with one's parents (Mahoney, Harris, & Eccles, 2006).

Other work shows that participation in community groups in one's youth predicts civic participation (voting, volunteering, joining and leading community groups) in adulthood (Duke, Skay, Pettingell, & Borowsky, 2009), suggesting that an ethic of civic participation or of social responsibility to the community is nurtured through such involvement. An ethic of social responsibility reflects values that transcend narrow self-interest. According to Schwartz's (1992, 2009) circumplex model, self-transcending values (benevolence and universalism) diverge from those at the opposite end of the continuum, i.e., self-enhancing values (power and achievement). Benevolence refers to values reflecting proactive responses to others that build relationships (e.g., loyalty, responsibility, honesty, kindness) and universalism to values that promote a more inclusive, peaceful world that protects all living things. In studies of late adolescents and young adults, these very self-transcending values as well as the youths' moral self-ideals increase as a result of their community involvement (Pratt, Hunsberger, Pancer, & Alisat, 2003).

We suggest several mechanisms that might explain why engagement in community-based organizations (CBOs) in one's youth may lead to self-transcending values and to lives of civic engagement in adulthood. First, CBOs provide a structured outlet for leisure time including a pro-social reference group of peers and adult mentors. Typically the latter (adults) are models of civic behavior insofar as many are volunteering their time to the organization. CBOs also fill the niche in the after school hours from

3:00–6:00 p.m. when many juvenile misdemeanors occur. These programs play a role in informal social control insofar as youth who participate in structured youth groups, particularly those that engage them in community service, are less likely to be involved in antisocial activities or substance abuse in later years (Barber, Eccles, & Stone, 2001). But the mechanism whereby CBOs contribute to later civic engagement goes beyond their role in keeping youth out of trouble.

As Verba et al. (1995) found in their study of adults, the very fact of being in a community organization increases the likelihood that one will be invited to join others. For youth, participating in a CBO increases the likelihood of recruitment into more community activities including activities such as community service. In other words, being in a CBO sets youth on a developmental pathway of continuing civic engagement. Moral development occurs in these settings through processes of informal social control, of negotiating shared moral norms with fellow members of one's community and with pro-social reference groups, of exposure to and engagement with a wider set of perspectives and people, and with a sense of social responsibility for that broader community of others.

Second, involvement in community organizations satisfied the human need to belong (Baumeister & Leary, 1995). The emotional ties to a community where young people feel that they belong are a foundation for nurturing morality. When young people feel wanted, feel that they count in the affairs of the community, they are less likely to violate its norms. In fact, youths' sense of "mattering" to others in the organization has been identified as the sine qua non of effective community-based youth organizations (Eccles & Gootman, 2001).

In contrast, the absence of such affective ties is considered a problem for the individual and for the community as well; we use terms like disaffected or alienated to capture that disconnect. The notion of reconnecting youth into the web of community relations is the thesis underlying restorative justice practices with juvenile offenders. Practices such as victim-offender mediation, community service, and conflict resolution are designed to repair relationships, to restore the youth's membership in the community through socially responsible actions. But it is not only the young offender who engages in reparation. Community members also are made aware of ways that they could make the youth feel more included (Bazemore & Walgrave, 1999). The focus here is less on youth breaking a law and more on the break from the community that needs repair. In contrast to a retributive framework in which the juvenile offender is held accountable to the state, restorative justice practices emphasize his/her obligation to repair the harm done to victims and to the broader community.

Developing the democratic dispositions of youth is a third way in which the routine practices of CBOs contribute to moral and character development. Concepts and beliefs about the self and society—about what *does* and what *should* occur—flow from participating with others in these routine practices (Goodnow, Miller, & Kessel, 1995). CBOs provide their members opportunities to work towards goals that are collectively defined in a context where the status of all members is relatively equal. When they engage in group projects, peers hold one another accountable to the group: If you promise to help, you had better show up or risk the likelihood that you will lose face in the eyes of your peers. Virtues of loyalty, team spirit, trust, and trustworthiness, dispositions that are foundational for citizenship, are nourished (Flanagan, 2004).

The political scientist C. Douglas Lummis (1996) notes that, not only do we learn about trust but that we also become trustworthy persons through the repeated commitments and honoring of promises we make to fellow human beings. Relations of trust

> are established in the web of human relations by thousands of promises and contracts, some explicit but most not, which people make in their daily dealings with one another over the years and over generations. Trust is not morality, but it produces virtuous behavior and virtuous persons.
>
> (p. 145)

Alluding to the social contract that binds members of a civil society together, Lummis adds that

> the act of making and keeping a promise is a conquest of the chaos that would come if each of us followed our individual passions from moment to moment wherever they lead. It is a conquest that establishes order without placing humankind under a punishing God, a punishing leviathan, a punishing conscience, or a punishing order of exploitative work.
>
> (p. 146)

In sum, keeping promises (i.e., keeping faith with one another) may be a means by which teens learn what it means to be part of a commons and about the ties that bind them to fellow members of their community.

A fourth way in which CBOs contribute to the moral and character development of younger generations is by developing their connections and relationships with adults who themselves are committed to the commons. In fact, positive relationships between adults and adolescents increase and negative group stereotypes break down when adolescents and adults work on shared issues in community-based youth programs (Jarrett, Sullivan, & Watkins, 2005; Zeldin, Camino, & Mook, 2005).

Activation of group identities. The process of moral identity formation in CBOs depends on the extent to which youth identify with the organization or group. But how does such group identity formation come about? According to social identity theory (Tajfel, 1981) one's social identity is the part of one's self-concept that derives from the knowledge of belonging to a group and the value and emotional attachment associated with being a member of that group. When a group identity is salient, moral development is shaped by norms about who "we" are and how "we" act (Thomas & Lewis, 2013). Furthermore, informal social control and peer pressure to conform will affect behavior within the group. Since collective action enhances well-being (Klar & Kasser, 2009), group identities will be reinforced. When people identify with a group and internalize its norms, they not only conform to those norms but also believe that choosing behavior consistent with the group is an authentic, freely chosen decision rather than a constraint on free will (Amiot, Sansfacon, Louis, & Yelle, 2011).

Discussions within a group reinforce the group's identity and increase the likelihood that members will engage in collective action. Discussions also increase the likelihood that people from diverse backgrounds and perspectives will find common ground (Thomas & Louis, 2013). In our own work with adolescents, we found that peer discussions in which different perspectives were aired and respected, increased adolescents' sense of group solidarity. Over the period of a year, these group processes increased youths' social trust or faith in humanity (Flanagan & Stout, 2010).

Our very standards for personal moral action and our beliefs about what constitutes a just world are shaped by the groups with which we identify. Hatano and Takahashi (2005) make this point when they contrast cognition about the natural world with societal cognition, arguing that, in the latter, "'how the entity is' is almost always associated with 'how it should be'" (pp. 290, 291). Morality itself is intertwined with our thinking about society, and Hatano and Takahashi contend that the nurturing of children's societal cognition is inevitably accompanied by emotions and morality. Ultimately, our theories about a moral and just community are not objective truths but are entangled with our affection for and allegiance to the groups with which we identify.

TYPES OF COMMUNITY INVOLVEMENT

We have noted common processes in community-based organizations that figure in the role they play as contexts for moral and character development. Next we turn to a discussion of two features of CBOs that differ with respect to the opportunities they afford for moral and character development—the degree to which they involve public action and the degree to which the CBO and its work exposes youth to a homogeneous or heterogeneous mix of others.

Public action. We know that opportunities for developing civic identities and commitments vary based on the kinds of community activities in which youth engage. For example, longitudinal analyses following a US sample of adolescents into young adulthood showed that involvement in community service, political action, and public performance in adolescence predicted voting, volunteering, and joining community organizations in adulthood (McFarland & Thomas, 2006). The authors point to the *public* quality of the adolescent activities of community service, political action, and public performance. Their reference to the *public quality* of these activities echoes Arendt's discussion of the public realm—where one's activities gain meaning because they are seen and heard by everyone. We would take this point a step further to note that, in the course of their actions in public, youth are *engaged in the commons* and are developing identities as members of the public.

Diversity. The potential for moral development in the community or public realm also depends on the extent to which experiences there meet the standards that Dewey (1916) posed for evaluating the democratic character of associations, i.e., how numerous and varied were the interests shared by members of a group and how full and free was the interplay of the group and its members with other groups. In other words, opportunities for moral development in community organizations are enhanced by the diversity of backgrounds and perspectives represented in the group. Diversity in groups may even motivate members to engage in more action for the common good.

Several studies have pointed to positive relationships between the diversity of a group and the civic commitments of its members. For example, in their in-depth interviews with 100 adults selected for their persistent involvement in community work, Daloz and colleagues (1996) point to what they refer to as an "enlarged engagement with the other" as the most important and consistent factor motivating commitments to the common good:

We had not anticipated this finding, but early in the study as people told us their stories, we began to hear about important encounters with others significantly different from themselves. On the surface, the forms of difference were variable. But when we examined this pattern more closely, the differences that were significant in the formation of commitment to the common good were differences defined by "tribe."

(p. 63)

In two of our own studies of adolescents' and young adults' commitment to the commons we also have noted the value of diversity in boosting young people's civic commitments. In the first study, we compared adolescents' perceptions of their local community, contrasting youth who had engaged in community service with peers who had participated in other forms of extracurricular activities. The most negative perceptions of fellow community members were voiced by those youth who had not engaged in either form of group activity. That is, adolescents were least likely to report that people in their community worked together to solve problems if the youth themselves were uninvolved in community affairs (either through extracurricular or community service work). But the most positive reports of the community's collective efficacy, i.e., the capacity of ordinary people to trust one another and work together to address the community's problems, were reported by those youth who engaged in community service. Their reports were more positive when compared to their peers who engaged only in extracurricular activities. In addition, adolescents' open-ended reports about what they had learned from engaging in community service pointed to its potential to diversify the networks of others with whom they interact. Challenging group stereotypes and realizing the interdependence and mutual obligations that bind members of communities together were common themes in the youths' responses.

We concluded that, in contrast to the more homogeneous interest-based groups that characterize most extracurricular clubs, community service offers adolescents opportunities to explore (individual and collective) identity with a more heterogeneous group of people in their community—people who may differ from them in age, ethnicity, religion, or social class. Consequently, it has the potential for extending their relationships with and understanding of others as well as the boundaries of the community for which they feel responsible (Flanagan, Kim, Collura, & Kopish, in press).

In a second study we looked at the elements of AmeriCorps national service programs that boosted the civic engagement of members over a period of one year. Based on baseline and post program data collected from a national sample of participants, we found that Corps members' reports of diversity in their experience (i.e., working with fellow Corps and community members who were from backgrounds different from their own) was the most significant predictor of *increases in civic engagement* (participation in community-based meetings and events, joining organizations that supported issues they cared about, voicing their views on issues via media or at public meetings, voting, and keeping informed about current events) over the one-year period. In addition, for those youth whose families had earned less than the median household income at the time the data were collected, civic engagement increased if the Corps member felt a sense of community in the AmeriCorps program, i.e., that s/he was part of a community and that s/he had made a contribution to that community (Flanagan, Gallay, & Kim, 2012).

In summary, we would argue that moral development is linked to an increasing understanding of society and one's relationship to others and the larger world—it depends on understanding one's role in the commons. The notion of the commons, and the sense of responsibility and care that accompanies it, compels one to notice and respond to the injustice that exists in one's community. The scope of the community with which one identifies—who is identified as part of the "we"—grows wider with more varied experiences, especially when grounded in intentional engagement with people and perspectives that differ from one's own.

THE NATURAL ENVIRONMENT: OUR COMMONS

In this final section, we turn to a discussion of the moral imperative of environmental action and of the unique possibilities for moral development afforded by an understanding of the environment as our commons through work in community-based organizations.

Climate change is arguably the biggest global challenge facing younger generations with implications for the very necessities of life. For example, water quality and availability is a major global public health concern that is likely to raise significant moral questions in coming decades. Is water a public good or can it be privatized? Does everyone deserve access to clean water and how should they get it? Regardless of where they live, there are profound implications of climate change for the decisions about consumption and lifestyle and the very definitions of well-being and success for younger generations (Giddens, 2009). Even the most optimistic scenarios of lowering carbon emissions and greenhouse gas temperatures suggest that major changes in lifestyles, values, and orientations of one's interests with those of a broader community will be needed.

Environmental issues have local, regional, and global manifestations, which give them a distinct moral advantage insofar as they lend themselves to the links between personal, local behavior and public, regional, and global cumulative impact. Environmental issues are, in fact, moral issues. Natural resources are essential for the survival of life on earth, so it is everyone's responsibility to preserve them and ensure they are maintained at an adequate level of quality to sustain life. As the environment is something we all share, it is part of a global commons.

A small but growing body of scholarship points to the moral foundations of environmental action. For example, research with young people across culturally and economically diverse communities shows that youth have a rich and diverse appreciation for nature and a moral responsiveness to it that extends beyond local community threats such as pollution (Kahn, 2003). Motivations to protect the natural world have both anthropocentric (based on its value to humans) and biocentric (nature has intrinsic value in and of itself) bases (Persing, 2007). Children as young as first grade employ both types of arguments in their environmental moral reasoning. Across diverse cultures young people's moral reasoning about the environment includes arguments about using nature as well as about the intrinsic value of nature and respect for living things (Kahn, 2003).

Compared to the research on youth, there is a larger body of work on the moral foundations of environmental action in adulthood. According to two meta-analyses of research with adults conducted 20 years apart, pro-environmental behavior is associated with moral dispositions and motivations including awareness of one's interdependence with other people and species and responsibility for the commons (Bamberg & Moser, 2007; Hines, Hungerford, & Tomera, 1986/87). These moral dispositions are identified as consistent psychosocial determinants of responsible environmental behavior. Other work shows that environmental action is correlated with generative concern in parents and adolescents—in their personal lifestyle decisions and in collective actions with groups to effect environmental policies (Pratt, Norris, Alisat, & Bisson, 2012).

Environmental concern is tied to a person's notion of self and the degree to which people define themselves as independent, interdependent with other people, or inter-dependent with all living things. Consistent with our argument about the role of group identities in the development of moral selves, scholars have focused on the role of an environmental identity underlying the moral motivation to transcend self-interest and preserve the environment in the interests of other people, species, and future generations (Schultz, 2001). An environmental identity has been described as a sense of belonging or connection to something larger than oneself, including the nonhuman world (Arnocky, Stroink, & De Cicco, 2007) and is correlated with the degree to which an individual associates with nature (Dutcher, Finley, Luloff, & Johnson, 2007). Whether for anthropocentric or biocentric reasons, an environmental identity reflects a belief that the environment is important to us as well as an important part of who we are. The psychological role of an environmental identity is similar to that of other collective identities—providing a sense of connection to a larger whole (Clayton, 2003).

Lacking an awareness of our interdependencies with other persons and species is a major reason why moral standards may not be activated in behavior. In fact, selective moral disen-gagement—a failure to identify with and take responsibility for the commons—underpins environmental degradation (Bandura, 2007). Moral disengagement from environmental responsibility occurs, in part, due to the phenomenon of "free riding," i.e., people absolve themselves of personal responsibility out of beliefs that "others" are taking care of the problem or because consumption of material goods has become so integral to people's identities and ways of life. In turn, consumer behaviors (and consciences) can be manipulated through "greenwashing" practices that convince the public that products are more eco-friendly than they actually are, creating false ethical reasons for their purchase.

Engagement in environmental community action projects can combat this disen-gagement in young people through two practices of progressive education outlined by John Dewey—hands-on learning about real world issues and work with fellow members of one's community. In environmental action projects, students are actively engaged in real-world issues through hands-on learning. Issues that students identify and tackle in collaboration with community groups are generally complex and thus require the exper-tise and perspectives of a diverse group of stakeholders.

In this model of environmental community action, young people are exposed to dif-fering points of view and learn that everyone's opinion and interest must be considered. In order to take concrete action that is a staple of these projects, deliberation as to the course of action must take place with consideration of the views of those on all sides of the issue. Young people can be active citizens through all parts of the process. The sense that they can get things done in their community if they work together can lead to a validation of commitment to collective work for common good.

The value of collective action is another lesson that youth learn. Solutions take time and require the commitments of many individual citizens working together to achieve a common goal. Because young people work on these projects in partnership with CBOs, gaining from the expertise and experience of adults in their community, they learn that they are not alone in solving environmental issues. Through collective action addressing common issues with members of their community, youth also gain a sense of the moral commitment of their fellow citizens. In this way, the meaning of "the commons" and the joint responsibility to preserve it deepens for the youth involved.

At the same time environmental projects lend themselves to consideration of larger issues. For example, nonpoint source pollution of a watershed is affected by the actions of many institutions and citizens in a large geographical area. There is not a single source to point to from which pollution originates; rather there are multiple contributors from many jurisdictions, all of which have both local and larger regional impact. Young people learn that it may not be fair or just, but it is the reality that outside forces have a great impact on everyday lives in local communities.

We believe that environmental community action projects are well suited to contribute to moral development both because such projects are easily accessible to young people and because of the unique features of such projects. Environmental community action projects are those that put young people into direct contact with the environment and ask them to work with others in their community to solve a local environmental problem or issue. Through these projects, young people can come to identify themselves as members of the public, see natural resources as public or shared resources, gain skills and dispositions that enable them to work collectively with others, and develop the motivation and commitment to act (Gallay & Flanagan, 2012).

As we noted earlier, Elinor Ostrom's (2010) description of the commons included both common pool resources and public goods. Aldo Leopold (1948) famously took the concept of common good and community further, to include "the land": soil, water, plants, and animals collectively. He recognized that ethical behavior ultimately was rooted in people's awareness of their interdependence: "All ethics evolved so far rest upon a single premise: that the individual is a member of a community of interdependent parts" (p. 204).

If awareness of the interdependence of human beings is part of the development of a moral self, environmental projects with community organizations are well suited for the challenge. Interdependence is a fundamental scientific concept within and between biological and physical environments as well as a key idea in the study of ecology. Ecosystems cannot survive or flourish unless all members of the community are in balance. Moral and ethical questions are logical extensions of these scientific concepts.

Through environmental projects, young people learn that their everyday actions have everyday (and cumulative) implications for the well-being of others whom they may never see. Because the environment is not circumscribed and an action in one space affects life and well-being in another (i.e., water pollution flowing downstream, etc.), "others" affected by our actions include other communities down river, other nations, peoples, and species (Gallay & Flanagan, 2012). The slogan, "an injury to one is an injury to all" is apt because of the ripple effects of environmental damage. Indeed, the very meaning of "community" is extended in environmental work insofar as the community isn't defined by political boundaries or property lines. A river flows through many towns, counties, states, etc.... Watersheds observe only the boundaries of natural features, not of politics. Environmental issues affect not just the local area, not just Americans, not even just human beings. In this way, environmental community action projects can help students gain an awareness of the idea of global citizenship, of empathy, and responsibility for a wide range of "others."

Interdependence also is implicated in the solutions to environmental issues. No one individual or group can address environmental preservation alone. Environmental groups have to work with others—coalitions need to form, stakeholders need to be brought to the table. Collective action is taken for a common good.

Protecting the commons, these public goods and spaces, even has a specific connection to generativity in environmental work. Environmental community action projects are often aimed at long-term goals, as sustainability is a core concept of ecology. Young people are introduced to the idea that the actions they are taking benefit their future, as well as the future of generations that come after them. This has moral development implications because youth are thinking of the well-being of others, including those not yet alive. The intergenerational commitment of environmental community action echoes Arendt's (1958) discussion of work in the public realm: "If the world is to contain a public space, it cannot be erected and planned for one generation only; it must transcend the lifespan of mortal men" (p. 50).

Environmental projects with community-based organizations offer opportunities for moral engagement. Through such projects youth come to appreciate that they are members of a community with a stake in solving issues shared by that community. As community members wrangle with issues, diverse perspectives are likely to be aired. Besides such heterogeneous encounters within a community, environmental decisions have implications beyond the geographical and political borders of communities as well as beyond the borders of generations and time. Consequently, when communities wrestle with environmental issues, there are moral questions concerning the implications of their actions and decisions for other people and species whom they do not know. Environmental questions, thus, have the potential to enlarge the moral community for which we feel responsible. Environmental projects create opportunities for homogeneous and heterogeneous encounters, a bonding and bridging with others that are essential components of moral development.

CONCLUSION

In this chapter, we have presented an overview of the concept of the commons and its continued relevance, shared empirical studies on the potential of CBOs to contribute to moral development and the variance between settings, and highlighted environmental community action projects as a type of engagement that is particularly rich for both moral development and understanding one's identity as a member of the interdependent, global commons. We conclude by recognizing that concepts such as "the commons" and "the common good" are useful in framing one's role in the world, but they are often too abstract as a starting point. Young people can come to understand the commons by participating in the concrete practices in CBOs in local contexts. The habits that develop via the routine practices of CBOs become integral to the youths' evolving identities. Ultimately, those identities (the who I am and what I stand for) are the bases from which their moral actions flow (Youniss & Yates, 1999). Beyond the dispositions and skills that youth develop in the present, the repeated enactments of routine practices in CBOs help to create a cache of memories, upon which people can draw throughout their lives, of people working together to address complex social and moral issues (Daloz et al., 1996; Nasir & Kirshner, 2003; Parks, 2000). This cache of memories, coupled with actual practice in mini-polities and reassurance that their contribution matters, equips young people to navigate moral ambiguity and complexity on an individual level, but more importantly, those practices equip them to collectively build moral environments.

REFERENCES

Amiot, C.E., Sansfacon, S., Louis, W.R., & Yelle, M. (2011). Can intergroup behaviors be emitted out of self-determined reasons? Testing the role of group norms and behavioral congruence in the internalization of discrimination and parity behaviors. *Personality and Social Psychology Bulletin, 38*(1), 63–76.

Arendt, H. (1958). *The human condition.* Chicago: University of Chicago Press.

Arnocky, S., Stroink, M., & De Cicco, T. (2007). Self-construal predicts environmental concern, cooperation, and conservation. *Journal of Environmental Psychology, 27*(4), 255–264.

Bamberg, S., & Moser, G. (2007). Twenty years after Hines, Hungerford, and Tomera: A new meta-analysis of psycho-social determinants of pro-environmental behavior. *Journal of Environmental Psychology, 27*, 14–25.

Bandura, A. (2007). Impeding ecological sustainability through selective moral disengagement. *International Journal of Innovation and Sustainable Development, 2*(1), 8–35.

Barber, B.L., Eccles, J.S., & Stone, M.R. (2001). Whatever happened to the Jock, the Brain, and the Princess? Young adult pathways linked to adolescent activity involvement and social identity. *Journal of Adolescent Research, 16*, 429–455.

Baumeister, R.F., & Leary, M.R. (1995). The need to belong: Desire for interpersonal attachments as a fundamental human motivation. *Psychological Bulletin, 117*, 497–529.

Bazemore, G., & Walgrave, L. (1999). *Restorative juvenile justice: Repairing the harm of youth crime.* New York: Criminal Justice Press.

Blum, L. (1999). Race, community and moral education: Kohlberg and Spielberg as civic educators. *Journal of Moral Education, 28*(2), 125–143.

Boyte, H.C. (2011). Constructive politics as public work: Organizing the literature. *Political Theory, 39*(5), 630–660.

Clayton, S. (2003). Environmental identity: A conceptual and an operational definition. In S. Clayton & S. Opotow (Eds.), *Identity and the natural environment* (pp. 45–65). Cambridge, MA: MIT Press.

Daloz, L.A., Keen, C.H., Keen, J.P., & Parks, S.D. (1996). *Common fire: Lives of commitment in a complex world.* Boston: Beacon Press.

Dewey, J. (1916). *Democracy and education: An introduction to the philosophy of education.* New York: The Free Press.

Dewey, J. (1927). *The public and its problems.* New York: Holt.

Duke, N., Skay, C., Pettingell, S., and Borowsky, I. (2009). From adolescent connections to social capital: Predictors of civic engagement in young adulthood, *Journal of Adolescent Health, 44*, 161–168.

Dutcher, D., Finley, J., Luloff, A., & Johnson, J. (2007). Connectivity with nature as a measure of environmental values. *Environment and Behavior, 39*, 474–493.

Eccles, J.S., & Gootman, J.A. (2001). *Community programs to promote youth development.* National Research Council and Institute of Medicine Committee on Community-Level Programs for Youth. Board on Children, Youth, and Families, Division of Behavioral and Social Sciences and Education. Washington, DC: National Academy Press.

Flanagan, C. (2004). Volunteerism, leadership, political socialization, and civic engagement. In R.M. Lerner & L. Steinberg (Eds.), *Handbook of adolescent psychology* (pp. 721–746). New York: Wiley.

Flanagan, C. (2013). *Teenage citizens: The political theories of the young.* Cambridge, MA: Harvard University Press.

Flanagan, C., Gallay, L., & Kim, T. (2012). *Political incorporation in emerging adulthood: The potential of national service.* Paper presented at the biennial meetings of the Society for Research on Adolescence, Vancouver, BC, March, 2012.

Flanagan, C., Kim, T., Collura, J., & Kopish, M.A. (in press). Community service and adolescents' social capital. *Journal of Research on Adolescence.*

Flanagan, C.A., & Stout, M. (2010). Developmental patterns of social trust between early and late adolescence: Age and school climate effects. *Journal of Research on Adolescence, 20*(3), 748–773.

Fung, A. (2003). Survey article: Recipes for public spheres: Eight institutional design choices and their consequences. *Journal of Political Philosophy, 11*(3), 338–367.

Gallay, E.E., and Flanagan, C. (2012). Civic environmentalism: Social responsibility for public resources. In P.M. Brown, M. Corrigan, & A. Higgins-D'Alessandro, (Eds.), *Handbook on prosocial education* (pp. 171–178). Lanham, MD: Rowan and Littlefield.

Giddens, A. (2009). *The politics of climate change.* Cambridge: Polity Press.

Goodnow, J., Miller, P.J., & Kessel, F. (1995). *Cultural practices as contexts for development.* San Francisco: Jossey-Bass.

Hatano, G., & Takahashi, K. (2005). The development of societal cognition: A commentary. In M. Barrett & E. Buchanan-Barrow (Eds.), *Children's understanding of society* (pp. 287–303). East Sussex, UK: Psychology Press.

Hines, J.M., Hungerford, H.R., & Tomera, A.N. (1986/87). Analysis and synthesis of research on responsible environmental behavior: A meta-analysis. *Journal of Environmental Education, 18*, 1–8.

Jarrett, R.L., Sullivan, P.J., & Watkins, N.D. (2005). Developing social capital through participation in organized youth programs: Qualitative insights from three programs. *Journal of Community Psychology, 33*(1), 41–55.

Kahn, P. (2003) The development of environmental moral identity. In S. Clayton & S. Opotow (Eds.), *Identity and the natural environment* (pp. 113–134). Cambridge, MA: MIT Press.

Klar, M., & Kasser, T. (2009). Some benefits of being an activist: Measuring activism and its role in well-being. *Political Psychology, 30*, 755–777.

Leopold, Aldo. (1948). *A Sand County almanac, and sketches here and there.* New York: Oxford University Press.

Lummis, C.D. (1996). *Radical democracy.* Ithaca, NY: Cornell University Press.

Mahoney, J.L., Harris, A.L., & Eccles, J.S. (2006). Organized activity participation, positive youth development, and the over-scheduling hypothesis. *Social Policy Report, 20*(4). Ann Arbor, MI: Society for Research in Child Development.

Marstin, R. (1979). *Beyond our tribal gods: The maturing of faith.* Maryknoll, NY: Orbis Books.

McFarland, D.A., & Thomas, R.J. (2006). Bowling young: How youth voluntary associations influence adult political participation. *American Sociological Review, 71*, 401–425.

Nasir, N.S., & Kirshner, B. (2003). The cultural construction of moral and civic identities. *Applied Developmental Science, 7*(3), 138–147.

Nucci, L.P. (2008). Social cognitive domain theory and moral education. In L. Nucci and D. Narvaez (Eds.), *Handbook of moral and character education* (pp. 291–309). New York: Routledge.

Ostrom, E. (1998). A behavioral approach to the rational choice theory of collective action. Presidential Address, American Political Science Association, 1997, *American Political Science Review, 92*(1), 1–22.

Ostrom, E. (2010). Beyond markets and states: Polycentric governance of complex economic systems. *American Economic Review, 100*(3), 641–672.

Parks, S.D. (2000). *Big questions, worthy dreams: Mentoring young adults in their search for meaning, purpose, and faith.* San Francisco, CA: Jossey-Bass.

Persing, J.A. (2007). *On environmental moral thinking: Outdoor recreation as a context for development.* Saarbrücken, Germany: VDM Dr. Müeller e. K. und Lizenzberger.

Power, F.C. (2004). Moral self in community. In D.K. Lapsley & D. Narvaez (Eds.), *Moral development, self and identity* (pp. 47–64). Mahwah, NJ: Erlbaum.

Pratt, M.W., Hunsberger, B., Pancer, S.M., & Alisat, S. (2003). A longitudinal analysis of personal values socialization: Correlates of a moral self-ideal in late adolescence. *Social Development, 12*(4), 563–585.

Pratt, M.W., Norris, J.E., Alisat, S., & Bisson, E. (2012). Earth mothers (and fathers): Examining generativity and environmental concern in adolescents and their parents. *Journal of Moral Education, 42*(1), 12–27.

Schultz, P.W. (2001). The structure of environmental concern: Concern for self, other people, and the biosphere. *Journal of Environmental Psychology, 21*, 327–339.

Schwartz, S.H. (1992). Universals in the content and structure of values: Theoretical advances and empirical tests in 20 countries. *Advances in Experimental Social Psychology, 25*, 1–65.

Schwartz, S.H. (2009). Culture matters: National value cultures, sources, and consequences. In R.S. Wyer, C. Chiu, & Y. Hong (Eds.), *Understanding culture: Theory, research, and application* (pp. 127–150). New York: Psychology Press.

Tajfel, H. (1981). *Human groups and social categories: Studies in social psychology.* Cambridge: Cambridge University Press.

Thomas, E.F., & Louis, W.R. (2013). Doing democracy: The social psychological mobilization and consequences of collective action. *Journal of Social Issues, 7*(1), 173–200.

Verba, S., Schlozman, K.L., & Brady, H.E. (1995). *Voice and equality: Civic voluntarism in American politics.* Cambridge, MA: Harvard University Press.

Watts, R.J., Diemer, M.A., & Voight, A.M. (2011). Critical consciousness: Current status and future directions. *New Directions for Child and Adolescent Development, 2011*(134), 43–57.

Youniss, J. (2009). When morality meets politics in development. *Journal of Moral Education, 38*(2), 129–144.

Youniss, J., & Yates, M. (1999). Youth service and moral identity: A case for everyday morality. *Educational Psychology Review, 11*(4), 361–376.

Zeldin, S., Camino, L., & Mook, C. (2005). The adoption of innovation in youth organizations: Creating the conditions for youth–adult partnerships. *Journal of Community Psychology, 33*, 121–135.

26

THE MORAL AND CIVIC EFFECTS OF LEARNING TO SERVE

Daniel Hart, M. Kyle Matsuba, and Robert Atkins

By 1999, 64% of all public schools had students participating in service activities, and then between 1984 and 1999 the number of high schools offering community service opportunities rose from 27% to over 80% (National Center for Education Statistics, n.d.). More recently, in a 2007–2008 survey of 1,190 colleges, it was found that nearly one-third of students participated in service (Campus Compact, 2009). And although slight declines have occurred over the past two years, close to 64.5 million people reported volunteering in 2012 (US Department of Labor, 2013), contributing 7.9 billion hours of service, which is estimated to be valued at $171 billion (Corporation for National and Community Service, 2013). Given the prevalence of volunteering and the economic and social value of volunteering to our nation, leaders continue to call the American people to service (United We Serve, 2013).

Service work may not only advantage the community, but also foster development among its participants. Recent reviews have claimed a multitude of benefits for students ranging from increases in academic performance to heightened self-esteem (Celio, Durlak, & Dymnicki, 2011; Conway, Amel, & Gerwien, 2009; Furco & Root, 2010; van Goethem, forthcoming). Given the prosocial, civic nature of community service, it is not surprising that the consensus among these reports is that community service also supports moral and character development. The multitude of benefits has led to the development of service-learning programs in schools and universities. This chapter explores the extent to which service-learning is associated with good outcomes, and the paths through which service might lead to these outcomes. We begin by selectively reviewing the service-learning literature highlighting the various theoretical paradigms and the empirical research findings as they relate to moral and civic attitudes and behaviors. We then explore the practical similarities between service-learning and community service programs as revealed in research and discuss possible implications of these similarities. Finally, we present recent research on volunteering that raises important issues for service-learning and community service practitioners.

THEORETICAL ROOTS TO SERVICE-LEARNING PROGRAMS

The theoretical roots to service-learning programs are diverse. Many service-learning researchers and practitioners cite the writings of John Dewey (1972). Dewey wrote extensively on the link between education and society. He envisioned communities of students working together to identify and respond to the social problems of their times (Kahne & Westheimer, 2001), and wrote of the transformative nature associated with these real-life educational experiences (Giles & Eyler, 1994). Through these continuous, interactive, and reflective experiences with the world—community service and service-learning—students gain new perspectives on and skills for solving social, moral, and civic problems.

Others have emphasized slightly different facets to service-learning. For example, Kenny, Simon, Kiley-Brabeck, and Lerner (2001), and Warter and Grossman (2001), emphasized the transactional reciprocity between student and context where each community in which participants volunteer provides a unique cultural, environmental, political, and historical context. Students learn about civic matters and social issues in each of these milieus and each of these contexts contribute to students' thinking on social issues. Yates and Youniss (2001) bring a developmental perspective to service-learning programs. Having youth interact with a broader network of people holding a diversity of values can cause students to reflect on, elaborate, and revise their beliefs about social justice, social institutions, and civic matters. This expansion of students' current ideological beliefs and socio-moral framework provides a path through which they may achieve identity as described by Erikson.

Still others view service-learning from a social learning perspective, having argued that students acquire their civic attitudes and behaviors through the modeling and expectations communicated by significant adults (e.g., Scales, Blyth, Berkas, & Kielsmeier, 2000; Switzer, Simmons, Dew, Regalski, & Wang, 1995). In the context of service-learning, witnessing adults engaged in serving others and discussing the significance of such actions facilitate the acquisition and internalization of similar socially responsible attitudes and behavior by students. Finally, some researchers have focused their work around Eisenberg's model of prosocial reasoning and behavior. According to Batchelder and Root (1994), service-learning experiences trigger empathic responses in students toward the people they serve, thus bringing conscientious attention to another's need and motivating them to respond. Having students discuss their service-learning experience may facilitate students' prosocial-reasoning development, which should, in turn, increase their motivation to respond to those in need (Blasi, 1995).

The diverse theoretical perspectives suggest that community service and service-learning may affect many psychological domains of children's and adolescents' lives—self-esteem, identity, academic achievement, moral and civic development have been identified by advocates as benefiting from the influence of community service—and may do so through cognitive, social, emotional, and cultural processes. The many claims regarding benefits together suggest that service-learning and community service may be the solution to the flaws and problems of children and adolescents.

Yet the diversity of outcomes and proposed mechanisms of influence suggests that the service-learning as a discipline lacks the kinds of compelling research findings that constrain theorizing in other academic fields. If a field lacks clear findings about mechanisms and routes of influence, then the relation of theory to findings cannot be judged, and all theories are equal. To a degree, this remains the current state of affairs in the study of community service to moral and character development. Theoretical perspectives on community service and service-learning are also curiously independent of many of the kinds of activities in which children and adolescents are actually engaged.

WHAT IS SERVICE-LEARNING?

While there is no specific consensus in how service-learning is defined in the literature, Furco (1996) sees service-learning as a combination of community service activities with learning through academic, elective, or vocational courses. Service-learning programs typically possess some or all of the following features (Pritchard, 2001): (1) clearly identified learning objectives; (2) student participation in selecting service activity; (3) a theoretical base; (4) integration of the service experience with an academic course; and (5) student reflection.

In contrast, community service typically refers to programs that focus on the recipients who benefit from the service activity (Furco, 1996). While these programs may foster the development of participants' moral and altruistic disposition, often these programs do not emphasize the formal integration of educational curriculums with service work, and so may not include formal reflection activities. Interestingly, some researchers differentiate between service-learning and community service programs based on the underlying goal of the service program. For example, Alt (1997) and Kahne and Westheimer (2001) distinguish between "change" and "charity" goals. Programs that have "change" as their goal hope to transform participants by enhancing their academic motivation and learning as it relates to civic issues associated with the service-learning experience. Programs that have "charity" as their focus hope to foster participants' altruistic and moral nature. This latter goal is more prevalent in community service programs (Pritchard, 2002).

Given the diversity of uses of the constructs service-learning and community service, it is unsurprising that an array of programs has been claimed as members of each. Consequently service-learning programs vary enormously from each other, differing substantially in program content (e.g., a focus on poverty or the environment), the intensity and duration of the program, the size of the student groups participating, and the degree of choice students have in selecting projects (Furco, 2003). Moreover, students enter these programs with different interests and abilities (Root, 2005). Finally, because service-learning programs take place in natural settings typically unobserved by researchers, it is difficult to know exactly what experiences students receive during service-learning (Waterman, 2003).

WHAT ARE THE EFFECTS OF SERVICE-LEARNING?

Articles reviewing the research on service-learning courses suggest positive, but not easily interpreted, results (Celio et al., 2011; Conway et al., 2009; Furco & Root, 2010; van Goethem, forthcoming). We review a few of these studies to highlight the benefits of, and theoretical issues associated with, service-learning.

Reduction of Negative Behaviors

In a large, well-designed study, Melchior (1999) investigated service-learning programs embedded in seven middle schools across the US. These programs involved intensive, hands-on service involvement plus opportunities to reflect on the experience through discussions, journal writing, research papers, and presentations. Melchior found that by the end of the program service-learning participants were less likely to be pregnant or have made someone pregnant, and less likely to have been arrested in the previous six months than students not enrolled in the service-learning program. Moreover, the effect was maintained for a year following the termination of the program. Finally, students who continued to be involved in organized service a year later consumed less alcohol compared to students who did not continue their involvement. These results suggest diverse and impressive positive benefits for community service.

Other studies have also reported positive behavioral effects on students as a result of participating in service-learning programs. For example, Switzer et al. (1995) compared junior high students who either tutored younger students or provided help at senior citizens facilities to students in a control group. They found that the boys in the "helper" program were more involved in school and community activities, had fewer problem behaviors in school, and were more likely to report that they felt like a better person. Allen, Philliber, Herrling, and Kuperminc (1997) had participants perform voluntary service, discuss their service experiences, and participate in classroom-based social skill development. At the completion of the academic year, participants in the program were less likely than adolescents in the control group to have failed a class, have been suspended, or to have become pregnant compared to those in the control group. While Allen et al. were not able to determine whether a specific element of the program—service, reflection, or social skill building—was responsible for the benefits of the Teen Outreach, they did report that number of hours spent in community service was a better predictor of benefits than was the number of classroom sessions attended. However, the theoretical mechanisms through which these programs effect such positive results are vague and mostly untested.

Impacts on Moral Development

In studies exploring the impact of service-learning on moral development the results have been generally positive (see Root, 2005). For example, Conrad and Hedin (1982) chose 30 "experiential education programs" that emphasized students learning by doing with associated reflection. The authors found that relative to students in the comparison group, students in the experiential programs showed significant gains in moral reasoning. These findings have been replicated in other studies (Boss, 1994; Lies, Bock, Brandenberger, & Trozzolo, 2012).

Leming (2001) compared three groups of high school students: Those enrolled in a community service elective course that featured a socio-moral "reflection" component, those enrolled in a community service elective course with a limited, more general reflection component, and students from the same high schools enrolled in English classes. At the end of the semester-long class, students enrolled in the socio-moral reflection community service class had made substantial gains relative to the other two groups (the community service with limited reflection, the comparison group of students enrolled in the English classes) on measures of identity and social responsibility. Leming's work suggests that the form of reflection may be an important consideration.

Billig (2000) also cited studies showing that service-learning programs influenced prosocial personality characteristics such as trustworthiness, empathy, and dependability. For instance, Scales et al. (2000) found that middle school students involved in service-learning programs have greater concern for the welfare of others compared to students in a control group. In addition, students who performed more than 30 hours of service during the year had a greater perceived efficacy in helping others compared to those students who performed less service. Finally, students involved in service-learning, and who reported that their participation made them more interested in their other classes, scored higher than comparison students in their concern for others' welfare, and their perceived efficacy in helping others. For Scales et al. (2000), the duration of service-learning experience and the reflection on this experience are important in maintaining students' concern for others and the belief they can effect change in helping others.

Service-learning's Effects on Civic Engagement

Many studies report a positive link between service-learning and civic engagement (Furco & Root, 2010). Yates and Youniss (1996), for instance, examined the essays of service-learning participants (described above) for "transcendent" ideological reflections, and found that service-learning experiences can stimulate change in students' ideological perspective. The authors noted a movement away from a concrete description of and judgmental attitude towards homeless people and a movement towards connecting their experience with abstract constructs such as social inequality and societal responsibility. Root (2005) reported that service-learning programs increase students' interest in politics, attitude toward community involvement, willingness to take political action, and political activity level. Similarly, Billig's (2000) review revealed that students in service-learning programs had an increased understanding of government function and were more likely to vote up to 15 years later. Billig also reported that students in service-learning programs were more likely to be aware of community needs, believed they could make a difference, and were committed to service now and later in life. Finally, Melchior (1999) found that students involved in service-learning programs showed an immediate increase in civic attitudes (e.g., "A good citizen to me is someone who puts back into the community"). However, this effect was not evident a year later. The absence of long-term longitudinal assessments leaves open important questions, including whether programs really have the transformational impacts claimed by theorists and whether financial and curricular investments in the programs are warranted by outcomes.

Meta-Analyses of Service-Learning Studies

In addition to the positive effects of service-learning on moral and civic attitudes discussed in the previous two sections, reviews generally find that service-learning has diffuse positive effects on various outcome measures. Celio et al. (2011) considered 62 service-learning studies involving 11,837 students to determine their outcomes in five areas including attitudes towards self, school and learning, civic engagement, social skills, and academic performance. To be included in the analysis, the service-learning program had to meet four objectives. Programs need to: (1) be linked to academic curriculum; (2) actively involve youth in its design; (3) involve community partners; and (4) provide opportunities for reflection. Programs involved students in elementary, secondary, or postsecondary level and included a control group. Celio et al. reported that the average effect sizes were small to medium (ranging from 0.27 to 0.43) for each of the five outcome areas suggesting that service-learning programs were successful in producing positive outcomes.

In another meta-analysis, Conway et al. (2009) considered 103 samples from 78 different studies. Each study included a pretest–post-test design with a community service component sandwiched in between. They reported that students showed improvement on academic and learning outcomes, personal outcomes (e.g., volunteer motivation, moral development), social outcomes (e.g., leadership and interpersonal skills), and citizenship outcomes (e.g., obeying laws, community involvement). Effect sizes ranged from small (e.g., $d = 17$ for citizenship outcomes) to moderate (e.g., $d = 0.43$ for academic outcomes). Further, Conway et al. reported that service-learning programs with a reflection component had a greater effect than those without on personal, social, and citizenship outcomes. However, intensity and duration of service made no difference on outcome measures.

Summary

The research evidence generally suggests that service-learning has beneficial effects on adolescents and their development. Reductions in problem behaviors have been reported, as have increases in school engagement, academic achievement, self-esteem, attitudes towards school, social skills, and so on. However, the fact that service-learning seems to influence equally so many psychological facets of young people makes the identification of specific causal mechanisms difficult; it appears that service-learning has benefits for domains of psychological functioning ordinarily thought to be relatively independent of each other. Nevertheless, researchers and educators have attempted to infer from the studies reviewed above how service-learning characteristics facilitate moral and civic development. Billig (2000), for example, lists the following program characteristics that she believes are necessary to maximize the effects of service participation: (1) a high degree of student responsibility for the service; (2) autonomy, student choice; (3) direct contact with the service recipient; and (4) reflection. Others have added that students must be involved in leadership positions, be directing the project themselves, and have a voice in the process (Melchior, 1999; Morgan & Streb, 2001). National standards have been promulgated by the National Youth Leadership Council that incorporates the criteria discussed above (National Youth Leadership Council, 2009).

While each of these program characteristics can be linked to one or more theoretical perspectives reviewed and to one or more empirical findings reported, the research support for each is ambiguous. In Celio and colleagues' (Celio et al., 2011) meta-analysis, they found that interventions that featured more of these national standards produced more development in students than did interventions with few or none of these characteristics. While this finding is of value—clearly, programs ought to include more of these standards and produce the best possible outcomes for students—they do little to clarify theoretical outcomes. For example, while reflection has been shown to be associated with positive outcomes in service-learning programs, these results do little to clarify the role reflection plays in scaffolding psychological development. In our view, based on the weight of the available evidence, we continue to be unclear which of the elements of community service and service-learning, or sum total, are critical to produce the beneficial outcomes observed. Moreover, the processes through which these effects occur have yet to be clearly identified.

THE EFFECTS AND CAUSES OF VOLUNTEERING CAN INFORM AN UNDERSTANDING OF COMMUNITY SERVICE AND SERVICE-LEARNING

Researchers and practitioners often presume that service-learning is fundamentally different from volunteering. Actions are considered volunteering if they: (1) are voluntary; (2) are deliberate; (3) occur over a period of time; (4) occur without expectation of rewards or punishments; (5) are serving others in need of help; and (6) are on behalf of people or causes (Snyder & Omoto, 2008). While there are many formal ways to distinguish between service-learning and volunteering, they are ordinarily treated distinct based on the degree to which entry into and duration of the activity is voluntary and by the extent of reflection that occurs. Yet while these conceptual distinctions theoretically make volunteering and service-learning substantially different activities, the limited research on the matter fails to substantiate the importance of these distinctions in terms of the activity's effect on children and adolescents.

Service-Learning and Volunteering have Similar Effects

Volunteering and service-learning show similar effects on participating children and adolescents. For instance, compared to non-volunteers, volunteers scored higher on measures of positive emotions, social skills, sympathy, self-esteem, and emotion regulation (e.g., Davis, Mitchell, Hall, Lothert, Snapp, & Meyer, 1999; Omoto & Snyder, 1995; Penner, Fritzsche, Craiger, & Freifeld, 1995; Unger & Thumuluri, 1997; Yogev & Ronen, 1982). In addition, research has found volunteering to be a protective factor for youth including fewer behavioral problems (Eccles & Barber, 1999; Uggen & Janikula, 1999). These results parallel those in the service-learning literature reviewed, thus making it difficult to draw distinctions between service-learning and community service programs based on outcome differences.

Comparisons of Service-Learning and Community Service Yield Few Differences

Research directly comparing service-learning and community service experiences also show few outcome differences. For example, Furco (2001) studied over 500 students at two high school sites. These students were enrolled in one of four classes/conditions: community service, service-learning, service-based internship program (in which students spent time learning about a particular career), and no service. The effects of the program were assessed in academic, career, ethical, social, personal, and civic domains. On most of these measures the two service-oriented groups scored significantly higher than the no service group. However, no outcome differences were found between service-learning and community service participants. If measurable differences between community service participants and those enrolled in service-learning programs are lacking, then perhaps the characteristics that distinguish them from each other have little effect on developmental outcome.

Recent evidence suggests that whether service activity is voluntary or mandated matters little for developmental outcome. Hart, Donnelly, Youniss, and Atkins (2007) used data from the National Educational Longitudinal Study (NELS:88) to compare the long-term civic outcomes of required and voluntary community service in high school. Grade 12 students who reported involvement in high school community service—whether required or voluntary—also reported higher levels of voting and community involvement in early adulthood. Metz and Youniss (2003, 2005) made use of a naturally occurring transition whereby a required service-learning program replaced a voluntary one within a high school to study the effects of such a change on students' later volunteering and civic engagement. Cohorts of students were followed longitudinally for two years before and after the imposition of the mandatory service requirement. Metz and Youniss found that rather than having a diminishing effect, requiring community service of students in this school *increased* interest in volunteering and civic participation.

The research by Hart et al. (2007) and Metz and Youniss (2003, 2005) suggest that researchers and theorists have over-emphasized the importance of voluntary entrance into community service for the effects of the activity on outcome. Critics of service-learning—who dismiss the value of service-learning—probably over-estimate the perceived coerciveness of service-learning to participants. There is so much about the role of student that is prescribed by law, regulation, and tradition that a service-learning requirement probably adds little discernible burden. Unless autonomy is seriously undermined by the requirement, the community service activity is likely to benefit its participants.

Researchers and theorists are also likely to over-emphasize the voluntary nature of volunteering. While it is true that some people are more likely to volunteer than others as a result of personality predispositions (Atkins, Hart & Donnelly, 2005; Matsuba, Hart, & Atkins, 2007), the fact is that most people become involved in volunteering because they are asked to do so by someone else (Matsuba et al., 2007) and that the activity usually occurs in the context of a social institution. No doubt participating in community service in order to fulfill a school requirement is somehow different than participating in the same activity because a friend or admired adult (e.g., minister, troop leader, teacher) asked one to do so. Nonetheless, it is important to recognize that in both cases there are external incentives to participation.

A second quality distinguishing service-learning from community service/volunteering is the former's emphasis on structured reflection on the activity. The idea is that only through discussion or written consideration of the service activity can adolescents derive the full benefit of participation. In our own research (e.g., Hart et al., 2004), we have used data from the US National Household Survey of 1999 (Nolin et al., 2000) (see Hart et al., 2004; McIntosh, Hart, & Youniss, 2007). When we regressed political efficacy scores on a set of variables corresponding to each participant's demographic statuses (age, gender, race), control variables (academic achievement, extracurricular participation), verbal discussion of service activities, and written reflection on service activities, we found that talking about the service activity in class was related to *lower* levels of political efficacy, while writing about service was a positive predictor. We have no compelling explanation for the positive associations between written reflection and political efficacy; however, research consistently confirms the psychological benefits associated with writing interventions (see Pennebaker, Mehl, & Niederhoffer, 2003). Our results, along with others (e.g., Kahne & Sporte, 2008), suggest that curricular activities have uncertain relations with the outcomes of service-learning.

On the other hand, recent meta-analysis of service-learning and community service programs conducted by Conway et al. (2009) and van Goethem (forthcoming) reach an entirely different conclusion. For example, Van Goethem identified 49 studies published since 1980 of service-learning/community service programs for adolescents, and used these studies to try and assess the importance of reflection and curricular components for the outcomes. The author used a coding system to characterize the types of reflection that were used in the service-learning program and contacted authors of studies in order to obtain information for this purpose when the reflection activities were poorly described. Her meta-analytic findings suggest that service activities by themselves mattered little; only adolescents involved in activities that featured reflection and co-curricular activities showed much development. Moreover, their analyses suggested that the *amount* of reflection was positively related to the benefits of service-learning, but that the *nature* of those reflection activities was not.

Summary

Distinctions made between service-learning and volunteering do not seem clearly linked to differences in outcomes. Both service-learning and volunteer studies are associated with positive developmental outcomes in the moral and civic domains. Some of the components assumed to be critical to service-learning programs, such as student autonomy and opportunities for reflection, do not seem essential for beneficial impacts. Unfortunately, even this conclusion is only tentative; there are some authors who claim that *only* reflection produces benefits from service-learning, a finding seemingly at odds from research on the benefits of volunteering.

Clearly, there is a real need for better research to determine the degree to which service-learning has effects distinct from those arising from volunteering and community service (see also Furco & Root, 2010). One direction that this research should take is to clarify the nature of "reflection." Reflection suggests a consideration of the experiences gained in the service activities. But in many studies (e.g. Leming, 2001) reflection is only one part of a set of co-curricular activities intended to foster social and personal growth. The consequence is that it can be difficult to discern whether the "reflection" activities are genuinely enhancing benefits of service or are better understood to have their own direct effects on development in different domains.

WHAT DOES THE RESEARCH ON VOLUNTEERING SUGGEST ABOUT LONG-TERM OUTCOMES AND DEVELOPMENTAL PROCESSES?

Long-Term Outcomes

Few studies have considered long-term consequences of service-learning as they related to moral and civic development. In contrast, studies of volunteering have considered its long-term impact. For example, using the National Educational Longitudinal Study data set, Hart et al. (2007) found that both voluntary and school-required community service were associated with volunteering in adulthood even after controlling for other relevant predictors and demographic variables. Other studies report similar findings (Astin, Sax, & Avalos, 1998; Wilson & Musick, 1997).

The Nature of Community Service Matters

Service-learning theory and research has tended to ignore the importance of the *nature* of community service that is performed by program participants. It is as if theorists and practitioners assume that what children and adolescents *do* matters less than *reflection on*, and *integration into the curriculum of* the activity. Youniss and his colleagues (e.g., Metz, McLellan, & Youniss, 2003) have been particularly persuasive in arguing for the centrality of activity for understanding the effects of community service on adolescents. They compared adolescents who performed "social cause service" (activities that put students in contact with people in need) to "standard service" (activities that did not involve contact with people in need) and to no service. Metz et al. (2003) found that students in the social cause service group had the greatest intentions of engaging in future, unconventional activities such as boycotting a product, demonstrating for a cause, and working for a political campaign.

To extend these findings, we (Hart, Matsuba, & Atkins, 2008) analyzed data from the National Education Longitudinal Survey of 1988 (NELS:88; for a description of this study, see Hart et al., 2007) to investigate the links between type of volunteering and civic attitude (i.e., "importance to help others in community"), locus of control, and self-worth among Grade 12 students. We regressed civic attitude on a set of demographic variables and on a set of dummy variables corresponding to eight volunteer service contexts. Controlling for demographic variables, service in service groups, political organizations, community groups, hospitals, and environmental contexts were associated with higher levels of valuing helping others in the community. We repeated the same type of analysis for locus of control, controlling for demographic variables and as well for Grade 10 locus of control. Adolescents reporting community service in the context of environmental groups had changed towards more internal locus of control between Grades 10 and 12 than those performing community services in other groups. Finally, we regressed Grade 12 self-esteem on demographic variables and Grade 10 self-esteem, and found that adolescents involved in community groups increased in self-esteem while those volunteering in environmental organizations declined in self-esteem.

These results suggest that some types of community service activities may be more beneficial than others in fostering the commitment to volunteer and to participate in civil society. Rarely discussed is the possibility that some types of community service may actually *depress* future volunteering and *retard* the development of qualities that service-learning aims to foster. Such a finding is suggested by our finding of an inverse relation between environmental group participation and self-esteem.

A particularly compelling example of the potentially retarding effect of community service on the development of civic qualities is described by Kahne and Westheimer (2006). They compared two school-based service-learning programs. Participants in one program worked in collaboration with the local government to improve the delivery of services. The various governmental offices in which students worked were interested in educating students about government, and had identified projects that ensured that students would both learn and succeed. Students in the other program chose their own projects based on a set of readings that emphasized social injustice and community problems. Projects included lobbying the county government to build a new health clinic to better serve women's health needs, lobbying the state legislature to introduce new legislation concerning juvenile delinquency, and efforts to investigate child labor and biased standardized testing. Students were pre and post tested on measures of political efficacy, political leadership, and civic knowledge. Perhaps not surprisingly, students in the first program—the one in which students worked in collaboration with government officials who were interested and prepared to offer meaningful community service experiences to adolescents—showed increases in political efficacy, political leadership, and civic knowledge compared to a control group not enrolled in the program. Of particular importance for our point in this section was the finding that adolescents in the other program—the one in which community service projects challenged the status quo and often failed in achieving change—had diminished political efficacy in comparison to those in the control group who did not participate in the program.

Kahne and Westheimer (2006) portray the second program not as a failure but as providing an opportunity for adolescents to learn about the challenges to effecting change in social structures. In a sense, students in the second program were acquiring a deep appreciation for the resistance to change that characterizes political systems. Whether Kahne and Westheimer are correct in that interpretation, our point is that *what* participants *do* in community service may matter in determining the effects of participation on developmental outcome.

Processes in Volunteering

There has been considerably more research on the processes that culminate in, and in turn are influenced by volunteering than is true in the service-learning domain (see Snyder & Omoto, 2008). Hart and colleagues (2007) have proposed a model of volunteering that synthesizes the literature on the roots of volunteering, and have tested the model in a representative sample of American adults. They propose that volunteering is the product of, and in turn influences, (1) moral judgment and civic attitudes, (2) self and identity, and (3) relationships and institutions. The research evidence indicates that those with sophisticated moral judgment and prosocial attitudes are most likely to volunteer. The service-learning research—reviewed in an earlier section—suggests that community service can, in turn, foster the development of moral development and heighten civic attitudes.

Identity and self-related cognitions are also associated with volunteering. Piliavin and colleagues (Lee, Piliavin & Call, 1999; Piliavin & Callero, 1991) studied the emergence of the role-identity of *blood donor* among those who regularly volunteered to give blood. They found that those volunteers for whom the identity was elaborated and salient were more likely to persist over time in blood donation. Matsuba, Hart, and Atkins (2007) reported that adults who think often about their contributions to the community and who believe themselves efficacious in helping others are more committed to volunteering than adults who do not hold these beliefs. Hart and Fegley (1995) found that adolescents deeply engaged in volunteer community service viewed their activities as integral components of themselves in the future and of their ideal selves, a constellation of self-representations suggesting that the volunteer activities had been synthesized into their identities. Finally, Kahne and Westheimer (2006) have documented how service-learning programs can affect beliefs about the self's political efficacy.

The third domain of psychological functioning related to volunteering is social capital or social networks (Hart, 2005; Snyder & Omoto, 2008). People typically enter into volunteering because they are asked to do so by family, friends, and the institutions to which they belong. Consequently it is not surprising that people who volunteer are also more likely to be attending church, meeting with friends, and so on (Matsuba et al., 2007). Omoto and Snyder (2002) reported that volunteers become increasingly connected into community over time as a result of their work. In our own work (Hart et al., 2008), we found that those students reporting participation in required community service became more involved in religious participation in Grade 12, even after controlling for Grade 10 participation, than were students not involved in community service. The same pattern was observed for extracurricular participation. The results suggest that even required community service is associated with the strengthening of bonds to social institutions in the community. In our view, future research ought to pay more attention to the possibility that one of the main benefits of service-learning is its effects on social capital.

CONCLUSION

Our goal in this chapter was to continue to raise important issues concerning service-learning and its effects on moral and civic functioning. Like many others, we are advocates for the potential developmental benefits of service-learning and community service. Yet our review cautions against complacent acceptance of the notion that service-learning is well-understood and always growth-facilitating. Our review suggests that theory concerning service-learning is only weakly tied to research findings. There are a number of consequences that follow from the lack of synthesis of theory and data. The first of these is that all theories are plausible, and consequently neither practice nor research can rely on a set of guiding principles. Moreover, the benefits that are claimed by advocates for service-learning seem little connected to theory or to the actual practice of service-learning. Finally, the disconnects among theory, practice, and research have resulted in very little evidence for any of the psychological processes that have been proposed to connect service-learning to the multitude of outcomes that are supposedly associated with the practice.

Although the state of theorizing concerning service-learning is very weak, there is good reason to correct this deficiency. The available evidence suggests that service-learning and community service are associated with development. There is solid evidence that service-learning influences moral development, civic attitudes, and civic participation and the sense of self and identity. Research also suggests that service-learning may be associated with decreases in risk behavior and increases in positive behavior (e.g., academic achievement).

Our review has been critical of claims by advocates that service-learning has distinct effects on development. In particular, the integration of service-learning with curriculum material, freedom of choice in the selection of service activities, and the opportunity to reflect on the service activity either through discussion or writing have been claimed by advocates to be essential elements of development-fostering educational practice. However, we find little compelling evidence for the importance and necessity of any one of these features. First of all, research comparing service-learning programs with curriculum integration to community service programs without curriculum integration yields a very mixed picture. While some meta-analyses (van Goethem, forthcoming) find strong support for the importance of reflection, the same study finds little evidence that the nature of the reflection matters. Consequently, even if reflection is beneficial there are few results available to date to indicate how such activities ought to be structured. Second, students required to participate in community service seem to benefit from it as much as do students given freedom of choice.

Indeed, our review suggests that there is little evidence to indicate that service-learning has different effects on adolescent development than does volunteering. Both are associated with changes in civic and moral reasoning and attitudes, and in the sense of self and identity. The parallels between service-learning and volunteering suggested to us that the former might increase social capital as has been observed with the latter. Our analyses of data from the NELS:88 were supportive of the idea that service-learning increases social capital, as those involved in required mandatory community service were characterized by increases in religious and extracurricular participation when compared to those not involved in any sort of community service.

Finally, our review suggests that more attention ought to be paid to the activities in which participants are involved. All community service is not alike; we have reported that community service in some institutional contexts seemed more advantageous than others (Hart et al., 2008). Moreover, we reviewed research by Kahne and Westheimer (2006) that suggested that community service in some contexts may actually be associated with decrements in qualities usually believed to increase as a result of service-learning. We know too little about how the nature of service activity influences adolescents, and we suspect that practitioners are too little concerned with this issue as well.

There are too many gaps in theory and research for an accurate appraisal of the value of service-learning to facilitate development. We cannot in good conscience at this time recommend service-learning as the answer to all problems and challenges faced by adolescents. However, there are real reasons to be optimistic. Most research finds that adolescents benefit from service-learning and we have a general idea about the areas that are influenced by service-learning. There are tremendous opportunities for theorists, practitioners, and researchers to contribute to adolescent development through the application and evaluation of service-learning.

REFERENCES

Allen, J. P., Philliber, S., Herrling, S., & Kupermine, G. (1997). Preventing teen pregnancy and academic failure: Experimental evaluation of a developmentally based approach. *Child Development, 64,* 729–742.

Alt, M. N. (1997). How effective an educational tool is student community service? *Nassp Bulletin, 81,* 8–16.

Astin, A., Sax, L., & Avalos, J. (1998). Long-term effects of volunteerism during the undergraduate years. *Review of Higher Education, 22,* 187–202.

Atkins, R., Hart, D., & Donnelly, T. M. (2005). The influence of childhood personality on volunteering during adolescence. *Merrill-Palmer Quarterly, 51,* 145–162.

Batchelder, T. H., & Root, S. (1994). Effects of an undergraduate program to integrate academic learning and service: Cognitive, prosocial cognitive, and identity outcomes. *Journal of Adolescence, 17,* 341–355.

Billig, S. H. (2000). Research on K-12 school-based service-learning: The evidence builds. *Phi Delta Kappan, 81,* 658–664.

Blasi, A. (1995). Moral understanding and the moral personality: The process of moral integration. In W. M. Kurtines & J. L. Gewirtz (Eds.), *Moral development: An introduction* (pp. 229–253). Boston, MA: Allyn and Bacon.

Boss, J. A. (1994). The effect of community service work on the moral development of college ethics students. *Journal of Moral Education, 23,* 183–191.

Campus Compact. (2009). *2008 service statistics: Highlights and trends of Campus Compact's annual membership survey.* Boston, MA. Retrieved December 4, 2009, from: www.compact.org/wp-content/uploads/2009/10/2008-statistics1.pdf.

Celio, C. I., Durlak, J., & Dymnicki, A. (2011). A meta-analysis of the impact of service-learning on students. *Journal of Experiential Education, 34*(2), 164–181.

Conrad, D., & Hedin, D. (1982). The impact of experiential education on adolescent development. *Child & Youth Services, 4,* 57–76.

Conway, J. M., Amel, E. L., & Gerwien, D. P. (2009). Teaching and learning in the social context: A meta-analysis of service learning's effects on academic, personal, social, and citizenship outcomes. *Teaching of Psychology, 36*(4), 233–245.

Corporation for National and Community Service. (2013). *Volunteering in America.* Retrieved March 11, 2013, from Corporation for National & Community Service: www.nationalservice.gov/about/volunteering/index.asp.

Davis, M. H., Mitchell, K. V., Hall, J. A., Lothert, J., Snapp, T., & Meyer, M. (1999). Empathy, expectations, and situational preferences: Personality influences on the decision to participate in volunteer helping behaviors. *Journal of Personality, 67,* 469–503.

Dewey, J. (1972). Ethical principles underlying education. In J. A. Boydston (Ed.), *John Dewey: The early works (1882–1989)* (Vol. 5, pp. 54–83). Carbondale: Southern Illinois University Press. (Original work published 1897.)

Eccles, J. S., & Barber, B. L. (1999). Student council, volunteering, basketball, or marching band: What kind of extracurricular involvement matters? *Journal of Adolescence Research, 14*, 10–43.

Furco, A. (1996). Service-learning: A balanced approach to experiential education. In B. Taylor (Ed.), *Expanding boundaries: Serving and learning* (pp. 2–7). Washington, DC: Corporation for National Service.

Furco, A. (2001). Is service-learning really better than community service? A study of high school service program outcomes. In A. Furco & S. H. Billig (Eds.), *Service-learning: The essence of the pedagogy* (pp. 23–50). Greenwich, CT: Information Age Publishing.

Furco, A. (2003). Issues of definition and program diversity in the study of service-learning. In S. H. Billig & A. S. Waterman (Eds.), *Studying service-learning: Innovations in education research methodology* (pp. 13–33). Mahwah, NJ: Lawrence Erlbaum Associates.

Furco, A., & Root, S. (2010). Research demonstrates the value of service learning. *Phi Delta Kappan, 91*(5), 16–20.

Giles, D. E., Jr., & Eyler, J. (1994). The theoretical roots of service-learning in John Dewey: Toward a theory of service-learning. *Michigan Journal of Community Service Learning, 1*(1): 77–85.

Hart, D. (2005). The development of moral identity. In G. Carlo & C. P. Edwards (Eds.), *Moral motivation through the life span* (pp. 165–196). Lincoln, NB: University of Nebraska Press.

Hart, D., Atkins, R., Markey, P., & Youniss, J. (2004). Youth bulges in communities: The effects of age structure on adolescent civic knowledge and civic participation. *Psychological Science, 15*, 591–597.

Hart, D., Donnelly, T. M., Youniss, J., & Atkins, R. (2007). High school predictors of adult civic engagement: The roles of volunteering, civic knowledge, extracurricular activities, and attitudes. *American Educational Research Journal, 44*(1), 197–219.

Hart, D., & Fegley, S. (1995). Prosocial behavior and caring in adolescence: Relations to self-understanding and social judgment. *Child Development, 66*, 1346–1359.

Hart, D., Matsuba, M. K., & Atkins, R. (2008). The moral and civic effects of learning to service. In L. P. Nucci & D. Narvaez (Eds.), *Handbook of moral and character education* (pp. 484–499). New York: Routledge.

Kahne, J., & Sporte, S. (2008). Developing citizens: The impact of civic learning opportunities on students' commitment to civic participation. *American Educational Research Journal, 45*(3), 738–766.

Kahne, J., & Westheimer, J. (2001). In the service of what? The politics of service learning. In J. Claus & C. Ogden (Eds.), *Service learning for youth empowerment and social change* (pp. 25–42). New York: Peter Lang.

Kahne, J. & Westheimer, J. (2006). The limits of political efficacy: Educating citizens for a democratic society. *PS: Political Science and Politics, 39*, 289–296.

Kenny, M., Simon, L. A. K., Kiley-Brabeck, K., & Lerner, R. M. (2001). Promoting civil society through service learning: A view of the issues. In M. E. Kenny, L. A. K. Simon, K. Kiley-Brabeck, & R. M. Lerner (Eds.), *Learning to serve: Promoting civic society through service learning* (pp. 1–14). Boston, MA: Kluwer.

Lee, L., Piliavin, J. A., & Call, V. R. A. (1999). Giving time, money, and blood: Similarities and differences. *Social Psychology Quarterly, 62*, 276–290.

Leming, J. S. (2001). Integrating a structured ethical reflection curriculum into high school community service experiences: Impact on students' sociomoral development. *Adolescence, 36*, 33–45.

Lies, J. M., Bock, T., Brandenberger, J., & Trozzolo, T. A. (2012). The effects of off-campus service learning on moral reasoning of college students. *Journal of Moral Education, 41*(2), 189–199.

Matsuba, M. K., Hart, D., & Atkins, R. (2007). Psychological and social-structural influences on commitment to volunteering. *Journal of Research in Personality, 41*, 889–907.

McIntosh, H., Hart, D., & Youniss, J. (2007). The influence of family political discussion on youth civic development: Which parent qualities matter? *PS: Political Science & Politics.*

Melchior, A. (1999). Summary report: National evaluation of learn and serve America. Unpublished manuscript, Center for Human Resources, Brandeis University.

Metz, E., McLellan, J., & Youniss, J. (2003). Types of voluntary service and adolescents' civic development. *Journal of Adolescent Research, 18*, 188–203.

Metz, E., & Youniss, J. (2003). A demonstration that school-based required service does not deter—but heightens—volunteerism. *PS: Political Science and Politics, 36*, 281–286.

Metz, E. C., & Youniss, J. (2005). Longitudinal gains in civic development through school-based required service. *Political Psychology, 26*, 413–437.

Morgan, W., & Streb, M. (2001). Building citizenship: How student voice in service-learning develops civic values. *Social Science Quarterly, 82*, 154–169.

National Center for Education Statistics. (n.d.). Service-learning and community service in K-12 public schools: Summary of key findings. Retrieved on December 4, 2006, from: http://nces.ed.gov/surveys/frss/publications/1999043/index.asp.

National Youth Leadership Council. (2009). *K-12 service-learning standards for quality practice.* Retrieved on January 2, 2013, from: www.nylc.org/sites/nylc.org/files/files/Standards_Oct2009-web.pdf.

Nolin, M. J., Montaquila, J., Lennon, J., Kleiner, B., Kim, K., Chapman, C., Chandler, K., Creighton, S., & Bielick, S. (2000). *National Household Education Survey of 1999: Data file user's manual, Volume I* (NCES Publication No. 2000–076). Washington, DC: US Department of Education, National Center for Education Statistics.

Omoto, A. M., & Snyder, M. (1995). Sustained helping without obligation: Motivation, longevity of service, and perceived attitude change among AIDS volunteers. *Journal of Personality and Social Psychology, 68,* 671–686.

Omoto, A. M., & Snyder, M. (2002). Considerations of community: The context and process of volunteerism. *American Behavioral Scientist, 45*(5), 846–867.

Pennebaker, J. W., Mehl, M. R., & Niederhoffer, K. G. (2003). Psychological aspects of natural language use: Our words, our selves. *Annual Review of Psychology, 54,* 547–577.

Penner, L. A., Fritzsche, B. A., Craiger, J. P., & Freifeld, T. R. (1995). Measuring the prosocial personality. In J. Butcher & C. D. Spielberger (Eds.), *Advances in personality assessment* (Vol. 10). Hillsdale, NJ: Lawrence Erlbaum.

Piliavin, A. J., & Callero, P. L. (1991). *Giving blood: The development of an altruistic identity.* Baltimore, MD: Johns Hopkins University Press.

Pritchard, I. A. (2002). Community service and service-learning in America: The state of the art. In A. Furco and S. H. Billig (Eds.), *Service-learning: The essence of the pedagogy* (pp. 3–21). Greenwich, CT: Information Age Publishing.

Root, S. C. (2005). School-based service: A review of research for teacher educators. In E. Zlotkowski (Series Ed.) & J. A. Erickson & J. B. Anderson (Vol. Eds.), *Learning with the community: Concepts and models for service-learning in teacher education* (pp. 42–72). Sterling, VA: Stylus.

Scales, P. C., Blyth, D. A., Berkas, T. H., & Kielsmeier, J. C. (2000). The effects of service-learning on middle school students' social responsibility and academic success. *Journal of Early Adolescence, 20,* 332–358.

Snyder, M., & Omoto, A. M. (2008). Volunteerism: Social issues perspectives and social policy implications. *Social Issues and Policy Review, 2*(1), 1–36.

Switzer, G. E., Simmons, R. G., Dew, M. A., Regalski, J. M., & Wang, C. (1995). The effect of a school-based helper program on adolescent self-image, attitudes, and behavior. *Journal of Early Adolescence, 15,* 429–455.

Uggen, C., & Janikula, J. (1999). Volunteerism and arrest in the transition to adulthood. *Social Forces, 78,* 331–362.

Unger, L. S., & Thumuluri, L. K. (1997). Trait empathy and continuous helping: The case of voluntarism. *Journal of Social Behavior and Personality, 12,* 785–800.

United We Serve. (2013). *United we serve.* Retrieved March 12, 2013, from United We Serve: www.serve.gov/.

US Department of Labor. (2013). *Volunteering in the United States, 2012.* Retrieved March 11, 2013, from the Bureau of Labor Statistics: www.bls.gov/news.release/volun.nr0.htm.

van Goethem, forthcoming.

Warter, E. H., & Grossman, J. M. (2001). An application of developmental-contextualism to service-learning. In A. Furco & S. H. Billig (Eds.), *Service-learning: The essence of the pedagogy* (pp. 83–102). Greenwich, CT: Information Age Publishing.

Waterman, A. S. (2003). Issues regarding the selection of variables for study in the context of the diversity of possible student outcomes of service-learning. In S. H. Billig & A. S. Waterman (Eds.), *Studying service-learning: Innovations in education research methodology* (pp. 72–90). Mahwah, NJ: Lawrence Erlbaum Associates.

Wilson, J., & Musick, M. (1997). Who cares? Toward an integrated theory of volunteer work. *American Sociological Review, 62,* 694–713.

Yates, M., & Youniss, J. (1996). Community service and political-moral identity in adolescents. *Journal of Research on Adolescence, 6,* 271–284.

Yates, M., & Youniss, J. (2001). Promoting identity development: Ten ideas for school-based service-learning programs. In J. Claus & C. Ogden (Eds.), *Service learning for youth empowerment and social change* (pp. 43–67). New York: Peter Lang.

Yogev, A., & Ronen, R. (1982). Cross-age tutoring: Effects on tutors' attributes. *Journal of Educational Research, 75,* 261–268.

27

EDUCATION FOR SUSTAINABILITY

Moral Issues in Ecology Education

Elisabeth Kals and Markus Müller

DEFINITIONS AND GUIDING PRINCIPLES OF EDUCATION FOR SUSTAINABILITY

There is no doubt that the pollution and destruction of the natural environment is one of the key sociopolitical problems of an increasingly industrialized world. Despite numerous attempts to reduce the threats of ecological damages, most of the global ecological problems and their long-term effects are not yet under control (for example, global warming, defor-estation, extinction of species, destruction of the ozone layer, exhaustion and pollution of natural resources; e.g., McKenzie-Mohr, 2002). For a long period of time, these problems have been considered primarily as technological challenges that can be managed by new, more energy-efficient technologies. However, to a large extent, ecological problems are due to maladapted human behavior. This is particularly evident with regard to the continuous growth of the human population on earth. Consequently, within social sciences, the eco-logical crisis has been called a "crisis of maladapted behavior" (Maloney & Ward, 1973) or a "crisis of culture" (Devall, 1982). As social scientists, we need to study the complexities of these maladapted behavior patterns and their moral implications not only in terms of the costs to human health and welfare, but also of the ethical aspects of our relationship as humans to the general welfare of the planet (see Kahn, 1999).

Efforts in "education for sustainability" attempt to partially address these environ-mental and moral concerns. Education for sustainability includes teaching and other intervention strategies to promote values, knowledge, skills, and motivation to help achieve ecological, economic, and social welfare (Jones, Selby, & Sterling, 2010). This is in line with the definition of "environmental education" as the "*curriculum encouraging understanding and appreciation of the environment through subjects such as local history, ecology, pollution etc.*" (Page, Thomas, & Marshall, 1980, p. 122).

The focus of this chapter is how environmental psychological research can inform education for sustainability. First, we describe the historical paradigm shift from the one-dimensional term "environmental protection" to the multidimensionality of "sustainability." Then we offer an overview of approaches for promoting sustainable behavior, reflecting the broad variety of target groups, aims, and frameworks of these intervention programs. Many successful intervention programs show that children can be introduced to sustainable behavior from an early age but these efforts must still be much more reinforced and established than is currently the case. We focus on the moral dimension of sustainable behavior by taking the socio-ecological dilemma into account, and we present a wide range of empirical findings on the moral dimension of ecological thinking, feeling, and behavior. We reflect the difficult question to what extent these findings are taken into account by intervention programs. Finally, we propose concrete suggestions for evidenced-based approaches to promoting sustainable thinking, feeling, and behavior.

FROM ENVIRONMENTAL PROTECTION TO SUSTAINABILITY

"Sustainability" and its synonymous term "sustainable development" were originally used in forestry and forest management. From the report of the Club of Rome (Meadows, Meadows, & Behrens, 1972), through the Brundtland Report (WCED, 1990) and the world summit for sustainable development in Rio de Janeiro in 1992, it has gained the status of a guiding principle in the discussion on ecological problems and necessary behavioral changes and is one of the most popular terms within the public discourse on ecological problems. Sustainability is discussed on all political levels and has now displaced the older principles of "pollution control" and "environmental protection" (De Haan & Kuckartz, 1998). In its original meaning, sustainability represented the normative demand to realize intergenerational justice so that the next generations could enjoy adequate opportunities for economic and social development (WCED, 1990). However, the global spread of the term has led to an increasingly inconsistent use and a multitude of definitions (see Kaufmann-Hayoz, 2006).

Consensus exists that sustainable development goes beyond environmental protection with its primary focus on pro-environmental aims and efforts. Instead, various socially accepted aims need to be balanced. In the relevant literature, ecological, economic, and social targets are discussed as three different dimensions of sustainability (see Jüdes, 1997; Kreibich, 1996):

- The ecological dimension, also called *ecological sustainability*, encompasses aims with regard to the natural environment, such as the protection of natural resources, the reduction of environmental pollution and contamination, climate protection, the protection of the ecosystems, the care for nature and landscape areas, the conservation of biodiversity, and so on. This part of sustainability is largely congruent with the older term of environmental protection.
- Sustainable *economic development* includes such things as economic welfare, protection of job security, economic freedom, and freedom of choice.
- The third dimension comprises *sustainable social development*, including, among other factors, the satisfaction of basic human needs so that future conflicts over the distribution of resources can be avoided. This explicitly embraces the need of intergenerational justice.

Although these fields define the most commonly cited dimensions of sustainability, the list is not exhaustive (see Valentin & Spangenberg, 2000).

The various dimensions of sustainability (ecological, economic, social), although closely interconnected, often compete with one another and cannot be easily reconciled. There is a complex transdisciplinary discussion on the right balance between the dimensions to achieve justice (see Kreibich, 1996): Should the ecological dimension be given priority? Or should all three dimensions be weighted equally? To what extent can economic welfare be achieved without putting ecological aims at risk? In the literature, only a few examples are reported where a balance between the three dimensions was explicitly sought. One of these examples includes an ecological village with about 30 households, where sustainable lifestyles were established bringing together ecological, social, and economic aims (Kirby, 2003).

Summing up, sustainability is a "*fuzzy set*" (Linneweber, 1998, p. 66) that leaves room for interpretation. Sustainable development is always the product of weighing competing aims and values against another. A justice perspective can offer a theoretical framework to this discourse by constructing ecological conflicts as conflicts of justice (Montada, 2007; Müller, 2012) that also concern the justice for future generations (Gethmann, 2008). Therefore, the concept of sustainability does not imply that there are "easy" technological solutions to the interlocking social, ecological, and economic problems. Rather, it shows that the greatest challenge of modern societies is to develop cultures of discourse, to find ways to consider the many issues involved, to respect the interests of stakeholders as well as the rights of nature. Individual competencies for conflict resolution, awareness of moral dilemmas, and a democratic culture of mutual understanding lie at the heart of an education for sustainability.

OVERVIEW OF APPROACHES FOR PROMOTING SUSTAINABLE BEHAVIOR

Globally, many efforts are underway to promote pro-environmental or sustainable behavior. Many non-governmental organizations (NGOs) point at education as a key instrument for promoting sustainable development (see Huckle & Sterling, 1996). Before going into detail, we will give an overview of the different scopes and dimensions of programs for promoting sustainability.

In terms of focus, education programs can follow two different approaches (see Kyburz-Graber, Hofer, & Wolfensberger, 2006): The first approach encompasses intervention programs that are aimed at the promotion of pro-environmental behaviors. These programs usually combine learning about nature and the environment with outdoor experiences. In contrast, the second approach explicitly refers to moral dilemmas and conflicts that arise when complexity of the issue is taken into account. In these programs, the human-environment relationship is a central theme, for example by studying the use and misuse of natural resources.

They can also vary on targeted audience (e.g., governments and intergovernmental bodies, non-governmental organizations, the mass media, and the private sector, see Leal Filho & Littledyke, 2004). An example for a broader approach would be community-based programs that aim at advancing concerns for sustainability in a municipality (e.g., educational programs in adult education centers).

Sustainable development in the context of businesses is also discussed as "greening of business" (see Huckle & Sterling, 1996)—a concept with increasing application, which is also due to stricter environmental laws and the fact that "sustainability" has become a key criterion for organizational evaluation. As such, it is applied as a criterion of "good work" in organizations, as a valuation standard of corporate culture, or as one of the dimensions of corporate citizenship (Habisch, Jonker, Wegner, & Schmidpeter, 2005).

Besides their context, other criteria for categorizing programs are defined by the following questions (for an overview, see Ahlberg & Leal Filho, 1998):

- Does the program focus on individuals, trying to modify their attitudes, values, emotions, or behaviors, or on the situational context, by changing the basic dilemma structure through incentive systems, such as lowered prices for mass transit systems or stricter laws to protect the environment?
- What is the target group? Is it individuals, who should rethink and change their individual behavior (e.g., decisions in their households, their consumer behavior, or political votes); multipliers, like people with high social standing, influence, and acceptance (teachers, leaders in organizations, etc.), or even mega-actors, who are especially influential by their decision-making, either in the political or the economic system?
- What specific aims, strategies, and means are implemented in the program, and on what theoretical base are they founded?
- On what level does the program take place (e.g., on the level of individuals or organizations)?
- Is the motivation to conduct the program mainly internal or external, and how and by whom is the program financed and evaluated?
- Is the program based on practical (social) or academic problem definitions and objectives (Scott, 2006)?

Many sustainability education programs are unpublished and, therefore, not part of the body of scientific knowledge. One reason might be that there are no research interests involved and that the programs do not meet any of the previously mentioned scientific standards. Concerning programs that are guided by standards of program implementation and evaluation, an important area is in post-secondary education, in particular university education. Sustainability is included in Bachelors and Masters programs in a broad variety of disciplines, such as education, environmental psychology and other environmental sciences, geography, economics, business, law, engineering, media and cultural studies, nursing and health sciences, art and design, languages, theology, etc. (for an overview, see Jones et al., 2010). The implementation of issues of sustainability in programs is discussed in almost all disciplines, and even in business-related degree programs (MacVaugh & Norton, 2012). A variety of different political, methodological, and didactical approaches is, for example, covered on the level of the UNESCO program "Higher Education for Sustainable Development" (for an overview, see Adomßent, Godemann, Leicht, & Busch, 2006). Academic teaching of sustainability at higher educational levels often goes together with processes of "greening the campus" (see Jones et al., 2010). In these processes, teams of college students, educational and technical staff work together to identify areas where the environmental balance of the campus can be improved, for example by developing monitoring systems for energy and water consumption, by using solar energy, or by using knowledge from psychology to change energy-using behavior at the university. Often, these projects are audited and become part of larger programs that also involve local and regional stakeholders, like transportation companies, utility companies, and many more.

In many countries, education for sustainability has become an institutional requirement on the level of primary and secondary schools (see Simonneaux & Simonneaux, 2012). Overviews for programs on this level have been published previously (see, for example, Krizek, Newport, White, & Townsend, 2012; Leal Filho, 2011) along with helpful materials for practitioners, scholars, and researchers in this field (see, for example, Satapathy, 2007). Ahlberg and Leal Filho (1998) have compiled examples from national experts for curricular school achievements from all over the world, such as the curricular endeavor to educate pupils aged 4–14 in sustainability in Scotland, teacher training in Mexico, environmental education centers in a National Park in South Africa, a Flemish green school project, environmental education on soil features in Slovenia as well as in the region of Poland, the Czech Republic, and Germany. Many more current examples of school programs aiming at promoting sustainable thinking and behavior are reported by Clarke (2012), such as Sweden's "Forest Schools," China's "Green Schools" program, the US "Green Ribbon Schools," or the "School of Sustainability." As Clarke explains, schools of sustainability should not follow the traditional path of education, asking "*what kind of young adults do we want to see as a result of this process?*" but rather ask "*what kind of sustainable community do we want our schools to build as they redefine their service to others?*" (Clarke, 2012, p. 107). As an example, he reports a project where the concept of urban farms is located in a school environment. Teachers, students, parents, and the local community work together to explore the space around the school buildings, come up with new ideas of how to use the space, create work groups to collaborate on many different projects (like the production of food, the redesign of a space as a small stage, etc.), make plans on the management of the spaces, etc. It is evident that this process should not be seen as yet another burden for school teachers who have to follow a strict learning curriculum, but as a resource and a place where learning can take place.

An overview of the international perspective in environmental education is also presented by means of collected examples (see Leal Filho & Littledyke, 2004). The number of specific examples for schools and other projects to promote sustainability by education is enormous. However, it seems to be an ongoing, dynamic process with networking or exchange between the various approaches being very difficult. Most texts, consequently, close with demands for further interventions on the level of curricula.

Although education for sustainable development needs to be established as a political aim on a societal level, schools are, without any doubt, the primary institutions for formal education. As schools contribute to the moral development of children (see Davidson, Khmelkov, Baker, & Lickona, 2011) they have the responsibility to promote sustainable behavior as well (for a further discussion of the role of primary and secondary schools, see Lange, 2012).

In the literature, several key concepts are defined that are the basis for acting and deciding in a sustainable way. The key competences, systematic thinking, anticipatory thinking, and critical thinking were empirically investigated (Rieckmann, 2012). If the moral dimension of sustainability is to be included, Kohlberg's moral stages (Kohlberg, 1984) need to be discussed besides cognitive abilities. The level of critical reflection rises by age and experience, and establishing education for sustainability on higher curriculum levels would allow more sophisticated intervention aims and the outlook that graduates, for example, could function as multipliers after their studies. Nevertheless, despite the definite statements of the original theories, in modern psychological and philosophical views knowledge seeking is integral at every phase of the process (see Kuhn, 2010) so that there is no necessary need for post-conventional moral reasoning to start with corresponding interventions programs. In line with this modern view there are many attempts which have successfully begun to establish sustainable development at an early age (see, for example, McNichol, Davis, & O'Brien, 2011; Zoller, 2011). As a conclusion of the theoretical and empirical findings, children can be introduced to principles of sustainability from an early age, but these principles need to be regularly reinforced and refined (see Huckle & Sterling, 1996).

THE MORAL DIMENSION OF SUSTAINABLE THINKING AND BEHAVIOR

The moral dimension of sustainable behavior is approached by various disciplines, such as moral sociology (with a focus on collective actors), moral philosophy (focusing on normative questions), moral education (aiming to change behavior), and moral psychology (mainly trying to explain behavior empirically, based upon individuals' perspectives). This section follows this last approach. Within this approach, Schnack (1998, p. 83) responds to the question "*Why focus on conflicting interests in environmental education?*" with a simple answer: "*Because environmental problems are constructed of conflicting human interests in relation to nature.*" More specifically, environmental issues can create a dilemma or conflict in which people must choose between short-term individual and long-term societal interests as well as interests in relation to nature. Typical for these kinds of dilemmas is that environmentally unfriendly behavior yields individual benefits in the short run: Far-distance travels for holidays, for example, are attractive and beneficial for an individual. However, the same behavior can contribute to environmental pollution in the long run, which causes harms to the society and the individual. On the other hand, environmentally friendly behavior is often considered as less attractive—for example, many people prefer using their car to using public transportation—but has, as is evident, positive long-term effects on society, the individual, and the environment. The very structure of these dilemmas can be found in many areas of environmental conflicts, be it on a local (for example, the question whether to build a beltway in a nature protection area) or a more complex global level (for example, behavior connected with the emission of greenhouse gases).

Behavioral changes are doubtlessly necessary to overcome the ecological crisis and thus sustainable action serves the community as a whole. The necessary decision-making includes behavior at a private as well as at political and economic levels in such a way that mega-actors in politics and industry take the ecological consequences of their decisions into account just as well as the economic and social consequences. A shift in cost–benefit outcomes of the decisions, however, facilitates a self-serving bias (Linneweber, 1998). This is described by the paradigm of the socio-ecological dilemma (also called "social trap" or "commons dilemma"; Hardin, 1968; Platt, 1973) and can be illustrated by individual private decisions, but is also applicable to the decisional structure of mega-actors: Environmental damages are side effects of productive, useful, or enjoyable activities serving various interests and values of people. Pro-environmental politics and behaviors imply restrictions on these interests and values. The various costs, however, like reduced comfort, the effort required to change behavior patterns, or financial shortages, are individualized: They directly and exclusively affect the acting individual, whereas society as a whole benefits from sustainable behavior.

On the other hand, environment-endangering decisions may have direct and personal benefits for the individual. Ecological risks and burdens that derive from these decisions are perceived to be external to the individual. Due to this externalization, environmentally risky decisions become a "rational choice" in cases in which an alternative environmentally relevant behavior could be chosen as well (Montada & Kals, 2000). This is not to say that every activity with negative ecological side effects is necessarily irresponsible or selfish. Rather, measures to protect the environment may interfere with other highly valued social objectives, such as freedom of choice. This is also reflected in the shift from the term "environmental protection" to the term of "sustainability" (see Schmuck & Schultz, 2002).

Further conditions may promote decisions that put the environment at risk. For instance, the causal chain from CO_2 emissions due to the use of fossil energy resources to the greenhouse effect is indirect, uncertain, complex, and delayed to an indeterminate point of time in the future (see Schmuck & Schultz, 2002). In this respect, the detrimental effects of one's own environmentally risky behaviors can easily be doubted or ignored. Moreover, the externalization of ecological costs is affected by time and geographical shifts (Opotow & Clayton, 1994; Pawlik, 1991): The effects of CO_2 emissions, for instance, are not restricted to the local area, but might affect people far away from the polluter in terms of place and time, such as people living in other countries or belonging to future generations. In this respect, it is a rational choice for many polluters to continue their polluting activities as long as they do not have to expect sanctions for their abusive behavior (Montada & Kals, 2000; Müller & Hiendl, 2012).

This explains why solely appealing to actors' long-term interests is not an effective intervention strategy for promoting sustainable behavior. Instead, pro-environmental behavior can be understood as moral behavior. The moral dimension of pro-environmental behavior was empirically confirmed on the level of cognitions as well as emotions: Concerning the cognitive level, it has been shown that experiencing moral obligations, accepting ecological responsibility, and perceiving ecological (in)justices form a strong motivational base for sustainable behavior (for an overview, see Stern, 2000) and help to overcome the socio-ecological dilemma. In general, the more the model variables are specifically tied to the ecological dimension, the more they become predictive for sustainable behavior. Dispositional constructs are less powerful. For instance, generalized social responsibility, often measured by the eight-item scale of Berkowitz and Lutterman (1968), evidences only low correlations with sustainable attitudes, and does not predict sustainable behavior (e.g., Arbuthnot, 1977; Tucker, 1978). A dispositional approach to explaining sustainable behavior therefore has been largely abandoned.

Similar result patterns can be found for egoism and altruism as personality traits. Often no significant correlations between egoistic or altruistic personality and various attitudes towards sustainability and sustainable behaviors can be found. This was, for example, examined by Russell (2001) in the context of climate protective behavior, like energy consumption in one's household.

However, many of the studies are quite old, reflecting the overall shift from generalized to environment-specific moral attitudes and thus avoiding possible lower correlations and effect sizes caused by different levels of specificity of predictors and behaviors.

Nevertheless, a few general attitudes have proven to be powerful predictors of sustainable behavior. These are, for example, the belief in a just world, empathy, and control beliefs, which are part of the model of prosocial personality (Bierhoff, 2008) and which were able to predict pro-social, including sustainable, behavior well. Following this tradition, the model of Stern (2000) distinguishes between egoistic, altruistic, and biospheric environmental concern. However, especially the biospheric concern seems to be positively related with sustainable behavior (e.g., Schultz, 2001).

Moral development in the context of ecological values, norms, and behavior represents another growing field of research. The development of an ecological ethics has been investigated referring to the change from materialistic to post-materialistic value orientations (Lantermann, Döring-Seipel, & Schima, 1992). Kohlberg's model of moral development (1984) has been applied to pro-environmental, respectively sustainable, behavior from the very beginning of the emergence of environmental psychology (see Dispoto, 1977). In this approach, sustainable behavior is interpreted as a function of different developmental levels of moral judgment (see Eckensberger, Breit, & Döring, 1999). This is mainly assessed by Rest's Defining Issues Test (DIT) to measure moral judgment (Rest, 1986; Rest, Narvaez, Bebeau, & Thoma, 1999). The test embraces various moral dilemmas which do not include ecological or socio-ecological dilemmas. The DIT has been used in environmental psychology studies (e.g., Karpiak & Baril, 2008) or a modified test has been developed to specifically gauge moral reasoning related to environmental issues (e.g., Axelrod, 1994; Ojala, in press).

At a glance, confirmative result patterns can be found for this Neo-Kohlbergian approach (see Axelrod, 1994; Karpiak & Baril, 2008; Ojala, in press). For example, Karpiak and Baril's (2008) study of college students showed that higher scores on moral judgment correlate positively with ecocentrism (belief in the intrinsic importance of nature) and negatively with environmental apathy. Even effects of moral judgment development on environmental behavior have been demonstrated (Ojala, in press). This reflects that more research needs to be done in this area.

In general, correlations between sustainable behavior and moral variables increase, when moral predictors are applied to ecological norms. For both Schwartz's Norm Activation Model (Schwartz & Howard, 1980) or Stern's Value-Belief-Norm Model (Stern, 2000), the acceptance of ecological norms and values as well as the internal attribution of environmental responsibility are the most decisive predictors of sustainable behavior (see Kaiser, Fuhrer, Weber, Ofner, & Bühler-Ilieva, 2001; Montada & Kals, 2000). The denial of environmental responsibility, or its exclusive attribution to powerful others, leads to environment-endangering decisions, for example, the promotion of economic interests regardless of their impact on nature, or an active engagement in motorsport activities (Montada & Kals, 2000).

The power of responsibility appraisals is bolstered by environment-specific justice appraisals. The more people perceive the socio-ecological conflict as a justice dilemma in which profits and sufferings are distributed unjustly, the more they are willing to contribute to the settling of this dilemma and to the (re-) establishment of justice (see Müller, 2012; Müller & Kals, 2007; Syme, Kals, Nancarrow, & Montada, 2006). This is particularly the case when ecological burdens affect future generations or people living in other geographical areas (e.g., in so-called underdeveloped countries), who have neither agreed to take the ecological risks nor profit in any way from taking these risks. A denial of these justice problems facilitates environmentally risky behavior (Horwitz, 1994; Opotow & Clayton, 1994; Syme et al., 2006).

In summary, across different action fields and heterogeneous samples, it has been shown that moral reasoning is a powerful motivational basis for overcoming interest shifts described in the socio-ecological dilemma. This is in line with normative approaches, such as the "integrity of creation" or the "principle of responsibility" according to Hans Jonas (2012).

The building of behavioral decisions is, however, not a purely cognitive process, but is flanked by responsibility- and justice-related emotions, such as blame or indignation about insufficient sustainable behavior (for an overview, see Kals & Maes, 2002). These moral emotions should not be misinterpreted as "by-products" of dominant cognitions in such a way that they impair an apparently cognitive process of decision-making, but they seem to be a chiefly independent source of motivation (Haidt & Kezebir, 2010). This shows that in the field of sustainable behavior emotions arouse behavior in addition to rational cognitions by their affective, cognitive, and motivational component.

Affective connection to nature, also called emotional commitment to nature, emotional affinity toward nature, nature-relatedness, or inclusion of nature in self, is one of the very powerful emotions (see Clayton, 2003; Dutcher, Finley, Luloff, & Johnson, 2007; Kals, 2012; Nisbet, Zelenski, & Murphy, 2009). This construct can be traced back to Wilson and Kellert's biophilia hypothesis (Kellert, 1997) and belongs to a completely different emotional category, which can explain sustainable behavior well—regardless of moral obligations (see Kals, Schumacher, & Montada, 1999). As the most strongly experienced and intimate of feelings, it is incompatible with the rational-choice theory referring to maximizing one's own benefit on a rational decision base (see Coleman & Fararo, 1993), and its motivational functions can also not be explained by the concept of the socio-ecological dilemma. Affective connection towards nature can be traced back to present and past experiences in nature (Müller, Kals, & Pansa, 2009) and is closely related to the development of an environmental identity (Clayton, 2003; Hinds & Sparks, 2008). Data from questionnaire surveys have shown that the time spent in nature in one's childhood as well as positive experiences in nature are strong predictors of the emotional connection to nature (Kahn & Kellert, 2002; Kals et al., 1999). In this respect, young people living in highly industrialized areas are not as emotionally connected to nature as people living in rural areas with a lot of nature surrounding them (see Hinds & Sparks, 2008; Müller et al., 2009). There is an ongoing debate as well as research on affective connection, increasingly confirming the power of this emotional bond with nature (Kals, 2012).

To what extent are the reported findings reflected in intervention programs? Aho (1984) presented a theoretical framework of education for sustainability with special focus on teaching pro-environmental action (concrete actions, decision-making, solutions, and choices). The author distinguishes between three psychological domains that need to be addressed in order to reach this aim: focusing (1) upon ethics and values (environmental values, ethics, responsibility, and attitudes), (2) upon cognitions (knowledge, understanding, cognitive processes, and skills), and (3) upon affections (experiences and emotions). These domains have significant overlap and interact with each other. Applying the previously reported findings to Aho's three psychological approaches for promoting sustainable education, the literature on motives for sustainable behavior provides support for all of them: Any education or intervention strategy should equally take into account individual ethics and values, environment-specific cognitions, as well as emotions and nature experiences. These approaches are described in the following section in further detail.

SUGGESTIONS FOR EVIDENCE-BASED APPROACHES TO PROMOTE SUSTAINABLE THINKING, FEELING, AND BEHAVIOR

In this chapter, we suggest that sustainable behavior be considered a category of moral action that competes with other socially accepted behaviors, such as pursuit of economic growth. Thus, the question "How can sustainable behavior be promoted?" should be reformulated into "How can the socio-ecological dilemma and the interest conflicts that result from the three-dimensional concept of sustainability be overcome?" Under what personal and situational conditions is sustainable action prioritized?

The promotion of sustainable thinking, feeling, and behavior has primarily been done under a moral perspective. Based upon Rest's four-component model (Rest, 1986), the perspectives of moral sensitivity, judgment, motivation, and moral character can be distinguished which all offer an important approach to promote sustainable behavior. Concerning these moral perspectives, cognitions and emotions with regard to ecological responsibility and justice seem to be most important. Models that refer to the specifics of these behaviors, such as Schwartz's Norm-Activation Model (Schwartz & Howard, 1980) or Stern's Value-Belief-Norm Model (Stern, 2000), successfully predict and explain sustainable decisions and behaviors. For intervention purposes, this result leads to the conclusion that responsibility- and norm-focused approaches should include a discourse on ecological, economic, and social responsibilities, and that ecological ethics, also called "green moral values" should be established (see Bassey, 1998). This could be done in families and institutions for early education (like kindergartens and elementary schools), high schools, post-secondary institutions, and the broader public.

Furthermore, the empirical findings on moral development suggest including discussions about environment-specific dilemma situations in intervention programs (see Thompson & Stoutemyer, 1991). The socio-ecological dilemma can be presented in many different forms. It may be experienced in fishing conflict games, either in a real or computerized learning environment (see, for example, Ernst & Spada, 1993). These approaches should address in the same way cognitions as well as emotions, like indignation about insufficient environmental protection shown by others in fishing conflict games.

As the dilemma situations are very complex, moral thinking should be combined with sustainable thinking (Spada, Opwis, Donnen, Schwiersch, & Ernst, 1990). Environmental psychology has contributed extensively to the body of knowledge on psychological barriers to promoting sustainable behavior (see Swim et al., 2010). One major barrier is the phenomenon of "limited cognition" (Gifford, 2011): Environmental problems are rather complex, and they involve many non-linear relations and a high degree of uncertainty about causes and effects. Individuals, however, as described, tend to act on a more short-term basis, neglecting the long-term effects of their behaviors. Moreover, perceived uncertainty can even serve as a justification for inactivity, and risks that are communicated as being uncertain tend to reduce willingness for action (Budescu, Broomell, & Por, 2009). Thus, education for sustainability has to face the double task of neither overwhelming individuals with too much uncertainty nor over-simplifying complex relations.

A supplementary way to fostering the moral perspective on sustainable behavior and to overcoming the gap between short-term self-interests and long-term interests of society is offered by positive nature experiences. Being in nature promotes the development of an affective connection to nature, feelings of empathy toward, and identification with it. Connection to nature varies between individuals. It is primarily instigated by direct experiences in nature, such as viewing and experiencing wilderness, observing phenomena of weather, or perceiving the change of the seasons (Lyons & Breakwell, 1994). Most authors agree that this relatedness to nature becomes stronger the more concretely nature is experienced, and that it is based on affective experiences rather than solely cognitive appraisals (Nisbet et al., 2009), for example, when knowledge of nature is transferred by experiencing nature consciously with one's five senses (Kaplan, 2001).

Connection to nature is especially promoted when nature experiences are shared with significant others (Kals et al., 1999). These joint experiences seem to facilitate the integration of this experience into one's own self-concept and identity (Clayton, 2003). These significant others (at first, one's parents) take on the role of transmitting nature values and enjoyment. The "significant others" change over one's life span in such a way that family members are more and more replaced by peers. Therefore, the fostering of positive experiences within nature, preferably shared with significant others, is, even in environmental education programs for adults, a potent way to provoke interest and an affective connection to nature and to overcome the interest conflicts between short-term self-interests and long-term ecological interests of the society as a whole.

This last finding demonstrates that the implementation of the education programs needs to be done with regard to the specific circumstances and the social context in which they take place. Internal and external motivators influence one another in their effects and efficacy. If, therefore, not only the individual is in the focus of interest but if the environment is also shaped in such a way that sustainable behavior is promoted, effects are strengthened. This can be done on the situational level (e.g., by using prompts reminding of sustainable behavior) or on the social level (e.g., by the modeling behavior of respected others who, for example, demonstrate sustainable behavior or who enjoy the natural environment). On a more global level, the change of general conditions of relevant behavior, such as stricter laws, or prize and reward systems, should also be taken into account.

Comparing the sections on the motive structure of sustainable behavior with a possible derivation of intervention programs on the one hand and the earlier overview on current intervention programs on the other, the reader will recognize a gap: On the one hand, a profound knowledge base on the motives and motivation for sustainable behavior has been established leading to specific recommendations for intervention; on the other hand, practical intervention programs consist of patchwork elements only. Reasons for this discrepancy and suggestions how to overcome it are discussed in the following section.

SUMMARY AND OUTLOOK

The term of "environmental education" (later partly changed into "education for sustainability," see above) was coined in the 1970s around the same time when environmental psychology was established as a scientific discipline. The beginnings of environmental education, however, can be traced back to the 1950s or 1960s (Eulefeld, 1990). A major contribution to the promotion of environmental education can be seen in the UNESCO conferences of the 1970s. They provided an impetus to make environmental education programs part of the general education process and to integrate it into school curricula.

Since then, many fine grained decisions of ministries of education in Europe have been made to achieve this aim (see Eulefeld, 1990). Parallel developments can be observed for the US, with some time lag, though.

Promoted by these political developments, many innovative programs have been developed all over the world, but mainly independently of the existing empirically confirmed knowledge base concerning motives and motivation for sustainable behavior. In environmental education, a research deficit has been recognized, concerning the content and implementation of programs as well as their effectiveness (see Bolscho & Hauenschild, 2006). This deficit needs to be overcome by focusing upon the specific competencies of the related disciplines. Two of the core contributions of environmental psychology can be seen in the provision of knowledge on the motivation base of sustainable behavior and on the effectiveness of intervention strategies. Environmental educators, on the other hand, are experts for the application of this knowledge in practical programs. Thus, environmental psychologists and educators need to collaborate for their mutual benefit, and they need to invite other disciplines such as sociology, political sciences, economy, nature sciences, engineering to achieve inter- or even transdisciplinarity (Schweizer-Ries & Perkins, 2012).

The relation between practice and science in the field of sustainability remains difficult, though. Two ways to justify environmentally related interventions can be differentiated: The first, basically scientific approach advises the traditional four steps of (1) formulating a problem definition (problem; P), (2) finding explanations for the problem (analysis; A), (3) developing and testing the process model (test; T), and (4) constructing an intervention program (help; H), which also includes the program's evaluation (PATH-model of Buunk & van Vugt, 2008). The second approach, which is related to action research, is based on practical problems, where scientific knowledge is derived from the intervention process itself (Schweizer-Ries & Perkins, 2012). Both strategies have specific advantages and disadvantages. It may be politically opportune to directly start action-oriented with interventions and education programs to promote sustainable behavior, but these interventions should nevertheless be evaluated in order to gather feedback about the effectiveness of such programs and to have an impact on further theorizing, research, and intervention planning in the field of education for sustainability.

A clarification of the core concepts is much needed, in particular a working consensus of what is meant by "sustainability" and "sustainable behavior" has to be achieved on the level of examples and concrete behavioral decisions, also in order to avoid the described inflationary use of the terms. The concept of interactional expertise for sustainability education has been introduced to address this need (Berardy, Seager, & Selinger, 2011). A special focus is on the communication of sustainable research (Scott, 2006) to overcome the gap between research and practice, that is between primarily academic and sociopolitical objectives. Additional core competencies on joined thinking and dealing with uncertainty can be learned.

One way to concretize this interdisciplinary approach would be to promote approaches aiming to link the current need for action with the existing knowledge base of environmental psychology. A combination of both intervention paths may result: The practical requirements should be answered directly by offering education programs; in parallel, the underlying motives of sustainable behavior and the critical demand of networking and the handling of uncertainty should be analyzed further. Thus, we do not follow the argumentation that further research on the underlying motives of sustainable behavior is necessary as a sine qua non to establish intervention programs. Of special help are the interventional approaches that aim to link theory and practice by founding their practical work on theories and psychological mechanisms. They help explain what sustainable thinking and behavior embrace on a meta-level (like valuing the different dimensions of sustainability and promoting a discourse to the individual case with respect to justice and necessary trade-offs) and they lead to the derivation of core competencies (like complex thinking). This practical work should be demand-driven (see Geesteranaus, 1998), which implies that the impulse for conducting the program should arise from practical needs and underlines that the call from people working in the field of environmental education should be heard.

On a more general level, education for sustainability should be understood as a lifelong process: It should begin in kindergarten and pre-school, should be followed up in primary and secondary schools as well as in universities, and finally be disseminated into other areas of life. In schools this education for sustainability has not yet reached the level it should have, as environmental protection and sustainability are not at the center of the curriculum of any school subject. As a vision, even a school subject "sustainability" could be introduced in curricula (see Ahlberg & Leal Filho, 1998). This would not only strengthen the moral discourse and moral development but also cognitive development of students by introducing them to complex thinking.

In his book *Education for Sustainability: Becoming Naturally Smart*, Paul Clarke (2012) argues for a full transformation of schools and schooling that is required to reach the aim of education for sustainability. He bases his argument on the assumption that such education needs to be grounded in a comprehensive understanding of our relationship with the natural world. Although examples for integrating the concept of sustainability on the level of the nation's or federal state's curricula can be found nearly everywhere, the majority of schools are still far away from being green schools, as a place where sustainability is exemplified (for example by teachers' or parents' thinking and behavior) and successfully taught. Walter Leal Filho speaks of a vision of education and of a long-term goal on the level of world trends (Leal Filho, 2011). On a theoretical level, many papers discuss this global dimension and its specific challenges (see, for example, Ahmad, Soskolne, & Ahmed, 2012).

On the applied level of educational practice, there are many solitary struggles and attempts to tackle these challenges, but they are not sufficiently linked on national or even international levels. Environmental psychology and educational sciences can provide the knowledge required to define goals and establish appropriate means and strategies for these programs. Yet, the final responsibility for the realization of this global task remains with educational policies.

REFERENCES

Adomßent, M., Godemann, J., Leicht, A., & Busch, A. (Eds.). (2006). *Higher education for sustainability. New challenges from a global perspective.* Frankfurt a.M.: VAS.

Ahlberg, M. & Leal Filho, W. (Eds.). (1998). *Environmental education for sustainability: Good environment, good life.* Frankfurt a.M.: Peter Lang.

Ahmad, W., Soskolne, C.L., & Ahmed, T. (2012). Strategic thinking on sustainability: Challenges and sectoral roles. *Environment, Development and Sustainability, 14*(1), 67–83.

Aho, L. (1984). A theoretical framework for research into environmental education. *International Review of Education, 30,* 183–191.

Arbuthnot, J. (1977). The roles of attitudinal and personality variables in the prediction of environmental behavior and knowledge. *Environment and Behavior, 9*, 217–232.

Axelrod, L.J. (1994). Balancing personal needs with environmental preservation: Identifying the values that guide decisions in ecological dilemmas. *Journal of Social Issues, 50*, 85–104.

Bassey, M. (1998). Greed, boredom, love and joy—and the ecological predicament: A call for educational research into the learning of green moral values. In M. Ahlberg & W. Leal Filho (Eds.), *Environmental education for sustainability: Good environment, good life* (pp. 149–162). Frankfurt a.M.: Peter Lang.

Berardy, A., Seager, T.P., & Selinger, E. (2011). Developing a pedagogy of interactional expertise for sustainability education. Proceedings of the 2011 IEEE. International symposium on sustainable systems and technology. Chicago.

Berkowitz, L. & Lutterman, K.G. (1968). The traditional socially responsible personality. *Public Opinion Quarterly, 32*, 169–185.

Bierhoff, H.W. (2008). Prosocial behaviour. In M. Hewstone, W. Stroebe, & K. Jonas (Eds.), *Introduction to social psychology. A European perspective* (pp. 176–195). Malden, MA: Blackwell.

Bolscho, D. & Hauenschild, K. (2006). From environment education to education for sustainable development in Germany. *Environmental Education Research, 12*(1), 7–18.

Budescu, D.V., Broomell, S., & Por, H. (2009). Improving communication of uncertainty in the reports of the intergovernmental panel on climate change. *Psychological Science, 20*, 299–308.

Buunk, A. P. & van Vugt, M. (2008). *Applying social psychology—from problems to solutions.* London: Sage.

Clarke, P. (2012). *Education for sustainability: Becoming naturally smart.* London: Routledge.

Clayton, S. (2003). Environmental identity: A conceptual and operational definition. In S. Clayton & S. Opotow (Eds.), *Identity and the natural environment. The psychology of nature* (pp. 45–65). Cambridge, MA: MIT Press.

Coleman, J.S. & Fararo, T.J. (Eds.). (1993). *Rational choice theory: Advocacy and critique* (2nd print). Newbury Park, CA: Sage.

Davidson, M., Khmelkov, V., Baker, K., & Lickona T. (2011). Values education: The Power2Achieve approach for building sustainability and enduring impact. *International Journal of Educational Research, 50*(3), 190–197.

De Haan, G. & Kuckartz, U. (Eds.). (1998). *Umweltbildung und Umweltbewusstsein—Forschungsperspektiven im Kontext nachhaltiger Entwicklung* [Environmental education and ecological awareness—research perspectives in the context of sustainable development]. Opladen: Leske & Budrich.

Devall, B. (1982). Ecological consciousness and ecological resisting: Guidelines for comprehension and research. *Humboldt Journal of Social Relations, 9*, 177–196.

Dispoto, R.G. (1977). Interrelationships among measures of environmental activity, emotionality, and knowledge. *Educational and Psychological Measurement, 37*, 451–459.

Dutcher, T.S., Finley, J.C., Luloff, A.E., & Johnson, J.B. (2007). Connectivity with nature as a measure of environmental values. *Environment & Behavior, 39*(4), 474–493.

Eckensberger, L.H., Breit, H., & Döring, T. (1999). Ethik und Barriere in umweltbezogenen Entscheidungen: Eine entwicklungspsychologische Perspektive. In V. Linneweber & E. Kals (Eds.), *Umweltgerechtes Handeln* [Environmentally justified behavior] (pp. 165–189). Berlin: Springer.

Ernst, A.M. & Spada, H. (1993). *Modeling actors in a resource dilemma: A computerized social learning environment* (Forschungsbericht Nr. 101). Freiburg: Psychologisches Institut der Albert-Ludwigs-Universität Freiburg.

Eulefeld, G. (1990). Umwelterziehung. In L. Kruse, C.-F. Graumann, & E.-D. Lantermann (Eds.), *Ökologische Psychologie* [Ecological psychology] (pp. 654–659). Weinheim: Psychologie Verlags Union.

Geesterenaus, C.M. (1998). Quality of environmental education. An emphasis on process development. In M. Ahlberg & W. Leal Filho (Eds.), *Environmental education for sustainability: Good environment, good life* (pp. 57–64). Frankfurt a.M.: Peter Lang.

Gethmann, C.F. (2008). Wer ist der Adressat der Langzeitverpflichtung? In J. Mittelstraß & C.F. Gethmann (Eds.), *Langzeitverantwortung. Ethik-Technik-Ökologie* [Long-term responsibility. Ethics-technology-ecology]. Darmstadt: Wissenschaftliche Buchgesellschaft.

Gifford, R. (2011). The dragons of inaction: Psychological barriers that limit climate change mitigation and adaptation. *American Psychologist, 66*, 290–302.

Habisch, A., Jonker, J., Wegner, M., & Schmidpeter, R. (Eds.). (2005). *Corporate social responsibility across Europe.* Berlin: Springer.

Haidt, J. & Kezebir, S. (2010). Morality. In S. Fiske, D. Gilbert, & G. Ginzley (Eds.), *Handbook of social psychology* (5th ed., pp. 797–832). Hoboken, NJ: Wiley.

Hardin, G. (1968). The tragedy of the commons. *Science, 162*, 1243–1248.

Hinds, J. & Sparks, P. (2008). Engaging with the natural environment: The role of affective connection and identity. *Journal of Environmental Psychology, 28*, 109–120.

Horwitz, W.A. (1994). Characteristics of environmental ethics: Environmental activists' accounts. *Ethics and Behavior, 4*, 345–467.

Huckle, J. & Sterling, S.R. (1996). *Education for sustainability.* London: Earthscan.

Jonas, H. (2012). *Das Prinzip Verantwortung* [The responsibility principle]. Berlin: Suhrkamp.

Jones, P., Selby, D., & Sterling, S.R. (2010). *Sustainability education. Perspectives and practice across higher education.* London: Earthscan.

Jüdes, U. (1997). Nachhaltige Sprachverwirrung. Auf der Suche nach einer Theorie des Sustainable Development [Sustainable language diffusion. Searching for a theory of sustainable development]. *Politische Ökologie, 52*, 26–29.

Kahn, P.H., Jr. (1999). *The human relationship with nature: Development and culture.* Cambridge, MA: MIT Press.

Kahn, P.H. Jr. & Kellert, S.R. (Eds.). (2002). *Children and nature: Psychological, sociocultural, and evolutionary investigations.* Cambridge, MA: MIT Press.

Kaiser, F.G., Fuhrer, U., Weber, O., Ofner, T., & Bühler-Ilieva, E. (2001). Responsibility and ecological behaviour. In A.E. Auhagen & H.W. Bierhoff (Eds.), *Responsibility. The many faces of a social phenomenon* (pp. 109–126). London/New York: Routledge.

Kals, E. (1996). Are proenvironmental commitments motivated by health concerns or by perceived justice? In L. Montada & M. Lerner (Eds.), *Current societal concerns about justice* (pp. 231–258). New York: Plenum Press.

Kals, E. (2012). Affective connection to nature. In A.C. Michalos (Ed.), *Encyclopedia of quality of life research.* Berlin: Springer (http://referencelife.springer.com).

Kals, E. & Maes, J. (2002). Sustainable behavior and emotions. In P. Schmuck & W. Schultz (Eds.), *Psychology of sustainable development* (pp. 97–122). Norwell, MA: Kluwer Academic Publishers.

Kals, E., Schumacher, D., & Montada, L. (1999). Emotional affinity toward nature as a motivational basis to protect nature. *Environment & Behavior, 31*(2), 178–202.

Kaplan, R. (2001). The nature of the view from home: Psychological benefits. *Environment & Behavior, 33*(4), 507–542.

Karpiak, C.P. & Baril, L.B. (2008). Moral reasoning and concern for the environment. *Journal of Environmental Psychology, 28*, 203–208.

Kaufmann-Hayoz, R. (2006). Human action in context: A model framework for interdisciplinary studies in view of sustainable development. *Umweltpsychologie, 10*(1), 154–177.

Kellert, S. R. (1997). *Kinship to mastery: Biophilia in human evolution and development.* Washington, DC: Island Press.

Kirby, A. (2003). Redefining social and environmental relations at the ecovillage at Ithaca: A case study. *Journal of Environmental Psychology, 23*, 323–332.

Kohlberg, L. (1984). *The psychology of moral development: The nature and validity of moral stages.* San Francisco: Harper & Row.

Kreibich, R. (Ed.). (1996). *Nachhaltige Entwicklung. Leitbild für die Zukunft von Wirtschaft und Gesellschaft* [Sustainable development. Guidance principle for the future of economy and society]. Weinheim: Beltz.

Krizek, K.J., Newport, D., White, J., & Townsend, A.R. (2012). Higher education's sustainability imperative: How to practically respond? *International Journal of Sustainability in Higher Education, 13*(1), 19–33.

Kuhn, D. (2010). What is scientific thinking and how does it develop? In U. Goswami (Ed.), *Handbook of childhood cognitive development* (pp. 497–523). Malden, MA: Blackwell.

Kyburz-Graber, R., Hofer, K., & Wolfensberger, B. (2006). Studies on a socio-ecological approach to environmental education—a contribution to a critical position in the education for sustainable development discourse. *Environmental Education Research, 12*, 101–114.

Lange, J.M. (2012). Education in sustainable development: How can science education contribute to the vulnerability perception? *Research in Science Education, 42*(1), 109–127.

Lantermann, E.-D., Döring-Seipel, E., & Schima, P. (1992). *Ravenhorst. Gefühle, Werte und Unbestimmtheit im Umgang mit einem ökologischen Szenario* [Ravenhorst. Feelings, values, and uncertainty in coping with an ecological scenario]. München: Quintessenz.

Leal Filho, W. (2011). *World trends in education for sustainable development.* Frankfurt a.M.: Peter Lang.

Leal Filho, W. & Littledyke, M. (Eds.). (2004). *International perspectives in environmental education.* Frankfurt a.M.: Peter Lang.

Linneweber, V. (1998). Nachhaltige Entwicklung als unscharfes Prädikat [Sustainable development as a fuzzy construct]. *Umweltpsychologie, 2*(1), 66–77.

Lyons, E. & Breakwell, G.M. (1994). Factors predicting environmental concern and indifference in 13- to 16-year-olds. *Environment & Behavior, 26*, 223–238.

MacVaugh, J. & Norton, M. (2012). Introducing sustainability into business education contexts using active learning. *International Journal of Sustainability in Higher Education, 13*(1), 72–87.

Maloney, M.P. & Ward, M.P. (1973). Ecology: Let's hear from the people. An objective scale for the measurement of ecological attitudes and knowledge. *American Psychologist, 28*, 583–586.

McKenzie-Mohr, D. (2002). The next revolution: Sustainability. In P. Schmuck & W.P. Schultz (Eds.). *Psychology of sustainable development* (pp. 19–36). Boston: Kluwer Academic Publishers.

McNichol, H., Davis, J.M., & O'Brien, K.R. (2011). An ecological footprint for an early learning centre: Identifying opportunities for early childhood sustainability education through interdisciplinary research. *Environmental Education Research, 17*(5), 689–704.

Meadows, D.H., Meadows, J.R., & Behrens, W.W. (1972). *The limits to growth*. New York: Universe Books.

Montada, L. (2007). Conflicts and the justice of conflict resolution. In K. Törnblom & R. Vermunt (Eds.), *Distributive and procedural justice. Research and applications* (pp. 255–268). Burlington, VA: Ashgate/Glower.

Montada, L. & Kals, E. (2000). Political implications of environmental psychology. *International Journal of Psychology, 35*(2), 168–176.

Müller, M.M. (2012). Justice as a framework for the solution of environmental conflicts. In E. Kals & J. Maes (Eds.), *Justice and conflicts: Theoretical and empirical contributions* (pp. 239–250). New York: Springer.

Müller, M.M. & Hiendl, B. (2012). Wahrgenommene Gerechtigkeit von Verteilungen der Kosten des Klimawandels und ihre Bedeutung für Handlungsbereitschaften zum Klimaschutz [Perceived justice of distributions of costs of climate change and their impact on commitments to protect the climate]. *Umweltpsychologie, 16*(2), 29–47.

Müller, M.M. & Kals, E. (2007). Interactions between procedural fairness and outcome favorability in conflict situations. In K.Y. Törnblom & R. Vermunt (Eds.), *Distributive and procedural justice* (pp. 125–140). Aldershot, UK: Ashgate.

Müller, M.M., Kals, E., & Pansa, R. (2009). Adolescents' emotional affinity towards nature: A cross-societal study. Special issue: Children and nature. *Journal of Developmental Processes, 4*, 59–69.

Nisbet, E.K., Zelenski, J.M., & Murphy, S.A. (2009). The nature relatedness scale: Linking individuals' connections with nature to environmental concern and behaviour. *Environment & Behavior, 41*, 715–740.

Ojala, A. (in press). The importance of different components of morality in environmentally friendly behaviour. In K. Helkama (Ed.), *Values, morality, and knowledge*. Helsinki: Department of Social Research, Helsinki University.

Opotow, S. & Clayton, S. (Eds.). (1994). Green justice: Conceptions of fairness and the natural world. *Journal of Social Issues, 50*(3), 1–12.

Page, G.T., Thomas, J.B., & Marshall, A.R. (1980). *International dictionary of education*. Cambridge: MIT Press.

Pawlik, K. (1991). The psychology of global environmental change: Some basic data and an agenda for cooperative international research. *International Journal of Psychology, 26*, 547–563.

Platt, J. (1973). Social traps. *American Psychologist, 28*, 641–651.

Raivio, K. (2011). Sustainability as an educational agenda. *Journal of Cleaner Production, 19*(16), 1906–1907.

Rest, J.R. (1986). *Moral development. Advances in research and theory*. New York: Praeger.

Rest, J.R., Narvaez, D., Bebeau, M.J., & Thoma, S.J. (1999). *Postconventional moral thinking*. Mahwah, NJ: Erlbaum.

Rieckmann, M. (2012). Future-oriented higher education: Which key competencies should be fostered through university teaching and learning? *Futures, 44*(2), 127–135.

Russell, Y. (2001). *Intergenerationelle Verantwortlichkeit und Gerechtigkeit im globalen Umweltschutz. Unveröffentlichte Dissertation* [Intergenerational responsibility and justice in global environmental protection. Unpublished Ph.D. thesis]. Trier: Universität Trier.

Satapathy, M.K. (2007). *Education, environment and sustainable development*. Delhi: Shipra Publications.

Schmuck, P. & Schultz, P.W. (Eds.). (2002). *Psychology of sustainable development*. Norwell, MA: Kluwer Academic Publishers.

Schnack, K. (1998). Why focus on conflicting interests in environmental education? In M. Ahlberg & W. Leal Filho (Eds.), *Environmental education for sustainability: Good environment, good life* (pp. 83–96). Frankfurt a.M.: Peter Lang.

Schultz, P.W. (2001). The structure of environmental concern: Concern for self, other people, and the biosphere. *Journal of Environmental Psychology, 21*, 327–339.

Schwartz, S.H. & Howard, J.A. (1980). Explanations of the moderating effect of responsibility denial on the personal norm-behavior relationship. *Social Psychology Quarterly, 43*, 441–446.

Schweizer-Ries, P. & Perkins, D.D. (2012). Sustainability science: Transdisciplinarity, transepistemology, and action research. *Umweltpsychologie, 16*(4), 6–10.

Scott, A. (2006). Communicating sustainability research. Theoretical and practical challenges. In W. Leal Filho (Ed.), *Innovation, education and communication for sustainable development.* Frankfurt a.M.: Peter Lang.

Simonneaux, J. & Simonneaux, L. (2012). Educational configurations for teaching environmental socioscientific issues within the perspective of sustainability. *Research in Science Education, 42*(1), 75–94.

Spada, H., Opwis, K., Donnen, J., Schwiersch, M., & Ernst, A. (1990). Ecological knowledge. Acquisition and use in problem solving and in decision making. *Western European Education, 22,* 49–72.

Stern, P.C. (2000). Toward a coherent theory of environmentally significant behavior. *Journal of Social Issues, 56*(3), 407–424.

Stern, P.C. & Gardener, G.T. (1981). The place of behavior change in the management of environmental problems. *Zeitschrift für Umweltpolitik, 2,* 213–239.

Swim, J., Clayton, S., Doherty, T.J., Gifford, R., Howard, G., Reser, J. et al. (2010). *Psychology and global climate change: Addressing a multi-faceted phenomenon and set of challenges.* Retrieved from www.apa.org/science/about/publications/climate-change-booklet.pdf [2012/07/05].

Syme, G.J., Kals, E., Nancarrow, B.E., & Montada, L. (2006). Ecological risks and community perceptions of fairness and justice: A cross-cultural model. *Human and Ecological Risk Assessment, 12,* 102–119.

Thompson, S.C. & Stoutemyer, K. (1991). Water use as a commons dilemma: The effects of education that focuses on long-term consequences and individual action. *Environment and Behavior, 23,* 314–333.

Tucker, L.R. (1978). The environmentally concerned citizen. *Environment and Behavior, 10,* 389–418.

Valentin, A. & Spangenberg, J.H. (2000). A guide to community sustainability indicators. *Environmental Impact Assessment Review, 20,* 381–392.

WCED (World Commission on Environment and Development). (1990). *Our common future.* Oxford: Oxford University Press.

Zoller, U. (2011). Science and technology education in the STES context in primary schools: What should it take? *Journal of Science Education and Technology, 20*(5), 444–453.

28

MORAL AND CHARACTER EDUCATION THROUGH SPORTS

F. Clark Power and Kristin K. Sheehan

Most adults who played sports as children assert without hesitation or qualification that sports build character. Asked to identify the specific virtues that sports build, the majority identify virtues related to achievement, such as hard work and perseverance. Some mention social virtues, such as teamwork and unselfishness. Sports likely instill a work ethic and teach life lessons about persistence and teamwork (Shulman and Bowen, 2002), but whether they help to develop morality is a question that is rarely investigated or even asked. No one brings up justice spontaneously. In fact, when asked whether participation in sports taught them fairness and other moral virtues, such as honesty, most athletes and coaches scratch their heads. It is instructive to note that in a 2010 blog while still at the height of his celebrity, Lance Armstrong listed three traits to describe his character: strong, helpful, and optimistic. He never included justice or honesty. What does this say about the virtues that we tend to emphasize in sports and the consequences of losing sight of morality as a component of character?

DO SPORTS BUILD CHARACTER?

School and sport administrators typically justify the inclusion of sports as an extracurricular activity by claiming that they promote character as well as physical development. For example, when challenged to demonstrate whether interscholastic athletics had any educational worth, a committee formed by the New York State Public High School Athletic Association (NYSPHSAA), drew up "An Educational Framework for Interscholastic Athletics," which recognized the teaching of virtue as the primary goal of sports participation (2001). The committee reaffirmed the NYSPHAA's mission statement that interscholastic athletics are to foster "the quest for excellence" and promote high standards of "competence, character, civility, and citizenship" (NYSPHAA, 2001). The NYSPHAA is not alone in justifying sports programs as contributing to character development. The mission statement of the

National Federation of State High School Associations states that sports "develop good citizenship and healthy lifestyles."

In spite of the pervasive belief, at least among administrators, that sports build character, there has been a dearth of empirical evidence to support the claim. Recently, several studies indicate youth sports may have a beneficial influence on indicators of Positive Youth Development (PYD) (e.g., Gano-Overway et al., 2009; Zarrett et al., 2009). Yet these studies also show that the sports experience can have negative effects as well. While there are studies showing that sports participation can prevent delinquency, there are other studies indicating that sports participation can increase it (Mahoney, Eccles, & Larsen 2004; Hartmann & Massoglia, 2007; Gardner, Roth, & Brooks-Gunn, 2009; Zarrett et al., 2009). As Bredemeier and Shields (2006) rightly assert, there is no univocal sports experience. Athletes' experiences of playing sports vary widely depending on the particular sport they are playing, the competitive level, the coaching style, the influence of parents, and so on.

SPORTS ARE PLAY

Before we can begin to analyze the ways in which the sports experience can build character, we must take into account the fact that sports are by nature play and, as such, have a critical role in child development. Huizinga (1955, p. 13) provides what has become the classical definition of play as a fundamental expression of human freedom:

> [Play]is a free activity standing quite consciously outside "ordinary" life as being "not serious" but at the same time absorbing the player intensely and utterly. It is an activity connected with no material interest, and no profit can be gained by it. It proceeds within its own proper boundaries of time and space according to fixed rules and in an orderly manner.

Huizinga's (1955) description of play as having the paradoxical quality of being "non-serious" but, at the same time, utterly engrossing captures sports at their best. Sports played well bring about pure joy and a release from the cares of everyday life. Play provides a wide range of cognitive, social, and emotional benefits to people of all ages, particularly to children (e.g., Elkind, 2007; Fisher, 1992; Pellegrini & Holmes, 2006). Piaget believed that through playing games, children developed a sense of fairness and understanding of rules. Initially, children find the rules of games to be arbitrary impositions that constrain their free play. Yet through the experience of playing games with their peers, children gain ownership of them as "the free product of mutual agreement and an autonomous conscience" (1932/1965, p. 28). Piaget found that as children become competent to make their own rules they base those rules on the "spirit of the game," making new rules to make their games more challenging and fair. In observing how children play games, Piaget found a model for moral education. The teacher, he proposed, should act as a "collaborator" and not a "master" (p. 404). Masters impose rules and expect obedience, while collaborators make rules based on reason and reciprocity.

Piaget's research has had surprisingly little influence on recent discussions of sports as a character-building activity. This may be because the games that Piaget studied, marbles and hopscotch, are more like children's informal pickup games than organized youth sports. Children's sports experience has changed dramatically over the last 40 years as adult-organized sports have almost completely replaced informal, children-controlled games (Chudacoff, 2007; Coakely, 2009; Scarlett, Naudeau, Salonius-Pasternak, & Ponte, 2005). This dramatic alteration of children's lives is not confined to sports alone. In fact, as Chudacoff (2007) and Gray (2011) among others have pointed out, children's play in general has been on the decline to the detriment of their well-being.

Most of the enjoyment that children experience in playing games comes from the fact they control their activity. Once young children have mastered the basic skills of a sport, like soccer, and understand the rules, they easily become engrossed in devising strategies on offense and defense. Yet in organized youth sports, coaches typically take charge of the strategic element of the game while leaving only the execution of their decisions to the children. In such cases, it would be more accurate to say it is the coaches who are playing rather than the children. This leads to two unfortunate consequences. First, the enjoyment of the game diminishes and second, the cognitive value of the game is reduced. Research in social cognitive development (Selman, 1980), suggests that competitive games encourage children to take the roles of others and to coordinate roles in developing strategies involving multiple players. Evidence from the study of youth sports suggests that the more children are involved in their games, the more likely they are to develop the creativity and the mastery needed to excel (Côté & Fraser-Thomas, 2007).

As Piaget found, games do more than help children acquire activity-specific expertise, games help children to develop a morality of cooperation in which they learn through direct experience not only how to compete but the value of playing by rules. In the marble games that Piaget studied, the children were responsible not only for their strategies but also for assuring that the rules of the game were upheld and enforced. In organized youth sports, adult officials, referees, and umpires are given that responsibility. Yet instead of respecting officials for ensuring fairness in games, coaches, even at the elementary school level, often angrily criticize officials in front of their players (Shields, Bredemeier, LaVoi, & Power, 2005).

Youth sports can never realize their character-building potential as long as adults control them. If children are to develop moral virtues through sports participation, character educators must address the fact that the adult-dominated structure of youth sports is inherently flawed. Ironically, adult control also undermines the development of athletic excellence because adult control creates a high pressured, authority-constrained environment that discourages the experimentation and innovation necessary in the development of great athletes (Coakley, 2009). Such an environment also undermines the single most important motivational factor in youth sports—love of the game itself. In their study of the factors that contributed to US Olympians' success, Gibbons et al. (2003) found that the "love of the sport," acquired in the early years when teaching and learning is "playful," is, as Bloom (1985) discovered in his pioneering educational research, the foundation for later excellence (p. 32).

It should not be surprising then that self-determination researchers are finding that when coaches support children's autonomy by giving them choices and power over making decisions, children enjoy sports more and experience greater intrinsic motivation (Conroy & Coatsworth, 2007; Hagger & Chatzisarantis, 2007). Although moral educators (Power & Higgins-D'Alessandro, 2008) and self-determination theorists (Ryan & Deci, 2007) argue that children and adolescents should be given greater power over decision-making to foster moral development and intrinsic motivation, coaches are sometimes reluctant to yield much power over decisions about play on the field or discipline off the field. Coaches tend to coach as they are coached, and few models are available that emphasize fostering athletes' autonomy by helping coaches to foster discovery learning, ask good questions, organize team meetings, and facilitate democratic decision-making (Beedy, 1997; Giancola, 2010; Power & Sheehan, 2012).

Coakley (2009) notes the rise of organized youth sports, which began in the postwar years of the 1950s and 1960s and was fueled by the following factors: 1) the need for supervised outside of school activities caused by the rise in the number of families with both parents working outside the home; 2) a redefinition of what it means to be a "good parent" that emphasizes involving children in structured activities with measurable markers of success; 3) a rising concern that left on their own, children will get in trouble; 4) a belief that organized sports will protect children from the dangers of the world; and 5) the rise in wealth, status, and esteem attained by elite and professional athletes. These factors combine to "professionalize" youth sports (e.g., Brower, 1979; Coakley, 2009). Youth sport programs have become increasingly dominated by adults who have imposed "big league" structures and expectations on children. Professionalized uniforms, fancy scoreboards, elaborate rules for drafting players, growing numbers of spectators, and the imperial presence of adult coaches have transformed children's play into highly pressured and carefully scrutinized work (see Farrey, 2008).

CHARACTER OR "CHARACTERS" DEVELOPED THROUGH SPORT

Shields et al. (2005) undertook a study of youth sport behaviors, which raised disturbing questions about the character-building qualities of the youth sport experience today. In a sample of children between the sixth and eighth grades, over one-quarter of the children reported that during their past sports season their coaches encouraged them to retaliate, angrily argued with a referee, yelled at a player for making a mistake, and berated an opponent. Not only did children witness coaches misbehaving, but also their parents. The same study revealed that spectator behavior was no better than that of the coaches. Approximately 40% of the children in the sample reported that fans teased them and their teammates; and over two-thirds of the children reported seeing fans angrily yell at an official. Given that this study focused only on one sport season, we can only imagine what children witness from adults over their entire youth sport careers.

In spite of the negative behavior that they witness, most children report that they have fun playing organized sports. Many children report that participating in sports teaches them about teamwork and about getting along with others (Power & Seroczynski, 2013). Yet to date, there is no empirical evidence that participation in organized sports develops moral judgment (e.g., Conroy, Silva, Newcomer, Walker, & Johnson, 2001; Shields, Bredemeier, & Power, 2002; Stoll & Beller, 2000; Weiss & Smith, 2002). Cross-sectional research (Bredemeier and Shields, 1986a; Kavussanu and Ntoumanis, 2003; Proios, Doganis, Arvanitidou, Unierzyski, & Katsagolis, 2004; Stevenson, 1998) indicates that increased athletic experience does not lead to higher moral reasoning. In fact, some studies with college level athletes suggest that sports experience can have a negative effect on moral thought (Bredemeier & Shields, 1986a; Priest, Krause, & Beach, 1999; Stoll & Beller, 2006). Similar results have been found in studies of high school sports (Beller & Stoll, 1995; Rulmyr, 1996). A failure to find that sports participation promotes moral judgment at the high school or college levels does not necessarily mean that sports participation cannot play a role in moral development at the youth level. It may be that, in spite of the lofty claims of their mission statements, the highly competitive nature of high school and college athletics compromises their effectiveness in fostering moral development. Yet the few studies that we have on the effects of organized youth sports on children's moral reasoning indicate that participation in moderate to high contact youth sports have a negative effect (Bredemeier, Weiss, Shields, & Cooper, 1986; Conroy et al., 2001).

It appears to us that the organization and professionalization of youth sports coupled with the lack of attention given to cultivating athletes' responsibility for fairness at all levels of all sports (with the notable exceptions of tennis, golf, and Ultimate Frisbee [Power & Sheehan, 2013]) has rendered sports to be a largely amoral activity. There has been a broad consensus for some time now that if organized sports are going to influence moral reasoning and behavior, those who serve as coaches are going to have to undertake the task of character education in a deliberate way that is informed by research in moral development (e.g., Shields and Bredemeier, 1995; National Association for Sport and Physical Education [NASPE], 2006).

THE RISE OF CHARACTER EDUCATION PROGRAMS IN SPORTS

Character development has been an important goal of organized sports as they took root in the 1920s and 1930s. For example, in its mission statement at the time of its founding in 1939, Little League Baseball described its purpose as designed "to develop superior citizens rather than superior athletes" (Chudacoff, 2007, p. 207). Founders of youth sports organizations believed that sports participation would teach the virtues of loyalty, hard work, and cooperation; virtues needed for success in the emerging economic order. At that time, both Protestant and Catholic evangelists also promoted "Muscular Christianity," an approach to physical education and sports that emphasized masculine virtues leading to physical as well as moral health (Putney, 2003). Although character development continues to be a major aim of youth sport organizations, character education is now also seen as a remedy for the perceived rise of bad behavior in youth and high school sports (e.g., Clifford & Feezel, 1997; Lumpkin, Stoll, & Beller, 2002; Martens, 2004; Power & Sheehan, 2012; Thompson, 1995; Yeager, Baltzell, Buxton, & Bzdell, 2001). Most character education programs do not present elaborate definitions of character, but offer lists of values and recommendations for coaches. Their content typically includes what Lickona and Davidson (2005) have described as two distinguishable types of character: ethical and performance. Ethical character includes relational virtues, such as justice and care, while performance character includes achievement virtues, such as effort and perseverance.

For example Jim Thompson (1995, 2003), the founder of the Positive Coaching Alliance, one of the largest coach education programs in the country, strongly advocates that coaches act as character educators. In his first book, *Positive Coaching: Building Character and Self-Esteem through Sports*, he describes character as made up of the following traits: 1) mental toughness; 2) having fun; 3) winning and losing with class; 4) courage; 5) setting and committing to goals (defined in terms of sports skills); and 6) effort and determination (Thompson, 1995, pp. 113–120). Most of these traits are related to achievement. The closest trait to a social or moral virtue in his list is winning and losing with "class," which means displaying sportsmanship and refusing to cheat to win. In his last book, entitled *The Power of Double-Goal Coaching: Developing Winners in Sports and Life*, Thompson (2010) puts the development of character on par with winning. He also gives more emphasis to the moral dimension of character by replacing the concept of showing "class" with "honoring the game," which means acting in positive ways that show respect for one's self, teammates, opponents, and officials.

In his popular Character Counts Sports, Michael Josephson uses the mantra "Victory with Honor" to temper the quest for winning with an appeal to virtue. Like Thompson, Josephson recognizes that winning is important, but he cautions that winning should not be pursued in ways that degrade the self, others, and the sport itself. Josephson and Thompson rightly frame their character education approaches to sport as an antidote to the corrosive pursuit of winning at all cost. Josephson's list of virtues, the "six pillars of character," concentrates on moral character virtues, such as "trustworthiness, respect, caring, and fairness." Yet Josephson also values performance character by including under the virtue of responsibility "habits and life skills that lead to success" (Josephson Institute, 2006).

Thompson and Josephson's understanding of character as consisting of virtues related to both high achievement and morality is typical of contemporary character education approaches (e.g., Lickona, 1992; Ryan & Bohlin, 1999; Vincent, 1999). These approaches regard moral education as a part of character education. Historically, however, the character and moral education approaches are somewhat different in the way in which they understand what virtues mean and how they are prioritized. They also differ in the emphasis that they give to moral reasoning and democratic deliberation. *Moral* education, as it is currently practiced, grounds itself in Piaget and Kohlberg's cognitive developmental approach and in domain theory (e.g., Nucci, 2001 and Turiel, 1983), which is focused on morality as fairness or justice (Lapsley & Narvaez, 2006; Power & Power, 2012; Nucci, 2009). This approach promotes the development of moral judgment by presenting children with moral problems involving conflicts of interest for discussion and democratic deliberation. The Play Like a Champion Today approach comes out of the moral education tradition as it also makes reference to the cardinal virtues of prudence, justice, fortitude, and temperance (Power & Sheehan, 2012).

In the 1980s, political conservatives, such as Secretary of State William Bennett, and traditionalist social scientists, such as Kevin Ryan and Edward Wynne, aligned to form the character education movement. Drawing on Aristotle's virtue theory, they opposed certain features of the moral education approach and espoused what they regarded as a more common sense, authority-centered approach to teaching values. Ryan (1989) noted that in contrast to moral education, the character education movement was eclectic: it embraced a wide range of moral theories and pedagogical approaches. He maintained, however, that character education was grounded in tradition and sought to "pass on" and "preserve" the wisdom of the past rather than "to change the social order" (p. 15). Finally and perhaps most significantly, Ryan noted that the character education movement viewed children as "more malleable" and, therefore, needing "formation" and "a strong environment" (p. 16). Neither Ryan nor Wynne (1989) saw much value in democratic class meetings or moral discussions.

Under the influence of Lickona (1992) and Berkowitz (Berkowitz & Bier, 2005) among others, the character education movement shifted from opposing the methods of moral education to endorsing them alongside the traditional methods of didactic instruction and modeling. Both Lickona and Berkowitz made key contributions to the development of moral education theory and practice, and both sought to add to the methods of moral education more traditional methods of direct instruction and modeling. This eclectic approach to character education exploded in popularity throughout the 1990s and into the 2000s as character education gained widespread popular acceptance in public as well as religious and private schools. The most significant challenge that the current character education movement faces is to maintain an eclectic embrace of different virtues and pedagogies while providing a coherent and meaningful moral stance. On the contrary, moral educators going back to Kohlberg (1981) put a clear priority on the virtue of justice before all other virtues (Power & Power, 2012). In fact, drawing from Aristotle as well as Kant, moral educators maintain that achievement virtues are only virtues if they are rooted in virtue of justice. The desire to win at sports can be so strong that achievement virtues that lead to success, such as hard work, perseverance, and self-sacrifice can easily become detached from justice.

One of the most sobering studies of the win-at-all cost mentality is a well-known study of cheating conducted by Bob Goldman in the mid-1990s (Bamberger & Yaeger, 1997). He asked 198 Olympic- or near-Olympic-level athletes to respond to two scenarios:

1. You are offered a banned performance-enhancing substance, with two guarantees: a) You will not be caught; b) You will win.

    Would you take the substance?

2. You are offered a banned performance-enhancing substance that comes with two guarantees: a) You will not be caught; b) You will win every competition you enter for the next five years and then you will die from the side-effects of the substance.

    Would you take it?

Goldman found that 193 of the athletes reported that they would cheat in the first scenario and over half would cheat in the second (Bamberger & Yaeger, 1997). Much attention has been focused on the fact that more than half of these athletes were willing to die for a medal. Yet should we be surprised that elite athletes who had already dedicated so much of their lives to attain the heights they had would be willing to make the ultimate sacrifice? Too little attention has been given to the fact that almost all of the athletes would be willing to cheat to win a medal if they could get away with it. How important is the virtue of honesty relative to other achievement-related virtues in sports? Is honesty the same kind of virtue as perseverance or courage?

Many of the character education programs that emphasize the development of virtues fail to take into account the distinctiveness of the virtue of justice and related moral virtues, such as honesty. The moral virtues bind categorically. Achievement related virtues are desirable in our culture but justice is obligatory in any culture. In the realm of sports where winning is so highly valued and rewarded, the achievement virtues are understandably emphasized. Character educators need to do more than advocate for lists of virtues. They need to put a priority on justice as the foundation for all virtue.

One implication of giving a priority to the virtue of justice is making clear that coaches should not allow injured athletes to risk further injury by continuing to practice or play. Under the guise of building virtue by "toughening up their athletes," coaches often encourage their players to shake off injuries or to conceal them so they are not considered "soft" or lazy. A study by the Minnesota State Athletic Union revealed that over 21% of the athletes said that they had been pressured to play with an injury. As we are learning more about the risks of concussions, increased efforts are being made to educate coaches about their responsibilities to protect their players. It is important, however, that these efforts be grounded in a moral concern (i.e., fairness to the athlete) and not simply in a prudential concern to avoid the legal ramifications of negligence.

Giving a priority to justice also means that, whatever motivational or disciplinary value coaches may think that physical punishments have, the infliction of pain is abusive and a violation of athletes' right to their physical integrity. Many coaches justify the use of such punishments as character-building and a time-honored part of sports culture. Yet the National Association for Sport and Physical Education (2009) calls them "inappropriate" and educationally "unsound" (p. 2).

Character educators face an even greater challenge in defending children's basic rights to play and to engage in activities that promote their health and physical development. The UN Convention on the Rights of the Child declares that children have a "right to engage in play and recreational activities appropriate to the age of the child" (Article 31). Recently the US Department of Education (2013) issued a directive declaring that sports are a "civil right" and that schools receiving federal aid should make accommodations to provide access to sports for children with disabilities. Secretary of Education Arnie Duncan (2013) argued that all children should be able to reap not only the health-related benefits of physical activity but the character benefits of sports participation:

> Sports can provide invaluable lessons in discipline, selflessness, passion and courage, and this guidance will help schools ensure that students with disabilities have an equal opportunity to benefit from the life lessons they can learn on the playing field or on the court.
>
> (p. 1)

At the most basic level, fairness demands that regardless of their abilities or disabilities athletes have an equal opportunity to participate in sports. Yet organized sports at all levels favor some children and adolescents at the expense of others. This is most obvious when considering the difference family income makes to children's access to playgrounds and athletic facilities as well as to sports equipment, clinics, summer camps, and, of course, sports teams. However, income is not the only factor in determining the opportunity to play sports in the United States. Many youth sport organizations permit children of perceived low ability to be cut from teams or given little or no playing time. Not only is it unfair to exclude children from sports participation, it is also unwise from a talent development perspective. Throughout childhood and into early adolescence, sports organizations should be taking a long-term perspective on athletic development by keeping sports fun, avoiding premature talent identification, and helping all children to achieve their potential (Balyi, 2001).

Perhaps the single most important contribution that character education can make to youth and high school sports in America is to confront the injustices built into the structure of organized youth and high school sports. All children deserve access to the psychological as well as physiological benefits of sports. All children deserve the opportunity to play and to develop the virtues of fairness and honesty as well as courage and friendship on the sports field. If character education through sport programs are to adequately address the win-at-all-cost mentality that corrodes the culture of sports today, they cannot emphasize performance character at the expense of ethical character.

THE ROLE OF THE COACH

Ideally, coaches should be mentor-teachers, who focus on developing each player. In the mentor-teacher role, the adult's responsibility is to introduce the experience of different sports to children so that children can play those sports on their own. Typically, parents serve as children's first mentor-teachers. They not only instruct their children by helping them to learn basic sports skills, such as throwing or kicking a ball, but they also initiate children into the culture of a particular sport by watching games with them on television, taking them to ball parks to cheer on local teams, and acquainting them with the lore and heroes of the sport. This mentor-teaching role is very different from the managerial role that coaches play from the earliest youth sport level through college. As managers, coaches become the primary participants in children's games. They compete along with their players and they experience all of the emotions of competitors, becoming elated when their team wins and dejected when they lose. In fact, many coaches often feel these emotions more poignantly than young athletes.

When coaches become managers, winning may become increasingly important to them. As managers, they exercise almost complete control of their players. They assign players to positions; they design strategies in practices and orchestrate their execution during games from the sidelines; they decide who plays and when in order to maximize their competitive advantage. It is no wonder that many coaches become so consumed by their role as managers that they become confused about who they are serving, the athletes or their own ego.

Youth sport coaches should be child-centered and focus on helping children to develop their skills and enjoy the sport. However, as managers, they often become demanding and imperious; even to the point of berating and punishing their own players (see Shields et al., 2005). Coaches do not always set out to be managers; they are often the victims of a sports culture gone amuck. For example, starting his youth sport coaching career determined to "do it the right way," "place sportsmanship ahead of winning," and "involve all the kids," volunteer Buzz Bissinger admitted that he quickly became the coach he vowed not to be:

> I could see the pathology that was overcoming me, the sickness of winning and having my stomach ache when we didn't win. The sickness of five-minute car rides home with my son that seemed like five hours, as I went through the litany of all the things he had done wrong. The sickness of seeing the frustration and tears in his eyes as he was forced to listen to my addled concept of what I thought it meant to be a coaching parent.
>
> (Bissinger, 2008, p. 1)

There are two ways in which character educators can respond to the toxic culture of organized sports: the way of compromise and the way of confrontation. Most coach education programs take the way of compromise, which accepts the legitimacy of the coach's managerial role and adds to it the role of character educator. This way, which is implicit in slogans like "Double-Goal Coaching" and "Victory with Honor" does not force coaches to choose between winning and meeting the needs of children but holds out the promise that they can pursue both.

We believe that coaches must take the less traveled way of confrontation. This means presenting coaches at the youth sport level with an either-or decision about their primary aim, either coach to win or coach to develop each child. Those who choose to coach to win or who do not want to have to choose between them are better suited to coach at the high school, college, and professional levels. Children at the youth sport level deserve coaches who are committed to player development before all else. This does not mean that they should not care about winning. It does mean that all of their decisions should be aimed at developing each player and that they should not put one player's development over another's.

The litmus test for whether youth sport coaches are mentor-teachers is how they distribute playing-time. Giving children equal playing-time is a matter of justice and must be the bedrock of any educational approach to character. We cannot in good conscience maintain that sports contribute to children's development and deny some children the opportunity to play. No child's well-being, health, possible future athletic attainments, and character development should be sacrificed for the sake of winning and success. The data very clearly shows that children rank playing for fun far ahead of winning as a reason for playing sports (Hyman, 2010; Seefeldt, Ewing, & Walk, 1992). Moreover, it makes little moral or educational sense to demand that children at an early stage of their athletic development "earn" the privilege of playing by demonstrating the very qualities (e.g., hard work, courage, and perseverance) that they are in the process of developing.

THE RELATION BETWEEN PERFORMANCE AND ETHICAL CHARACTER

Giving primacy to the virtue of justice and distinguishing moral from achievement virtues does not imply that what Lickona and Davidson call ethical and performance character are unrelated. Studies of athletes using achievement goal theory (Duda & Hall, 2001) find that athletes' goal orientations are correlated to socio-moral judgment and behavior (e.g., Duda, 2001; Duda & Balaguer, 2007; Kavussanu and Ntoumanis, 2003; Kavussanu and Roberts, 2001; Sage, Kavussanu, & Duda, 2006). Achievement goal theory identifies two contrasting motivational orientations: task and ego. An individual with a task orientation sets self-referenced goals, for example, to increase one's number of rebounds or decrease one's turnovers. A person with an ego orientation sets social comparison goals, such as demonstrating superiority over others by winning (or not losing). Research shows that ego-oriented athletes are more likely to cheat and to engage in reckless aggression than task-oriented athletes (Duda & Balaguer, 2007). Achievement goal research also shows while all athletes care about winning and losing, athletes vary on the extent to which they incorporate task and ego goals in their self-evaluations.

COMPETITION

Shields and Bredemeier (2009) argue there is a point in which an obsessive desire to win can actually undermine the competitive spirit itself. They define this willingness to do whatever it takes to win as decompetition, not "true competition." Decompetition undermines intrinsic motivation by substituting the enjoyment of the play of sports themselves for the tangible (e.g., money) or intangible (maintaining self-worth) extrinsic rewards that come from winning. Decompetition can also undermine moral motivation by detaching winning from fairness.

Far more research is needed to examine how athletes think about winning in relation to achieving mastery, and playing fairly. Duda (2001) finds that the task and ego orientations are not mutually exclusive. Athletes can be and often are high on both. Research is needed to determine how athletes achieve a balance between these goals and how considerations of fairness factor into both orientations. The task and ego measure, the Task and Ego Orientation in Sport Questionnaire (TEOSC), does not address issues of fairness or rule-following explicitly. The measure assesses the criteria that athletes use in assessing the conditions under which they feel the most successful. Moreover, the measure does not directly assess how athletes manage to balance these two orientations when competing. Presumably those who choose to participate in sports value competition and enjoy it. The orientations give us some insight into what athletes value about the sport and what it is about the competition that brings value. From the perspective of Aristotle's theory of ethics, competitiveness in sports is virtuous if athletes put the quality of their play ahead of the outcome. What is distinctive about performance character in sports as distinct from performance character in school is that the goal of playing well is inherently related to playing to win. For example, a task-oriented basketball player will feel most successful when she is putting forth her best effort and playing as well as she can.

Playing well in competition cannot be completely self-referenced; it will entail countering the moves of the opposition. In individual sports, like gymnastics, figure skating, and swimming, task-oriented athletes are able to focus on their own performance without having to pay much attention to what their opponents are doing. In either individual or team sports, striving to win does not take away from the virtue of competing well. In fact, in most situations striving to win is involved in playing well. Striving to win is actually a part of the implicit social contract that athletes enter into when they decide to play a competitive sport. In their review of the achievement goal literature, Duda and Balaguer (2007) find task but not ego orientation consistently predicts sport attitudes and behavior. One explanation for this is that there may be a positive and negative type of ego orientation. The positive type complements the task orientation by valuing competitive success as a way of demonstrating competence; the negative type is based on a fear that losing will reveal a lack of competence (Duda & Balaguer, 2007).

Although playing to win is a part of a virtuous competitive mindset, whether one actually wins is in an Aristotelian framework a consequent end or bonus. Aristotle makes this point in distinguishing a good craftsperson from a person of good character. The good craftsperson is judged exclusively by the quality of her or his product. The person of character, on the other hand, is judged by the quality of her or his actions and intentions, whether or not they achieve their desired results. Virtuous athletes understand playing well, which includes playing competitively, as their highest goal.

It is understandable that athletes who attach more importance to the outcome of competition than they do the quality of their performance may be more prone to cheat or engage in irresponsible aggressive play (Duda & Balaguer, 2007). On the other hand, many athletes with a high ego orientation still accept the constraints of rules and moral norms in competition. Rules are constitutive of games themselves and moral norms assure that games are safe for all parties. No matter how badly they want to win or hate to lose, when athletes enter into competition, they implicitly enter into a social contract in which they agree to abide by the rules and observe principles of fair play and mutual respect. Cultivating a performance character can help them to enjoy their athletic experience more by focusing their attention on what they can control and detaching their sense of worth from whether they win or lose.

Lickona and Davidson (2005) rightly argue that a task orientation is an important component of performance character. Achievement goal research demonstrates that coaches' goal orientations play a critical role in establishing the motivational climate on their team. This climate in turn has a significant influence on athletes' goal orientation, moral behavior, and attitudes (Duda & Balaguer, 2007; Kavussanu, 2007; Kavussanu & Ntoumanis, 2003; Miller, Roberts, & Ommundsen, 2005; Roberts, 2001).

Duda and Balaguer (2007) point out that coaches' ego orientation is a far more significant problem for moral functioning than athletes' ego orientation. Coaches with a strong ego orientation undermine athletes' pursuit of either achievement or moral virtues by focusing on winning rather than on their players' development. It is clear from a growing body of achievement goal research that if coaches are to be effective character educators they should curb their own ego orientation and cultivate a motivational climate with a high task orientation. Such a climate will directly promote the development of achievement-related virtues and indirectly support the development of moral virtues.

GAME REASONING AND MORAL IDENTITY

The competitive nature of sports can lead not only to a strong ego orientation but also to a negative sports identity. As Bredemeier and Shields (1986b) have argued, sports, particularly contact sports, may lead athletes to adopt two different identities, one for off the field and one for on the field. In a study comparing male and female college basketball players with college students who were not athletes, they found that the athletes' reasoning on moral sport dilemmas was significantly lower than their reasoning on non-sport moral dilemmas. They described those athletes using lower stage moral reasoning as engaging in "game reasoning," which allows them to operate in an almost "morality free zone." Bredemeier and Shields (1986b) also referred to the attenuated experience of moral norms within the context of a game as a "bracketed morality." A bracketed morality is one in which athletes feel free to act in self-interested and highly aggressive ways that would not be permissible outside of the game. Weiss, Smith, and Stuntz (2008) give a shocking example of this phenomenon from an interview with NFL football player Brian Cox:

> When I'm on the field, I think about causing as much pain to the person lined up across from me as possible. During the three hours of the game on Sunday evening, I figure I can commit as many crimes as I want without going to jail.
>
> (p. 198)

Although some sports can release some athletes from moral constraints and excuse cheating, reckless aggression, and even cruelty, sports need not necessarily lead to a split sense of identity or to anomie. Some athletes may be drawn to sports or recruited to play certain positions in contact sports because they are unusually aggressive, prone to anger, lacking in empathy, or uninhibited. In the absence of responsible coaches and a strong team moral atmosphere, sports, like football and rugby, can provide them with an outlet and even social approval for rough play. Sports clearly have the potential to lead athletes down a path that inhibits the development of their moral reasoning and of a moral identity. Sports can lead other athletes to think of themselves as playing a role on the field, which is different from who they are off the field. Blasi (1993, 2009) describes identity as a developmental process of self-integration, which underlies different social selves. Although individuals may describe themselves as having different selves in different social contexts, character education should help athletes to construct a core identity that unifies their athletic persona. For example, a college football player explained that although he was highly aggressive on the field, he was not the "kind of person" who would take a cheap shot to intimidate a receiver. Acknowledging that he had been guided by a morally principled coach, he said he took personal pride in trying to follow the "golden rule" by treating his opponents as he would like to be treated.

We have precious little research on how sports participation influences pre-adolescent and adolescent identity formation. This is surprising because sports play such a significant role in the lives of so many children and adolescents. It is also troublesome because in a sports-crazed society, children can become local and even national celebrities for their precocious athletic prowess. Early stardom comes with a price. Children and adolescents are not psychologically prepared to have adults fawning all over them because of their early athletic success. Character development becomes a challenge for children and adolescents, who may come to believe that they are so exceptional that they do not have to abide by the same rules as others. In order to help children and adolescents to develop a moral identity through participation, character educators must address the culture in which children and athletes develop their identities. In our view, children and adolescents are best served in a culture that de-emphasizes exceptional athletic achievements and focuses instead on helping all children to focus on how they can serve others and develop themselves.

ESTABLISHING A TEAM MORAL ATMOSPHERE

Research in moral education suggests that the key to developing individuals' moral identity and moral functioning more generally is to focus on the moral atmosphere of the sports team (Power & Higgins-D'Alessandro, 2005). As important as developing a proper motivational climate may be, care should be taken to distinguish a motivational climate from a moral atmosphere (Kavassanu, 2007; Power, Higgins, & Kohlberg, 1989). A motivational climate cannot substitute for a moral atmosphere. A moral atmosphere relates to those features of the social environment that directly influence athletes' moral functioning: their moral judgments, responsibility, and behavior. Extrapolating from what has been learned from studies of the just community schools (Power, 2002; Power et al., 1989; Power & Higgins-D'Alessandro, 2008; Power & Power, 2012; Shields et al., 2002) as well as what we are now learning from our Play Like a Champion coaching clinics, the key to establishing a moral atmosphere is to have coaches focus on issues of fairness and team building. Concretely this means taking time to address issues such as how to treat referees and opponents with respect and how to become a good citizen of the team. It also means giving athletes a significant role to play in decision-making about team rules and discipline.

Power et al. (1989) argued that the peer culture is a key component of moral atmosphere. The peer culture arises out of the interaction of the members of a group. As Power et al. (1989) showed, peer groups set expectations for how members should behave and these expectations vary in the extent to which they reflect moral values. For example, it is commonplace for adolescents to put pressure on each other to exclude those who are deemed "unpopular" or outside of their clique. On the other hand, many sports teams encourage players to be friendly to everyone. Sports teams provide an ideal environment for establishing norms of caring and shared responsibility because teams bring individuals together to pursue common goals. With proper direction and support from coaches, sports teams can become truly moral communities with shared norms of caring, trust, collective responsibility, and participation (Power & Power, 2012). Research on socio-moral development shows that somewhere between the ages of 11 and 14 most adolescents develop their first understanding of a group as a whole greater than the sum of its parts. Membership in a group offers a sense of purpose as well as a sense of belonging (Damon, 2008). Sports teams may well be the best resource character educators have for developing civic virtues, such as loyalty and sacrifice for the group. Coaches have a unique opportunity to help their players to experience what it means to be a responsible citizen by taking the time to deliberate with them about how to put the common good before their private interests while also respecting the rights of each member of the team.

THE EFFECTIVENESS OF COACH EDUCATION

Research has established that coach education significantly improves children's sports experience. Most of the existing research has been undertaken by Smoll and Smith and their colleagues (Barnett, Smoll, & Smith, 1992; Coatsworth & Conroy, 2006; Conroy & Coatsworth, 2004; Smith, Smoll, & Barnett, 1995; Smith, Smoll, & Curtis, 1979; Smith, Smoll, & Cumming, 2007; Smoll, Smith, Barnett, & Everett, 1993) using the Coach Effectiveness Training approach (CET) and a revision of CET, the MAC (Mastery Approach to Coaching), which is based on motivational climate research (e.g., Duda & Balaguer, 2007). This body of research indicates that coach training can be used effectively to increase the amount of encouragement and verbal rewards that coaches give their players. Young athletes perceived trained coaches as engaging in more positive verbal behaviors, in less negative verbal behaviors, and in more mastery behaviors than untrained coaches. In addition, youth playing for the trained coaches liked their coaches more, perceived their coaches as liking them more, reported sports improved their self-esteem, helped them to feel less anxious, had lower dropout rates, and demonstrated motivational gains.

In a study sponsored by the LA'84 Foundation, Power and Seroczynski (2013) investigated the effectiveness of a coach education program designed specifically for character development. Coaches of boys' and girls' basketball in public middle schools were instructed in the Play Like a Champion Today coaching approach, which emphasizes establishing teams as moral communities through conducting moral discussions before and after practice. The trained coaches were given a manual with sports-related moral scenarios addressing socio-moral issues, such as how to treat an unpopular player on the team or whether players should take the risk of trusting their teammates on "help defense." Players on the teams with trained coaches perceived their coaches as putting a greater emphasis on moral values and developing a sense of fairness than those on teams with untrained coaches. Players on the teams with trained coaches also described their experiences on the team as more fun. Most importantly, the players on teams with trained coaches reported that they thought more about fairness and learned more about taking responsibility over the season than did their peers on teams with untrained coaches. No significant differences were found in players' moral reasoning although the teams with coaches who held discussions lasting at least 20 minutes and involved most of their players showed modest gains in moral reasoning over a season lasting only two months. No differences were found in players' self-reports of their own moral behavior or sportsmanship. This is not surprising given that previous research indicated that moral discussions must generally be sustained over several months to be effective (Higgins, 1980; Schlaefli, Rest, & Thoma, 1985).

This study has important implications for character education for three reasons. First, it shows that a character-oriented coaching clinic can lead coaches to engage in deliberate practices designed to promote moral awareness and development. Second, it shows that coaches can be taught to help players have a more enjoyable and morally engaged experience. Although much can be accomplished in a three-hour clinic, more time was needed to communicate the concepts and develop the skills necessary to foster the development of moral reasoning and behavior. Ideally, shorter, follow-up clinics should be provided for coaches to achieve greater mastery of the discussion approach. Third, it demonstrates that in order for coaches to educate for ethical character, they need to set aside time for team meeting discussions. To date, the only successful moral education interventions have been most successful in physical education classes and camp settings that are removed from the pressures of a competitive sports season (e.g., Bredemeier, Weiss, Shields, & Shewchuck, 1986; Hellison, 2003; Romance, Weiss, & Brockovan, 1986). This study suggests that coaches can fruitfully incorporate team moral discussions into a competitive sports season. Future research is needed to investigate the effects of using moral discussions with different teams and over multiple seasons.

CONCLUSION

With direction and support from well-prepared coaches, participation in sports can and should help children and adolescents to develop moral as well as achievement virtues. In order for sports to realize their character education potential, coaches, particularly at the youth sport level, need to put the development of their players before winning. Character educators must confront a managerial mentality pervasive at all levels of sport in which coaches control children rather than teach or mentor them. Sports are meant to be played for the sheer fun of the experience, and children can reap the full benefits of sports only if they have control over their own games. Although character educators must focus on what virtues should be taught and how they should be taught, they also take responsibility for assuring that all children have a fair opportunity to play sports. At present, the income inequalities present in the adult society are reflected in youth and high school sports. While opportunities for affluent children to play sports are growing, opportunities for poor children are declining. Poor children are not the only children who are losing out. Children are cut from teams and sit on benches because they are perceived to lack the skills and abilities of others. Character educators ought to advocate for the rights of all children to enjoy playing sports and to develop their skills.

REFERENCES

Balyi, I. (2001). Sport system building and long-term athlete development in Canada. The situation and solutions, in Coaches Report. *The Official Publication of the Canadian Professional Coaches Association, 8* (1, Summer), 25–28.

Bamberger, M., & Yaeger, D. (1997). Over the edge. *Sports Illustrated, 14*, 62–70.

Barnett, N. P., Smoll, F. L., & Smith, R. E. (1992). Effects of enhancing coach-athlete relationships on youth sport attrition. *The Sport Psychologist, 6*, 111–127.

Beedy, J. P. (1997). *Sports PLUS: Positive learning using sports: Developing youth sports programs that teach positive values.* Hamilton, MA: Project Adventure.

Beller, J. M., & Stoll, S. K. (1995). Moral development of high school athletes. *Journal of Pediatric Science, 7*(4), 352–363.

Berkowitz, M. W., & Bier, M. C. (2005). *What works in character education: A research-driven guide for educators.* St. Louis, MO: Character Education Partnership.

Bissinger, B. (2008, August 22). Bench the parents. *New York Times.* Retrieved from www.nytimes.com/2008/08/23/opinion/23bissinger.html?pagewanted=all&_r=0.

Blasi, A. (1993). The development of identity: Some implications for moral functioning. In G. G. Noam & T. Wren (Eds.), *The moral self* (pp. 99–122). Cambridge, MA: The MIT Press.

Blasi, A. (2009). The moral functioning of mature adults and the possibility of fair moral reasoning. In D. Narvaez and D. K. Lapsley (Eds.), *Personality, identity, and character. Explorations in moral psychology* (pp. 396–440). New York: Cambridge University Press.

Bloom, B. S. (1985). *Developing talent in young people.* New York: Ballatine Books.

Bredemeier, B. J., & Shields, D. L. (1986a). Moral growth among athletes and nonathletes: A comparative analysis. *Journal of Genetic Psychology, 147*, 7–18.

Bredemeier, B. J., & Shields, D. L. (1986b). Game reasoning and interactional morality. *Journal of Genetic Psychology, 147*, 257–275.

Bredemeier, B. J., & Shields, D. L. (2006). Sports and character development. *Research Digest President's Council on Physical Fitness and Sports, 7*, 1–8.

Bredemeier, B., Weiss, M., Shields, D., & Cooper, B. (1986). The relationship of sport involvement with children's moral reasoning and aggression tendencies. *Journal of Sport Psychology, 8*, 304–318.

Bredemeier, B., Weiss, M., Shields, D., & Shewchuk, R. (1986). Promoting moral growth in a summer sport camp: The implementation of theoretically grounded instructional strategies. *Journal of Moral Education, 15*, 212–220.

Brower, J. J. (1979). The professionalization of organized youth sport: Social psychological impacts and outcomes. *The Annals of the American Academy of Political and Social Science, 1*, 29–46.

Chudacoff, H. P. (2007). *Children at play: An American history.* New York: York University Press.

Clifford, C., & Feezel, R. (1997). *Coaching for character: Reclaiming the principles of sportsmanship.* Champaign, IL: Human Kinetics.

Coakley, J. J. (2009). *Sport in society: Issues and controversies* (10th ed.). New York: McGraw-Hill.

Coatsworth, J. D., & Conroy, D. E. (2006). The effects of coach training on self-esteem in youth swimmers: Age and gender effects. *Psychology of Sport & Exercise, 7*, 173–192.

Conroy, D. E., & Coatsworth, J. D. (2004). The effects of coach training on fear of failure in youth swimmers: A latent growth curve analysis from a randomized controlled trial. *Journal of Applied Developmental Psychology, 25*, 193–214.

Conroy, D. E., & Coatsworth, J. D. (2007). Assessing autonomy-supportive coaching strategies in youth sport. *Psychology of Sport and Exercise, 8*, 671–684.

Conroy, D. E., Silvia, J. M., Newcomer, R. R., Walker, B. W., & Johnson, M. S. (2001). Personal and participatory socializers of the perceived legitimacy of aggressive behavior in sport. *Aggressive Behavior, 27*, 405–418.

Côté, J., & Fraser-Thomas. J. (2007). Youth involvement in sport. In R. Crocker (Ed.). *Sport psychology: A Canadian perspective* (pp. 270–298). Toronto: Pearson.

Damon, W. (2008). *The path to purpose: How young people find their calling in life.* New York: Simon and Schuster.

Duda, J. (2001). Achievement goal research in sport: Pushing the boundaries and clarifying some misunderstandings. In G. Roberts (Ed.), *Advances in motivation in sport and exercise* (pp. 129–182). Champaign, IL, Human Kinetics.

Duda, J. L., & Balaguer, I. (2007). The coach-created motivational climate. In S. Jowett & D. Lavalee (Eds.), *Social psychology of sport* (pp. 117–130). Champaign, IL: Human Kinetics.

Duda, J. L., & Hall, H. (2001). Achievement goal theory in sport: Recent extensions and future directions. In N. Robert, H. A. Hausenblas, & C. Janelle (Eds.), *Handbook of sport psychology* (pp. 417–443). New York: Wiley.

Duncan, A. (2013, January 25). We must provide equal opportunity in sports to students with disabilities. Home-room [Blog post of US Department of Education]. Retrieved from www.ed.gov/blog/2013/01/we-must-provide-equal-opportunity-in-sports-to-students-with-disabilities/.

Elkind, David. (2007). *The power of play: Learning what comes naturally.* Cambridge, MA: Da Capo Lifelong.

Farrey, T. (2008). *Game on: The all-American race to make champions of our children.* New York: ESPN Books.

Fisher, Edward P. (1992). The impact of play on development: A meta-analysis. *Play and Culture, 5*(2), 159–181.

Gano-Overway, L., Newton, M., Magyar, M., Fry, M., Kim, M. S., & Guivernau, M. (2009). The influence of the perception of caring climate on character developments among youth sport participants. *Developmental Psychology, 45,* 329–340.

Gardner, M., Roth, J. L., & Brooks-Gunn, J. (2009). Sports participation and juvenile delinquency: The role of the peer context among adolescent boys and girls with varied histories of problem behavior. *Developmental Psychology, 45,* 341–353.

Giancola, D. P. (2010). *Democratic coaching: Creating a culture of champions.* Saarbrücken, Germany: LAP LAMBERT Academic Publishing.

Gibbons, T., Hill, R., McConnell, A., Forster, T., Reiwald, S., & Peterson, K. (2003). *US Olympians describe the success factors and obstacles that most influenced their Olympic development.* Colorado Springs, CO: United States Olympic Committee.

Gray, P. (2011). The decline of play and the rise of psychopathology in children and adolescents. *American Journal of Play, 3*(4).

Hagger, M. S., & Chatzisarantis, N. L. D. (Eds.). (2007). *Intrinsic motivation and self-determination in exercise and sport.* Champaign, IL: Human Kinetics.

Hartmann, D. and Massoglia, M. (2007). Reassessing the relationship between high school sports participation and deviance: Evidence of enduring, bifurcated effects. *The Sociological Quarterly, 48,* 485–505.

Hellison, D. (2003). *Teaching responsibility through physical activity* (2nd ed.). Champaign, IL: Human Kinetics.

Higgins, A. (1980). Research and measurement issues in moral education interventions. In R. Mosher (Ed.), *Moral education: A first generation of research and development.* New York: Praeger.

Huizinga, J. (1955). *Homo ludens: A study of the play-element in culture.* Boston, MA: Beacon Press.

Hyman, M. (2010). *Until it hurts: America's obsession with youth sports and how it harms our kids.* Boston, MA: Beacon Press.

Josephson Institute. (2006). *A handy guide to strengthening athletes' character.* Los Angeles, CA: Josephson Institute.

Kavussanu, M. (2007). Morality in sport. In S. Jowett & D. E. Lavallee (Eds.), *Social psychology in sport* (pp. 265–278). Champaign, IL: Human Kinetics.

Kavussanu, M., & Ntoumanis, N. (2003). Participation in sport and moral functioning: Does ego orientation mediate their relationship? *Journal of Sport & Exercise Psychology, 25*(4), 1–18.

Kavussanu, M., & Roberts, G. C. (2001). Moral functioning in sport: An achievement goal perspective. *Journal of Sport & Exercise Psychology, 23,* 37–54.

Kohlberg, L. (1981). *The philosophy of moral development: Moral stages and the idea of justice.* San Francisco, CA: Harper & Row.

Lapsley, D. K., & Narvaez, D. (2006). Character education. In W. Damon & R. Lerner (Series Eds.), *Handbook of child psychology,* Vol. 4 (A. Renninger & I. Siegel, Vol. Eds.) (pp. 248–296). New York: Wiley.

Lickona, T. (1992). *Educating for character: How our schools can teach respect and responsibility.* New York: Bantam.

Lickona, T., & Davidson, M. (2005). *Smart & good high schools: Integrating excellence and ethics for success in school, work, and beyond.* Washington, DC: Character Education Partnership.

Lumpkin, A., Stoll, S. K., & Beller, J. M. (2002). *Sport ethics: Applications for fair play.* Boston, MA: McGraw-Hill.

Mahoney, J. L., Eccles, J. S., & Larson, R. W. (2004). Processes of adjustment in organized out-of-school activities: Opportunities and risks. In G. G. Noam (Ed.), *After-school worlds: Creating a new social space for development and learning: New directions for youth development, 101* (pp. 115–144). Hoboken, NJ: Wiley.

Martens, R. (2004). *Successful coaching* (3rd ed.). Champaign, IL: Human Kinetics.

Miller, B. W., Roberts, G. C., & Ommundsen, Y. (2005). Effect of perceived motivational climate on moral functioning, team moral atmosphere perceptions, and the legitimacy of intentionally injurious acts among competitive youth football players. *Psychology of Sport and Exercise, 6,* 461–477.

National Association for Sport and Physical Education (NASPE). (2006). *Quality coaches, quality sports: National standards for sports coaches.* Reston, VA: NASPE.

National Association for Sport and Physical Education (NASPE). (2009). *Physical activity used as punishment and/or behavior management.* Reston, VA: NASPE.

New York State Public High School Athletic Association. (2001). *An education framework for interscholastic athletic programs.* Latham, NY: NYSPHSAA.

Nucci, L. (2001). *Education in the moral domain*. Cambridge: Cambridge University Press.

Nucci, L. (2009). *Nice is not enough: Facilitating moral development*. Upper Saddle River, NJ: Merrill.

Pelligrini, A. D., & Holmes, R. M. (2006). The role of recess in primary school. In D. Singer, R. Golinkoff, & K. Hirsh-Pasek (Eds.), *Play-learning: How play motivates and enhances children's cognitive and socio-emotional growth*. New York: Oxford University Press.

Piaget, J. (1932/1965). *The moral judgment of the child*. London: Free Press.

Power, F. C. (2002). Building democratic community: A radical approach to moral education. In William Damon (Ed.), *Bringing in a new era in character education*. Stanford, CA: Hoover Press, Stanford University.

Power, F. C., Higgins, A., & Kohlberg, L. (1989). *Lawrence Kohlberg's approach to moral education*. New York: Columbia University Press.

Power, F. C., & Higgins-D'Alessandro, A. (2005). Character, responsibility, and the moral self. In D. K. Lapsley & F. C. Power (Eds.), *Character psychology and education*. Notre Dame, IN: University of Notre Dame Press.

Power, F. C., & Higgins-D'Alessandro, A. (2008). The just community approach to moral education and the moral atmosphere of the school. In L. Nucci & D. Narvaez (Eds.), *Handbook of moral and character education*. New York: Routledge.

Power, F. C., & Power, A. M. (2012). Moral education. In A. Higgins-D'Alessandro, M. W. Corrigan, & P. M. Brown (Eds.), *The handbook of prosocial education*. Lanham, MD: Rowan & Littlefield Publishing Group.

Power, F. C., & Seroczynski, A. (2013). Coaching for moral development. Report to LA'84 Foundation.

Power, F. C., & Sheehan, K. K. (2012). *Leading moral discussions on sports teams*. University of Notre Dame, IN: Play Like a Champion.

Power, F. C., & Sheehan, K. K. (2013). Moral motivation in sports. In K. Heinrichs, F. Oser, & T. Lovat (Eds.), *Handbook of moral motivation: Theories, models, applications* (pp. 405–436). Rotterdam, The Netherlands: Sense Publishers.

Priest, R. F., Krause, J. V., & Beach, J. (1999). Four-year changes in college athletes: Ethical value choices in sports situations. *Research Quarterly for Exercise and Sport, 70*, 170–178.

Proios, M., Doganis, G., Arvanitidou, V., Unierzyski, P., & Katsagolis, A. (2004). The ability of moral reasoning in stages in prediction of goal orientation in sports. *Studies in Physical Culture and Tourism, 11*(1).

Putney, C. (2003). *Muscular Christianity: Manhood and sports in Protestant America, 1880–1920*. Cambridge, MA: Harvard University Press.

Roberts, G. C. (2001). Understanding the dynamics of motivation in physical activity: The influence of achievement goals on motivational processes. In G. C. Roberts (Ed.), *Advances in sport and exercise motivation* (pp. 1–50). Champaign, IL: Human Kinetics.

Romance, T., Weiss, M., & Brockovan, J. (1986). A program to promote moral development through elementary school physical education. *Journal of Teaching in Physical Education, 5*, 126–136.

Rulmyr, R. (1996). Interscholastic athletic participation and the moral development of adolescents in Arizona high schools. Unpublished doctoral dissertation, Northern Arizona University.

Ryan, K. (1989). In defense of character education. In L. Nucci (Ed.), *Moral development and character education: A dialogue* (pp. 3–17). Berkeley, CA: McCutchan.

Ryan, K., & Bohlin, K. E. (1999). *Building character in schools: Practical ways to bring moral instructions to life*. San Francisco, CA: Jossey-Bass.

Ryan, R. M., & Deci, E. L. (2007). Intrinsic and extrinsic motivation in exercise and sport. In M. S. Hagger & N. L. D. Chatzisarantis (Eds.), *Intrinsic motivation and self-determination in exercise and sport* (pp. 1–19). Champaign, IL: Human Kinetics.

Sage, L., Kavussanu, M., & Duda, J. (2006). Goal orientations and moral identity as prosocial and antisocial functioning in male association football players. *Journal of Sport Sciences, 24*, 455–466.

Scarlett, W. G., Naudeau, S. C., Salonius-Pasternak, D., & Ponte, I. C. (2005). *Children's play*. Thousand Oaks, CA: Sage Publications.

Schlaefli, A., Rest, J. R., & Thomas, S. (1985). Does moral education improve moral judgment? A meta-analysis of intervention studies using the DIT. *Review of Education, Research, 55*, 319–352.

Seefeldt, V., Ewing, M. E., & Walk, S. (1992). *Overview of youth sport programs in the United States*. Washington, DC: Carnegie Council on Adolescent Development.

Selman, R. (1980). *The growth of interpersonal understanding: Developmental and clinical analyses*. Ann Arbor, MI: Academic Press.

Shields, D., & Bredemeier, B. (1995). *Character development and physical activity*. Champaign, IL: Human Kinetics.

Shields, D., & Bredemeier, B. (2009). *True competition: A guide to pursuing excellence in sport and society*. Champaign, IL: Human Kinetics.

Shields, D. L., Bredemeier, B. L., LaVoi, N. M., & Power, F. C. (2005). The sport behavior of coaches, parents, and athletes: The good, the bad, and the ugly. *Journal of Research in Character Education, 3*(1), 43–59.

Shields, D., Bredemeier, B., & Power, F. C. (2002). Character development and children's sport. In F. Smoll & R. Smith (Eds.), *Children and youth in sport: A biopsychosocial perspective* (2nd ed., pp. 537–559). Indianapolis, IN: Brown & Benchmark.

Shulman, J. L., & Bowen, W. G. (2002). *The game of life: College sports and educational values.* Princeton, NJ: Princeton University Press.

Smith, R. E., Smoll, F. L., & Barnett, N. P. (1995). Reduction of children's sport performance anxiety through social support and stress-reduction training for coaches. *Journal of Applied Developmental Psychology, 16*(1), 125–142.

Smith, R. E., Smoll, F. L., & Curtis, B. (1979). CET: A cognitive-behavioral approach to enhancing relationship skills in youth sport coaches. *Journal of Sport Psychology, 1,* 59–75.

Smith, R. E., Smoll, F. L., & Cumming, S. P. (2007). Effects of a motivational climate intervention for coaches on young athletes' sport performance anxiety. *Journal of Sport and Exercise Psychology, 29*(1), 39–59.

Smoll, F. L., Smith, R. E., Barnett, N. P., & Everett, J. J (1993). Enhancement of children's self-esteem through social support training for youth sport coaches. *Journal of Applied Psychology, 78*(4), 602–610.

Stevenson, M. J. (1998). Measuring the cognitive moral reasoning of collegiate student-athletes: The development of the Stevenson-Stoll Social Responsibility Questionnaire. Unpublished doctoral dissertation, University of Idaho.

Stoll, S. K., & Beller, J. M. (2000). Do sports build character? In J. R. Gerdy (Ed.), *Sports in school: The future of an institution.* New York: Teachers College.

Stoll, S. K., & Beller, J. M. (2006). Ethical issues in sport. In R. Lapchick (Ed.), *New game plans for college sport* (pp. 75–90). Greenwood, CT: Rowman & Littlefield.

Thompson, J. (1995). *Positive coaching: Building character and self-esteem through sports.* Portola Valley, CA: Warde Publishing.

Thompson, J. (2003). *The double-goal coach: Positive coaching tools for honoring the game and developing winners in sports and life.* New York: HarperCollins.

Thompson, J. (2010). *The power of double-goal coaching: Developing winners in sports and life.* Portola Valley, CA: Balance Sports Publishing.

Turiel, E. (1983). *The development of social knowledge: Morality and convention.* Cambridge, England: Cambridge University Press.

United Nations. (1989) Convention on the rights of the child (article 31).

US Department of Education. (2013). *US Department of Education clarifies schools' obligation to provide equal opportunity to students with disabilities to participate in extracurricular athletics.* Washington, DC: US Department of Education.

Vincent, P. F. (1999). *Developing character in students* (2nd ed.). Chapel Hill, NC: Character Development Publishing.

Weiss, M., & Smith, A. L. (2002). Friendship quality in youth sport: Relationship to age, gender, and motivation variables. *Journal of Sport & Exercise Psychology, 24*(4), 420–437.

Weiss, M. R., Smith, A. L., & Stuntz, C. P. (2008). Moral development in sport and physical activity: Theory, research, and intervention. In T. S. Horn (Ed.), *Advances in sport psychology* (3rd ed., pp. 187–210). Champaign, IL: Human Kinetics.

Wynne, E. (1989). Transmitting traditional values in contemporary schools. In L. Nucci (Ed.), *Moral development and character education: A dialogue* (pp. 6–25). Berkeley, CA: McCutchan.

Yeager, J. M., Baltzell, A. L., Buxton, J. N., & Bzdell, W. B. (2001). *Character and coaching: Building virtue in athletic programs.* Port Chester, NY: Dude Publications.

Zarrett, N., Fay, K. Li, Y., Carrano, J., Phelps, E., & Lerner, R. M. (2009). More than child's play: Variable- and pattern-centered approaches for examining effects of sports participation on youth development. *Developmental Psychology, 45*(2), 368–382.

29

A THEORETICAL AND EVIDENCE-BASED APPROACH FOR DESIGNING PROFESSIONAL ETHICS EDUCATION

Muriel J. Bebeau and Verna E. Monson

This chapter provides a guided reflection on the state of theory, research, and practice for ethics education in the professions. We begin with an evidence-based theoretical approach to ground professional ethics education, followed by an overview of the nature of professionalism in society that includes a brief history of the ethics education movement. We then review the general status of ethics education, including changes in accreditation standards followed by current educational practices in medicine, dentistry. law, nursing, and veterinary medicine. Next, alternative options for assessing and promoting the broadly defined capacities specified by psychological theory are cited and reviewed. Last, we offer recommendations for enhancing ethics and professionalism education in the health professions and law to meet emerging accreditation guidelines that focus on outcome assessment.

A THEORETICAL APPROACH TO PROFESSIONAL ETHICS EDUCATION

Rest (1983) extended Kohlberg's theory of moral reasoning development, first by designing an easy-to-score and administer measure of moral judgment (Rest, 1979) and then by defining the Four Component Model (FCM) of Morality to explain how cognition, affect, and social dynamics interact to influence moral action (Rest, Narvaez, Bebeau, & Thoma, 1999). Table 29.1 provides an operational definition for each component (we refer to them as capacities or abilities) and describes their interactive nature. Their particular relevance for professional ethical development is described below.

The Four Component Model (FCM): Implications for the Professions

MORAL SENSITIVITY

For individuals being socialized to professional practice, ethical sensitivity involves the ability to see things from the perspective of other individuals and groups (including other

Table 29.1 The Four Component Model of Morality

Starting with the question "How does moral behavior come about?" Rest (1983) suggested that the literature supports at least four component processes, all of which must be activated for moral behavior to come about. The four components are a useful way to conceptualize the capacities required for effective moral functioning.

Moral Sensitivity

Moral sensitivity focuses on the interpretation of a situation, the various actions that are available, and how each action might affect the self and others. It involves imaginatively constructing possible scenarios (often from limited cues and partial information), knowing cause–consequence chains of events in the real world, and having empathy and role-taking skills. Both cognitive processes (perception, appraisal, and interpretation) and affective arousal (e.g., anger, apathy, anxiety, empathy, and revulsion) contribute to the interpretation of problematic situations.

Moral Judgment

Once a person is aware that various lines of action are possible, one must ask which line of action is more morally justified. This is the process emphasized in the work of Piaget and Kohlberg. Even at an early stage, people have intuitions about what is fair and moral, and make moral judgments about even the most complex of human activities. The psychologist's job is to understand how these intuitions arise and what governs their application to real-world events. The educator's job is to understand how best to promote reasoning development, especially for students who have not developed the ability prior to professional education.

Moral Motivation and Commitment

Moral motivation and commitment involves prioritizing moral values over other personal values. People have many values (e.g., careers, affectional relationships, aesthetic preferences, institutional loyalties, hedonistic pleasures, excitement). Whether the individual gives priority to moral concerns seems to be a function of how deeply moral notions penetrate self-understanding, that is, whether moral considerations are judged constitutive of the self (Blasi, 1984). For behavior to occur, the moral agents must first decide on a morally correct action when faced with a dilemma, and then conclude that the self is responsible for that action. One is motivated to perform an action just because the self is at stake and on the line—just because the self is responsible. Moral motivation is a function of an internal drive for self-consistency. Blasi (1991) argues: "The self is progressively moralized when the objective values that one apprehends become integrated within the motivational and affective systems of personality and when these moral values guide the construction of self concept and one's identity as a person."

Moral Character and Competence

Moral character and competence is having the strength of your convictions, having courage, persisting, overcoming distractions and obstacles, having implementing skills, and having ego strength. A person may be sensitive to moral issues, have good judgment, and prioritize moral values; but if he or she is lacking in moral character and competence, he or she may wilt under pressure or fatigue, may not follow through, may be distracted or discouraged, and moral behavior will fail. This component presupposes that one has set goals, has self-discipline and controls impulse, and has the strength and skill to act in accord with one's goals.

It is noteworthy that the model is not conceived as a linear problem-solving model. For example, moral motivation may affect moral sensitivity, and moral character may constrain moral motivation. In fact, Rest (1983) makes clear the interactive nature of the components. Furthermore, and in contrast to other models of moral function that focus on the traditional three domains—cognitions, affect, and behavior—the Four Component Model of Morality assumes that cognition and affect co-occur in all areas of moral functioning. Thus, moral action is not simply the result of separate affective and cognitive processes operating as part of an interaction. Instead, each of the four components is a mix of affective and cognitive processes that contribute to the component's primary function.

Source: Adapted from Bebeau (2006); Bebeau, Rest, and Narvaez (1999).

cultural[1] and socioeconomic groups), and more abstractly, from legal, institutional, and organizational perspectives. It includes knowing the regulations, codes, and norms of one's profession, and recognizing when they apply. This process highlights the idea that moral behavior can only occur if the professional codes the situation as moral.

Moral Judgment

Because professional practice is essentially a moral enterprise in which new issues frequently arise with societal change and technological advances, the ability to reason carefully about the dilemmas of one's profession is an essential capacity for practitioners. Rest and colleagues (1999) advanced the application of Kohlbergian stage theory to professional education by defining and validating three schemas associated with moral thinking in adults: the *personal interest* schema, characterized by decisions motivated by self-interest and/or a concern for interpersonal reciprocity; *maintaining norms* schema, focused on enforcement of existing norms, rules, codes, and laws; and the *postconventional* schema, centered on concepts of justice, fairness, duty, and the evolutionary nature of morality in society and in the professions. Recent interest in applying schema theory to professional education has centered on providing the individual with a baseline profile indicating which moral schema is predominant for the individual at entry to professional school, then providing post-test information to show whether the educational program has facilitated development (Bebeau & Faber-Langendoen, 2014). Of particular interest in professions education is the documented relation between advances in moral reasoning measured by life-span measures like Rest's (1979) Defining Issues Test (DIT) and profession-specific measures of ethical reasoning (Bebeau & Thoma, 1999; Thoma, Bebeau & Bolland, 2008).

Moral Motivation and Commitment

Concerns for the development of a professional identity are the focus of two lines of research. One adapts Robert Kegan's (1982) theory of life-span identity formation to professional identity formation (Bebeau & Monson, 2012; Bebeau & Thoma, 2013; Forsythe, 2005; Hamilton & Monson, 2012; Rule & Bebeau, 2005). A second flows from philosophers' observations of models of professionalism that appear to guide moral action (Bebeau, Born, & Ozar; 1993; Thoma & Bebeau, 2013). Although applicants to the professions typically state their interest and commitment to becoming a professional, Bertolami (2004) notes that seldom during the course of professional education are students encouraged to reflect on this initial commitment to professionalism or to refine it based upon new understandings that emerge during professional education. Confirming this lack of attention to professional identity formation during professional education, Lee Shulman (2010) remarked in the preface to *Education Physicians*, the last of the Carnegie Foundation's recent studies of five professions (law, medicine, clergy, engineers, and nurses) that the most overlooked aspect of professional preparation was "the formation of a professional identity with a moral core of service and responsibility around which each student's habits of mind and practice are organized" (p. ix).

Moral Character and Competence

For the professional, technical competence, problem solving, interpersonal skills, and characterological dispositions must come together to implement an effective action. Bandura (1977) explains how cognition and affect interact when facing a challenging problem. A person who sees a task as "fun" or "challenging," is more likely to persist to resolve a problem. Conversely, if a problem is approached with dread, perseverance is less likely. Practice in resolving difficult and recurrent problems—like responding to an angry patient, or discussing a disciplinary issue with an offending peer—changes the expectations of efficacy, which in turn changes behavior. Apathy and cynicism arise when students can't figure out how to effectively implement professional expectations. In research ethics education, such "survival skills" are deemed critical to the responsible conduct of research (Institute of Medicine [IOM], 2002b, p. 105).

Dynamic Processes of the FCM

Rest saw the processes encompassed by the FCM as distinctive, yet dynamic in nature. A wide range of studies (e.g., Bebeau, 2002; Thoma, 1994) show that moral judgment development predicts pro-social behavior; yet it predicts only 10–15% of the variance. Other processes, particularly component 3 (moral motivation and commitment)—what Blasi (1984) refers to as the development of the moral self and Kegan (1994) refers to the development of an identity—appear to be the primary driver of moral action (Thoma & Bebeau, 2013). For example, when dental professionals who have been disciplined by a licensing board are compared with a sample of dental professionals who consistently demonstrate exemplary moral behavior, those disciplined not only exhibit shortcomings in one or more of Rest's Four Components, but with few exceptions illustrate only vague understanding of professional expectations. In contrast, exemplary dentists can and do spontaneously articulate professional values and expectations. In a similar vein, Walker and colleagues' (e.g., Frimer & Walker, 2009) studies illustrate the distinctiveness of moral exemplars' ability to integrate the personality traits of communion and agency—something that comparison group participants (ordinary citizens and the occasional moral hero) cannot do. Frimer and Walker's (2009) reconciliation model describes development as the shift from the person's conscious recognition of a tension between agency and communion to an active integration of the two. Taken together these two sets of findings suggest that moral motivation is furthered when individuals have a sense of connection between the self and others as well as a confidence in one's ability to affect change. The challenge for educators and researchers who wish to further establish the role each process contributes to moral action must first attend to the validity of measurement. Without well-validated measures, it is not possible to establish the role each process contributes to moral action.

THE NATURE OF PROFESSIONALISM

Many people in today's society refer to themselves as professionals, though society generally distinguishes among occupational groups based upon the presence or absence of particular attributes (Freidson, 1988; Hall, 1975). Whether a particular occupation actually qualifies as a "profession," based upon criteria sociologists advance, makes for interesting debate. In our view (Bebeau & Monson, 2012), such a debate needs to precede ethics instruction in a profession, as characteristics of a profession and the expectations of a professional are not well understood, especially at entry to a profession. We show how to assess and educate for these understandings. The need for such education is heightened by environmental and political factors that impact individuals and the professions collectively.

Many today (e.g., Benner, Sutphen, Leonard, & Day, 2009; Cohen, 2006; Hafferty, Brennan, & Pawlina, 2011; May, 1999; Rule & Welie, 2009) see professions in a state of crisis. In medicine, access to health care has been addressed through the Affordable Care Act (H.R. 3590–111th Congress: Patient Protection and Affordable Care Act. 2009), yet the gap in public health outcomes by level of education and race has widened in the last two decades (Olshansky et al., 2012), despite the steadily increasing amount the US spent on health care (Berwick & Hackbarth, 2012). Dentistry, having exempted itself from government programs such as Medicare, has neither addressed access to care or cost containment (Rule & Welie, 2009). In law, the failure to control costs has resulted in the outsourcing of legal services, which in turn results in a decline in available jobs for recent graduates—yet there is a paucity of affordable legal services for the nation's most poor and vulnerable (Landsman, 2009). Mann (2006) argues for "the development of a sociological consciousness, interdisciplinary thinking, and understanding of the economic and political dimensions of health care" (p. 167). Advancing the scholarship of teaching and learning in ethics education has as its first goal to develop good professionals, and as its second goal to develop good professionals who work collectively to advance the public good.

The Ethics Education Movement: A Brief History

In the health professions, the push for ethics education originated with technological advances in medicine that foreshadowed new and emerging problems for health care providers. The goals of professional ethics education were first articulated by Bok (1976), and promoted by the Hastings Center (1980)—one of the first centers organized to focus on applied ethics, and ethics at bedside. In 1982, Rest was invited to introduce his Four Component Model of Morality in the Hastings Center Report (Rest, 1982). Interestingly, the first three of Rest's components (sensitivity, reasoning, and motivation) are analogous to the goals Bok and the Hastings Center articulated—the need to develop moral perceptions and aspirations, in addition to moral reasoning. Absent from Bok's vision is emphasis on Rest's Fourth Component—variously described as character and competence or implementation.

In the early days of ethics education in the health professions, the predominant method for resolving ethical issues (Beauchamp & Childress, 1979—now in its sixth edition) was application of principles (autonomy, beneficence, nonmaleficence, and distributive justice) to the resolution of tough problems. If assessment of ethical decision making occurred, the methods were those typical of courses in philosophy—the analysis of written argument. Some alliances were formed between medical educators and moral psychologists in the late 1970s and a number of studies using Kohlbergian measures to assess moral judgment of medical students and physicians began to appear in the literature (e.g., Candee, Sheehan, Cook, Husted, & Bargen, 1982; Sheehan, Candee, Willms, Donnelly, & Husted, 1985). As we review the status of ethics education in the professions today, we see pockets of moral psychology's influence, sometimes in the structure and organization of ethics educational programs (e.g., Bebeau, 1994; Duckett & Ryden, 1994; Hamilton, 2008; IOM, 2002b), more often in efforts to assess the effects of instruction (Baldwin & Self, 2006; Bebeau 2002, 2006, 2009a, 2009b; Rest & Narvaez, 1994). What is quite clear, however, is that unlike moral education in elementary and secondary education where moral psychologists have been the driving force behind the design and assessment of moral education (Lapsley

& Narvaez, 2006), educators with grounding in moral philosophy and ethics have been the driving force behind much of professional ethics education (Doukas, McCullough, & Wear, 2010; 2012). As has been argued elsewhere (Bebeau, Rest, & Narvaez, 1999), grounding education and assessment in a view that knowledge, skills, and attitudes are the processes that give rise to morality is less helpful than a vision like the FCM that helps to define researchable variables and create authentic measures of professional ethical development and performance.

In contrast to the health professions, the impetus for ethics education in law was the egregious conduct of lawyers in the Watergate scandal (Graham, 1997). The typical approach to teaching professional responsibility courses in law (note they are not referred to as ethics courses) is to read opinions from appellate cases, judgments from the deliberations by association ethics committees, and to study state rules of professional responsibility or code of conduct (usually based on the American Bar Association Model Rules of Professional Conduct) in preparation for the required professional responsibility licensing examination. Egan, Kayhan, and Ramirez (2004, p. 309) note, such "courses suffer from three main shortcomings: they are mostly rule-based, they seldom venture into actual ethical analysis, and they are often not taken seriously by students." In addition, teaching to the profession's code perpetuates the notion that conduct not prohibited by the rules is ethically permissible. Thus, rather than promoting professional ideals to which one aspires, the rules serve as the prevailing ethical norms, rather than the minimum standards that keep you out of trouble.

As in elementary and secondary education, educators in the professions debate whether to focus on the individual's character or on reasoning and problem solving. This ongoing debate is evident in Volume 10 of *Advances in Bioethics* (Kenny & Shelton, 2006). As its title implies (*Lost Virtue…*), the concern is with character formation. Advantages for the character approach are presented by physician ethicist Ed Pellegrino (2006) whose work with ethicist David Thomasma (Pellegrino & Thomasma, 1993) provides rich and useful operational definitions of the virtues of medical practice. A cogent critique of virtue ethics as a guide to educational program development is presented by Robert Veatch (2006). Other chapters argue for other dimensions of development, with no real resolution to the debate. Of particular interest is the work of Beauchamp and Childress (2009; sixth edition) whose work over the decades has responded to critiques from the bioethics community on methods for moral justification—particularly the application of moral principles (referred to as principlism) to resolve moral issues. The current edition includes an expanded theory of common morality and a reworked theory of the ethic of care as a form of virtue ethics.

In the last edition of the *Handbook of Moral and Character Education* (Bebeau & Monson, 2008), the dominant concern for ethics educators had shifted the debate from questions of character or ethical competence to a concern for simple adherence to appropriate behaviors. Predicated on a series of studies (Papadakis, Hodgson, Teherani, & Kohatsu, 2004; Stern, Frohna, & Gruppen, 2005; Teherani, Hodgson, Banach, & Papadakis, 2005), educators were able to link behaviors exhibited during medical school with subsequent disciplinary action by a state licensing board. Such findings were noteworthy, as educators had been unable to link GPA and national board examinations (the available gatekeepers for incompetence) and professional behavior. The Accreditation Council for Graduate Medical Education (ACGME, 2013) defined professionalism "as manifested through a commitment to carrying out professional responsibilities, adherence to ethical principles, and sensitivity to a diverse patient population."

Even before the evidence linking behaviors exhibited in medical school with subsequent disciplinary actions, Papadakis, Loeser, and Healy (2001) argued for an administrative structure to remediate students' deficiencies in behaviors judged as unprofessional. Yet, it is simply not enough to focus only on the external manifestation of behavior. In fact, in a closing chapter in *Measuring Medical Professionalism*, Hafferty (2006) eloquently asserted our belief: that tying too much of the assessment of professionalism to observable behaviors would not address the internalization of professional expectations reflected in Rest's third component.

> [M]edicine must avoid the self-serving inconsistency of claiming to establish professionalism as an internalized and deep competency while willing to settle for graduates who manifest it only as a surface phenomenon. Such fence sitting, of course, calls into question just how core professionalism is to the nature and identity of medicine. A professionalism that is deep must exist at the level of identity. Surface professionalism … is nothing more than doing one's job in a "professional manner." Surface professionalism sidesteps issues of identity and treats professionalism as something physicians can put on and take off like one's stethoscope. Professionalism as a deep competency might generate the same behavior, but the behavior in question is more real/authentic because the behavior is consequentially linked to the social actor's underlying identity (as a professional) rather than to how the job was carried out (in a professional manner).
>
> (p. 283)

Today, we see medical educators (e.g., Jarvis-Selinger, Pratt, & Regehr, 2012) beginning to embrace Shulman's call to focus on the identity of the individual—a perspective that is consistent with the view of moral psychology that the moral self is the link between knowing and doing. Our work of identity formation (Bebeau & Monson, 2012) illustrates that the usual socialization process in the professions doesn't sufficiently develop either a basic understanding or an internalization of professional expectations.[2] This is not to suggest that the measurement of medical professionalism should not be included as a dimension of assessment of professional competence, but it should not be the only strategy that focuses students' attention on appropriate professional behaviors.

STATUS OF ETHICS EDUCATION

The early work of the Hastings Center (1980) defined goals for ethics education that are in concert with Rest's evidence-based model of morality. Yet, our reviews of the status of ethics education across professions (detailed below) reflects a surprising lack of consensus on goals and purposes—both across and within professions, significant variation in time devoted to instruction, significant variation in content and methods and limited attention to assessment. This finding was not surprising in the 1980s, but today nearly every major medical center has an affiliated bioethics center and accreditation organizations have for some time required instruction in ethics and/or professionalism. Accrediting bodies tend to refrain from prescriptive recommendations, thus few institutions included evidence of the outcomes of ethics education in their self-studies. Today, the accountability movement in the US appears to have influenced the latest accreditation guidelines for the five professions we studied.

The situation is similar for graduate medical education. Reviews of residency programs (Downing, Way, & Caniano, 1997; Mulvey, Ogle-Jewett, Cheng, & Johnson, 2000) indicated minimal attention to clinical ethics in either surgery or pediatrics, though such education was deemed desirable. Further, except for the recent appeal to fostering professional identity formation (Jarvis-Selinger et al., 2012)—which clearly appeals to Kegan's constructivist theory of identity formation, and occasional references to the use of the Defining Issues Test to assess moral judgment development (e.g., the work of Self and colleagues reviewed by Bebeau, 2002) and two recent studies stemming from Baldwin's (Baldwin, Adamson, Self, Sheehan, & Oppenberg, 1996) observation of the relation between malpractice and moral judgment development for orthopedic surgeons (Bohm et al., in press; Mercuri, Karia, Egol, & Zuckerman, 2013)—there simply isn't a consistent appeal to moral psychology for the framing of goals and purposes for ethics education. Our findings are confirmed by a team of medical ethics and humanities educators (Doukas et al., 2010, 2012) recently convened to advance education in medical ethics and humanities.

The Need for a Systematic Approach to Ethics Education

What happens if insufficient attention is paid to the theoretical grounding for ethical decisions? As Shulman concluded, "the moral core around which habits of mind are organized" is missing. Bebeau and Faber-Langendoen (2014) summarize defenses offered by advance-level medical students caught cheating in a medical education course (Clarke, 2011). A subsequent remedial course for these students revealed that most could not articulate basic expectations of a medical professional even though they were about to graduate. Others (Editorial, 2006; Rudavsky, 2007; Sherman & Margolin, 2006, 2007), describe similar breaches of integrity and the amazing justifications offered. Less blatant, but troubling because they reflect shortcomings in ethics education, two studies reveal shortcomings in ethical competence. Using four hypothetical cases involving end-of-life decision making, Wong, Eiser, Mrtek, and Heckerling (2004) observed that physicians were guided by (1) patient-focused beneficence; (2) a patient- and surrogate-focused perspective that included risk avoidance; and (3) best interests of the patient determined by ethical values, rather than self-interest concerns, such as (a) economic impact on the physician; (b) expediency in resolution of the situation; and (c) the expense of medical treatment. Whereas the values that appeared to be influential determinants of decisions were guided by biomedical principles, the participants' decision methods appeared to resemble casuistry more than principle-based decision making. Testing actual performance, Gisondi, Smith-Coggins, Harter, Soltysik, and Yarnold (2004) measured the uniformity of ethical decision making for 30 emergency medicine residents using five high-fidelity simulations. In only one ethical scenario did the residents perform all the critical actions. Residents performed the fewest critical actions for a patient confidentiality case. Whereas professional behaviors appeared to be learned through some facet of residency training— senior residents had better overall performance than incoming interns—this study, together with the Wong et al. study, highlight: (1) the need for more focused ethics instruction; (2) the value of performance-based assessment for providing authentic learning and testing experience; and (3) the importance of feedback that enables professionals to compare their performance with peers and against a standard (the criterion rating form).

Accreditation Guidelines for Professional Ethics Education

Accrediting bodies for the five professions we reviewed have required institutions to include education in ethics and professionalism for at least the last two accrediting cycles. For undergraduate medical schools, the accreditation standard states

> A medical education program must include instruction in medical ethics and human values and require its medical students to exhibit scrupulous ethical principles in caring for patients and in relating to patients' families and to others involved in patient care.
>
> (LCME, 2012)

What hasn't been required is that institutions specifically demonstrate the effectiveness of ethics and professionalism education—though some outcome-minded institutions have included such data at part of their accreditation self studies.

Responding to the accountability movement in the US, two accrediting bodies are requiring that institutions engage in the specification and assessment of competencies. Both the Accreditation Council of Graduate Medical Education (ACGME, 2013) and the Commission on Dental Accreditation (ADA, 2013) are phasing in new accreditation systems requiring schools to report attainment of educational outcomes. In medicine, seven of 26 specialties (emergency medicine, internal medicine, neurologic surgery, orthopedic surgery, pediatrics, diagnostic radiology, and urology) have articulated levels of resident physician competencies based on expert panels and existing literature (Nasca, Philibert, Brigham, & Flynn, 2012). Schools will assess residents at six-month intervals. The levels, referred to as milestones, suggest their developmental nature. One of the subcompetencies of professionalism concerns the ethics of patient care.[3]

The challenge, of course, is to design systems to demonstrate achievement of such competencies. The systematic use of behavior checklists completed by multiple raters— the likely method of monitoring competence achievement—is certainly preferable to simply claiming learning outcomes are achieved, or relying on the fact that few students fail national and regional board exams. The concern, expressed by medical education scholars, is that "competency is not enough" (e.g., Jarvis-Selinger et al., 2012). Jarvis-Selinger and colleagues, together with Hafferty et al. (2011), recommend a focus on the individual's inner psychosocial capacities associated with identity formation coupled with a focus on the professions' contractual obligations to society (Cruess & Cruess, 2008a). Others, Ginsburg, Regehr and Lingard (2004) stress the underlying reasons and justification for the behaviors, and Dyche and Epstein (2011) stress cultivating an attitude of curiosity. A balance must be sought between behavioral observations and the assessment of capacities such as those suggested by Rest's FCM.

Standards for law school accreditation state that the curriculum must include instruction in "substantive law" and "other professional skills" that are "generally regarded as necessary to effective and responsible participation in the legal profession" (ABA, 2013). Arguing that the standards generally refer only to the floor requirements needed to prepare students in legal rules and procedures, and professional skills, Hamilton (2008) offers a definition of professionalism that integrates legal knowledge and skill with a set of aspirational values and ideals to guide a lawyer's decisions and actions. Calling for a systematic empirical approach like the FCM for developing curriculum, assessment, and pedagogical methods to foster professionalism, Hamilton stresses professionalism's developmental nature which requires a lifelong commitment to learning and development. Currently, he is engaged in research to define specific competencies expected of law school graduates in the first year of their employment (Hamilton, 2013a). Whereas the American Bar Association Accreditation standards do not currently incorporate Hamilton's focus on outcome assessment, the ABA is expanding efforts to share knowledge of this, and similar approaches (Hamilton, 2013b).

The National League for Nursing Accrediting Commission, Inc. (NLNAC, 2013) Standards and Criteria state that programs being reviewed in January 2014 must have clearly articulated student learning outcomes and program outcomes consistent with contemporary practice. Student outcomes are defined as "statements of expectation written in measurable terms that express what a student will know, do, or think at the end of learning." Beyond requiring "clearly stated learning and program outcomes" the document does not specify reporting of the assessment of outcomes.

Responding to animal welfare concerns (Tonsor & Wolf, 2011), the American Veterinary Medical Association (AVMA, 2012a) Council on Education (COE) (AVMA, 2012b) mandates that schools teach ethics within the curriculum. Recently mandated is a requirement that schools develop outcome assessment of holistic competencies necessary for the professional practice. Unlike professions that specify particular ethics competencies, veterinary medicine appears to consider ethics integral to each of its competencies. How ethics outcomes will be assessed is unclear. However, the COE policy states that in order to meet accreditation standards, veterinary schools must provide

> opportunities throughout the curriculum for students to gain an understanding of professional ethics, delivery of professional services to the public, personal and business finance and management skills; and gain an understanding of the breadth of veterinary medicine, career opportunities and other information about the profession.

Its stance towards animal welfare ethics is reflected in the directive that veterinary schools provide students with the "knowledge, skills, values, attitudes, aptitudes and behaviors necessary to address responsibly the health and well being of animals in the context of ever-changing societal expectations."

Current Practices

Current practices in ethics education are documented to varying degrees. Methods range from surveys of school administrators or faculty to outcomes assessment with alumni.

MEDICINE

Medical education appears to distinguish ethics instruction (i.e., promoting reasoning) from promoting professionalism (i.e., behavior). In a survey of 126 US medical schools (Swick, Szenas, Danoff, & Whitcomb, 1999), 89.7% of the 116 responding schools offer formal instruction related to professionalism—teaching professionalism as a single course or incorporating it as part of multiple courses. Diverse strategies to promote professionalism include "white-coat ceremonies" and other orientation experiences. Earlier reviews focused on ethics instruction (Eckles, Meslin, Gaffney, & Helft, 2005; Lehmann, Kasoff, Koch, & Federman, 2004; Miles, Lane, Bickel, Walker, & Cassel, 1989). DuBois and Burkemper (2002) conclude (1) ethics teaching occurs during the first two years in the preclinical setting, and just over half of the medical schools teach ethics for one year; (2) no single source, reading, or code shapes the curricula; (3) 10 teaching objectives were identified, with the majority including these: to become familiar with medical ethics topics, and to develop ethical reasoning; (4) methods include discussion/debates, readings, writing exercises, and lectures; (5) evaluation methods described did not dispel the notion that courses are not rigorous; and (6) the most common method of grading is pass/fail and the most common criterion for grading is class attendance and participation. In sum, schools rarely engaged in formal assessment of the effectiveness of their courses—even when developing ethical reasoning is the most commonly-stated purpose. Eckles and colleagues (2005) concluded: It appears that the approach taken within a particular institution reflects the educator's preference or background, rather than a carefully crafted analysis of the educational and developmental needs of the students.

Some 40 years after programs in medical ethics and humanities were established, three medical ethics and humanities faculty (Doukas et al., 2010, 2012) confirm Eckles' observations, reporting the lack of a comprehensive critical appraisal of medical education in ethics and humanities. Doukas and colleagues organized an expert panel as part of The Project to Rebalance and Integrate Medical Education (PRIME), which convened an expert panel to specify a need for clear direction and academic support that should be based on clear objectives that can be reliably assessed. However, the panel did not get beyond affirming the importance of "two essential skill sets": patient-centered skills, and critical thinking skills. Their next publication promises to address learning objectives, sound assessment, critical appraisal of residency learning, and refinement of objectives and measurement based upon critical appraisal.

Dentistry

Lantz, Bebeau, and Zarkowski (2011) surveyed the status of ethics teaching and learning in US dental schools. All 56 schools responded. Compared with previous surveys conducted over the last 30 years, the researchers note little change in the mean number of contact hours (26.5), which represents 0.5% of the mean clock hours of instruction for dental education programs. However, positive changes are evident—from rules-based lectures merged with jurisprudence and practice management—typically presented in the fourth year until at least the mid 1980s—to a gradual introduction of case-based teaching as suggested by Bebeau (1985). Also influential in facilitating change were results of a task force of ethicists, dental educators, and practitioners commissioned to develop guidelines for the teaching of ethics. Grounded in Rest's FCM, the resulting 1989 Curriculum Guidelines on Ethics and Professionalism in Dentistry (Commission on Dental Education, 1989) specified goals for ethics education that subsequently informed accreditation standards requiring ethics instruction in undergraduate dental education. Today, all schools require ethics instruction, but after July 2013, the Commission on Dental Accreditation (CODA, 2013)—responding to the accountability movement—will require that schools report attainment of educational outcomes.

What has changed over time is what qualifies as ethics instruction, the pedagogies used, and the development and availability of norm-referenced learning outcome assessments used by a number of schools to demonstrate program effectiveness. More impressive, however, is the percentage of schools that say they use reflective writing and other assessment procedures that require students to demonstrate their ability to apply ethical principles to complex cases. To support ethics instruction and outcome assessment, the American Society for Dental Ethics, with support from the American College of Dentists, regularly sponsors Faculty Development Workshops at the Annual Meeting of the American Dental Education Association. Outcome measures and instructional materials developed for these workshops are available through the Center for the Study of Ethical Development (www.ethicaldevelopment.ua.edu/bebeau-materials). Thus, dentistry is well positioned to respond to CODA's (2013) requirements for outcome assessment.

Law

Contrasting legal education with medical education, Egan et al. (2004) noted that legal ethics did not attempt to teach foundational frameworks for making moral judgments, and did not concern itself with the development of altruism, integrity, or character. Courses focused on teaching legal rules to enable students to pass a professional responsibility examination required for licensure in all states[4] (National Conference of Bar Examiners [NCBE], 2013). Prior to the 2007 Carnegie report (Sullivan, Colby, Wegner, Bond, & Shulman, 2007), efforts to influence moral judgment such as those reported by Hartwell (1995), or to study the relation between moral judgment and professional characteristics (Landsman & McNeel, 2004) were exceptions in legal education.

Several initiatives have broadened the perspective of legal education scholars about the primacy of moral reasoning development and professional identity formation. Following the 2007 Carnegie report's recommendations, Neil Hamilton of the University of St. Thomas (Minnesota) School of Law, advanced a definition of professionalism in law (Hamilton, 2008) that incorporated the FCM as its core, and organized a national symposium on empirical professionalism in law inviting influential scholars affiliated with the Carnegie report to present position papers subsequently published in a special issue of the *University of St. Thomas Law Journal* (2008). The 2008 symposium inspired a subsequent series of a local and national symposia, that connected influential legal scholars with scholars outside the legal profession (e.g., Shulman, Colby, Sullivan, Bebeau) to address research and pedagogy regarding professionalism. These efforts inspired law schools to collaborate on curricular changes and pedagogic innovations to foster identity development (e.g., *Educating Tomorrow's Lawyers* at the University of Denver, a consortium of 28 law schools nationally, and the *National Institute for Teaching Ethics and Professionalism* at Georgia State, a consortium of seven law schools). He also arranged funding for educational research, engaged the authors in consultation (MJB and VEM) to plan and conduct research on identity formation of lawyers (Hamilton & Monson, 2012b), to engage educators in innovation in law students' moral reasoning development using team-based learning and academic controversy (Johnson, Johnson, & Monson, 2013), and also to analyze longitudinal and cross-sectional studies of law students' moral reasoning development (Hamilton, Monson, & Organ, 2013; Monson, Hamilton, & Organ, 2013).

Nursing

A recent critique of nursing education (Benner et al., 2009) argues for a radical transformation of nursing education to better prepare nurses to function in a chaotic and dysfunctional US health care system. Our review of the nursing education literature suggests that the current status of nursing ethics education is consistent with Woods' (2005) review, noting that schools employ many of the possible philosophical and theoretical approaches to teach ethics. Woods lists and references 14 philosophical approaches (e.g., traditional theoretical ethics, virtue ethics, values approaches, narrative ethics, casuistry, an ethic of care approach, codes of ethics) and an array of teaching methods (e.g., lectures, tutorials, debates, model emulation, cases studies, relational narratives, reflective practice, clinical supervision, or combinations of these). Yet, based on their extensive field research, Benner and colleagues (2009) cited "a significant difference between what educators and students articulate as their understanding of ethical comportment and the actual teaching of it." Whereas educators and students "describe 'ethics' in terms of learning the principles of bioethics, in everyday practice, [the focus] is with ethical comportment, on becoming good practitioners" (p. 11). Consistent with Shulman (2010), Benner and colleagues recommend that programs focus on the formation of professional identity rather than on socialization. However, the Benner critique does not suggest a theoretical model to guide the focus on identity formation. We found only a few studies (e.g., Park, Kjervik, Crandell, & Oermann, 2012; Ryden, Duckett, Crisham, Caplan, & Schmitz, 1989) that ground their educational programs in a theory of learning that is linked to an assessment of competence.

Veterinary Medicine

An increasing focus on animal welfare ethics in veterinary education (Tonsor & Wolf, 2011) parallels changing consumer attitudes regarding farm animal production as well as the laws and regulations defining humane treatment of companion and sport animals. In the past, ethics instruction typically focused on legal and practice management issues. To meet emerging concerns for animal welfare, farm animal veterinarians must be able to respond to advocacy groups who challenge animal production methods as well as regulations within companion or sport animal industries. Similarly, both large and small animal veterinarians must be able to competently assist law enforcement when called upon to provide expert consulting on cases of possible abuse or neglect.

Although some model courses (e.g., Michigan State University's long-standing required two-credit animal welfare course [Abood & Siegford, 2010]); and the UK's animal welfare ethics curriculum developed for veterinary schools through a partnership between the University of Bristol and the World Society for the Protection of Animals (WSPA) (Main, 2010) have been developed, we did not find current information on the status of ethics teaching, and only an announcement in 2011 that an AVMA committee has been organized to develop a model curriculum in veterinary ethics and animal welfare. Further, aside from Self's work on moral reasoning development of veterinarians (see Bebeau, 2002 for a review), studies do not provide outcome data on the effectiveness of instruction. Although Abood and Siegford (2012) provide student opinion data on their introductory course, they do not include an analysis of the effectiveness of student writing assignments, though a scoring rubric for analyzing student assignments is presented.

Reflections on Current Practices

Our review of reports on the status of ethics education across professions suggests that most articles in the literature are "much ado about what to do" with little evidence as to what works. When evidence is presented (e.g., Abood & Siegford, 2012; Jensen, 2003), it is student course evaluation data indicating whether students "like" the instructional strategies or "like" the professor. Like Jensen, in our experience, students "like" instruction when it is highly engaging, uses real cases with outstanding speakers/or commentators, but find fault with the professor and the instructional strategies when they are judged on the basis of the adequacy of their ethical arguments or on the adequacy of action plans and dialogs they design to demonstrate ethical competency (e.g., "respect for persons" or "informed consent") in real or simulated situations. Relying on student course evaluations as an indicator of the success or value of ethics instruction assumes that if students enjoy instruction, they will learn. This assumption is not supported by empirical evidence (Clayson, Frost, & Sheffet, 2006). For an extensive discussion of the relation between ratings and learning, see Bebeau and Monson (2008).

CAPACITIES AS THE FOCUS OF ETHICS EDUCATION: A REVIEW OF THE EVIDENCE

Ethical Sensitivity

Studies using well-validated measures of ethical sensitivity—as Rest defined it—demonstrate that sensitivity is a construct that is distinct from moral judgment (Bebeau, 2006). Similar to studies of moral reasoning (see next section), both professionals and professional school students vary greatly in their ability to interpret the characteristics of patients/clients and responsibilities of the professional embedded in tests of ethical sensitivity. Further, some studies (Bebeau, 2006, 2009b) show that sensitivity can be influenced by educational interventions, and in some settings (You, Maeda, & Bebeau, 2011) small but significant gender differences, favoring women, are evident.

In a meta-analysis of ethical sensitivity research, You et al. (2011) identified 37 studies in which 23 measures were described to assess ethical sensitivity in dentistry, medicine, nursing, counseling, business, science, and school settings. After classifying the measures along several dimensions, including the extent to which the construct was elicited by the stimulus materials, they concluded that only seven of the measures met criteria, and most have not been extensively validated. Examples of validated measures that elicit the process include the Dental Ethical Sensitivity Test (DEST; Bebeau & Rest, 1982; Bebeau, Rest, & Yamoor, 1985) designed for dentistry and the Racial Ethical Sensitivity Test (REST; Brabeck & Sirin, 2001; Sirin, Brabeck, Satiani, & Rogers-Serin, 2003) designed for counseling psychology.

What distinguished measures like the REST and DEST is the extent to which the stimulus presents clues to a moral problem without ever signaling what moral issue is at stake or what professional responsibility is called for. In contrast, some test designers seemed to conceptualize "ethical sensitivity" as the ability to name the moral issue when a condensed synopsis of a moral problem is presented. For example, in a case like Heinz and the Drug dilemma, one could argue that naming the moral conflict as a tension between the rights of the druggist to his property and the rights of Heinz's wife to her life is a matter of moral awareness or ethical sensitivity. In fact, Hebert, Meslin, and Dunn (1992) designed such a measure for assessing ethical sensitivity in medical education and observed wide variation in students' abilities, finding it a useful assessment tool.

Such findings no doubt are of interest. However, when ethical sensitivity is simply defined as the ability to name the moral issue (e.g., patient autonomy, informed consent, distributive justice, or practitioner autonomy), important dimensions of ethical sensitivity may be overlooked. In fact, Rest (1983) thought that naming the moral issue was part of the reasoning and judgment process, and that the ability to diagnose what was happening from ambiguous clues and putting these together with sometimes vaguely understood professional and societal expectations was an unmeasured capacity that provided insight into moral failings (Bebeau, 2009b).

Moral Reasoning and Judgment

Several approaches are used to assess moral reasoning and judgment, and each has its place in the design of ethics education. Following is a brief overview of the various techniques, their usefulness and appropriateness for assessing student learning, providing feedback, and assessing curricular effectiveness.

Classroom Assessment

In ethics and philosophy courses, the essay is the preferred method for assessing and providing feedback to students on their developing reasoning ability. Whereas it is possible to achieve agreement on criteria and standards for assessment of essays (e.g., Bebeau, Pimple, Muskavitch, Borden, & Smith, 1995), most ethics educators in professions find such assessments time-consuming or find themselves insufficiently equipped to develop criteria and standards to achieve sufficient interjudge agreement to use essays to assess learning outcomes across educational and institutional settings. What experience and evidence show (Bebeau, 1994, 2006) is that students in professional education are intellectually mature and though they may come to professional education with low P scores on measures such as the DIT, they often learn quickly[5] to construct well-reasoned arguments and to apply criteria for judging the adequacy of an argument. For sample cases and criteria for judgment, see www.ethicaldevelopment.ua.edu/bebeau-materials/.

Standardized Measures of Life-Span Development

Standardized tests like the DIT (Rest, 1979; Thoma, 2006) are frequently used to test the effects of professional education on moral judgment development. The interest is in establishing whether professional education adds value beyond the well-established finding—that moral judgment shows dramatic growth during college unless programs are narrowly focused on the technical aspects of career development or are dogmatic in their approach (McNeel, 1994; Pascarella & Terenzini, 2005). Findings from studies of moral judgment development in the professions typically do not show change in moral judgment development in the absence of a well-validated ethics intervention. For an extensive summary of studies describing education effects, intervention effects, subgroup differences, regression effects,[6] and climate effects across professions, see Bebeau (2002) and Bebeau and Monson (2008) for an update of findings.

Profession-Specific Measures of Reasoning and Judgment

The question for educators in areas like "integrity in scientific research," is whether to teach to the codes and policy manuals or to teach concepts particular to the discipline: intellectual honesty, humane care of animals, intellectual property, collegiality in scientific investigations, and so on (IOM, 2002a, pp. 36–40). Following Strike's (1982) suggestion that measures of life-span development may not be sensitive to learning of profession-specific concepts taught in an ethics curriculum, Bebeau and Thoma (1999) devised the Dental Ethical Reasoning and Judgment Test (DERJT) as a prototype measure of intermediate concepts. Such concepts are thought to reside between the more prescriptive directives of codes of professional conduct and the more abstract principles (e.g., autonomy, beneficence, and justice) described by ethicists (e.g., Beauchamp & Childress, 1994). The DERJT is sensitive to dental ethics education interventions, is a useful measure for diagnosing deficiencies in reasoning and judgment as displayed by dentists disciplined by a licensing board (Bebeau, 2009b), and is moderately correlated with DIT scores (Thoma et al., 2008).

In the past, ethics educators were typically limited to measures of life-span development (e.g., the DIT or the MJI) to demonstrate the effects of ethics education. Two recent studies support the added benefit of an intermediate concept measure (ICM) as an outcome measure for ethics education programs. Initially, the ICM was thought to be most applicable to professions education, where the acquisition of particular and often unique concepts is required. In concert with this expectation, Turner (2008) designed and validated an Army Leader Ethical Reasoning Test (ALERT) that provides information on ethical competence over and above what is provided by DIT scores. Whereas Thoma, Derryberry, and Crowson (2013) demonstrated that an ICM designed for adolescents can capture the transition from personal interest to conventional reasoning, Bebeau (2009b) demonstrated the dental ICM was particularly useful in helping disciplined dentists see how often they were unable to distinguish bad choices from better choices.

MORAL MOTIVATION AND IDENTITY FORMATION

Development of a professional identity is an important outcome of the professional education and socialization process. One approach is to use essays or interviews to elicit a sense of professional identity as it unfolds during the course of professional education. A second is to design sets of items to measure a professional's role concept (Bebeau et al., 1993).

Professional Identity Formation

Kegan (1982) proposed that one's identity is first embedded with close others (i.e., family, friends, and co-workers), and through life experiences (including education) can become more inclusive, with an increasing sense of self-authorship (Baxter Magolda & King, 2004) and moral responsibility to society. The developmental challenge of forging one's identity involves becoming authentic and shedding others' definitions of us that are self-limiting or leave us vulnerable to succumbing to pressures of self-interest or loss of autonomy. Forging a professional identity requires integration and meshing of professional values and expectations with personal ones. Validation studies of Kegan's model (Forsythe, Snook, Lewis, & Bartone, 2002) conducted within the military profession support the constructivist's view that individuals move from self-centered conceptions of identity through a number of transitions, to a moral identity characterized by the expectations of a profession—to put the interests of others before the self, or to subvert one's own ambitions to the service of society or to the nation. The fully integrated moral self (i.e., personal and professional values are fully integrated and consistently applied) tends not to develop until midlife—if it develops at all (Forsythe et al., 2002).

Explorations into the development of a professional moral identity (recently summarized by Bebeau & Monson, 2012; Hamilton & Monson, 2012a) ask students to compose essays on questions derived from Kegan's interviews. Essays reflect a wide range of commitment to and understanding of professional values and expectations, the extent to which societal obligation to underserved populations is expressed, and whether such expectations are a core part of the entering student's personal value system. As with Forsythe and colleagues' studies of entering professionals, the predominate mode of identity was a Stage 2/3 transition, meaning a focus on self-interest with professional expectations seen as external to the self, rather than a constituent of the moral self. Monson and Bebeau (2006) found that dental students at higher stages (about 37% of entering students) were more likely to incorporate issues of access to care, serving medical assistance patients, and volunteering to help those in need, as key expectations of the self.

Role Concept

The Professional Role Orientation Inventory (PROI; Bebeau et al., 1993) is designed to elicit a professional's conception of their professional role. Four 10-item scales assess dimensions of professionalism that are described in models of professionalism cited in the professional ethics literature. The PROI scales have been shown to consistently differentiate beginning and advanced student groups and practitioner groups expected to differ in role concept. The measure is sensitive to the effects of instruction and has performed well in construct validation studies. See Thoma and Bebeau (2013) for a recent summary of validation studies. Further, the measure has been adapted for other settings (e.g., physical therapy by Swisher, Beckstead, & Bebeau, 2004 and to Korean dentists by Choi & Kim, 2007).

Several studies confirm the need for professional socialization. Anderson (2001) concluded that graduate students do not intuit the values of the research discipline either from the curriculum or from their research mentors. Similarly, entering dental students (Bebeau, 1994) couldn't articulate professional expectation, sometimes even after explicit instruction. Further, whereas medical students (Feudtner, Christakis, & Christakis, 1994; Rennie & Crosby, 2002) believe they should report professional misconduct, most are unwilling or uncomfortable doing so. Both researchers cite situational factors that seem to work against professional self-regulation and point to the need for explicit professional socialization together with appropriate practice in confronting real or perceived misconduct. Based on the recent Carnegie reports, noting a deficiency in this area of professional socialization, and a recent report by Jarvis-Selinger and colleagues (2012), suggesting this is an area requiring attention, perhaps medical education will catch up with other professions (e.g., dentistry and the military) which are addressing this important aspect of professional development.

Character and Competence: Implementation of the Decision

The importance of practitioner attributes and practical skills is particularly evident when comparing physicians who have been sued for malpractice versus those who have not. Studies indicate that even a small increase in the amount of time spent in patient communication can reduce the likelihood of malpractice complaints (Ambady & Rosenthal, 1992; Levinson, 1994). As with the other capacities, both students and professionals vary considerably in the courage and capacity to address the tough problems they will likely encounter in practice. But sometimes what appears to be lack of courage is actually a manifestation of practical wisdom (Schwartz & Sharpe, 2005). Wading into a problem when you lack practical know-how may create a bigger mess than the failure to act.

Assessing fourth component capacities is commonly done through performance assessments or case simulations, and is routinely part of admissions processes where the individual's undergraduate co-curricular activities are used as a proxy for character. In medical education, Objective Structured Clinical Examinations (OSCEs) present the medical student with a "standardized patient" with whom they interact. Feedback on their effectiveness is provided.

In dental ethics education (Bebeau, 1994), students are presented with realistic case scenarios with patients that examine a number of challenging ethical dilemmas.[7] Taking the role of a professional, students analyze their responsibilities in complex clinical situations and develop action plans and dialogs that are critiqued for their potential effectiveness. This practice builds confidence and provides a template for situations in practice that the student will encounter. A recent analysis of the ability of 120 dental graduates to implement effective actions (You & Bebeau, 2012) indicated that women graduates developed substantially more effective dialogs and action plans than their male colleagues (effect size of 0.51). Consistent with the hypothesis that moral motivation would influence ethical implementation, the researchers noted that whereas male and female students had similar scores on the responsibility dimension of a measure of moral motivation (PROI scores) at entry to professional school, and both demonstrated growth in their commitment to professional responsibilities, women demonstrated significantly greater change, an effect size of 0.75 for women versus 0.5 for men.

APPYING THE FOUR COMPONENT MODEL TO REMEDIATE LAPSES IN PROFESSIONALISM

Whether habits/behaviors apparent during professional school are (1) reflective of character traits that are resistant to change, (2) are indicative of an underdeveloped professional identity, or (3) are associated with underdeveloped capacities in ethical sensitivity, reasoning, or implementation of defensible moral actions are questions of considerable interest to professions education. A retrospective analysis of performance data for 41 dentists referred for ethics instruction by a state dental board provides insight into actions judged by others to be unprofessional (Bebeau, 2009a, 2009b).

Of the 41 dentists referred for ethics assessment, two were exempt from instruction based on pretest performance on five well-validated measures of the FCM, and 38 completed an individualized course designed to remediate deficiencies in ethical abilities identified at the pretest. Statistically significant change (effect sizes ranging from 0.55 to

5.0) was observed for ethical sensitivity (DEST scores), moral reasoning (DIT scores), and role concept (essays and PROI scores). Analysis of the relations between ability deficiencies and disciplinary actions supports the explanatory power of Rest's FCM. Of particular interest is the way the model helped professionals deconstruct the usual summary judgments about character (unethical or unprofessional are some of the milder descriptors often used) and see themselves as lacking capacities that could be further developed. For example, in cases where disciplinary action was taken for insurance or Medicaid fraud, analysis of role concept and moral reasoning helped reinterpret what appeared to be acts to promote self-interest as an unbounded sense of responsibility toward others. The performance-based assessments (especially the DEST) were useful in identifying shortcomings in either ethical sensitivity or ethical implementation that accounted for the moral failing. Rather than trying to line his or her pocket—the usual attribution of such acts—the individual paternalistically manipulated the system in order to help the patient achieve much needed care.

In eight cases where disciplinary action was taken for providing specialty care below the standard of a specialist,[8] each dentist had acceptable ethical sensitivity scores, but seven of the eight had moral reasoning scores below the mean for dental graduates, and five of the eight had very low reasoning scores (DIT P scores in the low 30s). This finding is reminiscent of Baldwin and Self's (2006) observation showing a relation between low DIT scores and frequency of malpractice claims. Of all the examples of shortcomings in capacities observed, the most compelling was the inability of 39 of the 41 referrals to articulate key professional expectations (e.g., the responsibility for lifelong learning, for self-monitoring, and regulation of the profession), expectations that come tripping off the tongues of the 10 moral exemplars studied by Rule and Bebeau (2005). This finding argues for the importance of an explicit focus on professional identity formation—something the disciplined dentists said they had not received and something they said they highly valued about the remedial ethics program. In fact, three insights about the design of ethics curricula emerged from a qualitative analysis of the referrals' self-assessments of learning. First, beginning the instructional process with a discussion of the distinguishing features of a profession and the expectations that follow is uplifting and renewing. Second, practitioners highly valued the insight gained from the diagnostic assessment of their strengths and weaknesses across the four capacities that give rise to decision making. Third, practitioners highly valued the emphasis the course put on ethical implementation. Instead of stopping with "What is happening?" and "What ought to be done?" as is typical of much ethics instruction, the courses spent time focusing on how to implement an action plan, including what to say and how to say it.

Building an Environment to Support Ethical Development and Professionalism

Two general conclusions guide our recommendations. First, there is ample evidence that our capacities to recognize, reason about, commit to, and implement actions judged by others to be moral, continue to develop across the life span. Second, there is also ample evidence that professional growth and personal development is best accomplished in a cooperative and collegial learning environment—one that uses multiple educational paradigms and multiple methods of assessment. Given such evidence, professional schools must reflect carefully on their responsibility for promoting developmental growth and should be held accountable by accrediting bodies for the evidence of their program's educational effectiveness. Following are general recommendations for enhancing ethics education.

First, ground the goals and purposes of ethics education in the FCM and begin the socialization process by focusing on the identity of the individual and its congruence with both societal and professional expectations. Ethics education often begins with a focus on moral quandaries, sometimes preceded by a brief review of moral theories. Such an approach is sure to engage students—maybe not the theory part—but it also can do them a disservice. Asked to take a position on an ethical dilemma when the student has had little opportunity to become acquainted with professional and societal expectations may encourage a defensive stance on personal moral values, rather than open reflection upon what it means to become a professional and, in effect, exploring whether the profession's value system and one's own are congruent. No one has to become a dentist or physician or lawyer, but if one decides to do so, doesn't the profession have a right to expect that when the individual takes the oath of office that he or she not only means it, but knows what it means? Students rarely come to professional school with a clear vision of societal and professional expectations,[9] and do not intuit them from the general educational process. Professional education must be conveyed as an opportunity to reflect on this important commitment. It should not be assumed that if one is in professional school that one has resolved personal and professional expectations and integrated these into one's identity as a dentist, lawyer, or physician. In fact, our research (Bebeau & Monson, 2012) illustrates the developmental nature of professional identity formation, and our experience (Bebeau & Faber-Langendoen, 2014) with students who have violated professional norms indicates how challenging it can be to address unprofessional behavior in practice.

Second, design ethics curricula appropriate to the students' level of professional development. Genetic engineering and cloning may be intriguing value problems for medical ethicists, but seldom are such problems of central concern to the novice. Rather, students worry about problems that are more mundane (e.g., performing a physical examination on a very ill patent, speaking up when noticing a questionable practice performed by a superior, managing conflicting directives given by a resident and an attending physician, responding to an angry patient, deciding whether the physician has the right to assert his or her values with respect to filling prescriptions for "the morning after pill"). As we have argued, students need not only decide on an ethically defensible response, but need to work out how to effectively implement their good intentions.

Third, professional education is expected to define professional expectations and develop reflective self-directed learners (Knowles, Holton, & Swanson, 2005). Professional schools need to collaborate in order to design or utilize measures of ethical sensitivity, moral reasoning, and role concept, to provide students with insight about their own personal and professional development, thus enabling them to become reflective and self-directed. Tests of life-span development (e.g., DIT) can be used to provide students with personal insight as to how their skills at reasoning and judgment compare with those of their peers and with expert judgment. Likewise, profession-specific measures like the DERJT or the PROI can be used to counsel students about the development of their abilities so each can engage in more reflective practice. A part of reflective practice is to set personal learning goals.

Fourth, behavioral indicators of professionalism have been defined and validated (Papadakis et al., 2001; Platfoot Lacey, 2012). These may include such things as meeting commitments, treating others (including faculty) respectfully, or self-monitoring the use of mood-altering drugs. By defining professional expectations, we include bottom-up processes of empowering students to articulate their understanding of professional expectations. By this, we mean that program evaluation and student development efforts designed to glean the opinions of students and empower them are successful to the extent the students who are given leadership and power have the vision and values to advance professional expectations. Coaching student leaders to raise the bar for their peers on community service may be necessary, as opposed to allowing a *laissez-faire* approach to shape student culture and values.

Fifth, the institution must attend to the moral milieu. Because students learn from observing peers and faculty, requiring the assessment of professional behaviors within an environment where those behaviors are not the norms would present a considerable challenge and risk being perceived as organizational hypocrisy. There must be a whole school commitment that includes modeling the professional behavior we wish to promote. Modeling will also extend, from time to time, to confronting issues of intolerance, arrogance, entitlement, or paternalism. When brought to professional settings, such behaviors can be devastating—to clients, patients, and to careers. This dimension of personal development cannot be relegated to a single ethics course, but rather must be woven into the fabric of school culture. The ultimate respect we can accord students is to act as swiftly in confronting these issues as would a human resources officer with an employee.

Last, a professional ethics curriculum needs to promote a sense of the profession's collective responsibility for the welfare of society. Only when professionals exercise their collective responsibility to promote the public good will the trust society has carefully given be maintained. The role of the educator is to raise such consciousness.

NOTES

1. Ethical sensitivity embraces what is currently referred to as "cultural competency"—i.e., the knowledge and understanding of difference that enables a provider to deliver services that are respectful of and responsive to the health beliefs, practices, and cultural and linguistic needs of a particular patient.

2. Our approach is consistent with Cruess and Cruess (2008b) who recommend the integration of sociological and virtue-based approaches to defining professional expectations. A virtue-based approach is certainly acceptable, but unless the approach also reflects what medical sociologists have observed, the profession runs the risk of failing to meet legitimate societal expectations.

3. Five milestones of ethical competence are:

    1. Is aware of basic bioethical principles and is able to identify ethical issues in clinical situation.
    2. Consistently recognizes ethical issues in practice and is able to discuss, analyze, and manage such issues in common and frequent clinical situations.
    3. Is able to effectively analyze and manage ethical issues in complicated and challenging clinical situations.
    4. Consistently considers and manages ethical issues in practice and develops and applies a systematic and appropriate approach to analyzing and managing ethical issues when providing medical care.
    5. Demonstrates leadership and mentorship on understanding and applying bioethical principles clinically, particularly responsiveness to patients above self-interest and self-monitoring, and develops institutional and organizational strategies to protect and maintain these principles.

4. The Multistate Professional Responsibility Examination (MPRE) is a standardized exam of the National Conference of Bar Examiners (NCBE) and is required for admission to the bar in all but three US

jurisdictions. The MPRE assesses mastery of the rules, principles, and codes contained within the American Bar Association's (ABA) Model Rules of Professional Conduct (MRPC) and Model Codes of Judicial Conduct (MCJC).

5. Dental students in the Minnesota curriculum demonstrate significant growth in the ability to develop a well-reasoned moral argument following 10 hours of small group dilemma discussions. In addition to the discussions, students receive written feedback during the course on five written essays.

6. Whereas it is hard to imagine actual erosion in the ability to reason in the sense that individuals who are able to comprehend more advanced moral arguments and therefore prefer them (which is what selection of postconventional moral arguments on the DIT amounts to), suddenly lose the ability to comprehend such arguments. However, when students encounter the complexities of professional practice, some become disillusioned and cynical about the possibility of applying such ideals in real-life situations. Selecting more self-interest or maintaining norms arguments at post-test may simply reflect students' concerns about the practice environment.

7. Cases include how to manage a case of suspected child abuse, substandard work by a previous dentist, drug-seeking behavior of a patient, and patient requests for treatment that does not align with the dentist's values or judgment.

8. The Dental Practice Act does not prohibit the generalist from providing specialty care (e.g., endodontic or orthodontic care), but does hold the generalist to the standards of the specialist.

9. See Bebeau and Monson (2012) for an extensive discussion and list of citations.

REFERENCES

Abood, S. K., & Siegford, J. M. (2012). Student perceptions of an animal-welfare and ethics course taught early in the veterinary curriculum. *Journal of Veterinary Medical Education, 39*(2), 136–141.

Accreditation Council for Graduate Medical Education. (2013). *The next accreditation system.* Retrieved from www.acgme-nas.org/.

Ambady, N., & Rosenthal, R. (1992). Thin slices of behavior as predictors of interpersonal consequences: A meta-analysis. *Psychological Bulletin, 2,* 256–274.

American Bar Association (ABA). (2013). *American Bar Association Standards for Approval of Law Schools* [ABASALS]. Retrieved from www.americanbar.org/content/dam/aba/publications/misc/legal_education/Standards/2013_2014_final_aba_standards_and_rules_of_procedure_for_approval_of_law_schools_body.authcheckdam.pdf.

American Dental Association. (2013). Commission on Dental Accreditation (CODA) website. Available at www.ada.org/117.aspx.

American Veterinary Medical Association. (2012a). *Accreditation policies and procedures of the AVMA council on education, April 2012 (revised October 2012).* Retrieved from www.avma.org/ProfessionalDevelopment/Education/Accreditation/Colleges/Pages/coe-pp.aspx.

American Veterinary Medical Association. (2012b). *Council of education, changes to standards of Accreditation.* Retrieved from www.avma.org/ProfessionalDevelopment/Education/Accreditation/Colleges/Pages/coe-standard-newsletter-spring2012-changes-to-standards.aspx.

Anderson, M. (2001). What would get you in trouble: Doctoral students' conceptions of science and its norms. *Proceedings of the ORI Conference on Research on Research Integrity.* Washington, D.C.: Office of Research Integrity.

Baldwin, D. C., Jr., & Self, D. J. (2006). The assessment of moral reasoning and professionalism in medical education and practice. In D. T. Stern (Ed.), *Measuring medical professionalism* (pp. 75–94). New York: Oxford University Press.

Baldwin, D. C., Jr., Adamson, T. E., Self, D. J., Sheehan, T. J., & Oppenberg, A. A. (1996). Moral reasoning and malpractice. A pilot study of orthopedic surgeons. *American Journal of Orthopedics, 25*(7), 481–484.

Bandura, A. (1977). Toward a unifying theory of behavioral change. *Psychological Review, 84*(2), 191–215.

Baxter Magolda, M., & King, P. M. (2004). *Learning partnerships: Theory and models of practice to educate for self-authorship.* Sterling, VA: Stylus.

Beauchamp, T. L., & Childress, J. F. (1979). *Principles of biomedical ethics* (1st ed.). New York: Oxford University Press.

Beauchamp, T. L., & Childress, J. F. (1994). *Principles of biomedical ethics* (4th ed.). New York: Oxford University Press.

Beauchamp, T. L., & Childress, J. F. (2009). *Principles of biomedical ethics* (6th ed.). New York: Oxford University Press.

Bebeau, M. J. (1985). Teaching ethics in dentistry. *Journal of Dental Education, 49,* 236–243.

Bebeau, M. J. (1994). Influencing the moral dimensions of dental practice. In J. Rest & D. Narvaez (Eds.), *Moral development in the professions: Psychology and applied ethics* (pp. 121–146). New York: Erlbaum.

Bebeau, M. J. (2002). The Defining Issues Test and the Four Component Model: Contributions to professional education. *Journal of Moral Education, 31*(3), 271–295.

Bebeau, M. J. (2006). Evidence-based character development. In N. Kenny & W. Shelton (Eds.), *Advances in bioethics: Vol. 10. Lost virtue: Professional character development in medical education* (pp. 47–86). Oxford, UK: Elsevier.

Bebeau, M. J. (2008). Promoting ethical development and professionalism: Insights from educational research in the professions. *University of St. Thomas Law Journal, 5*(2), 366–403.

Bebeau, M. J. (2009a). Enhancing professionalism using ethics education as part of a dental licensing board's disciplinary action: Part 1 An evidence-based process. *Journal of the American College of Dentists, 76*(2), 38–50.

Bebeau, M. J. (2009b). Enhancing professionalism using ethics education as part of a dental licensing board's disciplinary action: Part 2 Evidence the process works. *Journal of the American College of Dentists, 76*(3), 32–45.

Bebeau, M. J., & Faber-Langendoen, K. (in press). Remediating lapses in professionalism. In A. Kalet and C. Chou (Eds.), *Remediation in Medical Education.* (pp. 103–127). New York: Springer Science.

Bebeau, M. J., & Lewis, P. (2004). *Manual for assessing and promoting identity formation.* Center for the Study of Ethical Development, University of Minnesota.

Bebeau, M. J., & Monson, V. E. (2008). Guided by theory, grounded in evidence: A way forward for professional ethics education. In L. Nucci & D. Narvaez (Eds.), *Handbook on moral and character education* (pp. 557–582). Hillsdale, NJ: Routledge.

Bebeau, M. J., & Monson, V. E. (2012). Professional identity formation and transformation across the life span. In A. Mc Kee and M. Eraut (Eds.), *Learning trajectories, innovation and identity for professional development* (pp. 135–163). New York: Springer.

Bebeau, M. J., & Rest, J. R. (1982). *The dental ethical sensitivity test.* Center for the Study of Ethical Development, University of Minnesota.

Bebeau, M. J., & Thoma, S. J. (1994). The impact of a dental ethics curriculum on moral reasoning. *Journal of Dental Education, 58*(9), 684–692.

Bebeau, M. J., & Thoma, S. J. (1999). "Intermediate" concepts and the connection to moral education. *Educational Psychology Review, 11*(4), 343–360.

Bebeau, M. J., & Thoma, S. J. (2013). Moral motivation and the Four Component Model. In K. Heinrichs, F. Oser, & T. Lovat (Eds.), *Handbook of moral motivation* (pp. 475–498). Rotterdam, The Netherlands: Sense Publishers.

Bebeau, M. J., Born, D. O., & Ozar, D. T. (1993). The development of a professional role orientation inventory. *Journal of the American College of Dentists, 60*(2), 27–33.

Bebeau, M. J., Pimple, K. D., Muskavitch, K. M. T., Borden S. L., & Smith D. L. (1995). *Moral reasoning in scientific research: Cases for teaching and assessment.* Bloomington, IN: Indiana University.

Bebeau, M. J., Rest, J. R., & Narvaez, D. F. (1999). Beyond the promise: A perspective for research in moral education. *Educational Researcher, 28*(4), 18–26.

Bebeau, M. J., Rest, J. R., & Yamoor, C. M. (1985). Measuring dental students' ethical sensitivity. *Journal of Dental Education, 49*, 225–235.

Benner, P., Sutphen, M., Leonard, V., & Day, L. (2009). *Educating nurses: A call for radical transformation.* San Francisco: Jossey-Bass.

Bertolami, C. N. (2004). Why our ethics curricula don't work. *Journal of Dental Education, 68*(4), 414–425.

Berwick, D. M., & Hackbarth, A. D. (2012). Eliminating waste in US health care. *JAMA, 307*(14), 1513–1516.

Blasi, A. (1984). Moral identity: Its role in moral functioning. In W. M. Kurtines & J. L. Gewirtz (Eds.), *Morality, moral behavior, and moral development* (pp. 129–139). New York: Wiley.

Blasi, A. (1991). Moral understanding and the moral personality: The process of moral integration. Unpublished manuscript.

Bohm, K. C., Van Heest, T., Gioe, T. J., Agel, J., Johnson, T. C., & Van Heest, A. E. (in press). Assessment of moral reasoning skills in the orthopedic surgery resident applicant. *Journal of Bone and Joint Surgery.*

Bok, D. (1976). Can ethics be taught? *Change, 8*, 26–38.

Brabeck, M. M., & Sirin, S. (2001). *The racial ethical sensitivity test: Computer disk version (REST-CD).* Chestnut Hill, MA: Boston College.

Candee, D., Sheehan, T. J., Cook, C. D., Husted, S. D., & Bargen, M. (1982). Moral reasoning and decisions in dilemmas of neonatal care. *Pediatric Research, 16*, 846–850.

Choi, J., & Kim, M. (2007). A study on the development of professionalism of dental students based on moral psychology. *The Korean Journal of Educational Psychology, 21*(1), 69–88.

Clarke, E. (2011, May 22). Upstate students put cheating scandal behind them. http://centralny.ynn.com/content/top_stories/544294/upstate-students-put-cheating-scandal-behind-them/.

Clayson, D. E., Frost, T. F., & Sheffet, M. J. (2006). Grades and the student evaluation of instruction: A test of the reciprocity effect. *Academy of Management Learning & Education, 5*(1), 52–65.

Cohen, J. (2006). Foreword. In. D. T. Stern (Ed.), *Measuring medical professionalism* (pp. v–viii). New York: Oxford University Press, Inc.

Commission on Dental Education. (1989). Curriculum guidelines on ethics and professionalism in dentistry. *Journal of Dental Education, 53*, 144–148.

Cruess, R. L., & Cruess, S. R. (2008a). Expectations and obligations: Professionalism & medicine's social contract with society. *Perspectives in Biology and Medicine, 51*(4), 579–598.

Cruess, S. R., & Cruess, R. L. (2008b). Understanding medical professionalism: A plea for an inclusive and integrated approach. *Medical Education, 42*, 755–757.

Doukas, D. J., McCullough, L. B., & Wear, S. (2010). Reforming medical education in ethics and humanities by finding common ground with Abraham Flexner. *Academic Medicine, 85*, 318–323.

Doukas, D. J., McCullough, L. B., & Wear, S. (2012). Medical education in medical ethics and humanities as the foundation for developing medical professionalism. *Academic Medicine, 87*, 341–344.

Downing, M. T., Way, D. P., & Caniano, D. A. (1997). Results of a national survey on ethics education in general surgery residency programs. *American Journal of Surgery, 174*(3), 364–368.

DuBois, J. M., & Burkemper, J. (2002). Ethics education in US medical schools: A study of syllabi. *Academic Medicine, 77*(5), 432–437.

Duckett, L. J., & Ryden, M. B. (1994). Education for ethical nursing practice. In J. R. Rest & D. F. Narvaez (Eds.), *Moral development in the professions* (pp. 51–69). Hillsdale, NJ: Erlbaum.

Dyche, L., & Epstein, R. M. (2011). Curiosity and medical education, *Medical Education, 45*, 663–668.

Eckles, R. E., Meslin, E. M., Gaffney, M., & Helft, P. R. (2005). Medical ethics education: Where are we? Where should we be going? A review. *Academic Medicine, 80*(12), 1143–2252.

Editorial. (2006, June 14). UNLV cheaters still get diplomas (editorial). *Las Vegas Review Journal.*

Egan, E. A., Kayhan, P., & Ramirez, C. (2004). Comparing ethics education in medicine and law: Combining the best of both worlds. *Annals of Health Law, 13*, 303–325.

Feudtner, C., Christakis, D. A., & Christakis, N. A. (1994). Do clinical students suffer ethical erosion? Students' perceptions of their ethical and personal development. *Academic Medicine, 69*, 670–679.

Forsythe, G. B. (2005). Identity development in professional education. *Academic Medicine, 80*, S112–S117.

Forsythe, G. B., Snook, S., Lewis P., & Bartone, P. T. (2002). Making sense of officership: Developing a professional identity for 21st century army officers. In D. M. Snider & G. L. Watkins (Eds.), *The future of the army profession* (pp. 357–378). Boston: McGraw-Hill.

Freidson, E. (1988). *Profession of medicine: A study of the sociology of applied knowledge.* Chicago: University of Chicago Press.

Frimer, J. A., & Walker, L. J. (2009). Reconciling the self and morality: An empirical model of moral centrality development. *Developmental Psychology, 45*, 1669–1681.

Ginsburg, S., Regehr, G., & Lingard L. (2004). Basing the evaluation of professionalism on observable behaviors: A cautionary tale. *Academic Medicine, 79*(10), S1–S4.

Gisondi, M. A., Smith-Coggins, R., Harter, P. M., Soltysik, R. C., & Yarnold, P. R. (2004). Assessment of resident professionalism using high-fidelity simulation of ethical dilemmas. *Academic Emergency Medicine, 11*(9), 931–937.

Graham, K. (1997, January 28). The Watergate watershed: A turning point for a nation and a newspaper. *Washington Post*, p. D01. Retrieved from www.washingtonpost.com/wpdyn/content/article/2002/06/11/AR2005112200811.html.

Hafferty, F. (2006). Measuring professionalism: A commentary. In D. T. Stern (Ed.), *Measuring medical professionalism* (pp. 81–306). New York: Oxford University Press.

Hafferty, F. W., & Castellani, B. (2010). The increasing complexities of professionalism, *Academic Medicine, 85*(2), 288–301.

Hafferty, F. W., Brennan, M., & Pawlina, W. (2011). Professionalism, the invisible hand, and a necessary reconfiguration of medical education. *Academic Medicine, 86*(11), 1329–1481.

Hall, R. H. (1975). The professions. In R. H. Hall, *Occupations and the social structure* (2nd ed., pp. 63–135). Englewood Cliffs, NJ: Prentice-Hall.

Hamilton, N. (2008). Assessing professionalism: Measuring progress in the formation of an ethical professional identity. *University of St. Thomas Law Journal, Vol. 5; U of St. Thomas Legal Studies Research Paper No. 08–10.* Retrieved from SSRN: http://ssrn.com/abstract=1118204.

Hamilton, N. W. (2012). Fostering professional formation (professionalism): Lessons from the Carnegie Foundation's five studies on educating professionals, *Creighton Law Review, 45,* 771–774.

Hamilton, N. W. (2013a). Law-firm competency models and student professional success: Building on a foundation of professional formation/professionalism. *U of St. Thomas (Minnesota) Legal Studies Research Paper No. 13–22.* Retrieved from http://ssrn.com/abstract=2271410.

Hamilton, N. W. (2013b). The qualities of the professional lawyer. In Paul Haskins (Ed.), *Essential qualities of the professional lawyer.* Chicago: ABA Standing Committee on Professionalism.

Hamilton, N. W., & Monson, V. E. (2012a). Legal education's ethical challenge: Empirical research on how most effectively to foster each student's professional formation (Professionalism). *University of St. Thomas Law Journal, 9*(2). Retrieved from http://ssrn.com/abstract=2004749.

Hamilton, N. W., & Monson, V. E. (2012b). Ethical professional (trans)formation: Themes from interviews about professionalism with exemplary lawyers (April 6, 2011). *52 Santa Clara L. Rev.* Retrieved from http://ssrn.com/abstract=1804419.

Hamilton, N. W., Monson, V. E., & Organ, J. M. (2013). Empirical evidence that legal education can foster student professionalism/professional formation to become an effective lawyer. *University of St. Thomas Law Journal,* 2013. Retrieved from http://ssrn.com/abstract=2205447.

Handehman, M. M., Knapp, S., & Gottlieb, M. C. (2009). Positive ethics: Themes and variations. In S. J. Lopez & C. R. Snyder (Eds.), *Oxford handbook of positive psychology* (2nd ed.). *Oxford library of psychology* (pp. 105–113). New York: Oxford University Press.

Hartwell, S. (1995). Promoting moral development through experiential teaching. *Clinical Law Review, 1*(3), 505–539.

Hastings Center. (1980). *The teaching of ethics in higher education.* Hastings-on-Hudson, NY: Hastings Center.

Hebert, P. C., Meslin, E. M., & Dunn, E. V. (1992). Measuring the ethical sensitivity of medical students: A study at the University of Toronto. *Journal of Medical Ethics, 18,* 142–147.

H.R. 3590–111th Congress: Patient Protection and Affordable Care Act. (2009). Retrieved from www.govtrack.us/congress/bills/111/hr3590.

Institute of Medicine (IOM). (2002a). *Integrity in scientific research.* Washington, D.C.: Institute of Medicine, National Research Council.

Institute of Medicine (IOM). (2002b). Promoting integrity in research through education. In NRC Committee on Assessing Integrity in Research Environments, Institute of Medicine (Ed.), *Integrity in scientific research* (pp. 84–111). Washington, D.C.: Institute of Medicine, National Research Council.

Institute of Medicine (IOM). (2002c). Outcome measures for assessing integrity in the research environment. In NRC Committee on Assessing Integrity in Research Environments, Institute of Medicine (Ed.), *Integrity in scientific research* (pp. 143–166). Washington, D.C.: Institute of Medicine, National Research Council.

Jarvis-Selinger, S., Pratt, D. D., & Regehr, G. (2012). Competency is not enough: Integrating identity formation into the medical education discourse. *Academic Medicine, 87*(9), 1185–1190.

Jensen, G. M. (2003, April). Exploration of critical self-reflection in the teaching of ethics: The case of physical therapy. In *Developing mindful professionals: A cross-disciplinary exploration.* A tape-recorded symposium presented at the Annual Meeting of the American Educational Research Association, Chicago.

Johnson, D. W., Johnson, R. T., & Monson, V. E. (2013). Cooperation-competition and constructive controversy in developing professional ethics in law school classes. *University of St. Thomas Law School Journal.*

Kegan, R. (1982). *The evolving self.* Cambridge, MA: Harvard University Press.

Kegan, R. (1994). *In over our heads: The mental demands of modern life* (pp. 188–196). Cambridge, MA: Harvard University Press.

Kenny, N., & Shelton, W. (Eds.). (2006). *Advances in bioethics: Vol. 10. Lost virtue: Professional character development in medical education* (pp. 47–86). Oxford: Elsevier.

Knowles, M. S., Holton, E. F., & Swanson, R. A. (2005). *The adult learner: The definitive classic in adult education and human resource development* (6th ed.). Burlington, MA: Elsevier.

Landsman, M., & McNeel, S. P. (2004). Moral judgment of law students across three years: Influences of gender, political ideology and interest in altruistic law practice. *South Texas Law Review, 45*(4), 891–920.

Landsman, S. (2009). The growing challenge of pro se litigation. *Lewis & Clark Law Review,* 439–460.

Lantz, M. S., Bebeau, M. J., & Zarkowski, P. (2011). The status of teaching and learning of ethics in US dental schools. *Journal of Dental Education, 75*(10), 1295–1309.

Lapsley, D. K., & Narvaez, D. (2006). Character education. In A. Renninger & I. Siegel (Vol. Eds.), W. Damon & R. Lerner (Series Eds.), *Handbook of child psychology* (Vol. 4, pp. 248–296). Hoboken, NJ: Wiley.

Lehmann, L. S., Kasoff, W. S., Koch, P., & Federman, D. D. (2004). A survey of medical ethics education at US and Canadian medical schools. *Academic Medicine, 79,* 682–689.

Levinson, W. (1994). Physician-patient communication: A key to malpractice prevention. *Journal of the American Medical Association, 273,* 1619–1620.

Liaison Committee for Medical Education (LCME). (2012). Functions and structure of a medical school: LCME accreditation standards. Retrieved from www.lcme.org/standard.htm.

Main, D. C. J. (2010). Evolution of animal-welfare education for veterinary students. *Journal of Veterinary Medical Education, 37*(1), 30–35.

Mann, K. V. (2006). Learning and teaching in professional character development. In N. Kenny & W. Shelton (Eds.), *Advances in bioethics: Vol. 10. Lost virtue: Professional character development in medical education* (pp. 145–184). Oxford: Elsevier.

May, W. F. (1999). Money and the professions: Medicine and law. In *The future of callings—An interdisciplinary summit on the public obligations of professionals into the next millennium. William Mitchell Law Review, 25*(1), 75–102.

McNeel, S. P. (1994). College teaching and student moral development. In J. R. Rest & D. Narvaez (Eds.), *Moral development in the professions: Psychology and applied ethics* (pp. 27–50). Hillsdale, NJ: Erlbaum.

Mercuri, J. J., Karia, R. J., Egol, K. A., & Zuckerman, J. D. (2013). Moral reasoning strategies of orthopaedic surgery residents. *The Journal of Bone and Joint Surgery, 95*(6), e361–369.

Miles, S. H., Lane, L. W., Bickel, J., Walker, R. M., & Cassel, C. K. (1989). Medical ethics: Coming of age. *Academic Medicine, 64*, 705–714.

Monson, V. E., & Bebeau, M. J. (2006, July). *Entering dental students' stages of identity formation: A replication study.* Paper presented at the Annual Meeting of the Association for Moral Education (AME), Fribourg, Switzerland.

Monson, V. E., Hamilton, N. W., & Organ, J. E. (2013, October). *Professional formation (professionalism) outcomes from matriculation to graduation in legal education.* Paper presented at the Annual Meeting of the Association for Moral Education (AME), Montreal, Canada.

Mulvey, H. J., Ogle-Jewett, E. A., Cheng, T. L., & Johnson, R. L. (2000). Pediatric residency education. *Pediatrics, 106*(2, Pt. 1, Aug), 323–329.

Nasca, T. J., Philibert, I., Brigham, T., & Flynn, T. C. (2012). The next GME accreditation system—rationale and benefits. *New England Journal of Medicine, Special Report.* Retrieved from www.acgme-nas.org/.

National Conference of Bar Examiners (NCBE). (2013). *NCBE website.* Retrieved from www.ncbex.com.

National League for Nursing Accrediting Commission, Inc. (NLNAC). (2013). *Accreditation manual.* Retrieved from www.acenursing.net/manuals/SC2013.pdf.

Olshansky, S. J., Antonucci, T., Berkman, L., Binstock, R. H., Boersch-Supan, A., Cacioppo, J. T. et al. (2012). Differences in life expectancy due to race and educational differences are widening, and many may not catch up. *Health Affairs, 31*(8), 1803–1813.

Papadakis, M. A., Hodgson, C. S., Teherani, A., & Kohatsu, N. D. (2004). Unprofessional behavior in medical school is associated with subsequent disciplinary action by state medical board. *Academic Medicine, 79*, 244–249.

Papadakis, M. A., Loeser, H., & Healy, K. (2001). Early detection and evaluation of professionalism deficiencies in medical students: One school's approach. *Academic Medicine, 76*(11), 1100–1106.

Papadakis, M. A., Paauw, D. S., Hafferty, F. W., Shapiro, J., & Byyny, R. L. (2012). Perspective: The education community must develop best practices informed by evidence-based research to remediate lapses of professionalism. *Academic Medicine, 87*(12), 1694–1698.

Park, M., Kjervik, D., Crandell, J., & Oermann, M. H. (2012). The relationship of ethics education to moral sensitivity and moral reasoning skills of nursing students. *Nursing Ethics, 19*(4), 568–580.

Pascarella, E. T., & Terenzini, P. T. (2005). Moral development. In E. T. Pascarella & P. T. Terenzini, *How college affects students: Vol. 2. A third decade of research. Findings and insights from twenty years of research* (pp. 345–371). San Francisco: Jossey-Bass.

Pellegrino, E. D. (2006). Character formation and the making of good physicians. In N. Kenny & W. Shelton (Eds.), *Advances in bioethics: Vol. 10. Lost virtue: Professional character development in medical education* (pp. 1–15). Oxford: Elsevier.

Pellegrino, E. D., & Thomasma, D. C. (1993). *The virtues in medical practice.* New York: Oxford University Press.

Platfoot Lacey, D. (2012). Embedding professionalism into legal education. *Journal of Law, Business & Ethics, 18*, 41. Retrieved from SSRN: http://ssrn.com/abstract=1975368.

Rennie, S. C., & Crosby, J. R. (2002). Students' perceptions of whistle blowing: Implications for self-regulation. A questionnaire and focus group study. *Medical Education, 36*(2), 173–179.

Rest, J. (1979). *Development in judging moral issues.* Minneapolis: University of Minnesota Press.

Rest, J. R. (1982). A psychologist looks at the teaching of ethics. *The Hastings Center Report, 12*(1), 29–36.

Rest, J. R. (1983). Morality. In P. H. Mussen, J. Flavell, & E. Markman (Eds.), *Handbook of child psychology: Vol. 3. Cognitive development* (4th ed., pp. 556–629). New York: Wiley.

Rest, J. R., & Narvaez, D. F. (Eds.). (1994). *Moral development in the professions: Psychology and applied ethics.* Hillsdale, NJ: Erlbaum.

Rest, J. R., Narvaez, D., Bebeau, M. J., & Thoma, S. (1999). *Postconventional moral thinking: A neo-Kohlbergian approach.* Hillsdale, NJ: Erlbaum.

Rudavsky, S. (2007, May 8). Cheating scandal snares nearly half of IU dental class. *The Indianapolis Star.*

Rule, J. T., & Bebeau, M. J. (2005). *Dentists who care: Inspiring stories of professional commitment.* Chicago: Quintessence.

Rule, J. T., & Welie, J. V. M. (2009). The access to care dilemma: Symptom of a systemic condition. *Dental Clinics of North America, 53*(3), 421–433.

Ryden, M., Duckett, L., Crisham, P., Caplan, A., & Schmittz, D. (1989). Multi-course sequential learning as a model for content integrations: Ethics as a prototype. *Journal of Nursing Education, 28*(6), 271–275.

Schwartz, B., & Sharpe, K. E. (2005). Practical wisdom: Aristotle meets positive psychology. *Journal of Happiness Studies, 7*, 377–395.

Sheehan, T. J., Candee, D., Willms, J., Donnelly, J., & Husted, S. D. (1985). Structural equation models of moral reasoning and physician performance. *Evaluation in the Health Professions, 8*, 379–400.

Sherman, T., & Margolin, J. (2006, May 16). Cheating scam rocks UMDNJ dental school. *Newark Star-Ledger.*

Sherman, T., & Margolin, J. (2007, February 16). New cheating scheme rocks dental school. UMDNJ plans to discipline eight linked to exam-copying scandal. *Newark Star Ledger.*

Shulman, L. (2010). Foreword. In M. Cooke, D. M. Irby, & B. C. O'Brien (Eds.), *Educating Physicians.* San Francisco: Jossey-Bass.

Sirin, S. R., Brabeck, M. M., Satiani, A., & Rogers-Serin, L. (2003). Validation of a measure of ethical sensitivity and examination of the effects of previous multicultural and ethics courses on ethical sensitivity. *Ethics and Behavior, 13*(3), 221–235.

Stern, D. T. (Ed.). (2006). *Measuring medical professionalism* (pp. 281–306). New York: Oxford University Press.

Stern, D. T., Frohna, A. Z., & Gruppen, L. D. (2005). The prediction of professional behavior. *Medical Education, 39*, 75–82.

Strike, K. A. (1982). *Educational policy and the just society.* Chicago: University of Chicago Press.

Sullivan, W. M., Colby, A., Wegner, J. W., Bond, L., & Shulman, L. S. (2007). *Educating lawyers: Preparation for the profession of law.* San Francisco: Jossey-Bass.

Swick, H. M., Szenas, P., Danoff, D., & Whitcomb, M. E. (1999). Teaching professionalism in undergraduate medical education. *Journal of the American Medical Association, 282*(9), 830–832.

Swisher, L. L., Beckstead, J. W., & Bebeau, M. J. (2004). Models of professionalism: Confirmatory factor analysis of the Professional Role Orientation Inventory among physical therapists. *Physical Therapy, 84*(9), 784–799.

Teherani, A., Hodgson, C. S., Banach, M., & Papadakis, M. A. (2005). Domains of unprofessional behavior during medical school associated with future disciplinary action by a state medical board. *Academic Medicine, 80(10 Suppl.)*, S17–S20.

Thoma, S. J. (1994). Moral judgments and moral action. In J. Rest & D. Narvaez (Eds.), *Moral development in the professions: Psychology and applied ethics* (pp. 199–211). New York: Erlbaum.

Thoma, S. J. (2006). Research on the Defining Issues Test. In M. Killen & J. G. Smetana (Eds.), *Handbook of moral development* (pp. 67–92). Mahwah, NJ: Erlbaum.

Thoma, S. J., & Bebeau, M. J. (2013). Moral motivation and the Four Component Model. In K. Heinrichs, F. Oser, & T. Lovat (Eds.), *Handbook of moral motivation* (pp. 49–68). Rotterdam, The Netherlands: Sense Publishers.

Thoma, S. J., Bebeau, M. J., & Bolland, A. (2008). Development phase as a moderator of the relationship between moral judgment and intermediate concepts in young professional students. In F. Oser & W. Veugelers (Eds.), *Getting involved: Global citizenship development and sources of moral values* (pp. 147–160). Rotterdam, The Netherlands: Sense Publishers.

Thoma, S. J., Bebeau, M. J., & Born, D. O. (1998). Further analysis of the Professional Role Orientation Inventory. *Journal of Dental Research, 77, Special Issue*, Abstract, 116–120.

Thoma, S. J., Derryberry, W. P., & Crowson, H. M. (2013). Describing and testing an intermediate concept measure of adolescent moral thinking. *European Journal of Developmental Psychology, 10*(2), 239–252.

Tonsor, G. T., & Wolf, C. A. (2011). Mandatory labeling of animal welfare attributes: Public support and considerations for policymakers. *Food Policy, 36*(3), 430–437.

Turner, M. E. (2008). The development and testing of an army leader intermediate ethical concepts measure. Unpublished dissertation, University of Alabama.

University of St. Thomas Law Journal, Special Issue. (2008). *Symposium: The formation of an ethical professional identity in the peer-review professions* (with Muriel J. Bebeau, Anne Colby, William M. Sullivan, Gary Lee Downey, Charles R. Foster, Neil Hamilton, David C. Leach, and Nicholas H. Steneck). Minneapolis, MN: University of St. Thomas School of Law.

Veatch, R. M. (2006). Character formation in professional education: A word of caution. In N. Kenny & W. Shelton (Eds.), *Advances in bioethics: Vol. 10. Lost virtue: Professional character development in medical education* (pp. 29–46). Oxford: Elsevier.

Wong, W., Eiser, A. R., Mrtek, R. G., & Heckerling, P. S. (2004). By-person factor analysis in clinical ethical decision making: Q methodology in end-of-life care decisions. *American Journal of Bioethics, 4*(3), W8–22.

Woods, M. (2005). Nursing ethics education: Are we really delivering the good(s)? *Nursing Ethics, 12*(1), 5–18.

You, D., & Bebeau, M. J. (2012). Gender differences in the ethical competence of professional school students. *Journal of Dental Education,* 76, 1137–1149.

You, D., Maeda, Y., & Bebeau, M. J. (2011). Gender differences in moral sensitivity: A meta-analysis. *Ethics and Behavior, 21*(4), 263–282.

NAME INDEX

A

Abood, S. K. 519
Adler, A. 279
Adolphs, R. 281
Ahlberg, M. 475, 483
Aho, L. 479
Ajzen, I. 424
Aknin, L. B. 230
Allen, J. P. 459
Alt, M. N. 458
Althof, W. 61, 101, 199, 207–8, 215, 256
Anderson, M. 523
Appiah, K. 25
Aquinas, T. 27, 45
Aquino, K. 87, 90
Aragaki, C. 315
Araki, N. 308, 309, 310, 314, 316, 320
Araujo, U. 192–3
Arendt, H. 443, 444, 448, 453
Aristotle 2, 14–18, 58n2, 142, 272, 274, 347, 354, 358
    collaborative thinking 23
    moral character 44, 84, 498
    practical wisdom 15–18, 24
    reason 14, 15
    self-authorship 152
    virtue theory 14–18, 25, 44, 85, 102, 493, 494
Arnold, M. L. 80
Arnold, T. 47
Arsenio, W. 123, 128, 230
Arthur, J. 47, 57
Atkins, R. 74, 89
Aufenanger, S. 217

B

Balaguer, I. 497, 498, 499
Baldwin, D. C. 514, 525
Bandura, A. 20, 147, 213, 279, 302, 391, 425, 428, 509–10
Bar-On, R. 275, 276
Barclay, J. 46

Bargh, J. A. 88, 141, 144
Barnard, H. C. 46
Barriga, A. Q. 91
Barton, K. C. 359
Batchelder, T. H. 457
Batson, C. D. 231, 233
Battistich, V. 263, 265
Beauchamp, T. L. 512
Bebeau, M. 68, 430–1, 509, 510, 511, 512, 513, 514, 517, 520, 521, 522, 523, 524, 525, 526
Becker, M. H. 424
Beckner, W. 102, 106
Benn, R. 234, 235
Benner, P. 519
Bennett, W. 15, 55, 187, 493
Benninga, J. S. 258
Benson, P. L. 429, 430
Bentham, J. 46
Bergem, T. 101
Berger, R. 302, 303–4
Bergman, R. 85
Berkowitz, L. 477
Berkowitz, M. 54, 61, 76, 106, 109, 113, 165, 249, 250, 251, 252, 254, 255, 256, 257, 258, 290, 303, 493–4
Berman, S. 274, 408
Beyer, L.E. 110, 111, 113
Bier, M. C. 54, 251, 252, 254, 255, 256, 257, 258, 290, 303
Billig, S. H. 459, 460
Bissinger, B. 496
Bitz, B. 130
Blair, R. 123
Blasi, A. 68, 85–7, 88, 92, 141, 144, 299, 500, 508
Blatt, M. 75, 76, 141, 165, 318–19
Bock, T. 152
Bohlin, K. E. 53, 106, 109, 110
Bok, D. 511
Bouffard, S. 268
Boyte, H. 442
Brabeck, M. M. 68

SUBJECT INDEX

Note: Page numbers in **bold** are for figures, those in *italics* are for tables.